Sustainability Reporting, Ethics, and Strategic Management Strategies for Modern Organizations

Ionica Oncioiu
Titu Maiorescu University, Romania

Sorinel Căpuşneanu
Titu Maiorescu University, Romania

Dan Ioan Topor
1 Decembrie 1918 University, Romania

Dana Maria (Oprea) Constantin
University of Bucharest, Romania

IGI Global
PUBLISHER of TIMELY KNOWLEDGE

A volume in the Advances in Business Strategy and Competitive Advantage (ABSCA) Book Series

Published in the United States of America by
IGI Global
Business Science Reference (an imprint of IGI Global)
701 E. Chocolate Avenue
Hershey PA, USA 17033
Tel: 717-533-8845
Fax: 717-533-8661
E-mail: cust@igi-global.com
Web site: http://www.igi-global.com

Library of Congress Cataloging-in-Publication Data

Names: Oncioiu, Ionica, 1972- editor.
Title: Sustainability reporting, ethics, and strategic management strategies for modern organizations / Ionica Oncioiu [and three others], editors.
Description: Hershey, PA : Business Science Reference, [2021] | Includes bibliographical references and index. | Summary: "This book explores various theoretical and practical approaches of ethical standards and sustainability reporting and their impact in the 21st century"-- Provided by publisher.
Identifiers: LCCN 2020013008 (print) | LCCN 2020013009 (ebook) | ISBN 9781799846376 (hardcover) | ISBN 9781799857006 (paperback) | ISBN 9781799846383 (ebook)
Subjects: LCSH: Sustainability development reporting.
Classification: LCC HD60.3 .S8735 2021 (print) | LCC HD60.3 (ebook) | DDC 658.4/08--dc23
LC record available at https://lccn.loc.gov/2020013008
LC ebook record available at https://lccn.loc.gov/2020013009

This book is published in the IGI Global book series Advances in Business Strategy and Competitive Advantage (ABSCA) (ISSN: 2327-3429; eISSN: 2327-3437)

British Cataloguing in Publication Data
A Cataloguing in Publication record for this book is available from the British Library.

For electronic access to this publication, please contact: eresources@igi-global.com.

Advances in Business Strategy and Competitive Advantage (ABSCA) Book Series

Patricia Ordóñez de Pablos
Universidad de Oviedo, Spain

ISSN:2327-3429
EISSN:2327-3437

MISSION

Business entities are constantly seeking new ways through which to gain advantage over their competitors and strengthen their position within the business environment. With competition at an all-time high due to technological advancements allowing for competition on a global scale, firms continue to seek new ways through which to improve and strengthen their business processes, procedures, and profitability.

The **Advances in Business Strategy and Competitive Advantage (ABSCA) Book Series** is a timely series responding to the high demand for state-of-the-art research on how business strategies are created, implemented and re-designed to meet the demands of globalized competitive markets. With a focus on local and global challenges, business opportunities and the needs of society, the **ABSCA** encourages scientific discourse on doing business and managing information technologies for the creation of sustainable competitive advantage.

COVERAGE

- Customer-Orientation Strategy
- Value Chain
- Adaptive Enterprise
- Differentiation Strategy
- Cost Leadership Strategy
- Resource-Based Competition
- Business Models
- Competitive Strategy
- Entrepreneurship & Innovation
- Joint Ventures

IGI Global is currently accepting manuscripts for publication within this series. To submit a proposal for a volume in this series, please contact our Acquisition Editors at Acquisitions@igi-global.com or visit: http://www.igi-global.com/publish/.

The Advances in Business Strategy and Competitive Advantage (ABSCA) Book Series (ISSN 2327-3429) is published by IGI Global, 701 E. Chocolate Avenue, Hershey, PA 17033-1240, USA, www.igi-global.com. This series is composed of titles available for purchase individually; each title is edited to be contextually exclusive from any other title within the series. For pricing and ordering information please visit http://www.igi-global.com/book-series/advances-business-strategy-competitive-advantage/73672. Postmaster: Send all address changes to above address.

Titles in this Series

For a list of additional titles in this series, please visit: www.igi-global.com/book-series

International Perspectives on the Youth Labor Market Emerging Research and Opportunities
Samir Amine (Université du Québec en Outaouais, Canada)
Business Science Reference • ©2020 • 217pp • H/C (ISBN: 9781799827795) • US $170.00

Open and Innovative Trade Opportunities for Latin America and the Caribbean
Pablo Alberto Baisotti (University of Costa Rica, Costa Rica)
Business Science Reference • ©2020 • 255pp • H/C (ISBN: 9781799835035) • US $215.00

Cases on Performance Improvement Innovation
Darlene M. Van Tiem (Capella University, USA & University of Michigan – Dearborn, USA) and Nancy Crain Burns (Crain Burns Associates LLC, USA)
Business Science Reference • ©2020 • 377pp • H/C (ISBN: 9781799836735) • US $195.00

Handbook of Research on Entrepreneurship Development and Opportunities in Circular Economy
Neeta Baporikar (Namibia University of Science and Technology, Namibia & University of Pune, India)
Business Science Reference • ©2020 • 696pp • H/C (ISBN: 9781799851165) • US $265.00

Digital Transformation and Innovative Services for Business and Learning
Kamaljeet Sandhu (University of New England, Australia)
Business Science Reference • ©2020 • 282pp • H/C (ISBN: 9781799851752) • US $235.00

Development and Implementation of Adaptive Trade Policy in the Era of Digital Globalization
Vardan Mkrttchian (HHH University, Australia) and Yulia Vertakova (Financial University Under the Government of the Russian Federation, Kursk, Russia)
Business Science Reference • ©2020 • 300pp • H/C (ISBN: 9781799831341) • US $215.00

Entrepreneurial Development and Innovation in Family Businesses and SMEs
Andreas Masouras (Neapolis University, Cyprus) Georgios Maris (University of the Aegean, Greece) and Androniki Kavoura (University of West Attica, Greece)
Business Science Reference • ©2020 • 312pp • H/C (ISBN: 9781799836483) • US $215.00

Dynamic Strategic Thinking for Improved Competitiveness and Performance
Georgette Andraz (CEFAGE, University of Algarve, Portugal) Helder Carrasqueira (University of Algarve, Portugal & CiTUR, Portugal) Rosaria Pereira (CiTUR, Portugal & University of Algarve, Portugal) and Rita Baleiro (University of Algarve, Portugal & CiTUR, Portugal)

IGI Global
PUBLISHER of TIMELY KNOWLEDGE

701 East Chocolate Avenue, Hershey, PA 17033, USA
Tel: 717-533-8845 x100 • Fax: 717-533-8661
E-Mail: cust@igi-global.com • www.igi-global.com

Editorial Advisory Board

Table of Contents

Detailed Table of Contents

ethics and corporate governance. South Africa too, has had its fair share of scandal that has had its legal fraternity, government, and business sector develop the Kings I, Kings II, Kings III, and Kings IV laws that stipulate corporate governance and ethics. Organisations have to be honest, professional, and transparent in their business practices.

The accounting profession has intensely witnessed compelling challenges in the 21st century. Due to increased number in stakeholders and huge informational need, the traditional model has become unsatisfactory in meeting this need and evaluating company's future performance. Apparently, companies trying to survive in globally competitive markets couldn't attain this goal by focusing merely on financial outcomes. Thus, sustainability reporting has emerged as a vital non-financial information demanded by stakeholders. However, ethical insights on credibility and accountability of this information have been documented and discussed in the literature. Tapping into behavioral finance paradigm and upper echelon approach, this chapter exerts an effort to link financial reporting/audit quality to sustainability reporting and discusses those ethical issues on these processes. Further, while drawing attention to overconfidence bias in individuals involved in reporting and assurance stages, it suggests influential role of decision-makers' personal traits on these mechanisms in a misleading way.

Values and strategies are two powerful drivers of business. Both of them have effects on the activities and practices of the firms. This chapter compares the relevance of values and strategy in Scandinavian business basing on the contents of the web pages for the largest firms in Sweden, Norway, Denmark, and Finland. The results show the importance of values in the forms of responsibility and sustainability in these web pages. The firms also provide complement information, how they will follow these topical contemporary values in their business. According to analysis, the role of strategy is still relatively important, but not so important as values especially in the headings of homepages or "about us" pages.

The presence of several legal entities within the same group entails the existence of as many independent accountants as there are companies. In accordance with IFRS 3 "business combinations," the result is goodwill that will be recognized as a non-current intangible asset in the consolidated balance sheet, being subjected annually to the impairment test; insofar as the investment cost is lower than the acquisition cost of the net assets, the negative goodwill will be obtained which will be recognized in the form a profit in the consolidated profit and loss account. In addition, national differences in accounting, taxation, and auditing are the sources of the various problems that arise in the process of controlling subsidiaries and consolidating accounts. This chapter aims to study the convergence and divergence regarding business combinations in the joint business as well as to analyze the managerial controversies that are presented in the conversion of the financial statements.

This integrated approach implies a broad approach to monitor the performance of the organization both during its life cycle and on the different social dimensions, from the perspective of the conformity of the management processes in relation to the economic, social, and environmental principles. Currently, the social responsibility reporting is a major challenge for the management of organizations in the context where honesty, transparency, business ethics, are values shared by an entire community. The research involves a process through which a series of correlations between the CSR reporting tools and the organization performance management can be analyzed by highlighting the role of the different reporting variables in the architecture of the performance indicators of the organization. The chapter addresses how a set of CSR reporting indicators can be identified and be integrated into the performance indicators which characterize the sustainability of a company.

In the trend of digital marketing, the back and front office activities are automized. For any business organization of various departmental activities, finance and marketing play a vital role. Finance and marketing are the most important functional areas of operations in any business organization, as they directly impact the financial growth as well as market steadiness of the business. As very crucial decisions taken in these functional areas of operations affect the other departments, the decisions in these financial marketing should be taken with utmost care. Henceforth, this results in greater impact on economic growth of the organization. Therefore, the decisions in finance and marketing activities should consider various factors (critical to quality) before arriving at a conclusion. In order to attain the final decision, multi-criteria decision-making (MCDM) methods can be applied. These MCDM methods consider the conflicting factors to evaluate the finance and marketing activities.

Preface

Current modern companies, which are also the key factors of a global economy, are subject to increasing pressures to conduct their business in an environmentally responsible manner, due to social and environmental problems. By integrating multiple processes and methods, sustainability reporting plays a key role by providing reliable, relevant, accurate, and timely information to managers. Improving long-term environmental performance can bring economic benefits to those companies that are innovative and environmentally sensitive, especially by integrating environmental information into their business strategies.

The identification of new models for presenting environmental information, of the specific indicators for certain sectors of the economy, as well as the use of sustainable business models are some of the topics covered in this book. The issue of sustainability is a current and future one that will open new horizons for specialists and those interested in sustainable development and environmental conservation, and are also the center of major interest for a large category of stakeholders in knowing the financial and non-financial performance of profitable or non-profit organizations.

On the other hand, in the 21st century, ethics fulfills both the role of moral judgment and decision-making in terms of balancing problems that can lead to conflict. In the same time, the business resources have been shaped by the needs of the past and are subsequently applied in the current sustainable process to respond to the needs of the future. Taking into account all the changes, management and financial accounting becomes a powerful information tool for executives, managers, and employee teams to gain insights and make better decisions. Based on this, the management becomes the main actor in whose role the success or the failure of the business carried out through the company he leads is decided. Along with concepts such as ethical, controlling, auditing, reporting, management and financial accounting provides value with the decision-making process. All these debates underline the major responsibility of users when configuring accounting and finance models and thereby in modeling business information.

Accounting professionals choose to respect the fundamental principles established by the ethical codes in order to maintain their credibility with the public and to demonstrate the honesty and correctness of the works they practice. Being affiliated with various specialized organizations, accountants are accredited and protect their professional reputation. Unfortunately, there are also people who violate public or private trust and solving ethical dilemmas does not always end favorably. Tax evasion, theft and corruption are the main negative effects of unethical actions of accountants and organizations. Ethics and practice in managerial and financial accounting include both strict adherence to the guidelines and careful evaluation of the unique situations in which professional judgment is required. Understanding ethics through the perspective of independence, integrity, confidentiality and professional competence can help and guide decision-making by helping to maintain professional reputation in the field.

The book *Sustainability Reporting, Ethics, and Strategic Management Strategies for Modern Organizations* proposes an interdisciplinary perspective and to explore various theoretical and practical approaches of ethical standards, management accounting and its impact on different areas of activity. It will contrast external financial accounting for government regulators and the investment community with internal management accounting for managers to leverage for decision making. Also, the book examines the role of management accounting from other concepts point of view such as: ethical standards, Corporate Social Responsibility, creative accounting, green accounting, environmental indicators, e-accounting, KPI, lean accounting, controlling, auditing, reporting, etc. offering a number of new insights into management and financial accounting.

The dimensions of strategic management accounting and operated interconnected tools used to make managerial decisions are presented by Sorinel Căpuşneanu, Dan Ioan Topor, Dana Maria (Oprea) Constantin, Cristian-Marian Barbu, Mihaela Ştefan Hint, the authors of the first chapter "Strategic Management Accounting: Dimensions and Strategic Tools". The main objectives of this chapter are to present the general approaches of the concept of strategic management accounting, the dimensions of the application of strategic management accounting and the strategic tools used by companies in establishing strategies and making decisions. Based on the specialized literature, the authors present the most significant theoretical-methodological approaches to strategic management accounting, the participation of management accountants in the decision-making process, the tools used by strategic management accounting. All aspects presented by the authors are based on existing literature, university studies and specialized literature from around the world. The chapter ends with the conclusions of the authors regarding the dimensions and implications of using the specific tools of strategic management accounting for decision making at managerial level.

An interesting perspective on the ethics in accounting and finance is provided by Vannie Naidoo, the author of the second chapter "Ethics in Accounting and Finance a South African Perspective". Ethics forms the corner stone of business and commerce today. It is the lifeblood of every institution be it private or public enterprise. Organizations' have to develop and implement a properly structured policy on ethics outlaying proper governance within the institution. Accounting and finance services are crucial in managing a company's finances and wealth. In the accounting, profession in order for there to be transparency and trust ethics is a crucial area that needs to be present. The many scandals and ethical dilemmas faced by countries organizations throughout the world has made us pause and take stock of what is happening in industry and has prompted action in law and governance towards ethics and corporate governance. South Africa too, has had its fair share of scandal that has had our legal fraternity, government and business sector develop the Kings I, Kings II, Kings III and Kings IV laws that stipulate corporate governance and ethics. Organizations have to be honest, professional and transparent in their business practice.

The answer to one of the paradigms of finance behavior related to financial reporting and environmental reporting is identified by Sibel Dinç, the author of the third chapter" Unseen Link Between Sustainability Reporting and Financial Reporting: Behavioral Finance Paradigm". Accounting profession has intensely witnessed compelling challenges in the 21st century. Due to increased number in stakeholders and huge informational need, traditional model has remained unsatisfactory in meeting this need and evaluating company's future performance. Apparently, companies trying to survive in globally competitive markets couldn't attain this goal by focusing merely on financial outcomes. Thus, sustainability reporting has emerged as a vital non-financial information demanded by stakeholders. However, ethical insights on credibility and accountability of this information have been documented and discussed in the literature. Tapping into behavioral finance paradigm and upper echelon approach, this chapter exerts an effort to link financial reporting/audit quality to sustainability reporting and discusses those ethical issues on these processes. Further, while drawing attention to overconfidence bias in individuals involved in reporting and assurance stages, it suggests influential role of decision-makers' personal traits on these mechanisms in a misleading way.

The business drivers of the company and their role are highlighted by a comparative study conducted by Rauno Rusko, the author of the fourth chapter "Values or Strategy? Comparative Study about the Roles of Values and Strategy in the Web Pages of the Largest Scandinavia". According to the author, values and strategies are two powerful drivers of business. Both of them have effects on the activities and practices of the firms. This chapter compares the relevance of values and strategy in Scandinavian business basing on the contents of the web pages for the largest firms in Sweden, Norway, Denmark and Finland. The results show the importance of values in the forms of responsibility and sustainability in these web pages. The firms also provide complement information, how they will follow these topical contemporary values in their business. According to analysis, the role of strategy is still relatively important, but not as important as values especially in the headings of homepages or "About us" -pages.

The business combinations present convergent and divergent that has been studied through the prism of IFRS 3 by Alin Eliodor Tănase, Traian Ovidiu Calotă, Gabriela Claudia Oncioiu, the authors of the fifth chapter "Convergence and Divergence Regarding Business Combinations". This chapter aims to study the convergence and divergence regarding business combinations in the joint business as well as to analyze the managerial controversies that they are presented the conversion of the financial statements. The presence of several legal entities within the same group entails the existence of as many independent accountants as there are companies. In accordance with IFRS 3 "Business combinations", the result is goodwill that will be recognized as a non-current intangible asset in the consolidated balance sheet, being subjected annually to the impairment test, insofar as the investment cost is lower than the acquisition cost of the net assets, the negative goodwill will be obtained which will be recognized in the form a profit in the consolidated profit and loss account. In addition, national differences in accounting, taxation and auditing are the source of the various problems that arise in the process of controlling subsidiaries and consolidating accounts.

The identification of a set of CSR reporting indicators and their influence on improving the performance of an organization are highlighted by Nicoleta Cristache, Daniel Constantin Diaconu, Razvan Catalin Dobrea, Cristina Dima, Cristian Constantin Draghici and Daniel Peptenatu, the authors of the sixth chapter" The role of CSR reporting instruments in increasing the Organization's Management Performance". The chapter addresses how a set of CSR reporting indicators can be identified and be integrated into the performance indicators which characterize the sustainability of a company. This integrated approach implies a broad approach to monitor the performance of the organization both during its life cycle and on the different social dimensions, from the perspective of the conformity of the management processes in relation to the economic, social and environmental principles. Currently, the social responsibility reporting is a major challenge for the management of organizations in the context where honesty, transparency, business ethics are values shared by an entire community. The research involves a process through which a series of correlations between the CSR reporting tools and the organization performance management can be analyzed by highlighting the role of the different reporting variables in the architecture of the performance indicators of the organization.

By using Multi Criteria Decision Making (MCDM) methods in digital marketing, a new direction for analyzing financial decisions is launched and presented by Prabadevi Boopathy, N Deepa, the authors of the seventh chapter "Decision Analysis in Financial Marketing Using Multi-Criteria Decision Making Methods". In the trend of digital marketing, the back and front office activities are atomized. For any business organization of various departmental activities, the Finance and Marketing plays a vital role. Finance and Marketing are the most important functional areas of operations in any business organization, as they directly impact the financial growth as well as market steadiness of the business. As very crucial decisions taken in these functional areas of operations which affects the other departments, the decisions in these financial marketing should be taken with almost care. Henceforth, this results in greater impact on economic growth of the organization. Therefore, the decisions in Finance and Marketing activities should consider various factors (critical to quality) before arriving at final conclusion. In order to attain the final decision, Multi criteria decision making(MCDM) methods can be applied. These MCDM methods consider the conflicting factors to evaluate the Finance and Marketing activities.

A short but comprehensive implementation guide of sustainability reporting and its benefits in the profitable and non-profit organizations was presented by Dana Maria Constantin (Oprea), Sorinel Căpuşneanu, Dan Ioan Topor, Elena Grigore, Adrian Amadeus Tişscovschi and Elena Bogan, the authors of the eighth chapter" Sustainability Reporting: Short Implementation Guide and Its Benefits". The main objectives of this chapter are to present a brief implementation guide of sustainability reporting, according to GRI requirements and the benefits of its use. Based on the specialized literature, the authors present various aspects encountered in implementing sustainability reporting, interpreting the information used for the internal management and the stakeholders through the sustainability indicators. All the aspects presented and analyzed are based on the existing specialized studies and on the higher education ones. The chapter ends with the authors' conclusions regarding the importance of implementing the guide of the sustainability reporting and its advantages and disadvantages in the short and long term. Through this contribution of the authors, new opportunities are opened in order to exploit the informational content specific to the sustainability reporting that is particularly relevant to all stakeholders.

The impact produced by CSR on small businesses and the value obtained by small companies is studied by Markku Vieru and Janne Peltoniemi, the authors of the ninth chapter "Effect of Corporate Social Responsibility on Pricing of Small Business Loans: Evidence from Finland". This study analyzes corporate social responsibility (CSR) issues in small business finance in Finland, especially within relationship banking. The study combines credit-file data obtained from a large local Finnish bank with a CSR questionnaire conducted with the bank's business loan managers. The credit-file data contain specific details of CSR characteristics, as well as relationship, collateral, firm, and loan-specific characteristics. CSR, typically considered as a non-financial item, contains value-relevant financial information which affects the loan pricing level. The results show that both overinvestment in CSR and the value created by CSR are valid, but connected to different CSR characteristics. Overinvestment is associated with the environment, and value creation with diversity and employees. The results contribute to the understanding of the characteristics of CSR in the context of small business bank lending, as well as more generally to important implications for small firms, banks and management practices.

The principles and possibilities of applying modern leadership are analyzed and presented by Lavinia Essen, Mirela Anca Postole and Marilena Ciobanasu, the authors of the tenth chapter "Future Directions in Leadership Development: Principles and Applications". The objective of this chapter is to demonstrate the role of leadership development in the digital economy. The problem of leadership, leader and leadership style has provoked a considerable number of theoretical and experimental researches, being one of the central themes of the psycho sociology of social groups. Being in front of a considerable volume of experimental data, obtained under very different conceptual and methodological conditions, the problem of leadership has a fragmentary character, being necessary a careful selection of the results that have a sufficient practical relevance.

In a sustainable economy, the management of certain risks and threats at company level are rendered by Ionica Oncioiu, Mircea Alecsandru Udrescu and Alina Gheorghe, the authors of the eleventh chapter" Strategic Management: Company's Management Strategies in Sustainable Economy". The material presented in this chapter aims to capture some particularities of the strategic management of the company in managing risks and threats, to detect some interference between the managerial strategy and the organizational culture, to bring to attention the correlations between the vision of the business, the strategic segmentation and the corporate strategies, through which strategic management ensures the behavioral change of the company on the market. The sustainable economy has put in front of the company's strategic management two directions of responsibility: the motivation of the change or the disappearance of the market. Because the sustainable economy imposed for the Romanian companies, at the same time, higher quality requirements for products and services, but also responsibilities strictly regulated by relations with the natural environment.

The impact of the development strategy of a company is highlighted by the value added to the company and this is presented by Lavinia Essen Yildirim and Diana Mândricel, the authors of the twelfth chapter "Importance of Value of the Company for Development Business". In this context, the action of the market contemporary forces determines certain behavior of the companies, which become more and more engaged in the resources, quality, customers and suppliers, in which the top role is played by the top quality management. At the same time, the value of an enterprise or rather of its shares is no longer calculated as the sum of the values of its assets, but determined by its ability to generate economic benefits, the balance sheet loses interest in the income statement. This chapter analysis the new research directions regarding the value of the company in managing business risks.

A new perspective on the role of controlling in the age of sustainability and digitalization is brought by Ibrahim Oba and Mirela Anca Postole, the authors of the thirteenth chapter "The Role of Controlling in the Business Environment". Environmental changes and especially the development of the digital economy have posed real existential questions to businesses, provoked strategic reflection and made the emergence of controlling efficient. The objective of this chapter was to explore the role of controlling in the business environment and generalizes a reflection on strategy and controlling in the life of companies. The results show that the controlling has a significant role in enhancing the corporate governance pillars in companies, and the successes of corporate governance requires compliance with all elements of internal control.

Through the age of digitalization, the role of the top management of an entity has changed and adapted to the future visions needed to improve performance. These aspects transposed by the leader's vision are presented by Ionica Oncioiu and Alina Stanciu, the authors of the fourteenth chapter "The Role of the Leader in Increasing the Performance of the Entity". Digital era has brought with the exponential growth of the economic and technological opportunities that entities can access and implement in the development of their own activities and a series of threats with strategic impact. At the same time, business excellence models represent the entity's framework for synchronizing vision with action decisions in a more systematic and structured manner, which results in an entity's performance increase. This chapter aims to open new research and deepen directions at the intersection of accounting and management, between science and practice, with the role of potentiating performance as a result of managerial accounting and leadership vision.

Due to the increase of the interest of the stakeholders in accessing the ESG information of a company, the effect of the information disclosure and the impact of the financial performance are evidenced by a study made by Ismail Cagri Ozcan, the author of the last chapter "Environmental, Social, and Governance Disclosure and Financial Performance-Evidence from the Rail Industry". The Environmental, Social, and Governance (ESG) disclosure performance of the companies is becoming a major criterion for significant stakeholders like shareholders, creditors, and customers. In line with the increasing interest in ESG activities, a growing respective literature emerges. Despite this evolving attraction, the ESG aspects the transport industry in general and rail industry in particular remain relatively untouched except for a small body of research on airlines. This study aims at filling this gap by analyzing how the ESG disclosure performance of the rail companies affect their financial performance, which we measure by return on assets (ROA), return on equity (ROE), and Tobin's Q. Based on a sample of 35 rail companies from 9 countries over the 2007-2017 period, our analyses show that ESG disclosure performance has a positive and statistically significant association with the ROA of the rail companies.

Acknowledgment

Looking back, we wish to thank all the persons who made the publishing of the present volume possible: Jan Travers, Melissa Wagner, Erin Wesser, Christina Henning, Nicole Elliott, Kristina Byrne, Lindsay Johnston, Joshua Witman, Nick Newcomer, Jaimie Watts, Josephine Dadeboe, Jordan Tepper, Sean Eckman, Marianne Caesar, Colby Conway and many other IGI Global team members, reviewers, collaborators, and all the contributing authors: without your efforts and dedication this editorial project would have never been possible.

Chapter 1
Strategic Management Accounting:
Dimensions and Strategic Tools

Sorinel Căpușneanu
https://orcid.org/0000-0003-3799-3993
Titu Maiorescu University, Romania

Dan Ioan Topor
1 Decembrie 1918 University, Romania

Dana Maria (Oprea) Constantin
https://orcid.org/0000-0002-5517-8151
University of Bucharest, Romania

Cristian Marian Barbu
Artifex University, Romania

Mihaela Ștefan Hint
1 Decembrie 1918 University, Romania

ABSTRACT

This chapter deals with some dimensions of strategic management accounting, including the instruments with which they operate and interconnect in order to make managerial decisions. The main objectives of this chapter are to present the general approaches of the concept of strategic management accounting, the dimensions of the application of strategic management accounting, and the strategic tools used by companies in establishing strategies and making decisions. Based on the specialized literature, the authors present the most significant theoretical-methodological approaches to strategic management accounting, the participation of management accountants in the decision-making process, the tools used by strategic management accounting. All aspects presented by the authors are based on existing literature, university studies, and specialized literature from around the world. The chapter concludes with the conclusions of the authors regarding the dimensions and implications of using the specific tools of strategic management accounting for decision making at managerial level.

DOI: 10.4018/978-1-7998-4637-6.ch001

INTRODUCTION

The computerization of the strategic management in the decision-making process is the main key in vitalizing the strategies and achieving the objectives proposed by an organization. An integrated strategic management system is based on management accounting, which is the creator and manager of these information flows needed especially for internal users to achieve the objectives pursued. Exceeding the internal information limits and the orientation towards the external environment is justified by determining the relationship between the strategy pursued and the information formation mode. By improving the methodology and strategic management needs, the efficiency of strategic management accounting is demonstrated. Thus, the entire information cycle of management accounting is oriented according to the strategic positioning of an organization. An organization is particularly interested in managing its cost structure, which is the subject of strategic management, but also the creation of the information flow necessary to optimize strategic decisions of senior management. The implementation of these problems determined the purpose of our study by clarifying some aspects related to the concept of strategic management accounting and its dimensions, but also to the strategic tools used in cost management and obtaining performance by an economic entity. The main objectives of this chapter consist in: *(1) presentation of the conceptual approaches of strategic management accounting; (2) presentation and explanation of the dimensions of strategic management accounting and of the competitive advantage; (3) the integrated application of ABC and BSC methods in an economic entity in the winemaking industry.*

Conceptual Approaches to Strategic Management Accounting (SMA)

The most important definitions of strategic management accounting focus on the components of marketing, control or strategic management, as evidenced by the following approaches of specialists: (1) "providing and analyzing management accounting data on their businesses and competitors in the view of developing and monitoring the business strategy "(Simmonds, 1981); (2)" providing and analyzing the financial information of the market of the firm's products and the costs of the competitors but also of the cost structures, including the monitoring of the strategy of the company and of the other competitors in these markets during certain periods of time "(Bromwhich, 1990); (3) "a generic approach to accounting for strategic positioning, defined by an attempt to integrate discoveries from management accounting and marketing management into strategic management" (Roslender & Hart, 2003), idea also shared by other specialists (Guilding et al., 2000; McManus & Guilding, 2008). (4) "identifying a set of information needed to support strategic decisions" (Agasisti et al., 2008). (5) "implies taking a strategic orientation for generating, interpreting and analysis of management accounting information and competitors' activities provide the key dimension for comparison "(Langfield-Smith, 2008). (6)" using management accounting systems to support strategic decision making "(Tilman & Goddard, 2008). (7)" part of the management accounting dedicated to strategically oriented information for decision making and control "(Ma & Tayles, 2009).

As it can be seen, the presented definitions highlight some clear aspects related particularly to the information about competitors, but do not question the customers or the business environment as this information is essential in developing and monitoring the business strategy but also for creating sustainable values (Carlsson-Wall et al., 2015; McManus, 2013). In addition to the limitations brought by the authors through the definitions presented, there are also other specialists who believe that non-financial information is a feature of strategic management accounting (Bhimani & Langfield-Smith, 2007; Cinquini & Tenucci, 2010; Langfield-Smith, 2008), accounting and control systems, exceeding the limits of financial information and identifying the main success and performance factors of a company (Baines & Langfield-Smith, 2003; Cadez & Guilding, 2008; Chenhall, 2008). The relevance and importance of strategic management accounting in strategic planning is essential (Cuganesan et al., 2012) being a part of strategic management along with strategy implementation and control (Nixon & Burns, 2012).

In our opinion, *strategic management accounting is that part of management accounting dedicated to developing and monitoring the business strategy by providing analysis documents based on internal (financial and non-financial) information of the company and external information from its other competitors.* In other words, strategic management accounting is dedicated to the strategic positioning of the company through the practice of strategic management.

Other specialists consider strategic management accounting as a set of strategic accounting practices, techniques or tools that support the strategic management process (Guilding et al., 2000; Cravens & Guilding, 2001; Cinquini and Tenucci, 2010). The object of strategic management accounting needs to be expanded by taking into account recent developments such as: focusing on internal resources and organizational capabilities to support external competitive bases (Tayles et al., 2007; Cummings & Daellenbach, 2009; Nixon & Burns, 2012), intensifying the active role in rethinking the strategy, developing new forms of management accounting and obtaining sustainable competitive advantages (Cuganesan et al., 2012).

The Dimensions of Strategic Management Accounting (SMA)

According to the above-mentioned specialists, the dimensions of the SMA include: (1) the involvement of the management accountant in the strategic decision-making process; (2) involvement of the management accountant in practicing the SMA. We consider that we can also add a third dimension called the *analysis of strategic investments* that has been debated and analyzed by other specialists in the field.

(1) *Involvement of the management accountant in the strategic decision-making process.* This dimension of the SMA entrusted to the management accountant was approached and analyzed through the prism of:
   - the active involvement of the managing accountant in the decision-making process of an organization (Simmonds, 1982; Bromwich and Bhimani, 1994; Brouthers & Roozen, 1999). According to the authors, the managing accountant can anticipate the reactions of the competitors and can act accordingly. Thus, the skills of the management accountant extend to general management, marketing, strategic management, etc.
   - presenting an expanded vision on business, sometimes playing the key role in promoting certain organizational changes needed under uncertain conditions (Fauré & Rouleau, 2011) or in adopting SMA (Tayles et al., 2007) and designing and implementing measurement systems of intellectual capital (Chiucchi, 2013). This aspect is explained by the greater use of contemporary SMA practices that take into account in the decision-making process both financial and non-financial information, business processes, human resources, markets, customers and competition (Roslender and Hart, 2003).
   - cooperation and understanding in an objective and transparent way of the alternatives that it offers to the management in order to make the best decisions (Dixon, 1998; Cravens and Guilding, 1999; Roslender and Hart, 2006; Tillmann & Goddard, 2008). Other studies have

been devoted to examining the characteristics, role and importance of the management accountant in cooperating with several management functions and implementing the accounting systems and management control with strategic orientation (Feeney & Pierce, 2007; Lambert & Pezet, 2011; Chiucchi, 2013; Hiller et al., 2014).

Taking into account the aspects related to the new attributions and qualities of the management accountant generated by the SMA dimension, the specialists came up with a new concept of professional accountant called strategic management accountant (Coad, 1996; Cadez and Guilding, 2008; Tillman and Goddard, 2008). It plays an important role in designing team-based structures (Chenhall, 2008), demonstrating flexibility, high quality and performance (Scott & Tiessen, 1999). Management accountant's skills are considered as advantages and far more objective than other categories of department managers directly involved and specialized in a particular field (Nixon and Burns, 2012). Its skills in financial guidance must be outpaced by adopting a non-financial orientation related to competition, markets and the internal and external environment in general (Nyamori et al., 2001; Feeney & Pierce, 2007; McManus & Guilding, 2008). He must have an interdisciplinary understanding, creativity and social skills, being able to communicate at an inter-relational level within a company (Coad, 1996; Feeney and Pierce, 2007; Tillmann and Goddard, 2008).

In the last decades, the role of the management accountant has changed from a simple information supplier to an active partner or advisor in strategic issues, in the foundation of the decision-making process (Nyamori et al., 2001), having a professional prestige by being involved in several activities and functions (Hiller et al., 2014). However, there are also conservative, contrary views that the managing accountant should only provide financial information (Lord, 1996), without his involvement in the use of SMA practices or strategic decision-making. In other words, the implementation of the SMA can be achieved with other organizational functions not only necessarily with the help of the managing accountant or the strategic accountant (Dixon and Smith, 1993; Dixon, 1998).

In our opinion, taking into account the evolution of the business environment and the impact of the innovative technology that is going on and which will increase in the near future, but also the complexity of the decision-making process, it is necessary to cooperate with the strategic management accountant in the SMA practices. His role has expanded and his duties have increased in comparison with his previous duties, as well as his responsibility.

(2) *Involvement of the management accountant in the practice of the SMA.* SMA practices are used in collecting, processing, analyzing and providing the information needed for decision makers for strategic management and other managerial and strategic functions (Pires et al., 2015). In the following, a series of concrete differences between the conventional practices of management accounting and strategic management accounting are presented (Table 1):

A list of SMA practices has been completed (starting from the list developed by Guilding et al., 2000) and presented by Cadez & Guilding (2008). According to this list, 16 practices of SMA classified into 5 broad categories were considered as follows:

(A) *The costs.* This category includes practices that are found in conventional management accounting, such as cost determination and analysis (Atkinson et al., 2012; Horngren et al., 2012). The other practices are found in strategic management accounting with an external orientation to the future and very important for planning: target cost and value chain cost (Cooper, 1996; Ewert & Ernst, 1999; Roslender & Hart, 2010; Cuganesan et al., 2012); the life cycle of the products or the quality costs that contribute to the development of strategies based on the life cycle of the products or services, respectively quality management (Pires et al., 2015).

Table 1. Differences between traditional management accounting and strategic management accounting

<table>
<tr><th>Traditional management accounting</th><th colspan="2">Strategic management accounting</th><th>SMA practice lists</th></tr>
<tr><td>Historical, internal orientation
Dimensional analysis (financial measurement)</td><td>Future-oriented, external
Multidimensional analysis (financial and non-financial measurement)</td><td>Coad (1996);
Guilding et al. (2000);
Cadez & Guilding (2008);
Cinquini & Tenucci (2010);
Cuganesan et al. (2012);</td><td rowspan="2">ABC, LCC, Quality costing
Target costing
Value chain costing
Benchmarking
Customer profitability analysis
Customer segment profitability analysis
Lifetime customer profitability analysis
Valuation of customers as assets
Customer accounting</td></tr>
<tr><td>Advantages: creating and realizing benefits to improve performance by providing cost information</td><td colspan="2">Advantages: it allows the creation and realization of competitive advantages and improves the organizational performance by providing strategic information about competition, customers, markets and the external environment.</td></tr>
<tr><td>Lack of focus on certain capabilities</td><td colspan="2">Orientation to internal and organizational resources (Nixon & Burns, 2012) with management focus (Furrer et al., 2008; Cummings & Daellenbach, 2009)</td><td rowspan="2">Costs
Performance planning, control and measurement
Making strategic decisions
Competition accounting
Customer accounting
Cadez & Guilding (2008)</td></tr>
<tr><td>Advantages: supporting managerial decision making</td><td colspan="2">Advantages: supporting competitiveness</td></tr>
</table>

Source: Authors' own processing

(B) *Performance planning, control and measurement.* This category includes two widely used practices with external and future orientations: (a) benchmarking consisting of identifying best practices used by competitors to improve organizational performance; and (b) integrating performance by using financial and non-financial measurement with internal or external perspectives that allow the practice of integrated performance management (Chenhall, 2008). The best example of an integrated performance measurement system is the balanced scorecard (Balanced Scorecard) used in performance planning, more specifically development, implementation and strategy control (Kaplan & Norton, 2001) or intellectual capital identification and management (Tan et al., 2008; Tayles et al., 2007).

(C) *Strategic decision making*. It is focused on three accounting practices with strategic orientation: prices, costs and evaluation of the brand. Strategic pricing focuses on defining the strategy taking into account the actions and reactions of competitors with direct implications on future external orientation issues (Simmonds, 1992). Strategic costs focus on strategic analysis and enable the creation and realization of competitive advantages (Shank & Govindarajan, 1992). As part of the management accounting evaluation, brand evaluation is a relevant source for obtaining competitive advantages of an organization (Dent, 1996; Roslender & Hart, 2010). The information provided by management accounting on brand assessment is particularly useful for strategic managers in allocating resources on profitable brands and gaining competitive advantages thus knowing the impact of their long-term decisions (Cravens & Guilding, 1999).

(D) *Competition accounting*. Information published by competing firms is an important source for formulating an organization's strategy (Dixon, 1998). Also information from the media, from research contracts with universities or scientific papers held at conferences or published in magazines is an important source in developing competitive strategies and monitoring competitors (Dent, 1996). In other words, competition accounting comprises three competencies focused on external-oriented competitors needed to plan, make decisions and monitor the strategy of an organization (Dent, 1996; Dixon, 1998).

(E) *Customer accounting.* It focuses on three important customer-centric practices: customer profitability analysis, customer lifetime profitability analysis, and customer evaluation. Customer profitability analysis refers to evaluating the profitability of a customer or customer segment, while customer lifetime profitability analysis refers to their lifetime, having a future orientation. Customer valuation is based on their valuation as assets and lifespan (Andon & Baxter, 2011; McManus & Guilding, 2008; Guilding & McManus, 2002) with future external horizons and generating future profits for a customer or customer segment. The benefits of these practices can be summarized as: (a) improving the development of strategies; (b) improving cooperation between management, accounting and other managerial functions by practicing strategic management or strategic marketing (Andon & Baxter, 2011; McManus & Guilding, 2008); (c) consolidation of decisions regarding the development of the product range; (d) pricing and managing customer resources.

(3) *Involvement of the management accountant in the strategic analysis of investments.* Not being included as an SMA practice, we will treat this dimension separately, as will the specialists who have previously analyzed this particularly important practice of an organization (Carr et al., 2010; Tillmann & Gooddard, 2008; Roslender & Hart, 2003; Carr & Tomkins, 1996; Bromwich & Bhimani, 1994). According to experts, strategic investment analysis consists of the process of identifying, evaluating and selecting between strategic projects that can contribute to improving the position of competitiveness and other non-financial or intangible benefits (related to quality, efficiency, flexibility, innovation and customer satisfaction) and which can have effects on the development of long-term sustainability (Carr et al., 2010; Alkaraan & Northcott, 2006; Adler, 2000). In other words, strategic investment analysis analyzes the market, the needs of customers and the ability of competitors to meet these needs. In order to reach the goal of strategic investment analysis, it may be necessary to resort to other SMA practices such as: benchmarking, balanced scorecard or value chain analysis (Alkaraan & Northcott, 2006). We are of the opinion that we can also add to the strategic analysis of investments and the adoption of orientations towards internal resources and intellectual capital as parts of the strategic management and sources generating competitive advantages with future sustainable value.

Competitive Advantage and its Dimensions

The competitive advantage consists in the formulation and implementation of strategies by a company in order to achieve a better competitive position, appealing to the physical, technical and organizational capabilities and resources it has and which allows it to design and implement its competitive strategies. According to the experts, the competitive advantage is closely linked to: (1) the ability of companies to meet the needs of customers and employees, as well as to obtain a greater profit from investments in the development and achievement of the proposed objectives (Anik et al., 2010); (2) the ability of the company to achieve the excellence and the value perceived by customers (Weinstein, 2012), having a direct and indirect relationship with the stability of the company on the market (Baroto et al., 2012); (3) the ability of companies to defend and maintain their competitive position on the market, improve management decisions, production and marketing skills, as well as strengthen customer relationships

(Sigalas et al., 2013); (4) the creative and innovative tool to produce and deliver goods and services more efficiently than other market competitors (Naliaka & Namusonge, 2015), or the strategy that develops certain business models, accelerating the growth and development of a company contributing also to improving its reputation (Ranjith, 2016).

Considering the ones listed above, we believe that the competitive advantage can be considered a dimension of the company that helps it to reach its competitive and reputational objectives, contributing significantly to meeting the requirements of internal and external customers. Among all these, the company ensures a certain market share and stability in the competitive market and future profitability. According to the experts' opinion (Brem et al., 2016; Diab, 2014), the basic dimensions of the competitive advantage are (Alamri, 2018):

(1) *The cost.* According to this dimension of competitive advantage, practicing low costs compared to competition allows companies to gain a higher market share, helps managers to support their strategy and ensure a leading position in the field of costs (Baroto et al., 2012; Ranjith, 2016). The reduction of the prices of the products also helps to increase the demand and to reduce the profit margin, in case the company does not incur low costs (Sachitra et al., 2016). Reduced costs can be achieved by: (a) efficient use of its production capacity; (b) improving the quality of the products; (c) innovation in the technological design of products (Baroto et al., 2012).

(2) *Quality.* This dimension of the competitive advantage focuses on the ability of a company to meet the demands and expectations of customers at the highest possible level in order to ensure a relaxed competitive position and a customized reputation. Other specialists agree with this statement too, (Chen et al., 2013; Daru, 2016) also emphasizing other aspects such as imposing higher prices on customers by delivering high quality products.

(3) *Flexibility.* This dimension of competitive advantage describes the ability of a company to rapidly produce a wide range of new or modified products as a result of customer requirements (Combe, 2012). Other authors consider flexibility as the ability of the company to change processes into methods, identifying 4 types: (a) product flexibility (the ability of processes to execute new or modified products); (b) the flexibility of the product mix (the ability of the processes to produce mixed products); (c) product size flexibility (the ability of the products to change the level of production or the level of production activity in order to adapt the products to the dimensions required by customers); (d) delivery flexibility (the ability of processes to adapt to changing delivery times of products) (Eryesil et al., 2015).

(4) *Delivery.* According to the experts' opinion (Prajogo & McDermott, 2011), delivery is the basic dimension of the competitive advantage that focuses on reducing the design and delivery time of new or modified products to customers. Other equally important issues related to delivery are mentioned by other specialists: (a) speed of delivery (it considers reducing the waiting time of a product or orders); (b) speed of development (envisages reducing the time between the design phase of the product and until the product is launched on the market); (c) timely delivery (Krajewsky & Ritzman, 2005).

Integrated Application of ABC and BSC in an Economic Entity in the Winemaking Industry

In order to apply the ABC method, it is necessary to divide the production process into its component activities. However, this division must be made in such a way that there is a balance between the information needs and the costs of obtaining and processing the respective information.

An important step in applying the ABC method is to identify the main activities, the associated costs as well as the cost drivers. As for the specific costs of each activity, they can be grouped into direct costs and specific costs necessary to carry out the respective activity. In the category of direct costs we will include labor costs regarding the manufacturing or control process, the consumption of auxiliary materials (sulfur dioxide, bentonite, etc.), the cost of using and maintaining specific equipment, the depreciation charges, the costs of energy and water consumption, and other costs that can be directly identified as being specific to the activities analyzed. Additional or ancillary costs include the costs of ancillary activities (pumping, cooling, storage etc.) that are required to carry out the main activity. Table 2 presents briefly the process-activities-associated costs - cost drivers scheme, which will be developed later in the case study by allocating the appropriate monetary values.

Table 2. Process-activities-associated costs - cost drivers scheme

<table>
<tr><th>Processes</th><th>Activities</th><th>Associated costs</th><th>Cost drivers</th></tr>
<tr><td rowspan="3">Grape harvesting, reception and quality testing</td><td>Grape selection, collection and transport</td><td>Direct costs: cost of grapes, cost of labor hours, transport cost</td><td rowspan="3">Kg grapes</td></tr>
<tr><td>Grape reception (quality testing, weighing, unloading)</td><td>Direct costs: hourly labor rate, equipment depreciation, energy</td></tr>
<tr><td>Ancillary activities</td><td>Auxiliary costs: the cost of auxiliary materials (shovels, buckets, etc.)</td></tr>
<tr><td rowspan="4">Wine production</td><td>Pre-fermentation activities:
- destemming
- crushing
- pumping in fermentation tanks</td><td rowspan="4">Direct costs:
- hourly work rate
- raw material cost (previously calculated)
- costs associated with the equipment (depreciation, maintenance, cleaning)
- electricity
Indirect costs associated with ancillary activities:
- equipment preparation</td><td rowspan="4">No of days
No. of types of wine made
Quantity of wine by types of wine</td></tr>
<tr><td>Fermentation</td></tr>
<tr><td>Post-fermentation, maturation, aging</td></tr>
<tr><td>Ancillary activities:
- equipment preparation
- wine cellar guard</td></tr>
<tr><td rowspan="3">Unpacking of wine</td><td>Mixing different varieties of wines</td><td rowspan="3">Direct costs: cost of mixed wines, hourly rate of direct workers, cost of equipment (depreciation, maintenance, energy consumption), cost of auxiliary materials</td><td rowspan="3">No. of bottles</td></tr>
<tr><td>Clarification and stabilization</td></tr>
<tr><td>Preparation for sale (bottling, plugging, labeling)</td></tr>
</table>

Source: Authors' own systematization

For the first activity, we will have the following relation of determining the cost of the raw material:

$$Cost\ of\ raw\ materials_i = Cg + Cpcrag \quad (1)$$

Table 3. Allocation of direct costs on activities according to ABC method

P1. Grape reception			**Unit**	**Quantity**	**Value (lei)**
A 1.1	Raw material collection	Grapes	wag.	365.8	**2926400**
A 1.2	Grape reception:	**Total manual work:**			**2898.54**
	- quality testing	direct wages	wag.	365.8	860.68
	- weighing	powering the screw	wag.	365.8	2,037.86
		Total materials from which:			**194.3**
A 1.3	Ancillary activities	Shovels	pcs	10	24.3
		Buckets	pcs	40	48.6
		straw brushes	pcs	50	60.7
		Brooms	pcs	100	60.7
	Total direct costs P1		wag.	365.8	**2929492.84**
P2. Wine production			**Unit**	**Quantity**	**Value (lei)**
A 2.1	Pre-fermentation activities	**Raw materials:**			**2929492.84**
	- destemming	- grapes	wag.	365.8	
	- crush	**Lucrări manuale total:**			**480.58**
	- pumping fermentation tanks	Feeding the screw	wag.	365.8	2,037.86
		serve crush clusters	wag.	365.8	1,272.81
		Directing the marc to the press	wag.	135.3	79.33
		Press service	wag.	135.3	318.35
		Placing the marc on the belt	wag.	58.5	130.00
		Sulfite grapes + must	wag.	365.8	898.91
		Service of decanted must pumps	wag.	65.9	40.78
		Transfer of decanting bulbs	wag.	54.9	101.18
		Transferred must over-sulphite	wag.	11	20.27
		Maintaining daily hygiene	wag.	850	934.47
		Total materials of which:			**5317.02**
		Bulbs	pcs	50	14
		Rivets	Kg	45	56.1
		sulfur balls	kg	200	59.4
		Rush	kg	400	93.4
		Paraffin	kg	500	336
		Calcined soda	kg	1000	179
		bentonite	kg	8000	2990
		Gauze	ml	30	1.12
		Donate oak	mc	10	1121
		Striped board	kg	500	467
	Total direct costs A2.1				**2935290.44**

continued on following page

Table 3. Continued

A 2.2	Ferment	Raw materials:			
		- must			**2935290.44**
		Total manual work:			**4527.22**
		Transfer of over-sulphite must	wag.	11	25.88
		Installation supervision must	wag.	274.5	432.21
		Quantitative/qualitative reception must	wag.	274.5	125.67
		Concentrated must transfer	wag.	274.5	505.91
		Conditioning vessels	wag.	530	1,165.34
		Maintaining daily hygiene	wag.	800	879.5
		Ready SO_2 solution	wag.	450	247.36
		Prepared vessels for winemaking	wag.	450	989.44
		Prepared inventory for winemaking	wag.	450	6.8
		Prepared spaces for winemaking	wag.	450	989.44
		Equipment transport + installation	wag.	450	765
		Transfer after fermentation	wag.	274.5	754.45
		Waste disposal	wag.	27.5	45.35
		Dishwashing	wag.	274.5	452.67
		Transferred yeast	to	274.5	905.34
	Total direct costs A2.2				**2939817.66**
A 2.3	Post-fermentation	Raw materials:			2939817.66
	Maturation and aging	Total manual work:			**4155.15**
		Preparation of sulfur filters	wag.	247.1	351.55
		Filling and correction with SO_2	wag.	247.1	607.22
		Treatment of wine with bentonite	wag.	247.1	351.55
		Laboratory sample collection	wag.	247.1	581.4
		Maintaining daily hygiene	wag.	225	247.36
		Fill and correct with SO_2	wag.	274.5	169.87
		Collected samples for the laboratory	wag.	248.7	273.41
		Transfer to decanting	wag.	274.5	606.98
		Waste disposal	to	274.5	60.47
		Dishwashing	wag.	274.5	603.56
		Transferred yeast	to	274.5	301.78
		Total materials of which:			**8152.34**
		Lamps	pcs		280.34
		Wire brushes	pcs		124
		Insulating gloves	pcs		56
		Fir timber	mc		1,240.00
		fir balls	mc		765
		lime balls	kg		125

continued on following page

Table 3. Continued

		Paint	kg		676
		Asbestos	pcs		345
		Galvanized sheet	kg		512
		Other materials			2256
		Overalls	per		1298
		PSI hose	ml		54
		Rubber boots	per		421
		Electricity	kw	1000	**1100**
	Total direct costs A2.3				**2953225.15**
A 2.4	Ancillary activities	Guard cellar	hours	2110	1200
	Total direct costs A 2.1-A 2.4				**2954425.15**
P3. Unpacking of wine			**Unit**	**Quantity**	**Value (lei)**
A3.1	Mixing of fermented wines	Raw materials:			2954425.15
		Total manual work:			**497.01**
		Quality wine reception	wag.	290	61.89
		Harvested average sample for the laboratory	t	290	95.11
		Download wine	t	290	178.16
		Wine blending	t	290	161.85
	Total A 3.1				**2954922.16**
A 3.2	Clarification and stabilization	Raw materials:			**2954922.16**
		Total manual work:			**4935.67**
		Treatment of wine with bentonite	t	290	206.29
		Homogenization of wine	t	290	226.92
		Drawing wine from the warehouse	t	290	142.53
		Evacuation of the deposit	t	290	127.53
		Treatment of wine with tannin and gel	t	290	206.29
		Wine mixing and blending	t	290	185.67
		Pulling the wine from the yeast	t	290	142.53
		Subjecting the wine to heat shock	t	290	742.65
		Filtration of wine for work	t	290	618.88
		Pulling wine under pressure vessels	t	290	168.79
		Making the full	t	290	79.70
		Performing the decanting	t	290	142.53
		Correction of alcohol blends + MC	t	290	1,155.65
		Correction of blends with sorbic acid+SO_2	t	290	1,155.65
		Reception of concentrated must		290	57.84
		Yeast transfer and shipment	t	14.5	47.82
		Conditioning of vessels	t	530	1,165.34
		Ready SO_2 solution	t	450	247.36

continued on following page

Table 3. Continued

		Sulfite wines with SO_2	t	365.8	1,005.38
		Electricity:			**24,274.80**
		Pump	kw	90	7,499.94
		ventilation	kw	201.3	16,774.86
		Total materials of which:			**34,213.28**
		Filter board	pcs	30	4,680.90
		EC sterile plates	pcs	30	20,163.90
		Sulfur powder	kg	0.6	5.4
		Trisodium phosphate	kg	0.03	3.6
		Calcined soda	kg	0.03	4.86
		bentonite	kg	10	286.86
		Gelatine	kg	0.05	28.51
		Citric acid	kg	5	1,500.29
		Sorbic acid	kg	2	6,601.28
		K ferocyanide	kg	0.15	58.51
		Bicarbonate K	kg	1.5	801.15
		SO_2	kg	1	78.02
	Total A 3.2				**3,018,345.91**
A 3.3	Preparing for the sale	Raw materials:			3018345.91
		Total manual work:			**33193.39**
	- bottling	Foremen and shift managers			2376.88
	- plugging	Suply of empty bottles on the conveyor belt	mb	2500	417.33
	- labeling	Powered washing machine with detergent and lye water	mb	2500	378.23
		Mechanical washing of bottles	mb	2500	575.63
		Check the washed bottles	mb	2500	546.68
		Filled bottles with mechanical wine	mb	2500	1604.53
		Control full bottles	mb	2500	546.68
		Returned bottles with impurities	mb	2500	521.72
		Mechanically stapled or doped	mb	2500	575.63
		Applied thermo caps	mb	2500	518.36
		Mechanical tagging	mb	2500	758.1
		Applied flyers (contra-labels)	mb	2500	575.63
		Leveling content bottles	mb	2500	758.1
		Aesthetic control of bottles	mb	2500	758.1
		CTC control - belt end	mb	2500	546.73
		Retrieved bottles from the belt-laid shuttles	mb	2500	1555.07
		Sorting shuttles	mb	2500	417.33
		Transport of broken and palletized shuttles	mb	2500	417.33

continued on following page

Table 3. Continued

		Empty shuttles on the belt - received	mb	2500	575.63
		Washed and sanitized softened water	mb	2500	539.24
		Washing/sanitizing sterilization bottling plants	mb	2500	539.24
		Filtered wine (filter format-plates removed)	mb	2500	523.38
		Pasteurized wine	mb	2500	628.05
		Sorting and dating labels	mb	2500	518.69
		Quantitative/qualitative bottles receiption	mb	2500	582.86
		Removed the chunks and took them to the container	mb	2500	7.56
		Hygiene washing Filling	mb	2500	518.36
		Supply material	mb	2500	417.33
		Place the bottles in cardboard	mb	2500	758.10
		Closing and sealing the boxes	mb	2500	518.36
		Place the box on the conveyor belt	mb	2500	1236.85
		Handling full packaging	mb	2500	4785.58
		Handling empty packaging	mb	2500	4785.58
		removed the plugs manually	mb	2500	46.96
		Wash stained bottles manually	mb	2500	352.22
		Preparation and closing Act.	mb	2500	758.1
		Energy and water:			**16490.63**
		Energy	kw	150000	16,490.63
		Total materials of which:			**123781.07**
		Spare parts			5002.16
		brooms pvc	pcs	30	21.87
		Brushes for washing bottles	pcs	100	36.44
		PVC brushes	pcs	20	10.93
		Illuminating lamps	pcs	10	11.66
		Different paint	1	100	388.74
		Caustic soda	Kg	7000	3,061.32
		Calcined soda	Kg	3500	1,020.44
		Trisodium phosphate	kg	3000	1,749.33
		Metal staples	pcs	2000000	9,146.80
		Cork plugs	pcs	320000	14,955.02
		Thermo caps	pcs	680000	7,094.49
		Filter board	pcs	16000	28,583.76
		Cardboard boxes	pcs	25000	11,433.50
		Gelux rolls	pcs	800	291.55
		Label wine 0.75	pcs	310000	1,196.23
		Label winw 1/1	pcs	1930000	7,447.50

continued on following page

Table 3. Continued

		armbands	pcs	2230000	18,141.89
		PVC shuttles		500	824.53
		Bottles 1/1		70000	11,004.75
		Bottles 0.75		15000	2,358.16
	Total A3.3				**3,191,811.00**
	Total P3				**3191811**

Source: Authors' own calculations

In which: Cg = the cost of grapes; i = the current period; and Cpcrag = the proportional costs related to the activities rendered for the collection of grapes.

For the other activities, the relationship will be a recurring one, as follows:

$$Cost\ of\ raw\ materials_i = Crm_{i-1} + Cpcrsa_{i-1} \quad (2)$$

Unde: Crm_{i-1} = cost of raw $material_{i-1}$; i-1 = previous period;

$Cpcrsa_{i-1}$= the proportional costs related to the specific $activities_{i-1}$.

Following the allocation of direct costs on the activities identified under the ABC method, the following situation resulted in Table 3.

The next step is to allocate indirect costs to cost drivers. For this purpose, following the discussions with the employees, the percentages of the allocation of resources by activities were decisive. The final results of the application of the percentages previously determined on the expenses incurred by the auxiliary departments are presented in Table 4.

In order to calculate the unit cost by activities and by products, it is necessary to quantitatively determine the cost drivers, which is made based on the production technological records, and the accounting data (Table 5).

Applying the ABC method is not easy due to the large volume of calculations and the need for information obtained from both the accounting documents, the technology sheets and the discussions with the staff, but the use of specialized software fit to the company specific, even if it involves an initial investment that it may seem significant, it brings significant benefits in the area of managerial accounting.

Another utility of applying the ABC method is to use the data provided by it, in applying the Balanced Scorecard (BSC) method, the second part of the case study aiming to demonstrate how the two methods can be integrated in order to achieve the entity's strategic goals.

The purpose of implementing the Balanced Scorecard (BSC) method consisted in: (1) facilitating the achievement of the economic entity's mission and achieving the set objectives; (2) aligning the activity of the economic entity with the standards existing in the winemaking industry; (3) ensuring coherence between existing activities redefined in the context of the strategic managerial approach; (4) offering a tool for evaluating the activity and measuring the progress. Synthetically, the key objectives pursued by

Table 4. Allocation of indirect costs by activities

Activities	A1.1	A1.2	A1.3	A2.1	A2.2	A2.3	A2.4	A3.1	A3.2	A3.3
Administrative dep										
- salaries	2,204.56	2,204.56	2,204.56	6,613.69	8,818.26	6,613.69	4,409.13	4,409.13	2,204.56	4,409.13
- metrological checks	-	465.90	-	931.80	1,397.70	931.80	931.80	-	-	-
- advertising expenses and protocol	-	-	-	-	-	-	-	-	-	56,780.00
- licenses	-	-	-	1,552.50	1,552.50	1,552.50	1,552.50	-	-	-
-expenses sanitation	514.51	257.25	257.25	1,029.02	257.25	257.25	771.76	514.51	514.51	771.76
- expenses different materials	1,236.00	1,236.00	1,236.00	1,236.00	1,236.00	1,236.00	1,236.00	1,236.00	1,236.00	1,236.00
Mechanical workshop										
- salary	-	-	-	1,255.70	1,883.55	1,883.55	1,883.55	3,767.10	1,883.55	-
-electricity	-	-	-	65.80	98.70	98.70	98.70	197.40	98.70	-
-expenses workshop maintenance	-	-	-	93.50	140.25	140.25	140.25	280.50	140.25	-
- mat. repairs	-	-	-	378.60	567.90	567.90	567.90	1,135.80	567.90	-
- exp. repair and maintenance sections	-	-	-	421.90	632.85	632.85	632.85	1,265.70	632.85	-
The boiler										
-salary	-	-	-	114.89	689.34	689.34	344.67	344.67	114.89	-
- exp. repairs	-	-	-	67.53	405.17	405.17	202.59	202.59	67.53	-
- water	-	-	-	71.30	427.80	427.80	213.90	213.90	71.30	-
- electric	-	-	-	646.43	3,878.60	3,878.60	1,939.30	1,939.30	646.43	-
-fuel	-	-	-	4,141.79	24,850.72	24,850.72	12,425.36	12,425.36	4,141.79	-
-consumables	-	-	-	137.28	823.71	823.71	411.85	411.85	137.28	-
-mat. auxiliary	-	-	-	282.98	1,697.88	1,697.88	848.94	848.94	282.98	-
Technological water station										
- salaries	-	-	-	201.47	302.21	302.21	302.21	302.21	302.21	302.21
-exp. repairs	-	-	-	40.02	60.03	60.03	60.03	60.03	60.03	60.03
- raw materials	-	-	-	116.00	174.00	174.00	174.00	174.00	174.00	174.00
- energy	-	-	-	1,649.06	174.00	174.00	174.00	174.00	174.00	174.00
-mat. auxiliary	-	-	-	48.59	72.89	72.89	72.89	72.89	72.89	72.89
Refrigeration plant										
- salaries	-	-	-	-	-	402.94	402.94	402.94	402.94	402.94
- electric energy	-	-	-	-	-	10,995.42	10,995.42	10,995.42	10,995.42	10,995.42
- raw-materials	-	-	-	-	-	1,539.40	1,539.40	1,539.40	1,539.40	1,539.40
- consumables	-	-	-	-	-	752.32	752.32	752.32	752.32	752.32
TOTAL	**3,955.07**	**4,163.72**	**3,697.82**	**21,095.86**	**50,141.30**	**61,160.92**	**43,084.26**	**43,665.96**	**27,213.74**	**77,670.10**

Source: Authors' own calculations

Table 5. Calculation of the unit cost of production by ABC method for the Riesling Italian assortment

Activities	Direct costs	Indirect costs	Overall cost	Value driver	Cost/ driver	UNIT	Value inductor/ variety	UNIT
A1.1	2,926,400.00	3,955.07	2,930,355.07	365.8 wag.	8,010.81	lei/wag.	0.8011	lei/kg
A 1.2	2,898.54	4,163.72	7,062.26	365.8 wag.	19.31	lei/wag.	0.0019	lei/kg
A 1.3	194.30	3,697.82	3,892.12	365.8 wag.	10.64	lei/wag.	0.0011	lei/kg
	2,929,492.84	**11,816.61**	**2,941,309.45**		8,040.76	lei/wag.	0.8041	lei/kg
A2.1	5,797.60	21,095.86	26,893.46	9 wine varieties	2,988.16	lei/variety		
A2.2	4,527.22	50,141.30	54,668.52	6 days	9,111.42	lei/day	2,024.76	lei/variety
A2.3	13,407.49	61,160.92	74,568.41	30 days	2,485.61	lei/day	1,104.72	lei/variety
A2.4	1,200.00	43,084.26	44,284.26	120 days	69.04	lei/day	3,690.35	lei/variety
	2,954,425.15	**187,298.94**	**3,141,724.09**					
A3.1	497.01	43,665.96	44,162.97	100000 bottles	0.44	lei/bottle	0.44	lei/bottle
A3.2	63,423.75	27,213.74	90,637.49	100000 bottles	0.91	lei/bottle	0.91	lei/bottle
A3.3	173,465.09	77,670.10	251,135.19	100000 bottles	2.51	lei/bottle	2.51	lei/bottle
	3,191,811.00	**335,848.74**	**3,527,659.74**		35.28			
	Total cost of production						**6,825.2996**	
	Quantity						**1,000.00**	
	Unit cost of production						**6.83**	

Source: Authors' own calculations

implementing the Balanced Scorecard (BSC) method were: (1) the focus on creating Value and developing new business opportunities; (2) focus on the quality of the products offered; (3) increasing investor confidence by ensuring greater transparency of activities and their results; (4) the focus on the personal development of employees in the context of sustainable economic development.

Stage (1) Define the vision, the mission and the strategy. The purpose of defining the vision, mission and strategy is to ensure the coherence between the developed performance measures (indicators) characteristic of each BSC perspective and the strategic objectives of the economic entity. Also, a clear definition of the above elements allows employees to both visualize and understand the links between performance indicators and the achievement of strategic goals. In this sense, it is necessary to determine the point that the economic entity is expected to reach the near future.

Defining the company's vision: Due to the fast changes and the evolution of the winemaking industry from a fragmented agricultural activity to a professional industry, as well as changing the demand of customers, the success of the economic entity can only be achieved by managing these changes, by continuously adapting to innovation, to the demands of the market and its complexity as well as to the needs of the consumers.

The mission of the company: (1) reaching a market share that will ensure the economic entity the leading position at national level, as well as positioning in the first ten European wine producers; (2)

strengthening the position on the local market by offering quality wines and expanding the distribution network, especially exports; (3) the sustainable growth of the business both from the perspective of the turnover and of maximizing the value for the shareholders.

Company strategy: (1) expanding the distribution network; (2) the introduction of new varieties of wine in the production process; (3) maintaining and consolidating the position held on the market of wine producers; (4) rapid adaptation to changes in the local and international wine market; (5) reducing dependence on certain markets or product groups.

The main values of the company refer to: (1) the focus on consumer requirements; (2) customer loyalty; (3) focus on quality and sustainability of the business; (4) maintaining a friendly atmosphere in the relations with the employees; (5) practicing the business respecting the ethical values, with honesty and integrity.

Stage 2. Development of operational objectives that characterize the performance, of indicators to quantify their achievement and of targets to be achieved. The operational objectives that characterize the performance concern those aspects of the activity that must be efficient and effective in order to achieve the vision. Based on these objectives, the performance indicators to be calculated are defined and their measures are established over a period of time (3-5 years).

In creating performance measures, the link between them and the strategic vision of the economic entity was considered. Also, at least one objective defined by the four perspectives was associated with at least one performance characterization indicator associated with that objective. The indicators have been precisely defined, including the object of the calculation, the method of quantification, the source of the data and the time period during which the evaluation is done. In defining or choosing indicators, we considered the inclusion of both quantitative and qualitative sizes.

Even if quantitative sizes provide objective information that can serve to justify managerial decisions related to resource allocation, qualitative measurements are equally important, even if they have a high degree of subjectivity being based on the experiences of customers, managers or employees. What is essential, however, is to ensure a balance between qualitative and quantitative indicators. Table 6, table 7, table 8 and table 9 present the four specific BSC dimensions that are highlighted: the objectives, indicators, targets to be achieved, as well as the actions to be taken.

Table 6. The financial dimension

Objectives	Indicators	Targets	Actions/initiatives
Maintaining a certain level of current liquidity to ensure normal activity	Cash flows	- maintaining a constant level of cash flows	- tracking of receivables
Keeping the turnover at a level at least equal to that of the previous year	Turnover; Change in turnover	- increase in turnover by at least 5% compared to the previous year	- bi-monthly analysis of turnover
Increased profit	Market share; Financial rates: ROI, ROE	- 10% increase in market share; - the existence of a positive change in the value of the financial rates calculated in comparison with the previous year	- monthly market share analysis - monthly calculation of financial efficiency indicators

Source: The economic entity's vision

Table 7. The customer dimension

Objectives	Indicators	Targets	Actions/initiatives
Development of new varieties of wine	Percentage of sales of new varieties of wine from total sales; The ratio of new varieties / existing varieties	-Value of the indicator of at least 5%; - growth of new products by 10% compared to the previous year	-monitoring the research-development activity - permanent analysis of the market, especially of the main competitors
Developing partnerships with important clients	Change in the number of permanent customers	- increase of permanent customers by 20%; - attracting a minimum of 4 clients from the international market	- Permanent contact with potential clients from the internal and external market - extension of distribution channels - efficiency of the activity of the sales department
Ensure continuous distribution	Timely distribution of products (appreciated by customers)	- obtaining a score of minimum 4 offered by customers (on a scale from 1-5) on the speed of order fulfillment	- drawing up questionnaires and completing them by the main clients
Actions for improving the client fidelity	The situation of sales by customers and periods	- increased sales by at least 5% on each customer over one year old	- the bi-monthly preparation of the sales reports and the analysis of their dynamics

Source: The economic entity's vision

Table 8. Internal processes

Objectives	Indicators	Targets	Actions/initiatives
Improvement of operation lines	The value of investments in relation to turnover	- increase of investments with respect to the previous year by a minimum of 10%	- analysis of investment needs
Enhanced efficiency of process lines	The time value of the production cycle on wine varieties The unit cost of each variety of wine Operational profit on wine varieties	- decrease of the production cycle - decrease of the production cost by at least 5% - increase of operating profit by at least 5%	- the re-technologization of the processing lines - the analysis of the production costs by the ABC method - monthly analysis of the operational profit by categories of activities and products and identification of the areas that can be made more efficient
Product design	Number of changes made to the labels	- modification of at least 25% of the product labels	- the existence of a permanent concern for product design
Introducing new products	The ratio new products/ existing products	- introduction of at least 2 new products	- monitoring the progress related to the development of new products - permanent analysis of the competitors' market

Source: The economic entity's vision

Table 9. Growing and learning

Objectives	Indicators	Targets	Actions/initiatives
Increasing the qualification and specialization of the personnel	Number of trainings /No. of employees Percentage of employees trained periodically	- increase by 15% of the trainings carried out compared to the previous year - 40% increase in the number of employees participating in the training activities	- development of a human resources development plan by the specialized department - identification of training needs of staff - monitoring the performances of the employees participating in training activities
Focus on product quality	No. of scrap / Production value	- weekly analysis of the number of rejections Decreasing the number of rejects by at least 10% compared to the previous year	- identification of the causes of the existence of rejects
Introducing new products	Number of products introduced/number of products introduced by the main competitor	- the introduction of a minimum of two new products	- permanent analysis of the market - efficiency of the activity of the R&D department - identifying potential market opportunities for niche products

Source: The economic entity's vision

As can be seen from the analysis of the elements contained in the four dimensions designed for the implementation of the BSC method, the method aims at the future of the economic entity, and what it wants to achieve. The central point of the method refers to strategy and vision, and not to the exercise of excessive control, and the central premise is that the employees will adopt the necessary behaviors and exercise their attributions to achieve them. Therefore, defining concrete measures to evaluate the four dimensions is very important in order to provide employees with a basis for self-evaluation and subsequently for evaluation.

The dashboard is an important tool in obtaining numerous reports and situations widely used by the management of an economic entity. The entity does not use an efficient computer system and therefore no component related to the dashboard. With the help of the dashboard, it could generate reports such as: (1) analysis of the commercial flow for customers and suppliers (it presents the situation of the invoices received, respectively paid, and the differences determined by the exchange rate variation); (2) sales analysis (by agents, counties, localities, months, partners, products, etc.); (3) evolutions of cash flows, exchange rates, stocks; (4) the situation of the invoices received, respectively paid; (5) the situation of the orders. The analysis can be performed both on the basis of graphs and reports.

A very important report that is confined to the dashboard is that concerning the sales agents. The report presents the total and average points obtained during the current month, respectively year by an agent. This report was generated after a number of visits to potential customers had previously been made. The report presents information taken from the Visits forms, grouped by partners. The data refer to the following characteristics: sales agent, date of visit, number of visit, duration of the visit, purpose of the visit, start and end time of the visit, date of the next visit, future purpose, kilometers traveled, rating awarded, tasks, self-assessment of the activity, problems encountered, activity evaluation, observations. An example of this report is shown in Table 10. The report was designed starting from two objectives: on the one hand the supervision of the activity carried out by the agents of the company as well as their monitoring according to the individual achievements.

Table 10. Sales agents report

Visits made to the client	
Partner: S.C. SERIC S.A.	
Sales agent name	Iftimoaie Costel
Date	20.05.2012
Nr. visit	1
Travel time	110 minutes
Purpose	Product presentation
Visiting start time	09:00
Time to visit	15:00
Next visit date	25.05.2012
Aim for future visits	Catalog presentation
Km traveled	120
Rating	Not granted
Self-evaluation	Promoter (potential customer)
Problems	They were not identified
Remarks	Company with a very large retail market, customers and very select products sold.

Source: authors' own vision

Another report circumscribed to the dashboard is that concerning the commercial flow of customers. This situation calculates the commercial addition related to the products whose value was received from the customers, relating the invoices received with those issued. The report displays information related to a complete business cycle, from the issuance of the offer to the receipt of the invoice (Table 11). The report is particularly important for the commercial department of the company for assessing the contracts and clauses obtained by each agent individually. Also, the report tracks the collection time on each client, and it is subsequently used to forecast cash flows based on the average collection time that can be calculated on each client. The information provided by this report is especially useful to the legal department because they allow the compliance of the contractual clauses regarding the payment terms by each client.

Table 11. Customer commercial flow

Agent	Partener	Invoice no.	Series	Date	Paid	Total value	Paid	Rest	Date of collection	Duration of collection
Iftimoaie Costel	Simeco S.R.L.	1108894	BYVDJ	15.02.08	Yes	1120	1120	0	18.02.12	3 days
Duda Ionuţ	Amadeus S.R.L.	1108895	BYVDJ	16.02.08	No	2425	2000	425	20.02.12	
Florescu Angel	PIV S.R.L.	1108896	BYVDJ	17.02.08	Yes	1310	1310	0	17.02.12	0 days

Source: Authors' own synthesis

Another report concerns the analysis of sales. The analysis of sales by agents, counties, localities, months, partners, regions or stocks is presented graphically, using as quantity, average price and value (Figure 1). This report is needed to establish future directions of action regarding target customers and how they can be attracted.

Figure 1. The situation of sales by geographical areas
Source: authors' own calculations

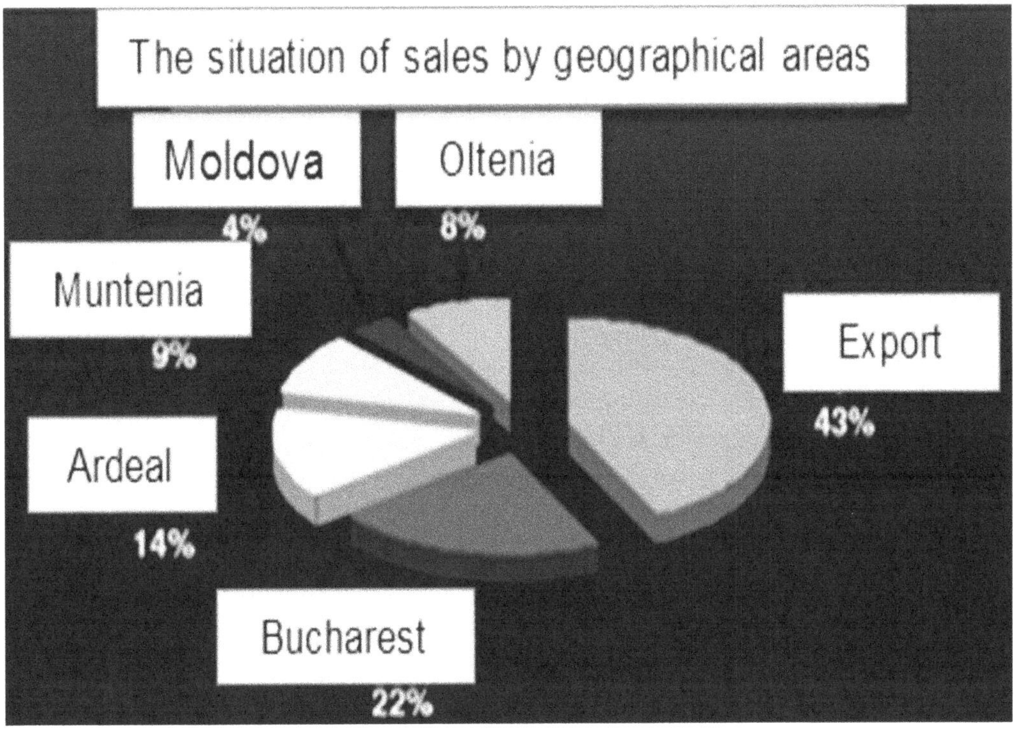

It is noted that a large share (43%) have exports during the period analyzed, which means that the company must make a series of investments necessary to expand international trade relations (appearance in foreign profile magazines, investment in the company's website, appearance on foreign specialized sites etc.).

One of the most interesting reports included in the dashboard is the one regarding the calculation of *performance indicators*. Within the report the indicators are grouped according to the type of indicator (eg performance indicator, structure indicator). The data presented are the following: (1) indicator name (the name is entered in formulas); (2) the minimum limit (is the limit that can be defined when introducing the calculation formula); (3) Value (is the calculated value of the indicator); (4) the maximum limit (is the limit that is defined when introducing the calculation formula). The initialization was made based on the information obtained from the financial statements for the years 2010, 2011 and 2012. For example, we considered the evolution of three indicators, namely: net result, expenses with raw materials at 1000 lei turnover and current liquidity (Table 12).

The report calculates a series of indicators considered relevant by the entity's management. Moreover, if the indicators do not fall between the minimum and the maximum set level, then it will be written in the report in red color, meaning that the entity has to take a series of measures to enter in optimal parameters.

Table 12. Evolution of economic and financial indicators by the economic entity (winemaking)

Indicator name	Minimum limit	2017	2018	2019	Maximum limit
Result of the exercise (Euro)	0	499.946	424.193	452.757	n/a
Depreciation expenses at 1000 lei turnover	0	21,63	31,78	29,77	25
General liquidity	1,4	1,22	1,35	1,49	2

Source: Authors' own calculations

The presented report analyzes in the first part the evolution of the net result in real sizes (Euro), pointing to a decrease in 2018 compared to 2017 and a recovery in the year 2019. This fluctuation is due to the change in the range of products offered to the market in 2018, in the sense that this year the entity focused on the production expected to have a much larger market in the future. Regarding the second calculated indicator, Expenses with depreciation at 1,000 lei Turnover, it is observed that it had a negative evolution during the analyzed period, fact evidenced by "entering the red zone". The entity registered an increase of this indicator due to the investment plan, which contributed to an increase in the value of fixed assets, a situation that did not materialize in a significant increase in turnover. Finally, the general liquidity had a favorable evolution, moving from the "red zone" to the normal area. Both limits (minimum and maximum respectively) were set based on the particularities existing in the winemaking industry, with the existence of a safety stock to prevent stock breaks. The size of this indicator in the financial year 2019 signifies that the company has the capacity to cover its short-term liabilities by realizing short-term assets (cash, debt collection and stock trading respectively).

Another important situation for the choice of future accounting methods regarding stock valuation is the comparison of the discharge methods. This report allows a comparison between the values used for the discharge through different models of valuation of the outgoing stocks (FIFO, Weighted average cost, LIFO respectively). The situation is necessary in order to choose the optimal accounting method for the discharge. Currently, the entity uses the FIFO method for discharge, a method which, under the conditions of an inflationary economy, leads to an underestimation of expenses and, therefore, to an overestimation of profit. Thus, it is recommended to the management to use the LIFO method for the unloading from the management of the stocks, obviously to the extent that this method will be allowed by the international reference accounting standards.

SOLUTIONS AND RECOMMENDATIONS

In view of the issues addressed during this chapter, we propose to the specialists and to all those interested, the following improvement solutions:

- adopting strategic management in formulating strategies, and implicitly the use of strategic management accounting as the main source of information needed to formulate strategic decisions.
- development of current management accounting systems through their integrated use, which guarantees obtaining complete information, the efficiency of strategic decisions and improving the performance of an organization;
- implementation of information technology (IT) type Big Data Analytics or software packages dedicated to strategic management accounting methods such as: Activity-Based Costing/Activity-Based Management (ABC/ABM), (Anghelache et al., 2019; Căpușneanu et al., 2019; Constantin et al., 2019), Economic Resource Planning (ERP), Balanced Scorecard (BSC) etc.

Based on the concepts discussed above, we recommend to the specialists and to all those interested in deepening the strategic management accounting the following aspects:

- research of specialized literature regarding the successful adoption and implementation of new innovative technologies along with other strategic management accounting tools such as ABC/M, ERP, Balanced Scorecard, LCC, Target costing, etc.
- research at national and global level of the impact produced by the new innovative technologies on the strategic management accounting at the level of the entities/organizations that have implemented them.
- adapting and extending the culture of management accountants regarding the advantages and limitations offered by strategic management accounting.
- Extending the culture of information technology within companies/organizations that have adopted or wish to adopt software packages dedicated to strategic management accounting and improving the performance of an organization.

FUTURE RESEARCH DIRECTIONS

Through the objectives set out in this chapter, we consider that we have reached our target in the business or academic environment. The chosen topic is current and of future interest for all categories of interested specialists. The amount of information presented covers a wide range of international specialty literature dedicated to strategic management accounting.

This amount of information was synthesized in an attempt to present segments with real future research directions. By this, we suggest to the specialists and to all those interested the following research directions:

- analyzing the possibilities of adapting and implementing the new innovative technologies to other strategic management accounting methods, existing or to the integrated methods used;
- analysis of the position of the management accountants regarding the new concepts and tools of the strategic management accounting within an entity/organization;
- analysis of the impact of the strategic managerial decisions resulted by adapting or implementing other strategic management accounting tools, as well as their impact on the cost or performance management of an entity/organization.

CONCLUSION

Due to its structure, this chapter covers some segments dedicated to the conceptual approaches of strategic management accounting and its dimensions, as well as the impact produced by the use of integrated methods on the cost and performance management of an economic entity. As strengths of this chapter, the following can be mentioned:

- it fills some existing gaps in the field of strategic management accounting and the influence of its dimensions on the management accountants by interpreting the debated conceptual approaches, including their advantages;
- analyzes some hypotheses of strategic management and strategic management accounting and of the role of the management accountant in the conditions of their application within an organization;
- presents a case study on the integrated use of strategic management accounting tools (ABC and BSC) within an economic entity in the winemaking industry and some proposals for generating reporting situations that can be starting points in the future analysis of research undertaken.

Through the contribution made to the realization of this chapter and through the challenges launched along the lines of adopting and implementing strategic management accounting tools, we are confident that new research directions have been launched. All that remains is the involvement of the specialists in the extension of the research framework launched and the continuation of the effort started in identifying new opportunities to substantiate the managerial strategic decisions with direct effect on the improvement of the performance of an entity/organization.

REFERENCES

Adler, R. W. (2000). Strategic investment decision appraisal techniques: The old and the new. *Business Horizons*, *43*(6), 15–22. doi:10.1016/S0007-6813(00)80017-8

Agasisti, T., Arnaboldi, M., & Azzone, G. (2008). Strategic management accounting in universities: The Italian experience. *Higher Education*, *55*(1), 1–15. doi:10.100710734-006-9032-6

Alamri, A. M. (2018). Strategic Management Accounting and the Dimensions of Competitive Advantage: Testing the Associations in Saudi Industrial Sector, *International Journal of Academic Research in Accounting*. *Finance and Management Sciences*, *8*(2), 48–64.

Alkaraan, F., & Northcott, D. (2006). Strategic capital investment decision-making: A role for emergent analysis tools? A study of practice in large UK manufacturing companies. *The British Accounting Review*, *38*(2), 149–173. doi:10.1016/j.bar.2005.10.003

Andon, P., & Baxter, J. (2011). Introducing and contextualising customer lifetime valuation: A management accounting teaching resource. *Accounting Education*, *20*(1), 39–61. doi:10.1080/09639284.2010.543342

Anik, R., Nadjadji, A., & Suwignjo, P. (2010). Analysis of internal and external factors for competitive advantage of Indonesian contractors. *Journal of Economics and Engineering*, *2*(4), 51–68.

Atkinson, A. A., Kaplan, R. S., Matsumura, E. M., & Young, S. M. (2012). *Management accounting – Information for decision-making and strategy execution* (6th ed.). Pearson Prentice Hall.

Baines, A., & Langfield-Smith, K. (2003). Antecedents to management accounting change: A structural equation approach. *Accounting, Organizations and Society, 28*(7-8), 675–698. doi:10.1016/S0361-3682(02)00102-2

Baroto, M. B., Abdullah, M. M. B., & Wan, H. L. (2012). Hybrid strategy: A new strategy for competitive advantage. *International Journal of Business and Management, 7*(20), 120–133.

Bhimani, A., & Langfield-Smith, K. (2007). Structure, formality and the importance of financial and nonfinancial information in strategy development and implementation. *Management Accounting Research, 18*(1), 3–31. doi:10.1016/j.mar.2006.06.005

Brem, A., Maier, M., & Wimschneider, C. (2016). Competitive advantage through innovation: The case of Nespresso. *European Journal of Innovation Management, 19*(1), 133–148. doi:10.1108/EJIM-05-2014-0055

Bromwich, M. (1990). The case for strategic management accounting: The role of accounting information for strategy in competitive markets. *Accounting, Organizations and Society, 15*(1-2), 27–46. doi:10.1016/0361-3682(90)90011-I

Bromwich, M., & Bhimani, A. (1994). *Management accountant pathways to progress.* The Chatered Institute of Management Accountants.

Brouthers, K. D., & Roozen, F. A. (1999). Is it time start thinking about strategic accounting? *Long Range Planning, 32*(3), 311–322. doi:10.1016/S0024-6301(99)00035-7

Cadez, S., & Guilding, C. (2008). An exploratory investigation of integrated contingency model of strategy management accounting. *Accounting, Organizations and Society, 33*(7-8), 836–863. doi:10.1016/j.aos.2008.01.003

Carlsson-Wall, M., Kraus, K., & Lind, J. (2015). Strategic management accounting in close interorganisational relationships. *Accounting and Business Research, 45*(1), 27–54. doi:10.1080/00014788.2014.965128

Carr, C., Kolehmainen, K., & Mitchell, F. (2010). Strategic investment decision making practices: A contextual approach. *Management Accounting Research, 21*(3), 167–184. doi:10.1016/j.mar.2010.03.004

Carr, C., & Tomkins, C. (1996). Strategic investment decisions: The importance of SCM. A comparative analysis of 51 case studies in U.K., U.S. and German companies. *Management Accounting Research, 7*(2), 199–217. doi:10.1006/mare.1996.0012

Chen, Y., Hsu, J., Huang, M., & Yang, P. (2013). Quality, size, and performance of audit firms. *The International Journal of Business and Finance Research, 7*(5), 89–105.

Chenhall, R. H. (2008). Accounting for the horizontal organization: A review essay. *Accounting, Organizations and Society, 33*(4-5), 517–550. doi:10.1016/j.aos.2007.07.004

Chiucchi, M. S. (2013). Intellectual capital accounting in action: Enhancing learning through interventionist research. *Journal of Intellectual Capital, 14*(1), 48–68. doi:10.1108/14691931311289011

Cinquini, L., & Tenucci, A. (2010). Strategic management accounting and business strategy: A loose coupling? *Journal of Accounting and Organizational Change*, *6*(2), 228–259. doi:10.1108/18325911011048772

Coad, A. (1996). Smart work and hard work: Explicating a learning orientation in strategic management accounting. *Management Accounting Research*, *7*(4), 387–408. doi:10.1006/mare.1996.0022

Combe, A. (2012). Marketing and flexibility: Debates past, present and future. *European Journal of Marketing*, *46*(10), 1257–1267. doi:10.1108/03090561211248116

Cooper, R. (1996). Costing techniques to support corporate strategy: Evidence from Japan. *Management Accounting Research*, *7*(2), 219–246. doi:10.1006/mare.1996.0013

Cravens, K. S., & Guilding, C. (1999). Strategic brand valuation: A cross-functional perspective. *Business Horizons*, *42*(4), 53–62. doi:10.1016/S0007-6813(99)80064-0

Cravens, K. S., & Guilding, C. (2001). An empirical study of the application of strategic management accounting techniques. *Advances in Management Accounting*, *10*, 95–124.

Cuganesan, S., Dunford, R., & Palmer, I. (2012). Strategic management accounting and strategy practiceswithin a public sector agency. *Management Accounting Research*, *23*(4), 245–260. doi:10.1016/j.mar.2012.09.001

Cummings, S., & Daellenbach, U. (2009). A guide to the future of strategy? The history of Long Range Planning. *Long Range Planning*, *42*(2), 234–263. doi:10.1016/j.lrp.2008.12.005

Daru, M. (2016). Total Quality Management (TQM): A strategy for competitive advantage. *International Journal of Research in IT and Management*, *6*(9), 51–55.

Dent, J. F. (1996). Global competition: Challenges for management accounting and control. *Management Accounting Research*, *7*(2), 247–269. doi:10.1006/mare.1996.0014

Diab, S. M. (2014). Using the competitive dimensions to achieve competitive advantage: A study on Jordanian private hospitals. *International Journal of Academic Research in Business and Social Sciences*, *4*(9), 138–150. doi:10.6007/IJARBSS/v4-i9/1136

Dixon, R. (1998). Accounting for strategic management: A practical application. *Long Range Planning*, *31*(2), 272–279. doi:10.1016/S0024-6301(98)00011-9

Dixon, R., & Smith, D. (1993). Strategic Management Accounting. *Omega*, *21*(6), 605–618. doi:10.1016/0305-0483(93)90003-4

Eryesil, K., Esmen, O., & Beduk, A. (2015). The role of strategic flexibility for achieving sustainable competition advantage and its effect on business performance. *World Academy of Science, Engineering and Technology*, *9*(10), 587–593.

Ewert, R., & Ernst, C. (1999). Target costing, co-ordination and strategic cost management. *European Accounting Review*, *8*(1), 23–49. doi:10.1080/096381899336131

Fauré, B., & Rouleau, L. (2011). The strategic competence of accountants and middle managers in budget making. *Accounting, Organizations and Society*, *36*(3), 167–182. doi:10.1016/j.aos.2011.04.001

Feeney, O., & Pierce, B. (2007). Today's management accountant: Honest bean counter and savvy business advisor? *Accountancy Ireland*, *39*, 16–21.

Furrer, O., Thomas, H., & Goussevskaia, A. (2008). The structure and evolution of the strategic management field: A content analysis of 26 years of strategic management research. *International Journal of Management Reviews*, *10*(1), 1–23. doi:10.1111/j.1468-2370.2007.00217.x

Guilding, C., Cravens, K. S., & Tayles, M. (2000). An international comparison of strategic management accounting practices. *Management Accounting Research*, *11*(1), 113–135. doi:10.1006/mare.1999.0120

Guilding, C., & McManus, L. (2002). The incidence, perceived merit and antecedents of customer accounting: An exploratory note. *Accounting, Organizations and Society*, *27*(1-2), 45–59. doi:10.1016/S0361-3682(01)00030-7

Hiller, K., Mahlendorf, M. D., & Weber, J. (2014). Management accountants' occupational prestige within the company: A social identity theory perspective. *European Accounting Review*, *23*(4), 671–691. doi:10.1080/09638180.2013.849204

Horngren, C. T., Datar, S. M., & Rajan, M. V. (2012). *Cost accounting – A managerial emphasis* (14th ed.). Pearson Prentice Hall.

Kaplan, R. S., & Norton, D. P. (2001). Transforming the balanced scorecard form performance measurement to strategic management: Part II. *Accounting Horizons*, *15*(2), 147–160. doi:10.2308/acch.2001.15.2.147

Krajewski, L. J., & Ritzman, L. P. (2005). *Operations Management* (7th ed.). Prentice Hall.

Lambert, C., & Pezet, E. (2011). The making of the management accountant – Becoming the producer of truthful knowledge. *Accounting, Organizations and Society*, *36*(1), 10–30. doi:10.1016/j.aos.2010.07.005

Langfield-Smith, K. (2008). Strategic management accounting: How far have we come in 25 years? *Accounting, Auditing & Accountability Journal*, *21*(2), 204–228. doi:10.1108/09513570810854400

Lord, B. R. (1996). Strategic management accounting: The emperor's new clothes? *Management Accounting Research*, *7*(3), 347–366. doi:10.1006/mare.1996.0020

Ma, Y., & Tayles, M. (2009). On the emergence of strategic management accounting: An institutional perspective. *Accounting and Business Research*, *39*(5), 473–495. doi:10.1080/00014788.2009.9663379

McManus, L. (2013). Customer accounting and marketing performance measures in the hotel industry: Evidence from Australia. *International Journal of Hospitality Management*, *33*, 140–152. doi:10.1016/j.ijhm.2012.07.007

McManus, L., & Guilding, C. (2008). Exploring the potential of customer accounting: A synthesis of the accounting and marketing literatures. *Journal of Marketing Management*, *24*(7-8), 771–795. doi:10.1362/026725708X345515

Naliaka, V. W., & Namusonge, G. S. (2015). Role of inventory management on competitive advantage among manufacturing firms in Kenya: A case study of UNGA Group Limited. *International Journal of Academic Research in Business and Social Sciences*, *5*(5), 87–104.

Nixon, B., & Burns, J. (2012). The paradox of strategic management accounting. *Management Accounting Research, 23*(4), 229–244. doi:10.1016/j.mar.2012.09.004

Nyamori, R. O., Perrera, M. H. B., & Lawrence, S. R. (2001). The concept of strategic change and implications for management accounting research. *Journal of Accounting Literature, 20*, 62–83.

Pires, R.A.R., Alves, M.C.G., & Rodrigues, L. L. (2015). Strategic management accounting: definitions and dimensions. In XVIII Congreso AECA Innovación y internacionalización: factores de éxito para la pyme. *Cartagena*, 1-17.

Prajogo, C., & McDermott, P. (2011). Examining competitive priorities and competitive advantage in service organisations using Importance-Performance Analysis matrix. *Managing Service Quality, 21*(5), 465–483. doi:10.1108/09604521111159780

Ranjith, V. (2016). Business Models and Competitive Advantage. *Procedia Economics and Finance, 37*, 203–207. doi:10.1016/S2212-5671(16)30114-9

Roslender, R., & Hart, S. J. (2003). In search of strategic management accounting: Theoretical and field study perspectives. *Management Accounting Research, 14*(3), 255–279. doi:10.1016/S1044-5005(03)00048-9

Roslender, R., & Hart, S. J. (2006). Interfunctional Cooperation in progressing accounting for brands: The case for brand management accounting. *Journal of Accounting & Organizational Change, 2*(3), 229–247. doi:10.1108/18325910610690072

Roslender, R., & Hart, S. J. (2010). Taking the customer into account: Transcending the construction of the customer through the promotion of self-accounting. *Critical Perspectives on Accounting, 21*(8), 739–753. doi:10.1016/j.cpa.2010.04.002

Sachitra, V., Chong, S. C., & Khin, A. A. (2016). Sources of competitive advantage measurement in the minor export Crop Sector in Sri Lanka result from pilot study. *Asian Journal of Agricultural Extension. Economia e Sociologia, 12*(2), 1–15.

Scott, T. W., & Tiessen, P. (1999). Performance measurement and managerial teams. *Accounting, Organizations and Society, 24*(3), 263–285. doi:10.1016/S0361-3682(98)00060-9

Shank, J. K., & Govindarajan, V. (1992). Strategic cost management: The value chain perspective. *Journal of Management Accounting Research, 4*, 179–198.

Sigalas, Ch., Economou, V. P., & Georgopoulos, N. B. (2013). Developing a measure of competitive advantage. *Journal of Strategy and Management, 6*(4), 320–342. doi:10.1108/JSMA-03-2013-0015

Simmonds, K. (1981). Strategic management accounting. *Management Accounting, 59*, 26–30.

Simmonds, K. (1982). Strategic management accounting for pricing: A case example. *Accounting and Business Research, 47*(47), 206–214. doi:10.1080/00014788.1982.9728809

Tan, H. P., Plowman, D., & Hancock, P. (2008). The evolving research on intellectual capital. *Journal of Intellectual Capital, 9*(4), 585–608. doi:10.1108/14691930810913177

Tayles, M., Pike, R. H., & Sofian, S. (2007). Intellectual capital, management accounting practices and corporate performance: Perceptions of managers. *Accounting, Auditing & Accountability Journal*, *20*(4), 522–548. doi:10.1108/09513570710762575

Tillmann, K., & Goddard, A. (2008). Strategic management accounting and sense-making in a multinational company. *Management Accounting Research*, *19*(1), 80–102. doi:10.1016/j.mar.2007.11.002

Weinstein, A. (2012). *Superior customer value: strategies for winning and retaining customers* (3rd ed.). CRC Press-Taylor & Francis Group.

ADDITIONAL READING

Anghelache, C., Căpuşneanu, S., Topor, D. I., & Marin-Pantelescu, A. (2019). Target Costing and Its Impact on Business Strategy: Computer Program for Cost Accounting and Administration. In I. Oncioiu (Ed.), *Network Security and Its Impact on Business Strategy* (pp. 20–43). IGI Global, USA. doi:10.4018/978-1-5225-8455-1.ch002

Căpuşneanu, S., Topor, D. I., Türkeş, M. C., & Rakoş, I.-S. (2019). Throughput Accounting: Decisional Informational Support for Optimizing Entity's Profit. In I. Oncioiu (Ed.), *Throughput Accounting in a Hyperconnected World* (pp. 27–56). IGI Global, USA. doi:10.4018/978-1-5225-7712-6.ch002

Constantin, D. M., Topor, D. I., Căpuşneanu, S., Türkeş, M. C., & Anghel, M.-G. (2019). Green Reporting and Its Impact on Business Strategy: Computer Program for Evidence and Green Reporting. In I. Oncioiu (Ed.), *Network Security and Its Impact on Business Strategy* (pp. 91–109). IGI Global, USA. doi:10.4018/978-1-5225-8455-1.ch006

KEY TERMS AND DEFINITIONS

Activity-Based Costing (ABC): An accounting method that identifies the costs of (indirect) activities and then allocates these costs to the products. The allocation of the costs of the activities on the products is realized through the cost drivers.

Balanced Scorecard (BSC): Tool for measuring the performance of strategic management used to provide a feedback on identifying and improving internal business functions and external results.

Strategic Management Accounting (SMA): Part of the management accounting dedicated to developing and monitoring the business strategy by providing analysis documents based on the internal and external information of the other competitors of the company.

Chapter 2
Ethics in Accounting and Finance:
A South African Perspective

Vannie Naidoo
University of KwaZulu-Natal, South Africa

ABSTRACT

Ethics forms the cornerstone of business and commerce today. It is the lifeblood of every institution be it private or public enterprise. Organisations have to develop and implement a properly structured policy on ethics outlaying proper governance within the institution. Accounting and finance services are crucial in managing a company's finances and wealth. In the accounting profession, in order for there to be transparency and trust, ethics is a crucial area that needs to be present. The many scandals and ethical dilemmas faced by countries organisations throughout the world has made us pause and take stock of what is happening in industry and has prompted action in law and governance towards ethics and corporate governance. South Africa too, has had its fair share of scandal that has had its legal fraternity, government, and business sector develop the Kings I, Kings II, Kings III, and Kings IV laws that stipulate corporate governance and ethics. Organisations have to be honest, professional, and transparent in their business practices.

INTRODUCTION

In today's business environment, the area of ethics is a very contentious issue that is becoming a major driver for responsible business practices world- wide. Corporate scandals have rocked economies throughout the world, which has resulted in us relooking at ways to improve the area of finance, and accounting, which have in recent years been plagued with issues of unethical behaviour. This unethical behaviour perpetuate within the organization, can have serious consequences to the shareholders' and other stakeholders of the organization and can affect the local and international economy in which the business operates. This ripple effect can have a catastrophic effect and ruin business relationships with

DOI: 10.4018/978-1-7998-4637-6.ch002

current and future investors. No economy can survive, if investors' perceptions about a countries business is poor.

The auditors and financial accountants within the organization have a moral obligation to the public to aspire to a strong ethical mind-set that they should consciously practice in their daily business dealings. Fostering goodwill in the business environment with stakeholders specifically is high on the agenda, in order to receive continued support and investment. It is important to reiterate that a strong investment climate depends on investors' having a high regard for the ethical standards implemented by business and confidence and trust in the organization. It is imperative for accountants and financial directors to take the lead in being vigilant in upholding a strong ethical code of conduct. If we turn to South Africa, this country has also been shamed in the media for unethical scandals that have soured investor trust.

To improve the country's business climate and attract foreign direct investment it is the duty and responsibility of the accounting and financial practitioners' to uphold and practise a strong code of ethics that can uplift, develop and sustain a positive business climate that investors can feel proud and confident to invest in. Transparency, honesty, good business practice and social responsibility should be the guiding principles to uphold the accounting and financial fraternity.

The discussion will start by firstly, highlighting different theorists' views on ethics in accounting and finance.

ETHICS IN ACCOUNTING AND FINANCE

To gain an understanding of ethics in accounting and finance, theorists have provided different views and insights on the subject. From all the different theorists' views explored by the researcher, an important realization has emerged namely; that ethics is crucial to the survival and growth of the accounting profession. A synergistic approach should be followed within the organization, in order for ethics to permeate the relevant structures of the organisation in a holistic manner. Since the main aim is to instil a high moral code of ethics in accounting and finance, this means that all accounting and finance staff at all levels within the organization should implement this in their daily business practices.

The discussion will now turn to defining ethics. The word "ethics" is etymologically derived from the Greek word "ethos", which means "character" or "manners" (Skorupski, 2003). Brinkmann (2002), defined ethics "as a discipline in which matter of right and wrong, good and evil, virtue and vice are methodically examined. Ethics looks at human behaviour, moral principles and the attempt to distinguish good from bad. When trying to identify common issues being dealt with within the business environment, professional bodies' codes of ethics is the right place to look. These codes represent what we can consider to be the reflection of business ethics. Codes of ethics should mainly address the particularities of high risk activities and are built on the collective conscience of a profession as a proof for the group's acknowledgment of the moral dimension". In a South African tertiary business ethics education module, Rossouw and Van Vuuren (2010) define ethics as: "Ethics concerns itself with what is good or right in human interaction. It revolves around three central concepts: 'self', 'good' and 'other'. Ethical behaviour results when one does not merely consider what is good for oneself, but also considers what is good for others. It is important that each of these three central concepts be included in a definition of ethics".

Ethical standards are thought to first be introduced and developed at the home front, by the family members or guardians. Later in the life of an individual, ethical principles can be strongly influenced by the standards of an individual's surrounding community, with the improper or even criminal behaviour of others influencing some individuals' behaviour, (O'Leary, 2009). Shaw (2008) claimed that the personal standards that people adopt is formed in a large part from the influence of others in their lives, and that ethics and moral judgements involve the application of basic guidelines of societal values and standards. Painter-Morland and Werhane (2008) argue that character is never fully formed, but always vulnerable to circumstances, and that people are malleable, responding in fascinating ways to their environment, peers and pressures around them. Jackling, Cooper, Leung and Dellaportas (2007) adds that in their study, the majority of the adult population, including accountants, possess conventional levels of moral reasoning. They go on further to add that evidence suggests that these can be influenced by external factors, including religion, legal systems, the political system and specific regulations, rather than universal principles.

Theorist argue that the area of ethics in recent years have emerged more prominent because of corporate and political scandals that have surfaced in recent years. Egham and Mhedhbi (2016) argue that the question of integrity within the accounting profession has been challenged stemming from the global scandals, such as Enron, WorldCom, Bank of Credit, Global Crossing, Commerce International, Cadbury, Parmalat, and Polly Peck.

Accountants have a duty to the public to ensure that the public entities, be it a company or public enterprise have transparent, honest and accurate recording of their respective transaction incurred. Ogbonna and Ebimobowei (2012) investigated how ethical accounting standards had affected Nigerian banks financial reports. The study's findings indicated that standards of ethical accounting had been extensively linked with the financial reports of the Nigerian banks. The findings indicated that there was a positive relationship relating ethics in accounting and financial reporting quality concerning return on investment, dividend per share, and earnings per share.

Langlois and Lapointe (2010) indicates that ethical skills can be enhanced through teaching and learning. Haberman (2003) argues that the issue of accounting fraud has to be tackled from the root of it-, which is education. The detection of accounting fraud alone will not end the problem; he further argues that to tackle unethical behaviour requires that one have to look at the prevention of it as well. Kelly (2004) posits that the challenges to the accounting profession, which had included the Enron bankruptcy scandal that resulted in the indictment and conviction of Arthur Andersen, had reinforced the requirement that accountants must adhere to the highest ethical standards. It is important to note that the personal beliefs and ethical perceptions of accounting students are attributes that can indicate the respective students' moral reasoning ability. This should be the rationale in teach accounting students at universities on salient areas that constitutes unethical behaviour and the punishment that goes with it.

The accountancy, professional body SAICA, in South Africa, responded to the challenge of ethics by putting in practice in 2007 that all universities affiliated with SAICA must have in place a formalised ethics education curriculum, in addition to the study of the profession's codes of ethics, as a mandatory curriculum requirement (SAICA, 2011). It is important to note that this step taken by the accounting board in South Africa, served to strengthen the profession in terms of their commitment in upholding a solid code of ethics in their profession. Accountants and financial practitioners should aspire to performing their duties and tasks with utmost professional courtesy and integrity based on a high moral compass of transparency and honesty. Jamnik (2011) suggests that a professional accountant must have a high degree of professional integrity. Professional accountants and financial practitioners should have an ethical responsibility to gain specialist knowledge before offering their professional services. They need to improve their knowledge by continuous training so that they develop a strong mental attitude to serve the public the best way possible. Accountants, auditors and financial practitioners have a duty and responsibility to the public like no other profession in the world.

Professional behavior requires that accountants and auditors refrain from any actions that may place the profession in a bad light (SAICA 2006). The five fundamental principles in the IFAC code are: integrity; objectivity; professional competence and due care; confidentiality; and professional behaviour (IFAC, 2006). In the discussion that follows the international ethical standards developed for accounts will be put forward and discussed in detail:

- Integrity: Integrity is not a set of guidelines or a development of achievement, but rather a state of awareness oriented near honesty and an obligation to acting a succeeding principle rather than for the sake of personal gain.
- Objectivity: to the degree, that it is physically possible, the interests or outlooks of the individuals or companies who hire them should not prejudice accountants. An accountant also should not let individual biases or benefits influence either the numbers that go into a bookkeeping system or the fallouts that come out of it. Facts and results should at all times be taken at face value and result in the accountant making the necessary assumptions and decisions accordingly.
- Professional Competence and Due Care: The arena of accounting is a body of an evolving frame of situation that changes as regulation and best practices are re-defined over different periods. It is the duty of an ethical accountant to stay well-informed of these expansions and provide clients with up-to-date material and the highest eminence of service.
- Confidentiality: Accountants are privy to sensitive information. It is the duty and responsibility of an accountant to never disclose any of this information to outside parties, friends or family members who may stand to advance from it. Likewise, an accountant should not use any information gotten while performing his/her professional services for the sake of individual gain, such as vending stock in a business whose books appear doubtful.
- Professional Behaviour: As with any living, an accountant should ensure that he fulfils his/her designated tasks and activities to the highest personal and specialized standards. These include completing tasks methodically and on time, subsequent though on commitments and only putting through compliant expenditures for services that have been rendered, (IFAC, 2006).

In the discussion, that follows ethical dilemmas in the South African context involving accounting and finance will be unpacked and explored in detail.

ETHICAL DILEMMAS IN SOUTH AFRICA INVOLVING ACCOUNTING AND FINANCE

South Africa has also had major financial, bribery and corruption scandals in recent years, which has reared its ugly head and soiled the foundation of the countrys'good business practice. Motlanthe, (2011) the former South African Deputy President, stated that corruption was "cancerous" and "the pestilence of corruption menacing the soul of our democracy is a life-and-death matter on which our future depends". He further stated: "what we need is a conscious intervention at the level of education to enable our nation to appreciate the devastation corruption is causing in the long term".

The current political struggle is fuelled by corruption in government that has reduced a once rich country like South Africa to a 'junk" status. In view of corruption and bribery scandals in South African politics, Olifant (2009) states that the South African government is very clear on the amount that should be declared as acceptable gifts and they should not exceed a rand value of a thousand rand (R1000). It is not known whether this standard rate set, of a thousand-rand value is a South African or an international standard set. Sbu Ndebele, a former Member of Executive Council (MEC) for transport in Kwa-Zulu Natal made world-wide news, when he was given a gift worth R1.1 million (a Mercedes-Benz) and some cattle by a group of contractors who benefitted from government contracts during his term of office. This blatant disregard of power can cripple a good country like South Africa, when politician choose to line their pockets instead of championing the cause of the hard working people of South Africa. Calhoun (2011) indicates in guanxi in China what the Western countries might call corruption (bribe) is indeed a form of acceptable business practice as it is seen as a gift. This raises the question of a countries culture and how it can be interpreted within the context of ethical standards. The author advocates that a universal principle be followed by all countries when it comes to upholding a high moral code of ethics in business.

An international ethical code of business conduct should be standardised and mandated across the world. Therein lies the challenge, as countries pride themselves in following their own ethical standards, principles and codes that is conducive to that specific country's culture. According to Transparency International (2010) in a study they conducted in 2010 in which members of the South African public were asked how they thought the level of corruption in the country had changed in the last 3years. The results indicated that 24% of respondents said it had decreased, 14% felt it had stayed the same and the remaining 62% of respondents said it had increased.

South Africa faced another scandal in 2011, when accusations of corruption by officials of the Department of Mineral Resources (DMR) in their handling of the mineral rights debacle involving Kumba and Imperial Crown Trading (ICT) erupted. Roberts (2012) indicated that Kumba accused ICT, a politically connected company with shareholders such as President Jacob Zuma's son Duduzane and Deputy President Kgalema Motlanthe's partner, Gugu Mtshali, of paying a bribe to a government official at the DMR and of forging parts of its prospecting rights application so that they could benefit from the deal. This shows how political figures reputations are brought into disrepute if they allow their family members to manipulate the government departments for their own person gain. This again is a blatant disregard of power. The author feels strongly that this situation could be avoided if proper policy be legislated and put in place, to prevent such abuses from occurring. The policy must mandate that no persons should stand to benefit financially in business dealings if their family is politically connected in government. If evidence is made available and the persons are found guilty, the said persons be it politician or family member must pay a heavy fine and be prevented from making such business dealings again. This is the only way corruption can be rooted out in South Africa, as it is crippling the very foundation of our democracy and contaminating our economy from prospective growth opportunities.

Now, we would turn to reviewing the Telkom scandal in South Africa. After a decade-long investigation into Telkom's practices, the partially government- owned company was fined R449 million in 2012 by the Competition Tribunal for abusing its dominance in the telecommunications market in South Africa between 1999 and 2004 (Motaung, 2012).

In South Africa, reports on the "moral-ethical" crisis in the country and the country losing its "moral compass" appear on a regular basis (Raga & Taylor, 2005). Various issues influence ethics within an organisation. According to Carroll and Buchholtz (2006) the following issues in ethics is present within South African organisation. They are presented below and discussed in detail:

- Conflicts of interest - Companies and Public owned enterprises must have policy in place that stipulates implicitly that accountants, auditors, employees, and stakeholders must declare conflict of interest or they will be in breach of their contacts and face fines and other penalties.
- Receiving gifts, gratuities and entertainment- The accountants, auditors, directors, CEO and employee's and stakeholders must disclose receiving gifts, gratuities and entertainment from the companies' clients or suppliers or future suppliers, as these "gifts" cannot be construed by the public as being made in a dubious manner to "bribe" or have a tender allocated to their company or public enterprise.
- Protecting company proprietary information- The Company or Public owned enterprise has sensitive information that its staff at all levels of management need to protect. Management or staff cannot leak sensitive information, to family or friends to make a personal profit as this could be construed as unethical business practices.
- Giving gifts, gratuities, entertainment – A Company or Public enterprise cannot give gifts etc. in order to gain new clients and contracts. This is unethical business practice that can ruin the reputation of the company or public enterprise. These organizations if found guilty of such unethical misconduct can be subject to fines and penalties.
- Discrimination- the Company or Public enterprise has to uphold the country's law. This means that discrimination at any level should not be tolerated. Discrimination of staff, discrimination in handing out tenders, discrimination of sourcing suppliers etc. is an example of unprofessional business practice. South Africa has a strong Labour law and Constitution that strongly rejects discrimination within any organisation or public enterprise. Since the country comes from a past regime based on apartheid, great in-roads in terms of legal statute was crafted and mandated by laws and legislation in South Africa, to protect the rights of men, women, people of colour and sexual orientation.
- Sexual harassment – sexual harassment within any Company or Public enterprise should not be tolerated. Specific South African Labour laws advocates a safe work environment be present for both men and women who are employed by the Company or Public enterprise. The Company or Public enterprise is responsible for its employees and any unethical behaviour of this nature, needs to be reported and dealt with according to Company or Public enterprise policy that is in keeping with the country's laws.
- Kickbacks – If management, accountants, auditors or any other stakeholder of the organization receive or give kickbacks to gain tenders, is an example of unethical business practice and aside from damaging the reputation of the respective Company or Public enterprise, these organizations can face the strong arm of the law and be prosecuted for this unethical practice in business.
- General conduct – The general conduct of business must be professional, honest and transparent at all times. If it is not, then the Company or Public enterprise is guilty of unethical behaviour and should be prosecuted by law accordingly.
- Employee theft- the money and assets of a Company or Public enterprise must be safeguarded at all times. Staff at any level, who steal money or assets from the organization, is guilty of unethical business practice and this should be considered a crime. In terms of the South African law, once evidence is gathered, the person or persons if found guilty should be prosecuted accordingly.
- Proper use of company assets – Staff within an organization must not intentionally neglect or damage with malicious intent the assets of an organization. If evidence reveals that the person be found guilty, then he or she should be prosecuted by the full extent of the law.

Many organisations are developing policies or programs to perpetuate strong ethical behaviour within their organisation. According to Ferrell and Ferrell (2009), the following seven steps represents a brief summary of an effective ethics programme that Companies and Public enterprises in South Africa can aspire to, to combat unethical behaviour. They are:

1. Assessing risks and putting in place standards and codes of ethical conduct.
2. Providing high-level managerial oversight to ensure compliance with these standards (for example, the appointment of a dedicated ethics officer within the organization).
3. Taking due care not to place individuals with a propensity to engage in misconduct in a position of authority where they can influence others.
4. Using training programmes to communicate the agreed standards to all employees. (On- the- job training can take place within the organization every year to establish, reaffirm or sustain a culture of a strong ethical code of conduct within the organization).
5. Establishing systems to monitor conduct and allow employees to report abuses. (Having an anonymous tip off line for example, that employees or the public can call to report abuses).
6. Enforcing standards, rewards, and punishments consistently across the company. (A strong code of ethical conduct should be included in the organizations' culture so that everyone is holistically called upon to uphold a strong ethical code of conduct, when representing the organization or during the staffs' daily activities).
7. Constantly reviewing the system, and taking steps to revise and improve the way it works, (Ferrell & Ferrell,2009)

In the discussion, that follows the need and importance of ethics education to accounting students will be reflected on and discussed.

ETHICS EDUCATION DELIVERED TO ACCOUNTING STUDENTS

To ground a good code of conduct in our accountants, auditors and financial managers there needs to be strong educational curriculum in place at university level that guides students on what is construed as right or wrong behaviour. The curriculum should be designed to illustrate the implications of unethical business practices and unethical behaviour on the professional, the profession and the business organization.

Milanzi's study (1997) found an information deficit in the field of Business Ethics. This prompted many universities to redesign their programs and curriculum in recent years to include ethics in business to accountants and financial managers. Sager (2003) is of the opinion that the ideal education of a professional individual is not complete without an examination in ethics. Armstrong, Ketz and Owsen (2003) determined that educators play a pivotal role in the development of ethical character and behaviour by increasing the students in accounting to moral sensitivity, moral reasoning and moral motivation. Low, Davey and Hooper (2008) posit that it is important to have ethics as part of an education programme and it is also still possible to mold the thinking of the accounting students who will enter the business environment once they graduate. On the other hand another construct by theorists Ghaffari, Kyriacou and Brennan (2008), reflects that whether students can actually apply what they have learnt from ethics education to specific practical business situations depends on the prevailing cultural norms.

Academics within South African universities are charged with a huge responsibility to teach and train students in accounting in what is good business ethics. The sad reality sometimes within South African universities, is that the accounting ethics curriculum focuses more on cases of poor ethics from Europe, America and other countries abroad than cases from Africa and South Africa specifically. It is therefore imperative that academics at South African universities are trained accordingly in developing curriculum. The curriculum should focus on key themes, some of them should include; what is ethics, the rationale behind why accounting students should subscribe to it, the relevance and importance of ethics to accountants, South African ethical dilemmas and the South African culture of ethics. It is important when designing curriculum to include both local and international case study.

Kerr and Smith (1995) argue that although great effort is expended on teaching Accounting students the technical aspects of accounting, the development of ethical values generally seems to be left to chance, because these students' exposure to ethical issues is often limited to a discussion of the ethical code of the profession in Auditing courses or Tax courses for example. The same tendency appears in South Africa, because the Accounting students who want to become auditors and public accountants follow a curriculum based on the requirements of SAICA and the PAAB, which does not make provision for a separate course on business ethics and limits these students' exposure to ethical issues concerned with the profession's ethical code. According to Chan and Leung (2006), Accounting students who are exposed to a core course of 'Ethics in Accounting', in their Accountancy degree curriculum, have higher ethical sensitivity ability, compared to the students who are given only a few hours of integrated ethical interventions of their entire curriculum coverage.

Rothenburg (2003) promotes the offering of mandatory courses in Business Ethics and the integration of the subject into introductory Accounting courses because prospective Accounting students should realise that accountants can and must make decisions independently of their client's or employer's wishes. He goes on further to argue that such courses should make Accounting study a more dynamic field, with grey areas to be explored through case studies, and that in the long run this would attract more and better-qualified candidates to the profession (Rothenburg 2003:8).

Within the South African context, Smit and Steenkamp (2015) summarised the challenges to incorporating pervasive qualities and skills such as ethics and ethical behaviour into the CA(SA) curriculum as follows:

- The traditional nature of the CA(SA) curriculum is that a large proportion of time and focus is placed on technical knowledge, with limited time available to develop pervasive qualities and skills;
- Pervasive qualities and skills are more difficult to develop than technical skills. Pervasive skills are implicit skills and furthermore, these skills are more easily developed with working experience and small groups; and
- It is more difficult to assess pervasive skills in a theoretical environment compared to a practical environment.

The difficulty in teaching ethics is that many Tax, Auditing and Accounting academics are subject experts and not trained educators. To close this gap, the University of KwaZulu- Natal requires academics to enrol on the Academic Development Program (UEIP) that assists academics to embrace proper teaching pedagogy, teaching paradigms, curriculum development and supervision skills. This training can assist Accounting academics to redesign their curriculum and teach ethics in a more appropriate style to their students.

DePaul University's vision includes the objective to 'provide opportunities for all students to learn ethical systems and demonstrate ethical practice' and, in line with this vision which is akin to the SAICA competency framework, (DePaul, 2007). De Paul (2007) indicates that the following key aspects on ethics should be included in curriculum. They are:

- To develop and enhance awareness of ethical issues in the discipline, subject or profession.
- To challenge students to understand basic principles of ethics, to think and write critically, and to confront inconsistencies in their own ethics and values systems.
- To develop a decision model for reasoning through ethical issues; and
- To enable students to apply ethics traditions and their decision model to new ethical issues they encounter (De Paul, 2007).

CONCLUDING REMARKS

The author put forth a lively academic discussion on ethics. The key theme filtering through is that ethics in accounting and finance is crucial to the business environment in South Africa. Accountants and financial practitioners have a duty and obligation to uphold a high moral code of conduct and practice their work with integrity, honesty and professional courtesy. A way forward for the accounting discipline to prosper and sustain itself in years to come, is if the fraternity continues to ensure that proper education in ethics be delivered to their students at university level. The Accounting curriculum needs to reflect current ethical scandals in South Africa and the world. Training Accounting academics to be better teachers is also a crucial factor to consider. Accounting students need to understand the consequences of unethical business practice and how they will be persecuted if they are found in preach of this ethical code of conduct.

FUTURE RESEARCH AREAS

There should be research conducted on how African culture impacts on ethics. Studies in this research area can assist Accounting academics to understand different African countries take on ethics. Since South Africa does business in Africa, understanding how accountants from Africa are influenced by their culture can enhance the current knowledge on the subject.

Another area of future interest; is embarking on comparative studies on developed and developing countries and their views on the ethical code of conduct amongst accounting practitioners in various industries. Africa and its Western counterparts have different approaches to ethics that can be explored. The pros and cons on the ethical code of conduct amongst accountants can bring interesting dialog and relevant information that can reveal possible gaps.

A critique and review of the existing accountants ethical code of conduct in South Africa needs to also be investigated to provide insights into the gaps present.

REFERENCES

Armstrong, M. B., Ketz, J. E., & Owsen, D. (2003). Ethics education in accounting: Moving toward ethical motivation and ethical behavior. *Journal of Accounting Education*, *21*(1), 1–16. doi:10.1016/S0748-5751(02)00017-9

Brinkmann, J. (2002). Marketing ethics as professional ethics: Concepts, approaches and typologies. *Journal of Business Ethics*, *41*(1/2), 159–177. doi:10.1023/A:1021318710382

Carroll, A. B., & Buchholtz, A. K. (2006). Business & Society: Ethics and Stakeholder Management (6th ed.). Mason: Thomson South-Western.

Chan, Y. S. S., & Leung, P. (2006). The Effects of Accounting Students' Ethical Reasoning and Personal Factors on Their Sensitivity. *Managerial Auditing Journal*, *21*(4), 436–457. doi:10.1108/02686900610661432

De Paul University. (2007). *Ethics 101*. Viewed 8 April 2017. Retrieved from https://business.depaul.edu/about/centers-institutes/institute-business-professional-ethics/ Documents/EthicsManual.pdf

Ferrell, L., & Ferrell, O. (2009). *Essential Managers: Ethical Business*. Dorling Kindersley.

Ghaffari, F., Kyriacou, O., & Brennan, R. (2008). Exploring the Implementation of Ethics in U.K. Accounting Programs. *Issues in Accounting Education*, *23*(2), 183–198. doi:10.2308/iace.2008.23.2.183

International Federation of Accountants (IFAC). (2006). *Approaches to the Development and Maintenance of Professional Values, Ethics and Attitudes in Accounting Education Programs*. Information Paper. New York. Retrieved from http://www.ifac.org

Jackling, B., Cooper, B. J., Leung, P., & Dellaportas, S. (2007). Professional Accounting Bodies' Perceptions of Ethical Issues, Causes of Ethical Failure and Ethics Education. *Managerial Auditing Journal*, *22*(9), 928–944. doi:10.1108/02686900710829426

Jamnik, A. (2011). Ethical code in the public accounting profession. *Journal of International Business Ethics*, *1*(1), 80–90.

Kelly, P. T. (2004). *An Examination of the Moral Reasoning of Accounting Students* (Doctor of Philosophy Thesis). University of Connecticut.

Kerr, D. S., & Smith, L. M. (1995). Importance of and approaches to incorporating ethics into the accounting classroom. *Journal of Business Ethics*, *14*(1), 987–995. doi:10.1007/BF00872114

Langlois, L., & Lapointe, C. (2010). Can ethics be learned? Results from a three-year action-research project. *Journal of Educational Administration*, *48*(2), 147–163. doi:10.1108/09578231011027824

Low, M., Davey, H., & Hooper, K. (2008). Accounting Scandals, Ethical Dilemmas and Educational Challenges. *Critical Perspectives on Accounting*, *19*(1), 222–254. doi:10.1016/j.cpa.2006.05.010

Milanzi, M. C. (1997). Business Ethics in Eastern and Southern Africa. *Journal of Business Ethics*, *16*(14), 1549–1553. doi:10.1023/A:1005811014294

Motlanthe, K. (2011). *Address at the University of the Witwatersrand, Johannesburg (February 17, 2011): The Presidency Republic of South Africa*. Available: http://www.thepresidency.gov.za/pebble.asp?relid=4682

O'Leary, C. (2009). An Empirical Analysis of the Positive Impact of Ethics Teaching on Accounting Students. *Accounting Education, 18*(4–5), 505–520. doi:10.1080/09639280802532158

Ogbonna, G. N., & Ebimobowei, A. (2012). Effect of Ethical Accounting Standards on the Quality of Financial Reports of Banks in Nigeria. *Current Research Journal of Social Sciences*, *4*(1), 69–78.

Olifant, N. (2009). *S'bu Ndebele's R1, 1-million gift*. https://www.iol.co.za/news/politics/sbundebele

Painter-Morland, M., & Werhane, P. (2008). *Cutting Edge Issues in Business Ethics Continental challenges to Tradition and practice*. Springer.

Rothenburg, E. (2003). Incorporating business ethics into introductory accounting courses. *The CPA Journal*, *6*(8).

Sager, W.H. (2003, June 14). Professional conduct: symbol of a profession. *National Public Accountan*t.

SAICA. (2011). *CA (SA) Training Programme*. Available: https://www.saica. co.za/Training/Training/CASATrainingProgramme/tabid/1657/language/enUS/Default.aspx

Shaw, W. H. (2008). *Business Ethics*. Wadsworth Inc.

Smit, S., & Steenkamp, G. (2015). The competencies developed in an undergraduate accounting course before SAICA's SAICA competency framework was effective: A student's perspective. *Journal of Economic and Financial Sciences*, *8*(2), 666–688. doi:10.4102/jef.v8i2.115

South African Institute of Chartered Accountants (SAICA). (2006). *Code of professional conduct*. https://www.saica.co.za/documents/Code_of_Professional_Conduct_2006.pdf

Transparency International Global Corruption Barometer. (2010). Available at http: www transparency.org/policy research/survey indices/gcp/2010/

Zeghal, D., & Mhedhbi, K. (2016). An analysis of the factors affecting the adoption of international accounting standards by developing countries. *The International Journal of Accounting*, *41*(4), 373–386. doi:10.1016/j.intacc.2006.09.009

KEY TERMS AND DEFINITIONS

Accounting: Accounting is the reliable, systematic, and transparent recording and communication of economic information in accordance with Generally Accepted Accounting Principles (GAAP).

Corporate Governance: Is grounded by three principles namely transparency, accountability, and security. Organisations have to conform to the necessary laws and legislations in South Africa that govern corporate governance.

Ethics: Is a moral philosophy or code of conduct practiced by a person or group of people within the business world.

Finance: Refers to the management of money and includes activities like investment, borrowing, lending, budgeting, saving, and future forecasting of shares or financial issues.

South Africa: Refers to a country on the southernmost tip of the African continent. It includes dessert, beaches, animal and plant life and a well- built infrastructure and business district.

Chapter 3
Unseen Link Between Sustainability Reporting and Financial Reporting:
Behavioral Finance Paradigm

Sibel Dinç Aydemir
https://orcid.org/0000-0003-1897-0913
Sabanci University, Turkey

ABSTRACT

The accounting profession has intensely witnessed compelling challenges in the 21st century. Due to increased number in stakeholders and huge informational need, the traditional model has become unsatisfactory in meeting this need and evaluating company's future performance. Apparently, companies trying to survive in globally competitive markets couldn't attain this goal by focusing merely on financial outcomes. Thus, sustainability reporting has emerged as a vital non-financial information demanded by stakeholders. However, ethical insights on credibility and accountability of this information have been documented and discussed in the literature. Tapping into behavioral finance paradigm and upper echelon approach, this chapter exerts an effort to link financial reporting/audit quality to sustainability reporting and discusses those ethical issues on these processes. Further, while drawing attention to overconfidence bias in individuals involved in reporting and assurance stages, it suggests influential role of decision-makers' personal traits on these mechanisms in a misleading way.

INTRODUCTION

In an increasingly changing and complex world, information, already important issue, has made a world of difference in early 2000s. Accounting and auditing scandals, market collapses following bubbles starting from US markets and expanding into nearly those of all financial markets have amplified the significance of the all relevant information, let alone financial information. This is because that companies trying to survive in a globally competitive markets couldn't attain this goal by focusing merely on

DOI: 10.4018/978-1-7998-4637-6.ch003

financial outcomes. Therefore, suggesting a tool for companies to survive in this challenging environment, sustainability reporting (SR) has emerged as a vital non-financial information demanded by stakeholders. At the same time, the efforts to reduce information asymmetry, to deal with agency problems and further to improve stakeholder engagement/relation have let to discussing credibility and accountability of all this information meticulously.

On the other hand, extant research has heavily concentrated on quality, credibility of companies' financial reporting (FR) systems for two main reasons. First, audit quality (AQ) has been defined in terms of FR systems and measured frequently through FR indicators since traditional accounting approach toward reducing information asymmetry and dealing with principal-agent problems has predominantly overvalued financial information, shareholders and present investors. Therefore, AQ and FR quality have been used interchangeably. Second, accounting/auditing scandals, frauds occurred unprecedentedly in the 2000s have directed efforts of not only researchers but also businesses and regulatory bodies on this issue. Researchers started to explore audit/financial reporting quality, its determinants and consequences. Thereby, governments, accounting associations and other significant regulatory bodies all over the world have been striving to reconstruct confidence in the auditing/financial reporting functions through a series of ethical, disciplinary and institutional arrangements. However, on the other side, crucial sustainability issues such as climate change, human rights, governance and social well-being as mostly pronounced themes have urged companies in all countries to understand sustainability and empower their decisions concerning sustainability aspects both at national and also at international level. As such, in addition to financial information, non-financial information has gained prominence and stakeholders, future investors have been added as new counterparties in addition to shareholders and present investors for corporate communications and relations. Successively, sustainability indexes have been appeared in both developed and also developing countries' capital markets due to the investors who seek for sustainability components and apply to this criterion in their investment decisions. Ultimately, SR has come to the fore as common practice and worldwide trend in the 21st century.

These two substantial issues do not definitely compete in a horse race. Rather, there are both similarities and also key differences between them. First, both FR and SR systems share essentially the same mission; (1) reducing information asymmetry between counterparties in the markets and (2) showing how the reporting companies are functioning economically and to which degree this disclosed information –financial or non-financial is credible and to what extent these companies pay regard to their stakeholders, (3) dealing with principal-agent phenomenon, or currently deemed as stakeholder engagement. Second, both two reporting processes have some global guidelines or standards released by international regulatory bodies. Yet, as mentioned above, there are some major differences between them. In the first place, FR process addresses relatively narrower scope in terms of the limited nature of financial information and hence the span of stakeholder engagement while SR process appeals to broader scope and the increased number of outside users because of the wide and diversified nature of economic, environmental and social aspects. Second, FR is mandatory whereas SR is still voluntary. That's why, it can be said that independent auditors as assurance providers have engaged in an established audit market. Yet, assurance providers of SR have still been performing in an unsettled area. Third, extant research on financial reporting/auditing could be recognized as relatively matured and most popular whereas SR is ever-developing research area, compared to the former.

However, this matured research body lacks in delineating FR/AQ through audit partner specific or individual attributes since it has highly argued audit firm specific characteristics' role on it. This is interesting since this process is entirely decision-making process and the role of decision-makers seems crucial, considering the studies suggesting that the research design overwhelmed by the firm-level attributes should be carried down to the individual-level characteristics (Lennox & Wu, 2018). Through behavioral finance suggestions on systematic biases such as overconfidence, the comprehension of auditing outcomes could extend into audit partner specific attributes thoroughly. First, managerial overconfidence has been documented on various organizational decisions. Second, the audit profession principles such as professionalism and skepticism in addition to international standards have remained unsolved or unsatisfactory in explaining many auditing frauds and failures in more recent times. Although there are key differences between FR and SR, they are similar regarding their mission. Also, both the two mechanisms fully represent a thoroughly decision-making process including too much information to be searched, to be processed and hence to be assured by assurance providers in those decision-makers' hands. More importantly, upper echelons (Hambrick, 2016; Hambrick & Mason, 1984) approach suggests that corporate behaviors reflect the personal attributes of top executives. Then, it isn't surprising to assume that responsible managers, assurance providers of both FR and also SR could view the decisional information concerning these reporting processes with their highly personalized and less standardized and sometimes client-guided decision-making styles. Some research arguing the credibility of SR and the independency of assurance providers has documented a considerable amount of management control on assurance providers' verification processes and management "readership" on these reports (Owen & O'Dwyer, 2004). Briefly, FR and SR seem to carry a significant manipulative risk of being prepared by their reporters in a misleading way at all stages of these processes. First, managers could manipulate this process in order to gain access to financial instruments, to improve the company's reputation and to maintain or attract the present and future investors respectively since the extant research has provided evidence of the relation between overconfident managers and unethical behaviors (e.g., Hsieh et al., 2018; Schrand & Zechman, 2012). When the managerial overconfidence exists, these overconfident managers think optimistically and couldn't see the outcomes of future's uncertain events and take risk easily and even improperly. Or, their overconfidence would increase the likelihood of occurrence of unethical corporate behaviors as manifested above by the extant research. Second, when the assurance providers are overconfident, they would not exploit all decision-specific information and they would ignore some of them due to the fact that the verification process is knowledge intensive task and that individuals have limited capabilities in information gathering, information processing and risk evaluation as suggested by behavioral finance paradigm (Kahneman & Tversky, 1979). Or due to their overconfidence-inopportune optimism- they would not anticipate some material risks or hence they would engage in risky activities in this process. Or due to their familiarity with the reporting company, their perspective would probably be highly client-guided and less standardized, etc. Third, the worst, when both the top managers and also assurance providers are inopportune optimists, the likelihood of occurrence of unexpected risky events and/or unethical behaviors in reporting and assurance providing processes would be higher. In a study, it is found that companies tend to engage in tax-avoidance activities more when their CEOs and CFOs are overconfident (Hsieh et al., 2018).

This chapter could bring novelty to the extant literature on both FR and also SR for several reasons. First, prior studies on FR/AQ have overwhelmingly put emphasis on the audit or client firm specific attributes in understanding it. Limited part of research has focused on mostly observed features of these reporting actors. This chapter strongly suggests that individual and psychological aspects of these actors of reporting processes should be examined. Due to some behavioral biases such as overconfidence, these reporting and assurance processes could deviate from the expected and actual form, making these reports dubious and untrustworthy for all stakeholders or outside users. Particularly in SR realm, there is a great body of research on ethical and problematic issues such as the credibility and trustworthy of this huge information. Then, this behavioral perspective could enable this research body which has heavily focused on process-specific factors such as compatibility with the global standards or guidelines to extend into both the reasons and the solutions of these ethical lapses. Amount of the information disclosed by the companies every day couldn't definitely decrease. Then, striving to ensure the accuracy and credibility of this immense information seems a vital task and this task requires first to know what's actually going on.

Second, from interdisciplinary perspective, this chapter discusses the ignored link between FR and SR. Through the ideas of upper echelon theory and the tenets of behavioral finance paradigm, this study first suggests that reporters could reflect their personal traits into reporting task and that assurance providers view the reports with their highly personalized, less standardized and sometimes client-guided lenses. Additionally, due to (1) their limited capabilities of information gathering and processing, (2) subjective probabilities attributed to the uncertain outcomes, (3) overconfidence bias in decision-making process, these reporters and assurance providers could (1) not include and evaluate all the information in decision environment, (2) not assess the likelihood of future events properly and (3) tend to think optimistically and hence to ignore decision-specific information and to engage in risky activities more, easily and improperly.

Third, prior studies seem to have evaluated reporting and assurance processes with the observed characteristics, and under the lights of the global guidelines. Through drawing attention to the importance of unobserved components of these processes, this chapter endeavors to break the routine in order to understand both FR/AQ and SR. Fourth, this chapter integrates two research areas- immature SR and mature FR- which are seemingly different and unlinked and therefore enables the researchers to transfer of the accumulated knowledge on the latter into the former and ultimately to make the former's comprehension clear.

BACKGROUND

DeFond and Zhang (2014) define audit quality as "*greater assurance that the financial statements faithfully reflect the firm's underlying economics, conditioned on its FR system and innate characteristics*". By implying its attestation function whereby audit partners render an opinion as to fair presentation of their clients' financial statements, thus lending credibility to the FR system, this definition makes auditing institution valuable and important. Furthermore, the effort to define it in this manner seems to have encouraged overwhelmingly audit quality research body to focus on FR quality perspective. At the same time, reducing information asymmetry while the individuals make their investment decisions has enabled the scholars to delineate audit quality through FR quality. That is why, in the accumulated research, firstly, these two concepts are used interchangeably or audit quality is deemed as the component of FR quality since it is documented that the first improves the credibility of the latter. Second, in the studies, AQ has been measured by FR quality indicators such as discretionary accruals (Al-Thuneibat et al., 2011; Campa, 2013; Choi et al., 2010; Hoitash et al.,2007; Jackson et al., 2008; Jenkins & Velury, 2012; Kumar & Lim, 2015; Nagy, 2012), accounting conservatism and value relevance of earnings (Campa, 2013) for a long time. Unprecedented and unexpected audit and accounting scandals have leaded the researchers to reconsider audit quality concept and alter its operationalization or their research design. Then, audit quality has been started to be measured as audit firm's or auditor's industry expertise (Jensen & Payne, 2005; Muttakin et al., 2017), audit firm size (Chen et al., 2005; Johl et al., 2007; Lee & Lee, 2013; Muttakin et al., 2017), audit time (Leventis & Caramanis, 2005), auditor's propensity to issue going concern opinion (Carey & Simnett, 2006; Jackson et al., 2008; Knechel & Vanstraelen, 2005), auditor ligitation outcomes (Fuerma & Kraten, 2009), the frequence of Accounting and Auditing Enforcement Releases (Kumar & Lim, 2015) and even twenty-eight audit quality indicators issued by Public Company Accounting Oversight Board (PCAOB) (Brown et al., 2016).

Ultimately, by the virtue of the immense changes in dynamics of the audit market trivet (i.e. audit firms, client firms and regulatory bodies), there has been a great body of research on audit quality. Specifically, due to accounting and auditing errors, misrepresentations, frauds and unexpected and unprecedented corporation collapses starting in early 2000s, researchers started to explore audit/financial reporting quality, its determinants and consequences. Not only researchers but also governments, accounting associations and other significant regulatory bodies all over the world have been striving to reconstruct confidence in auditing/financial reporting functions through a series of ethical, disciplinary and institutional arrangements. Companies have also strived for persuading their present or future investors or other stakeholders about the credibility of their FR mechanism and hence for reducing information asymmetry. Prior literature on audit quality has found that firm size (Choi et al., 2010; Francis & You, 2009), audit firm's industry expertise (Carson, 2009; Craswell et al., 1995; Francis & Yu, 2009;), audit fees (Hoitash et al., 2007) have contributed to improving audit quality while audit tenure (Almutairi et al., 2009; Bazerman et al., 1997; Carey & Simnett, 2006) has a negative impact. However, the findings have been controversial for the relationship between audit fees and audit quality and on the role of auditor rotation in enhancing auditor independence and hence in improving auditing quality (Bazerman et al., 1997; Carey & Simnett, 2006; Hoyle, 1978; Jackson et al., 2008). For example, Al-Thuneibat et al. (2011) found that audit firm tenure had an adverse effect on audit quality while Jackson et al. (2008) showed that audit quality increased with audit tenure.

Although there is a consensus on the importance of reconstructing the trust in both audit and also financial reports from the views of the all stakeholders in order to obviate frauds, corruptions and scandals all over the world, countries differ in attaining this crucial goal or providing auditor's independence due to nonuniformity in terms of their law, regulatory and governmental systems. For example, only French law applies joint-auditing in ensuring audit quality for the reason that this system enables cross-review, reciprocal monitoring. Also, the presence of two auditors enhances auditor independence (Piot, 2007). Additionally, countries vary across available or disclosed data concerning both supply and also demand dynamics of the market. Specifically, while audit fees are available data in US, it isn't disclosed in Turkey. In spite of international common regulations and requirements such as International Financial Reporting Standards (IFRS), to a great extent, research body in countries has been motivated by market functioning, rules of regulatory and advisory institutions, auditing/accounting events and even the jurisdictions, all of which are peculiar to the countries.

For good or ill, it is obvious that extant research has documented too much evidence for the drivers of audit quality in the years that followed unprecedented accounting scandals. Yet, these studies have implicitly assumed that audit partners distribute a uniform audit quality level, by putting excessive emphasis on audit firm-specific factors in explaining auditing quality. Some studies have drawn attention and suggested that the research design overwhelmed by the firm-level attributes should be carried down to the individual-level characteristics. Lennox and Wu (2018) review this archival literature and provide valuable insights into how this kind of research strand would extend the existing literature beyond the knowledge overly accumulated at firm or office level.

On the other hand, the limited research taking auditing partner specific or individual level attributes into consideration doesn't focus on psychological components of audit procedures, and the final decision-making process in itself. Yet, due to the fact that audit process is completely a decision making process in which capabilities, personalities, competencies of auditing partners impact their professional judgment and hence the audit opinion they ultimately render, some researchers have suggested that auditing partner level characteristics should be taken into consideration in audit quality research. Moreover, peculiar knowledge and competencies of the audit partners couldn't be carried to neither the firm nor the office level (Goodwin & Wu, 2014).

Reheul et al. (2007) have observed the relationship between individual auditor characteristics and audit opinion. They found that auditors with sector expertise tended to provide better assurance by disclosing financial statement errors in their reports. Similarly, some researchers found presence of restatements to be negatively related with some auditor attributes such as auditor industry expertise (Chin and Chi 2009; Romanus et al. 2008) and client tenure (Stanley & DeZoort, 2007). While Zerni (2012) provided evidence of industry expertise's positive effect on audit fees, Knechel et al. (2014) find that audit partners' style (agressive vs. conservative) had an influence on audit fees. There are a few behavioral studies in accounting that examine (1) the role of auditors' time pressure on their judgments (Svanberg & Ohman, 2013), and (2) the relationship between organizational error climate and auditor's propensity to handle errors (Gronewold & Donle, 2011), and (3) appearance of dysfunctional behaviors in auditors (Donnelly et al., 2003). However, the research linking the behavioral and attitudinal characteristics of audit partners and key managers with audit quality is interestingly rare.

All in all, it seems immensely precious to extend the audit quality literature into a more comprehensive manner through psychological and attitudinal aspects of audit outcomes including both this critical decision-making process and also those decision-makers with plentiful and complex information which has to be searched, processed and ultimately assured in their hands. For this purpose, it is necessary to wear behavioral finance lenses and to tap into these generous tenets in understanding auditing which basically puts place professionalism and skepticism on a pedestal, both by definition and by legislation.

BRINGING THE INVISIBLE INTO VIEW

Behavioral Finance

What would I eliminate if I had a magic wand? Overconfidence. (Kahneman, 2018)

Classical finance has assumed that people are rational, that even if there're some deviations from rational behavior, these are random, adding up to zero. Freely operating markets favor rational people and organizations. In this perspective, choice has been described as a maximization process (Tversky & Kahneman, 1986). Calculating stochastic probabilities of possible outcomes of decision alternatives, people make a choice of the alternative with most expected utility value. Briefly, this process inherently necessitates engagement of individual's statistical/computational capabilities into decision making process. Hence, these arguments in classical finance enable rational behavior assumption more conceivable. Certainly, in the markets, classical paradigm assumes that there could exist some people behaving irrationally.

Yet, in time, they could learn from their past experiences and their behaviors would converge to the rational. With the advent of prospect theory (Kahneman & Tversky, 1979), there's been a confounding shift regarding classical paradigm assumptions. Although its proponents have claimed that they don't negate tenets of classical finance, it has been necessary to change researchers' lenses according to new extended assumptions. According to them, classical paradigm does not describe actual choice behavior enough. First, people aren't rational. Due to bounded rationality (Simon, 1955) and limited information processing capacity (Dolinsky & Feinberg, 1986), people don't behave rationally in every time. They're human beings and could make errors in both perceiving decision environment as a whole and also calculating possibilities and expected value of each decision alternative. They could make computational errors and evaluate stochastic probabilities improperly. They even don't have the information enough regarding decision alternatives. Moreover, deviations from the rational behavior are systematic, not random. Due to some biases, they behave irrationally in a systematic way. Second, unlike classical finance, probabilities aren't stochastic. Individuals perceive the likelihood of decision outcomes subjectively (Kahneman & Tversky, 1972). People assign subjective probabilities to occurrence of some uncertain events. Third, it's asserted that prospect theory is "*a description of the behavior of real people*" (Tversky & Kahneman, 1986). Unlike classical view describing normative or idealized behavior of decision makers, it tries to explain actual individual behavior. Again, it should be stated that the new paradigm doesn't negate expected utility theory, by extending its assumptions. Principally, these two paradigms can be considered as "separate enterprises". It actually presents a descriptive choice model for anomalies in expected utility theory setting (Tversky & Kahneman, 1986).

Since classical finance approach supposes that people are "bayesian statisticians", rational, the extant literature has preponderantly focused on and tapped into demographics and sociodemographic factors in order to explain the individual financial behavior (Aren & Aydemir, 2015). At the institutional side, the case isn't different (please see Aren, Aydemir, Sehitoglu, 2016 for a review). Objective measures have been used to understand institutional behavior. However, the behavioral finance highlights the psychological and emotional aspects of the financial behavior. Seeing that people are irrational, error-prone and that they have limited information processing capacity and that the probabilities are subjective, all individual characteristics could then be important in understanding the financial decisions. In other words, relatively ignored factors which could probably influence a financial decision have been highlighted in the light of behavioral finance axioms.

Starting from this point of view, deep-rooted concepts in psychology, have been articulated and discussed again in the financial context. Decision making theories have been argued with these psychological and attitudinal factors for every stage of the decision making processes. Expected utility theory prioritizes the amount of information in order to make a wise, reasonable decision. Yet, having too much information doesn't ensure a plausible financial decision in behavioral finance view. People have limited information processing capacity and they may perceive the same information differently owing to their different attributes and psychological/emotional levels. Or, differences in the framing of the same decisional information could lead people to make diverse choices. Briefly, the perception may be different from the reality, hence they may exhibit biased behaviors in a systematic way. Thus, behavioral finance researchers have manifested many behavioral biases and delineated them thoroughly. As a matter of fact, these biases have been found as substantial in explaining the actual behavior of both individual and institutional investors.

Cognitive vs. Affective Bias

These biased behaviors exhibited by the individuals can be grouped into two main categories. Some could be originated from cognitive factors whereas the others may have an emotional origin. Put it differently, the cognitive factors such as perceiving the information incorrectly, evaluating the accurate information improperly, calculating the possibilities wrongly may make the observed behavior biased. These behaviors are recognized as cognitive biases. On the other hand, people may attach some positive or negative affects to some images (Finucane et al. 2000). They encode the given situations with different feelings and emotions. The same image may be perceived as favorable by someone, while it reminds the other person of negative feelings. More importantly, they are generally used to make quick evaluation. Due to their affects, feelings and emotions, people may display some biased behaviors. These are known affective biases. More explicitly, in cognitive biases, there is an information leading the decision, however, this information is wrong or perceived or processed improperly, whereas in affective biases, that is the positive/negative affect or feeling which drives a person to make a decision.

A great number of biases have been articulated and documented in behavioral finance studies such as availability, representativeness and anchoring (Tversky & Kahneman, 1974) yet in this chapter, overconfidence bias as most common and salient phenomenon in complex decision-making processes will be highlighted.

Overconfidence Bias

The claim that the probability judgements of people are susceptible to systematic biases and that the most prevalent one is overconfidence bias has been documented by Lichtenstein and Fischhoff (1977). First delineated by Oskamp (1965), overconfidence bias is the tendency of which people perceive their judged probabilities higher than actually they are. Through general-knowledge questions, people are asked firstly to select the most probable answer and later to express the certainty degree about their answers' accuracy (Fischhoff et al., 1977). Interestingly, those participants in the study are consistently overconfident.

Overconfidence bias is recognized as a cognitive limitation in behavioral finance literature and it exists when people are greatly optimistic in their initial assessment of a situation and hence are not good at taking the new additional information into their consideration due to their starting overconfident thinking (Fischhoff et al., 1977). Overconfident people are generally said to think optimistically about uncertain outcomes, about themselves and their decisions and hence they are able to ignore the relevant information about the possible outcomes pertaining to their decision-making tasks. There has been a proliferation of research manifesting the impact of overconfidence on various decision-making contexts. In the managerial context, top level managers tend to make more corporate investments since they are more likely to overestimate the expected returns of their investment alternatives (Malmendier & Tate, 2004). In a later study, they also provided evidence for the relationship between greater likelihood of merger decisions and overconfident CEOs (Malmendier & Tate, 2008). Further, Busenitz and Barney (1997) showed that entrepreneurs are more likely subject to decision-making biases (i.e., overconfidence) than managers in large organizations.

More importantly, there are some studies reviewing the research emphasizing the importance of CEO/CFO characteristics on reporting outcomes (Habib & Hossain, 2013). This study reviews the research documenting the significant role of managerial overconfidence on FR outcomes. It refers that some research has found that overconfident managers used earnings management strategies more than the others. Similarly, Presley and Abbott (2013) have drawn evidence of positive relation between CEO overconfidence and financial restatements. More interestingly, CEO overconfidence remained significant both pre- and post-date SOX periods, suggesting overconfidence bias as a permanent phenomenon in financial restatement setting. Moreover, Schrand and Zechman (2012) have found that overconfident managers were more likely to appeal to financial misreporting. Duellman, Hurwitz, & Sun (2015) have documented a negative relation between managerial overconfidence and audit fees and also found a lower likelihood for their use of industry-specialist auditors. An experimental study has manifested that managerial overconfidence caused an increase in the auditor's perceived risk of client fraud behavior (Johnson et al., 2013). Hsieh et al. (2018) have showed that companies were more likely engaged in tax avoidance activities when they had both overconfident CEO and also overconfident CFO, compared to other combinations in their study.

Considering the agency theory in which managers become agents of shareholders or rather stakeholders-they are principals-, the evidence of managerial overconfidence on FR outcomes could turned into a critical question in terms of all corporate communications, let alone to FR. Huge amount of data including financial and non-financial information are being disclosed by companies almost every day. Briefly, when resorting to upper echelons perspective (Hambrick & Mason, 1984), the likelihood of manipulation of this disclosed information by managers with some specific personal attributes which drive them to behave differently than the reasonable, expected behavior seems as easy as pie. Upper echelons theory is the idea that organizational strategies and decisions are greatly shaped by top executives' personal background since top executives assess their organizational situations through their own heavily individualized lenses (Hambrick, 2016). Then, it is suggested that "strategists" should be understood first in order to comprehend organizational "strategies". Also, Hambrick and Mason (1984) state that the upper echelon model entails both the psychological and also observable characteristics of upper echelons yet it is articulated that the observable characteristics have been focused on. Perhaps, regarding upper echelons model, researchers should put emphasis on psychological aspect more in order to understand organizational strategies thoroughly.

Furthermore, similar to top management decisions on hand, auditing process also accommodates gathering and processing a lot of information simultaneously and ultimately making a professional decision which greatly concerns outside users, including themselves since they are also liable for the outcomes of this weighty decision. Yet, the studies concentrating the relation between the auditing partners' overconfidence and auditing quality directly is rare. And all arguments about managerial overconfidence are still valid for audit processes. And inspired by this upper echelon perspective suggesting focusing on "strategists" to understand corporate "strategies", this chapter purports that reporters, auditors and assurance providers of these financial and non-financial reporting processes should be understood first if these processes are determined to be understood well.

Sustainability Reporting

In an increasingly changing and complex world, information-already important issue- has actually made a world of difference in the 2000s. As mentioned above, accounting and auditing scandals, market collapses following bubbles starting from US markets and expanding into nearly those of all financial markets have amplified the significance of the all disclosed information, let alone financial information. This is because that companies trying to survive in a globally competitive markets couldn't attain this goal by focusing merely on their financial outcomes. Therefore, as a tool for companies to survive in this challenging and demanding competition environment, SR has emerged as a vital non-financial information demanded increasingly by all stakeholders. At the same time, the efforts to reduce information asymmetry, to deal with agency problems and further to improve stakeholder engagement and relations have let to discussing credibility and accountability of all this information in detail and meticulously. Although sustainability concept's environmental component was mentioned first in the 1980s and its definition has been made in terms of ecosystem sustainability (Chapin et al., 1996), Dyllick and Hockerts (2002, p.131) have defined corporate sustainability as "*meeting the needs of a firm's direct and indirect stakeholders (such as shareholders, employees, clients, pressure groups, communities, etc.), without compromising its ability to meet the needs of future stakeholders as well*". For this goal to be attained, companies should keep and grow economic, social and environmental capital. By the way, it should be stated that sustainability has sometimes been deemed as "Corporate Sustainability (CR)" and "Triple Bottom Line (TBL)" in the literature (Aggarwal, 2013).

According to Global Reporting Initiative (GRI) (2011), SR is defined as *"the practice of measuring, disclosing, and being accountable to internal and external stakeholders for organizational performance towards the goal of sustainable development''*. Global Reporting Initiative is "*an independent international organization that has pioneered SR since 1997*" (GRI, 2019). This initiative has been the pioneer of worldwide practice in SR, helping both governments and businesses to understand this issue and to empower their decisions concerning crucial sustainability issues such as climate change, human rights, governance and social well-being through "*the first and most widely adopted global standards for SR*".

KPMG Survey of Corporate Responsibility Reporting (2017, p.9) declared that the world's largest 250 companies' SR ratio had increased from 35% in 1999 to 93% in 2017. Accordingly, the discourse which there has been a worldwide movement on SR doesn't seem an exaggerated phrase. Moreover, rapid increase in the number of investors attaching importance to social responsibility and/or sustainability issues has urged capital markets to construct sustainability index in both developed countries (e.g. Dow Jones US Sustainability Index, first in 1999) and also developing countries (e.g. Borsa Istanbul Sustainability Index, first in 2014). Actually, the first index was The Domini 400 Social Index (DSI) which represents a meticulously constructed portfolio of socially responsible common-stocks due to demands of socially responsible investors applying social criteria as well as the financial outcomes (Sauer, 1997). In spite of the critics that socially responsible investments would have poor investment performance, Herremans et al. (1993) manifested that socially responsible manufacturing companies financially predominated companies with poor corporate sustainability reputation during the six-year period 1982–1987. What's more, some research has manifested a link between corporate social responsibility (CSR) strategies and better access to finance. Companies with better CSR strategies (stakeholder engagement and increased transparency) have faced with lower capital constraints (Cheng et al., 2014). Actually, socially responsible investing isn't easily apprehensible issue. The studies (McLachlan & Gardner, 2004; Williams, 2007) have already manifested that in terms of observed features such as demographics, socially responsible investors are not different from the conventional investors, drawing attention to unobserved drivers of socially responsible investing. Therefore, studies attempting to classify investors as socially responsible have come under criticism by some research (Pasewark & Riley, 2010) due to (1) the multitude of social issues that individuals seek for, (2) the differences in the intensity of social feelings that they have, and (3) the socially responsible people's variability in their degree of financial commitment, remarkably pointing to psychological and personal motives for socially responsible investing.

To get to the main point, a wave of socially responsible investment thoughts in the 1990s has given way to sustainability in the 2000s. Indeed, sustainability concept has been in the limelight in this century or *"...become a mantra for the 21st century"* as stated by Dyllick and Hockerts (2002). Through its reporting standards, GRI, as a global stakeholder institution, has started a worldwide movement in sustainability realm. There are a wide range of international disclosure formats for companies to reveal what they do about their sustainability strategies in their reports (Camilleri, 2018) and fortunately GRI has also global strategic partnerships with other disclosure format providers such OECD (Organisation for Economic Co-operation and Development), UNEP (The United Nations Environment Programme), The Global Compact. Also, GRI guidelines have also synergies with UNCTAD (United Nations Conference on Trade and Development), IFC (International Finance Corporation), aiming to help companies in presenting all these required non-financial information in an integrated way (GRI, 2019). These efforts have also aimed to stress the inadequacies in corporate communications.

In spite of these efforts to integrate the non-financial information, academic conservation has a great consensus on that the credibility and trustworthy of this information is of vital importance. In a study examining the quality of sustainability reports from the view of assurance providers, it is observed that their assurance statements have seemed to have an optimistic and deliberative wording in that problematic issues and weaknesses were not explicitly expressed (Boiral et al., 2019). Additionally, some previous research has revealed that verification process by assurance providers seems preponderantly to consist of internal stakeholders, hindering full stakeholder engagement (Manetti & Toccafondi, 2012). However, the research body has predominantly put emphasis on the normative structure of SR and it lacks in the studies which strive to focus on actual, unobservable idiosyncratic mechanisms occurred in these processes. Second, there is a need for research designs which include influential role of decision-makers who are apt to delude involved counterparties on these decision-making processes.

The Link Between Sustainability and Financial Reporting

Actually, in general terms, the link between SR and FR isn't confounding and invisible in some manner. There are some joint constituents between them. First, both reporting mechanisms share essentially the same mission; (1) reducing information asymmetry between counterparties in the markets and (2) showing how the reporting companies were functioning economically and to which degree this disclosed information –financial or non-financial was credible and to what extent these companies pay regard to their stakeholders, (3) dealing with principal-agent phenomenon, or currently deemed as stakeholder engagement. Second, two reporting processes have some global guidelines or standards released by international regulatory bodies. Yet, there are some major differences between them. For example, FR process addresses relatively narrower scope in terms of the limited nature of financial information and hence narrower span of stakeholder engagement while SR appeals to broader scope and the increased number of outside users because of wide and diversified nature of economic, environmental and social issues. Above all, FR is mandatory whereas SR is voluntary. That's why integrated reporting exists, improving the legitimacy of companies' sustainability reports (Camilleri, 2018), in addition to suggesting a solution to the drawbacks of traditional FR (Dumay et al., 2016). Due to its voluntary basis, the assurance of the latter is much more important than the former. Yet, FR research has been the most popular research area, outperforming SR/accounting studies (Sharma & An, 2018). Perhaps, one reason is that FR has taken part in the literature much earlier than SR. It would be fruitful to link this matured literature to newly developing SR research. Although limited, there are some current studies focusing on this relationship

(Canning et al., 2019). Yet, this research has examined how financial audit concepts such as materiality could be transferred to sustainability assurance process. Or, they have mostly argued the credibility and assurance of sustainability reports in financial auditor context. In other words, they have referred that the big4 (PwC, KPMG, EY, and Deloitte) have increasingly been operating in SR assurance market both at national level (Sierra-García et al., 2013) and also at international setting (Fernandez-Feijoo et al., 2018). The research in international setting has provided evidence of higher disclosure level and more credibility in sustainability reports when the assurance provider and the financial auditor is the big4. On the other hand, prior research also has manifested that assurance process has been exposed to the management control to a greater degree due to the fact that (1) assurance providers have been reluctant to stressing the statements involving certain stakeholder constituencies, (2) assurance process has not captured stakeholder participation enough, (3) assurance statement has been directed at management's "readership" since assurance providers were appointed by management and this statement was reported to them (Owen & O'Dwyer, 2004). These findings refer apparently to the probable risk of employing SR communication in an abusing way, as proposed by this chapter. Further, Li (2019) has found that some managers had a tendency to apply to repetitive disclosures in order to suppress disclosures, providing evidence for management's manipulative power on these reports. Interestingly, repetitive disclosures have been used more if company had a new CEO, a high level of new disclosures in the notes, newly issued equity, and if it couldn't catch the prior year's return level. This is remarkably interesting. Eventually, under certain conditions, it seems that managers and/or assurance providers of SR could frame these reports in a misleading way. Overconfident individuals tend to think optimistically, to ignore risk-specific or decision-specific information and hence to take more and improper risks. Prior research has already showed that this inopportune optimism could hinder the individual's ability to evaluate the outcomes of uncertain events in the future and therefore could lead them to undertake unreasonable risks. Moreover, these people tend to display some unethical behaviors in diverse settings as mentioned above. Information asymmetry and agency theory really help the researchers and regulatory bodies in guiding them to delineate why and what should be done in terms of all corporate communications. However, behavioral finance paradigm and upper echelon perspective greatly enable to understand all these reporting processes thoroughly and actually and provide insights into why and what is really going on in this wide realm.

In the first place, focusing on merely FR/SR, when top or middle level managers are overconfident, they tend to think overly optimistic about their companies, not to be able to see some probable risks concerning uncertain future events and hence to ignore the important decision-specific information, due to their hubris. Therefore, they would make these reports be prepared in an optimistic rhetoric or more hazardously in a misleading way. Even if the middle managers or responsible managers with these reporting processes are not overconfident, they will obey to the instructions by overconfident top managers, driving the reports to reflect the tone of top managers. At the end of the day, they would admit that they have just done their duty. Let's remember Milgram experiment.

In the second place, the auditors and/or assurance providers stand for decision-makers of their attestation or verification functions. Interestingly, it is found that Andersen's audit quality was not materially different from other Big-Five auditors in the years before its failure. Yet, Andersen's independence seems to have suffered due to issuing less going-concern opinions in its audit reports in the years before its collapse (Kumar & Lim, 2015). This finding is really important since it manifested that there is no difference in observed indicators of audit quality yet unobserved factors harming auditor's independence or good sense could lead to failures or frauds. In this chapter's context, when the auditors of FR and/or assurance providers of SR are overconfident, they would examine these reports with their optimistic lenses. They would not exploit all information sources concerning their decision - audit opinion or assurance statement. Their hubris would hinder themselves from catching some material errors or fallacies or could harm their good sense. On the other hand, remembering the literature manifesting the link between overconfidence and unethical behaviors, both managers as reporting actors and also assurance providers seem to be apt to display unethical or dysfunctional behaviors concerning corporate communications at the expense of stakeholders' interests. Although both reporting mechanisms have been wrapped up with a series of ethical, disciplinary and institutional arrangements, financial auditors are also liable for the decision they render through legislation such as Sarbanes-Oxley Act, etc. However, SR mechanism seems vulnerable due to its voluntary basis. Unfortunately, SR mechanism, manifesting company's means of the end of sustainable development, appeals to broader scope (e.g., environmental, economic and social issues) and hence has more audiences (e.g., internal-external stakeholders, communities, pressure groups, etc.).

SOLUTIONS AND RECOMMENDATIONS

The previous section has strived to manifest how the actors of FR and SR mechanisms have an important role in these processes. Amidst the research preponderantly putting emphasis on normative structure of these mechanisms, there is a need for the research aiming at arguing these actors' role on credibility and trustworthy of this information. Additionally, the decision environment in both reporting mechanisms seems to be exposed to misdetections, inadequate information gathering and processing facilities and erroneous evaluations. Through the studies linking overconfidence bias in managers to unethical behavior in organizational decision-making setting, this chapter contributes to the extant research through drawing attention to the impact of idiosyncratic factors on these reports as well.

In terms of SR, firstly, it is proposed that some material principles and practices could be transferred from matured FR function to this immature mechanism since traditional FR approach has learned too much from its inadequacies and unprecedented accounting/auditing scandals and hence adapted itself and its devices as necessitated by the challenging and demanding global environment. Well established methods in financial audit process could serve as a beneficial tool for SR and its verification process. Second, in verification process, assurance providers should not prepare their statements individually. Rather, based on unanimity, let alone plurality, a team should express their opinion about the credibility of this information. Particularly, their statements should be as clear and explicit. The team work could hinder these reports from being dominated by an overconfident assurance provider's manipulative power.

Third, companies could submit their reports to one regulatory body at national level and this institution could randomly deliver these anonymous reports to randomly chosen assurance providers, just as anonym as paper evaluation. This could prevent assurance process from management control or other weaknesses. Fourth, depending on the prevalent measures suggested by literature, assurance firms could detect whether overconfident bias in reporting company's managers exists. Due to increase in perceived risk of reporting company when it has overconfident managers, they should view this company' reports more meticulously.

FUTURE RESEARCH DIRECTIONS

This chapter presents new research areas for academicians. First, they could include overconfidence and other most common bias (e.g., representativeness, availability, anchoring) in decision-making processes into their research models. Extant research on FR/SR has overly focused on normative and/or observed constituents in these processes. That's why, the research design aiming to highlight this relatively unstudied area could greatly contribute the literature. Second, it is better for researchers to focus on the individual factors' role on these mechanisms since reporters, assurance providers are ultimately human-being, prone to making errors. Understanding the role of invisible factors on reporting mechanisms could help in defining actual functioning of the processes and hence solving the peculiar problems.

CONCLUSION

Accounting profession has intensely witnessed compelling challenges in the 21st century. In the presence of increased number in stakeholders and hence of immense informational needs, traditional FR model has remained unsatisfactory in meeting this need and more importantly evaluating a company's future performance. On the other hand, the companies' SR activities in accordance with GRI guidelines have increasingly been common practice since SR is considered as a tool for improving their decisions concerning sustainability. Additionally, for the sake of improving their reputation, fame and maintaining and/or increasing their investors, companies have certainly seized the power of SR for stakeholder engagement and corporate communications. Yet, this power is a mixed blessing. SR could be turned into a misleading way of conveying the information to the stakeholders for gaining access to financial capital, getting an overrated impression, and deluding both the direct and indirect investors, etc. In fact, in terms of assurance providers, some current studies refer to major ethical debates on SR such as (1) interdependence between audit and consulting activities, (2) familiarity with the audit companies, (3) symbolic nature of assurance process, (4) commercial pressures on assurance providers (Boiral et al., 2019). More importantly, another prior study draws attention to management control on assurance processes and hence value-added to corporate management, not to the stakeholders (Owen & O'Dwyer, 2004).

In spite of these critics on SR, it is obvious that these global disclosure formats or standards have encouraged companies to change themselves and empower their strategies and corporate communications concerning sustainability aspects increasingly. Further, socially responsible investors' concerns about the companies' sensitivity to sustainability matter could have put pressure on them, as suggested by Sauer (1997). Hence, companies in both developing and developed countries have placed emphasis on sustainability indexes of capital markets. Consequently, the investors have been the most important stakeholder group which have evidently linked financial outcomes to SR to a large extent. As such, SR process carries an invisible risk in that firms could drive this process in a misleading way at the expense of stakeholders' interests. That's why, credibility and assurance of this huge non-financial information is very substantive for all stakeholders. Unfortunately, these corporate communication ways would not become proper and clear unless the actors' manipulative power is impeded. Through (1) transferring the accumulated knowledge on FR into SR sphere, (2) enabling FR and SR of anonymous companies being judged by anonymous auditors or assurance providers, (3) establishing an assurance process based on unanimity by an assurance team and (3) developing devices which could ameliorate the peculiar problems (i.e., overconfidence in responsible people) and ethical debates, value added to all stakeholders could be guaranteed.

ACKNOWLEDGMENT

I am deeply grateful to Associate Professor Mine AKSU for her generous and precious support and mentorship in the course of my postdoctoral research at Sabanci University. I also want to express my sincere thanks to Sabanci University (School of Management) for granting me use of their prosperous research sources as a visiting scholar.

REFERENCES

Aggarwal, P. (2013). Sustainability reporting and its impact on corporate financial performance: A literature review. *Indian Journal of Commerce & Management Studies*, *4*(3), 51–59.

Al-Thuneibat, A. A., Al Issa, R. T. I., & Baker, R. A. A. (2011). Do audit tenure and firm size contribute to audit quality? Empirical evidence from Jordan. *Managerial Auditing Journal*, *26*(4), 317–334. doi:10.1108/02686901111124648

Almutairi, A. R., Dunn, K. A., & Skantz, T. (2009). Auditor tenure, auditor specialization, and information asymmetry. *Managerial Auditing Journal*, *24*(7), 600–623. doi:10.1108/02686900910975341

Aren, S., & Aydemir, S. D. (2015). The moderation of financial literacy on the relationship between individual factors and risky investment intention. *International Business Research*, *8*(6), 17–28. doi:10.5539/ibr.v8n6p17

Aren, S., Aydemir, S. D., & Sehitoglu, Y. (2016). Behavioral biases on institutional investors: A literature review. *Kybernetes*, *45*(10), 1668–1684. doi:10.1108/K-08-2015-0203

Bazerman, M., Morgan, K., & Loewenstein, G. (1997). The impossibility of auditor independence. *Sloan Management Review*, *38*(4), 89–94.

Boiral, O., Heras-Saizarbitoria, I., Brotherton, M., & Bernard, J. (2019). Ethical issues in the assurance of sustainability reports: Perspectives from assurance providers. *Journal of Business Ethics*, *159*(4), 1111–1125. doi:10.100710551-018-3840-3

Brown, V. L., Gissel, J. L., & Neely, D. G. (2016). Audit quality indicators: Perceptions of junior-level auditors. *Managerial Auditing Journal*, *31*(8/9), 949–980. doi:10.1108/MAJ-01-2016-1300

Busenitz, L. W., & Barney, J. B. (1997). Differences between entrepreneurs and managers in large organizations: Biases and heuristics in strategic decision-making. *Journal of Business Venturing*, *12*(1), 9–30. doi:10.1016/S0883-9026(96)00003-1

Camilleri, M. A. (2018). Theoretical insights on integrated reporting: The inclusion of non-financial capitals in corporate disclosures. *Corporate Communications*, *23*(4), 567–581. Advance online publication. doi:10.1108/CCIJ-01-2018-0016

Campa, D. (2013). "Big 4 fee premium" and audit quality: Latest evidence from UK listed companies. *Managerial Auditing Journal*, *28*(8), 680–707. doi:10.1108/MAJ-11-2012-0784

Canning, M., O'Dwyer, B., & Georgakopoulos, G. (2019). Processes of auditability in sustainability assurance – The case of materiality construction. *Accounting and Business Research*, *49*(1), 1–27. doi:10.1080/00014788.2018.1442208

Carey, P., & Simnett, R. (2006). Audit partner tenure and audit quality. *The Accounting Review*, *81*(3), 653–676. doi:10.2308/accr.2006.81.3.653

Carson, E. (2009). Industry specialization by global audit firm networks. *The Accounting Review*, *84*(2), 355–382. doi:10.2308/accr.2009.84.2.355

Chapin, F. S. III, Torn, M. S., & Tateno, M. (1996). Principles of ecosystem sustainability. *American Naturalist*, *148*(6), 1016–1037. doi:10.1086/285969

Chen, K. Y., Lin, K. L., & Zhou, J. (2005). Audit quality and earnings management for Taiwan IPO firms. *Managerial Auditing Journal*, *20*(1), 86–104. doi:10.1108/02686900510570722

Cheng, B., Ioannou, I., & Serafeim, G. (2014). Corporate social responsibility and access to finance. *Strategic Management Journal*, *35*(1), 1–23. doi:10.1002mj.2131

Chin, C., & Chi, H. (2009). Reducing restatements with increased industry expertise. *Contemporary Accounting Research*, *26*(3), 729–765. doi:10.1506/car.26.3.4

Choi, J., Kim, C. F., Kim, J., & Zang, Y. (2010). Audit office size, audit quality, and audit pricing. *Auditing*, *29*(1), 73–97. doi:10.2308/aud.2010.29.1.73

Craswell, A., Francis, J., & Taylor, S. (1995). Auditor brand name reputations and industry specializations. *Journal of Accounting and Economics*, *20*(3), 297–322. doi:10.1016/0165-4101(95)00403-3

DeFond, M., & Zhang, J. (2014). A review of archival auditing research. *Journal of Accounting and Economics*, *58*(2-3), 275–326. doi:10.1016/j.jacceco.2014.09.002

Dolinsky, C., & Feinberg, R. A. (1986). Linguistic barriers to consumer information processing: Information overload in the Hispanic population. *Psychology and Marketing*, *3*(4), 261–271. doi:10.1002/mar.4220030405

Donnelly, D. P., Quirin, J. J., & O'Byran, D. (2003). Auditor acceptance of dsyfunctional audit behavior: An explanatory model using auditors' personal characteristics. *Behavioral Research in Accounting*, *15*(1), 87–110. doi:10.2308/bria.2003.15.1.87

Duellman, S., Hurwitz, H., & Sun, Y. (2015). Managerial overconfidence and audit fees. *Journal of Contemporary Accounting & Economics*, *11*(2), 148–165. doi:10.1016/j.jcae.2015.05.001

Dumay, J., Bernardi, C., Guthrie, J., & Demartini, P. (2016). Integrated reporting: A structured literature review. *Accounting Forum*, *40*(3), 166–185. doi:10.1016/j.accfor.2016.06.001

Dyllick, T., & Hockerts, K. (2002). Beyond the business case for corporate sustainability. *Business Strategy and the Environment*, *11*(2), 130–141. doi:10.1002/bse.323

Fernandez-Feijoo, B., Romero, S., & Ruiz, S. (2018). Financial auditor and sustainability reporting: Does it matter? *Corporate Social Responsibility and Environmental Management*, *25*(3), 209–224. doi:10.1002/csr.1449

Finucane, M. L., Alhakami, A., Slovic, P., & Johnson, S. M. (2000). The effect heuristic in jodgements of risk and benefits. *Journal of Behavioral Decision Making*, *13*(1), 1–17. doi:10.1002/(SICI)1099-0771(200001/03)13:1<1::AID-BDM333>3.0.CO;2-S

Fischhoff, B., Slovic, P., & Lichtenstein, S. (1977). Knowing with certainty: The appropriateness of extreme confidence. *Journal of Experimental Psychology. Human Perception and Performance*, *3*(4), 552–564. doi:10.1037/0096-1523.3.4.552

Flower, J. (2015). The international integrated reporting council: A story of failure. *Critical Perspectives on Accounting*, *27*, 1–17. doi:10.1016/j.cpa.2014.07.002

Francis, J., & Yu, M. (2009). The effect of Big 4 office size on audit quality. *The Accounting Review*, *84*(5), 1521–1552. doi:10.2308/accr.2009.84.5.1521

Fuerman, R. D., & Kraten, M. (2009). The big 4 audit report: Should the public perceive it as a label of quality? *Accounting and the Public Interest*, *9*(1), 148–165. doi:10.2308/api.2009.9.1.148

Global Reporting Initiative. (2011). Sustainability Reporting Guidelines. Global Reporting Initiative. *G3*, 1.

Global Reporting Initiative (GRI). (2019). *Information About GRI*. Retrieved from https://www.globalreporting.org/information/about-gri/Pages/default.aspx

Goodwin, J., & Wu, D. (2014). Is the effect of industry expertise on audit pricing an office-level or a partner-level phenomenon? *Review of Accounting Studies*, *19*(4), 1532–1578. doi:10.100711142-014-9285-8

Gronewold, U., & Donle, M. (2011). Organizational error climate and auditors' predispositions toward handling errors. *Behavioral Research in Accounting*, *23*(2), 69–92. doi:10.2308/bria-10061

Habib, A., & Hossain, M. (2013). CEO/CFO characteristics and financial reporting quality: A review. *Research in Accounting Regulation*, *25*(1), 88–100. doi:10.1016/j.racreg.2012.11.002

Hambrick, D. C. (2016). Upper echelons theory. *The Palgrave Encyclopedia of Strategic Management*. https://link.springer.com/referenceworkentry/10.1057/978-1-349-94848-2_785-1

Hambrick, D. C., & Mason, P. (1984). Upper echelons: The organization as a reflection of its top managers. *Academy of Management Review*, *9*(2), 193–206. doi:10.5465/amr.1984.4277628

Herremans, I., Akathaporn, P., & McInnes, M. (1993). An Investigation of Corporate Social Responsibility Reputation and Economic Performance. *Accounting, Organizations and Society*, *18*(October- November), 587–604. doi:10.1016/0361-3682(93)90044-7

Hoitash, R., Markelevich, A., & Barragato, C. A. (2007). Auditor fees and audit quality. *Managerial Auditing Journal*, *22*(8), 761–786. doi:10.1108/02686900710819634

Hoyle, J. (1978). Mandatory auditor rotation: The arguments and an alternative. *Journal of Accountancy*, *145*(5), 69–78.

Hsieh, T., Wang, Z., & Demirkan, S. (2018). Overconfidence and tax avoidance: The role of CEO and CFO interaction. *Journal of Accounting and Public Policy*, *37*(3), 241–253. doi:10.1016/j.jaccpubpol.2018.04.004

Jackson, A. B., Moldrich, M., & Roebuck, P. (2008). Mandatory audit firm rotation and audit quality. *Managerial Auditing Journal*, *23*(5), 420–437. doi:10.1108/02686900810875271

Jenkins, D. S., & Velury, U. K. (2012). Auditor tenure and the pricing of discretionary accruals in the Post-SOX Era. *Accounting and the Public Interest*, *12*(1), 1–15. doi:10.2308/apin-10204

Jensen, K. L., & Payne, J. L. (2005). Audit procurement: Managing audit quality and audit fees in response to agency costs. *Auditing*, *24*(2), 27–48. doi:10.2308/aud.2005.24.2.27

Johnson, E., Kuhn, J. R., Apostolu, B., & Hassell, J. M. (2013). Auditor perceptions of client narcissism as a fraud attitude risk factor. *Auditing*, *32*(1), 203–219. doi:10.2308/ajpt-50329

Kahneman, D. (2018). *An Interview with Daniel Kahneman*. Retrieved from https://www.theguardian.com/books/2015/jul/18/daniel-kahneman-books-interview

Kahneman, D., & Tversky, A. (1972). Subjective probability: A judgement of representativeness. *Cognitive Psychology*, *3*(3), 430–454. doi:10.1016/0010-0285(72)90016-3

Kahneman, D., & Tversky, A. (1979). Prospect theory: An analysis of decision under risk. *Econometrica*, *47*(2), 263–291. doi:10.2307/1914185

Knechel, W. R., & Vanstraelen, A. (2005). The relationship between auditor tenure and audit quality implied by going concern opinions. *Auditing*, *26*(1), 113–131. doi:10.2308/aud.2007.26.1.113

Knechel, W. R., Vanstraelen, A., & Zerni, M. (2014). Does the identity of engagement partners matter? An analysis of audit partner reporting decisions. *Contemporary Accounting Research*, *32*(4), 1443–1478. doi:10.1111/1911-3846.12113

KPMG Survey of Corporate Responsibility Reporting. (2017). Retrieved rom https://home.kpmg/xx/en/home/insights/2017/10/the-kpmg-survey-of-corporate-responsibility-reporting-2017.html

Kumar, K., & Lim, L. (2015). Was Andersen's audit quality lower than its peers? A comparative analysis of audit quality. *Managerial Auditing Journal*, *30*(8/9), 911–962. doi:10.1108/MAJ-10-2014-1105

Lennox, C. S., & Wu, X. (2018). A review of the archival literature on audit partners. *Accounting Horizons*, *32*(2), 1–35. doi:10.2308/acch-51942

Leventis, S., & Caramanis, C. (2005). Determinants of audit time as a proxy of audit quality. *Managerial Auditing Journal*, *20*(5), 460–478. doi:10.1108/02686900510598821

Li, H. (2019). Repetitive disclosures in the MD&A. *Journal of Business Finance & Accounting*, *46*(9-10), 1063–1096. doi:10.1111/jbfa.12405

Lichtenstein, S., & Fischhoff, B. (1977). Do those who know more also know more about how much they know? *Organizational Behavior and Human Performance*, *20*(2), 159–183. doi:10.1016/0030-5073(77)90001-0

Malmendier, U., & Tate, G. (2004). *CEO overconfidence and corporate investment.* NBER Working Paper, No. 10807.

Malmendier, U., & Tate, G. (2008). Who makes acquisitions? CEO overconfidence and the market's reaction. *Journal of Financial Economics, 89*(1), 20–43. doi:10.1016/j.jfineco.2007.07.002

Manetti, G., & Taccofondi, S. (2012). The role of stakeholders in sustainability reporting assurance. *Journal of Business Ethics, 107*(3), 363–377. doi:10.100710551-011-1044-1

McLachlan, J., & Gardner, J. (2004). A Comparison of Socially Responsible and Conventional Investors. *Journal of Business Ethics, 52*(1), 11–25. doi:10.1023/B:BUSI.0000033104.28219.92

Muttakin, M. B., Khan, A., & Mihret, D. G. (2017). Business group affiliation, earnings management and audit quality: Evidence from Bangladesh. *Managerial Auditing Journal, 32*(4/5), 427–444. doi:10.1108/MAJ-01-2016-1310

Nagy, A. (2012). Audit partner specialization: The case of Andersen followers. *Managerial Auditing Journal, 27*(3), 251–262. doi:10.1108/02686901211207483

Oskamp, S. (1965). Overconfidence in case-study judgments. *Journal of Consulting Psychology, 29*(3), 261–265. doi:10.1037/h0022125 PMID:14303514

Owen, D., & O'Dwyer, B. (2004). *Assurance statement quality in environmental, social and sustainability reporting: A critical evaluation of leading edge practice.* ICCSR Research Paper Series, No. 23-2004.

Pasewark, W. R., & Riley, M. E. (2010). It's a Matter of Principle: The Role of Personal Values in Investment Decisions. *Journal of Business Ethics, 93*(2), 237–253. doi:10.100710551-009-0218-6

Piot, C. (2007). Auditor concentration in a joint-auditing environment: The French market 1997-2003. *Managerial Auditing Journal, 22*(2), 161–176. doi:10.1108/02686900710718663

Presley, T. J., & Abbott, L. J. (2013). AIA submission: CEO overconfidence and the incidence of financial restatement. *Advances in Accounting, Incorporating. Advances in International Accounting, 29*(1), 74–84. doi:10.1016/j.adiac.2013.03.007

Reheul, A. M., Van Caneghem, T., Van den Bogaerd, M., & Verbruggen, S. (2017). Auditor gender, experience and reporting in nonprofit organizations. *Managerial Auditing Journal, 32*(6), 550–577. doi:10.1108/MAJ-01-2016-1296

Romanus, R. N., Maher, J. J., & Fleming, D. M. (2008). Auditor industry specialization, auditor changes, and accounting restatements. *Accounting Horizons, 22*(4), 389–413. doi:10.2308/acch.2008.22.4.389

Sauer, D. A. (1997). The Impact of Social-Responsibility Screens on Investment Performance: Evidence from the Domini 400 Social Index and Domini Equity Mutual Fund. *Review of Financial Economics, 6*(2), 137–149. doi:10.1016/S1058-3300(97)90002-1

Schrand, C. M., & Zechman, S. L. C. (2012). Executive overconfidence and the slippery slope to financial misreporting. *Journal of Accounting and Economics, 53*(1-2), 311–329. doi:10.1016/j.jacceco.2011.09.001

Sharma, U., & An, Y. (2018). Accounting and accountability in Fiji: A review and synthesis. *Australian Accounting Review, 28*(3), 421-427.

Sierra-García, L., Zorio-Grima, A., & García-Benau, M. A. (2013). Sustainable development and assurance of corporate social responsibility reports published by Ibex-35 companies. *Corporate Social Responsibility and Environmental Management*, *20*(6), 359–370. doi:10.1002/csr.1303

Simon, H. A. (1955). A behavioral model of rational choice. *The Quarterly Journal of Economics*, *69*(1), 99–118. doi:10.2307/1884852

Stanley, J. D., & DeZoort, F. T. (2007). Audit firm tenure and financial restatements: An analysis of industry specialization and fee effects. *Journal of Accounting and Public Policy*, *26*(2), 131–159. doi:10.1016/j.jaccpubpol.2007.02.003

Svanberg, J., & Ohman, P. (2013). Auditors' time pressure: Does ethical culture support audit quality? *Managerial Auditing Journal*, *28*(7), 572–591. doi:10.1108/MAJ-10-2012-0761

Tversky, A., & Kahneman, D. (1974). Judgement under uncertainty: Heuristics and biases", *Science. New Series*, *185*(4157), 1124–1131. PMID:17835457

Tversky, A., & Kahneman, D. (1986). Rational choice and framing of decisions. *Journal of Business*, *59*(4), 251-278.

Williams, G. (2007). Some determinants of the socially responsible investment decision: A cross-country study. *Journal of Behavioral Finance*, *8*(1), 43–57. doi:10.1080/15427560709337016

Zerni, M. (2012). Audit partner specialization and audit fees: Some evidence from Sweden. *Contemporary Accounting Research*, *29*(1), 312–340. doi:10.1111/j.1911-3846.2011.01098.x

ADDITIONAL READING

Akerlof, G. A., & Schiller, R. J. (2009). *Animal Spirits*. Princeton University Press.

Aydemir, S. D., & Aren, S. (2017). Do the effects of individual factors on financial risk-taking behavior diversify with financial literacy? *Kybernetes*, *46*(10), 1706–1734. doi:10.1108/K-10-2016-0281

Kahneman, D. (2015). *Thinking Fast and Slow*. Farrar, Straus and Giroux.

KEY TERMS AND DEFINITIONS

Audit Quality: It refers to degree of attestation function whereby auditing partners render an opinion as to fair presentation of their clients' financial statements, thus lending credibility to the financial reporting system.

Behavioral Finance Paradigm: It is a paradigm that gives a delineation of actual choice behavior under the assumptions that people are not rational, that sum of the deviations from rational behavior doesn't sum up to zero and that subjective probabilities rather than stochastic probabilities determine the decision weights.

Financial Reporting: It is a form of mandatory corporate communication through which represents fair presentation of the company's financial statements and which discloses the information to the stakeholders about the company's economic functioning.

Overconfidence: Overconfidence bias is recognized as a cognitive limitation in psychology literature and it exists when people are greatly optimistic in their initial assessment of a situation and hence are not good at taking the new additional information into their consideration due to their starting overconfident thinking.

Prospect Theory: A choice theory in which value function is determined by gains, losses, and concave for gains and convex for losses, and in which stochastic probabilities are replaced by decision weights derived from. subjective probabilities. This theory also suggests that individuals make inconsistent preferences when the same choice is presented through different framing due to the isolation effect.

Sustainability Reporting: It is a form of corporate communication through which the company discloses to all stakeholders (internal-external or present-future investors or pressure groups) for the company's corporate strategies and practices about sustainable development.

Upper Echelon Theory: It is the idea that organizational strategies and decisions are greatly shaped by top executives' personal background since top executives assess their organizational situations through their own heavily individualized lenses.

Chapter 4
Values or Strategy?
Comparative Study About the Roles of Values and Strategy in the Web Pages of the Largest Scandinavian Firms

Rauno Rusko
University of Lapland, Finland

ABSTRACT

Values and strategies are two powerful drivers of business. Both of them have effects on the activities and practices of the firms. This chapter compares the relevance of values and strategy in Scandinavian business basing on the contents of the web pages for the largest firms in Sweden, Norway, Denmark, and Finland. The results show the importance of values in the forms of responsibility and sustainability in these web pages. The firms also provide complement information, how they will follow these topical contemporary values in their business. According to analysis, the role of strategy is still relatively important, but not so important as values especially in the headings of homepages or "about us" pages.

INTRODUCTION

The contemporary public discussions about business and enterprises emphasize the responsible themes of business, such as corporate social responsibility (CSP), ethics and sustainable development. The popularity of these responsible themes of business are based on the several reasons, but especially climate change, which has changed and will change in the several ways the tool and practices to carry on business in the forms of energy use, travelling, recycling, among others (Jones, & Levy, 2007; Wells, Ponting, & Peattie, 2011).

These responsible themes of business emphasize the role of values. This development is based on the changes in the natural environment. Also, the changed business environment, such as the changed attitudes of stakeholders, have effects on how to make business in the firms.

DOI: 10.4018/978-1-7998-4637-6.ch004

Strategy as a concept leans on military history, such as Sun Zu and writings of Clausewitz. Sun Zu describes the strategy and tactics of Chinese military leaders 300-400 B.C. and Clausewitz strategy and tactics of Napoleon during his wars. Gradually term "strategy" has also used in the context of business and planning. (See, e.g. Mintzberg et al., 1998). However, this kind of history has effects on the connotations of strategy even today.

This study focuses on the roles of values and strategies in the firms. And especially, this study focuses on Scandinavian firms, which are known, according to some researches (Vidaver-Cohen & Brønn, 2015), relatively responsible firms among other firms in the world.

According to several studies (Goodpaster, 1991; Graafland, Van de Ven, & Stoffele, 2003; Collis & Rukstad, 2008) both strategies and values are important guidelines of business. Even everyday activities and practices of the firms might follow these guidelines (Rossouw et al., 2010). On the contrary, both strategies and values are often relatively general umbrella terms, which are difficult to follow exactly in the business activities. However, the connotations of strategy compared to value is harder and more competitive (c.f. Llewellyn & Tappin, 2003; Verenich, 2014). Term value might easily have connotations with CSR, ethics and sustainable development, but connotations of strategy are generally far away from the concepts.

It is possible to define strategy in a way, which is linked with CSR, ethics or sustainable development, but without this kind of direct definition of strategy the linkage between strategy and these terms of responsibility is relatively weak.

The content and structure of the public documents for the firm, such as official webpages and annual reports, hints the attitudes of the firm about values, corporate social responsibility (CSP), ethics and sustainable development, among others. Therefore, the fact whether the emphasis of these public documents is on strategy or on values, will tell something about aims, routines and practices of the firm.

This study compares the relative importance of values and strategies of the largest Scandinavian firms using official public documents, such as webpages and annual reports as an empirical source. It is possible to define Scandinavian in several ways: the smallest area of these definitions covers Norway, Sweden and part of Finland and the largest area covers Norway, Sweden, Finland, Denmark, Island and even Faroe Islands. This study follows the definition, where Norway, Sweden, Denmark and Finland are included in the Scandinavian countries (Alestalo & Kuhnle, 1986).

Practically, this study is directed in 80 Scandinavian firms, 20 Norwegian, 20 Swedish, 20 Danish and 20 Finnish firms. All of these firms are among top 100 firms in each country. They are coming from different industries and geographically their headquarters are in different parts of these countries. Many of these firms are internationally oriented and they have large activities even in all Scandinavian countries – and often all over the world.

Literature Review: Values and Strategies

Values

In the context of business values, arise several possible themes for study: decision-maker, decision-making process and content of business values. Empirical part of this study focuses on the content business values and especially their relationship and position to the content of strategies. This sub-chapter mainly contains these other themes associated with business values.

Values of business, or "business values" have connotation with corporate social responsibility (CSR) and business ethics (Joyner, Payne & Raiborn, 2002) - and also with corporate social opportunity (CSO) (Jenkins, 2009). According to Grayson & Hodges (2004, 13) CSO mentality can be achieved "in achieving alignment of business values, purpose and strategy with the social and economic needs of customers and consumers, while embedding responsible and ethical business policies and practices throughout the company". This perspective shows also the linkage between business values and strategy.

However, business values are, compared to strategy, more strongly linked with CSR and business ethics. Term "strategy" itself do not reflect or have any direct ethical connotations, such as CSR or business ethics. That is, in order to have ethical reflections term "strategy" need adjective or further definitions, such as "legal compliance strategy" or "integrity strategy" (Joyner et al., 2002).

Values and especially "business values" are popular themes of literature, which is often focused on family firms. However, several variables have effects on the values of the firms. Age and size of the firm and the structure of the ownerships, for example, affects the prevailing values of the firm. Koiranen (2002) has studied over 100 years old Finnish family firms with the following research question: 'How do certain firms that have been involved in business for over one century perceive and rank their business values?' The data of his study based on self-assessments of the active family executives working at the top level (response rate 39.7%). The top values were honesty, credibility, obeying the law, quality, and industriousness, but the values of yielding good economic return to owners, willingness to grow, and to get social recognition all scored surprisingly low. According to Koiranen (2002), the adjectives best describing the characteristics of owning families were: committed, responsible, fair, hardworking, and successful.

Several studies have compared the business values of family firms to non-family firms (e.g. Erdem and Gül Başer, 2010; Adams, Taschian and Shore, 1996). Erdem and Gül Başer (2010) study family and business values of regional family firms. According to them, family values are rather traditional hand, which the value of business are innovating. The family values and business values are a synergistic construct. Erdem and Gül Başer (2010) notice that the founders are dominant factors in the formation of values of the family firms and the second generation voluntarily continues this effect.

Adams et al. (1996) study ethics in family business and especially whether family firms are more, less or equally as ethical as non-family controlled firms. Comparing structured interview data from 214 respondents in family firms with a proportionally matched sample of 230 respondents in non-family-owned firms, they found some differences in ethics-related attitudes, behavior and experiences: fewer family-owned businesses had formal codes of ethics. Family-firms were more likely to employ informal methods to promote ethical behavior, with role modeling of expected behaviors regarded as more important than in non-family firms. (Adams et al., 1996)

In addition to business values of family firm versus non-family firm, also business values of small firms related to large firms have been studied. According to Spence and Lozano (2000), in the small firms (from Spain and USA) the importance of informal mechanisms such as the influence of friends, family and employees are highlighted, and the likely ineffectiveness of formal tools such as codes and social and ethical standards. Thus, it seems that the features of the emphasized values of family firms and small firms resembles each other. In both cases informal mechanism of values are especially important. However, this chapter focuses on the values and strategies of (Scandinavian) large, international, firms.

In international firms the business values differ from the value of small firms. Among large Scandinavian firms, however, are some family-owned firms. Ciulla (2007) emphasizes the leaders' role in the content of business values. However, she sees that the more important question is not "Whose values?"

but "What values?" Important is, what a leader actually does to demonstrate his or her values (Ciulla, 2007). Ciulla (2007) studies how leaders translate values into action and actions into enduring organizational values. She emphasizes what theories of leadership say about how leaders influence follower and looks at the leadership of P. Roy Vagelos of Merck & Company to illustrate the how the values of founders and current leaders shape the values of their own organizations, and can shape the values of the industries in which they operate.

Strategies

History of the term "strategy" stem from military activities in China. The most famous old military strategy book is Sun Tzu's "The Art of War". However, there are altogether seven early books about military strategy in China dated to the periods of Spring and Autumn (722-481 BC) and Warring States (403-221 BC) (McCaffrey, 2015, 23). According to McCaffrey (2015), "the reason for this strategic attention is that Art of War contains a system of strategic thought that lends itself to social science interpretations. In particular, there is an emphasis in Sun Tzu's thought on universal principles of strategy that are often cast in essentially economic terms." McCaffrey (2015) interprets, that numerous other early Chinese works are included in the canon of classic Chinese strategic thought. Also, the book of Clausewitz has been mentioned among initial strategic books. According to Kitchen (2010, 119), "the early history of strategy is concerned solely with military campaigns, and was distinguished by Clausewitz from tactics, which 'is the art of using troops in battle; strategy is the art of using battles to win the war'."

Gradually term "strategy" launched into the management and business-making discussions. However, due to history of term strategy, connotations of strategy easily linked with war and (hard) competition, not with values. However, strategic discussions have developed and diversified to the various directions. In strategy-as-practice (SAP) discussions, for example, strategy making is based – not only on the managers of the firms – but also on the practitioners of the organization (Jarzabkowski, 2004; Jarzabkowski, & Spee, 2009).

Methodology

Methods

This study is possible to interpret as some kind of comparative case study, because it compares the relative importance of values and strategies of the largest Scandinavian firms using official public documents, such as webpages and annual reports as an empirical source (cf. Zitzler & Thiele, 1998, September). However, the cases are these countries and announcements of their largest firms related to values and strategies. The main point is not to compare these countries, but generally the positions of values and strategies in the firms of Scandinavian. Scandinavian is possible to define in several ways: the smallest area of these definitions covers Norway, Sweden and part of Finland and the largest area covers Norway, Sweden, Finland, Denmark, Island and even Faroe Islands. This study is focused on the 20 large firms in Norway, Sweden, Denmark and Finland, that is altogether 80 firms. All of these firms are among top 100 firms in each country and they are not purposely focused on any particular industries and their headquarters are not specific parts of the countries. Mostly these firms have multinational activities.

Though values and strategies are the main point of the chapter this study has also reflections of multi-case study because of several studied firms, which are informants of the study. In other words, four Scandinavian countries form the sampling base for multi-case study (cf. Otero-Neira, Lindman, & Fernández, 2009).

Data

Data contains 80 Scandinavian (Nordic) firms and their official web pages. The main focus is on their ways to consider values and strategies – and especially the hierarchic order between these two concepts in each company. (Largest Companies, 2020) http://www.largestcompanies.com/toplists.

Data covers 20 largest companies (basing on turnover in year 2017) from Denmark, Finland, Sweden and Norway. Analysis is based on webpages of the companies and especially the position and context of the values and strategy in the webpages. Analysis focuses on homepage/main pages and pages "About us" or "About company". In addition to word "value(s)", also Corporate Social Responsibility (CSR),

Table 1. Largest companies of Denmark and their turnover and main industry.

Firm	Turnover (1000 euros)	Main Industry
A.P. Møller – Mærsk A/S	192 168 000	Water transport
Centrica Energy Trading A/S	69 259 259	Electricity, gas, steam and air conditioning supply
Danske Bank A/S	48 149 000	Financial service activities
Ørsted Salg & Service A/S	43 134 000	Electricity, gas, steam and air conditioning supply
Ørsted Wind Power A/S	42 581 928	Electricity, gas, steam and air conditioning supply
Vestas Manufacturing A/S	36 637 686	Manufacture of machinery and equipment n.e.c.
Lego A/S	36 391 000	Financial service activities, except insurance and pension
Coop Danmark A/S	35 541 000	Retail trade
Energi Danmark A/S	32 541 064	Electricity, gas, steam and air conditioning supply
Lego System A/S	27 354 841	Other manufacturing - Manufacture of games and toys
Equinor Refining Denmark A/S	23 007 458	Manufacture of coke and refined petroleum products
Pandora A/S	22 806 000	Wholesale trade, except of motor vehicles and motorcycles Wholesale of watches and jewellery
Siemens Gamesa Renewable Energy A/S	21 460 302	Manufacture of electrical equipment
Danish Crown A/S	21 406 000	Manufacture of food products
Lundbeck A/S, H	18 117 000	Manufacture of basic pharmaceutical products and pharmaceutical preparations
Reitan Distribution A/S	16 978 596	Wholesale trade, except of motor vehicles and motorcycles
Coloplast A/S	15 528 000	Manufacture of medical and dental instruments and supplies
Bestseller A/S	13 859 805	Wholesale of clothing and footwear
Dansk Shell, A/S	13 082 700	Manufacture of coke and refined petroleum products
Velux A/S	12 772 000	Wholesale of wood and other construction materials, Wholesale of sanitary equipment

Table 2. Largest companies of Finland and their turnover and main industry.

Firm	Turnover (1000 euros)	Main Industry
Nokia Oyj	23 147 000	Activities of head offices; management consultancy activities, Manufacture of computer, electronic and optical products and communication equipment
Neste Oyj	13 217 000	Manufacture of coke and refined petroleum products
Kesko Oyj	10 675 900	Wholesale trade, except of motor vehicles and motorcycles
Stora Enso Oyj	10 045 000	Manufacture of paper and paper products
UPM-Kymmene Oyj	10 010 000	Manufacture of paper and paper products
KONE Oyj	8 942 400	Manufacture of machinery and equipment n.e.c. - Manufacture of lifting and handling equipment
Outokumpu Oyj	6 363 000	Financial service activities, Manufacture of basic metals
Sampo Oyj	5 815 000	Financial service activities
Metsäliitto-konserni	5 040 000	Forestry and logging
Wärtsilä Oyj Abp	4 923 000	Manufacture of machinery and equipment
Fortum Oyj	4 520 000	Activities of head offices; management consultancy activities, Electricity, gas, steam and air conditioning supply
Cargotec Oyj	3 280 100	Manufacture of machinery and equipment Manufacture of lifting and handling equipment
Valmet Oyj	3 159 000	Activities of head offices; management consultancy activities Manufacture of machinery and equipment ..for paper and paperboard production
Konecranes Oyj	3 136 400	Manufacture of machinery and equipment Manufacture of lifting and handling equipment
Huhtamäki Oyj	2 988 700	Activities of head offices; management consultancy activities Manufacture of rubber and plastic products
Metso Oyj	2 706 000	Manufacture of machinery and equipment
Amer Sports Oyj	2 685 200	Financial service activities, Wholesale trade, except of motor vehicles and motorcycles Wholesale of sporting equipment
Finnair Oyj	2 568 400	Air transport - Passenger air transport
Kemira Oyj	2 486 000	Manufacture of chemicals and chemical products
Caverion Oyj	2 282 800	Architectural and engineering activities; technical testing and analysis

"Responsibility" and "Sustainability" are interpreted to be in the category of Values. Strategy in the analysis is exactly in the form of "Strategy", "Strategies" or with some other complementing word (However, e.g. "Sustainable strategy is mainly interpret to be part of "Values".

These webpages were checked 9.-11. January 2020. In the case of some firms it was difficult to determine the importance/position of values or strategy following these criterions above, In these cases data was missing (--) in the analysis.

Tables 1-4. introduces these firms of the analysis with turnover and main industry.

Table 3. Largest companies of Sweden and their turnover and main industry.

Firm	Turnover (1000 SEK)	Main Industry
Volvo, AB	390 835 000	Manufacture of motor vehicles, trailers and semi-trailers
Volvo Car AB	252 653 000	Manufacture of motor vehicles, trailers and semi-trailers
Ericsson, Telefon AB LM	210 838 000	Manufacture of computer, electronic and optical products
H & M Hennes & Mauritz AB	210 400 000	Retail sale of clothing in specialised stores
Skanska AB	171 730 000	Construction of buildings
Vattenfall AB	156 824 000	Electricity, gas, steam and air conditioning supply
Scania CV AB	137 126 000	Manufacture of motor vehicles, trailers and semi-trailers
Electrolux, AB	124 129 000	Manufacture of electrical equipment
Essity AB	118 500 000	Manufacture of paper and paper products
ICA Gruppen AB	115 354 000	Wholesale trade, except of motor vehicles and motorcycles
Corral Petroleum Holdings AB	103 641 000	Financial service activities
Securitas AB	101 466 700	Security and investigation activities
Sandvik AB	100 072 000	Manufacture of basic metals
Atlas Copco AB	95 363 000	Manufacture of machinery and equipment
Nordea Bank AB	93 269 650	Financial service activities,
SKF, AB	85 713 000	Manufacture of machinery and equipment
Assa Abloy AB	84 048 000	Manufacture of fabricated metal products, except machinery and equipment
Telia Company AB	83 559 000	Telecommunications
Axel Johnson Holding AB	82 354 000	Retail trade

RESULTS OF THE ANALYSIS

Results are based on 80 Scandinavian firms, 20 from Denmark, Finland, Norway and from Sweden. The main research question leans on the hierarchic position between values and strategy, that is whether values or strategy is in the most important driver of firm. In other words, whether values, such as sustainability or responsibility among others, are the main point and strategy perhaps supports values in the (webpages of the) firm or vice versa.

The results mainly focus on the physical place of values and strategy in the webpages of the firms. The results are placed in the Tables 5.-8. These Tables contain some details about the pages of the company (or details/problems of the analysis) and answer to the question whether strategy or values are more important in these webpages, basing on the criterions of the analysis. This column has remarks "Strategy", "Values", or Values(Strategy), which means that Values are more important, but these pages emphasize (somehow) also the Strategy. "Strategy & Values" or "Values/Strategy" mean, that these two concepts are equally important in these webpages.

In the case of Denmark 16 out of 20 companies emphasize more Values in the webpages. One firm emphasize strategy and in one of the companies these two are equally important (or actually unimportant). In Finland 11 out of 20 firms emphasize values clearly compared to strategy, in six Finnish cases

Table 4. Largest companies of Norway and their turnover and main industry.

Firm	Turnover (1000 SEK)	Main Industry
Norsk Hydro ASA	160 914 000	Manufacture of basic metals
Telenor ASA	110 425 000	Telecommunications
Helse Sør-Øst RHF	81 755 329	Public administration and defence; compulsory social security
Equinor ASA	79 593 000	Extraction of crude petroleum and natural gas
Odd Reitan Private Holding AS	72 042 000	Financial service activities
Reitangruppen AS	72 042 000	Wholesale trade
Rema 1000 AS	54 359 000	Rental and leasing activities
Coop Norge SA	49 297 000	Wholesale trade
The Resource Group Trg AS	42 176 000	Financial service activities
Aker ASA	42 163 000	Manufacture of other transport equipment - Building of ships and boats
Orkla ASA	40 837 000	Manufacture of food products
Norwegian Air Shuttle ASA	40 265 000	Air transport
Norsk Tipping AS	38 134 000	Gambling and betting activities
Veidekke ASA	35 667 000	Construction of buildings
Total E&P Norge AS	35 091 000	Extraction of crude petroleum and natural gas
Atea ASA	34 709 000	Wholesale trade
Esso Norge AS	31 061 000	Manufacture of coke and refined petroleum products
Axis-Shield AS	30 578 000	Research and experimental development on biotechnology
Exxonmobil Exploration And Production Norway AS	30 239 000	Extraction of crude petroleum and natural gas
Laco AS	29 537 000	Water transport

Values seems to be more important compared to Strategy, but Strategy is, however, mentioned in the webpages, but not so strongly as Values. In two Finnish cases both Values and Strategy have been emphasized equally in the webpages.

Among the webpages of the largest Swedish companies Values are more important compared to Strategy. Only in two cases their importance seems to be equal. In six cases out of 20 both values and strategy are emphasized, but Values seems to be more important. Table 8 contains the information about largest firms of Norway. In the case of Norway, the analysis met more problems compared to other countries. The webpages of several companies do not have English versions and do not have reflections of Values or Strategy even in Norwegian. However, in nine cases Values are clearly more important compared to strategy and in one case strategy complements Values. In three cases the ownership is the same and their pages Values have been mentioned, but not in the headings.

Generally speaking, the largest Scandinavian firms resembles each other in the use of values and strategy in their webpages – and especially in the headings of their webpages. There is not any remarkable differences between these four countries, Denmark, Finland, Sweden and Norway. In all of these countries the headings, such as “responsibility”, “CSR” or “sustainability” are very important.

Values or Strategy?

Table 5. Denmark. Values or Strategy?

Firm	Details	Strategy or values more important?
A.P. Møller – Mærsk A/S	Strategy used in the context of sustainable strategy (e.g. values)	Values
Centrica Energy Trading A/S	Strategy listed before values	Strategy
Danske Bank A/S	Strategy used in the context of sustainable process (e.g. values)	Values
Ørsted Salg & Service A/S	Sustainability one of the headlines of the homepage	Values
Ørsted Wind Power A/S	Sustainability one of the headlines of the homepage	Values
Vestas Manufacturing A/S	in About –page Sustainability one of the headlines of the homepage	Values
Lego A/S	--	--
Coop Danmark A/S	"Ansvarighed" (responsibility in English) one of the headlines in main page.	Values
Energi Danmark A/S	Corporate Social Responsibility is one of the headlines in "om os" (about us) page.	Values
Lego System A/S	--	--
Equinor Refining Denmark A/S	"Our values" is one of the headlines in "About us" –page.	Values
Pandora A/S	Sustainability is one of the headlines in the main page	Values
Siemens Gamesa Renewable Energy A/S	Sustainability is one of the headlines in the main page	Values
Danish Crown A/S	Sustainability is one of the headlines in the main page	Values
Lundbeck A/S, H	Sustainability is one of the headlines in the main page	Values
Reitan Distribution A/S	"Social ansvarlighed" one of the headlines in the homepage	Values
Coloplast A/S	In "About coloplast" page "Vision and values" and "Corporate Responsibility" among headlines of the page.	Values
Bestseller A/S	in "about" –page "BRINGING SUSTAINABLE FASHION FORWARD" is one of the headlines	Values
Dansk Shell, A/S	Do not contain values or strategy in homepage or in About us -page	(Values/strategy)
Velux A/S	CSR &Sustainability one of the headlines in the Our Company -page	Values

CONCLUSION AND DISCUSSIONS

The analysis of the chapter based on public announcements of the firms, and especially their webpages. This kind of analysis do not reveal the actual activities and attitudes of the managers and planners of the firms. It only reflects the public message of the firm and these announcements and heading of them is possible interpret part of the marketing and image & brand activities of the firms. Basing on the theoretic perspectives about the content of the announcements, it is important to consider the questions of theory in use and espoused theory.

Table 6. Finland. Values or Strategy?

Firm	Details	Strategy or values more important?
Nokia Oyj	About Us –page contain "Sustainability" as one of the headlines. Main page contains headline: "Three strategies to help you capture the 5g opportunity"	Values/Strategy
Neste Oyj	Sustainability is one of the headlines in homepage. Name of the homepage is "Creating a healthier planet for our children"	Values
Kesko Oyj	Responsibility is one of the headlines in "Company"-page. Three themes of sustainability in the news of the homepage.	Values
Stora Enso Oyj	The renewable materials company in main headline of the homepage	Values
UPM-Kymmene Oyj	About us page contains "Strategia" as one of the headlines (In Finnish)	Values
KONE Oyj	Sustainability is one of the headlines in homepage.	Values
Outokumpu Oyj	Sustainability is one of the headlines in homepage.	Values
Sampo Oyj	"Responsibility" is one of the headlines in the main page, in the About Us- page Strategy and Objectives is one of the headlines.	Values (Strategy)
Metsäliitto-konserni (Metsä Group)	Sustainability is one of the headlines in homepage. In the About Us-page Strategy and Objectives is one of the headlines.	Values (Strategy)
Wärtsilä Oyj Abp	"Enabling sustainable societies with smart technology" is in the headline of web (search engine), sustainability is in the headline of homepage, Strategy and purpose is the first headline in the About –page.	Values (strategy)
Fortum Oyj	Join the change for a cleaner world -is in the headline of web (search engine), Sustainability is one of the headlines in About -page.	Values
Cargotec Oyj	Sustainability is one of the headlines in all pages, About Us –page contains also "strategy"	Values (strategy)
Valmet Oyj	In the homepage below About Valmet is Sustainability one of the headlines. In the About Us –page "Valmet's value creation" is before "Strategy"	Values (strategy)
Konecranes Oyj	About Konecranes –page contains e.g. following headlines: Mission, Vision and Values; Corporate Responsibility	Values
Huhtamäki Oyj	"Responsibility" is one of the headlines in the main page, in the About –pages contain headline "values and Direction"	Values
Metso Oyj	"About Us"- page includes e.g. following headlines: Strategy, Sustainability. Sustainability is also one of the headlines after "Explore more">Metso Corporation.	Strategy & Values
Amer Sports Oyj	Responsibility is one of the headings in homepage, strategy is ones of the headings in About Us -page	Values (Strategy)
Finnair Oyj	Corporate responsibility is one of the headings (in Finnish) homepage. Values of Finnair (In Finnish is one of the heading in About Finnair.	Values
Kemira Oyj	About Us –page "Corporate responsibility" in hweadings up of the page; Strategy the first heading middle of the page	Values/Strategy
Caverion Oyj	In About Caverion –page (In Finnish) is heading "Sustainable development" (In Finnish)	Values

There is dilemma between theory-in-use and espoused theory: there is often a gap between what is genuinely valued (espoused theory) and what actually occurs in practice (theory-in-use) (Argyris, 1990; Laiken, 2001; Rusko et al., 2017). In other words, it is difficult to know exactly, what the ACTUAL role

Values or Strategy?

Table 7. Sweden. Values or Strategy?

Firm	Details	Strategy or values more important?
Volvo, AB	About Us-page contains headings "Strategy" and "CSR and sustainability"	Strategy/Values
Volvo Car AB	--	--
Ericsson, Telefon AB LM	In "More" –page contains "Sustainability & CR" and "About us"; About us –page contains also "Sustainability & CR"	Values
H & M Hennes & Mauritz AB	H & M Group -homepage contains heading: Sustainability. About us –page contains Our Values	Values
Skanska AB	Sustainability is one of the headings of the mainpage. About us –page contains heading "Strategy"	Values (Strategy)
Vattenfall AB	Main page contains heading "See also", which contains subheading "Sustainability"	(Values)
Scania CV AB	--	--
Electrolux, AB	Homepage contains heading "sustainability". About -page contains "Strategy"	Values (Strategy)
Essity AB	Homepage contains heading "sustainability". Company -page contains "Strategy"	Values (Strategy)
ICA Gruppen AB	Homepage contains heading "sustainability About ICA Gruppen -page contains "Goals and strategy"	Values (Strategy)
Corral Petroleum Holdings AB	About Corral Petroleum Holdings AB - Preem.se -page contains "Sustainability" (upper heading) and "Strategy" (Left heading)	Values and strategy
Securitas AB	Homepage contains heading "Our responsibility" and About us- page has heading "Our values"	Values
Sandvik AB	About us- page contains sustainable business	Values
Atlas Copco AB	In the homepage is heading "More about" and there sub-heading "Social responsibility: Water for all" also in homepage.	Values
Nordea Bank AB	In the homepage is heading "sustainability" up of the page and end of the page.	Values
SKF, AB	About SKF -page is the main heading: "The values that drive us". In the down of the main page is heading Organization and the subheading "Sustainability"	Values
Assa Abloy AB	In the homepage is heading "Sustainability" ad About us-page contains heading "Strategy"	Values (Strategy)
Telia Company AB	"Sustainability is one of the headings in the homepage. About the company -page contains heading "Strategy"	Values (Strategy)
Axel Johnson Holding AB	"Sustainability is one of the headings in the homepage. Homepage contains also heading: "Sustainable ambitions"	Values

of values and strategies are in the practices of the large Scandinavian firms. Now values, such as CSR, responsibility, sustainability, SEEM to be more important compared to strategy. This might be fact in espoused theory, but not necessarily in theory in use.

Official announcements, such as webpages reflect the perspectives of espoused theory. In order to study actual practices, that is theory in use, it is necessary to have other sources of data, such as inter-

Table 8. Norway. Values or Strategy?

Firm	Details	Strategy or values more important?
Norsk Hydro ASA	"Sustainability" is one of the headings in the homepage.	Values
Telenor ASA	"Sustainability" is one of the headings in the homepage. About us-page contains headings: "Our strategy" and "Our culture"	Values (Strategy)
Helse Sør-Øst RHF	--(No pages in English)	--
Equinor ASA	Homepage contains large heading: Towards a sustainable energy future in Norway. About us-heading contains subheading: Ethics and compliance in Equinor	Values
Odd Reitan Private Holding AS	Values or strategy are not in the headlines of the webpages. There are, however, contents focused on values: "...Our values govern everything we do – and they define who we are."	(Values?)
Reitangruppen AS	Values or strategy are not in the headlines of the webpages. There are, however, contents focused on values: "...Our values govern everything we do – and they define who we are."	(Values?)
Rema 1000 AS	Values or strategy are not in the headlines of the webpages. There are, however, contents focused on values: "...Our values govern everything we do – and they define who we are."	(Values?)
Coop Norge SA	--	--
The Resource Group Trg AS	--	--
Aker ASA	Homepage contains heading: Corporate responsibility. About Aker -page has heading "Values"	Values
Orkla ASA	"Sustainability" is one of the headings in the homepage. About Orkla -page contains heading "Sustainability"	Values
Norwegian Air Shuttle ASA	Everything about our company – page contains e.g. following headings: "A sustainable business model" and "Corporate responsibility"	Values
Norsk Tipping AS	Homepage contains "samfunnsansvar" (Social responsibility in English)	Values
Veidekke ASA	Verdigrunnlag is one of the headings in om oss (About us) page.	Values
Total E&P Norge AS	Our Group -page contains heading "Our identity", which contains e.g. heading "Values" and "Etics policy"	Values
Atea ASA	"Corporate responsibility" is one of the headings of the homepage. Homepages contains also heading "Values"	Values
Esso Norge AS	--	(Values in international ESSO -pages)
Axis-Shield AS	--	--
Exxonmobil Exploration And Production Norway AS	--	(Values in international ESSO -pages)
Laco AS	(Specific homepage is difficult to find; according to several sources, e.g. Bloomberg Markets) this company has only one worker)	--

views or observations about the actual practices, routines and culture of the firms. This fact provides interesting theme for further studies of strategy and values.

However, the analysis revealed the importance of values in the contemporary actions of the firms. Firms do not necessarily to use term "values", but several connotations of this term, such as "sustainability", "responsibility" or CSR", among others in their headings of the homepage or "About us"-pages. "Strategy" is still important term in business, but not so often used heading as it might be expected to be in the official announcements.

It seems that at least large Scandinavian firms have adapted the perspectives of New Economy and Green Economy (cf. Pop, Dina & Martin, 2011) in their official announcements. Furthermore, these terms reflecting new values are HEADINGS of these announcements, which means that there are plenty of content in the pages, which describe the details, how the ideas sustainability/responsibility are followed in this particular company. Actually this detailed content might confirm more about these values based practices of the firm than just the headings.

It is important to understand some restrictions of the study: empirical analysis focused on large Scandinavian firms. It is difficult to enlarge these results to the SMEs (Small and Medium-sized enterprises) in Scandinavian. Furthermore, it is possible that the emphasis of strategies and values is different from the results of this study in other parts of world.

REFERENCES

Adams, J. S., Taschian, A., & Shore, T. H. (1996). Ethics in family and non-family owned firms: An exploratory study. *Family Business Review*, *9*(2), 157–170. doi:10.1111/j.1741-6248.1996.00157.x

Alestalo, M., & Kuhnle, S. (1986). 1 The Scandinavian Route: Economic, Social, and Political Developments in Denmark, Finland, Norway, and Sweden. *International Journal of Sociology*, *16*(3-4), 1–38. doi:10.1080/15579336.1986.11769909

Argyris, C. (1990). *Overcoming organizational defences: Facilitating organizational learning*. Allyn and Bacon.

Ciulla, J. B. (2007). The importance of leadership in shaping business values. In *Corporate Ethics and Corporate Governance* (pp. 67–77). Springer. doi:10.1007/978-3-540-70818-6_5

Collis, D. J., & Rukstad, M. G. (2008). Can you say what your strategy is? *Harvard Business Review*, *86*(4), 82-90.

Erdem, F., & Gül Başer, G. (2010). Family and business values of regional family firms: A qualitative research. *International Journal of Islamic and Middle Eastern Finance and Management*, *3*(1), 47–64. doi:10.1108/17538391011033861

Goodpaster, K. E. (1991). Business ethics and stakeholder analysis. *Business Ethics Quarterly*, *1*(1), 53–73. doi:10.2307/3857592

Graafland, J., Van de Ven, B., & Stoffele, N. (2003). Strategies and instruments for organising CSR by small and large businesses in the Netherlands. *Journal of Business Ethics*, *47*(1), 45–60. doi:10.1023/A:1026240912016

Jarzabkowski, P. (2004). Strategy as practice: Recursiveness, adaptation, and practices-in-use. *Organization Studies*, *25*(4), 529–560. doi:10.1177/0170840604040675

Jarzabkowski, P., & Paul Spee, A. (2009). Strategy-as-practice: A review and future directions for the field. *International Journal of Management Reviews*, *11*(1), 69–95. doi:10.1111/j.1468-2370.2008.00250.x

Jenkins, H. (2009). A 'business opportunity' model of corporate social responsibility for small-and medium-sized enterprises. *Business Ethics (Oxford, England)*, *18*(1), 21–36. doi:10.1111/j.1467-8608.2009.01546.x

Jones, C. A., & Levy, D. L. (2007). North American business strategies towards climate change. *European Management Journal*, *25*(6), 428–440. doi:10.1016/j.emj.2007.07.001

Joyner, B. E., Payne, D., & Raiborn, C. A. (2002). Building values, business ethics and corporate social responsibility into the developing organization. *Journal of Developmental Entrepreneurship*, *7*(1), 113.

Kitchen, N. (2010). Systemic pressures and domestic ideas: A neoclassical realist model of grand strategy formation. *Review of International Studies*, *36*(1), 117–143. doi:10.1017/S0260210509990532

Koiranen, M. (2002). Over 100 years of age but still entrepreneurially active in business: Exploring the values and family characteristics of old Finnish family firms. *Family Business Review*, *15*(3), 175–187. doi:10.1111/j.1741-6248.2002.00175.x

Laiken, M. (2001). *Models of organizational learning: Paradoxes and best practices in the post industrial workplace*. NALL Working Paper, 25. University of Toronto. Retrieved January 12, 2020, from https://nall.oise.utoronto.ca/res/25MarilynLaiken.pdf

Llewellyn, S., & Tappin, E. (2003). Strategy in the public sector: Management in the wilderness. *Journal of Management Studies*, *40*(4), 955–982. doi:10.1111/1467-6486.00366

McCaffrey, M. (2015). The economics of peace and war in the Chinese military classics. *Economics of Peace and Security Journal*, *10*(1), 23–31. doi:10.15355/epsj.10.1.23

Mintzberg, H., Ahlstrand, B. W., & Lampel, J. (1998). *Strategy Safari: The Complete Guide Through the Wilds of Strategic Management*. Harlow, UK: Financial Times.

Otero-Neira, C., Tapio Lindman, M., & Fernández, M. J. (2009). Innovation and performance in SME furniture industries: An international comparative case study. *Marketing Intelligence & Planning*, *27*(2), 216–232. doi:10.1108/02634500910944995

Pop, O., Dina, G. C., & Martin, C. (2011). Promoting the corporate social responsibility for a green economy and innovative jobs. *Procedia: Social and Behavioral Sciences*, *15*, 1020–1023. doi:10.1016/j.sbspro.2011.03.232

Rossouw, D., Prozesky, M., du Plessis, C., & Prinsloo, F. (2010). *Ethics for accountants & auditors*. OUP Catalogue.

Rusko, R., Hietanen, L., Kohtakangas, K., Kemppainen-Koivisto, R., Siltavirta, K., & Järvi, T. (2017). Educational and Business Co-Operatives: The Channels for Collective Creativity and Entrepreneurial Teams. In Collective Creativity for Responsible and Sustainable Business Practice (pp. 242-259). IGI Global.

Spence, L. J., & Lozano, J. F. (2000). Communicating about ethics with small firms: Experiences from the UK and Spain. *Journal of Business Ethics, 27*(1-2), 43–53. doi:10.1023/A:1006417425446

Verenich, V. (2014). The Splendors and Miseries of Constitutional Reasoning in Times of Global Crisis: A Critical Look from the Realist Perspectives of Semiotics. *International Journal for the Semiotics of Law-Revue internationale de Sémiotique juridique, 27*(4), 687-711.

Vidaver-Cohen, D., & Brønn, P. S. (2015). Reputation, responsibility, and stakeholder support in Scandinavian firms: A comparative analysis. *Journal of Business Ethics, 127*(1), 49–64. doi:10.100710551-013-1673-7

Wells, V. K., Ponting, C. A., & Peattie, K. (2011). Behaviour and climate change: Consumer perceptions of responsibility. *Journal of Marketing Management, 27*(7-8), 808–833. doi:10.1080/0267257X.2010.500136

Zitzler, E., & Thiele, L. (1998, September). Multiobjective optimization using evolutionary algorithms—a comparative case study. In *International conference on parallel problem solving from nature* (pp. 292-301). Springer.

Chapter 5
Convergence and Divergence Regarding Business Combinations

Alin Eliodor Tănase
Titu Maiorescu University, Romania

Traian Ovidiu Calotă
Titu Maiorescu University, Romania

Gabriela Claudia Oncioiu
Titu Maiorescu University, Romania

ABSTRACT

The presence of several legal entities within the same group entails the existence of as many independent accountants as there are companies. In accordance with IFRS 3 "business combinations," the result is goodwill that will be recognized as a non-current intangible asset in the consolidated balance sheet, being subjected annually to the impairment test; insofar as the investment cost is lower than the acquisition cost of the net assets, the negative goodwill will be obtained which will be recognized in the form a profit in the consolidated profit and loss account. In addition, national differences in accounting, taxation, and auditing are the sources of the various problems that arise in the process of controlling subsidiaries and consolidating accounts. This chapter aims to study the convergence and divergence regarding business combinations in the joint business as well as to analyze the managerial controversies that are presented in the conversion of the financial statements.

INTRODUCTION

Intangible assets acquired in a business combination, including a project represented by an internal research and development process, are recognized in accordance with IFRS 3 as assets separated from goodwill if they meet the definition and criteria for recognizing assets, if they are separable or result

DOI: 10.4018/978-1-7998-4637-6.ch005

from contractual or legal rights, and the fair value of the assets can be measured reliably (Ball, Li & Shivakumar, 2015; Iatridis, 2010; Guthrie & Parker, 2016).

Also, the same Standard stipulates that "in some circumstances, the acquirer may be required to make a subsequent payment to the seller, as compensation for a reduction in the value of the assets given, the equity instruments issued or the debts existing or assumed by the acquirer in exchange for control on the acquired company. This is the case when, for example, the acquirer guarantees the market price of the issued capital or debt instruments as part of the cost of the business combination and is required to issue additional capital or debt instruments to recover the initially determined cost. In such situations, no increase in the cost of the business combination is recognized. in the case of equity instruments, the fair value of the additional payment is offset by an equal reduction in the value attributed to the instruments originally issued. in the case of debt instruments, the additional payment is regarded as a reduction of the premium or an increase of the discount at the initial issue" (Choi, Peasnell & Toniato, 2013; Barth, Landsman & Lang, 2008;).

The high degree of competitiveness of an entity depends fundamentally on the degree of structuring, optimization and relationship between its processes. If the management of the entity wants lower production costs, lower delivery times and high quality of works, it must necessarily change its business processes. All the issues related to the mentioned issues are centralized and analyzed by a specialist, called a business analyst who will prepare two situations regarding the business processes of the entity: a current situation and a future situation that is desired. The business analyst also has the responsibility to facilitate, aggregate and monitor the business processes, while the management responsibility only includes providing the information necessary to guarantee the entire process. Ensuring success on the line of business process optimization can be translated by permanently optimized internal processes or by a methodology of permanent improvements.

The emphasis in this standard is on the accounting treatment at the date of purchase. In particular, it provides that all business combinations will be accounted for by applying the acquisition method (Schleicher, Tahoun & Walker, 2010).

There may be situations where more investors are interested in investing in the same entity (Ball, Li & Shivakumar, 2015). They may at any time have a greater or lesser influence on the entity, but only one of them may have control (Iatridis, 2010). Other investors may have the right to participate in decision-making on the activities of the entity, which may eventually constitute evidence of significant influence, but not of control (Cairns, Massoudi, Taplin & Tarca, 2011).

The so-called acquisition cost and the cost of the business combination represent the sum of the fair values of the transferred assets, the acquired debt and the equity instruments issued by the acquirer, in exchange for the control over the acquired entity, at the date of the transaction. It also includes direct costs, directly attributable (such as professional fees), but not the costs of issuing equity or debt used to pay the obligation. When a contract for a business combination provides for an adjustment of the cost of the combination based on future events, the acquirer will include the value of that adjustment in the cost of the combination at the date of purchase, if the adjustment is probable and can be reliably evaluated (Allen & Ramanna, 2013; Bozec, 2008; Chen, Tang, Jiang & Lin, 2010; Tendeloo & Vanstrelen, 2005).

Despite the solid principles embodied in IFRS 3, many analysts believe that determining fair value implies a considerable degree of managerial flexibility. Intangible asset values, such as computer software, may not be easily validated when analyzing acquisitions.

The managerial reasoning can be evident especially in the allocation of the purchase price surplus (after all other allocations to assets and liabilities). If, for example, the remaining excess purchase price is allocated to goodwill, the net profit of the firm will not be affected because goodwill is not amortized (but tested for impairment). If the surplus (positive difference) were to be allocated to the fixed assets, the amortization would increase, thus reducing the net profit and generating incorrect financial statements (Fu, Kraft & Zhang, 2012).

Over time, goodwill has become one of the most controversial topics in accounting. Goodwill cannot be evaluated directly. Its value is generally determined by evaluation, which is based on the evaluator's assumptions. As such, the value of goodwill is subjectively determined (Alzola, 2017).

According to IFRS 3, goodwill must be capitalized and tested annually for impairment. Goodwill is not amortized. Impairment of goodwill is a non-cash expense. However, impairment of goodwill affects the reported net profit. When the fund is deducted from the current period profit, the reported current profit decreases, but the future reported profit should increase when the asset's value is reduced to zero or when it is no longer impaired (Mechelli & Cimini, 2014).

The Standard specifies that an entity's functional currency reflects the transactions, events and underlying conditions that are relevant to it (Xiong, 2006; Leuz, Nanda & Wysocki, 2003). Consequently, once determined, the functional currency changes only if there is a change in those transactions, events and underlying conditions.

Foreign currency transactions are those transactions that are denominated or which provide for settlement in foreign currency (Zeghal, Chtourou & Fourati, 2012; Dechow, Sloan & Sweeney, 1996). They include, in accordance with IAS 21, the resulting transactions: when an entity buys or sells goods or services the price of which is denominated in foreign currency; borrows or lends funds when the due amounts are denominated in foreign currency; or otherwise acquires or disables assets, supports or repots debts denominated in foreign currency.

A foreign currency transaction - once the functional currency is established - may be recorded in the functional currency according to the two moments, initial recognition and subsequent recognition, as follows: initial recognition - the foreign currency exchange rate of the functional currency and the foreign currency, at the time of the transaction; the subsequent recognition (at the end of each reporting period) - the items will be converted according to their nature, monetary or non-monetary items (Ahmed, Neel & Wang, 2013; Thong, Ding & Lim, 2008; DeFond, 2010).

Enron, HealthSouth, Kmart, Parmalat, Tyco, WorldCom, Waste Management, Sunbeam, Adelphia Communications or Xerox represent just a few examples of companies that were subject to profound debates regarding the manipulation of financial information, with undesirable effects upon the investors' community. As a result of the accounting fraud unrevealed within these corporations, investor confidence has been seriously shaken, which has led to the collapse of trading prices (Fan, Li & Zheng, 2016).

The interest in an associate or a joint venture is the carrying amount of the investment in the associate or joint venture established by using the equity method, and any long-term interests that, in fact, part of entity's net investment in the associate or joint venture (Barth, 2013; Kothari, Leone & Wasley, 2005). After the holding entity is reduced to zero, additional losses are accounted for and a liability is recognized only to the extent that the entity has incurred legal or constructive obligations or made payments on behalf of the associate or joint venture. If the associate or joint venture subsequently reports profits, the entity resumes recognizing its share of those profits only after its share of the profits equals the share of losses not recognized.

This chapter aims to study the convergence and divergence regarding business combinations in the joint business as well as to analyze the managerial controversies that they are presented the conversion of the financial statements.

Background

Effective functioning of joint enterprise is ensured only when accurate and reliable information is disseminated between stakeholders who have invested in the performance and financial perspectives of an entity. IFRS 10 Consolidated financial statements, consolidated financial statements are the financial statements of a group presented as if it were a single economic entity (Barth, Landsman & Lang, 2008). It is assumed that the consolidated financial statements are more useful for management, owners and lenders entity acquirer. Separate financial statements are those presented by a parent, an investor in an associate or a venture in a jointly controlled entity, in which investments are accounted rather on the basis of the direct equity than on reported results and net assets of the investee (Alzola, 2017; Houque, Zijl, Dunstan & Karim, 2012; Jeanjean & Stolowy, 2008). A complete set of consolidated financial statements include: consolidated statement of financial position at the end of the period; consolidated statement of comprehensive income in the period; consolidated statement of changes in equity over time; consolidated cash flow period and notes, comprising a summary of significant accounting policies and other explanatory information (Lang, Raedy & Wilson, 2006; Fu, Kraft & Zhang, 2012).

The consolidated financial statements are prepared in accordance with IFRS 10, taking into account the following rules: individual financial statements of the main and its subsidiaries, which are used to prepare consolidated financial statements will be prepared for the same reporting date (Messier, Glover & Prawitt, 2008). If the end of the reporting period of a subsidiary is different from that of the main company, the subsidiary prepares, for consolidation purposes, additional financial statements on the same date as the financial statements of the main unless it is impracticable to do so. In these circumstances, the subsidiary will make some adjustments for the effects of significant transactions or events that occur between that date and the date the financial statements of the main company. However, the difference between the end of the reporting period of the subsidiary and the end of the reporting period of the parent company shall not be less than three months (Fan, Li & Zheng, 2016; Klein, 2002). During the reporting periods and any difference between the endings of the reporting periods shall be the same from period to period.

With regard to non-controlling interests (INC), IFRS 10 makes the following statement: INC will be presented in a consolidated statement of financial position within equity, separately from the equity of the owners of the parent; profit or loss and each component of other comprehensive income are attributed to owners of the parent and non-controlling interests. Total comprehensive income must be attributed to owners of the parent and non-controlling interests even if this results in a deficit balance in the non-controlling interests (Rittenberg & Schwieger, 2005).

If the INC is holding the cumulative preference shares classified as equity owned by a subsidiary, then the main company computes its share of profits or losses after adjusting for the dividends on such shares, whether or not dividends have been declared (Louwers, Ramsay, Sinason & Strawser, 2007).

If modifications in the capital shares of the main company in a subsidiary appear, but it did not result in the loss of control, then like the operations they are accounted like transactions with own capital (meaning transactions with the stockholders). Also, the carrying amounts of controlling interests (ICI) and the non-controlling (INC) should be adjusted to reflect changes related holdings in the subsidiary. Any difference between the amount by which the adjusted non-controlling interests (INC) and the fair value of consideration paid or received is recognized directly in equity and attributed owners of the main company.

A group share an associate or a joint venture - IAS 28 - is given by amount of packages of shares held by the parent company and its subsidiaries in that associate or joint venture (Whittington & Pany 2008; Lin, Riccardi & Wang, 2012). Shareholdings of the group in other associates or joint ventures are not taken into account for this purpose. When an associate or joint venture has subsidiaries, associates or joint ventures, profit or loss, other comprehensive income and net assets taken into account in applying the equity method are those recognized in the financial statements of the associate or joint venture (including share of associate or joint venture of profit or loss and other comprehensive income and net assets of its associates and joint ventures).

On the other hand, the financial asset is investment made by the main company in the net assets of the subsidiary (Iatridis, 2012). The net assets of the subsidiary is equivalent to its equity. Since the elements of assets and debt of the subsidiary are added to those of the main company in the consolidated balance sheet, it is normal to remove the asset representing investment the main company in a subsidiary, in return for the subsidiary's equity to avoid counting double of these assets net (Brüggemann, Hitz & Sellhorn, 2013; Beasley, M.S., Buckless, Glover & Prawitt, 2009). The consolidated financial statements will be included only equity belonging to the main company. Any non-controlling interests (ICN) will be presented separately, separately from the equity of the owners of the main company.

THE IMPACT OF BUSINESS COMBINATION ON THE CONSOLIDATED STATEMENT

Any transaction in which a company obtains control of entities may qualify as a joint enterprise (Jones & Smith, 2012). An entity shall determine whether a transaction or other event is a joint enterprise by applying the definition in IFRS 3 Joint Enterprises, which requires that the assets acquired and liabilities assumed constitute a business (Houque, Dunstan & Karim, 2012). If the assets acquired are not a business, the reporting entity shall account for the transaction or other event as an asset acquisition.

An enterprise is defined as a set of active and integrated activities that can be directed and managed in order to provide a return (Iatridis, 2010). Profitability can be in various forms such as, for example, dividends, lower costs or other economic benefits directly to investors or other owners, members or participants.

For each business combination, one of the combining entities shall be identified as acquirer (Lang, Raedy & Wilson, 2006). Determining the acquirer has implications from an accounting perspective, meaning that it will prepare consolidated financial statements. Determining the acquirer is considering the provisions of IFRS 10, meaning that the entity that obtains control is deemed to be the acquirer.

The conversion occurs when the currency in which the financial statements are prepared is different from the presentation currency (Zéghal, Chtourou & Mnif, 2011; Lobo & Zhou, 2001). With respect to the conversion of financial statements, it should be noted that this standard applies only if the entity whose financial statements are converted has a functional currency that is not a hyperinflationary economy (Jones & Smith, 2012; Watts & Zimmerman, 1978; Richardson, 2011).

Potential voting rights that are currently exercisable or convertible must be taken into account because an entity may own warrants on shares, options to purchase equities, debt or equity securities that are convertible into ordinary shares or other financial instruments - if exercised or converted - and that can lead: either providing an entity that holds more voting rights; or reduce the voting rights of another party's financial and operating policies (i.e. potential voting rights).

A joint venture type of shared commitment where the parties have joint control of the undertaking and also of the rights to the net assets of the undertaking (Daske & Gebhardt, 2006; Marra, Mazzola & Prencipe, 2011). There may be joint commitments which the parties have rights to the assets and obligations for liabilities related to commitment (Ghosh & Olsen, 2008; Landsman, Maydew, & Thornock, 2012). This type of commitment is called joint venture operation and it is not covered by this material, nor do we apply the equity method (Pope & McLeay, 2011; Pieper, Trevor, Weller & Duchon, 2017).

The method to be used for converting foreign entities' financial statements and the amount of resulting conversion adjustments depends on the determination of the functional currency (Balachandran & Faff, 2015). Taking into account the three types of coins that may arise in the discussion, such as the local currency in which the foreign entity operates, the functional currency and the presentation currency, there may be the following three cases: Local currency = Functional currency # Presentation currency; Local currency # Functional currency = Presentation currency; Local currency # Functional currency # Presentation currency (Barth, M. E., Landsman, Young & Zhuang, 2014).

Case 1 assumes that the entity carries out its accounting records and keeps its books in local currency, which is the same as the functional currency, and will therefore need to convert - where necessary - those records, expressed as financial statements, into presentation currency. In this case, the method known in the literature will be used as the current course method. Gains or losses resulting from conversion are recognized in other comprehensive income or equity.

Case 2 assumes that the entity carries out its accounting records and keeps its bookkeeping accounts in the local currency, which is different from the functional currency, and recalculates these values into equivalent units of functional currency, the result obtained being - in fact - the same as the currency of presentation because of the fact that the functional currency and the presentation currency are the same. The recalculation term is used as these values have already been initially calculated in the local currency. This recalculation should provide results comparable to those that would have been obtained if the entity had used its functional currency from the outset when recording its foreign currency operations. In this case, the method known in the literature will be used as a temporal method. Gains or losses resulting from recalculation are recognized in profit or loss for the period.

IAS 21 does not explicitly use these terms, but it can be inferred from their scope of application (Barth & Konchitchki, 2013). Thus, account will be taken of the provisions of the section on how to register at the level of each individual entity, whether or not a member of a group, the foreign currency transactions in its functional currency or how the financial statements denominated in foreign currency are converted into currency functional; the section on the conversion to the presentation currency of financial statements denominated in another currency.

The temporal method treats balancing items by their nature: monetary and non-monetary items that are translated as follows: monetary items (e.g. cash, receivables or trade payables) are translated using the closing rate and the resulting differences in differences are recognized in profit or loss; non-monetary items (e.g. tangible, intangible, etc.) are converted: using the exchange rate at the transaction date if they are valued on the historical cost basis or using the exchange rate from the date they were measured at fair value if valued based on fair value, and the resulting differences in profit or loss are recognized either in profit or loss because, when a gain or loss on a non-monetary asset is recognized in profit or loss, any exchange component of that non- the gain or loss must be recognized in profit or loss; or in other items of the comprehensive income because, when a gain or loss associated with a non-monetary item is recognized in other comprehensive income (e.g. revaluation of assets), any component of that gain or of that loss must be recognized directly in other items of comprehensive income (Chebaane & Othman, 2014).

Regarding non-controlling interests (ICN) standard makes the following statement regarding the fair value at the acquisition date: acquirer may measure a non-controlling interest held in the acquire at fair value at the acquisition date; if available prices in an active market for shares - the acquirer can measure the fair value at the acquisition date of INC given these prices; if not available in an active market prices for shares - the acquirer shall measure the fair value at the acquisition date of INC using other valuation techniques; fair values per share of the acquirer's interest in the acquire and the non-controlling interest calculated per share may be different. It is possible that the main difference is the inclusion of a first control in the fair value per share of the acquirer's interest or, conversely, the inclusion of a discount for lack of control (also called reducing minority) in the fair value per share of interest in controlling.

Sum of the first three components (VJ of the consideration transferred, INC and VJ of acquisition of ownership interest held previously) is the default (VI) in the transaction (Doukakis, 2010).

It should also be borne in mind that the financial statements of previous years should be translated at the exchange rates that were duly applied at the time when the conversion was made. In other words, they will not update at the closing rate or at the current average rate used in the financial statements of prior periods. If this update takes place, then these items would have different chair values and if they did not record movements.

The use of exchange rates and income from transaction dates in the case of income and expenditure is quite difficult to achieve (Horton, Serafeim & Serafeim, 2013). Consequently, from practical reasoning, a conversion rate can be used to convert exchange rates from transaction dates, for example, an average of the courses for that period. However, if exchange rates fluctuate significantly, the use of the average rate over a period is inadequate

SOLUTIONS AND RECOMMENDATIONS

The cumulative amount of exchange rate differences is presented in a separate component of equity until the disposal of the foreign operation. If these differences are related to a foreign operation that is not wholly owned (i.e. there are non-controlling interests) and which is reinforced, then the share of these differences for non-controlling interests is recognized as part of the non-controlling interest of the consolidated statement of financial position.

The difference between the involved in the transaction value and the accounting values will be allocated in the purchased assets and assumed liabilities from the acquisition date in order to obtain the fair value of them. The excess is allocated to the commercial background. It is important to bear in mind that this table of allocation will be established only once, at the purchasing date, and will remain unchanged. The revenue and expenses of a subsidiary are included beginning with its date of acquisition and until the date when the mother society doesn't control anymore. It is important to know that the value of the assets and the liabilities from the acquisition date will affect the consolidated result.

When talking about the fixed assets that are not depreciable (land), the values that are reported by the subsidiary don't take into account of the fair values from the acquisition date. The difference between the accounting values and fair values from the business combination date will be reflected only in mother society and in the worksheet that is necessary to obtain the consolidated financial situations. This difference, however, doesn't make any of the objects of an adjustment because the land is not depreciable.

Anyway, in the situation in which the land is not sold or it is noticed a temporary depreciation, we must make adjustments in the worksheet as well.

The commercial background registered as a consequence from the business combination won't be registered by any of the entities in the own individual financial situations. The commercial background will appear only in the consolidated financial situations of the mother society for an unlimited period of time.

Its value will be adjusted only if – a consequence of the depreciation test- we will notice depreciation. This depreciation will be registered as expenses, and there will be like a discount of the consolidated result. We observe that in the first year there is no depreciation, unlike the following years where the depreciation is present.

An enterprise should disclose, in its financial statements, information about the exchange differences' value either included in net profit or net loss for the period, or classified as equity. It should also reconcile the opening and closing balance to the cumulative exchange difference recorded as part of equity. Other information on functional currency should be included in the financial statements, including: if the functional currency is different from the currency of the country where the enterprise has its headquarters, the reason for using a different currency should be mentioned; the reason that was considered when making the decision to change the presentation or functional currency; if the financial statements are presented in a currency other than the functional currency, the enterprise must present, together with a description of the method used in the conversion process, the reason for using a different presentation currency and certify that the functional currency reflects the substance economic circumstances and the circumstances underlying this.

FUTURE RESEARCH DIRECTIONS

Business process management is a management approach focused on adapting the activities of an entity to the constantly growing and diversifying needs of customers. This approach is based on the flexibility and integration of computer applications that help to increase the efficiency of the economic entity, leaving a clear horizon for innovation. The most important aspect is that of contributing to the reduction of the operational costs by automating the operations with the help of computer programs, by attracting information from a process in order to understand and make the process more efficient and to eliminate the intermediaries within it.

We reiterate the following explanations regarding the statement of equity and the position of other items of comprehensive income: the cumulative amount of exchange rate differences is presented in a separate component of equity to the disposal of the foreign operation; the position of other elements of the overall result includes adjusting the conversion as an increase or decrease.

When a contract for a business combination provides for an adjustment of the cost of the combination based on future events, the acquirer will include the value of that adjustment in the cost of the combination at the date of acquisition, if the adjustment is probable and can be reliably evaluated.

The fair value of long-term debt, taken over by a combination of companies, is the present value of the capital payments and the interest for the remaining period up to the maturity, the update being made at the current interest rate on the market. Therefore, the fair value of the debt of the acquired entity, which was issued at an interest rate below the current rate, will be lower than the value recognized in the balance sheet of the acquired entity. Conversely, the fair value of the debt of the acquired entity will be greater than the value recognized in the financial statements of the acquired entity if the interest rate related to the debt is higher than the current interest rate.

Another challenge would be to extend and adapt this research to the specifics of different national economic systems, to generalize the relationship between business combination and company performance and other countries and industries, and not go on forever with examples and studies.

CONCLUSION

Societal groups must keep in mind that their efforts: to apply IFRS changes will be reported by investors - many managers consider confidentially management and consider discovery to be far too far (Mechelli & Cimini, 2014). They also have a positive attitude about the high degree of transparency and comparability that IFRSs apply.

It may be a priority for a group's management team to maintain that confidentiality - such as the progress made in implementing IFRS, on the day-to-day business of societies, more special projects.

Most of the managers interviewed are aware that they are well informed and understand the impact of IFRS.

Goodwill can significantly affect the comparability of financial statements between companies using different accounting methods. As such, the analyst must eliminate any distortion that the goodwill may create, its recognition, depreciation or impairment, by adjusting the company's financial statements. Adjustments must be made by: calculating financial indicators using balance sheet data without goodwill; examining operational trends using data that exclude depreciation of goodwill or impairment; evaluating future acquisitions of enterprises, taking into account the price paid in relation to the net assets and the profit possibilities of the acquired company.

A summary of the above-mentioned conversion rules on the financial statements of a foreign entity would show: income and expenses are translated to the average exchange rate of the period and thus the converted value of the current period result (profit or loss) ; all assets and liabilities are converted to the closing rate; social capital accounts are converted to the historical exchange rate from the date of acquisition; accounts that comprise accumulated profits: initial balance accrued profits - the amount carried forward from the previous year; dividends - are converted at the exchange rate from the reporting date; the current result of the period (profit or loss); Conversion differences - a distinct category in equity (balance amount of the active equation - debt = equity).

Much of the criticism of the benefits and limitations presented in the literature is universal in all sources. Unlike other elements, there were also contradictions and the dispersion of anomalies was extremely rare (i.e. most of the benefits / limitations were repeated throughout the literature). Despite this, three criticisms were identified: (1) lack of strong empirical evidence as a basis; (2) the departure from the specific perspectives of the key actors and, (3) the absence of a close connection with other elements (for example: approaches or types of adaptability).

REFERENCES

Allen, A., & Ramanna, K. (2013). Towards an understanding of the role of standard setters in standard setting. *Journal of Accounting and Economics*, *55*(1), 1–66. doi:10.1016/j.jacceco.2012.05.003

Alzola, M. A. (2017). Beware of the watchdog: Rethinking the normative justification of gatekeeper liability. *Journal of Business Ethics*, *140*(4), 705–721. doi:10.100710551-017-3460-3

Balachandran, B., & Faff, R. (2015). Corporate governance, firm value and risk: Past, present, and future. *Pacific-Basin Finance Journal, 35*(A), 1-12.

Ball, R., Li, X., & Shivakumar, L. (2015). Contractibility and transparency of financial statement information prepared under IFRS: Evidence from debt contracts around IFRS adoption. *Journal of Accounting Research*, *53*(5), 915–963. doi:10.1111/1475-679X.12095

Barth, M., Landsman, W., & Lang, M. (2008). International accounting standards and accounting quality. *Journal of Accounting Research*, *46*(3), 467–498. doi:10.1111/j.1475-679X.2008.00287.x

Barth, M. E. (2013). Global comparability in financial reporting: What, why, how, and when? *China Journal of Accounting Studies*, *1*(1), 2–12. doi:10.1080/21697221.2013.781765

Barth, M. E., Konchitchki, Y. L., & Landsman, W. R. (2013). Cost of capital and earnings transparency. *Journal of Accounting and Economics*, *55*(2–3), 206–224. doi:10.1016/j.jacceco.2013.01.004

Barth, M. E., Landsman, W. R., & Lang, M. H. (2008). International accounting standards and accounting quality. *Journal of Accounting Research*, *43*(3), 467–498. doi:10.1111/j.1475-679X.2008.00287.x

Barth, M. E., Landsman, W. R., Young, D., & Zhuang, Z. (2014). Relevance of Differences between Net Income based on IFRS and Domestic Standards for European Firms. *Journal of Business Finance & Accounting*, *41*(3-4), 297–506. doi:10.1111/jbfa.12067

Beasley, M. S., Buckless, F. A., Glover, S. M., & Prawitt, D. F. (2009). *Auditing Cases. An Interactive Learning Approach* (4th ed.). Prentice Hall.

Bozec, Y. (2008). Ownership Concentration, Separation of Voting Rights from Cash Flow Rights, and Earnings Management: An Empirical Study in Canada. *Canadian Journal of Administrative Sciences*, *25*(1), 1–15. doi:10.1002/cjas.52

Brüggemann, U., Hitz, J.-M., & Sellhorn, T. (2013). Intended and unintended consequences of mandatory IFRS adoption: A review of extant evidence and suggestions for future research. *European Accounting Review*, *22*(1), 1–37. doi:10.1080/09638180.2012.718487

Cairns, D., Massoudi, D., Taplin, R., & Tarca, A. (2011). IFRS fair value measurement and accounting policy choice in the United Kingdom and Australia. *The British Accounting Review*, *43*(1), 1–21. doi:10.1016/j.bar.2010.10.003

Chebaane, S., & Othman, H. B. (2014). The Impact of IFRS Adoption on Value Relevance of Earnings and Book Value of Equity: The Case of Emerging Markets in African and Asian Regions. *Procedia: Social and Behavioral Sciences*, *145*, 70–80. doi:10.1016/j.sbspro.2014.06.012

Chen, H., Tang, Q., Jiang, Y., & Lin, Z. (2010). The role of international financial reporting standards in accounting quality: Evidence from the European Union. *Journal of International Financial Management & Accounting, 21*(3), 220–278. doi:10.1111/j.1467-646X.2010.01041.x

Choi, Y.-S., Peasnell, K., & Toniato, J. (2013). Has the IASB been successful in making accounting earnings more useful for prediction and valuation? UK evidence. *Journal of Business Finance & Accounting, 40*(7–8), 741–768. doi:10.1111/jbfa.12025

Daske, H., & Gebhardt, G. (2006). International financial reporting standards and experts' perceptions of disclosure quality. *Abacus, 42*(3/4), 461–498. doi:10.1111/j.1467-6281.2006.00211.x

Dechow, P., Sloan, R., & Sweeney, A. (1996). Causes and consequences of earnings manipulation: An analysis of firms subject to enforcement actions by the SEC. *Contemporary Accounting Research, 13*(1), 1–36. doi:10.1111/j.1911-3846.1996.tb00489.x

DeFond, M. L. (2010). Earnings quality research: Advances, challenges and future research. *Journal of Accounting and Economics, 50*(2-3), 402–409. doi:10.1016/j.jacceco.2010.10.004

Doukakis, L. C. (2010). The persistence of earnings and earnings components after the adoption of IFRS. *Managerial Finance, 36*(11), 969–980. doi:10.1108/03074351011081286

Fu, R., Kraft, A., & Zhang, H. (2012). Financial reporting frequency, information asymmetry, and the cost of equity. *Journal of Accounting and Economics, 54*(2–3), 132–149. doi:10.1016/j.jacceco.2012.07.003

Ghosh, A., & Olsen, L. (2008). Environmental uncertainty and managers' use of discretionary accruals. *Accounting, Organizations and Society, 34*(2), 188–205. doi:10.1016/j.aos.2008.07.001

Horton, J., Serafeim, G., & Serafeim, I. (2013). Does mandatory IFRS adoption improve the information environment? *Contemporary Accounting Research, 30*(1), 388–423. doi:10.1111/j.1911-3846.2012.01159.x

Houque, M. N. (2012). The effect of IFRS adoption and investor protection on earnings quality around the world. *The International Journal of Accounting, 47*(3), 333–355. doi:10.1016/j.intacc.2012.07.003

Iatridis, G. (2010). International Financial Reporting Standards and the quality of financial statement information. *International Review of Financial Analysis, 19*(3), 193–204. doi:10.1016/j.irfa.2010.02.004

Iatridis, G. (2012). Hedging and earnings management in the light of IFRS implementation: Evidence from the UK stock market. *The British Accounting Review, 44*(1), 21–35. doi:10.1016/j.bar.2011.12.002

Jeanjean, T., & Stolowy, H. (2008). Do accounting standards matter? An exploratory analysis of earnings management before and after IFRS adoption. *Journal of Accounting and Public Policy, 27*(6), 480–490. doi:10.1016/j.jaccpubpol.2008.09.008

Jones, D. A., & Smith, K. J. (2012). Comparing the value relevance, predictive value, and persistence of other comprehensive income and special items. *The Accounting Review, 86*(6), 2047–2073. doi:10.2308/accr-10133

Klein, A. (2002). Audit committee, board of director characteristics and earnings management. *Journal of Accounting and Economics, 33*(3), 375–400. doi:10.1016/S0165-4101(02)00059-9

Kothari, S. P., Leone, A. J., & Wasley, C. E. (2005). Performance matched discretionary accrual measures. *Journal of Accounting and Economics*, *39*(1), 163–197. doi:10.1016/j.jacceco.2004.11.002

Landsman, W. R., Maydew, E. L., & Thornock, J. R. (2012). The information content of annual earnings announcements and mandatory adoption of IFRS. *Journal of Accounting and Economics*, *53*(1-2), 34–54. doi:10.1016/j.jacceco.2011.04.002

Lang, M., Raedy, J. S., & Wilson, W. (2006). Earnings management and cross listing: Are reconciled earnings comparable to US earnings? *Journal of Accounting and Economics*, *42*(1-2), 255–283. doi:10.1016/j.jacceco.2006.04.005

Leuz, C., Nanda, D., & Wysocki, P. D. (2003). Earnings management and investor protection: An international comparison. *Journal of Financial Economics*, *69*(3), 505–527. doi:10.1016/S0304-405X(03)00121-1

Lin, S., Riccardi, W., & Wang, C. (2012). Does accounting quality change following a switch from U.S.GAAP to IFRS? Evidence from Germany. *Journal of Accounting and Public Policy*, *31*(6), 641–657. doi:10.1016/j.jaccpubpol.2012.10.006

Lobo, G. L., & Zhou, J. (2001). Disclosure quality and earning management. *Asia-Pacific Journal of Accounting & Economics*, *8*(1), 1–20. doi:10.1080/16081625.2001.10510584

Louwers, T. J., Ramsay, R. J., Sinason, D. H., & Strawser, J. R. (2007). *Auditing and Assurance Services* (2nd ed.). McGraw-Hill Irwin.

Marra, A., Mazzola, P., & Prencipe, A. (2011). Board Monitoring and Earnings Management Pre- and Post-IFRS. *The International Journal of Accounting*, *46*(2), 205–230. doi:10.1016/j.intacc.2011.04.007

Mechelli, A., & Cimini, R. (2014). Is comprehensive income value relevant and does location matter? A European study. *Accounting in Europe*, *16*(25), 1–35. doi:10.1080/17449480.2014.890777

Messier, W. F., Glover, S. M., & Prawitt, D. F. (2008). *Auditing and Assurance Services. A Systematic Approach* (5th ed.). McGraw-Hill Irwin.

Pope, P., & McLeay, S. (2011). The European IFRS experiment: Objectives, research challenges and some early evidence. *Accounting and Business Research*, *41*(3), 233–266. doi:10.1080/00014788.2011.575002

Richardson, A. (2011). Myth, Paradigms and Academic Accounting Research: A Comment on Reading and Understanding Academic Research in Accounting. *Global Perspectives on Accounting Education*, *8*, 67–77.

Rittenberg, L. E., & Schwieger, B. J. (2005). *Auditing. Concepts for a Changing Environment* (5th ed.). Thomson South-Western.

Schleicher, T., Tahoun, A., & Walker, M. (2010). IFRS adoption in Europe and investment-cash flow sensitivity: Outsider versus insider economies. *The International Journal of Accounting*, *45*(2), 143–168. doi:10.1016/j.intacc.2010.04.007

Tendeloo, B., & Vanstrelen, A. (2005). Earnings management under German GAAP versus IFRS. *European Accounting Review*, *14*(1), 155–180. doi:10.1080/0963818042000338988

Thong, T. Y., Ding, D. K., & Lim, C. Y. (2008). Firm diversification and earning management: Evidence from seasoned equity offerings. *Review of Quantitative Finance and Accounting*, *30*(1), 69–92. doi:10.100711156-007-0043-x

Watts, R., & Zimmerman, J. (1978). Towards a Positive Theory of the Determination of Accounting Standards. *The Accounting Review*, *53*(1), 112–134.

Whittington, O. R., & Pany, K. (2008). *Principles of Auditing & Other Assurance Services* (16th ed.). McGraw-Hill Irwin.

Xiong, Y. (2006). Earning management and its measurement; a theoretical perspective. *The Journal of American Academy of Business, Cambridge*, *9*(1), 214–219.

Zeghal, D., Chtourou, S., & Fourati, M. Y. (2012). The effect of mandatory adoption of IFRS on earning quality: Evidence from the European Union. *Journal of International Accounting Research*, *11*(2), 1–25. doi:10.2308/jiar-10221

Zéghal, D., Chtourou, S., & Mnif, S. Y. (2011). An analysis of the effect of mandatory adoption of IAS/IFRS on earnings Management. *Journal of International Accounting, Auditing & Taxation*, *20*(2), 61–72. doi:10.1016/j.intaccaudtax.2011.06.001

ADDITIONAL READING

Ahmed, A., Neel, M., & Wang, D. (2013). Does mandatory adoption of IFRS improve accounting quality? Preliminary evidence. *Contemporary Accounting Research*, *30*(4), 388–423. doi:10.1111/j.1911-3846.2012.01193.x

Ball, R., Li, X., & Shivakumar, L. (2015). Contractibility and transparency of financial statement information prepared under IFRS: Evidence from debt contracts around IFRS adoption. *Journal of Accounting Research*, *53*(5), 915–963. doi:10.1111/1475-679X.12095

Fan, J. P. H., Li, J., & Zheng, G. (2016). Revisiting the bright and dark sides of capital flows in business groups. *Journal of Business Ethics*, *134*(4), 509–528. doi:10.100710551-014-2382-6

Guthrie, J., & Parker, L. D. (2016). Whither the accounting profession, accountants and accounting researchers? Commentary and projections. *Accounting, Auditing & Accountability Journal*, *29*(1), 2–10. doi:10.1108/AAAJ-10-2015-2263

Pieper, J. R., Trevor, C. O., Weller, I., & Duchon, D. (2017). Referral Hire Presence Implications for Referrer Turnover and Job Performance. *Journal of Management*, *19*, 14–20.

KEY TERMS AND DEFINITIONS

Accounting Estimates: Are often made under uncertainty in terms of determining their value as it involves the use of judgment. As a result, the risk of material misstatement is greater when these estimates are involved and in some cases the auditor may determine that the risk of material misstatement is greater and it requires special attention in the audit.

Equity: Total debts and owners' rights claimed for a specific period of time.

Fair Value: The amount at which an asset is bought or sold in an arm's-length transaction, in which neither party is forced to act.

Joint Business: Is defined as a transaction or other event in which an acquirer obtains control of one or more businesses. After completion of the combined entity as transferee undertaking and acquire continues its existence as a separate legal entity. In practice, some transactions sometimes called "true mergers" or "mergers between equal entities" are also business combinations.

Performance: The ability of an organization to exploit its environment to access scarce resources.

Chapter 6
The Role of CSR Reporting Instruments in Increasing the Organization's Management Performance

Nicoleta Cristache
Dunarea de Jos University of Galati, Romania

Daniel Constantin Diaconu
https://orcid.org/0000-0002-0468-6703
University of Bucharest, Romania

Razvan Catalin Dobrea
Bucharest University of Economic Studies, Romania

Cristina Dima
Bucharest University of Economic Studies, Romania

Cristian Constantin Draghici
University of Bucharest, Romania

Daniel Peptenatu
University of Bucharest, Romania

ABSTRACT

This integrated approach implies a broad approach to monitor the performance of the organization both during its life cycle and on the different social dimensions, from the perspective of the conformity of the management processes in relation to the economic, social, and environmental principles. Currently, the social responsibility reporting is a major challenge for the management of organizations in the context where honesty, transparency, business ethics, are values shared by an entire community. The research involves a process through which a series of correlations between the CSR reporting tools and the or-

DOI: 10.4018/978-1-7998-4637-6.ch006

ganization performance management can be analyzed by highlighting the role of the different reporting variables in the architecture of the performance indicators of the organization. The chapter addresses how a set of CSR reporting indicators can be identified and be integrated into the performance indicators which characterize the sustainability of a company.

INTRODUCTION

The performance of a business, in the context of economic globalization, should be approached from a multidimensional perspective, which should address at least the organization and community levels, as well as the resulting correlated social impact. This new integrated approach involves an ample effort to ensure and monitor the performance of the organization throughout its life cycle, across the different social dimensions, with the management processes complying with the economic, social and environmental principles.

Currently, Corporate Social Responsibility (CSR) reporting is a major challenge for the management of organizations in the context where truth, transparency, business ethics are values shared by the whole community. The parties involved in corporate social responsibility processes must outline their own strategies, adapted to their field of activity and the needs of the communities, building and promoting their long-term ideas, approaches and projects, assuming a real role to inform and educate in order to support the performance level.

CSR reporting was subject to an accelerated assimilation process. While initially it was imposed as a trending phenomenon, it results now from the awareness for the need to perform at the level of any organization. In this dynamic economic, social and political context, but also difficult to predict, corporate social responsibility was valued in the business environment more for its commercial valences than for the ethical ones. In a highly competitive market, the organizations quickly discovered the potential of this dimension, in the process of image building and reputation strengthening, as a prerequisite for a performant management.

Generally, the approaches in the specific literature provide a broader dimension when assuming the concept of CSR reporting as a guarantee for the success of an organization's business and for improving the performance of the management system. However, corporate social responsibility is not only an instrument of maximizing the value of the image, but also an essential element in the long-term success of the business, directly linked to the economic, social and environmental performance as well as the proper use of the reporting instruments (Li, Kim, Wu & Yu 2019).

Integrating an organization into the evolving environment and the use of CSR reporting instruments may generate value and contribute to strengthening the links with the stakeholders, and finally, generate a sustainable competitive edge based on elements of differentiation from the competition.

Organizations should be aware that a proactive approach to CSR reporting may generate benefits by creating and promoting a positive image on the market, which argues for the inclusion of appropriate reporting systems as priority instruments to ensure business sustainability.

The assessment of each of the criteria defining the measure of Social Responsibility and, finally, the sustainability of a business, may be carried out by different methods, which also allow to identify options for improvement. Also, the existing instruments enable the definition of the ways wherein the performance concerned organizations have to take into account all the economic, social and environmental impacts, while taking into account the importance of the communication process with the various stakeholders in order to raise the level of awareness of employees, suppliers, customers, consumers and the community with respect to issues of corporate social responsibility and sustainable development.

BACKGROUND

Literature Review

Corporate Social Responsibility programs of different organizations are frequently affected by lack of internal and external credibility and recognition. Given the wide range of actions falling within the category of corporate social responsibility, the assessment processes, respectively communication have also gone through various phases, relative to the level of acceptance and recognition, at least at the community level, and the immediate external environment.

The impact of a pro-active approach of the CSR reporting system on the financial performance of an organization, has been studied and researched (Hammann, Habisch & Pechlaner, 2009; Rhoua & Signal 2020), and numerous studies have been published showing a positive correlation (Torugsa &O'Donohue, 2012).

A first direction targeted by the organizations concerning their visibility in the social environment wherein they operate, was the creation and the strategic management of their communication with the stakeholders. CSR reporting has practically become a voluntary activity aimed at two major objectives: assessing the current condition of the company and communicating to the stakeholders the company's efforts and progress in the field of CSR practices (Dalal-Clayton & Bas, 2002).

The use of CSR reporting instruments represents a complex process (Elkington, 2017), involving changes of attitude at the company's management level, changes in the organizational structure and management processes (Waddock, 2015). The decision to implement the CSR reporting instruments is influenced by the size of the company, the corporate governance factors and the intrinsic motivation of the management (Koerber, 2015). In recent years, more and more companies have voluntarily engaged in the process of designing and implementing Corporate Social Responsibility standards, in particular those related to the environment. Due to their increased responsibility to the society, the organizations have started to publish information on corporate social responsibility in separate reports, which often accompanied their financial statements (Schwindenhammer, 2013).

As regards the existing reporting instruments, Prado-Lorenzo, Gallego-Alvarez and Garcia-Sanchez (2009) say that a large part tries to capture the results of the organizations in social terms. Clarkson, Overell and Chapple (2011) also say that recent studies show a significant relationship between the Information voluntarily reported by companies and their performance.

The European Commission, in 2011, revised the previous definition of Corporate Social Responsibility through a new approach, meaning that it represents "the responsibility of companies for their impact on society" (European Commission, 2011). In fact, the organizations are given a partner position with rules-setting skills, namely entities that have technical expertise or important financial resources that can help solve environmental problems.

Ligteringen and Zadek (2015) recommend that companies take the following actions leading to the convergence around a set of CSR reporting instruments:

- adoption of instruments to constitute the overall global framework on corporate social responsibility;
- promoting these CSR reporting instruments;
- supporting the actions enabling entities to integrate the use of CSR reporting instruments to increase effectiveness and create value.

Social reporting generates benefits in terms of the direct effects in the assessment and communication of the conditions wherein different entities act but also contribute to building internal and external credibility. In a climate dominated by the distrust of others, it is difficult for organizations to prove their social and environmental performance, and for this reason an appropriate response was to focus on social and environmental reporting practices.

A first Corporate Social Responsibility Reporting Initiative belongs to the Global Reporting Initiative (GRI) that has launched a complex tool covering the economic, social and environmental performance aspects of organizations. In this context, GRI provided a unitary instrument that turned CSR reporting into an agreed and recognized practice in companies worldwide (Orlitzky, Schmidt & Rynes, 2003). According to the statistics, at present, the number of instruments for CSR reporting reached 413, distributed worldwide on 4 axes: environment, sustainability, governance, social, out of which approx. 65% are mandatory (Lozano, 2019; Shada, Laia, Fatt, Klemeš & Bokhari, 2019). Basically, these CSR reporting instruments allowed the organizations to provide to whom it may concern information about the activities carried out, and facilitated the possibility to be actively involved in designing solutions to improve the processes of corporate social responsibility, transparency and social image (Margolis, Elfenbein & Walsh, 2007; Hickman & Cote, 2019; Morsing & Spence 2019).

In this context, managers also realized that it is important for companies to ensure the public transparency of information on practices and performance in the areas of Social Responsibility and sustainability. There are other theories of literature, which refer to the fact that the formal reporting mechanisms, reflecting the levels of commitment in corporate social responsibility, such as the annual reports may also become issues for the organization, for the interpretation of the interested parties, being potentially inconsistent from one organization to another (Bachmann & Ingenhoff, 2016; Burns, Houghton & Stewart 2019; Abbas 2020). In addition, if CSR reporting does not reflect corporate social responsibility practices, it could only act to enhance the image and to promote inefficient or symbolic CSR practices (Greg, Fernie & Dainty, 2018; Argento, Culasso & Truant 2019).

Current Framework of CSR Reporting in Romania

At national level the organizations initiated the first actions of Corporate Social Responsibility, mostly in response to the challenges of the external environment or to the pressure of communities. Started in the form of support or aid actions, the intentions of corporate social responsibility evolved significantly in terms of complexity, diversity, but particularly of budgetary allocation.

With the expansion of Corporate Social Responsibility actions and the relevant increase in budgets allocated to such interventions, domestic organizations faced a new problem, namely that of objective recognition and transparency relative to the needs of communities and business interests of owners or investors.

The first CSR reporting exercises were carried out by regional and national organizations as part of their international affairs or by the National representatives of transnational entities. In 2003, the first report on social involvement was published by a telecommunications company, followed by an increasing number of international organizations, operating at national level.

Corporate Social Responsibility reports were published and disseminated in a first phase with the aim of strengthening the image in relation to the different categories of stakeholders, without ensuring a high degree of uniformity and recognition.

Spreading of GRI standards at European level determined in the national organizations a quick assimilation process, in the context of concerns for non-financial performance. The main reason that has led to an increased number of reports as compared to the previous experience, is the commitment of the multinational companies conducting business in Romania to increase the level of transparency of the results. Currently, the organizations are at the stage of understanding and increasing awareness for the need for CSR reporting, to identify and capitalize on potential alternatives, as well as developing integrated strategies for training consumers and employees.

The year 2014 was a major reference in CSR reporting through the entry into force of Directive 2014/95 / EU on the obligation of large organizations to report annually a number of non-financial issues and information related to the diverse CSR actions and sustainability.

This directive compels "public interest enterprises" having more than 500 employees to publish a non-financial statement, including "information on at least environmental, social and personnel aspects, the observance of Human Rights and fighting corruption and bribery". The entities within the scope of the directive must publish, on an annual basis, beginning with the year 2017, a statement that contains a brief description of the business model, a description of the policies adopted in terms of the non-financial said aspects, the results of such policies, the main risks related to the said aspects, resulting from the operations of the business, and the manner wherein the company manages such risks, performance indicators relevant to the company's business, as well as a description of the diversity policy as applied to the administration and management bodies.

The organizations in Romania that got involved in CSR reporting have a clear preference for separate reports, to the detriment of including non-financial information in their annual financial reports, while integrated reporting has not become common practice. In a study conducted in 2018 by the company "the Azores Sustainability & CSR Services", a number of 696 companies were identified that published CSR reports, the areas most frequently quoted in the reporting being the food industry, chemical industry and telecommunications (Romania CSR Index, 2018).

For the medium and long term, the involvement in CSR reporting of Romanian companies will intensify and mature considerably in the conditions of more stringent legal requirements, increased market pressure and awareness, with direct effects on the number and quality of Corporate Social Responsibility reports.

RESEARCH ON MANAGERS' PERCEPTION OF THE ROLE OF CSR REPORTING INSTRUMENTS IN INCREASING ORGANIZATION'S MANAGEMENT PERFORMANCE

The completeness of the scientific endeavor on CSR reporting is ensured by the design of a quantitative research, with the objective of finding the extent to which the Romanian managers know, apply and develop operational instruments in organization management. This quantitative research aimed to test and validate objectives and assumptions formulated by means of appropriate statistical instruments and methods.

The purpose of research conducted with Romanian managers was to study the notoriety of these concepts, the evolution stage of CSR at the level of Romanian organizations, the way wherein the approach of the CSR policy influences the attitude of stakeholders towards the organization and implicitly the management performance from their perspective. According to the definition of the research subject matter, the following *research objectives* were established:

- Establishing the notoriety of the CSR reporting instruments;
- The extent to which CSR is considered as having a favorable or unfavorable role in the business environment and the impact on the performance of the company's management;
- Identifying the evolution stage of CSR reporting: incipient-growth-maturity;
- Differentiating CSR reporting across different types of organizations;
- Determining the perception of managers regarding the impact on the relations with the stakeholders

In addition to these research objectives the *research hypotheses* were defined and will ultimately be validated or disproved by the results obtained. Based on these considerations regarding the subject matter of the research, the following *assumptions* were formulated:

1. CSR reporting at the level of the Romanian business environment is in its infancy;
2. Romanian managers' perception of CSR reporting is favorable;
3. The impact of the CSR reporting instruments on the performance of the organization's management varies depending on the size of the organization, the sector of activity, year of establishment.

The variables submitted for research considered the conceptual and operational definition of the main aspects, that may be addressed from the perspective of the relationship between CSR reporting and the organization's management performance. Table 1 lists the main variables/analytical indicators and the respective approach perspective.

The approaches associated with the variables for analyzing the performance of the management processes from the perspective of CSR reporting are represented by:

- *The operational approach* - aims to identify the extent to which certain activities in the CSR reporting field can contribute to achieving an optimal profile of socially responsible organizations according to the existing international standards;
- *Conceptual approach* - it reflects the way CSR policies and existing reporting instruments support the management processes within the organization, respectively the strategic guidelines.

In the context of the objectives and assumed assumptions, we designed a questionnaire, structured in two parts, respectively Part 1- Identification of the role of CSR reporting instruments in increasing the organizations' management performance and Part 2- Company Profile, which included 19 questions. The questions were formulated based on known scales in quantitative and qualitative research, mainly using the previously defined variables.

The data were collected between November 15 and December 15, 2019, and the sample submitted for research included 172 willing managers as follows: 36 - managers from the South-East Region; 21-managers from the Center Region; 32-managers from the South Region; 30-managers from the

Table 1. Research variables/analytical indicators and associated approach

No. CRT.	VARIABLE / ANALYTICAL INDICATORS	CONCEPTUAL APPROACH	OPERATIONAL APPROACH
1.	**Notoriety of CSR reporting instruments**	Knowledge level of Romanian managers of CSR reporting instruments	Great extent Average extent Low extent Unknown
2.	**Evolution stage**	Consistency of CSR approach in organization's policy	Incipient Growth Maturity
3.	**Problems/areas of interest**	Diversity of issues that can be addressed by organizations in CSR policies and providing viable solutions	total agreement agreement neither agreement nor disagreement disagreement total disagreement
4.	**Transparency at organization level**	Highlighting the degree of education and the existing framework for strategic Management at Organization level/relationship with stakeholders	Very high High Doesn't matter A little Very little
5.	**CSR reporting standards**	Opportunities to increase the involvement of the organization and strengthen ties with stakeholders in terms of non-financial performance	Very high High Doesn't matter Small Very small
6.	**Competitive advantage**	Aspect that influences the performance of the organization, the extent to which the organization can differentiate itself from competition	Very much Much Doesn't matter A little Very little
7.	**Public confidence**	The extent to which the public has a perception that results in a benefit for the organization	Very high High Doesn't matter A little Very little
8.	**Integration into society**	The way the organization can join the value chain	Very high High Doesn't matter A little Very little
9.	**Cost-benefit ratio**	The extent to which the investment in CSR meets the expectations of managers	Very favorable Favorable Doesn't matter Unfavorable Very unfavorable
10.	**CSR communication instruments**	Ways in which organizations make their CSR projects known	Appropriate Not appropriate
Eleven	**Organization Size**	Category to which it belongs	SME Multinational
Twelve	**Field of activity**	The field in which each researched organization operates	-
Thirteen	**Seniority on the market**	Number of years after the appearance on the market	<10 years 10-20 years > 10 years

North-East Region; 20-managers from the North-West Region; 15-managers from the West Region and 18-managers from the South – West Region.

The first question was a filter question, so that managers who do not know about the CSR concept could not answer the questions of the questionnaire. As a result of the filtering there were 160 valid respondents, whose results were centralized and processed accordingly.

From the collected answers we selected those related to 6 questions, considered relevant to the research objectives. Thus, to question number 5, respectively: "Identify to what extent the following aspects are opportunities leading to an increased need to use CSR reporting instruments to increase the performance of the organization?" the synthesis of the collected answers (Figure 1).

Figure 1. Synthesis of answers to the question: "Identify to what extent are the following opportunities leading to an increase in the need to use CSR reporting instruments to increase the performance of the organization?"

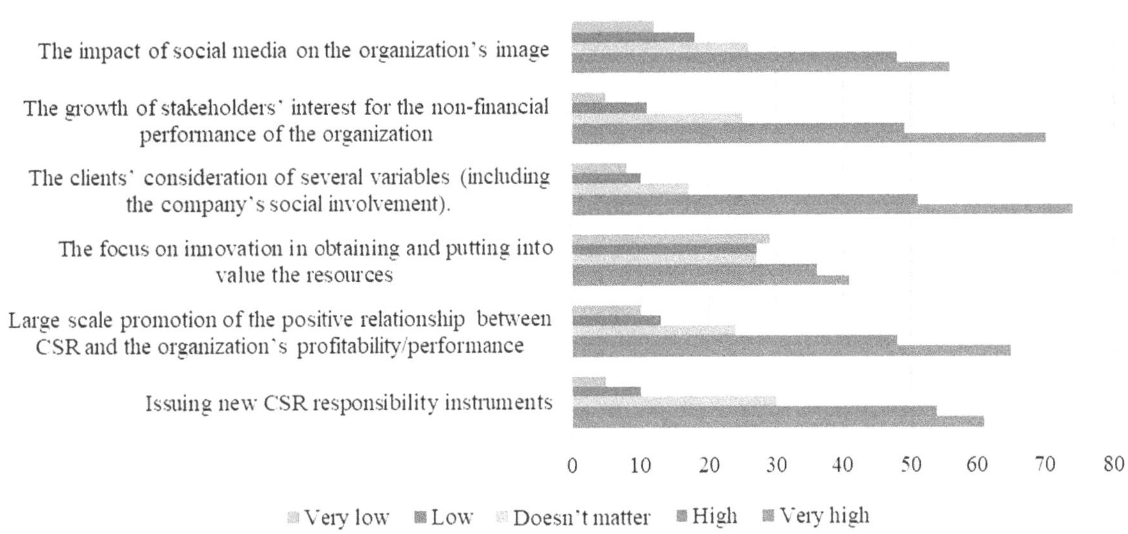

From the data collected it is noted that social involvement influences the decision to buy to a very large extent and that the major interest of stakeholders for the non-financial performance increases significantly. The social impact on the image of the organization, has the lowest percentage of "Very high" answers, reflecting the fact that the corporate social responsibility does not guarantee a quality image of the organization.

In Figure 2 we presented the synthesis of the collected answers to the question " mention to what extent do you think CSR reporting generates benefits at the level of the organization."

Figure 2. Synthesis of answers to the question: „To what extent do you think that CSR reporting benefits the organization."

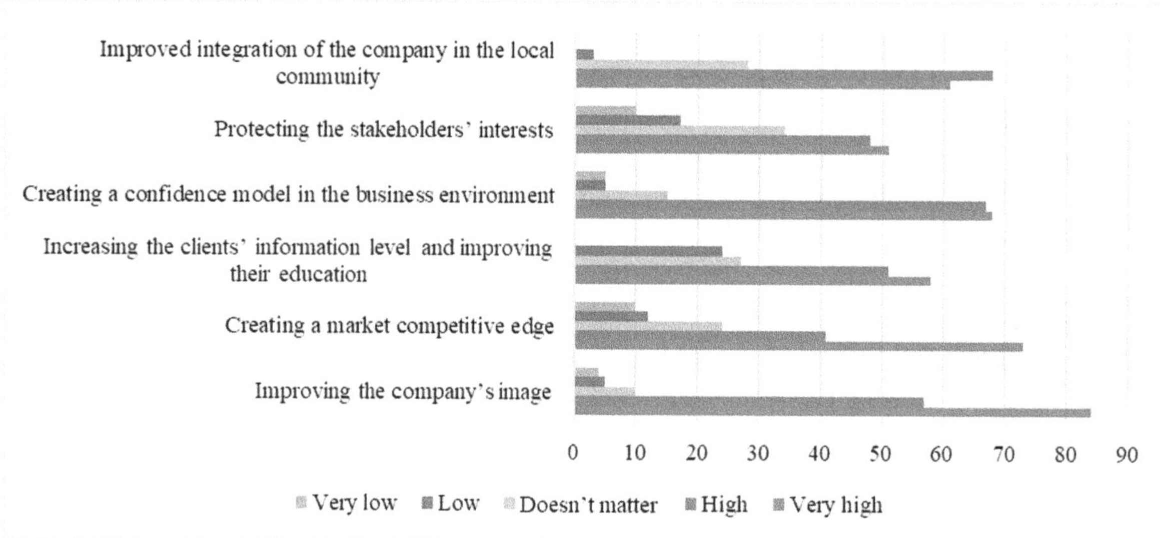

Most responses, classified in the "very high" category were focused in the area of the option on improving the image of the company by CSR reporting, while in the response variant "better integration of the organization in the local community", the share of responses was focused in the variant: "High" (Figure 3).

Figure 3. Synthesis of answers to the question: "To what extent do you consider the following issues to be challenges for CSR reporting?"

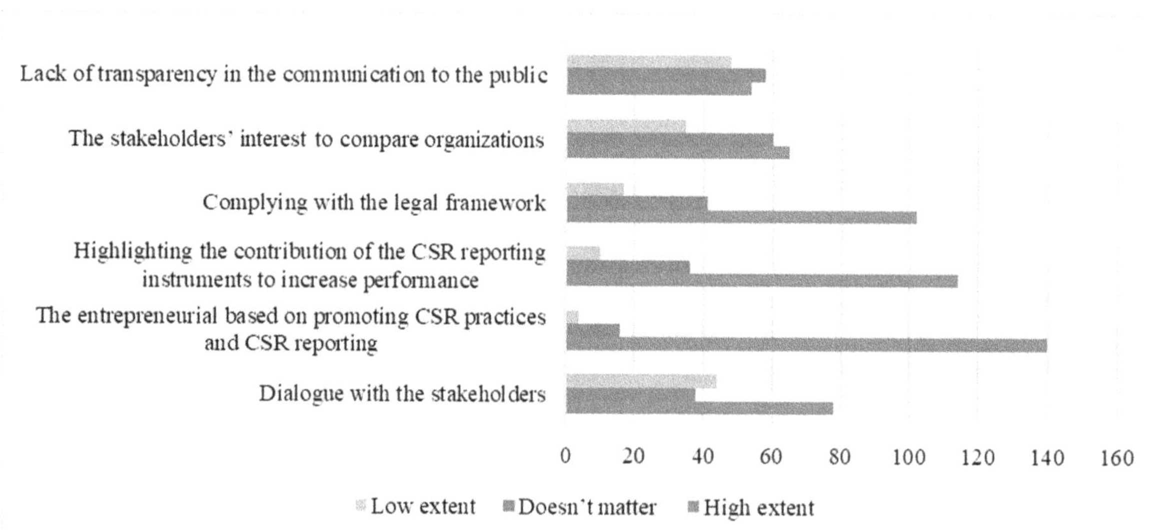

To the question about the challenges of reporting corporate social responsibility, the responses in the category of "Influence, to a large extent", focused on the possible answers on the entrepreneurship education, the contribution of the reporting system to improve the organization's performance and compliance with the legislative framework (Figure 4).

Figure 4. Synthesis of answers to the question: "What do you consider to be the role of CSR reporting instruments?"

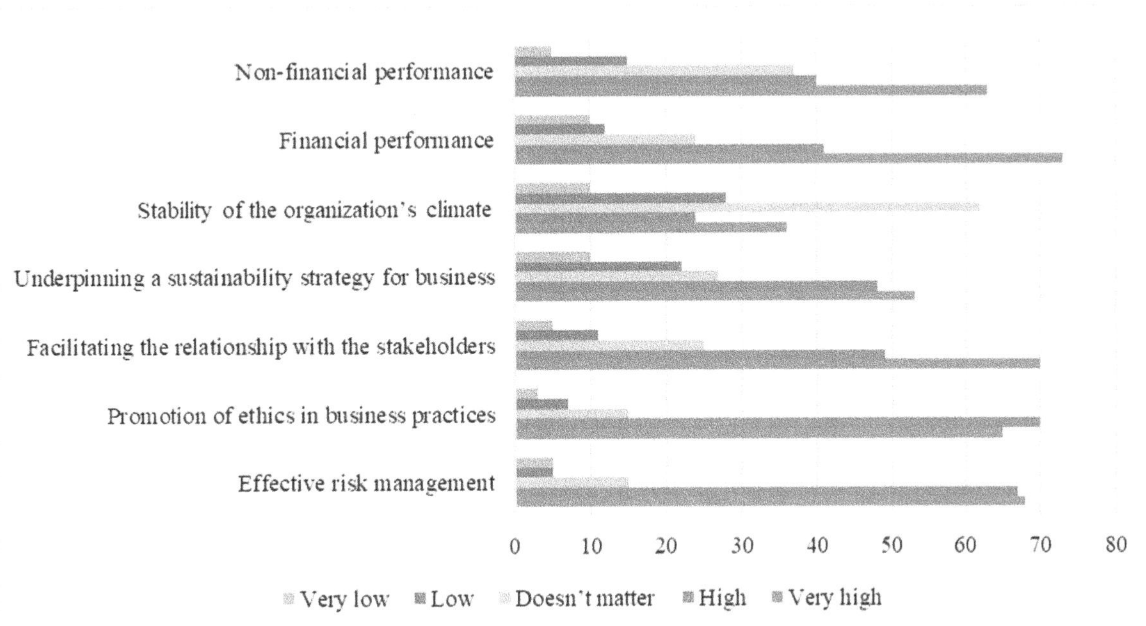

According to the responses, the major part of the CSR instruments is related to increased financial and non-financial performance, followed by the alternative of improved relations with stakeholders. In all the answers we have noticed that CSR reporting may support effective risk management. In the synthesis of the collected responses, a correlation is noted between the aim, objectives and hypotheses of the research, and the preparation of the questionnaire and the responses collected from managers involved in the research.

For a broader analysis of the impact of CSR reporting at the level of organizations in Romania, we proceeded to research the analytical indicators of their CSR profiles.

In order to test the hypotheses formulated we used the IBM SPSS Statistics Program, through which correlations were determined and a regression analysis was performed.

From the perspective of hypothesis H1: Is the competitive edge of the company influenced by the notoriety of CSR reporting instruments, the results of correlation analysis are presented in Table 2.

Table 2. Results of correlation analysis for hypothesis H1

Chi-Square Tests			
	Value	*df*	*Asymptotic Significance (2-sided)*
Pearson Chi-Square	4,779[a]	4	0.311

According to the information in Table 2 the value of the asymptotic significance is higher than the acceptable threshold (0.311>0.05), while the value of the Pearson Chi-Square coefficient is less than the threshold for the 4 degrees-of-freedom (4,779<9,488), which means that there is no statistically significant relationship between the two variables, and the hypothesis is disproven. The competitive edge of the organization is not influenced by the extent to which managers know the CSR reporting instruments, most of the managers questioned being informed about the reporting process and the instruments currently available on the market.

For hypotheses H2: The trust of the public is influenced by the transparency at the organization level, the results of the correlation analysis are presented in the Table 3.

Table 3. Results of correlation analysis for H2 hypothesis

Chi-Square Tests			
	Value	*df*	*Asymptotic Significance (2-sided)*
Pearson Chi-Square	13,291[a]	4	0.010

The asymptotic significance does not exceed the acceptable threshold (0.010<0.05), and the Pearson Chi-Square value is higher than the value in the distribution table for df = 4 (13,291>9,488), which means that the hypothesis is *validated* and there is a relationship between the two variables. According to the contingency table for this hypothesis, the managers of the analyzed organizations are convinced that the public is prone to trust those who are transparent and clearly transmit information of interest regarding their social responsibility initiatives and projects.

For the hypothesis *H3: The favorable perception of Romanian managers on CSR reporting is influenced by the size of the organization,* the results obtained from processing with IBM SPSS Statistics (Table 4).

Table 4. Results of correlation analysis for hypothesis H3

Chi-Square Tests			
	Value	*df*	*Asymptotic Significance (2-sided)*
Pearson Chi-Square	11,863[a]	6	0.065

The table shows that the value of asymptotic significance is higher than the acceptable threshold (0.065>0.05), and the value of Pearson Chi-Square coefficient is lower than its value in the distribution table for df=6 (11,863<12,592), which means that the hypothesis is invalidated and the size of the organization does not influence the favorable perception of the managers.

Hypotheses H4: The impact of using the reporting instruments on the organization's management performance depends on the age of the company, it has also been tested adequately, and the results are shown in the Table 5.

Table 5. Results of correlation analysis for hypothesis H4

Chi-Square Tests			
	Value	*df*	*Asymptotic Significance (2-sided)*
Pearson Chi-Square	120,928[a]	36	0.000

The value of asymptotic significance is within the acceptable range (0.000<0.05), and the Pearson Chi-Square coefficient is higher than the acceptable threshold (120,928>50,998), the hypothesis being validated. Basically, the longer the tradition on the market of the companies, the more their involvement in CSR projects is more efficient and transparency, visibility may provide the prerequisites for a better management.

For hypothesis H5: The competitive edge of a company generated by the involvement in CSR projects is influenced by its field of activity, the results were properly processed, their synthesis being presented in Table 6.

Table 6. Results of correlation analysis for H5 hypothesis

Chi-Square Tests			
	Value	*df*	*Asymptotic Significance (2-sided)*
Pearson Chi-Square	10,127[a]	6	0.119

This hypothesis is also invalidated, which is inferred from Table 6. The value of asymptotic significance exceeds the acceptable threshold (0.119>0.05) and the Pearson Chi-Square coefficient is lower than the value in the distribution table (10,127<12,592). The field wherein the company operates does not generate competitive edges in the CSR policy field.

Hypothesis H6: The trend of adopting CSR reporting standards is influenced by the cost-benefit ratio, has been properly tested and the results are centralized in Table 7.

Table 7. Results of correlation analysis for H6 hypothesis

Chi-Square Tests			
	Value	*df*	*Asymptotic Significance (2-sided)*
Pearson Chi-Square	18,953[a]	6	0.004

The data in the table indicates that the asymptotic significance is within the acceptable range (0.004<0.05), while the Pearson Chi-Square coefficient exceeds the value in the table for distribution (18,953>12,592), which means that the hypothesis is valid, and that the decision of the managers to select certain CSR reporting instruments is influenced by the cost-benefit analysis.

From the perspective of hypothesis H7: The evolution stage that marks the consistency in the approach of CSR reporting policies influences the diversity of areas of interest approached by the company, the results obtained after testing are presented in Table 8.

Table 8. Results of correlation analysis for H7 hypothesis

Chi-Square Tests			
	Value	*Df*	*Asymptotic Significance (2-sided)*
Pearson Chi-Square	8,882[a]	6	0.180

The value of asymptotic significance exceeds the acceptable threshold (0.180>0.05) and the value of Pearson Chi-Square is lower than that in the distribution table (8,882<12,592), as shown in the table. The assumption is disproven, which means that areas and issues of interest to a company do not generate different degrees of consistency in the non-financial reporting of the companies.

The testing of the hypothesis H8: The use of CSR communication instruments influences public confidence, generated the results presented in Table 9.

Table 9. Results of correlation analysis for H8 hypothesis

Chi-Square Tests			
	Value	*df*	*Asymptotic Significance (2-sided)*
Pearson Chi-Square	30,097[a]	18	0.037

According to the results in the table, the hypothesis is validated, the value of the asymptotic significance is less than the maximum value (0.037<0.05), and the value of the Pearson Chi-Square coefficient is greater than that of the table of distribution for df=18 (30,097>28,869), which demonstrates that the public confidence may be influenced by the use of the adequate instruments for the communication of CSR at the company level.

For hypothesis H9: The notoriety of CSR reporting instruments among managers influences the CSR performance, the results obtained are presented in Table 10.

Table 10. Results of correlation analysis for H9 hypothesis

Chi-Square Tests			
	Value	*df*	*Asymptotic Significance (2-sided)*
Pearson Chi-Square	30,786[a]	18	0.030

According to the table data, the hypothesis is *validated,* the value of asymptotic significance is lower than the maximum threshold (0.030<0.05), and the Pearson Chi-Square coefficient is higher than the value in its distribution table for df=18.

The managers' knowledge of the CSR reporting instruments influences the change in the policy of addressing CSR practices within the organization, including reporting practices with effects over the performance in this field.

In the regression analysis: the variable "aggregate CSR management performance" was considered dependent and the variable "Organization Size" was assessed as independent.

In Table 11 we presented the synthesis of the results of the regression analysis carried out in the research.

Table 11. Synthesis of regression analysis results

Model	R	R Square	Adjusted R Square	Std. Error of the estimated
1	0.309[a]	0.095	0.089	9,230

(a. Predictors: constant "Organization Size")

Table 12 integrates the results of the ANOVA analysis test, conducted for this research.

Table 12. ANOVA test results

Model		Sum of Squares	df	Mean Square	F	Sig.
1	Regression	1231,564	1	1231,564	14,455	.000[b]
	Residual	11672,450	137	85,200		
	Total	12904,014	138			
(a. Dependent Variable: All variables "aggregate CSR management performance"; b. Predictors: constant "Organization Size")						

The analysis coefficients for the results obtained in the conducted research are presented in Table 13.

Table 13. Coefficients of analysis

Model		Unstandardized Coefficients		Standardized Coefficients	t	Sig.
		B	Std. Error	Beta		
1	(Constant)	14,568	2,018		7,218	0.000
	Organization size	2,335	0.614	0,309	3,802	0.000
(a. Dependent Variable: All variables CSR management performance aggregated)						

According to the data in the table a value of R= 0.309 is indicated, less than 0.5, which means that the size of the organization is not a strong predictor. R Square = 0.089 or 8.9%, signifying the proportion of the variation of the dependent variable (performance) explained by the regression model, this being very small. The 0.00 significances in the table are lower than 0.05, which reflects the fact that the model is statistically significant.

Some of the hypotheses formulated following the research carried out and the tests applied have been validated. Thus, we can conclude that managers who know the CSR reporting instruments are concerned with the transparency of the organization and their integration into the organization. At the same time, they tend to become more concerned with CSR reporting with the confidence that all these initiatives offer the organization new opportunities to improve management practices and increase performance regardless of the company's size. The positive correlations between the CSR reporting level and financial and non-financial performance results could encourage more firms to engage in CSR activities and report these activities objectively and transparently.

Strategic Guidance Based on the SWOT: AHP Related Analysis of the Role of CSR Reporting in Increasing the Performance of the Organizations' Management

The CSR reporting has become not just an option but a necessity for the Romanian business environment and, in particular, for organizations that want to be more efficient. In this case, the components identified in the SWOT analysis are evaluated using the AHP (Analytic Hierarchy Process) method to measure their strengths and impacts. Analytic Hierarchical Processes represent decision modeling techniques, in which both tangible, quantitative and intangible, qualitative aspects may be evaluated, with the purpose of determining the comparative importance of several implementation alternatives.

AHP is the method that allows taking complex decisions using several criteria for managing critical aspects of a hierarchically structured problem or solving unstructured problems (Coyle, 2004). By applying the AHP method, one can obtain the best decision accompanied by a justification of the choices made, by presenting the weight of the criteria chosen in the final solution. This method integrates in a systematic approach both quantitative and qualitative aspects, and from their interaction the final decision is grounded (Ayag, 2005). Thus, a complex problem is divided into a hierarchy structure consisting of a goal and a set of objectives, criteria are assigned to the different levels of alternatives for decision, which may be addressed in terms of the comparisons in pairs.

Modeling and optimizing by using this technique allows also to achieve a controlled and quantified consensus of the decision makers with respect to the problem in case, it provides the possibility of a relapse; and the adjustment/correction of the model, based on the latest developments in the context wherein the issue of decision-making is placed.

The priority in this research is to identify the accessibility of CSR reporting instruments for Romanian managers and their role in increasing the organizations' management performance.

In this section, the elements of the SWOT analysis will be assessed and ranked according to the AHP method, which can provide a quantitative measure for the significance of each factor. The SWOT analysis of the social responsibility framework in Romania offers, through an integrated approach, the possibility to create a first image of the CSR reporting phenomenon in the Romanian business environment.

Subsequent to this image we will determine the effects of implementing CSR reporting instruments that may have an impact on the organizations' management performance, highlighted by the analytical hierarchy process (AHP). Practically every single factor of the four categories will be compared to the others, resulting in a cross-analysis of the strategies agreed upon by the managers who participated in the study. The final assessment involved determining the weights for each strategic alternative using the K. Goepel version 9.5.2012 software. The decision-making process at the corporate level often involves the analysis of all the relations and interests of the parties involved. In this context, the implementation of the analytical hierarchy process as a standard method for multicriterial problems requires a deeper perspective offered by the K. Goepel version 9.5.2012 software. Thus, in the case of a group of decision-making elements for each pair, the consensus indicator calculated in the form of a matrix is identified. In the next step, according to the consensus indicator, the decision sequence is rearranged to find groups with a high Consensus Index. Finding high consensus groups generates the development of new alternatives for a given decision issue.

SWOT Analysis of CSR Reporting System in Romania

SWOT analysis is a tool used for the simultaneous analysis of the internal and external environment, used as a support for substantiating decisions. The use of SWOT analysis in the decision-making mechanisms having a strategic scope facilitates the choice and application of a strategic variation leading to an optimal correlation between the elements of the internal environment and those of the external environment. Based on the conducted studies and research we presented a synthesis of SWOT analysis matrix for the CSR reporting system in Romania:

Table 14. SWOT Matrix

Strengths	**Weak points**
S1- Existence and availability of CSR reporting instruments (GRI, ISO 26000, etc.) S2 - Large diversity of activities in the CSR area that can be reported according to standards S3 - Increased interest of the Romanian managers for CSR reporting S4 - Relatively low input cost level according to CSR standards S5- CSR reporting in line with recognised standards is a tool to create a sustainable competitive advantage	W1 - Lack of reporting facilities for organizations involved in CSR campaigns W2- Poor monitoring of existing reporting initiatives W3- Weak promotion of the CSR reporting concept W4- Lack of an integrated CSR Development Strategy and of the requirement for CSR reporting at organization level W5- Lack of a strategic vision at the level of organizations' management related to CSR
Opportunities	**Threats**
O1- Increasing CSR reporting initiatives at company level O2- Increased interest for CSR at the level of the Romanian business environment and at the international level O3- Registration of the non-financial performance as criteria for additional evaluation of organizations O4- Compulsory non-financial reporting O5- The possibility to connect Romanian organizations to an international CSR reporting platform	T1- Lack of studies on the impact of CSR reporting on the organizations' management performance, approached from a qualitative and quantitative perspective T2 - The behavior of stakeholders (reluctance for such initiatives) T3- Lack of Education on CSR reporting T4- No motivation/reward system for reporting organizations according to CSR standards

The AHP process is applied to the SWOT Matrix and virtually every preference of the responding managers is turned into a numerical value that can be compared and evaluated on a scale of 1-9. In the comparison of two preferences, a linguistic scale with nine categories is used, where the indifference relationship is expressed by the phrase "equally important" and the relation of extreme preference is expressed by the phrase "extremely important". For example, if the words "equally important" are associated to the number 1 and the words "extremely important" are associated to the number 9, then, the term "not at all important" may be associated to the number 1/9. All the comparisons were made after processing the data collected in the study and the results are presented in Table 15.

Table 15. Comparison of the pairs between the SWOT elements

SWOT elements	S	W	O	T	Weight
S	1,000	2,000	0.500	0.250	0.220
W	2,000	1,000	3,000	0.333	0.290
O	0.500	3,000	1,000	0.500	0.320
T	0.250	0.333	0.500	1,000	0.170
CR=0.06					

CR (Consistency Ratio) is an index that enables measuring the validity of the respondents' answers in the survey. The consistency ratio must be lower than 0,1 (10%) in order to have an improved level of consistency. In other words, the consistency index is important for the decision maker to verify that its decisions are consistent, and the final decision is the right one (Saaty, 2004). Next, we calculated the local and global values of the SWOT Matrix elements presented in Table 16:

The need for an integrated approach to CSR reporting behavior at the level of Romanian companies is justified by the systemic perspective on CSR in the business environment, which allows highlighting the influential elements from economic, social and environmental points of view.

Thus, an integrated model of the CSR reporting process can target three major objectives, namely: promoting the importance of CSR reporting, developing CSR reporting instruments for companies, sustainable CSR reporting. In this context, we will consider the possibility of analyzing five strategic alternatives with the following structure (Table 17):

S1-monitoring strategy of Romanian companies that have so far opted for a form of CSR reporting activities
S2-information strategy aimed at accessing information for CSR reporting instruments
S3-implementation strategy focused on a process of implementing CSR reporting instruments
S4-the integration strategy that aims at horizontal and vertical integration of the CSR reporting process in the organization's management.

The relationships between the elements of the SWOT analysis and the proposed strategic alternatives are presented in Table No. 18, depending on the way they were assessed on a scale from 1-5 by the managers who participated in the study. The AHP method determined the importance value of the criteria in the SWOT analysis. The degree of relations (rij) represents the opinions of the questioned managers related to the way each element in the SWOT quadrant can contribute or not to each strategic alternative and how they can be integrated subsequently to establish an optimal strategic variation. The footprint of each element may be positive (S, A) or negative (W, T) and contribute with different rates to the overall assessment of the strategic alternatives. The values of the strategic alternatives (St_i) were calculated using the following formula (Eq. 1):

Table 16. Local and global values for SWOT Matrix elements

SWOT Elements/Weight	ID	Content SWOT Matrix	Local values	Global values
Strengths 0.220	S1	Existence and availability of CSR reporting instruments (GRI, ISO 26000, etc.)	0.301	0.069
	S2	Large diversity of activities in the CSR area that can be reported according to standards	0.246	0.056
	S3	Increased interest of the Romanian managers for CSR reporting	0.153	0.034
	S4	Relatively low input cost level according to CSR standards	0.145	0.028
	S5	CSR reporting in line with recognized standards is a tool to create a sustainable competitive advantage	0.155	0.033
Weak points 0.290	W1	Lack of reporting facilities for organizations involved in CSR campaigns	0.266	0.077
	W2	Poor monitoring of existing reporting initiatives	0.259	0.075
	W3	Weak promotion of the CSR reporting concept	0.200	0.058
	W4	Lack of an integrated CSR Development Strategy and of the requirement for CSR reporting at organization level	0.166	0.048
	W5	Lack of a strategic vision at the level of organizations' management related to CSR	0.109	0.032
Opportunities 0.320	O1	Increasing CSR reporting initiatives at company level	0.260	0.083
	O2	Increased interest for CSR at the level of the Romanian business environment and at the international level	0.213	0.068
	O3	Registration of the non-financial performance as criteria for additional evaluation of organizations	0.200	0.064
	O4	Compulsory non-financial reporting	0.197	0.063
	O5	The possibility to connect Romanian organizations to an international CSR reporting platform	0.130	0.042
Threats 0.170	T1	Lack of studies on the impact of CSR reporting on the organizations' management performance, approached from a qualitative and quantitative perspective	0.350	0.068
	T2	The behavior of stakeholders (reluctance for such initiatives)	0.285	0.043
	T3	Lack of Education on CSR reporting	0.229	0.039
	T4	No motivation/reward system for reporting organizations according to CSR standards	0.136	0.02

Source: Processing by authors with the K. Goepel V. 9.5.2012 software.

$$St_i = \sum_{j=1}^{n} wj\ rij\left(-1\right)^k \quad (1)$$

k, can take the value 2 - for the elements in the S, O quadrants and the value 1-for the elements in the W, T quadrants where:

St_i - The total value of the strategic alternative *I;*

Table 17. Strategic alternatives assessment matrix

SWOT Elements	ID	K Factor	Global values	S1	S2	S3	S4
Strengths	S1	2	0.069	5	4	3	2
	S2	2	0.056	4	3	2	1
	S3	2	0.034	5	3	1	3
	S4	2	0.028	5	4	4	1
	S5	2	0.033	4	2	5	3
Weaknesses	W1	1	0.077	1	2	3	3
	W2	1	0.075	4	2	2	1
	W3	1	0.058	5	4	2	3
	W4	1	0.048	2	2	3	2
	W5	1	0.032	1	2	3	2
Opportunities	O1	2	0.083	2	2	3	3
	O2	2	0.068	2	3	2	5
	O3	2	0.064	1	2	4	5
	O4	2	0.063	5	2	2	3
	O5	2	0.042	3	3	2	2
Threats	T1	1	0.068	1	3	1	2
	T2	1	0.043	1	1	3	2
	T3	1	0.039	1	2	4	2
	T4	1	0.020	2	3	4	2

Source: Processing by authors with the K. Goepel V. 9.5.2012 software.

wj - the global weight of a J element in the SWOT analysis;
rij- the degree of relations between the strategic alternative *i* and SWOT elements *j*
n - number of elements in the SWOT analysis;
k - factor of positive or negative contribution of the elements in the SWOT Matrix.

The value of each factor for each strategic alternative can be multiplied considering the overall values of SWOT analysis elements and the degree of relations with the SWOT elements (Table 18).

Table 18 - Values of strategic alternatives

	Strategic alternatives			
	S1	S2	S3	S4
Total value	0.008(4.)	0.159(3.)	0.268(2.)	0.419(1.)

Source: Processing by authors with the K. Goepel V. 9.5.2012 software.

It may be seen that by applying the calculation formula in order to quantify the impact of each strategic alternative, variant S4-which involves horizontal and vertical integration of CSR reporting in the management of the organization is the most attractive for Romanian managers. Even when the ensemble of elements in the SWOT analysis is not very large, the analysis of strategic alternatives based on the evaluation matrix is consistent. Following the evaluation of strategic alternatives, the following correlations were obtained (Table 19).

Table 19. Correlations of the evaluation of strategic alternatives

Variables	**Total values**	**S1**	**S2**	**S3**	**S4**	*k Factor*
Total values	1.00	-0.10	-0.32	- 0.49	- 0.56	- 0.25
S1	-0.10	1.00	- 0.18	- 0.29	- 0.61	- 0.29
S2	-0.32	- 0.18	1.00	0.20	- 0.76	- 0.33
S3	-0.49	- 0.29	- 0.20	1.00	- 0.38	- 0.48
S4	-0.56	- 0.61	- 0.76	- 0.38	1.00	0.68
K Factor	-0.25	- 0.31	- 0.33	- 0.48	0.58	1.00

Source-processing by authors with the K. Goepel V. 9.5.2012 software.

It can be seen that there is a consistent margin of the S4 strategic alternative for SO-type elements, as factors able to increase the organizations' management performance and a consistent marking for the WT-type elements (r=0.68), which indicates a positive perspective on the strategy aiming to the horizontal and vertical integration of CSR reporting within the management processes of the organization. For the strategic alternative S1 denotations generated by the value r = -0.29 are recorded. Also, the evaluation of strategies aimed at interaction and development (S2 and S3) relative to all factors involved in the analysis generated certain similarities (r = 0,20).

CONCLUSION

The results of this analysis highlight the need for the development of an integrated approach of CSR reporting in the framework of the Romanian organizations involving, on one hand, current management practices, and, on the other hand, to exploit the existing reporting instruments, with an impact on the performance of the organizations' management.

Most of the problems of managing the CSR reporting process target combating its complexity through methods to optimize the decisions related to costs and objectives. Optimization in this case targets, as a strategic alternative, the integration of CSR reporting in the management of the organization both horizontally and vertically.

For companies measuring their social impact it is essential to be able to demonstrate the non-financial results of their business. This practically facilitates their meeting with investors and to easier obtain targeted financing. From the perspective of the internal dimension we can talk about the internal function of measuring the social impact as CSR reporting instruments are used in a planned and efficient way.

CSR reporting can be an open and collaborative process that provides companies the opportunity to create new social relations, of cooperative actions and improves the participation of stakeholders (Milne & Grey 2013; Mukherjee & Nuñez 2018, Watts, Fernie & Dainty 2019).

The major challenge currently faced by Romanian managers is the need to ensure, for the beginning, a minimum of performance at the management level of the organization and in this respect the impact of an integrated strategic approach must be acknowledged. The results of this study can be a useful support in the decision-making process for the validation of strategic alternatives, in order to accelerate the conversion of CSR reporting policy towards a sustainable form of business management.

Basically, the adhesion of the managers to the strategic alternatives and to a behavior directed to CSR reporting, can also have the effect of bottom-to-top harmonization, and from an operational point of view, the implementation of these strategies is a necessary option in order to achieve a level of performance. Identifying the expectations of Romanian managers regarding the results of implementing strategies related to CSR reporting will help to focus attention on those elements that can proactively influence the performance of the organizations' management.

CSR reporting can be a relevant source for complex decision support, in which the elements of strategic scale are both a success factor and an element of differentiation. It can also be the major challenge faced by managers of Romanian companies, who want to implement the various CSR reporting instruments in response to ever increasing competitiveness.

REFERENCES

Abbas, J. (2020). Impact of total quality management on corporate green performance through the mediating role of corporate social responsibility. *Journal of Cleaner Production*, *242*, 118458. doi:10.1016/j.jclepro.2019.118458

Argento, D., Culasso, F., & Truant, E. (2019). From Sustainability to Integrated Reporting: The Legitimizing Role of the CSR Manager. *Organization & Environment*, *32*(4), 484–507. doi:10.1177/1086026618769487

Ayağ, Z. (2005). A fuzzy AHP-based simulation approach to concept evaluation in a NPD environment. *IIE Transactions*, *37*(9), 827–842. doi:10.1080/07408170590969852

Bachmann, P., & Ingenhoff, D. (2016). Legitimacy through CSR disclosures? The advantage outweighs the disadvantages. *Public Relations Review*, *42*(3), 386–394. doi:10.1016/j.pubrev.2016.02.008

Burns, C.J.M., Houghton, L., & Stewart, H., (2019). Sustainability – A key to Australian finance directors improving their organisation's CSR culture. *Corp Soc Resp Env Ma.*, 1– 13.

Clarkson, P. M., Overell, M. B., & Chapple, L. (2011). Environmental Reporting and its Relation to Corporate Environmental Performance. *Abacus*, *47*(1), 27–60. doi:10.1111/j.1467-6281.2011.00330.x

Coyle, G. (2004). *The Analytic Hierarchy Process (AHP).* Available from: http://www.booksites.net/download/coyle/stuent_files/AHP_Technique.pdf

Dalal-Clayton, D. B., & Bass, S. (2002). *National Sustainable Development Strategies: Experience and Dilemmas. Environmental Planning Issues, 6.* IIED.

Elkington, J. (2017). Towards the sustainable corporation: Win-win-win business strategies for sustainable development. *California Management Review, 36*(2), 90–100. doi:10.2307/41165746

European Commission. (2011). *A renewed EU strategy 2011-14 for corporate social responsibility*. Available from: https://www.europarl.europa.eu/meetdocs/2009_2014/documents/com/com_com(2011)0681_/com_com(2011)0681_en.pdf

Hammann, E., Habisch, A., & Pechlaner, H. (2009). Values that create value: Socially responsible business practices in SMEs: Empirical evidence from German companies. *Business Ethics (Oxford, England), 18*(1), 37–51. doi:10.1111/j.1467-8608.2009.01547.x

Hickman, L., & Cote, J. (2019). CSR reporting and assurance legitimacy: A client–assuror dyad investigation. *Journal of Applied Accounting Research, 20*(4), 372–393. doi:10.1108/JAAR-01-2018-0009

Koerber, C.P. (2015). Corporate responsibility standards: current implications and future possibilities for peace through commerce. *Journal of Business Ethics, 89*(4), 461–480.

Li, X., Kim, J. B., Wu, H., & Yu, Y. (2019). Corporate Social Responsibility and Financial Fraud: The Moderating Effects of Governance and Religiosity. *Journal of Business Ethics*. Advance online publication. doi:10.100710551-019-04378-3

Ligteringen, E., & Zadek, S. (2005). The Future of Corporate Responsibility Standards. *Business and the Environment, 16*(6), 121–123.

Lozano, R., (2019). Analysing the use of tools, initiatives, and approaches to promote sustainability in corporations. *Corp Soc Resp Env Ma.*, 1– 17.

Margolis, J. D., Elfenbein, H. A., & Walsh, J. P. (2002). *Does It Pay to Be Good? A Meta-Analysis and Redirection of Research on the Relationship between Corporate Social and Financial Performance*. Available from: https://books.google.com.hk/books/about/Does_it_Pay_to_be_Good.html?id=hE3OnQAACAAJ&redir_esc=y

Milne, M. J., & Gray, R. (2013). W(h)ither Ecology? The Triple Bottom Line, the Global Reporting Initiative, and Corporate Sustainability Reporting. *Journal of Business Ethics, 118*(1), 13–29. doi:10.100710551-012-1543-8

Morsing, M., & Spence, L. J. (2019). Corporate social responsibility (CSR) communication and small and medium sized enterprises: The governmentality dilemma of explicit and implicit CSR communication. *Human Relations, 72*(12), 1920–1947. doi:10.1177/0018726718804306

Mukherjee, A., & Nuñez, R. (2018). Doing well by doing good: Can voluntary CSR reporting enhance financial performance? *Journal of Indian Business Research, 11*(2), 100–119. doi:10.1108/JIBR-07-2018-0199

Orlitzky, M., Schmidt, F. L., & Rynes, S. L. (2003). Corporate Social and Financial Performance: A Meta-analysis. *Organization Studies, 24*(3), 403–441. doi:10.1177/0170840603024003910

Prado-Lorenzo, J. M., Gallego-Alvarez, I., & Garcia-Sanchez, I. M. (2009). Stakeholder engagement and corporate social responsibility reporting: The ownership structure effect. *Corporate Social Responsibility and Environmental Management, 16*(2), 94–107. doi:10.1002/csr.189

Rhoua, Y., & Singal, M. (2020). A review of the business case for CSR in the hospitality industry. *International Journal of Hospitality Management*, *84*, 102330. doi:10.1016/j.ijhm.2019.102330

RomaniaC. S. R. Index. (2018). Available from: https://www.theazores.ro/wp-content/uploads/2018/02/Romania_CSR_Index_Detailed_Report.pdf

Saaty, T. L. (2004). Decision making— The Analytic Hierarchy and Network Processes (AHP/ANP). *Journal of Systems Science and Systems Engineering*, *13*(1), 1–35. doi:10.100711518-006-0151-5

Schwindenhammer, S. (2013). Patterns and Explanations of Corporate Voluntary Norm Compliance: Results from a Structured Focused Comparison of German G500 in the Global Reporting Initiative. *German Policies Studies*, *9*(2), 123–160.

Shada, M. K., Laia, F. W., Fatt, C. L., Klemeš, J. J., & Bokhari, A. (2019). Integrating sustainability reporting into enterprise risk management and its relationship with business performance: A conceptual framework. *Journal of Cleaner Production*, *208*, 415–425. doi:10.1016/j.jclepro.2018.10.120

Sinthupundaja, J., Chiadamrong, N., & Kohda, Y. (2019). Internal capabilities, external cooperation and proactive CSR on financial performance. *Service Industries Journal*, *39*(15-16), 1099–1122. doi:10.1080/02642069.2018.1508459

Torugsa, N. A., O'Donohue, W., & Hecker, R. (2012). Capabilities, proactive CSR and financial performance inSMEs: Empirical evidence from an Australian manufacturing industry sector. *Journal of Business Ethics*, *109*(4), 483–500. doi:10.100710551-011-1141-1

Waddock, S. (2015). Building a new institutional infrastructure for corporate responsibility. *The Academy of Management Perspectives*, *22*(3), 87–108. doi:10.5465/amp.2008.34587997

Watts, G., Fernie, S., & Dainty, A. (2019). Paradox and legitimacy in construction: How CSR reports restrict CSR practice. *International Journal of Building Pathology and Adaptation*, *37*(2), 231–246. doi:10.1108/IJBPA-05-2018-0037

Chapter 7
Decision Analysis in Financial Marketing Using Multi-Criteria Decision-Making Methods

Prabadevi Boopathy
Vellore Institute of Technology, India

N. Deepa
Vellore Institute of Technology, India

ABSTRACT

In the trend of digital marketing, the back and front office activities are automized. For any business organization of various departmental activities, finance and marketing play a vital role. Finance and marketing are the most important functional areas of operations in any business organization, as they directly impact the financial growth as well as market steadiness of the business. As very crucial decisions taken in these functional areas of operations affect the other departments, the decisions in these financial marketing should be taken with utmost care. Henceforth, this results in greater impact on economic growth of the organization. Therefore, the decisions in finance and marketing activities should consider various factors (critical to quality) before arriving at a conclusion. In order to attain the final decision, multi-criteria decision-making (MCDM) methods can be applied. These MCDM methods consider the conflicting factors to evaluate the finance and marketing activities.

INTRODUCTION

As financial areas of operation are the lifeblood for determining whether a business is profitable or not, decision making in Financial Marketing plays a crucial role in Business World. The business executives can able to assess the financial allegations of investments and other activities related to business, only after understanding the financial analysis and valuation. Effective marketing involves understanding the needs of customers, demands of customers from season to season, cost negotiation to meet and

DOI: 10.4018/978-1-7998-4637-6.ch007

withstand in the market, advertisements to please and attract customer, retaining existing customers, planning and implementing. Finance and marketing are directly proportional, with a good marketing strategy in place one can effectively attain a decent financial value in their business. For an organization to survive in the recession period, it must have control over its cost incurred in various operations. So most of the contemporary business organization maintain a project team at each division to manage the cost incurred. To address the needs of customers, identify the various cost control parameters criteria relevant to the requirement of customers on various occasion and cost parameters at various divisions has to be identified. For developing such marketing decision models, a finite number of alternate decisions and the elements or attributes which influence to take correct decisions should be recognized. The limited set of alternatives (alternate decisions) are evaluated with respect to the identified set of attributes. There are many complexities in taking decisions in various activities of marketing in large businesses. Therefore marketing executives need decision support models for taking suitable decisions in order to gain more profit. Several Multi-criteria decision making (MCDM) methods have been used so far to build reliable decision-making models. There are various steps in taking reliable decisions using such MCDM methods. A decision matrix is constructed with a set of alternatives and attributes which are used to evaluate those alternatives. It is important to find the relative importance of the attributes as it plays a very significant role in decision making. Multi-criteria decision-making methods are used to find the assessment scores by considering the relative importance of the attributes. The assessment scores are then used for appropriate decision making.

Also, these MCDM methods can help the finance manager to make decisions on profit planning as profit is determined by various factors like pricing in the market, analysing demands in market, demand-supply chain and cost. Finance manager needs to manage the fund's allocation and fundraising from various sponsors for predicting the profit. Marketing managers play a greater role in promoting the product to the customer with attractive designs and trending patterns. They have to focus on right product delivery with zero per cent damage to right customers, identifying various price drivers to fix the product price, product promotion channels, location identification for the business, identifying best distribution networks and mapping products to customers (identifying right customers for the product). Altogether Financial marketing has to take various decisions from framing a budget plan to deliver the right product to the customers. So, here we discuss the decision making in various financial marketing services using MCDM approaches.

In the world of technological advancements, various functional areas of operation in business must adapt to the technological advancement for surviving in the market. The standard and vital functional areas of operation in any business is finance and marketing. Though automated software is prevailing in the market to automate the back-office activities and functional areas of the business, there are no best software tools for assisting in decision making. These software tools automize the manual operations, thus alleviating the manpower or labour costs involved. The financial and marketing researchers acknowledge that there is wide requirement for better decision making systems to address the decision problems in finance and marketing. Each functional areas of operation such as marketing & sales, Supply chain management, Accounting & finance and Human resources are interdependent among each other, for instance, accounting and finance module collaborates with other functional areas of operation as shown in Table 1. Table 1 also portrays the collaborative activities of Marketing and Finance with other functional areas of operation.

Table 1. Collaborative activities of Finance and Marketing with other functional areas of the organization

Functional Areas of operation	Collaboration Activities	
	From Finance and Accounting	**To Finance and Accounting**
Customer	Invoices and Credit memoranda	Payments
Human Resources	Gathering Hiring needs and personnel information in Finance and Accounting	Legal requirements and Job details, Employee Payroll and profit – expense data
Supply Chain Management	Sale data forecasting and manufacturing cost analysis	Determining Production plans, stock maintenance, materials procurement
Marketing and Sales	Cost/profit analysis	Sales order data
Collaboration activities of Marketing and Sales		
Functional Areas of operation	**From Marketing and Sales**	**To Marketing and Sales**
Customer	Status of the customer orders	Sales orders to be processed
Human Resources	Hiring requirement and personal information needed in Marketing and Sales	Legal requirements and Job details of recruited candidates
Supply Chain Management	Sales forecasts and sales orders	Product Availability data and order status
Finance and Accounting	Sales order data	Cost /profit analysis

A business process is the set of activities that intakes some input from the resources available and produces an outcome that is of value to the customer. A sample business process initiated by Marketing and Sales functional area of operation is depicted in Figure 1.

Figure 1. A sample Business Process

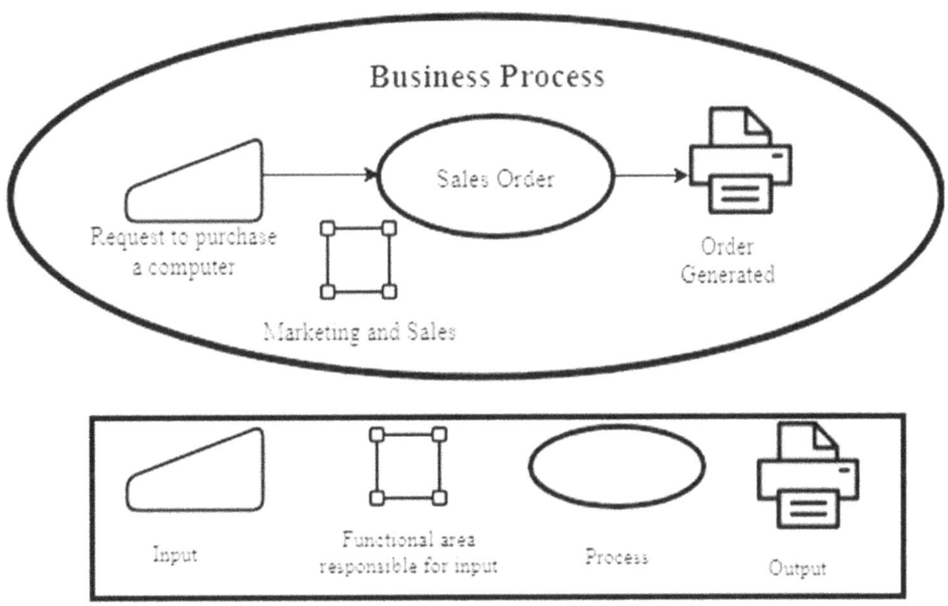

Any business process has four components, namely input, output, a functional area of the operation responsible for the input and the process done. The business process helps the manager to look at their organization from the perspective of the customer. Consequently, to stay on demand in the market with satisfied customers.

Background

This section provides broad discussion on financial marketing functional area of operation and various parameters to be considered while making marketing and financial decisions.

Decision Making in Finance Functional Area of Operation

Finance is the major functional area of operations in Banks, institutions, public accounting and corporation. Corporate finance is responsible for various decision making in an organization, which is of greater importance for value promotion in an organization. Financial managers need to decide on funding, profit analysis and tools for prioritizing financial resources (for assisting in effective utilization of financial resources). The organization should have proper perceptions of different investments made and their Return on Investment (ROI). Also, they should decide on various risk factors to be considered. Therefore, the activities of finance include deciding on investments, financing, dividends (among Shareholders) and the ROI. They must decide on what to invest, how to manage or fund the investment decision, and when to return ROI. All the above, they should ensure the highest possible risk factors are addressed with organization's optimized financial structure. The optimized financial structure refers to maximizing the organization's market value by minimizing the capital cost involved by the effective utilization of funds.

Financial Activity: Investment Management and Capital Budgeting

This activity must decide on the following:

1. *Treasury*: They must choose where to place or what can be done with the long term assets, i.e. whether to pursue investment opportunity. Also, decide on how to effectively manage short, medium payment flows and risk involved. Better analysis on realized and planned financial tractions in treasury impacts an organization's success. To assess market risk, they maintain an integrated central risk control system.
2. *Financial Accounting Tools*: The organization must decide on best accounting tools in the market because with which they will identify the capital expenditures, estimated cash flows, budget, cost allocation exploration, financial statements, forecasting, general ledger, special ledger, accounts payable/receivable, fixed asset accounting, legal consolidation and for comparative analysis of planned versus projected outcome.
3. *Financial Modelling:* To estimate the economic impact of the investment opportunity, it makes use of the Internal Rate of Return-IRR and the Net Present Value-NPV to evaluate the proposals on investment and compare various projects.

Financial Activity: Capital Financing

This activity makes decisions on how to finance investments optimally through equity and debts. If they decide on equity, they must ensure that the massive equity plans do not dilute their earnings and value of their investors. If they decide on the latter one, then they should be aware of increased risks with repayments of the enormous number of debts. Their goal must be to optimize the company's capital structure by reducing the Weighted Average Cost of Capital (WACC).

The optimal capital structure must have control on overhead cost, overhead orders, cost centre accounting (analyse the places where overhead incurs), Activity-based costing (controlling cross-departmental functions), product cost, cost object and profitability analysis (source of returns). The profitability analysis helps in decision making on selecting customers, determining prices, developing constraints and choosing distribution channels.

Financial Activity: Dividends and ROI

This activity has to decide on whether to retain excess business earnings for future funds and operational requirements or to dispense the earnings to the shareholders in the form of dividends.

The retained earnings help to fund a business extension. Retained earnings for business expansion is recommended if done without incurring additional debts nor diluting the value of equity by issuing more shares. If the Rate of Return (RoR) is more significant than Capital cost incurred, return the earnings to shareholders(i.e. make dividends among shareholders) or share buyers, else retain for future funds.

In addition to the above mentioned activity, some other criteria must be considered. The most important one is investment banking, which is used for evaluating financial needs and then raising appropriate capital to fulfil the need.

Thus to make financial decisions, the following criteria must be considered:

Decision Making in Marketing Functional Area of Operation

Marketing means not just advertisement its making people aware of the organization's evolution, its product, offers and services. For this to happen, an organization will involve in outreach activities like connecting customers through a phone call (call existing customers or new via the numbers obtained through the campaign), a punchy newsletter on every update, appearing on user searches of similar products in search engine, Promoting products or reaching the customer trade shows and product placement during game shows, movies, reality shows. Better decisions in marketing help the organization to retain the existing customers, attracts new customers and empowers longer-term customer relationship. The marketing managers must plan and execute all the marketing activities, thus maximizing the efficiency of the marketing resources in the organization. The marketing activities help to understand an organization's products, places, prices, promotion methodologies and market demands. An organization producing different products uses different types of strategies for each product type. The standard set of marketing activities for each product include: Selection of product/service, Product /service pricing, product placement, Incentive and promotion management, Segments and list management (attractive User Interface), Web-based marketing surveys, Email marketing, search engine marketing, campaign management, marketing resource management, self service portal for marketing and marketing analytics. The marketing module often gets input and assists other modules of an organization.

Table 2. Criterion to be considered for decision making in financial decisions

S.No	Criterion	Subcriterion
1	Investment management and Capital budgeting	Treasury • Long term Assets • Short term asset • Medium-term asset • Market risk Financial accounting tool • Capital expenditure • Cost estimation • Planned versus projected outcome • Ledger • Cost allocation forecast Financial modelling • IRR • NPV
2	Capital Financing	Asset • Equity • Debts • WACC Cost controlling • Overhead cost • Activity-based costing • Cost object • Accounts payable/receivable o Elcetronic Data Interchange (EDI) o Electronid fund transfers (EFT) • Fixed asset accounting • Legal consolidation • Profitability analysis o Pricing o Customer selection o Distribution channel selection o Developing constraints
3	Excess Earnings	Business Expansion Dividends RoR
4	Enterprise Controlling	Executive information system Business plan Profit centre accounting • Business transactions like Financial accounting, Materials management, Asset Management and Sales, which affects profit are included in profit centre accounting.
5	Other Criteria	Credit risk assessment Valuation methods Financial Plan Investment banking Risk management • Insurance • Business • Reputational risk • Interest rate risk • Liquidity risk • Operational risk • Volatility risk • Settlement risk

Marketing Activity: Selection of Product or Service

The organization or the manufacturer must first decide on what type of product or service to be delivered with the consent from the customer because, without a customer, better quality product produced has no value. They have analysed or *predict customer buying patterns* (Eg: consider a supermarket in Educational Institute, the student during admission will buy amenities for a hostel. So the supermarket set up will be rearranged showcasing a different type of products to be used in the hostel rooms (such as bed, cosmetics, new sim cards and so), whereas remaining groceries will be shifted to another corner of the supermarket. This setup will change when the admission time closes, and now groceries will be showcased.), *research market trends* (understanding the demands of the product or service in the market), *identify the various competitors in the race* (identifying the business people delivering same product or service) *and learning their way of approach to the customers to bring out the best.* This activity requires details about customers which require better segment and list management containing the organization's customer profile data and personalized marketing messages. The organization may adopt some techniques to learn *marketing analytics* for predicting customer behaviour.

Marketing Activity: Product Price Fixing

To decide or fix the product or service's price, an organization has to consider the following *market of the commodity*, compare and analyse the *price chart of similar product/ services* by various competitors, *commodity's status* within the market. E.g., when introducing a new type of same products existing in the market, an organization will plan for an initial discount to promote the product and lure the customers. If a product's demand is saturated in the market, the organization has to move the product to inventory, thus reducing the price.

Marketing Activity: Product Placement

The organization uses *direct or indirect sales* method to decide on where to distribute its product so that it will reach the marketplace. Through former one, the organization sells the product to customers directly, e.g., franchise, while with later one, the organization will approach the retailer and in turn, the retailer will sell the product. This depends on the nature of the product and its customer. Email marketing (effective means for communicating and distributing essential details) and Lead management (automizing leads distribution) are the sub-activities in the product placement.

Marketing Activity: Product Promotion

For better sales, an organization must create customer demand in the market. To attain it, an organization will promote its product through media advertisements (Newspaper, TV, Radio, web portals) and incentives on the product (customer card, product discounts, gifts and so). This will be followed by sales promotion. For instance, a hotel business can be promoted by adding hotel ads in railway ticket booking system based on the forecast of different tourist spots in the Journey. They conduct an effective public relations management campaign to promote the organization and its commodity. *Trade Promotion Management* must inculcate effective promotions to increase brand equity for attaining sales objectives and enables a closed-loop process depicted in figure 2.

Figure 2. The closed-loop trade promotion process

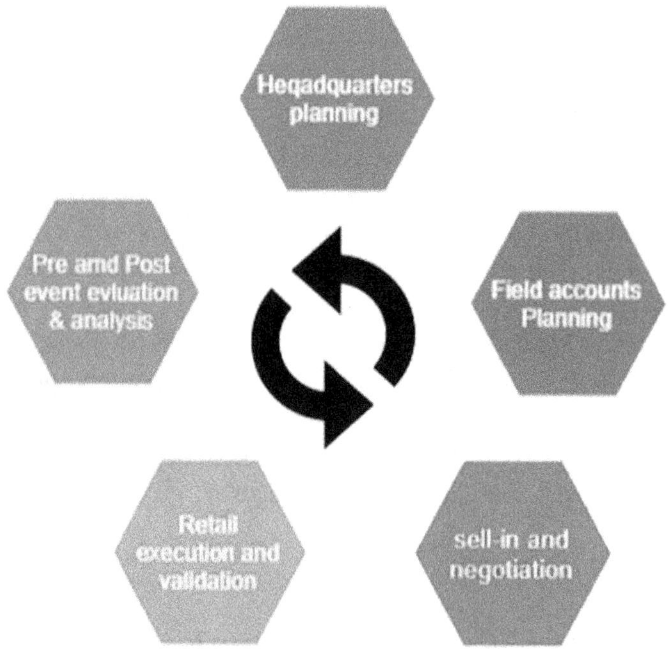

Campaign management for long term profitable relationship (for analyzing the activities via various inbound and outbound interaction channels) and may showcase their company through a volunteered donation towards the charity. A user-friendly self-service portal can be launched for customer interaction and organization's loyalty. Through which they can conduct a web-based marketing survey for better customer feedback on brand value and the distribution of promotional offers to the customers.

Alexis Leon states that the stages of the product life cycle are determined based on the marketing strategies viz., Product, Price, Distribution, Advertising and Sales Promotion (Zolfani, S. H et al., 2013). The stages of the product life cycle are

1. **New Product development**: In this stage, the organization has just started to develop a new product based on the idea generated. So here, the values for the marketing strategies will be:
    a. Product – no product is developed; the only purpose is evolved.
    b. Price- No price is fixed, Sales is zero. But investment costs will be high now.
    c. Distribution- No production to distribute.
    d. Advertising- No advertising will be entertained.
    e. Sales Promotion- Profits are negative now, so no promotion.
2. **Introduction:** The product has just developed, and now the strategies will be:
    a. Product-The company offers a *primary product* (to forecast the customer demand).
    b. Price- Set low to achieve the market strategy.
    c. Distribution- Build a selective distribution, because overproduction may be wasted before reaching the customer
    d. Advertising- create awareness about the product among early adopters, wholesalers/ retailers.
    e. Sales Promotion- Incurs massive expenditure to create a trial.

3. **Growth:** The product has reached the market or has created its customers and strategies will be:
    a. Product- The manufacturer offers product extensions, service and product warranty.
    b. Price- Now penetration pricing, because it has its place in the market
    c. Distribution- Build intensive distribution
    d. Advertising- Build awareness and interest among people through ads in media (i.e., mass market)
    e. Sales Promotion- Lower the expenditure to take advantage of customer demand
4. **Maturity:** The product is on-demand in the market with a trend set for its brand, and the strategies will be:
    a. Product- The manufacturer diversifies the brand and the models, among others.
    b. Price- Set the price to beat the market demand or match with the top competitors.
    c. Distribution- Build more intensive distribution.
    d. Advertising- Focus more on brand differences and benefits.
    e. Sales Promotion- Increases to encourage brand switching for adapting this product.
5. **Decline:** The product's demand is lost, and customers are switching to other brands, and the strategies will be:

Table 3. Criterion to be considered for decision making in financial decisions

S.No	Criterion	Subcriterion
1	Selection of product or service	customer buying patterns market trends competitors in the race • competitors approach customer marketing analytics • predict customer behaviour
2	Product price fixing	The market of the commodity price chart of similar product/ services commodity's status within the market
3	Product Placement	Sales method • direct sales • indirect sales Email marketing Lead management
4	Product Promotion	media advertisements Product incentives • Customer card • Discounts • Gifts • Lucky draw Trade Promotion Campaign • Inbound and out bound channels Self-service portal • Web-based marketing
5	Marketing strategies	Product Price Distribution Advertising and Sales Promotion

a. Product- Phase out the delicate items from the inventory.
b. Price- Cut price to attract customers based on price.
c. Distribution- Use selective distribution and phase out unprofitable outlets or distribution centre.
d. Advertising- Reduce to retain at least hard-core loyalists.
e. Sales Promotion- Promote to minimal level, spend less.

So while making decisions on marketing the criterion and sub-criteria specified in table 3 must be considered.

The Literature on MCDM Approaches in Finance and Marketing

A comprehensive decision model was developed to find the location for the construction of a shopping mall to attain maximum profit. The model was developed using two MCDM approaches, namely Step-wise Weight Assessment Ratio Analysis (SWARA) and Weighted Aggregated Sum-Product Assessment (WASPAS) (Zolfani, S. H et al., 2013). A Fuzzy, TOPSIS based hybrid model was developed for the selection of the location in group decision making (Chu, T. C., 2002, Deepa et al., 2019). An intelligent decision tool was developed for self-assessment in business innovation, and the tool can handle incomplete and uncertain data (Xu & Yang, 2006). An MCDM based model was proposed using three MCDM methods and six clustering algorithms for financial risk analysis (Kou et al., 2014). A hybrid approach was developed for the assessment of credit risk in Enterprise using Support Vector Machine (SVM) algorithm (Wang & Ma, 2012).

An approach was presented for the evaluation of classification algorithms for the prediction of Financial Risk, and a final ranking of the classification algorithms are provided using MCDM approaches such as Technique for Order of Preference by Similarity to Ideal Solution (TOPSIS), Preference Ranking Organization METHod for Enrichment of Evaluations PROMETHEE and VIKOR (Peng et al., 2011; Deepa and Ganesan, 2018). A prediction model was developed to select the best classification algorithm for analysis of credit risk using Analytical Hierarchy Process (AHP) method (Kou & Wu, 2014). An approach was proposed to rank financial sectors for stock selection using Grey Relational Analysis (GRA) method, and three weight calculation methods were used namely Heuristic, AHP, and Learning via a sample (Hamzaçebi & Pekkaya, 2011; Deepa and Ganesan, 2019). An enhanced decision model was proposed using Relevance vector machine and decision tree algorithm to forecast the credit risk (Wu & Hsu, 2012). A decision support system was presented to find credibility scoring for banks to calculate the credibility of manufacturing companies in Turkey using the TOPSIS method and Fuzzy approach (Ic & Yurdakul, 2010). PROMETHEE II, a Multi-criteria decision-making method, was applied for the selection of portfolio manager in which nine criteria were identified for the selection process (Hababou & Martel, 1998).

An integrated model was built using MCDM methods such as Dominance based rough set approach, Analytic Network Process and VIKOR to improve the operational and financial performance of Airlines by extracting the necessary critical factors (Pineda et al.,2018). An MCDM based approach was developed for the evaluation of imbalanced classifiers in the prediction of bankruptcy and credit which are characterized by multiple performance metrics using the TOPSIS method (Song & Peng, 2019). A group decision model was proposed for credit granting based on Strategic Choice Approach (SCA) in Financial marketing organization and the developed model showed many advantages in terms of transparency, goals of the organization, decision-makers' security and minimization of organization conflicts (Schotten, P. C., & Morais, 2019). An MCDM based hybrid Evaluation model was built for Corporate Governance to rank the financial companies by integrating Decision-making trial and evaluation laboratory (DEMATEL), VIKOR, ANP and Fuzzy evaluation technique (Huang et al., 2019). A multiple rule-based decision-making model was proposed using variable consistency dominance-based rough set approach with a multi-graded preferential degree of each Decision class and the model was validated by evaluating the performance of the group of financial holding companies in Taiwan (Shen et al., 2019).

An integrated fuzzy MCDM model was developed to rank the alternative distribution channels of the Turkish banking sector in corporate governance using Fuzzy DEMATEL and Fuzzy TOPSIS. The consumer needs and other internal, as well as external factors of the corporate government, were considered to build the model. Fuzzy DEMATEL was applied for the calculation of weights of the factors and Fuzzy TOPSIS was applied to rank the distribution channels (Dinçer et al., 2019). A forecasting model was developed using MCDM method namely Data Envelopment Analysis (DEA) to provide sophisticated corporate operating performance for managers in order to reach the objective of sustainable development. In order to present the overall characteristics of the data, a fuzzy visualization technique using Fuzzy robust principal component analysis was presented. The results were given to the restricted Boltzmann machine to develop a model for forecasting the operating performance of firms (Zhang & Lee, 2019). A hybrid decision model was developed to assess the performance of given public and private banks using Combinative Distance-based Assessment (CODAS) method. An Entropy method was deployed for the calculation of weights of the criteria and K-Means clustering algorithm was applied to check the consistency of ranking performance with the efficiency of asset management (Laha & Biswas, 2019). A framework was developed to identify and evaluate the barriers in the supply chain and also investigates the Sustainable Production and Consumption initiatives. Fuzzy Analytical Network Process was applied for evaluation purpose and the framework categorizes the key barriers into internal dimensions such as organization and supply chain and external dimensions such as regulation and customer (Torkabadi et al., 2018).

A methodology was developed for the assessment of the market value of companies based on their financial and social responsibility aspects using Analytical Hierarchy Process and Goal Programming. A set of variables from sustainability reports representing relative and absolute economics such as liquidity, leverage or solvency were considered for the assessment (Gómez et al., 2018). A model was developed to establish a performance evaluation model for corporate sustainability practices of Turkish banks. TOPSIS method was applied for the assessment and weights were calculated using Entropy method (Aras et al., 2018). A decision model was developed using MCDM approach namely Fuzzy Analytical Hierarchy Process in order to identify and rank the key factors which affect the financial position of the airline companies. The results of the decision model showed that the sustainability of the airlines plays major role in the annual inflation and GDP growth of the country (Mahtani & Garg, 2018). A study was proposed to calculate the relative importance of relevant factors that inspire the customer choice in Mobile Financial Services (MFS) namely mobile banking and mobile payments.

Fuzzy Analytical Process was applied for ranking the critical factors for the selection and evaluation of various MFSs (Gupta & Manrai, 2019). A model was developed using Fuzzy approach and MCDM methods to design and select products by integrating fuzzy Quality Function deployment(QFD) and the prototype product selection model. Various characteristics and factors required for the development of product were considered in prototype product development and the best prototype product was selected using Fuzzy Multi-criteria decision-making approach (Liu, 2011). An approach was developed using

Fuzzy Multi-criteria decision making for evaluating the performance of banks using three MCDM methods namely SAW, TOPSIS and VIKOR. The approach selected 23 parameters for evaluation purpose through literature and experts and ranked the performance of banks (Wu et al., 2019).

A decision model was built for online reputation management in Internet Marketing to evaluate and improve the performances of professional marketing services using hybrid MCDM models such as Decision-making Trial and Evaluation Laboratory and Analytical Network Process (Hung et al., 2012). A decision model was developed using a hybrid Multi-criteria decision-making method based on Fuzzy Multi-Objective Optimization approach to select the sustainable supplier and to allocate the order by considering various criteria such as social, economic and environment. The model was built using Fuzzy AHP and Fuzzy TOPSIS for ranking the suppliers based on three parameters such as social, green and conventional (Mohammad et al., 2019).

Hence it is evident from the literature that MCDM models provide better support in making Financial and marketing decisions. The MCDM approaches like TOPSIS, SAW, AHP, VIKOR, GRA, ELECTRE, PROMETHEE, ANP etc., are prominent approaches for various business decisions. From the literature, it is obvious that the MCDM approach TOPSIS provides better results in varied applications like crop disease prediction, crop classification, agriculture land suitability analysis (Vincent et al., 2019), crop yield prediction, ranking universities, predicting market trends, product distribution, resume scrutinization and more. So TOPSIS can be preferred over other MCDM approaches for making better financial decisions.

CONCLUSION

This chapter presents a brief discussion on various activities involved in Financial and Marketing decisions. Also, the decision models developed using MCDM approaches for Finance and Marketing in Business functional areas are discussed. The various conflicting factors required for taking decisions in Finance such as investments, capital budgets, accounting tool selection, treasury management, asset management, profit analysis, planning on excess earnings and Financial risk are identified. Some of the MCDM approaches can be applied to find the relative importance of these factors. Similarly the factors to be considered for making decisions in marketing activities like product selection, price fixation, product distribution or product placement are customer buying patterns, marketing trends, marketing analytics, commodities status in the market, trade promotion etc., In order to develop decision models, there is no specific method. Based on the problem, appropriate MCDM approaches can be applied or integrated for taking better decision in Finance and Marketing. MCDM methods are currently applied for prediction and ranking. In future, further research can be enhanced for classification problems in financial marketing by integrating with soft computing techniques such as rough set approach, soft set approach and evolutionary algorithms. MCDM approaches can be applied to financial marketing for group decision making. Based on the problem, it can be decided whether to include or exclude criteria for financial decision making. Thus the MCDM approaches are recommended to develop reliable decision models which helps to obtain better decisions in business. So the financial practitioners can predict and make better financial decisions by making use of various MCDM approaches in future.

REFERENCES

Aras, G., Tezcan, N., & Furtuna, O. K. (2018). Multidimensional comprehensive corporate sustainability performance evaluation model: Evidence from an emerging market banking sector. *Journal of Cleaner Production, 185*, 600–609. doi:10.1016/j.jclepro.2018.01.175

Chu, T. C. (2002). Facility location selection using fuzzy TOPSIS under group decisions. *International Journal of Uncertainty, Fuzziness and Knowledge-based Systems, 10*(06), 687–701. doi:10.1142/S0218488502001739

Deepa, N., & Ganesan, K. (2018). Multi-class classification using hybrid soft decision model for agriculture crop selection. *Neural Computing & Applications, 30*(4), 1025–1038. doi:10.100700521-016-2749-y

Deepa, N., & Ganesan, K. (2019). Hybrid Rough Fuzzy Soft classifier based Multi-Class classification model for Agriculture crop selection. *Soft Computing, 23*(21), 10793–10809. doi:10.100700500-018-3633-8

Deepa, N., Ganesan, K., & Sethuramasamyraja, B. (2019). Predictive mathematical model for solving multi-criteria decision-making problems. *Neural Computing & Applications, 31*(10), 6733–6746. doi:10.100700521-018-3505-2

Dinçer, H., Yüksel, S., Kartal, M. T., & Alpman, G. (2019). Corporate Governance-Based Evaluation of Alternative Distribution Channels in the Turkish Banking Sector Using Quality Function Deployment with an Integrated Fuzzy MCDM Method. In *Intergenerational Governance and Leadership in the Corporate World: Emerging Research and Opportunities* (pp. 39–77). IGI Global. doi:10.4018/978-1-5225-8003-4.ch003

Gómez-Navarro, T., García-Melón, M., Guijarro, F., & Preuss, M. (2018). Methodology to assess the market value of companies according to their financial and social responsibility aspects: An AHP approach. *The Journal of the Operational Research Society, 69*(10), 1599–1608. doi:10.105741274-017-0222-7

Gupta, K. P., & Manrai, R. (2019). Prioritizing Factors Affecting the Adoption of Mobile Financial Services in Emerging Markets—A Fuzzy AHP Approach. In *Performance Prediction and Analytics of Fuzzy, Reliability and Queuing Models* (pp. 55–81). Springer. doi:10.1007/978-981-13-0857-4_4

Hababou, M., & Martel, J. M. (1998). A multicriteria approach for selecting a portfolio manager. *INFOR, 36*(3), 161–176. doi:10.1080/03155986.1998.11732354

Hamzaçebi, C., & Pekkaya, M. (2011). Determining of stock investments with grey relational analysis. *Expert Systems with Applications, 38*(8), 9186–9195. doi:10.1016/j.eswa.2011.01.070

Huang, J. Y., Shen, K. Y., Shieh, J. C., & Tzeng, G. H. (2019). Strengthen Financial Holding Companies' Business Sustainability by Using a Hybrid Corporate Governance Evaluation Model. *Sustainability, 11*(3), 582. doi:10.3390u11030582

Hung, Y. H., Huang, T. L., Hsieh, J. C., Tsuei, H. J., Cheng, C. C., & Tzeng, G. H. (2012). Online reputation management for improving marketing by using a hybrid MCDM model. *Knowledge-Based Systems, 35*, 87–93. doi:10.1016/j.knosys.2012.03.004

Iç, Y. T., & Yurdakul, M. (2010). Development of a quick credibility scoring decision support system using fuzzy TOPSIS. *Expert Systems with Applications*, *37*(1), 567–574. doi:10.1016/j.eswa.2009.05.038

Kou, G., Peng, Y., & Wang, G. (2014). Evaluation of clustering algorithms for financial risk analysis using MCDM methods. *Information Sciences*, *275*, 1–12. doi:10.1016/j.ins.2014.02.137

Kou, G., & Wu, W. (2014). An analytic hierarchy model for classification algorithms selection in credit risk analysis. *Mathematical Problems in Engineering*, *2014*, 2014. doi:10.1155/2014/297563

Laha, S., & Biswas, S. (2019). A hybrid unsupervised learning and multi-criteria decision making approach for performance evaluation of Indian banks. *Accounting*, *5*(4), 169–184. doi:10.5267/j.ac.2018.11.001

Liu, H. T. (2011). Product design and selection using fuzzy QFD and fuzzy MCDM approaches. *Applied Mathematical Modelling*, *35*(1), 482–496. doi:10.1016/j.apm.2010.07.014

Mahtani, U. S., & Garg, C. P. (2018). An analysis of key factors of financial distress in airline companies in India using fuzzy AHP framework. *Transportation Research Part A, Policy and Practice*, *117*, 87–102. doi:10.1016/j.tra.2018.08.016

Mohammed, A., Harris, I., & Govindan, K. (2019). A hybrid MCDM-FMOO approach for sustainable supplier selection and order allocation. *International Journal of Production Economics*, *217*, 171–184. doi:10.1016/j.ijpe.2019.02.003

Peng, Y., Wang, G., Kou, G., & Shi, Y. (2011). An empirical study of classification algorithm evaluation for financial risk prediction. *Applied Soft Computing*, *11*(2), 2906–2915. doi:10.1016/j.asoc.2010.11.028

Pineda, P. J. G., Liou, J. J., Hsu, C. C., & Chuang, Y. C. (2018). An integrated MCDM model for improving airline operational and financial performance. *Journal of Air Transport Management*, *68*, 103–117. doi:10.1016/j.jairtraman.2017.06.003

Schotten, P. C., & Morais, D. C. (2019). A group decision model for credit granting in the financial market. *Financial Innovation*, *5*(1), 6. doi:10.118640854-019-0126-4

Shen, K. Y., Sakai, H., & Tzeng, G. H. (2019, June). Multi-graded Hybrid MRDM Model for Assisting Financial Performance Evaluation Decisions: A Preliminary Work. In *International Joint Conference on Rough Sets* (pp. 439-453). Springer. 10.1007/978-3-030-22815-6_34

Song, Y., & Peng, Y. (2019). A MCDM-Based Evaluation Approach for Imbalanced Classification Methods in Financial Risk Prediction. *IEEE Access: Practical Innovations, Open Solutions*, *7*, 84897–84906. doi:10.1109/ACCESS.2019.2924923

Torkabadi, A. M., Pourjavad, E., & Mayorga, R. V. (2018). An integrated fuzzy MCDM approach to improve sustainable consumption and production trends in supply chain. *Sustainable Production and Consumption*, *16*, 99–109. doi:10.1016/j.spc.2018.05.008

Vincent, D. R., Deepa, N., Elavarasan, D., Srinivasan, K., Chauhdary, S. H., & Iwendi, C. (2019). Sensors Driven AI-Based Agriculture Recommendation Model for Assessing Land Suitability. *Sensors (Basel)*, *19*(17), 3667. doi:10.339019173667 PMID:31450772

Wang, G., & Ma, J. (2012). A hybrid ensemble approach for enterprise credit risk assessment based on Support Vector Machine. *Expert Systems with Applications*, *39*(5), 5325–5331. doi:10.1016/j.eswa.2011.11.003

Wu, H. Y., Tzeng, G. H., & Chen, Y. H. (2009). A fuzzy MCDM approach for evaluating banking performance based on Balanced Scorecard. *Expert Systems with Applications*, *36*(6), 10135–10147. doi:10.1016/j.eswa.2009.01.005

Wu, T. C., & Hsu, M. F. (2012). Credit risk assessment and decision making by a fusion approach. *Knowledge-Based Systems*, *35*, 102–110. doi:10.1016/j.knosys.2012.04.025

Xu, D. L., & Yang, J. B. (2006). Intelligent decision system and its application in business innovation self-assessment. *Decision Support Systems*, *42*(2), 664–673. doi:10.1016/j.dss.2005.03.004

Zhang, Y., & Lee, M. (2019). A Hybrid Model for Addressing the Relationship between Financial Performance and Sustainable Development. *Sustainability*, *11*(10), 2899. doi:10.3390u11102899

Zolfani, S. H., Aghdaie, M. H., Derakhti, A., Zavadskas, E. K., & Varzandeh, M. H. M. (2013). Decision making on business issues with foresight perspective; an application of new hybrid MCDM model in shopping mall locating. *Expert Systems with Applications*, *40*(17), 7111–7121. doi:10.1016/j.eswa.2013.06.040

Chapter 8
Sustainability Reporting:
Short Implementation Guide and Its Benefits

Dana Maria (Oprea) Constantin
https://orcid.org/0000-0002-5517-8151
University of Bucharest, Romania

Sorinel Căpuşneanu
https://orcid.org/0000-0003-3799-3993
Titu Maiorescu University, Romania

Dan Ioan Topor
1 Decembrie 1918 University, Romania

Elena Grigore
University of Bucharest, Romania

Adrian Amadeus Tişcovschi
University of Bucharest, Romania

Elena Bogan
University of Bucharest, Romania

ABSTRACT

This chapter approaches some issues related to the implementation of sustainability reporting and its benefits within an economic entity. The main objectives of this chapter are to present a brief implementation guide of sustainability reporting, according to GRI requirements and the benefits of its use. Based on the specialized literature, the authors present various aspects encountered in implementing sustainability reporting, interpreting the information used for the internal management and the stakeholders through the sustainability indicators. All the aspects presented and analyzed are based on the existing specialized studies and on the higher education ones. The chapter ends with the authors' conclusions regarding the importance of implementing the guide of the sustainability reporting and its advantages

DOI: 10.4018/978-1-7998-4637-6.ch008

and disadvantages in the short and long term. Through this contribution of the authors, new opportunities are opened in order to exploit the informational content specific to the sustainability reporting that is particularly relevant to all stakeholders.

INTRODUCTION

In the last decades, the sustainability reporting has undergone a significant expansion both among the profitable entities and among the non-profit organizations. The companies have recognized the importance of information transparency about the sustainability profitability and their ability to run their business in a sustainable manner, as the expectations of the stakeholders increase from year to year.

In order to implement sustainability in companies, it is necessary to use an implementation guide that will provide users the information needed to complete this process step by step. This guide will be the starting point in the implementation of sustainability reporting, establishing, among other things, the resources involved, but also the tools and guidelines necessary to achieve the goal.

In order to achieve the goal of implementing sustainability reporting, there were mainly taken into consideration the GRI Sustainability Reporting (Guidelines on Economics, Environmental and Social Performance) and the Global Reporting Initiative: G4 Sustainability Reporting Guidelines - principles, standard disclosures and implementation handbooks.

BACKGROUND

Implementation Guide: Considerations, Aim and Phases

What is an implementation guide? This is the first question that each individual asks to start in adopting a method or methodologies, models etc. The implementation guide is an introduction to the implementation process that contains certain phases or steps that are taken in order to achieve it, offering the necessary help that will guarantee its success. Starting from the general purpose of the chapter, namely sustainability reporting, there have been tried to achieve two objectives: (1) *presenting a short implementation guide of the sustainability reporting in accordance with the GRI requirements* and (2) the *benefits of using the implementation guide within entities.*

The proposed guide will describe the general modalities necessary for the adoption of sustainability within an economic entity, offering also the necessary guidance for its achievement by: (1) facilitating, supporting and promoting corporate and social value; (2) improving awareness of certain risks and opportunities; (3) identifying, evaluating and managing material risks for the economic entity and stakeholders in order to create long-term value; (4) improving the quality and depth of the information disclosed according to the expectations of the sustainability information users.

This guide is addressed to all categories of entities or specialists interested in implementing sustainability practices and sustainability reporting in accordance with the GRI requirements, offering assistance and encouragement in achieving this endeavor. Worldwide, many organizations have gone beyond the CSR borders, adapting to the knowledge about sustainability and developing management models that integrate sustainability. The interested parts want to understand the approaches of the organizations in managing their risks and their economic, social and environmental opportunities. This is due to the climate change, resource scarcity, changing of the social expectations and environmental legislative requirements which mean increasing the impact of sustainability risks that determine the organizations to incorporate all of its considerations and long-term challenges.

GRI Reporting Principles

The sustainability reporting principles are the fundamental principles needed to report the activities of an organization and their impact, as well as their expectations by providing reliable information to all the stakeholders. According to GRI (2016), the reporting principles comprise two categories of principles:

- *Reporting principles needed to define the content of the sustainability report* (include: the principle of stakeholders' inclusion, the principle of the sustainability context, the principle of materiality, the principle of completeness), and
- *Reporting principles necessary to define the quality of the sustainability report* (include: the principle of accuracy, the principle of balance, the principle of clarity, the principle of comparability, the principle of reliability, the principle of punctuality).

(1) The *principle of stakeholders' inclusion*. According to this principle, the body which sets sustainability report must identify the interested stakeholders and to offer explanations to the expectations of the stakeholders. According to GRI (2016), the stakeholders are defined as '*entities or natural persons that can reasonably be expected to be significantly affected by the activities, products or services of the reporting organization or whose actions can reasonably be expected to affect the organization's ability to implements its strategies or the achievement of its objectives*'. The stakeholders include: shareholders, customers, suppliers, vulnerable groups, local communities, NGOs, employees or other workers, civil societies etc., whose rights are in accordance with the international law or conventions and which provide legitimate claims towards the organization.
The sustainability report must specify (in its content) information about: (a) the stakeholders considered responsible; (b) the results of the stakeholders' involvement processes in the activities of the organization in accordance with the legal and institutional framework.

(2) The *principle of sustainability context*. According to this principle, the entity that prepares the sustainability report must present the broadened framework of sustainability, which includes information on the entity's performance and its future contributions to the economic, social and environmental improvement or deterioration at local or global level. Also, the relationship between sustainability and the expected organizational strategy can be included in the context of the disclosures.
The sustainability report will specify (in its content) information related to: (a) its performance with a focus on the sustainable development in accordance with the objectives set at district, local, regional or global level; (b) their impacts and contributions in appropriate geographical contexts reflected in the entity's performance; (c) description of the economic, social and environmental elements of the entity's long-term strategies, including the risks, opportunities and objectives of the entity.

(3) The *principle of materiality*. According to this principle, the entity that prepares the sustainability report must include its most significant economic, social and environmental impacts or that which substantially influence the evaluations and decisions of investors or other stakeholders. The prin-

ciple of materiality is the one that determines the degree of relevance of the material subjects that deserve to be part of the sustainability reporting.

When assessing the sustainable material subjects, there can be taken into consideration the competitive mission and strategy of the organization, the expectations of the suppliers and customers, the compliance with the expectations expressed in laws, regulations, standards and international or the voluntary agreements of strategic importance, the main topics and future challenges for a certain sector, the basic competences of the organization and the way to contribute to sustainable development etc. For the assessment of the significant economic, social and environmental impacts, specific tools such as the Life Cycle Assessment can be used.

(4) The *principle of completeness.* According to this principle, the entity that prepares the sustainability report should include the coverage of the material topics and their limitations in order to allow the interested parts to evaluate the performance of the reporting organization during the reporting period, regarding the most significant economic, social and environmental impacts.

By covering the sustainable material subjects, the information provided is expected to reflect, in a sufficient and correct manner, the most significant economic, social and environmental impacts of the entity that will allow the interested parts a better evaluation based on the commitment process and in accordance with their expectations. The limits of the sustainable topics refer to the description of those material topics that have a direct impact on the entity and how it resolves it, as a result of the business relationships. In other words, the entity must present the significant impact, the causes that contributed to the impact and how they are resolved. The information in the report includes all those significant impacts from the reporting period and the reasonable appraisals of the predictable, inevitable or irreversible impacts.

(5) The *principle of accuracy.* In accordance with this principle, the information provided to the stakeholders should be sufficiently accurate and detailed to enable them to better evaluate the performance of the entity that has prepared the sustainability report. The characteristics of the provided information can vary, and they can be expressed quantitatively or qualitatively so that they might give their accuracy in the sustainability report.

The database, as well as the method of measuring them (quantitative or qualitative) should be adequately described, explaining the results obtained. The basic assumptions and techniques used to estimate the data, as well as the sources of provenance should be indicated. For quantitative data, the margin of error should be sufficient not to lead to wrong conclusions from the stakeholders. The qualitative statements in the report are in accordance with other reported information and other available evidence.

(6) The *principle of balance.* In accordance with this principle, the information in the sustainability report prepared by the reporting entity must contain both its negative and positive aspects in order to allow the interested parts to carry out a balanced assessment of the entity's performance. Emphasis should be placed on priority issues.

(7) The *principle of clarity.* In accordance with this principle, the information in the sustainability report prepared by the reporting entity must be accessible and easily understood by the stakeholders. In other words, the information should be presented in a readable format (in the form of tables of contents, maps, links etc.), avoiding the technical terms (acronyms, jargons or other terms unknown to the general public), offering explanations in a relevant section (glossary), being available to the interested parts (written, online etc.).

(8) The *principle of comparability*. According to this principle, the information presented in the sustainability report of the reporting entity must have been selected and reported in such a way as to enable the stakeholders to perform comparisons of the performance over time or with other organizations. In other words, the information collected, selected and reported can be analyzed and compared annually by the stakeholders, thus, being able to detect any significant changes during the reporting period of the addressed topics or of the obtained performances.

(9) *The Principle of reliability*. According to this principle, the information in the sustainability report of the reporting entity can be certified by examining the quality and materiality of the information presented as a result of the collection, registration, preparation, analysis and reporting processes. In other words, the external insurance is insured, the entity can identify the original source of the information, can provide reliable evidence, can support the assumptions or calculations. Also, the internal insurance is given by the owners of the information provided, which guarantees their accuracy.

(10) The *principle of punctuality or periodicity*. According to this principle, the entity that draws up the sustainability report must regularly present the information of the interested parts so that they can make informed decisions. In other words, the information disclosed in the sustainability report should refer to the reporting period, to the most recent updates, indicating possible retractions of the previous presentations and their motivation.

General Disclosures of the Sustainability Reporting

According to GRI (2019), the sustainability reporting must disclose the following information regarding the reporting entity in the GRI 102 Standard '*General Disclosures*': (1) organizational profile, (2) strategy, (3) ethics and integrity, (4) governance, (5) stakeholders engagement, (6) practical reporting.

(1) *The organizational profile* will provide information on: the name of the entity, the activities, brands, products or services of the entity, the location of the entity's headquarters, the location of the operations, the right of ownership and the legal form, the markets, the scale of the organization/entity, the employee information and other workers, the supply chain, the significant changes in the organization and its supply chain, the preventive principles or approaches, the external initiatives, the membership of associations.

(2) The *strategy* will provide information on: the statement of the senior decision-maker and the key impacts, risks and opportunities of the entity.

(3) *Ethics and integrity* will provide information on: the values, principles, standards and norms of behavior, including mechanisms for advice and concerns regarding the application of ethics within the entity.

(4) *The Governance* will provide information on: the governance structure, delegating authority, accountability level for economy, environment and social issues, the stakeholder consultation on economic, social and environmental, President and the composition of the highest governing body including its committees, the way of designating and selecting the highest governing body, including its role in establishing the purpose, values and strategy, conflicts of interest. GRI (2016) also refers to the evaluation of the performances of the highest governing body, but also its role in reporting the sustainability, the economic and environmental identification and management, the social impact, the efficiency of risk management processes, the review of economic, the social

topics and environment, the communication of critical concerns, the nature and total number of critical concerns, the remuneration policies, the involvement of stakeholders in the remuneration process, the annual compensation report, the percentage increase of the total compensation year report.

(5) *The stakeholders' engagement* will provide information on: the list of stakeholder groups, the collective bargaining agreements, the identification and selection of stakeholders, the stakeholder engagement approach, the key issues and critical concerns.

(6) *The practice report* will provide information on: the entities included in the consolidated financial statements, defining the content and limit of the topics report, the list of material topics, the information statements, the change in reporting, the reporting period, the latest data of the report, the reporting cycle, dates of contact for questions regarding the report, reporting claims in accordance with the GRI standards, the GRI content index, the external insurance.

The Importance of Integrating Sustainability and Sustainability Reporting

The stakeholders (investors, customers, employees, suppliers, NGOs, local communities etc.) have become more aware of the positive or negative impact that the entities have on the economy, the environment and society. The problems on sustainability can significantly affect the risk profile of the organization, the potential liabilities and its value. Therefore, it is necessary for the business community to respond appropriately and recognize the key benefits obtained from the integration of sustainability in business, such as: (1) improving the risk management; (2) promoting innovation and attracting new customers; (3) maintaining an operating license; (4) answering to the responsible investments and ensuring the capital; (4) improving productivity and optimizing costs; (5) improving the value and reputation of the brand (UNEP, 2012).

(1) *Improving risk management.* The entities need to consider integrating the economic, social and environmental risks because by sustainability reporting, the entities must present, evaluate significant risks with impact on their business. In other words, the management of the social and environmental economic risks is important for three major aspects, concerning the entity: (a) reducing exposure to the sustainability risks; (b) avoiding emerging risks and disclosures due to the legislative regulations; (c) reducing the capital costs.

  (a) *Reducing the exposure to the sustainability risks.* Given the increased exposure to the social conditions (population growth) and the environmental conditions (climate change, floods, high rainfall etc.), the entities must be able to proactively manage their sustainability risks. The lack of proper management of these sustainability risks can lead to negative effects for the entity, such as: increased costs, interruptions of the production cycle, financial losses, strikes etc. Also, the financial and non-financial risks can have a direct impact (exposure to the credit risks due to the economic, social and environmental problems) or indirectly, on an entity (increasing the unpredictability of the customers related to the assessment of fossil fuels that can become blocked assets).

  (b) *Avoiding emerging risks and disclosures due to the legal regulations.* The entities must consider in advance all changes to be applied, in particular those related to the environment, such as the greenhouse gas (GHG) emissions. In this way, the entities are already keeping pace with all the changes that appear and are even one step ahead of those that are undecided.

(c) *Reduction of the capital costs*. The investors are attracted to investing in those entities that practice very good sustainability risk management. This aspect determines the increase of the corporate value and diminish the capital costs by adding the capital premiums to these entities.

(2) *Promoting innovation and attracting new customers*. The entities that have already been prepared for the sustainability and have introduced products and services based on sustainability have conquered new market segments, thus, contributing to the growth of their business, but also stimulating the circular economy.

(3) *Maintaining an operating license*. This consists in obtaining the organizational legitimacy in the vision of the company or more correctly said the implicit approval of the local community on the commercial operations of an entity. The operating license can help an entity in achieving the opportunities and the management of the business risks, but the local community as an interested party can support the entities that engage in effective communication with them, especially on the management of the economic, social and environmental problems.

(4) *Answering to the responsible investments and capital assurance*. The investment decisions are made based on the analysis of the financial performance of an entity, as a result of the assessment of the economic, social and governmental factors. In this respect, the approach of *a responsible social investment* or *sustainable investment* is used and it aims to incorporate the economic, social and governmental factors in the investment decisions. There are very important the TCFD (2017) and Accenture (2016) recommendations in terms of encouraging the sustainable investments. Thus, the entities will have to adapt their business strategies to the sustainability strategies, to manage the sustainable performances or the lack of transparency in the sustainability reports.

(5) *Improving the productivity and optimizing the costs*. Improving the productivity can be achieved by recruiting and retaining the model employees, very capable and determined in carrying out efficient activities. Through this aspect, an entity can improve its reputation, attract new customers and suppliers, optimize its capital costs, increase the operating profit etc. The negative effects of not applying the sustainability considerations within an entity can lead to production disruptions, investigations by government agencies, fines or a bad reputation.

(6) *Improving the value and reputation of the brand*. Identifying the factors with high impact on the value and the reputation of an entity's brand can be achieved by analyzing the aspects related to the energy and water consumption, the raw material supplies, the human rights etc. (KPMG & ACCA, 2011; Environmental Leader, 2008). Increasing the confidence of the stakeholders in the entities that comply with the presented ones can lead to an increase in the value and reputation of the brand, but also to a customer loyalty.

The Analysis of the Sustainability Implementation Aspects Within a Profitable Entity

Based on the importance of sustainability and of the sustainable reporting described in the first part, the aim is to detail the most important aspects for which an entity wishes to integrate sustainability into its business strategy and use it to reduce its risks and take advantage of business opportunities. These are: (1) *supporting the senior management*; (2) *identifying and prioritizing the sustainable material problems;* (3) *managing or solving the sustainable material problems;* (4) *ensuring the credibility of a sustainable performance, the disclosure of information by sustainability reporting.*

(1) *Supporting a senior management.* The effective integration of sustainability within an entity involves ensuring the responsibility of the senior management. The decisions taken by the Board of Directors establish the strategic direction of adoption and implementation of sustainability. This commitment also involves providing the adequate resources, systems and processes that support the incorporation of sustainability, the risk management of the entity. The sustainability governance must be aligned with the corporate strategy. The entities or organizations which master a corporate organizational culture and a strong leadership can better manage the sustainability risks and opportunities. According to UNEP FI (2014), the itinerary for integrating sustainability at the Board of Directors is the following:
   (a) *Sustainability is not one of the priority topics in the Board of Directors' agenda.* At this stage, the sustainability is treated by the Board of Directors only as a common problem and not as a priority. From this stage, the members of the Board of Directors consider the integration of sustainability in order to achieve the sustainability objectives by integrating it into the business strategy and its governance.
   (b) *Sustainability issues are included on the agenda of the Board of Directors.* At this stage, the entity must present a commitment to present to the stakeholders the sustainable material problems in a comprehensive and strategic manner. In other words, the entity must create a way of presenting this sustainable information in the form of an autonomous sustainability report that will accompany its annual financial report. The entities may also option for integrated reporting that provides sustainable information to stakeholders by explaining how to obtain the value over time. These reports contain information on: the financial capital, the manufactured capital, the human capital, the social and relational capital, the intellectual and natural capital.
   (c) *Monitoring the integration of sustainability in the strategy of the Board of Directors.*

(2) *Identifying and prioritizing the sustainable material problems.* The sustainable material problems refer to the risks and opportunities arising from the impact of the economic, social and environmental factors on the operations and activities of an entity (examples: pollution, diversity, energy, depletion of natural resources, human rights etc.). These sustainable material problems are important because, on the one hand, they reflect the significant impact of the economic, social and environmental factors on the entity, and on the other hand, they substantially influence the assessment and decisions of the stakeholders.

   By considering the sustainable material problems from the internal (entity) and external (stakeholders) point of view, an effective sustainable evaluation on the materiality can be carried out, providing information with positive or negative impact on the vision and strategy of the analyzed entity. An entity may consider the economic, social and environmental factors with significant impact on the entity or stakeholders when evaluating the sustainable material problems, such as: the business model or strategy, the availability of products and services, the types of stakeholders, the size of entity, the geographic location, the financial impact, the reputation etc.

   In assessing the sustainable material problems, the impact of the products and services on the parts of the value chain of the entity or organization must also be determined. The nature of the operations carried out by the entity and their location can create problems with impact on the economic, social and environmental factors of the entity, but also within the value chain, especially if some of these are related to the application of the environmental legislation. International bodies such as GRI, SASB and IIRC provide information on how to apply the sustainability materiality. Although these bodies have different interpretations on the sustainable materiality, they are addressed to different categories of users, as it follows: GRI is addressed to stakeholders, while SASB and IIRC are addressed to investors.

'*The report should cover aspects that reflect the organization's significant economic, environmental and social impacts or substantively influence the assessments and decisions of stakeholders*' (GRI, 2013). SASB has drawn a map of materiality, identifying 26 issues of sustainability that could affect the financial condition or operating performance of the companies within an industry and which comprise a series of disclosures and associated accounting methods (SASB, 2018). In the recent years, there has been a fierce fight for the transparency of sustainability between the three bodies: GRI, SASB and IIRC. There is no collaboration for adopting a common concept regarding the sustainable materiality or its integration, transparency or creation of a reporting framework.

The procedure for evaluating and applying the sustainability materiality can be simplified by going through the following steps: (1) setting the objectives; (2) understanding the context of the entity; (3) the stakeholder engagement; (4) prioritizing problems; (5) reviewing the problems.

Phase 1: *Setting the objectives.* There must be considered the target audience for the assessment of the material sustainability (the stakeholders) so that the entity may develop a more strategic evaluation process. Thus, among the objectives targeted may be included: reviews of the business strategies of the Board of Directors, the investment decisions of the shareholders, facilitating commitments with stakeholders etc.

Phase 2: *Understanding the context of the entity.* Knowing the problems the entity is facing is essential in the context of the material sustainability. Thus, the entity proceeds to collect internal and external information with an impact on the achievement of the material sustainability objectives such as: reports of the Committee or the Administrative Council, the risk management assessment, minutes of meetings, standards of international organizations qualified in the field of sustainability (GRI standards, sustainability indexes), NGO reports, internal reports of colleagues, internal or external complaints, the stakeholders' opinions etc. The scope to apply the material sustainability must take into account the membership of the sector and the limits of the geographical location, including the organizational membership (within or outside the organization).

Phase 3: *Stakeholders' engagement.* The stakeholders have an interesting and at the same time very important point of view for the assessment of the material sustainability, i.e.: local communities, NGOs, customers, suppliers, investors, employees, regulators, government etc. When identifying the stakeholders and those most relevant to the entity in question, you can take into account their location, the types of activities carried out, the complexity of the value chain etc. The interested parts can provide real insights into the material sustainability of an entity, thus helping the entity to identify its activities with impact on the economic, social and environmental factors and to properly assess the economic, financial and environmental performance. The way of collecting information from the stakeholders is different and needs to be adapted in order to facilitate communication as easy as possible and also an understanding of the issues that will be examined.

Phase 4: *Prioritizing problems.* After identifying the issues of the material sustainability with significant impact on the economic, social and environmental factors of the entity and which also reflect the point of view of the stakeholders, they are confirmed by the management of the entity. From this stage, these problems are prioritized and the focus is on solving them.

This is achieved by concentrating the efforts and resources needed to achieve this strategic objective. The degree of information disclosure that will be part of the final sustainability report must also be taken into account here.

Phase 5: *Reviewing the problems.* After the approval received from the management, it is passed to the approval from the Board of Directors, because it bears the responsibility for the degree of disclosure of the information specified in the sustainability report. On this occasion, there is also established the periodicity of updating and reporting the sustainability which should be at least annual. The updating of the data should be carried out periodically and must take into account all the aforementioned aspects in order to maintain the truthfulness and the degree of interest in the business environment, but also the alignment with the needs of the stakeholders.

(3) *Managing or solving the sustainable material problems.* With all the necessary approvals and available resources, the entity will continue to resolve the material sustainable problems by adopting the best practices: (a) adopting ISO 14001 or ISO 45001; (b) developing internal policies and procedures; (c) implementing the various initiatives, measures or action plans; (d) establishing a set of indicators and long-term objectives, in line with the strategic objectives of the entity; (d) changing the existing system, adapting or implementing the new system according to the requirements of sustainable reporting.

In developing the set of sustainability indicators must be taken into account some criteria: the degree of importance or relevance to the objective pursued the quality indicator in the sustainability report and the relevance and usefulness in providing the information related to the sustainable categories of the concerned users. The data collection, the processing and interpretation are essential in the process of identifying and analyzing the sustainable indicators.

The management of the sustainable material problems will be carried out in accordance with the entity's goals and in alignment with the existing management approaches and processes and with the international environmental reporting standards. Through the sustainability report, the entity will provide the users with the interested information, information needed in order to understand the investment risks or its future investment strategies.

(4) *Ensuring credibility of the sustainable performance, the disclosure of information through the sustainability reporting.* In order to ensure an efficient communication of information to the categories of the targeted users (especially investors and other stakeholders), it is advisable for the entity to use a content index to disclose the sustainability information. The content index is a summary of the sustainability report, which provides the main information (governance structure and pages found within the document) in order to facilitate the users' easier access to that information.

The degree of accuracy and reliability of the information related to sustainability affects the quality of the decision-making process in the business environment. The entities need to know very well the information requirements of the stakeholders for the types of insurance (internal or external) they need. The financial information related to sustainability influences the internal and external decision-making process in terms of performance reporting. The assurance of the credibility of this information is given by the Board of Directors and the superior management of the entity through a declaration of sustainability assurance regarding the soundness of its management system of sustainability problems. The entity has two types of insurance:

(a) Internal- based on the responsibility of the governing body of the entity;
(b) External- based on the independent opinions regarding the sustainability disclosures.

The Analysis of the Sustainability Implementation Aspects in the Non-Profit Organizations

By accepting the stakeholder theory, the organizations were forced to redefine their competitive strategies and the way they manage their social issues as the public evaluates them and determines how non-profit is legitimized for new subject groups (Freeman, 1984).

Through communication, an entity capitalizes on certain intelligible, objective and verifiable information regarding its point of view related to certain economic, social and environmental aspects. Due to this opportunity, the entity increases its social acceptance by the stakeholders. Being a '*central activity for strengthening relationships within organizations*' (Kim and Reber, 2008), the corporate social responsibility has contributed to increasing the benefits for the non-profit organizations by: (1) increasing the level of volunteering and positivism in the working environment; (2) reducing costs and (3) displaying a much better public image (Jo, 2011; Lim & Lee, 2011); (4) increasing the organizational value and the stakeholder loyalty (Bortree, 2009; Gomez & Chalmeta, 2011).

The non-profit organizations have an ethical obligation towards the stakeholders to carry out responsible and transparent activities (Gazzola & Ratti, 2014) and to regularly and openly transmit information to the stakeholders on: vision, objectives, activities, achievements, processes for taking action, decisions and the organizational structure (Freeman, 1984). In order to adopt sustainability in the non-profit entities, they must develop the following aspects: the persons within the entity, the stakeholders, the mission and values of the entity, transparency, the environmental management, communication and social involvement (Vidal et al., 2005). The non-profit organizations have the responsibility to respect the impact produced on stakeholders and to increase the trust, the relationships and involvement in improving the business processes with a global sustainable impact (Zbuchea, 2013). The transparency of this information can be ensured through the annual sustainability report (Meyer et al., 2012), which may contain the views of the financial achievements, services and records in various graphic forms which are available to the interested parts through media or by publishing online (Zainon et al., 2013).

Nowadays, it is no longer sufficient for a non-profit organization to declare itself as such, but it must incorporate its core values into the strategic plans, work plans, individual performance review processes and general evaluations of its activities. The success and long-term development of a non-profit organization are given by the communication with the stakeholders that contribute to increasing its value.

Advantages and Disadvantages of Implementing Sustainability Reporting

Among the internal benefits of reporting sustainability offered to the non-profit companies or organizations may include: (1) a more accurate and faster understanding of risks and opportunities; (2) streamlining business processes, reducing costs and improving efficiency; (3) attracting, motivating and retaining employees; (4) understanding the connections between the financial and non-financial performance; (5) the possibility of performing comparisons of the internal performances with those of other organizations or sectors of activities; (6) the possibility of performing comparative analysis (benchmarking) and the evaluation of the sustainability performances regarding the performance standards; (7) developing the vision and strategy on sustainability; (8) influence of the business strategies and long-term management policies; (9) avoiding involvement in various social and governance failures (GRI, 2014).

Among the external benefits of reporting sustainability offered to the companies or non-profit organizations may be mentioned: (1) the understanding by the stakeholders of the real value of the company or organization, but also of their fixed assets; (2) understanding how a company or organization influences and is influenced by the expectations of the sustainable development; (3) possibilities to mitigate or reverse the negative impact on sustainability; (4) improving the reputation of the company or organization and/or brand loyalty; (5) gaining the trust and respect of the stakeholders and business partners; (6) increasing transparency and dialogue with the stakeholders; (7) gaining competitive advantage and leadership (GRI, 2014).

According to experts, the companies and organizations have found the following disadvantages of reporting sustainability: (1) the absence of the set of common practices design component that give the regulatory power of a standard (Slager et al., 2012); (2) the difference in the application of sustainability reporting in terms of its optionality, including the veracity of informational disclosures (Coram et al., 2009); (3) limitations on the measurement of the sustainability responsibilities.

SOLUTIONS AND RECOMMENDATIONS

Given the issues addressed during this chapter, there are proposed to the specialists and to all those interested, the following solutions for improvement:

- analyzing the GRI guide and consulting the literature before continuing the steps for adopting and implementing sustainability reporting (Căpuşneanu et al., 2020; Constantin et al., 2019a);
- analyzing the impacts of adopting sustainability reporting on the stakeholders (Constantin et al., 2019b) and on the economic, social and environmental performance of the companies (Oncioiu et al., 2019; Căpuşneanu et al., 2015);
- adopting the GRI guide for formulating strategies and management policies of the companies (Constantin et al., 2020).

Based on the concepts discussed above, we recommend the specialists and all those interested in deepening the GRI standards and reporting the sustainability of the following aspects:

- research of the specialized literature regarding the adoption and implementation of sustainability reporting of the GRI guide;
- research at national and global level of the impact produced by the adoption of the implementation guide on the strategic managerial accounting at the level of the entities/organizations (including the non-profit ones) that have implemented them;
- adapting and extending the company's culture among the employees regarding the advantages offered by the sustainability reporting, internally but also externally.
- increasing the publicity of the process of adoption and implementation of sustainability reporting among the companies and non-profit organizations.

FUTURE RESEARCH DIRECTIONS

Through the objectives set out in this chapter, we consider that we have reached our target in the business or academic environment. The chosen topic is current and future interest for all categories of specialists or non-specialists interested. The amount of information presented covers a wide range of international literature dedicated to adopt sustainability reporting and the GRI guide. This amount of information was synthesized in an attempt to present significant benchmarks in adopting sustainability reporting with real future research directions. By this, we suggest to the specialists and to all those interested the following research directions:

- analyzing the possibilities of adapting and implementing the sustainability reporting and the GRI guide to the specifics of companies, entities, organizations (including non-profit ones);
- analyzing the position of the companies, entities, organizations (including non-profit ones) on the concepts, environmental legislation and stakeholders' views in reporting sustainability;
- analyzing the impact of the strategic managerial decisions resulted by implementing the sustainability reporting, the environmental performance, the audit of the sustainability reporting (Ivan et al., 2017).

CONCLUSION

By its structure, this chapter covers some segments dedicated to briefly describing the steps required for the sustainability reporting by presenting a short guide to implement sustainability reporting and the advantages and disadvantages offered by this process. As strengths of this chapter, the following can be mentioned:

- it brings some clarifications on the adoption and implementation of sustainability reporting through the steps in the guide;
- it analyzes aspects of implementing sustainability in profitable companies, including the non-profit organizations;
- it presents the advantages and disadvantages of implementing sustainability reporting.

Through the contribution made in writing this chapter and through the challenges launched along the lines of adopting and implementing the sustainability reporting, we are confident that new research directions have been launched. There must be intensified the involvement of the specialized organizations and specialists from the companies with extensive experience in the financial and non-financial reporting in order to extend the launched research framework. The efforts must be continued towards identifying new opportunities for designing, deepening and diversifying the modalities of non-financial reporting at the level of the companies and organizations, including the non-profit ones.

REFERENCES

Accenture. (2016). *The United Nations Global Compact. CEO Study on Sustainability. Transforming Partnerships for the SDGs*. Author.

Bortree, D. S. (2009). The impact of green initiatives on environmental legitimacy and admiration of the organization. *Public Relations Review*, *35*(2), 133–135. doi:10.1016/j.pubrev.2009.01.002

Coram, P. J., Monroe, G. S., & Woodliff, D. R. (2009). The Value of Assurance on Voluntary Nonfinancial Disclosure: An Experimental Evaluation. *Auditing, 28*(1), 137–151. doi:10.2308/aud.2009.28.1.137

Environmental Leader. (2008). Retrieved from http://www.environmentalleader.com/2008/09/28/sustainability-and-its-impact-on-brand-value/

Freeman, R. E. (1984). *Strategic management: a stakeholder approach*. Pitman Publishing Inc.

Gazzola, P., & Ratti, M. (2014). Transparency in Italian non profit organizations. *The Annals of the University of Oradea – Economic Sciences, 23*(1), 123-133.

Gomez, L. M., & Chalmeta, R. (2011). Corporate responsibility in US corporate websites: A pilot study. *Public Relations Review, 37*(1), 93–95. doi:10.1016/j.pubrev.2010.12.005

GRI. (2016). Retrieved from https://www.globalreporting.org/standards/media/1036/gri-101-foundation-2016.pdf

GRI. (2019). Retrieved from https://www.globalreporting.org/standards/gri-standards-download-center/

GRI G4. (2013). Sustainability Reporting Guidelines, Reporting principles and standard disclosures. Author.

Jo, S. (2011). Factors shaping activists' perceptions of corporate organizations: An empirical case from South Korea. *Public Relations Review, 37*(2), 178–180. doi:10.1016/j.pubrev.2011.01.002

Kim, S., & Lee, Y. J. (2011). The complex attribution process of corporate social responsibility motives. *Public Relations Review, 38*(1), 168–170. doi:10.1016/j.pubrev.2011.09.024

Kim, S., & Reber, B. H. (2008). Public relations' place in corporate social responsibility: Practitioners define their role. *Public Relations Review, 34*(4), 337–342. doi:10.1016/j.pubrev.2008.07.003

KPMG & ACCA. (2011). *Business briefing series – 20 issues on building a sustainable business*. Author.

Meyer, B., Ferrari, D., & Zoebeli, D. (2012). *Transparency of NPOs' financial reporting: A quantitative study of annual reports (Switzerland)*. Retrieved from https://www.ffhs.ch/?action=get_file&id=583&resource_link_id=7bc

SASB. (2018). Retrieved from https://materiality.sasb.org/

Slager, R., Gond, J.-P., & Moon, J. (2012). Standardization as Institutional Work: The Regulatory Power of a Responsible Investment Standard. *Organization Studies, 33*(5-6), 763–790. doi:10.1177/0170840612443628

TCFD. (2017). *Final Report: Recommendations of the Task Force on Climate-related Financial Disclosures*. Retrieved from https://www.fsb-tcfd.org/publications/final-recommendations-report/

UNEP. (2012). *The Business Case for the Green Economy*. Sustainable Return on Investment.

UNEP FI Asset Management Working Group Support. (2014). *Integrated Governance, A New Model of Governance for Sustainability*. Author.

Vidal, P., Torres, D., Guix, B., & Rodríguez, M. P. (2005). *The Social Responsibility of Non-Profit Organisations. A conceptual Approach and Development of SRO model*. Observatori del Tercer Sector.

Zainon, S., Hashim, M., Yahaya, N., & Atan, R. (2013). Annual Reports of Non-profit Organizations (NPOs): An Analysis. *Journal of Modern Accounting and Auditing*, *9*(2), 183–192.

Zbuchea, A. (2013). Are customers rewarding responsible businesses? An overview of the theory and research in the field of CSR. *Management Dynamics in the Knowledge Economy*, *1*(3), 367–385.

ADDITIONAL READING

Căpuşneanu, S., Ivan, R., Topor, D. I., Oprea, D.-M., & Muntean, A. (2015). Environmental Changes and their Influences on Performance of a Company by Using Eco-dashboard. *Journal of Environmental Protection and Ecology*, *16*(3), 1091–1100.

Căpuşneanu, S., Topor, D. I., Constantin, D.-M., Manole, A., & Ştefan Hint, M. (2020). Environmental Management Accounting: A Business Perspective on the Policies, Analyzes and Benefits of its Implementation. In I. Oncioiu, G. Cokins, S. Căpuşneanu, & D. I. Topor (Eds.), *Management Accounting Standards for Sustainable Business Practices* (pp. 27–51). IGI Global, USA. doi:10.4018/978-1-7998-0178-8.ch002

Constantin, D. M., Topor, D. I., Căpuşneanu, S., & Anica-Popa, A. (2019b). Throughput Accounting and Green Reporting: Decision Support for Enhancing Environmental Performance. In I. Oncioiu (Ed.), *Throughput Accounting in a Hyperconnected World* (pp. 94–119). IGI Global, USA. doi:10.4018/978-1-5225-7712-6.ch005

Constantin, D.-M., Topor, D. I., Căpuşneanu, S., & Manole, A. (2020). Sustainability Reporting: Stakeholders and Reporting of Sustainability Accounting Information. In I. Oncioiu, G. Cokins, S. Căpuşneanu, & D. I. Topor (Eds.), *Management Accounting Standards for Sustainable Business Practices* (pp. 92–117). IGI Global, USA. doi:10.4018/978-1-7998-0178-8.ch005

Constantin, D. M., Topor, D. I., Căpuşneanu, S., Türkeş, M. C., & Anghel, M.-G. (2019a). Green Reporting and Its Impact on Business Strategy: Computer Program for Evidence and Green Reporting. In I. Oncioiu (Ed.), *Network Security and Its Impact on Business Strategy* (pp. 91–109). IGI Global, USA. doi:10.4018/978-1-5225-8455-1.ch006

Ivan, O.R., Căpuşneanu, S., & Ioan Topor, D. I., & Oprea (Constantin), D.-M. (2017). The auditing of the eco-dashboard of a company in the aluminum industry and its impact on sustainability. *Journal of Environmental Protection and Ecology*, *18*(1), 399–409.

Oncioiu, I., Căpuşneanu, S., Oprea Constantin, D.-M., Türkeş, M. C., Topor, D. I., Bîlcan, F. R., & Petrescu, A. G. (2019). Improving the Performance of Entities in the Mining Industry by Optimizing Green Business Processes and Emission Inventories. *Processes (Basel, Switzerland)*, *7*(8), 543. doi:10.3390/pr7080543

KEY TERMS AND DEFINITIONS

Disclosure of Sustainability: The act or process by which some sustainability information is made known (discovered) to stakeholders.

Guidance on Sustainability Reporting: Part of the Sustainability Reporting Handbook, with the role of facilitating a unitary understanding of the process of implementing sustainability reporting based on GRI standards and familiarizing beneficiaries of sustainability reports with basic requirements, rules and recommendations for the implementation of sustainability.

Sustainability Report: A report prepared by an organization (including the non-profit ones) that provides information on the economic, social and environmental performance to stakeholders.

Chapter 9
Effect of Corporate Social Responsibility on Pricing of Small Business Loans:
Evidence From Finland

Markku Vieru
https://orcid.org/0000-0002-8833-5248
University of Lapland, Finland

Janne Peltoniemi
https://orcid.org/0000-0002-0943-0424
Centria University of Applied Sciences, Finland

ABSTRACT

This study analyzes corporate social responsibility (CSR) issues in small business finance in Finland, especially within relationship banking. The study combines credit-file data obtained from a large local Finnish bank with a CSR questionnaire conducted with the bank's business loan managers. The credit-file data contain specific details of CSR characteristics, as well as relationship-, collateral-, firm-, and loan-specific characteristics. CSR, typically considered as a non-financial item, contains value-relevant financial information which affects the loan pricing level. The results show that both overinvestment in CSR and the value created by CSR are valid but connected to different CSR characteristics. Overinvestment is associated with the environment and value creation with diversity and employees. The results contribute to the understanding of the characteristics of CSR in the context of small business bank lending, as well as more generally to important implications for small firms, banks, and management practices.

DOI: 10.4018/978-1-7998-4637-6.ch009

INTRODUCTION

Debt financing opportunities are crucial, especially for small companies. Large body of literature refers to the strong role of debt financing, even being more important to small businesses than equity financing (Berger & Udell, 1998; Frame, Srinivasan & Woosley, 2001; Hyytinen & Pajarinen, 2002; Wu & Chua, 2012). Because most of the debt in small firms is financed by banks, it is important to understand how banks take into account the variety of information available of the company when making loan decisions and its terms. Previous research has demonstrated that financial performance of the bank client and characteristics of the bank/firm relationship have important effects on loan decisions (see e.g. Elyasiani & Goldberg, 2004). However, the effects of non-financial information, especially firms' corporate social responsibility (CSR) on loan decisions, are unclear (Goss & Roberts, 2011; El Ghoul, Guedhami, Kwok & Mishra, 2011; Rosa, Libratore, Mazzi & Terzani 2018).

Previous research suggests that the relationship between CSR and financial performance is not straightforward. On the one hand, costly CSR initiatives of a firm can be understood as a deviation from the goal of shareholder wealth maximization (Barnea & Rubin 2010). On the other hand, CSR can have a risk mitigation role preventing externalities of irresponsible acts of a firm to the society not shift back to the explicit costs of the firm (Heal 2004; Goss & Robers 2011). Finally, CSR can signal firm operation to outsiders (Dhaliwal, Li, Tsang & Yang, 2014; Michelon, Pilonato & Ricceri, 2014). This suggests that the CSR initiatives can have either positively, neural or even negatively associated with financial performance. Goss and Roberts (2011) suggest loan securitisation signals whether lender posit CSR activities coming from high or low-quality borrowers. However, Hoepner, Oikonomou, Scholtens and Schröder (2016) did not find conclusive evidence CSR effect of the interest rates of bank loans.

This study enters the topic from unique perspective by collecting information of firms CSR performance by questionnaire conducted with the bank's business loan managers in small businesses. Since the banks often demand access to proprietary information about the firms that may not be available to other outsiders (Goss & Roberts, 2011) it is possible that bank can have information about, among other things, clients' environmental and social performance. Thus, banks can exploit their unique position to client's private information (Armstrong, Guay & Weber, 2010, p. 214) by pricing CSR in terms and conditions of loan agreement. Second, our study complements research by using non-US data with different institutional setting. Unique credit-file data from a large local Finnish bank are explored. The data contain specific details of corporate social responsibility characteristics, and relationship-, collateral-, firm-, and loan-specific characteristics between 1995 and 2001. Finally, our study complements Goss and Roberts's (2011) study, which focus on multiple banks and larger firms by examining loan pricing for smaller firms and single local bank. Local banks may have better access to customers' financial and non-financial information than distant lenders.

The rest of the paper is organized as follows. In the next section, overinvestment and value-creation contexts and hypothesis are discussed. Section 3 describes the methodology and data. Section 4 reports results and Section 5 concludes the paper.

BACKGROUND

Prior research suggests several theoretical underpinnings how the cost of debt is associated with CSR. They involve (i) the overinvestment view arguing that CSR investments represent increased costs, resulting in decreased earnings and higher default risk and (ii) the value-creation view regarding CSR efforts as a way to increase competitive advantage, resulting in increased earnings and less risky financial returns to the lender. It is assumed that the lenders having information about manager motivation for CSR initiatives can take into account both type of views.

Overinvestment View

Overinvestment can result from two different sources. First, CSR investments can stem from agency conflict from managers and stockholders. Consequently, insiders (managers, directors or even large blockholders) can enjoy private benefits from CSR paid by stockholders (Barnea & Rubin 2010; Goss & Roberts 2011). Private bank lender can discourage overinvestment especially if the firm has a cash shortage or having high financial leverage but the firm with lot of cash banks governance role is limited. However, as discussed by Barnea & Rubio (2010) it is extremely hard to quantify CSR expenditure level since they are not separately reported in financial accounts.

Second, borrower can have behavioural pitfalls. The benefit of CSR practices is not straightforward since it produces extra costs but their outcomes are highly uncertain. Under these circumstances borrower can prone to overinvestment assuming optimistic cash flows. This type of prediction bias was explored and explained by Kahneman & Tversky (1973). For example, Shefrin (2007, 44-47) has reasoned causes of widespread excessive optimism in investments decisions. In addition, Malmendier & Tate (2005) perform cross-sectional tests of the effects of optimism on investment. Also, bounded rationality (Simon, 1957) appears to be a plausible explanation for overinvestment in CRS. For example, while the net present value criterion is the normative rule (in efficient markets), real managers tend to employ simpler rules. One of the rules can be imitation which involves an attempt to copy or mimic the actions of another decision maker (Pingles & Day, 1996). Pingle (1995) summarizes that imitation as one form of non-rational decision making economizes on decision making-resources. He explains that the likelihood to imitation increases when a decision is being made for the first time, after a change in the decision making environment and when the decision making environment is particularly complex. Since CSR investments can be fashionable resulted from imitations of trend-setters (Abrahamson, 1991, 1996; Aerts, Cormier & Magnan, 2005) CSR overinvestment is possible.

Several studies have evidences that the relationship between the CSR performance and the market value of equity can be negative (Hassel, Nilsson & Nyquist, 2005; Preston & O'Bannon, 1997; Freedman & Jaggi, 1982; Aupperle et al., 1985; Horst, Zhang & Renneboog, 2007). Horst et al. (2007) find that if the firm participates in other social and ethical issues than ones related to corporate governance, environmental standards or management, the shareholder value seems to be decrease. Some investors may be willing to pay a premium on securities related to socially responsible firms (Anderson & Frankle, 1980; Richardson & Welker, 2001). Hong (2008) concludes that firms with lowering stock performance or increasing exit level of institutional investors seem to increase their CSR practices. More specifically within overinvestment domain, Barnea & Rubin (2010) present evidence suggesting that insiders induce firms to overinvest in CSR.

Value-Creation View

According to value-creation view CSR actions can decrease the variability of earnings (i.e. risk mitigation effect) and/or increase earnings (i.e. sustained competitive advantage effect). In the first case, CRS can be viewed as put option (Goss & Roberts 2011). Under uncertain future cash flows proactive CSR investments can decrease down-side risk. If CSR affects the perceived riskiness of a firm, then socially responsible firms should benefit from lower financing costs. E.g. Feldman, Soyka & Ameer (1997) and El Ghoul et al. (2011) find supportive evidence. In particular, Feldman et al. (1997) show that firms adopting more environmentally pro-active posture experience a significant reduction in perceived riskiness to investors. Also El Ghoul et al. (2011) use risk mitigating effect of CRS find that firms with better CSR scores exhibit lower cost of equity.

In the second case, CSR investments can be understood being among intangibles (e.g., R&D, franchise, brand development, human capital, etc.). Intangibles are vital for many firms (Zingales 2000; Andayani, Atmini, Sadewo & Mwangi, 2008) and their valuation impacts are widely recognized. For example, Amir & Lev's (1996) findings support the notion that financial information of fast-changing technology-based industries is of limited use to investors. Commitment to socially responsible activities can lead to sustained competitive advantage (Hart, 1995; Russo & Fouts, 1997) and better financial performance (Margolis & Walsh, 2001; Orlitzky, Schmidt & Rynes, 2003). In addition, Eccles et al. (2012) find out that high sustainability firms significantly outperform their counterparts over the long-term, both in terms of stock market and accounting performance.

The fundamental problem faced by management is that investments in intangibles tend to reduce earnings in the short run (Bushee 1998; Graham, Harvey & Rajgopal 2005). However, there is some evidence that intangibles provide benefits for long term investors. For example, Edmans (2008) finds that employee satisfaction improves corporate stock performance rather than represents inefficient excessive non-pecuniary compensation. Also, the costs of maintaining a high level of CSR seem to be lower than the benefits reaped by the morale and productivity of employees (Soloman & Hansen, 1985).

CSR can be understanding also one form of trust creation (Perrini & Castaldo, 2008), and generally, long-term relationships with a high level of mutual trust can easily turn into a business advantage. According to the mutual dialogue and engagement between firms and stakeholders, they are able to generate trust in a long-term perspective; but in a short-term relationship, the creation of trust may be difficult (Burchell & Cook, 2008; Pivato et al., 2008). Thus CSR commitment can signal forward-looking information for stakeholders.

Previous studies have supported positive effects on CSR on financial performance and cost of capital. According to Martin (2002) firms are inclined to commit in social responsibility because of their positive effect on shareholders' value and creative factor of goodwill among consumers. Margolis & Walsh (2001) review the results of 80 studies (over the past 30 years) to determine whether CSR has predictive power on financial performance of the firms. Out of 42 studies, there is a positive relationship between CSR and financial performance, 19 find no relationship, 15 studies report mixed results, and only 4 studies show a negative relationship. Orlitsky et al. (2003) concludes that the corporate social and environmental performance is slightly positively correlated with the corporate financial performance.

The relationship between CSR and financial performance is positive (Pava & Krausz, 1996; Preston & O'Bannon, 1997; Lougee & Wallace, 2008; Rodgers, Choy & Guiral-Contreras, 2008). Also, CSR is positively related with growth in sales and returns on sales (Ruf et al., 2001) and with absolute abnormal returns (Becchetti et al., 2007). However, no significant relation is found between CSR and financial performance (profitability, stock returns) according to Aupperle, Carroll & Hatfield (1985) and McGuire, Sundgren & Scheeweis (1988).

Hypotheses

It is not clear whether CSR has a positive or negative relationship on the level of the loan premium. However, overinvestment and value-creation views are reasonable prediction how CRS activities affect cost of credit. Whether bank considers borrower's CSR activities having positive, neutral or even negative effect on the likelihood to keep the promise to repay depends on the management motivation and skills. However, it is assumed that local bank can effectively screen the quality of their customers and weight the costs and benefits of borrowers engaging CRS activities.

Consequently, lender considers that CSR activities for the low-quality borrower are more prevalent to be too costly without offsetting payoffs (*overinvestment hypothesis*):

H1: There is positive association between CSR and loan premium.

Oppositely, CRS activities can create value including e.g. greater product differentiation, reputation or image enhancement, the use of CRS to recruit and retain high-quality employees, and maintaining good relations with key stakeholders (*value-creation hypothesis*):

H2: There is negative association between CSR and loan premium.

The CSR context, in general, is broad and research-specific. This paper applies the general framework in order to define hypotheses and estimated models suitable for the combination of CSR and a relationship banking theme.

METHODOLOGY AND SAMPLE

Corporate Social Responsibility Metric

To determine the association between a loan premium and CSR, we construct a CSR variable based on manually gathered questionnaires sent to business loan managers in the bank. The questionnaire includes 20 questions (*Q*) of corporate social responsibility in seven components, including social (*G1*), corporate governance *(G2)*, diversity (*G4*), employees (*G5*), environment (*G6*), individual rights and products (*G7*), which are applied from the Kinder, Lydeberg & Domini & Co. (KLD) rankings for U.S. firms (Sharfman, 1996; Goss & Roberts, 2006). Each CSR component includes two to three questions with five alternative answers per question. The answers are classified from "totally disagree" (=0) to "totally agree" (=4). Value which equals one refers to low CSR orientation and value which equals five refers to high CSR orientation.

First, the aggregate CSR variable *Q* (*Score*) for a firm is computed using the data from the questionnaire. A scoresheet was designed for scoring firms on the performance of CRS based on assessment of business loan managers. A translated copy of the questionnaire is reported in Table 5 of the Appendix. Companies can score a maximum of 100 (=20 × 5) and a minimum zero points based on the listed items in the scoresheet. For convenience the variable is scaled to vary between zero and one. Thus, score for firm *i* is

$$Score_i = \sum_{j=1}^{21} Q_{ji}\ [0,1]$$

Table 1. Definition of variables.

Variable	Definition
Explanatory variable	
Loan premium	Negotiated marginal effective interest rate which includes the total loan arrangement fees and provisions for the lender. See the effective loan premium in the Appendix for the equation used to calculate the effective interest rate.
CSR variables (Questionnaire)	
Q_n	Aggregate questionnaire variable which is constructed by calculating the mean of all of the answers on the 21 questions. After analysing the frequency of *Q*, the values are adjusted to the nearest integer. Subscript (n) refers to the CSR –orientation (answer value in the questionnaire). Integers (n) from one to four are observed and used in the estimated models.
G_n (Sub-group)	Sub-group questionnaire variable with the subscript (n) referring to the CSR –orientation (answer value in the questionnaire). The sub-groups are social, governance, management, employees, environment, individual rights and products. The variables are constructed consistently with the aggregate questionnaire variable Q, but within the sub-group.
Control variables	
Duration	Length of the relationship between bank and firm (measured in years).
Financial Services	Number of the subject bank's financial services used by the firm.
Loans	Number of currently active loans from the subject bank.
Multiple	Dummy variable indicating (=1) whether the firm owner has multiple client-bank relationships with the subject bank or not (=0). Client-bank relationships can include either firms or individuals.
Commitment	Ratio of firm's total liabilities to the subject bank per total assets of the firm (=total liabilities/total assets). The liabilities of the firm to the subject bank equal the sum of all performing loans and bank guarantees.
Collateralization	Coverage of pledged total collateral over the total liabilities of the firm to the subject bank after the current loan (measured in percentages). [=(total collateral/liabilities)*100].
Non-bank Guarantee	Dummy variable indicating (=1) whether the loan is guaranteed by a Finnish non-bank financial institution or not (=0).
Leverage	Debt per assets of the firm. (=debt/assets)
Firm Age	Age of the firm (measured in years).
Firm Size	Total assets of the firm.
Legal Form	A dummy variable indicating (=1) whether the legal form of the firm is partnership/proprietorship. Otherwise limited liability (=0).
R3_5	Bank's internal risk-rating classification. (lower risk=R1_2, higher risk= R3_5). Financial risk classes are internally rated by the subject lender. Two risk classes are formed of five risk rating levels.
Industry	Nine industry dummies.
Maturity	Maturity of the loan (measured in years).
Loan Size	Amount of the loan (in thousand FIM).
Year	A dummy variable for each year in the data.

Second, the aggregate variable is spitted to seven CSR components by computed similarly to the aggregate variable and scaled to vary between zero and one. The general symbol for the sub-group is noted as *G*. As indicated in the Table 1, the G_n can have integer values between one and five, depending on the range of adjusted sub-group specific means. In the models of the results section, the questionnaire variables (Q, G) are referred as the *CSR variables*.

Models

The overinvestment and value-creation hypotheses are tested with the following OLS model:

$$\text{EffectiveRate} = \alpha + \gamma_0\text{Score} + \gamma_1\text{Duration} + \gamma_2\text{FinancialServices} + \gamma_3\text{Loans} + \gamma_4\text{Multiple} + \gamma_5\text{Commitment} + \gamma_6\text{Non-BankGuarantee} + \gamma_7\text{Leverage} + \gamma_8\text{FirmAge} + \gamma_9\text{FirmAge} + \gamma_{10}\text{FirmSize} + \gamma_{11}\text{LegalForm} + \gamma_{12}\text{R3\_5} + \gamma_{13}\text{LoansSize} + \Sigma\text{Year} + \Sigma\text{Industry} + \varepsilon \quad (1)$$

where the *Score* represent a firm's corporate social responsibility score based on the questionnaire to the business loan managers where high values indicate the good CSR performance and low values poor CSR performance, correspondingly. Depending on hypothesis *Score* can have either positive or negative effect on loan spread. More specially, if parameter γ_1 is positive it indicates CSR-related overinvestment by business loan managers and if parameter γ_1 is negative, it indicates value-creation.

The rest of the variables are control variables and they are related to the bank-firm relationship, commitment, firm characteristics and loan characteristic. Debt yields are essentially determined by i) the probability that the firm will not be able to meet its debt obligations and ii) by the degree of protection afforded to the lenders in such an event (Bhojraj & Sengupta, 2003: 455). Existing research has documented several firm-related financial risk characteristics and debt-related characteristics (e.g., Fisher, 1959; Cohen, 1962; Horrigan, 1966; West, 1970; Kaplan & Urwitz, 1979; Weinstein, 1981) influencing debt yields. However, a firm's likelihood of default would also depend on the availability of useful non-financial information for accurately evaluating the default risk and agency costs (Diamond & Verrecchia, 1991). Firm social and environmental performance can influence the assessment of default likelihood and agency costs.

This study uses the length of the relationship in years to analyze relationship duration (*Duration*). The other relationship variables deal with relationship scope, such as the number of financial services used (*Financial Services*), the number of performing loans (*Loans*), group of firms under the same ownership (*Multiple*), and the level of commitment (*Commitment*). Collateral effects are proxied by the value of a firm's total collateral over total liabilities to the bank (*Collateralization*). It is also controlled whether the loan is guaranteed by the major non-bank financial institution, or not (*Non-BankGuarantee*). This non-bank often works closely with banks by giving external guarantees to loans. Typically, banks require this type of guarantee for loans which are requested by start-ups or high-risk firms. There are five firm-specific variables that are associated with the leverage of the firm (*Leverage*), the age of the firm (*FirmAge*), the size of the firm (*Firm Size*), the legal form of the firm (*Legal Form*) and the internal risk rating of the firm (*R3_5*). Maturity (*Maturity*), the size of the loan (*LoanSize*) and year dummies (*ΣYear)* are used as loan-specific control variables. For each year, there is a dummy variable indicating the year when the loan was granted. Ten industries (*ΣIndustry*) are also controlled.

Sample

In this study, data consist of manually gathered questionnaires and credit-file data from a Finnish bank. The questionnaires are addressed to the same business loan managers who have granted the loans in the data. A survey is conducted in order to measure the level of CSR among the firms in the data. An application of CSR definitions and framework is implemented and analysed with the questionnaire, which is a survey distributed to the banks' business loan managers concerning the firms which have received bank financing. The Questionnaire is reported in Table5 in the Appendix. Totally 134 completely filled evaluations were received. These where matched with credit-file data from 1995 to 2001.

The estimation models are OLS-regressions computed by the mixed-procedure applying the maximum likelihood (ML) method with the SAS (Statistic Analysis Software). Several question groups, as explanatory variables, are formed from the questionnaire; and in addition, relationship-, collateral-, firm-, and loan-characteristics are used as control variables. The dependent variable is the loan premium, i.e., the marginal effective interest premium of the loan. The questionnaire variables (CSR) and control variables are defined in Table 1.

Descriptive Statistics

The summary statistics are presented in Table 2. The variable Q_n *(Score)*, representing the aggregate CSR variable, has the mean of 0.464 with standard deviation of 0.334. The mean value, slightly below the middle answer option (scaled between 0 and 1), refers to the description of the overall modest orientation for the CSR in the aggregate level. When compared to the components of CSR, the mean variables of G_n are between 0.049 (*Social*) and 0.473 (*Individual rights*). The sub-groups of social and products are represented with the largest variation of CSR –orientation with the standard deviations of 0.336 and 0.311, respectively.

Table 2. Summary statistics, period 1995-2001.

Variables	Unit	Mean	Std
Explanatory variable			
Log (Loan premium)	Log Ratio	0.950	0.501
CSR variables			
Q_n (Score)	Class n=1-4	0.464	0.334
G_n (Social)	Class n=1-4	0.049	0.336
G_n (Governance)	Class n=2-5	0.425	0.309
G_n (Management)	Class n=2-5	0.376	0.261
G_n (Employees)	Class n=1-4	0.405	0.276
G_n (Environment)	Class n=2-5	0.420	0.276
G_n (Individual rights)	Class n=2-4	0.473	0.286
G_n (Products)	Class n=1-4	0.381	0.311
Control variables			
Log (Duration)	Log Ratio	2.069	0.832

continued on the following page

Table 2. Continued

Variables	Unit	Mean	Std
Log (Financial Services)	Log Ratio	2.350	0.693
Loans	Quantity	1.463	1.520
Multiple	0,1	0.754	0.432
Log (Commitment)	Log Ratio	-1.604	3.534
Collateralization	%	99.668	23.009
Pergua	0,1	0.284	0.452
Non-bank Guarantee	0,1	0.172	0.378
Log (Leverage)	Log Ratio	-0.406	0.815
Log (Firm Age)	Log Ratio	2.338	0.715
Log (Firm Size)	Log Ratio	7.475	1.355
Legal Form	0,1	0.194	0.397
R3-5	0,1	0.381	0.487
Maturity	Years	4.695	3.451
Log (Loan Size)	Log Ratio	5.685	1.140
Year:			
1995	Year	0.022	0.148
1996	Year	0.090	0.287
1997	Year	0.112	0.316
1998	Year	0.127	0.334
1999	Year	0.291	0.456
2000	Year	0.172	0.378
2001	Year	0.187	0.391
Industry:			
Agriculture	n/a		
Industrial	0,1	0.127	0.334
Electronics	0,1	0.007	0.086
Construction	0,1	0.261	0.441
Wholesale, retail	0,1	0.224	0.418
Hotel & restaurants	0,1	0.037	0.190
Transportation	0,1	0.060	0.238
Financing	n/a		
Real estate	0,1	0.209	0.408

For control variables, the mean of log (*Duration*) is 2.069 and log (*Financial services*) is 2.350. The firms have an average of 1.463 outstanding loans, and the average collateralization coverage is almost 100 percent (99.668). Loans are personally guaranteed in 28 percent of the total number of loans in the sample, and the mean duration of the loan is 4.69 years (*Maturity*). It is notable, that personally guaranteed loans are handled as a proxy for the risk factor Peltoniemi & Vieru (2013).

Table 6 in the Appendix reports the correlation matrix for the CSR –variables. It is notable that correlation probabilities are statistically significant, and varies between 0.146 and 0.681. Nine of the correlations are below the 0.50 value. The highest value of correlation between two CSR –variables is reported between Environment and Product –based variables. However, the Product variables shows no statistical significance in the CSR regressions (Table 3 and Table 4).

RESULTS

Results on the Association Between Loan Premium and Aggregated CSR

The main results are reported using aggregate questionnaire variable Q_n *(Score)* in Tables 3. As indicated, the estimated regression coefficient for categorical variables Q_n is positive, which indicates that the effect on the loan premium is slightly increasing with the increasing orientation of CSR practices of the firm. However, the coefficient of Q_n is statistically insignificant (0.870). This suggest that CSR on the aggregate level is not associated with loan premium.

When analysing the control variables, many effects on the loan premium are found. The duration of relationship, and the maturity and size of the loan seem to be negatively associated with the loan premium. Firms benefit by the lower cost of credit by maintaining long-term relationships and/or if they are able to negotiate longer maturities for loans and for larger loans. However, it seems that the loan premium increases with number of loans and loans which are personally guaranteed, which also indicate the riskiness of the firm (Peltoniemi & Vieru, 2013).

Results on the Association Between Loan Premium and CSR Components

In order to examine whether the aggregation itself diminishes significant association, the aggregated CSR is split into CSR components (social, governance, diversity, employees, environment, individuals, and products) and tested with the OLS regression model. Table 4 presents the results for aggregated questionnaire answers within the sub-groups. Control variables are also regressed and reported in the table.

The results show significantly negative effects on the loan premium for the sub-groups of diversity (p<0,10), employees (p<0,05) and positive effect on the environment (p<0,05). The sub-groups of social, governance, individual rights and products do not show any statistical significance in the parameter values.

Keeping in mind that negative association between CSR component and loan premium indicates a support for value creation hypothesis the results suggest that high firm performance in diversity and employees' components are acknowledged by bank managers with lower loan premium. According to this result, firms which emphasize CSR –orientation activities among these dimensions, seem to be compensated by lower loan premiums in their loan contracts. These outcomes support the hypotheses of value-creation in this study. Similar type of value-creation association in the CSR framework is reported in Feldman et al. (1997) and El Ghoul et al. (2011). Also, in the larger framework, the value-creation in CSR is supported by Amir & Lev (1996), Hart (1995), Russo & Fouts (1997), Margolis & Walsh (2001), Orlitzky et al. (2003) and Eccles et al. (2012).

The only sub-group with negative and significant parameter value, towards lower CSR–orientation is the environment with the magnitude of 0.524, and the effect is rather large at the level of statistical significance (*p-value* = 0.013). Firms which practice more beneficial actions towards the environment

Table 3. The effect of CSR on the cost of the credit. Aggregated questionnaire data.

Variables	Estimate	p-value
Intercept	**3.020**	**<0.001**
CSR variables		
Q_nScore	0.039	0.870
Control variables		
Log(Duration)	**-0.146**	**0.032**
Log(Financial Services)	0.064	0.376
Loans	0.040	0.141
Multiple	-0.065	0.494
Log(Commitment)	0.001	0.951
Collateralization	-0.003	0.163
Pergua	0.072	0.663
Non-bank Guarantee	-0.031	0.755
Log(Leverage)	-0.060	0.310
Log(Firm Age)	0.038	0.642
Log(Firm Size)	-0.020	0.668
Legal Form	-0.076	0.491
R3-5	0.060	0.484
Maturity	**-0.039**	**0.008**
Log(Loan Size)	**-0.191**	**<0.001**
Year 1995	Ref.	
Year 1996	-0.075	0.809
Year 1997	-0.117	0.705
Year 1998	-0.214	0.498
Year 1999	-0.325	0.289
Year 2000	-0.358	0.238
Year 2001	-0.356	0.237
Obs.	134	
Adj.R-Sq.	0.424	

Dependent variable: Effective loan premium. Q_nScore represents the aggregate CSR –variable as described and formed in section 3.2. Control variables are combined from relationship-, collateral-, firm- and loan-based characteristics, and also yearly based dummies and industries are controlled (not reported here)

seem to pay higher loan premiums than other firms in the data. This specific part of our research results support the overinvestment hypothesis. An analogically similar result is found in Hassel et al. (2005), where the market value of firms is negatively related with the value- creation (for stakeholders). Similar results representing the CSR with some negative effects can be found in Preston and O'Bannon (1997), Freedman & Jaggi (1982), Aupperle, Caroll & Hatfield (1985) and Horst, Zhang & Renneboog (2007).

These results indicate two main implications. Firstly, the CSR issue seems to be value-relevant to the bank even after financial factors of the loan decision are controlled. This indicates that CSR, as identified

Table 4. The effect of CSR on the cost of the credit. Sub-group questionnaire data.

Variables	Estimate	p-value
Intercept	**3.180**	**<0.0001**
CSR variables (G_n)		
Social Score	0.129	0.347
Governance Score	-0.057	0.709
Management Score	**-0.366**	**0.059**
Employees Score	**-0.394**	**0.040**
Environment Score	**0.524**	**0.013**
Individual Score	-0.144	0.423
Product Score	-0.030	0.886
Control variables		
Log(Duration)	-0.100	0.131
Log(Financial Services)	0.076	0.289
Loans	0.034	0.194
Multiple	-0.133	0.164
Log(Commitment)	0.003	0.194
Collateralization	**-0.003**	**0.081**
Pergua	0.135	0.174
Non-bank Guarantee	-0.091	0.348
Log(Leverage)	-0.072	0.206
Log(Firm Age)	-0.020	0.806
Log(Firm Size)	-0.021	0.654
Legal Form	-0.072	0.495
R3-5	0.064	0.441
Maturity	**-0.043**	**0.003**
Log(Loan Size)	**-0.188**	**<0.001**
Year 1995	Ref.	
Year 1996	-0.073	0.808
Year 1997	-0.037	0.900
Year 1998	-0.183	0.543
Year 1999	-0.317	0.286
Year 2000	-0.374	0.227
Year 2001	-0.344	0.257
Obs.	134	
Adj.R-Sq.	0.493	

Dependent variable: Effective loan premium. *CSR variables (G_n)* represents the seven CSR groups: social, government, management, employees, environment, individual and products. Control variables are combined from relationship-, collateral-, firm- and loan-based characteristics, and also yearly based dummies and industries are controlled (not reported here) as a non-financial factor in a bank lending contract, does have financial value similarly to other financial factors of the lending in affecting the loan premium. Secondly, the value of CSR in bank loans may not be consistent among different components. As previous studies has also shown, the CSR link to cost of capital can be either positive (costly) or negative (beneficiary). When the bank evaluates the CSR positively in some components (diversity, employees), the bank may evaluate other components of CSR (environment) negatively in the same loan contract of the firm. The explanation for this type of practice can be found in the bank's approach to the repayment potential of the firm. The bank has an incentive to value items which are positively linked to the repayment outcomes. According to the results in this paper, the significant components closely related to a firm's own operations are management and employees. The environment –component may not be seen as strictly increasing the possibilities of the repayment of the loan. It may well be that the bank evaluates the environment–component as an additional cost, which can even be an unwanted burden for the firm from the bank's point of view.

Robust Tests

In addition to the main estimation results, two robust test are reported. First, an interaction term *Highq,* represents high-quality borrower, was included into model in the spirit of Goss and Roberts (2006). Since it is possible that bank manager may judge the borrower's CSR orientation based on the its quality, the CSR can have either positive or negative effect on loan spread. When testing the hypothesis of overinvestment / value-creation, the aggregate result of Q_n *(Score) x highq* supports the value-creation hypothesis, with the negative parameter value of -0.164. The p-value is, however, 0.531, which indicates to the insignificant statistical value.

Second, the chi-squared test is conducted for the normality of variables. For the two main regressions, Table 3 and Table 4, chi-squared test value is 126.83 with the probability of 0.780 (Table 3) and 132.73 with the probability of 0.678 (Table 4). Thus, the null hypothesis for the normality of the variable distributions is valid (not rejected).

CONCLUSION

This study is one of the first studies in the field researching the link between CSR and bank loan pricing where the main factors of bank lending, e.g., relationship-, collateral-, firm-, and loan-characteristics, are controlled. In this paper, Finnish credit-file data are analysed in the corporate social responsibility context.

The results show that interestingly both hypotheses were supported and connected with different CSR factors. The overinvestment hypothesis is valid with the CSR factor of environment and the value-creation hypothesis is valid with the CSR factors of management diversity orientation and employees' relation. Environmental CSR efforts of companies seem to bring economic costs and CSR activity with management and employees implicate financial benefits in terms of the cost of loan.

The main results of this study have important implications for small firms, banks and management practices. As analysed, it is observed that the CSR–factor, considered as a non-financial item, contains both overinvestment and value-relevant financial information affecting the loan pricing level. This practical relevance is important especially noting that the CSR–factor is financially meaningful after other financial factors, such as risk and relationship-specifics, are controlled.

REFERENCES

Abrahamson, E. (1991). Managerial fads and fashions: The diffusion and rejection of innovations. *Academy of Management Review*, *16*(3), 586–612. doi:10.5465/amr.1991.4279484

Abrahamson, E. (1996). Management fashion, academic fashion, and enduring truths. *Academy of Management Review*, *21*(3), 616–618.

Aerts, W., Cormier, D., & Magnan, M. (2005). Intra-industry imitation in corporate environmental reporting: An international perspective. *Journal of Accounting and Policy*, *25*(3), 299–331. doi:10.1016/j.jaccpubpol.2006.03.004

Al-Tuwaijri, S. A., Christensen, T. E., & Hughes, K. E. II. (2004). The relations among environmental disclosure, environmental performance, and economic performance: A simultaneous equations approach. *Accounting, Organizations and Society*, *29*(5-6), 447–471. doi:10.1016/S0361-3682(03)00032-1

Amir, E., & Lev, B. (1996). Value-relevance of nonfinancial information: The wireless communication industry. *Journal of Accounting and Economics*, *2*(1-3), 3–30. doi:10.1016/S0165-4101(96)00430-2

Andayani, W., Atmini, S., Sadewo, D., & Mwangi, J. (2008). *Corporate social responsibility, good corporate governance and the intellectual property: An external strategy of the management to increase the company's value*. National Conference on Management Research, Makassar. Retrieved from https://ssrn.com/abstract=1327513

Anderson, J. C., & Frankle, A. W. (1980). Voluntary Social Reporting: An Iso-Beta Portfolio Analysis. *The Accounting Review*, *55*(3), 467–479.

Angelini, P., Di Salvo, R., & Ferri, G. (1998). Availability and cost of credit for small businesses: Customer relationships and credit cooperatives. *Journal of Banking & Finance*, *22*(6-8), 925–954. doi:10.1016/S0378-4266(98)00008-9

Armstrong, C. S., Guay, W. R., & Weber, J. P. (2010). The role of information and financial reporting in corporate governance and debt contracting. *Journal of Accounting and Economics*, *50*(2-3), 179–234. doi:10.1016/j.jacceco.2010.10.001

Aupperle, K. E., Carroll, A. B., & Hatfield, J. B. (1985). An Empirical Examination of the Relationship between Corporate Social Responsibility and Profitability. *Academy of Management Journal*, *28*, 446–463.

Barnea, A., & Rubin, A. (2010). Corporate Social Responsibility as a conflict between shareholders. *Journal of Business Ethics*, *97*(1), 71–86. doi:10.100710551-010-0496-z

Bassen, A., Meyer, K., & Schlange, J. (2006). The Influence of corporate social responsibility on the cost of capital. *SSRN Electronic Journal*. Retrieved from https://ssrn.com/abstract=984406

Becchetti, L., Rocco, C., & Hasan, I. (2007). *Corporate Social Responsibility and Shareholder's Value: An Event Study Analysis*. Working Paper. Federal Reserve Bank of Atlanta. Retrieved from https://www.frbatlanta.org/research/publications/wp/2007/06.aspx

Berger, A., & Udell, G. F. (1995). Relationship lending and lines of credit in small business finance. *The Journal of Business*, *68*(3), 351–381. doi:10.1086/296668

Berger, A., & Udell, G. F. (1998). The economics of small business finance: The roles of private equity and debt markets in the financial growth cycle. *Journal of Banking & Finance*, *22*, 613–673. doi:10.1016/S0378-4266(98)00038-7

Berger, A., & Udell, G. F. (2003). Small business and debt finance. In Z. Acs & D. Audretsch (Eds.), *Handbook of entrepreneurship*. Kluwer Academic Publishing.

Bhattacharya, S., & Thakor, A. V. (1993). Contemporary banking theory. *Journal of Financial Intermediation*, *3*(1), 2–50. doi:10.1006/jfin.1993.1001

Blackwell, D., & Winters, D. (1997). Banking relationships and the effect of monitoring on loan pricing. *Journal of Financial Research*, *20*(2), 275–289. doi:10.1111/j.1475-6803.1997.tb00249.x

Bodenhorn, H. (2003). Short-term loans and long-term relationships: Relationship lending in Early America. *Journal of Money, Credit and Banking*, *35*(4), 485–506. doi:10.1353/mcb.2003.0025

Boot, A. W. (2000). Relationship banking: What do we know? *Journal of Financial Intermediation*, *9*(1), 7–25. doi:10.1006/jfin.2000.0282

Boot, A. W., & Thakor, A. V. (1994). Moral hazard and secured lending in an infinitely repeated credit market game. *International Economic Review*, *35*(4), 899–920. doi:10.2307/2527003

Botosan, C. A. (1997). Disclosure level and the cost of equity capital. *The Accounting Review*, *72*, 323–349.

Brevoort, K. P., & Wolken, J. D. (2008). *Does Distance Matter in Banking? Finance and Economics Discussion Series, Division of Research & Statistics and Monetary Affairs*. Federal Reserve Board. Retrieved from https://www.federalreserve.gov/Pubs/FEDS/2008/200834/200834pap.pdf

Burchell, J., & Cook, J. (2008). Stakeholder dialogue and organisational learning: Changing relationships between companies and NGOs. *Business Ethics (Oxford, England)*, *17*(1), 35–46. doi:10.1111/j.1467-8608.2008.00518.x

Bushee, B. J. (1998). Do institutional investors prefer near-term earnings over long-run value? *Contemporary Accounting Research*, *18*(2), 207–246. doi:10.1506/J4GU-BHWH-8HME-LE0X

Carlson, J. R., Carlson, D. S., & Ferguson, M. (2010). Deceptive Impression Management: Does deception pay in established workplace relationships? *Journal of Business Ethics*, 497–514.

Caves, R., & Uekusa, M. (1976). *Industrial organization in Japan*. Brookings Institution.

Cho, C. H., Guidry, R. P., Hageman, A. M., & Patten, D. M. (2012). Do actions speak louder than words? An empirical investigation of corporate environmental reputation. *Accounting, Organizations and Society*, *37*(1), 14–25. doi:10.1016/j.aos.2011.12.001

Cho, C. H., Michelon, G., & Patten, D. M. (2012). Impression management in sustainability reports: An empirical investigation of the use of graphs. *Accounting and the Public Interest*, *12*(1), 16–37. doi:10.2308/apin-10249

Cho, C. H., & Patten, D. M. (2007). The role of environmental disclosures as tools of legitimacy: A research note. *Accounting, Organizations and Society*, *32*(7-8), 7–8, 639–647. doi:10.1016/j.aos.2006.09.009

Cho, C. H., Phillips, J., Hageman, A. M., & Patten, D. M. (2009). Media richness, user trust, and perceptions of corporate social responsibility. An experimental investigation of visual website disclosures. *Accounting, Auditing & Accountability Journal*, *22*(6), 933–952. doi:10.1108/09513570910980481

Cho, C. H., Roberts, R. W., & Patten, D. M. (2010). The language of US corporate environmental disclosure. *Accounting, Organizations and Society*, *35*(4), 431–443. doi:10.1016/j.aos.2009.10.002

Cohen, A. (1962). Yield on new underwritten corporate bonds. *The Journal of Finance*, *42*, 585–605.

Collins, D. W., & Kothari, S. P. (1998). An analysis of intertemporal and cross-sectional determinants of earnings responses coefficients. *Journal of Accounting and Economics*, *11*(2-3), 143–181. doi:10.1016/0165-4101(89)90004-9

D'Auria, C., Foglia, A., & Reedtz, P. M. (1999). Bank interest rates and credit relationships in Italy. *Journal of Banking & Finance*, *23*(7), 1067–1093. doi:10.1016/S0378-4266(98)00131-9

Deegan, C. (2002). The legitimizing effect of social and environmental disclosures: A theoretical foundation. *Accounting, Auditing & Accountability Journal*, *15*(3), 282–311. doi:10.1108/09513570210435852

Degryse, H., & van Cayseele, P. (2000). Relationship lending within a bank-based system: Evidence from European Small Business Data. *Journal of Financial Intermediation*, *9*(1), 90–109. doi:10.1006/jfin.1999.0278

Dell'ariccia, G., & Marquez, R. (2004). Information and bank credit allocation. *Journal of Financial Economics*, *72*(1), 185–214. doi:10.1016/S0304-405X(03)00210-1

Dhaliwal, D., Li, O. Z., Tsang, A., & Yang, Y. G. (2014). Corporate social responsibility disclosure and the cost of equity capital: The roles of stakeholder orientation and financial transparency. *Journal of Accounting and Public Policy*, *33*(4), 328–355. doi:10.1016/j.jaccpubpol.2014.04.006

Diamond, D. W. (1984). Financial intermediation and delegated monitoring. *The Review of Economic Studies*, *51*(3), 393–414. doi:10.2307/2297430

Diamond, D. W., & Verrecchia, R. E. (1991). Disclosure, liquidity, and the cost of capital. *The Journal of Finance*, *46*(4), 1325–1359. doi:10.1111/j.1540-6261.1991.tb04620.x

Dowling, J., & Pfeffer, J. (1975). Organizational legitimacy: Social values and organizational behavior. *Pacific Sociological Review*, *18*(1), 122–136. doi:10.2307/1388226

Eccles, R. G., Ioannou, I., & Serafeim, G. (2014). The Impact of a Corporate Culture of Sustainability on Corporate Behavior and Performance. *Management Science*, *60*(11), 2835–2857. doi:10.1287/mnsc.2014.1984

Edmans, A. (2008). Does the stock market fully value intangibles? Employee satisfaction and equity prices. *SSRN Electronic Journal*. Retrieved from http://ssrn.com/abstract=985735

Edwards, J., & Fischer, K. (1994). Banks, finance and investment in Germany. *Econpapers*. Retrieved from https://EconPapers.repec.org/RePEc:cup:cbooks:9780521566087

El Ghoul, S., Guedhami, O., Kwok, C. C. Y., & Mishra, D. V. (2011). Does corporate social responsibility affect the cost of capital? *Journal of Banking & Finance, 35*(9), 2388–2406. doi:10.1016/j.jbankfin.2011.02.007

Elsas, R., & Krahnen, J. P. (1998). Is relationship lending special? Evidence from creditfile data in Germany. *Journal of Banking & Finance, 22*(10-11), 1283–1316. doi:10.1016/S0378-4266(98)00063-6

Elyasini, E., & Goldberg, L. G. (2004). Relationship lending: A survey of the literature. *Journal of Economics and Business, 56*(4), 315–330. doi:10.1016/j.jeconbus.2004.03.003

Fama, E. G. (1985). What's different about banks. *Journal of Monetary Economics, 15*(1), 29–36. doi:10.1016/0304-3932(85)90051-0

Feldman, S. J., Soyka, P. A., & Ameer, P. G. (1997). Does improving a firm's environmental management system and environmental performance result in a higher stock price? *Journal of Investing, 6*(4), 87–97. doi:10.3905/joi.1997.87

Fisher, L. (1959). Determinants of risk premiums on corporate bonds. *Journal of Political Economy, 67*(3), 217–237. doi:10.1086/258172

Fombrun, C., & Shanley, M. (1990). What's in a name? Reputation building and corporate strategy. *Academy of Management Journal, 33*, 233–258.

Frame, W. S., Srinivasan, A., & Woosley, L. (2001). The Effect of credit scoring on small business lending. *Journal of Money, Credit and Banking, 33*(3), 813–825. doi:10.2307/2673896

Freedman, M., & Jaggi, B. (1986). An analysis of the impact of corporate pollution disclosures included in annual financials statements on investors' decisions. *Advances in Public Interest Accounting, 1*, 193–212.

Gertler, M., & Gilchrist, S. G. (1994). Monetary policy, business cycles and the behaviour of small manufacturing firms. *The Quarterly Journal of Economics, 109*(2), 309–340. doi:10.2307/2118465

Godfrey, P. C. (2005). The relationship between corporate philanthropy and shareholder wealth: A risk management perspective. *Academy of Management Review, 30*(4), 777–798. doi:10.5465/amr.2005.18378878

Gore, A. (1993). *Earth in the balance*. Houghton Mifflin Company.

Goss, A., & Roberts, G. S. (2006). The cost of virtue: corporate social responsibility and the cost of debt Financing. *SSRN Electronic Journal*. Retrieved from http://ssrn.com/abstract=955041

Goss, A., & Roberts, G. S. (2011). The impact of corporate social responsibility on the cost of bank loans. *Journal of Banking & Finance, 35*(7), 1794–1810. doi:10.1016/j.jbankfin.2010.12.002

Graham, J. R., Harvey, C. R., & Rajgopal, S. (2005). The economic implications of corporate financial reporting. *Journal of Accounting and Economics, 40*(1-3), 3–73. doi:10.1016/j.jacceco.2005.01.002

Greenbaum, S., Kanatas, G., & Venezia, I. (1989). Equilibrium loan pricing under the bank-client relationship. *Journal of Banking & Finance, 13*(2), 221–235. doi:10.1016/0378-4266(89)90061-7

Hart, S. (1995). A natural-resource-based view of the firm. *Academy of Management Review, 20*(4), 986–1014. doi:10.5465/amr.1995.9512280033

Hassel, L., Nilsson, H., & Nyquist, S. (2005). The value relevance of environmental performance. *European Accounting Review*, *14*(1), 41–61. doi:10.1080/0963818042000279722

Heal, G. M. (2004). *Corporate social responsibility – an economic and financial framework*. SSRN Electronic Journal. Retrieved from doi:10.2139srn.642762

Hong, H. G. (2008). What Drives Corporate Social Responsibility? *SSRN Electronic Journal*. Retrieved from http://ssrn.com/abstract=1212645

Horrigan, J. (1966). The determination of long-term credit standing with financial ratios. *Journal of Accounting Research*, *4*(Supplement), 44–62. doi:10.2307/2490168

Hoshi, T., Kashyap, A., & Scharfstein, D. (1990). The role of banks in reducing the costs of financial distress in Japan. *Journal of Financial Economics*, *27*(1), 67–88. doi:10.1016/0304-405X(90)90021-Q

Hughes, K. II. (2000). The value relevance of nonfinancial measures of air pollution in the electric utility industry. *The Accounting Review*, *75*(2), 209–228. doi:10.2308/accr.2000.75.2.209

Hyytinen, A., & Pajarinen, M. (2002). *Small business finance in Finland. A Descriptive study*. ETLA, The Research Institute of the Finnish Economy, Discussion papers 812: 1-59.

Ittner, C. D., & Larcker, D. F. (1998). Innovations in Performance Measurement: Trends and Research Implications. *Journal of Management Accounting Research*, *10*, 205–238.

Kahneman, D., & Tversky, A. (1973). On the psychology of prediction. *Psychological Review*, *80*(4), 237–251. doi:10.1037/h0034747

Kaplan, R., & Urwitz, G. (1979). Statistical models of bond ratings: A methodological inquiry. *The Journal of Business*, *52*(2), 231–261. doi:10.1086/296045

KPMG. (2013). *The KPMG survey of corporate social responsibility reporting 2013*. Retrieved from https://assets.kpmg.com/content/dam/kpmg/pdf/2015/08/kpmg-survey-of-corporate-responsibility-reporting-2013.pdf

Lindahl, F. W., & Schadewitz, H. (2008). Accounting quality and the law. *SSRN Electronic Journal*. Retrieved from https://ssrn.com/abstract=1275971

Longhofer, D., & Santos, J. (2000). The importance of bank seniority for relationship lending. *Journal of Financial Intermediation*, *9*(1), 57–89. doi:10.1006/jfin.1999.0272

Lougee, B., & Wallace, J. (2008). The Corporate Social Responsibility (CSR) Trend. *Journal of Applied Corporate Finance*, *20*(1), 96–108. doi:10.1111/j.1745-6622.2008.00172.x

Malmendier, U., & Tate, G. (2005). CEO overconfidence and corporate investment. *The Journal of Finance*, *60*(6), 2661–2700. doi:10.1111/j.1540-6261.2005.00813.x

Margolis, J. D., & Walsh, J. P. (2001). *People and Profits*. Lawrence Erlbaum Associates. doi:10.4324/9781410600622

Martin, R. L. (2002). The virtue matrix: Calculating the return on corporate responsibility. *Harvard Business Review*, *80*, 68–75. PMID:11894384

McAdam, P., & Rummel, O. (2004). Corruption: A non-parametric analysis. *Journal of Economic Studies (Glasgow, Scotland)*, *31*(6), 509–523. doi:10.1108/01443580410569253

McGuire, J. B., Sundgren, A., & Scheeweis, T. (1988). Corporate social responsibility and firm financial performance. *Academy of Management Journal*, *31*, 354–372.

McWillams, A., & Siegel, D. (2001). Corporate Social Responsibility: A theory of the firm perspective. *Academy of Management Review*, *26*(1), 117–127. doi:10.5465/amr.2001.4011987

McWilliams, A., & Siegel, D. (2001). Corporate social responsibility and financial performance: Correlation or misspecification? *Strategic Management Journal*, *21*(5), 603–609. doi:10.1002/(SICI)1097-0266(200005)21:5<603::AID-SMJ101>3.0.CO;2-3

Menz, K.-M. (2009). Corporate social responsibility: Is it rewarded by the corporate bond market? A critical note. *SSRN Electronic Journal*. Retrieved from http://ssrn.com/abstract=1332349

Michelon, G., Pilonato, S., & Ricceri, F. (2014). CSR reporting practices and the quality of disclosure: An empirical analysis. *Critical Perspectives on Accounting*, 33.

Mörttinen, L. (2000). *Essays on loan pricing and the credit channel of monetary policy. Research Reports. Kansantaloustieteen laitoksen tutkimuksia, 85.*

Nakatani, I. (1984). The role of financial corporate grouping. In M. Aoki (Ed.), *Economic analysis of the Japanese firm* (pp. xx–xx). North Holland.

Orlitzky, M., Schmidt, F. L., & Rynes, S. L. (2003). Corporate social and financial performance: A meta-analysis. *Organization Studies*, *24*(3), 403–441. doi:10.1177/0170840603024003910

Pava, L., & Krausz, J. (1996). The Association between Corporate Social Responsibility and Financial Performance. *Journal of Business Ethics*, *15*(3), 321–357. doi:10.1007/BF00382958

Peltoniemi, J., & Vieru, M. (2013). Personal Guarantees, Loan Pricing and Lending Structure in Finnish Small Business Loans. *Journal of Small Business Management*, *51*(2), 235–255. doi:10.1111/jsbm.12015

Perrini, F., & Castaldo, S. (2008). Editorial introduction: Corporate social responsibility and trust. *Business Ethics (Oxford, England)*, *17*(1), 1–2. doi:10.1111/j.1467-8608.2008.00514.x

Petersen, M., & Rajan, R. (1994). The benefits of lending relationships: Evidence from small business data. *The Journal of Finance*, *49*(1), 3–37. doi:10.1111/j.1540-6261.1994.tb04418.x

Petersen, M., & Rajan, R. (1995). The effect of credit market competition on lending relationships. *The Quarterly Journal of Economics*, *110*(2), 407–433. doi:10.2307/2118445

Pingle, M. (1995). Imitation Versus Rationality: An Experimental Perspective on Decision Making. *Journal of Socio-Economics*, *24*(2), 281–315. doi:10.1016/1053-5357(95)90023-3

Pingle, M., & Day, R. H. (1996). Modes of economizing behavior: Experimental evidence. *Journal of Economic Behavior & Organization*, *29*(2), 191–209. doi:10.1016/0167-2681(95)00059-3

Pivato, S., Misani, N., & Tencati, A. (2008). The impact of corporate social responsibility on consumer trust: The case of organic food. *Business Ethics (Oxford, England)*, *17*(1), 3–12. doi:10.1111/j.1467-8608.2008.00515.x

Porter, M. E. (1991). Essay: America's green strategy. *Scientific American*, *264*(4), 4. doi:10.1038cien tificamerican0491-168

Preston, L., & O'Bannon, D. (1997). The Corporate Social-Financial Performance Relationship. *Business & Society*, *36*(4), 5–31. doi:10.1177/000765039703600406

Renneboog, L., Horst, J., & Zhang, C. (2007). *Socially responsible investments: methodology, risk exposure and performance*. Finance Working Paper No. 175/2007. Retrieved from http://ssrn.com/abstract_id=985267

Richardson, A., & Welker, M. (2001). Social disclosure, financial disclosure and the cost of equity capital. *Accounting, Organizations and Society*, *26*(7-8), 597–616. doi:10.1016/S0361-3682(01)00025-3

Rodgers, W., Choy, H., & Guiral-Contreras, A. (2008). Do investors value a firm's commitment to social activities? The Moderating Role of Intangibles and the Impact of the Sarbanes-Oxley Act. *SSRN Electronic Journal*. Retrieved from http://ssrn.com/abstract=1311473

Rodriguez, P., Siegel, D. S., Hillman, A., & Eden, L. (2006). Three Lenses on the Multinational Enterprise: Politics, Corruption and Corporate Social Responsibility. *Journal of International Business Studies*, *37*(6), 733–746. doi:10.1057/palgrave.jibs.8400229

Ruf, B. M., Muralidhar, K., Brown, R. M., Janney, J. J., & Paul, K. (2001). An Empirical Investigation of the Relationship between Change in Corporate Social Performance and Financial Performance: A Stakeholder Theory Perspective. *Journal of Business Ethics*, *32*(2), 143–156. doi:10.1023/A:1010786912118

Russo, M. V., & Foults, P. A. (1997). A resource-based perspective on corporate environmental performance and profitability. *Academy of Management Journal*, *40*, 534–559.

Sengupta, P. (1998). Corporate disclosure quality and the cost of debt. *The Accounting Review*, *73*, 459–474.

Sharfman, M. P. (1996). The Construct Validity of the Kinder, Lydenberg & Domini Social Performance Ratings Data. *Journal of Business Ethics*, *15*(3), 287–296. doi:10.1007/BF00382954

Sharpe, S. (1990). Asymmetric information, bank lending, and implicit contracts: A stylized model of customer relationship. *The Journal of Finance*, *45*, 1069–1089.

Shefrin, H. (2007). *Behavioral corporate finance: Decisions that create value*. McGraw-Hill/Irwin.

Simnett, R., Vanstrealen, A., & Chua, W. F. (2009). Assurance on sustainability reports: An international comparison. *The Accounting Review*, *84*(3), 937–967. doi:10.2308/accr.2009.84.3.937

Simon, H. (1957). *Administrative Behavior: A Study of Decision-making Processes in Administrative Organization*. Macmillan.

Soloman, R., & Hansen, K. (1995). *It's Good Business*. Atheneum.

Spicer, B. H. (1978). Investors, Corporate Social Performance and Information Disclosure: An Empirical Study. *The Accounting Review*, *53*, 94–111.

Stanwick, P. A., & Stanwick, S. D. (1998). The Relationship Between Corporate Social Performance, and Organizational Size, Financial Performance, and Environmental Performance: An Empirical Examination. *Journal of Business Ethics*, *17*(2), 195–204. doi:10.1023/A:1005784421547

Thakor, A. V. (1995). Financial intermediation and the market for credit. *Handbooks in OR and MS, 9, 1073-1103.*

Thakor, A. V., & Callaway, R. (1983). Costly Information Production Equilibria in the Bank Credit Market with Applications to Credit Rationing. *Journal of Financial and Quantitative Analysis*, *18*(2), 229–256. doi:10.2307/2330921

Verschoor, C. C. (1998). A Study of The Link Between Corporation's Financial Performance and Its Commitment to Ethics. *Journal of Business Ethics*, *17*(13), 1509–1516. doi:10.1023/A:1006020402881

Weinstein, D., & Yafeh, Y. (1998). On the costs of a bank centered financial system: Evidence from the changing main bank relations in Japan. *The Journal of Finance*, *53*(2), 635–672. doi:10.1111/0022-1082.254893

Weinstein, M. (1981). The systematic risk of corporate bonds. *Journal of Financial and Quantitative Analysis*, *41*(3), 257–278. doi:10.2307/2330238

Welch, I. (1997). Why is bank debt senior? A theory of asymmetry and claim priority based on influence costs. *Review of Financial Studies*, *10*(4), 1203–1236. doi:10.1093/rfs/10.4.1203

West, R. (1970). An alternative approach to predicting corporate bond ratings. *Journal of Accounting Research*, *7*(1), 118–127. doi:10.2307/2674717

Wu, Z., & Chua, J. H. (2012). Second-order gender effects: The case of U.S. small business borrowing cost. *Entrepreneurship Theory and Practice*, *36*(3), 443–463. doi:10.1111/j.1540-6520.2012.00503.x

Zingales, L. (2000). In search of new foundations. *The Journal of Finance*, *55*(4), 1623–1653. doi:10.1111/0022-1082.00262

Zorn, T., & Collins, E. (2006). Green is the new black: are CSR and sustainable business just fads? *Proceedings of the 20th ANZAM (of Management) Conference on "Management: Pragmatism, Philosophy, Priorities*". Retrieved from http://library-resources.cqu.edu.au:8888/access/detail.php?pid=cqu:961

APPENDIX

Questionnaire

There are five alternative answer choices from "Totally disagree" to "Totally agree". The questions cover both firms' internal and external operations for the time period of 1995-2001.

Table 5.

Questions in seven sub-groups	Totally disagree Totally agree				
	n=1 .... n=5				
1. Social					
1a) The management of the firm actively participates the development of the its business environment and social networks.	O	O	O	O	O
1b) The firm is acknowledged from its social or environmental activities.	O	O	O	O	O
1c) The firm commits to charitable actions more than an industry average.	O	O	O	O	O
2. Corporate governance					
2a) The management of the firm operates fairly to its stakeholders and developes the stakeholder network.	O	O	O	O	O
2b) The responsibilities of the firm are clearly identifiable	O	O	O	O	O
2c) The organizational structure of the firm is light and transparent.	O	O	O	O	O
3. Management					
3a) The work practices of the firm are fair and do not discriminate the freedom of religion, gender, nationality, race, disability or age.	O	O	O	O	O
3b) The organization culture of the firm indicates transparency and clear practices in internal and external operations and management.	O	O	O	O	O
4. Responsibility of employees					
4a) The firm actively seeks to employ motivated employees and the firm is a respected employer.	O	O	O	O	O
4b) The firm applies and develops various kinds of incentive programs for employees, which enhance commitment and conduct practices.	O	O	O	O	O
4c) The firm provides excellent work terms and conditions to its employees.	O	O	O	O	O
5. Environment					
5a) The firm actively observes the condition of the environment and seeks to decrease the pollutive actions and is commitment to energy saving practices.	O	O	O	O	O
5b) The firm applies sustainability in order to maintain good life conditions for the current generation and generations to come.	O	O	O	O	O
5c) Ths firm responds to the needs of the stakeholders and environment, and innovates the business according to these needs.	O	O	O	O	O
6. Individual rights					
6a) The firm acknowledges the individual rights in the international business by avoiding injustice, illegality and corruption, regardless of the country where the business partner or firm customer is operating.	O	O	O	O	O
6b) The firm operates in countries with low social responsibility levels.	O	O	O	O	O
6c) The employees are aware of the ethical norms the firm expects their employees to follow.	O	O	O	O	O

continued on the following page

Table 5. Continued

Questions in seven sub-groups	Totally disagree Totally agree				
	n=1 .... n=5				
7. Products					
7a) The firm respects its customers' right to good quality and reaches for high customer satisfaction.	O	O	O	O	O
7b) The firm provides economically profitable products/services which benefit individuals in socially weak positions.	O	O	O	O	O
7c) The marketing and pricing practices of the firm are aggressive.	O	O	O	O	O

Note: The question 7c) is intentionally formed in contradictive positioning, where n=1 (n=5) indicates high (low) CSR orientation, for "consistent answers" check-up purposes.

Correlation

Table 6. Correlation matrix of CSR –variables used in empirical models.

	Soc	Gov	Mgt	Emp	Env	Inv	Pro
Soc	1.00	0.282 <0.001	0.142 0.022	0.442 <0.001	0.502 <0.001	0.314 <0.001	0.293 <0.001
Gov		1.00	0.532 <0.001	0.516 <0.001	0.507 <0.001	0.323 <0.001	0.609 <0.001
Mgt			1.00	0.550 <0.001	0.549 <0.001	0.146 0.041	0.555 <0.001
Emp				1.00	0.672 <0.001	0.309 <0.001	0.508 <0.001
Env					1.00	0.360 <0.001	0.681 <0.001
Inv						1.00	0.578 <0.001
Pro							1.00

CSR –variables represent the seven CSR groups: social, government, management, employees, environment, individual and products.

The Effective Loan Premium

Equation for the calculation of the effective interest premium

$$A_K = \sum_{K'=1}^{m} \frac{A'_{K'}}{(1+i)^{t_{K'}}}$$

A_K = amount of the loan K (after fees charged)
$A'_{K'}$ = amount of the payment K′

m = number of the last payment
$t_{K'}$ = time period between the payment n:o 1 and payments n:o 2 → m
i = effective interest premium

Chapter 10
Future Directions in Leadership Development:
Principles and Applications

Lavinia Essen Yildirim
Ankara University, Turkey

Mirela Anca Postole
Titu Maiorescu University, Romania

Marilena Ciobanasu
Titu Maiorescu University, Romania

ABSTRACT

The problem of leadership, leader, and leadership style has provoked a considerable number of theoretical and experimental research, being one of the central themes of the psycho sociology of social groups. Being in front of a considerable volume of experimental data, obtained under very different conceptual and methodological conditions, the problem of leadership has a fragmentary character, being necessary a careful selection of the results that have a sufficient practical relevance. The objective of this chapter is to demonstrate the role of leadership development in the digital economy.

INTRODUCTION

The leadership process is a fundamental component of group life, a necessary condition for coordinating group members in order to pursue common goals. Indeed, the notion of leadership seems to be one of the few universals of human behavior (Islam, A. (2015). There is also anthropological evidence that indicates that societies without leadership are not known in at least some aspects of social life. The manifestation of leadership depends both on the existence of a leadership role and on some qualities of the individuals suitable for this role (Lloret, 2015).

DOI: 10.4018/978-1-7998-4637-6.ch010

Furthermore, leadership is influenced and determined by organizational culture and life experience. He demands integrity and obedience, responsibility, stability and change, visions and results. Effective leadership can be measured and modeled in at least three ways: through business results, organizational structure and organizational culture (Bula, 2012).

Anyway, it is the leader who controls and influences the organization, establishing the cultural framework in which decisions are made, supporting and demonstrating values, establishing goals and responsibilities (Velilla, Molina & Ortega, 2018). A successful leader understands that the organization is supported by values, beliefs and norms of behavior. These will allow him to rise above the difficulties and give him the tone, character and ability to resist.

Even if the manager is willing to initiate change, he must take into account the diagnosis of the organizational culture and a number of elements that can influence the results of the improvement process. The secret is to create procedures of the organization by which a behavior is rewarded or sanctioned, such as: the benchmarks for promotion, bonuses and salary facilities, professional appreciation assessments, disciplinary procedures (Nair & Saiz-Alvarez, 2019).

During the implementation of change, in general, resistance to change appears both on the part of the employees, and sometimes on the part of the managers. Often the sources of resistance to change are of the company or individual. Of the individual sources of resistance to change the most commonly encountered are: the time available for change; selective perception; social and economic losses; dependence on group members; the uncertainty of the future.

Numerous people think that leadership and management have the same meaning, but in fact they are different (Lazear, Saiz-Alvarez, Coduras & Cuervo-Arango, 2013). Leadership is the key active force that motivates and coordinates an organization to accomplish its objectives (Sarasvathy, 2001). A leader creates a vision for the others and then directs them towards achieving that vision. To be a leader you must have followers who have confidence in you and who give you their support and commitment to a goal (Alvarez & Barney, 2005). On the other hand, management is the process of getting things done, effectively and efficiently, through and with other people (Douglas & Shepherd, 1997).

Managers deal with difficulty through planning and budgeting (Gaglio & Katz, 2001). They put goals, determine how to meet those goals and gather resources to meet those goals. Leaders start with the vision and put strategies to meet this vision (Saiz-Alvarez, 2015). Managers organize and staff their employees to meet their goals. They create jobs to achieve the requirement of plans. Leaders try to recruit and keep the employees who participate their vision. Finally, managers control the employees' behaviour to ensure that employees meet the goals (Baron, 2007).

Some contemporary motivation issues facing today's leaders include motivating a diversified workforce, pay for performance programs, motivating minimum wage employees, motivating professional and technical employees, and flexible work schedule options (Saiz-Alvarez, 2018).

Management needs to think in terms of flexibility to motivate a diversified workforce. For instance, studies tell us that men place considerably more importance on autonomy in their jobs than do women (Anna, Chandler, Jansen & Mero, 2000; Johnson, 1990). In contrast, the opportunity to learn, good interpersonal relations, and convenient work hours are more important to women than to men. Managers need to recognize that the motivation of a single mother with two dependent children, who are working full time to support her family, may be quite different from the needs of a young, single part time worker or the needs of the older employee who is working to supplement his or her pension income. Employees have different personal needs and goals that they're hoping to satisfy through their jobs (Audretsch, 2003).

However, it is also important to look at the fact that doing a job that is the same day in and day out can become quite boring (Silva, 2007). When employees are given a job with different tasks and ability to grow, they tend to stay more motivated. Unfortunately, many workers are unused and do not get challenged or the ability to show their creativity to its potential. Leaders can motivate their work force by improving design of jobs, empowerment, assess fairness through the implementation of the equity theory and finally by implementing a quality of work life by providing safe and healthy environment and fair treatment of their workforce and designing a psychological contract that is used in exchange for the employees' contributions (Wagner, 2003).

The economic environment of the Digital Age, characterized by the acceleration of technology innovation, fierce competition in gaining competitive advantage, increasing consumer expectations, emerging market pressure, leads leadership to adapt Vision and Entity Strategy to new performance standards. Thereby, Leadership is the key active force that motivates and coordinates an organization to accomplish its objectives. A leader creates a vision for the others and then directs them towards achieving that vision. To be a leader you must have followers who have confidence in you and who give you their support and commitment to a goal. The objective of this chapter is to demonstrate the role of contemporary leader in the digital economy.

BACKGROUND

A review of the leadership literature shows an evolving sequence of schools of thought from Great Man and Trait theories to "Transformational" leadership (Barnes, Dang, Leavitt, Guarana & Uhlmann, 2018). Although early theories focused on the characteristics and behaviors of successful leaders, later theories begin to consider the role of followers and the related nature of leadership (Drucker,1985; Gnyawali & Fogel, 1994).

One of the first studies of leadership behaviour explore three leadership styles: autocratic, democratic, and laissez-faire (Schumpeter, 1942; Schumpeter, 1934; Kirzner, 1979).

Autocratic style where a leader has centralized authority, state work methods, makes independent decisions, and puts limit on employee's participation.

Democratic style where the leader involves his employees in the decision making, share his authority with employees, and share the decision making with his subordinates. Democratic style is divided into two other styles, consultative and participative.

Laissez-faire style where the leader gives complete freedom to his employees to do their job and make decisions. Laissez-faire leader basically provide material to employees and answer questions only.

On the other hand, to promote empowerment, leaders must create an environment in which employees feel that they have influence over performance and effective in the areas of their responsibility (Thorton & Yang, 2012). By empowering employees, leaders should expect some problems, at least in the short term because of the change and change takes time for employees to adopt to the new roles (Shane & Venkataraman, 2000). People might make mistakes at first, because of lack of training and more training is needed, the cost are going to be higher because higher skills employees make great contribution to the organization and demand higher wages (Schultz, 1980). Table 1 will illustrate the leadership theories in order (Bula, 2012).

Table 1. Leadership theories and the main subject of each theory

Leadership Theory(ies)	Main Subject
Great man Theories	Based on the belief that leaders are extraordinary people, born with great qualities and destined to lead. The use of this term 'Man' was intentional since until the later part of the twentieth century leadership was thought of as a concept which is primarily male, military and western. This led to the next school of trait theory
Trait Theories	The list of traits qualities associated with leadership exists in abundance and continues to be produced. They draw on virtually all the adjectives in the dictionary which describes some positive or virtuous human attribute, from ambition to zest for life
Behaviourist Theories	These concentrate on what leaders actually do rather than on their qualities, different patterns of behaviour are observed and categorised as styles of leadership. This theory attracted most attention from practising managers
Situational Leadership	This approach sees leadership as specific to the situation in which it is being exercised. For example, whilst some situations may require an autocratic style, others may need a more participative approach. It also proposes that there may be differences in leadership styles at different levels in the same organisation
Contingency Theory	This is a refinement of the situational viewpoint and focuses on identifying the situational variables which best predict the most appropriate or effective leadership style to fit the circumstances
Transactional theory	This approach emphasises the importance of the relationship between leader and follower, focusing on the mutual benefits derived from a form of 'contract' through which the leader delivers such things as rewards or recognition in return for the commitment or loyalty of the followers
Transformational theory	The concept here is change and the role of leadership in envisioning and implementing the transformation of organisational performance

Three contemporary approaches have been emerged lately: charismatic leadership, visionary leadership, and entrepreneurial leadership (Saiz-Alvarez, Coduras & Cuervo-Arango, 2014; Velilla, Molina & Ortega, 2018).

A Charismatic leader is one who provides an environment full of energy and positive reinforcement. Charismatic leaders encourage others and inspire them to be their best. Group members and employees want to impress a charismatic leader, so they work hard and strive to succeed. Under charismatic leadership, group members may view success in relation to their leaders. A group success tends to center on the leader that is a major problem with charismatic leadership. The charismatic leader is the glue that holds a group together. So, what happens if the leader should have to step down or transfer? Normally, the group dynamic will fizzle and individual members will lose enthusiasm.

Visionary leadership is the ability to create and articulate a realistic, credible attractive vision of the future for an organization or organizational unit that grows out of an improves on the present. Visionary leaders characterized by his ability to clarify his vision in term of actions and goals verbally. Second is the ability to express his vision through his behavior. Finally, the ability to extend his vision to different leadership context.

Entrepreneurial leadership the entrepreneur has certain leadership responsibility in the organization (Stephan, Uhlaner & Stride, 2015). Today's successful entrepreneur must be like the leader of a jazz ensemble that excels in improvisation, innovation, and creativity. Drawing out the best of other individuals even given the unpredictability of the situation (Agboli & Ukaegbu, 2006).

Later studies of leadership styles showed mixed results (Saiz-Alvarez, 2018; Velilla, Molina & Ortega, 2018). For example, democratic style sometimes created higher performance level than autocratic style of leadership, but at other times they created group performance that was lower than or equal to that of autocratic style.

In general, groups need leaders when interpersonal processes need to be improved or when each individual member's efforts need to be better coordinated.

There are several determining factors in the emergence of a group leader, including physical characteristics such as height, weight, age and gender, intelligence, personality traits, task skills and participation. It seems that the manifestation of leadership depends largely on the perceptions of the members of the group.

A lot of studies argue that those behaviors that build the leadership role generally fall into two categories: relationship behaviors and work behaviors.

Relationship behaviors are addressed to the attitudes, feelings and satisfaction of the members of the group, therefore it corresponds closely with the functions performed by the socio-emotional specialist. Even in groups that have tasks or problems to be solved, leaders often have to meet the personal needs of members. Relationship leadership involves strengthening morale, increasing group cohesion, reducing interpersonal conflicts, establishing the leader / member relationship, and expressing concern and consideration for all group members.

Working behaviors, on the other hand, deal with the actual problem rather than the personal satisfaction of the group members. Leaders must lead, lead the group in the direction of successfully achieving the proposed goal. Key aspects of working leadership can be defining group problems, establishing a communication network, providing evaluative feedback, planning, motivating action, coordinating member actions, and facilitating meeting goals by proposing solutions and removing obstacles.

Approaching the leader's traits has the merit of giving the logical approach to the idea that successful entrepreneurs have unquestionable chances to be successful leaders either through certain personality traits and physical characteristics, or as a result of their ability to practice effective leadership. strongly mobilize subordinates to achieve superior performance.

The behavior of successful leaders is part of the directive-permissive, antonymic autocratic-democratic and task-oriented-person pairs. Although formulated distinctly, the three pairs signify the behavioral characteristic of the leader: behavior focused on accomplishing tasks, production.

FUTURE DIRECTIONS IN LEADERSHIP DEVELOPMENT: PRINCIPLES AND APPLICATIONS

Fundamental to the achievement of entrepreneurial success, in the view of the author of this chapter, is the technological idea, closely related to its degree of commercial innovation. The degree of innovation is closely correlated with the size of the profit this entrepreneur can get it. Thus, it can be assumed that an entrepreneur who purchases the factors of production on the market, including the technological idea, will obtain a profit that can not exceed the natural rate of profit in that economy. The most researchers also fall into one of the common mistakes made by theoreticians in social sciences, namely to make a parallel between social and biological processes (Saiz-Alvarez, Muñiz & Huezo, 2016; Aldrich, 2011; Ireland, Hitt & Sirmon, 2003).

The essence of entrepreneurial spirit is the speculative nature of the extent to which the action of the human individual, in a broader sense, by bearing present costs, aims at satisfying future desires as the most intense (Cuervo et al., 2007). The temporal element necessary for human action and the implicit risk of action in time disappears from models that consider economics in a state of equilibrium, and consequently the role of the entrepreneur is not visible: entrepreneurial judgments are the substitute in the world real forecasts by producers in static equilibrium models (Frese & Gielnik, 2014).

Gaglio's (1997) approach seeks to identify a set of environmental factors that correlate with a set of human factors to explain where complex contracts depending on a set of events subsequent to their signing are onerous to be negotiated, applied. In the face of these difficulties, the firm may decide to avoid the market and make use of the internal arrangements for the transaction. But this analysis, although seemingly rational, frizzes a functionalist and behavioral approach to human behavior which, under the same conditions, is supposed to have the same reaction. Objectives and subjective judgments of value of individuals and entrepreneurs do not take place in such an analysis but in terms of their rationality.

The idea that companies spend all the resources by ignoring the relative structure of prices on the market is completely erroneous or can only be valid for some entrepreneurs who do not aim to obtain the profit from the activity they are doing (Ahmad & Seymour, 2008). Equally ignorant of the market prices may be an individual who initiates a market transaction.

First, any business is subject to the final profit test. If the shooter receives a financial loss, it is obvious that the allocation of resources was wrong. If the result is positive, it appears that the allocation of resources by the entrepreneur was more efficient than other entrepreneurs than the relative structure of the prices of all inputs and outputs on the market. This structure, however, always the term of comparison and the way of establishing the profits of entrepreneurship.

Entrepreneurial action always requires an innovative technological idea and the degree of innovation can be defined in a broad sense (Shepherd & Patzelt, 2011). If this is not the case, it is likely that the profit margin would not be higher than the normal profit in the economy or the extraordinary profit would be in the short term. The entrepreneur who buys all the inputs on the market does not make any contribution to the combination of these resources, at least technologically, is likely to get in just the natural rate of interest. Getting a higher profit than this natural rate of interest implies a new technological idea, which may well be those who view this activity as an arbitrary allocation of resources.

An entrepreneur who sells his services is not an entrepreneur in the sense used by Knight but is a manager (Feeser & Dugan, 1989). The entrepreneur becomes in this case the one who buys the services of that entrepreneur. Secondly, those employees who are paid a fraction of the profits become entrepreneurs in the broad sense because the rewarding of the production factor that they have the labor is no longer realized by present salary goods but by the side of uncertain future profit. These employees bring their own professional skills to their business and are rewarded with a share of profit. If the profit is 0, it is obvious that they will not be rewarded and will even bear losses that are of an entrepreneurial nature.

Thus, Kirzner (1979) offers an argument that will later see a significant development in company growth theory. Companies grow when entrepreneurs internalize previously traded transactions through the market and decrease when outsourcers outsource transactions that they previously coordinated within firms. Thus, by hierarchically allocating resources within the firm, the entrepreneurs manage to save existing trading costs due to the operation of those transactions through the market. The saving of these transaction costs is the main motivation to extend the limits of organizations to the detriment of market trades.

Another perspective opened by Coase later developed into what is called the theory of incomplete contracts (Stevenson & Jarillo, 1990). Observing that the more a contract for the supply of products or services over a longer period of time is, the less likely and less desirable, to specify what is expected of at the time of signing the contract. Thus, the two parties may agree only to broadly specify their obligations, and then to set out in more detail what is expected of each. To the extent that the behavior of one of the parties is influenced / directed by the other, the inclination for integration and hence the exercise of control is obvious. Given that short-term market-specific short-term contracts are insufficient, a form of integration is more likely.

Perhaps the most revolutionary view in Schumpter's writings is the idea that one did not need to be rich in order to have the opportunity to start as an entrepreneur/innovator (Scheinberg & McMillan, 1988). Schumpter (1911, 1997) stated that someone else's could equally support by his own wealth as well as an entrepreneur. If they are supported by their own wealth, then the entrepreneur actually fulfills two jobs: he is the banker and the entrepreneur at the same time. In any event, it is the banker not the entrepreneur, whether the two are the same or not, who truly bears the fruit of the financial risk pertaining to any innovation. Schumpter's theory was the first to treat innovation as an ingenious process. He turned down the predominant paradigm of an entrepreneur as a manager of the firm and replaced it with the alternative that the entrepreneur is the leader and innovator, or what Schumpter called the "primary mover of the economic system." Schumpter integrated the dynamics of technology into the business process when he defined the entrepreneur as an innovator. Schumpter's main contribution was a word picture that he offered in the above-mentioned book where he contrasted two worlds. The first was a world without the entrepreneur and with the circular flow of processes and technologies. In this picture Schumpter painted a static, repetitive process where everyday was the same as the one before and every firm in an industry was like the next one.

The second world was one where the entrepreneur entered the stage (Hébert & Link, 1989). By seeking an opportunity for profit, the entrepreneur introduces new economic combinations or innovations to reach his goal. This innovative capacity of the entrepreneur was seen as the prime endogenous cause of change or "the development of new economic systems." New combinations destroy the equilibrium of the economy (the circular flow) and create a new equilibrium. Continuous innovation therefore implies permanent change and permanent equilibrium readjustment. Perhaps more so than any other economist, Schumpter realized there was an age to come where the only constant would be constant discontent of the economic process.

Schumpter (1942) does not necessarily view the entrepreneur as the director or independent owner of a business. An entrepreneur can be any person who carries out a new economic combination and tries out new possibilities in order to achieve innovation. In most cases, the one who ends up producing these new combinations does not necessarily carry them out. Often the people who are already engaged in the production process have a natural tendency to fight innovation because innovation typically destroys their equilibrium process.

The complex task of forecasting and providing direction and control to the factors of production at the same time is concentrated on a narrow class of economic agents: the entrepreneurs (Carroll, G.R., & Khessina, O.M. (2005). In a sense, business decisions are never concrete calculated probabilities. With time and experience, the entrepreneur will specialize in directing, controlling, and bearing uncertainty while locating other economic agents to furnish him with the necessary productive services needed in exchange for a fixed fee. In that sense, other economic agents will not bear any of the uncertainty (changing technology, changing consumer preferences, or changing purchasing power) since the entrepreneur bears it all.

In Silva's view, the other major contribution by the entrepreneur is overall economic progress. In pursuing his/her goals, the entrepreneur will invariably improve the existing technologies and business organizations. In that context, entrepreneurs are the bottlenecks of economic growth: they determine the rate at which the economy grows and the new technologies that evolve. In addition, the entrepreneur is responsible for guaranteeing the pre-agreed remuneration to all interested parties in the firm (Silva, 2007).

The Austrian view of the world economy differs significantly from the standard view of the economist (Woo, Cooper & Dunkelberg, 1988). The neo-classical economist views the worldwide economic system in a general equilibrium, while the neo-Austrian economists see the world economy from a "dynamics of discovery" point of view. That is, the world economy is almost never at an equilibrium position since it is in a constant dynamism with constant changes. This, in their view, gives rise to constant opportunities for making pure profit. Omitting such opportunities arises only from what neo-Austrian economists coined "utter ignorance:" an unawareness of basic economic information ().

Regarding the Chicago and Austrian traditions, Lazear (2004) also notes the mistaken use of political and military terminology in politics: if this idiom would be just an innocent metaphor, it would not need his criticism. But he is the source of serious errors that play a sinister role in contemporary doctrines. The economic calculation specific to the entrepreneurial action does not require the establishment of a hierarchy to be put into practice. The entrepreneur will carry out his work according to the economic calculation he will translate into the transactions he runs through the market. It is obvious that all the exchanges in the market where an entrepreneur engages are made after a certain plan and they all compete for the achievement of a certain objective. The idea that only in a hierarchy can be organized production is free and is such a parallel wrong with military and political activity.

Discovery of profit-making opportunities is not accidental, but is stimulated by the prospect of personal reward. Therefore, the entrepreneur is either by nature (intrinsic motivation) or profit incentive the most alert member of the economic society. This view of entrepreneurship underpins theories and policies of economic development that include location theory, human resource development, and financing. Once outside of the interlocking modern theory of the firm, economic development makes great use of entrepreneurial decision-making. Much of this depends upon the sociological aspects of entrepreneurship.

Moreover, another tool of economic analysis, much used by some economists, is that of game theory (Astebro & Thompson, 2009; Sijbom, Janssen & Van Yperen, 2015). However, the parallel between human and game behavior is absolutely simplistic, deterministic and reductive, creating at the same time the impression of a closed system in which, ex ante, the decision tree is given.

Based on the assessment of the general situation, their ability to choose the most appropriate type of behavior and careful analysis of subordinates, leaders must always selectively adapt to the concrete situations they face.

The first behavior, the one focused on the accomplishment of the tasks, is specific to the leaders concerned with the timely and qualitative performance of the tasks, with the development according to the plans and the programs of the activities, with the precise definition of the quantitative and qualitative performances that each subordinate must realize. The leader must have the necessary competence to plan and organize the work of his subordinates so as to maximize their performance. The subordinates are renumbered in an incentive manner for each qualitatively acceptable result unit.

The second mentioned behavior, the person-oriented one, aims to create an efficient working team by supporting subordinates in their efforts, the wide use of the ways and means of harmonizing their needs with the organization's needs.

Approaching the leader's traits has the merit of giving the logical approach to the idea that successful entrepreneurs have unquestionable chances to be successful leaders either through certain personality traits and physical characteristics, or as a result of their ability to practice effective leadership. strongly mobilize subordinates to achieve superior performance. The behavior of successful leaders is part of the directive-permissive, antonymic autocratic-democratic and task-oriented-person pairs. Although formulated distinctly, the three pairs signify the behavioral characteristic of the leader: behavior focused on accomplishing tasks, production.

However, the concept of information asymmetry starts with a hypothesis that strikes a balance: the idea that between all operators on the market there must be an informational parity, that is, each of the same information, indifferent of its quality. Thus, both insiders and outsiders should have the same information at all times (Islam, 2015).

The information asymmetry exists, according to Mariotti and Glackin (2010), when the true circumstances characterizing a transaction or set of transactions are known by one or more parties but can not be obtained or identified by others at no cost. The information asymmetry, in its view, makes the transactions on the market subject to the risk, to favor the emergence of opportunistic behavior, see below - from those who have access to this information. In this sense, information asymmetry as limited rationality is tautological and can only be the basis of a circular argument. They are essentially the attributes of a normal state, which can not in itself constitute a scientific argument.

In the digital economy, both information asymmetry and limited rationality were the arguments used by some economists to try to explain the behavior of certain economic actors whose actions could not be explained by the mainstream analysis models (Nair & Saiz-Alvarez, 2019). In this respect, one of the topics in which these arguments were used is that of capital market investors, where even irrational investors have spoken. This perspective on economic behavior is also scientific: the irrational individuals do not operate in the economic sphere and the less can be done. What seems irrational to the outside observer is, however, perfectly rational for the individual who, according to the praxeological theory, uses his limited resources (including his or her own information and abilities) to pursue goals subjectively formulated by him. Some investors, for various reasons (such as the cost of information, the lack of analytical means, trust in others' abilities, etc.), can perfectly duplicate the trading strategy of other investors who have a good reputation and have registered in the past performance superior to the market. This strategy, which can be an observer of a tournament spirit, is as rational as to ignore the whole of the flock, considering that it possesses superior analytical and prognostic skills, adopt a contrarian strategy (opposed, in essence, to market movements).

SOLUTIONS AND RECOMMENDATIONS

As demonstrated above, entrepreneurship has many dimensions ranging from individual risk-taking to collective action and from economic theory to social development. The qualities and characteristics associated with each of these dimensions differ. On this basis, we now shall have a historical view on entrepreneurship theory. The intent was to illustrate the relations and significant differences within the literature of entrepreneurship, thus providing a framework to explain its diffusion.

Also, it is relevant to point out the mistake of many to personify the organisation: seeing the firm as a set of contractual relationships between individuals helps us to clarify that the personalization of the firm involved in formulating such questions as: What should be the company's objective function? or Does the company have a social responsibility? Is totally misleading and confusing.

FUTURE RESEARCH DIRECTIONS

The paradox of planning an economy is that the inputs of this process are purely arbitrary and have no economic significance. Thus, the paradox of economic activity is that anarchic production on the free market is the only one that allows individuals to assess their economic situation according to the realities of free prices, give an idea of the amount of capital they have at their disposal, and thus try to make as much information as possible on the evolution of consumer wishes.

For the future research directions, it is relevant to distinguish between those things that are within the firm. There is, in a very real sense, a multitude of complex (contractual) relationships between the legal fiction (the company) and the owners of the production factors (labor, raw materials, capital) and the consumers of the products made.

The consequence of these trends is that the entity of the future, as well as the industry of the future, can be reshaped in very meaningful ways, in which leaders can recombine in more effective ways the resources existing in the process of creating value.

CONCLUSION

Companies are having a high level of business growth and motivation, influence positively on the formation of new business ideas. It is therefore essential that emotional characteristics close to the ability to work and enthusiasm must be developed to take forward the company. Without passion, mainly in start-ups, it is impossible for firms to survive in the global market.

At the level of decision-making, the leader influences the quality of the decisions made by the entity's manager, decisions that have the purpose of obtaining the performance that can result only by meeting the objectives set and by influencing the decision-making and operational behavior of other people.

At the level of the information system, the leadership determines the data and information circuit, the information flows and circuits, the information procedures and the means of processing the information to substantiate, adopt and apply the decisions. From an information point of view, the technological revolution and the complexity of the information processing and storage variants have made a temporary leap, the entities today existing more in the virtual environment than in the physical space, almost as a condition sine qua non of resistance to the phenomena of globalization and disruption. This fact was also managed by the attitude of the managers of these entities who understood and adopted the technological and informational know-how and directed it at the level of the entity as a whole by creating on-line Intranet networks and Internet interfaces. and Social.

Business success is positively related to the level of training, participation in previous projects, business experience, and the number of founders. These factors, however, can change by other endogenous variables, such as debt, product prices, stakeholders' attitudes and investments, purchases, rotation sales, and wages, and exogenous factors, such as energy prices, external shocks, and country risk, among others.

REFERENCES

Agboli, M., & Ukaegbu, C. C. (2006). Business environment and entrepreneurial activity in Nigeria: Implications for industrial development. *The Journal of Modern African Studies*, *44*(1), 1–30. doi:10.1017/S0022278X05001394

Ahmad, N., & Seymour, R. G. (2008). *Defining Entrepreneurial Activity: Definitions Supporting Frameworks for Data Collection.* OECD Statistics Working Papers. OECD Publishing.

Aldrich, H. E. (2011). *An Evolutionary Approach to Entrepreneurship: Selected Essays by Howard E. Aldrich*. Edward Elgar.

Alvarez, S. A., & Barney, J. B. (2005). How Do Entrepreneurs Organize Under Conditions of Uncertainty? *Journal of Management*, *31*(5), 776–793. doi:10.1177/0149206305279486

Anna, A. L., Chandler, G. N., Jansen, E., & Mero, N. P. (2000). Women business owners in traditional and non-traditional industries. *Journal of Business Venturing*, *15*(3), 279–303. doi:10.1016/S0883-9026(98)00012-3

Astebro, T., & Thompson, P. (2009). *Entrepreneurs: Jacks of All Trades or Hobos?* Economics Research Working Paper Series, 48. Miami, FL: Florida International University.

Audretsch, D. B. (2003). *Entrepreneurship. A Survey of the Literature. Enterprise Papers, 14*. European Commission.

Baron, R. A. (2007). Entrepreneurship: A Process Perspective. In J. R. Baum, M. Frese, & R. A. Baron (Eds.), *The Psychology of Entrepreneurship* (pp. 19–39). Erlbaum.

Bula, H. O. (2012). Evolution and Theories of Entrepreneurship: A Critical Review on the Kenyan Perspective. *International Journal of Business and Commerce*, *1*(11), 81–96.

Carroll, G. R., & Khessina, O. M. (2005). The Ecology of Entrepreneurship. In S. A. Alvarez, R. Agarwal, & O. Sorenson (Eds.), *Handbook of Entrepreneurship Research: Disciplinary Perspectives* (pp. 167–200). Springer. doi:10.1007/0-387-23622-8_9

Cuervo, A., Ribeiro, D., & Roig, S. (Eds.). (2007). Entrepreneurship: Concepts, Theory, and Perspective. Springer.

Douglas, E. J., & Shepherd, D. (1997). *Why entrepreneurs create businesses: a utility maximizing response. Frontiers of Entrepreneurship Research*. Babson College.

Drucker, P. F. (1985). *Innovation and Entrepreneurship: Practice and Principles*. Harper Business.

Dubini, P. (1988). *Motivational and environmental influences on business start-ups: some hints for public policies. Frontiers of Entrepreneurship Research*. Babson College.

Feeser, H. R., & Dugan, K. W. (1989). *Entrepreneurial motivation: a comparison of high and low growth high tech founders. Frontiers of Entrepreneurship Research*. Babson College.

Frese, M., & Gielnik, M. M. (2014). The Psychology of Entrepreneurship. *Annual Review of Organizational Psychology and Organizational Behavior*, *1*(1), 413–438. doi:10.1146/annurev-orgpsych-031413-091326

Gaglio, C., & Katz, J. (2001). The Psychological Basis of Opportunity Identification: Entrepreneurial Alertness. *Small Business Economics*, *16*(2), 95–111. doi:10.1023/A:1011132102464

Gaglio, C. M. (1997). Opportunity recognition: review, critique, and suggested research directions. In J. Katz (Ed.), *Advances in Entrepreneurship, Firm Emergence and Growth* (pp. 139–202). JAI Press.

Gnyawali, D., & Fogel, D. (1994). Environments for entrepreneurship development: Key dimensions and research implications. *Entrepreneurship Theory and Practice*, *18*(4), 43–62. doi:10.1177/104225879401800403

Hébert, R. F., & Link, A. N. (1989). In Search of the Meaning of Entrepreneurship. *Small Business Economics*, *1*, 39–49. doi:10.1007/BF00389915

Ireland, R. D., Hitt, M. A., & Sirmon, D. G. (2003). A Model of Strategic Entrepreneurship: The Construct and its Dimensions. *Journal of Management*, *29*(6), 963–989. doi:10.1016/S0149-2063(03)00086-2

Islam, A. (2015). Entrepreneurship and the Allocation of Government Spending Under Imperfect Markets. *World Development*, *70*, 108–121. doi:10.1016/j.worlddev.2015.01.002

Johnson, B. R. (1990). Toward a multidimensional model of entrepreneurship: The case of achievement motivation and the entrepreneur. *Entrepreneurship Theory and Practice*, *14*(3), 39–48. doi:10.1177/104225879001400306

Kirzner, I. M. (1979). *Perception, Opportunity, and Profit: Studies in the Theory of Entrepreneurship*. The University of Chicago Press.

Lazear, E. P. (2004). Balanced Skills and Entrepreneurship. *The American Economic Review*, *94*(2), 208–211. doi:10.1257/0002828041301425

Lazear, E. P. (2005). Entrepreneurship. *Journal of Labor Economics*, *23*(4), 649–680. doi:10.1086/491605

Lloret, A. (2015). Modeling corporate sustainability strategy. *Journal of Business Research*, *69*(2), 418–425. doi:10.1016/j.jbusres.2015.06.047

Mariotti, S., & Glackin, C. (2010). *Entrepreneurship*. Prentice Hall.

Saiz-Alvarez, J. M. (2015). Solidarity Entrepreneurship in the European Knowledge Economies: Keys for a New Paradigm to Be Applied into Developing Nations. In Entrepreneurship in the Contemporary Knowledge-based Global Economy. Hershey, PA: Information Science Reference (IGI Global).

Saiz-Alvarez, J. M. (2018). *Business Strategies and Advanced Techniques for Entrepreneurship 4.0*. IGI Global. doi:10.4018/978-1-5225-4978-9

Saiz-Alvarez, J. M., Coduras, A., & Cuervo-Arango, C. (2013). Entrepreneurial Strategy, Innovation, and Cognitive Capabilities. What Role for Intuitive SMEs? *Journal of Small Business Strategy*, *21*(2), 25–35.

Saiz-Alvarez, J. M., Coduras, A., & Cuervo-Arango, C. (2014). An Entrepreneurial Well-being Model based on GEM Data for Spain. *International Journal of Interactive Multimedia and Artificial Intelligence*, *2*(5), 38–47. doi:10.9781/ijimai.2014.255

Sarasvathy, S. D. (2001). *Effectuation. Elements of Entrepreneurial Expertise*. Edward Elgar.

Scheinberg, S., & McMillan, I. C. (1988). *An all country study of motivations to start a business, Frontiers of Entrepreneurship Research*. Babson College.

Schultz, T. W. (1980). Investment in Entrepreneurial Ability. *The Scandinavian Journal of Economics, 82*(4), 437–448. doi:10.2307/3439676

Schumpeter, J. A. (1934). *The Theory of Economic Development: An Inquiry into Profits, Capital, Credit, Interest, and the Business Cycle*. Harvard University Press.

Schumpeter, J. A. (1977). *Capitalism, Socialism, and Democracy*. Harper Collins Publishers. (Original work published 1942)

Schumpeter, J. A. (1997). *Theorie der wirtschaftlichen Entwicklung: Eine Untersuchung über Unternehmergewinn, Kapital, Kredit, Zins und den Konjunkturzyklus*. Duncker Humblot. (Original work published 1911) doi:10.3790/978-3-428-07725-0

Shane, S., & Venkataraman, S. (2000). The Promise of Entrepreneurship as a Field of Research. *Academy of Management Review, 25*(1), 217–226. doi:10.5465/amr.2000.2791611

Shepherd, D. A., & Patzelt, H. (2011). The New Field of Sustainable Entrepreneurship: Studying Entrepreneurial Action Linking "What Is To Be Sustained" with "What Is To Be Developed?". *Entrepreneurship Theory and Practice, 35*(1), 137–163. doi:10.1111/j.1540-6520.2010.00426.x

Sijbom, R. B. L., Janssen, O., & Van Yperen, N. W. (2015). Leaders' Receptivity to Subordinates' Creative Input: The Role of Achievement Goals and Composition of Creative Input. *European Journal of Work and Organizational Psychology, 24*(3), 462–478. doi:10.1080/1359432X.2014.964215

Silva, O. (2007). The Jack-of-All-Trades entrepreneur: Innate talent or acquired skill? *Economics Letters, 97*(2), 118–123. doi:10.1016/j.econlet.2007.02.027

Stephan, U., Uhlaner, L. M., & Stride, C. (2015). Institutions and Social Entrepreneurship: The Role of Institutional Voids, Institutional Support, and Institutional Configurations. *Journal of International Business Studies, 46*(3), 308–331. doi:10.1057/jibs.2014.38

Stevenson, H. H., & Jarillo, J. C. (1990). A Paradigm of Entrepreneurship: Entrepreneurial Management. *Strategic Management Journal, 11*, 17–27.

Thorton, P. H., & Yang, L. (2012). *Entrepreneurship*. Oxford University Press.

Velilla, J., Molina, J. A., & Ortega, R. (2018). Why Older Workers Become Entrepreneurs? International Evidence Using Fuzzy Set Methods. *The Journal of the Economics of Ageing, 12*, 88–95. doi:10.1016/j.jeoa.2018.03.004

Wagner, J. (2003). Testing Lazear's jack-of-all-trades view of entrepreneurship with German micro data. *Applied Economics Letters, 10*(11), 687–689. doi:10.1080/1350485032000133273

Woo, C. Y., Cooper, A. C., & Dunkelberg, W. C. (1988). *Entrepreneurial typologies: definitions and implications, Frontiers of Entrepreneurship Research*. Babson College.

ADDITIONAL READING

Barnes, C. M., Dang, C., Leavitt, K., Guarana, C., & Uhlmann, E. L. (2018). Archival data in micro organizational research: A toolkit for moving to a broader set of topics. *Journal of Management*, *44*(4), 1453–1478. doi:10.1177/0149206315604188

KEY TERMS AND DEFINITIONS

Entrepreneur: Individual who starts a new business or adopt new business strategies in existing organizations.

Entrepreneurship: Business strategy focused on the creation of jobs, social wealth, and profit by optimizing the use of productive and commercial resources.

Chapter 11
Strategic Management:
Company Management Strategies in a Sustainable Economy

Ionica Oncioiu
Titu Maiorescu University, Romania

Mircea Alecsandru Udrescu
Artifex University, Romania

Alina Gheorghe
Artifex University, Romania

ABSTRACT

The material presented in this chapter aims to capture some particularities of the strategic management of the company in managing risks and threats, to detect some interference between the managerial strategy and the organizational culture, and to bring to attention the correlations between the vision of the business, the strategic segmentation, and the corporate strategies through which strategic management ensures the behavioral change of the company on the market. The sustainable economy has put in front of the company's strategic management two directions of responsibility: the motivation of the change or the disappearance of the market.

INTRODUCTION

Romanian companies prior to Romania's acceptance into the European Union considered the natural environment as a "one time getting", in relation to which they had only exploitation rights and very few responsibilities. Since Romania became part of the community of the western civilized world, it has committed itself to act in all media in full accordance with the European Union strategy for sustainable development, a document that has also become a framework for Romanian legislation. The general objective of the European strategy calls on the European states to act responsibly in order to improve the quality of life of its inhabitants by using environmental resources efficiently, by employing the potential

DOI: 10.4018/978-1-7998-4637-6.ch011

of ecological and social innovation of the economy, in order to ensure general prosperity in harmony with the natural environment. At the same time, the demands of the sustainable economy have become a turbulent environment for the Romanian companies, and their strategic management has been put in a position to adopt visions and strategies meant to maintain them and to affirm them fully in the new conditions required by the new market specific to the sustainable economy.

LITERATURE

Strategic management particularities of the company within the sustainable economy The defining peculiarity of the strategic management of the company consists in defining the full connection of the company to a new philosophy of political and social development, namely sustainable development, which represents the central element of the company's competitive environment.

The company's management can be in the situation either to notice the meanings in which the general environmental policies will evolve, and in such cases it is necessary to adapt the lucrative processes to the predictable constrictive perspectives of the environment, or to have the vision of a qualitative change of the lucrative domain with obvious implications in terms of competitive advantage (Armstrong, 2004). In principle, most companies are surprised by the terrible changes in the sustainability plan, which are generated by major political decisions or superstate arrangements. Such companies are always in a situation to recover considerable gaps compared to companies that have already implemented processes suitable for sustainable development (Newton, 2009). With all the advances in the technological field, such companies always find that they are characterized by poor efficiency indicators, by quite high specific consumption, by the proliferation of threats to the functional security and by the deepening of vulnerabilities in the level of decision-making sovereignty (Druker, 2010). In the situations where the strategic management of the company has the vision of sustainable development, it has all the chances to position them in the top of the powerful companies of progress and to offer products and services that support a harmonious coexistence with the environment (Eppler, 2007). They tend to be a model of sustainable development, characterized as being a generator of high added value, centered on knowledge, innovation and coexistence, focused on the continuous improvement of the people' s life quality inside the company, but also of the adjacent social systems, in harmony with nature (Gresoi & Gheorghe, 2011). For the companies that will always adapt to the requirements of sustainable development, their strategic management aims, as the case may be, to impose the following strategies in the short, medium or long term, as follows: the organic incorporation of the practices of sustainable development, according to the exigencies that have their origin in the environment externally, reaching an acceptable level according to the consideration of some basic indicators of sustainable development, generally accepted indicators, or the proximity, equalization, even exceeding, of the leading companies in the field, also based on the established indicators of sustainable development (Udrescu et al, 2016). Since the sustainable development becomes a fundamental option, the strategic management of the company is obliged to focus on the following directions of action, as follows: the acquisition of the conceptual framework with which the sustainable development operates at the zonal, national and global level; assessing the current situation of natural, anthropic, human and other capital according to which the performances of sustainable development are measured; materializing a vision of perspectives, over time horizons, strictly following the logic of the challenges that come from the companies and institutions that are dedicated to sustainable development; analyzing the specific problems that the current company faces in this way of development in the process of moving to sustainable development, by eliminating the existing gaps in relation with the performance levels of the modern companies; formulation of concrete strategies meant to ensure the implementation, monitoring and confirmation of the results in relation with the experience and practice established in the social reference and political environment (Jenson, 2004). Essentially, strategies for pursuing sustainable development standards can identify processes that can receive increased attention in the following periods, such as: rationally correlating development objectives in the cross-sectoral and zonal profile with the capacity to support natural capital; accelerated modernization of own education and training systems; firm introduction of eco-efficiency criteria in all company-specific activities; creating a functional mechanism to ensure the use of the best available technologies in investment decisions from public funds and beyond; anticipating the foreseeable effects of the changes in the external environment, as well as in the competitive environment, and developing contingency measures plans, including portfolios of alternative solutions for crisis situations; protection and enhancement of the material, financial, cultural and natural heritage of the company (Prahalad, 2010). Acquiring the conceptual framework with which sustainable development operates at the local, national and global level is concerned with the local adoption of multiple international conventions that establish precise obligations on the part of the states, with strict deadlines for implementation, aiming at climate change, biodiversity conservation, protection of wetlands, limiting the use of certain chemicals, according to a generally valid principle: "what is thought globally, is adopted at national level and is carried out at local level". The paradigm shift is justified by the perceived and mostly recognized reality, according to which climatic changes, erosion and desertification phenomena, habitat pollution, endanger the existence of a large number of plant and animal species, etc. it acts destructively on the quality of life of people in large areas of the planet.

This is why the phrase "sustainable development" is supported by the finding that human civilization expresses itself as a subsystem of the sphere, dependent on the general flows of production and reproduction, which decisively influence the future of social existence. The harmony between human-specific actions and the need to maintain a responsible balance with the natural environment are aspects that make more responsible than ever human action, which must be positioned somewhere at the confluence of economic, social and environmental factors. The strategic management of the company can at any time be inspired by the European Union's Sustainable Development Strategy, adopted by the EU Council on June 9th, 2006, which has the general objective of „carrying out actions that allow the European Union to achieve a continuous improvement of quality life for present and future generations by creating sustainable communities, able to manage and use resources efficiently and capitalize on the potential of ecological and social innovation of the economy to ensure prosperity, environmental protection and social cohesion" (The European Union's Sustainable Development Strategy, adopted by the European Union's Council on June 9th, 2006). Of course, the responsibility for the strategy's implementation lies with the European Union, through the signatory states and through the direct contribution of each national economic actor. In order to ensure the transposition of the European Union's Sustainable Development Strategy at national level, the States that have signed the undertakings are obliged to follow and detail the following guiding principles, as follows: promotion and protection of fundamental human rights; solidarity within and between generations; cultivating an open and democratic society, informing and actively involving citizens in the decision-making process; involvement of the business environment and social partners; policy coherence and quality of governance at local, regional, national and global levels; integration of economic, social and environmental policies through impact assessments and cultivation of stakeholders; use of modern knowledge to ensure economic and investment efficiency; applying the precautionary principle in the case of uncertain scientific information; applying the „polluter pays" principle (NCSD, 2008). Romania was welcomed in the European Union, pledging that it will respect in good faith the European Union's Sustainable Development Strategy. But it is easy to understand that, at the time of signing the accession agreements, the member states of this European organization had overcome some aspects of sustainable development, aspects that became for Romania real objectives to be met under acute conditions. For example, the complex issues of agricultural properties, access to drinking water, transport infrastructure, labor productivity, health system, which at a certain level of resolution in the European Union, were suddenly transformed into strategic vulnerability factors for the management of all the companies operating in the territory, but also into strategic risk factors for any management team that wanted to start business in the light of new development coordinates. As a consequence, the national framework for registration and operation of economic agents in the Romanian market has become more restrictive, the dynamics of sustainable development becoming dependent, to a large extent, both on the availability of resources and on a real system of circumstances (Gheorghe & Udrescu, 2019). On the working agenda of the strategic management of any Romanian company began to become increasingly threatening risk factors of an exogenous nature, among which some have acquired sharpening aspects, such as: amplification of the tendencies of increase in prices for petroleum products, increasing of uncertainties with regarding the attitude of the big foreign investors performing towards the new market that has become extremely emergent for them, the insufficient control of the negative, but predictable influences, on the national currency rate and on the inflation, with repercussions on the exchange rate, the accentuation, beyond the limits of the sustainability, of the phenomenon of specialized labor force migration from Romania to the rich states of Europe, regional constraints on the quality standards of all domestic products and services, etc. In close correlation with these exogenous risk factors, the strategic management of the company was besieged by a lot of other endogenous risk factors, among which they could be individualized: the short-term adjustment of the economic policies generated by the governmental conjunctions, the multiplication of the acts norms and the development of government bureaucracy, the accentuation of distrust in the impartiality of justice, the immoral conditional cooperation between public institutions and the entrepreneurial sector, the proliferation of client actions of the financial allocation priorities of the funds in the public interest, the reduction of the accessibility of the European funds, the unjustified delay state in the payment of the accumulated debts, disinterest in the management of extreme weather phenomena, the stimulation of the increase of the wage incomes outside an economic correlation with the corresponding increase of the labor productivity, by articulating the vocational training process at national level. With this pressure of the risk factors on the strategic management of the company, it was placed in the situation of forming a structure, group or contingent for urgent evaluation of risks, crises, etc., as decision support structures meant to diminish the unwanted economic effects. As the economic life became relatively unpredictable, and the constraints of sustainable development became a philosophy of competitive advantage, the strategic management of the company was forced to prepare contingency plans for anticipating system vulnerabilities and evaluating within the business visions, the possible effects of crisis situations that also include solution portfolios. Since the national normative framework implemented European provisions for sustainable development, the strategic management of the companies acted in two totally opposite directions: either it ignored the importance of the change, it continued to float on a more and more agitated sea, leaving the company to the constraints, until the bankruptcy was reached, either it founded a new lucrative vision, which would lead to unlocking the human potential and own material. With the focus on the new mission of the company, in close correlation with the new entrepreneurial vision, the strategic management of the company is obliged to focus first on releasing the latent potential of the company, in order to produce effective and efficient. Of course, this process does not exclude finding new and improved human resources, but thinking of the productive assembly so that the company can live in the new market conditions. At this moment of the opposite managerial activities, the traditional management has reached the limit of competence, while the innovative strategic management, which qualitatively reorients the running of the business, proves the professional competence, having competitive success.

The analysis of the majority of bankruptcies in the last period accuses the strategic management of the following shortcomings, even though it suggested, but unconvincingly, a certain vision of business, as follows: risky strategies, inadequate planning, inadequate procedures and superficial control. Risky strategies result directly from illusory visions, from choosing an unclear orientation of the future activity of the company. Such uncertainties generate a state of unclearness in the managed systems located on the managerial intermediate levels, which are seen in front of decisions that are not predictable, but also assume responsibility. Inadequate planning usually comes from visions without adequate strategies. Even if the figures and levels established by plan elements are met, usually with great weight, the results of planning are increasingly found in the waiting position, or in the market rejection. What has been planned and achieved no longer meets the criteria of effectiveness, even if through special efforts what has been done meets the requirements of efficiency. Thus, *strategic management* continues to produce what the market no longer accepts, because the market has also adopted sustainable development standards. Inappropriate procedures appear immediately in the context where, even if reasonable planning is available, strategic management does not impose technical, technological and quality procedures designed to ensure the completion of products and services. The lack of procedures is specific to the strategic management that is characterized by actions according to the principle "let us see." Superficial control stems from the uncertainty of the strategic management of the company. Since the vision is unfounded, the strategies are general, the plans are unclear, and the procedures are left to chance, and the control is carried out in the same note, superficiality and without finality. At the same time, it is possible that good vision, correct planning and appropriate procedures may be sabotaged by the absence of the necessary controls, the absence of which results in procedural slippages and biased division of responsibilities (Ciobanu & Roman, 1997). On the contrary, the *strategic management (S.M.)* that is committed to *sustainable development* clarifies its business vision, responsibly plans the available resources, names the working procedures and adequately controls the entire flow of products, initially from the consumer to the producer, as an understanding of the needs of the buyers, and then from the producer to the final consumer, as a competitive involvement in satisfying the needs of the buyer with the lowest costs. Such management establishes adequate financial structures, designs minimum profitability levels, strictly controls the management of inventories, operationally resolves the tendencies of gifting, pays attention to the mirage of expansion, minimizes lost sales, cultivates a responsible and empathetic attitude towards its customers, which they are trying to retain. *Responsible strategic management* (R.M.) keeps under constant control the proportion of its own outstanding payments and the size of its debtors, being reasonable financial relationships, reducing the risks and financial difficulties and opening the way for a predictability of doing business over time. Also, a strategic performance management pays all the attention of the company's own communication system, making it possible for the company's vision and strategy to be clearly communicated to all staff, the middle managers clearly understand their responsibilities in the new steps, so that all employees to come to understand the new tasks and the concrete ways in which they must get involved and, above all, how they will be controlled and appreciated. Announcing a new strategy, strategic management proceeds to a new distribution of material and human resources, who obviously aims to make it possible to translate the new strategy into reality, knowing that technology and human resources can change rapidly, but management has the heavy mission to inspire the new sense of urgency and responsibility that did not exist before. In this way, the road to success is defined. On the contrary, traditional strategic management focuses on increasing sales, the turnover invariably leading to the myopia of ineffective management of additional products, hence, the inconsistency of the control of the expenses on the product leads to the loss of losses caused by the introduction of new products, as well as to the lack of concern by the efficient use of the own capital used in the business. *Responsible strategic management* plans its activity not only in relation to the volume of profits and sales, but also in relation to their market share, aiming responsibly for long-term profitability. In general, the strategic management of the company is placed in the situation to decide between achieving a large market share, long term, and achieving a maximum profit, in the short term. The dynamics of market entry and exit tends to support the idea of achieving an optimal market report, when any deviation from a product / market relationship negatively changes the long-term profitability of the company. In order to determine the optimum weight of the company on the market, the strategic management is invited to go through the following steps: to estimate the relationship between the market share and profitability, to estimate the risk at different levels of the loss and to determine the value from which an increase of the market share it does not make enough profit to offset the additional risks the company would be exposed to (Thompson Jr., 1987). There may also be situations where the profitability may drop even to a large share of the firm in the market, especially when: some customers remain loyal to the competition, and the expenses for attracting them may far exceed the expenses incurred in attracting new customers, the needs of these clients wear unique aspects and do not deserve high levels of cost, companies looking to increase their market share are obliged to make additional expenses for various legal actions. It is considered that when these additional expenses equal the additional gains, the market share is reached. Strategic management is obliged to keep market risk under control. The risk is high for companies that have a low level of market share because the company is not competitive with the other stronger competitors. The risk decreases as the market share of the company increases, as it gains more consumer confidence and different consumer protection bodies. In a market with many competitors, companies with a dominant position become mobilizing targets for current and potential competitors, but the miracle of growth can be a risk. Standard methods of highlighting market results tend to encourage the view that higher profits are an automatic result of higher volumes of sales, but indirect costs are ignored at some point.

The success or failure of the companies in the conditions of the sustainable economy is strongly conditioned by the particularities in which their strategic management is manifested. It shows the direction in which the available resources are mobilized, under the conditions of national and regional environmental regulations, but also how they are coming to an end. **Strategic interference in organizational culture** *Organizational culture* (O.C.) constitutes the concrete form of manifesting the public personality of a company, a personality that is built on the sustainable assembly of its specific symbols, rituals and ceremonies, public rules of behavior and own values, a coherent system of public manifestation, which acts as a company to be different from another (Neagu & Udrescu, 2008). Of course, the personality of a company, as a manifestation in the relations with the external environment, expresses the quintessence of its internal environment, a system giving values, ideals, beliefs and common rules of conduct that unite the members of the organization as a whole (Neagu, 2017).

The specialized literature accepts a wide range of definitions, such as: “consistent application of an internal model that determines the behavior, values and schemes of thinking, action and speech in an organization"(Pascale, 1985) or "a system of material elements, values, norms and beliefs shared by the members of a group" (Schein, 1985).

In our own vision, we can appreciate the *organizational culture* of a company as being the whole of the principles, material and moral values, beliefs, rituals, competences and attitudes by which an organization presents itself in its competitive environment, its own model of being, acting, thinking and feel, for the company to exist and to assert itself in a highly regulated competitive environment. Therefore, the *organizational culture* represents the invisible force behind the easily observable and tangible things of an organization, the social energy that determines the employees act to create goods and services and the customers appreciation for it through a high level of satisfaction felt through its use.

Each company has its own *organizational culture*. This derives from its predictable past, present and future, from its current employees, from its material endowment, from its sustained reputation on the market, as well as from the goals, objectives and values with which its future trajectory is sustained. In order to achieve a high degree of performance, the organizational culture of a company must be simultaneously strong, appropriate and adaptive. Or this is only possible if there is adequate strategic management, capable of directing general energies in such directions. And strategic management is powerful when it has the ability to base future actions through appropriate visions, it adapts the company through mobilizing strategies and adapts the company through rigorous control of the follow-up of the roadmap (Gheorghe & Udrescu, 2017). Thus, strategic management becomes the vital center of the gear that guarantees the existence and evolution of the company in an increasingly turbulent environment. *Organizational culture* becomes the cause and work of *strategic management (S.M.)*. It is the cause of strategic management which formulates and communicates the vision, objectives and strategies to be followed and it is its work insofar as it ensures that things happen, but with the help of its employees. Through the organizational culture the rules, procedures, decisions of strategic management are interpreted by employees, thus becoming sources of behavioral motivation, or sources of negative motivation, at which strategic management must find concrete measures to eradicate. Strategic management basically aims to harmonize the values, beliefs, individual symbols with the objective directions of change, so that the company continues to represent a force on the market.

Strategic management (S.M.) and *organizational culture (O.C.)* appear as interdependent elements, with a close link between management, leadership, current and future performance and organizational culture. As soon as a new company is established, as soon as a new management strategy is implemented, conditions are created for the formation of a new organizational culture, which reflects the way of thinking and action of all, but under the authority of strategic management. In such circumstances, we appreciate that the strategic management has the duty that, with the formulation of the new visions and strategies, it will also express its own work conduct, a process by which it transmits on the managerial and execution stages subordinated the own belief of what is to be done.It happens, for the company to survive the changes and enjoy success. It is acknowledged that managers must be true role models for those they come in contact with, so they must have a great capacity for empathy, be able to understand and become understood, but pragmatically supporting the sense of becoming a company. This sense may require sacrifices from the employees, but also major behavioral changes, which are found throughout the organizational culture as factors of pressure on the adoption of change. The power to convince strategic management lies in its own cultural basis, in its level of professional competence, in the belief systems and values that decisively mark its actions for change.

Generally speaking, the cultural values that characterize the strategic performance management we appreciate that it aims, in a synergistic way: the orientation towards the teamwork, the sincerity, the

Figure 1. Traditional company surprised by the demands/constraints of the sustainable economy
Source: Manfred Kets de Vries, 2001

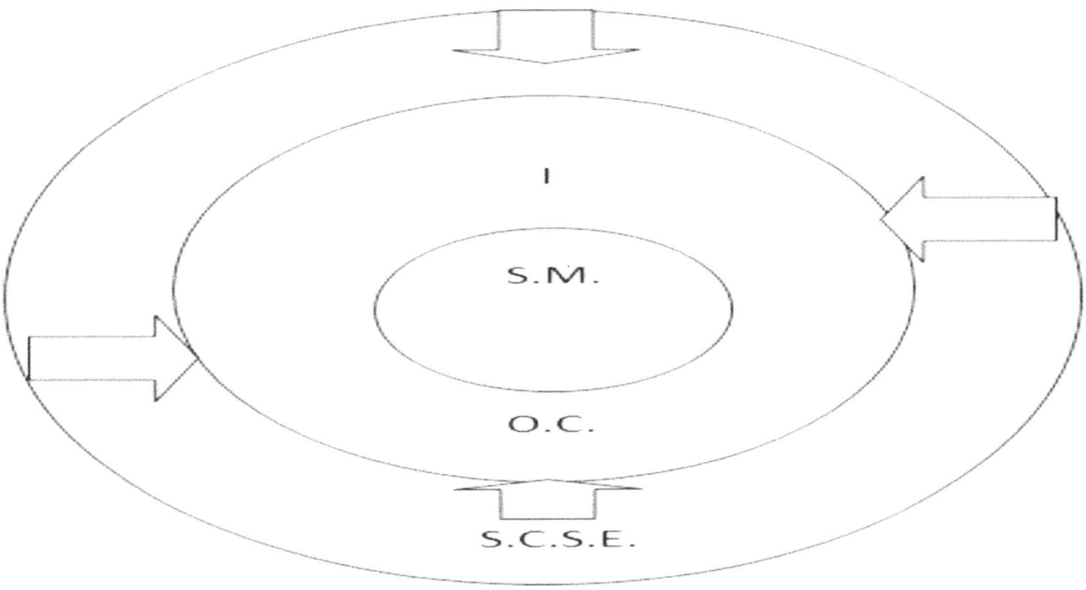

empowerment, the authority and the responsibility, the delegation with confidence, the respect for each employee, the orientation towards the client, the entrepreneurial attitude, pleasant atmosphere, taking responsibility, continuous learning, openness for qualitative change, confidence in vision and strategy (Manfred Kets de Vries, 2001). If a wise "anonymous" stated that "There are five types of companies: those who act, those who think they act, those who watch how others act, those who wonder what happens and who have no idea what happens", under the conditions of the sustainable economy, strategic management must have a clue as to what is to happen and believe in what is acting. And this belief of strategic management is aimed at two major coordinates: the elaboration of strategies meant to harmonize the goals of the company with the requirements of sustainable development and catalyzing the internal synergy in order to transpose the strategies into the work.

Hypothetically, as the demands of the sustainable economy become more and more obviously, the company, its strategic management and its organizational culture are under pressure from the risk factors coming from the external environment specific to the sustainable economy, as shown in Figure 1.

O.C. – traditional organizational culture
S.M.- company's strategic management
I- the basic interests of the organizational culture
SCSE- specific constraints of the sustainable economy

It is the strategic management's duty to find the new directions of action meant to transform the organizational culture of the company and bring the company into a state in which the sustainable economy specific environment becomes a friendly environment, in which the company finds resources to exist and to develop, so as suggested in Figure 2.

Figure 2. Adapted company to the requirements of the sustainable economy

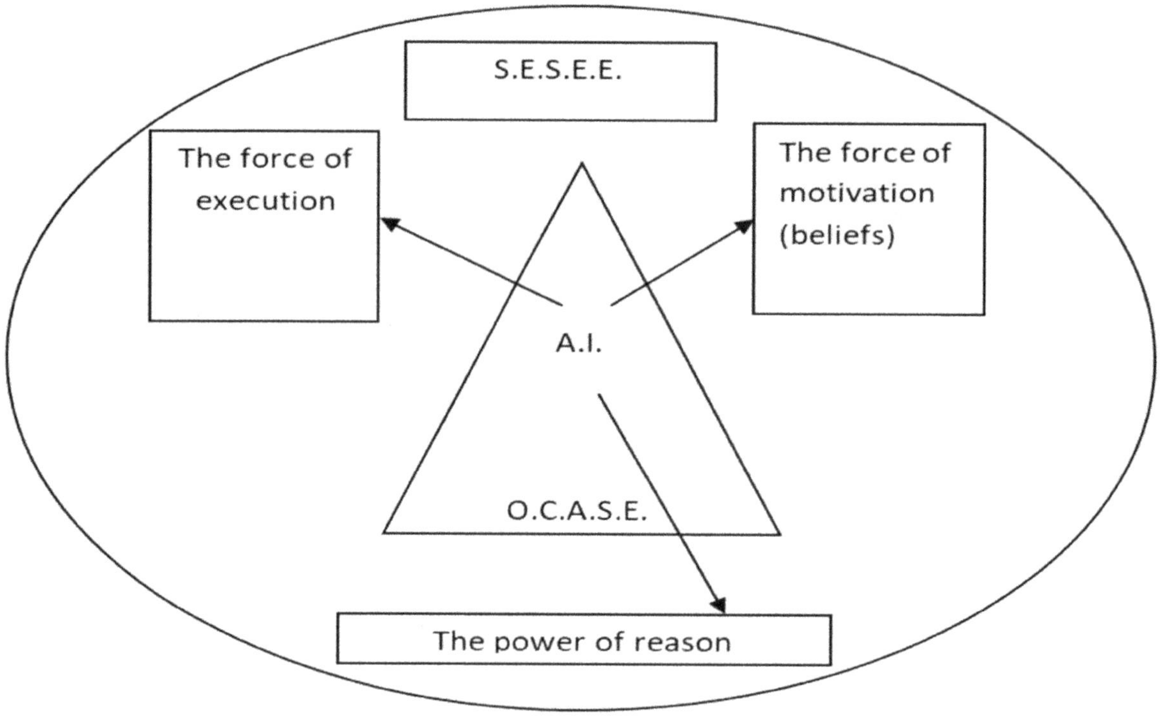

A.I.-adopted interests
O.C.A.S.E.- organizational culture adjusted to the sustainable economy
S.E.S.E.E.- the sustainable economy's specific external environment

Understanding the vulnerabilities to which the company is exposed under the conditions of increasingly obvious imposition of risk factors that have as a source the political and social support of the sustainable economy requires its strategic management to find answers to two major questions: "What should be undertaken (the meaning of change) in order to „Does the company continue to remain competitive in the market?"and" What must be done to make the sense of change known, believed and followed by the internal structures and subsystems of the company?"

The meaning of change is relatively easy to formulate. The audit of the company from several points of view can put at the disposal of the strategic management rational variants of action. And this field is widely analyzed by the specialized literature, formulating directions of action supported by solid mathematical calculations. As such, the strategic management is put in the situation to establish the variant of action mainly according to the degree of acceptance of the change by the different parties involved in this extremely complex process. As in medicine, a well-established diagnosis also requires appropriate therapy. But the appropriate therapy must be accepted and followed precisely by the patient. If this does not happen, the good intention of the doctor does not lead to the expected results: the recovery of the patient, but, on the contrary, the worsening of his health. For the strategic management of the company, once the action strategy is established, which guarantees the survival and development of the company as a whole, another process is initiated, as complicated, with both external and internal actors, which must be convinced or forced to supports the steps arising from the strategies adopted.

Figure 3. Correlating aspects between current strategies, policies and tactics for carrying out management strategies

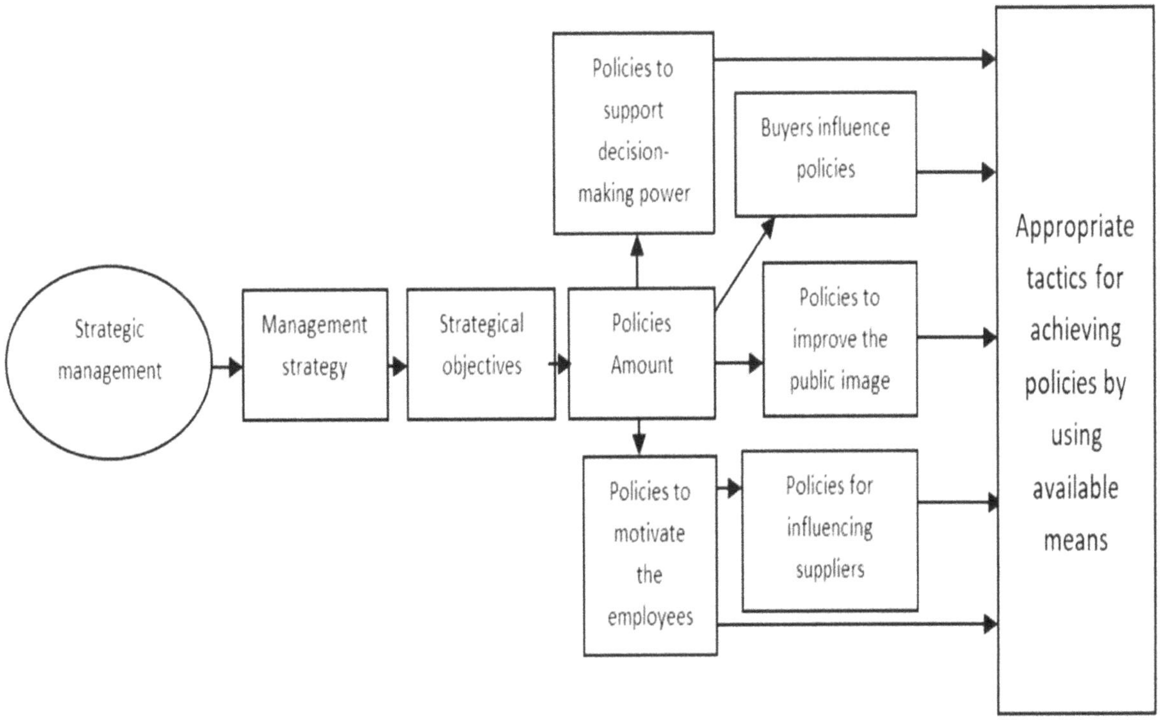

Strategic management becomes convinced of the need for change, but it is necessary to take into account that, in relation to the expected change, the shareholder pronounces, the suppliers, the buyers, the financial environment and the competition are manifested, the public administration, political and non-governmental organizations are positioned, it employs the structures and subsystems that define the internal environment of the company, s. o. In all directions, the strategic management of the company is placed in a position to support appropriate policies that make possible the realization of the action strategy. As such, the correlation of the strategic management's actions with the adopted strategy and the policies to be followed, which materialize in tactics to be followed, are suggested by those presented in Figure 3.

Of course, a strategic objective does not have the image of an order that is necessarily to be achieved, but it is the result of a rational process of involving resources under the conditions of major restrictions, from which a quantified definition (quantity, qualitative standards, alignment reached, level results), a clear responsibility, a coverage with resources available of human, financial, material and other nature), a calendar of terms, a delegation of authority, a system of reporting and control of the execution and, especially, a system for adjusting the course of its execution, in correlation with its vision of implementation desired to be optimal (Ziglar, 2011). A strategic objective can be formulated as: "10% reduction of indirect costs on the product by December 10, 2007" or "Introducing a new production line by December 10, 2010" or "increasing the turnover on product X by December 10th. Ofcourse, when establishing a strategic objective, strategic management analyzes the internal and external factors that can influence its achievement. For example, the attainment of the turnover of a particular product may be influenced by the following internal factors, such as: non-competitive prices, insufficient quantities on the market, decreased perceived quality, deficiencies in the activity of sales agents, deficiency of post-sale services, degradation of the brand image. Among the external factors, we can find: the unfavorable local situation, the decrease of the clients' incomes, the aggressive competition, the inadequate distribution channel, the phenomena related to fashion. Or the strategic management of the company must set such objectives so that they become mobilizing, otherwise they become illusory objectives, which have negative implications on their own organizational culture (Dumitrescu, 2002).

Strategic management is the mobilizing inner core that puts at the disposal of the company, the strategy that constitutes the basis of the organizational culture manifestation. For example, in the military, the strategy is the responsibility of the commander-in-chief to win the war. Basic dictionaries define strategy as "the art of using all the available means to ensure success in a fight (Marcu & Manea, 1978) and Igor Ansoff defines the managerial strategy as the set of decision criteria that guide the behavior of an economic agent, which results: the criteria that allow the measurement of the current and future performance of the company (quality criteria being referred to as guidelines, and quantitative ones, objectives), the rules governing the relations of the company with its environment, that is the integrated product-market system, which manages the vital correlations between production techniques and technologies, the market served and the preservation of the competitive advantage on it; the rules that govern the internal relations of conduct and managerial administration, the rules that the company follows on the potential market, as an expression of the great operational orientations, which derive from the basic content of the strategies (Ansoff, 1989).

Strategic management deserves its reputation if it focuses the entire organizational culture of the company towards market success, using courage and timely assets strategy at hand, among which is detached: production costs, quality of products and services, price flexibility, familiarity of customers with products and the services offered and the consolidation of their reputation, the modernization of the supply and sale chains, the consolidation of a favorable image of the market.

The objective requirements of the sustainable economy are just as strategic objectives. Formulating the implementation of the basic requirements of the sustainable economy becomes a major task of the strategic management to keep the company in the competitive environment thus adjusted. After the strategy is grounded, the task of strategic management is to implement it, generating new synergistic actions of the company's internal environment. In this direction, the company's strategic management is forced to conceive a new management structure, to modify it in the direction of efficiency, by using general managerial schemes that are carried out according to the principle of authority - budget-reward, to motivate the company's internal energies and resources around the strategical objectives, to be convinced that it enjoys the support of the conserved reserves specific to the organizational`s culture, to make decisive pressures, at least in the following directions: market, business environment and internal structuring. And so the sustainable economy becomes a turbulent environment for the company's organizational culture and alerts its strategic management, so that it reacts in the direction of change, which engages a new organizational culture, aimed at managing change.

Business Vision and Strategic Segmentation

Vision, missions and values are the way in which strategic management communicates its change strategy. The vision expresses the central core that underpins the path of choice, aspects that are found in the proposed strategy. Vision becomes a source of inspiration and motivation for employees who appreciate the expected change (Tracy, 2010). When the competitive environment is dominated by the requirements of sustainable development, the purpose of the business aims not only profit thresholds, but its thresholds in conditional correlation with responsibilities assumed towards the environment and with the next generations (Collins, 2010). Therefore, the vision in such conditions is a specific process of life; it is always dynamic, meant to satisfy the clients, the employees, the public administration, especially the environment. As the new business takes power, the business vision acquires new qualitative nuances, preserving the essence of the business and building confidence in the efforts made (Adamson, 2010).

A vision in the conditions of the *sustainable economy* emanates entrepreneurial aspects open towards: rigorous and safe compatibility of the business with the natural environment, responsibility towards the future generations, conditioning the maximization of the ecological security's profit, the compatibility between own strategies with the local, regional and national ones, that target the ecosystems, ensuring general well-being, developing an educational and professional system that puts the economy of exhausted natural resources on the foreground, diversification of specific indicators after which the quality of economic development is correlated with the quality of human life and the protection of the natural environment (Christensen, 1997).

The vision in the context of the pressures of the sustainable economy becomes a positive process, with an anticipatory character, aimed at modeling and reshaping the activities in a structured manner, which will lead both to obtaining efficient economic results, as well as to an improvement of the company's relations with the natural environment. The demands of the *sustainable economy* became the cause of entrepreneurial change, but also a fundamental criterion for appreciating the competitive advantage (Covey, 2006).

Strategic management has the duty to first notice the threats of the new environment on the company, and by raising awareness of its strengths and weaknesses, to devise renewal strategies, so it can minimize the obvious vulnerabilities, as well as the possible ones. The knowledge of the competitive situation and the awareness of the vulnerabilities are premises from which the strategic management can fulfill its forecasting purpose. The new state of affairs, at least at the national level, may suggest strategic management to resort to benchmarketing techniques, to learn from the leaders and competitors of the field, to discover best practices, to copy or adapt them, increasing their effectiveness (Udrescu & Gheorghe, 2016).

The general process of forecasting the change imposed by the demands of the sustainable economy is presented in Figure 4.

The vision and the strategy, as indispensable actions for the strategic management, have as a starting point the understanding of the environmental constraints and the evaluation of their own activity, as well as that of the competitors. But these are only achieved through adequate communication and motivating the employees, as long as they synergistically support the changes that are required (Udrescu & Gheorghe, 2017).

Before being a pioneer in the field, strategic management finds that on the market there are companies that have a leading position in the field of implementing the demands of the sustainable economy (Sexton, 2012). This is why strategic management has the chance to carry out benchmarking investigations, from which new possibilities of incorporating good production and commercial practices can be identified, as well as motivating employees to implement change directions. The incorporation of the benchmarketing's specific techniques in the strategic management's managerial processes of the company's adaptation to the sustainable economy's demands are synthetically presented in Figure 5.

Thus, the vision and strategy of change, demanded by the sustainable economy, transform themselves into a range of adjacent processes designed to position the company among the best performing in the field, which reflects its effort to achieve excellence in the field. Of course, a company presents itself as

Figure 4. The general process of awareness regarding a new vision and business strategies, and also, of achieving a new organizational culture through sustainable economy's specific performances

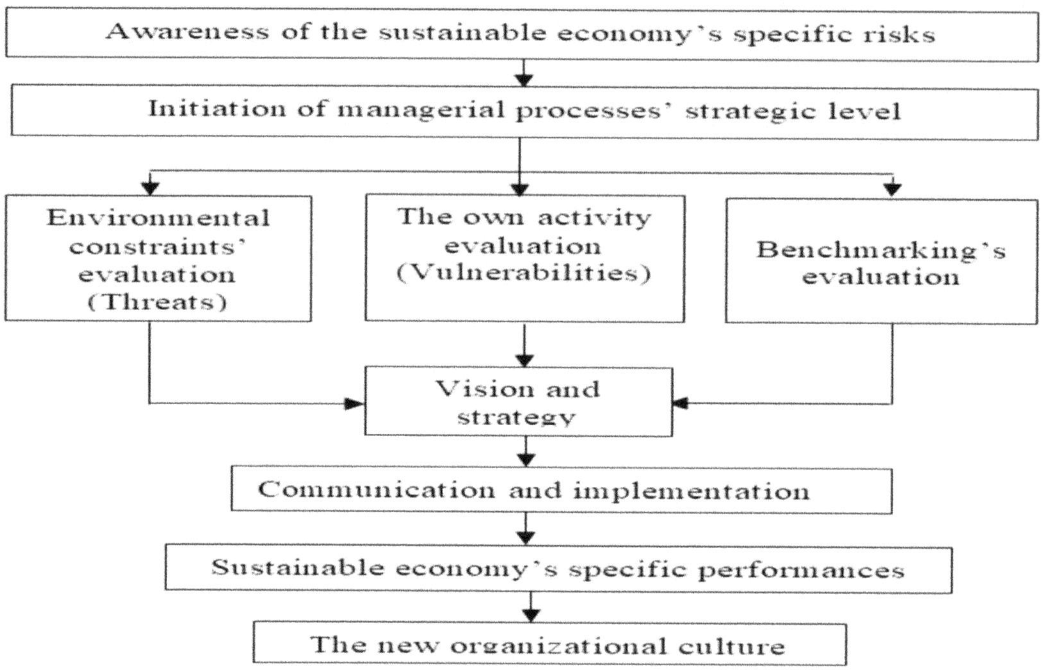

Figure 5. The managerial process of possible strategies' implementation

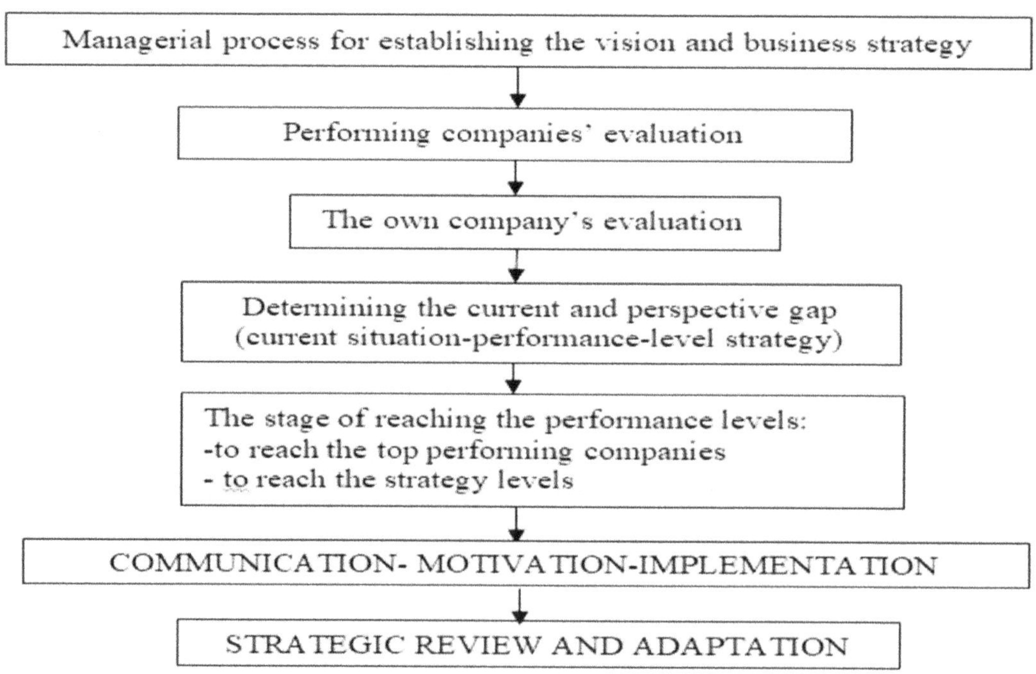

an aggregated set of products, functions and departments. The organization of a company can group and regroup several fields of activity, or it can divide fields of activity in autonomous decision centers. Under these conditions, the strategic segmentation is analyzed distinctly from the marketing segmentation, but both types of segmentation are found on the strategic management work table when a new business strategy dictated by the pressures of the sustainable economy is required.

Mainly, the marketing segmentation studies the activity sectors of the company in relation to the main competitors, it follows the structuring of the customers according to the behavior and motivation of purchase, suggests the adaptation of products and services to different groups of customers, usually causes short and medium term changes, while the strategic segmentation aims at the systemic analysis of the company's activities as a whole, it aims to divide the activities into homogeneous groups, according to social division of labor' s firm criteria (same technology, same markets, same competitors, same suppliers), it allows to highlight the employment of new business opportunities or giving up current activities, usually causes changes in the medium and long term in the company's internal structure (Fisk, 2008). In essence, the marketing segmentation aims to bring together the products and services

Table 1. Strategic segments' criteria

Strategic criteria	Identification elements	Content	
		Marketing segmentation	**Company's strategic segmentation**
Consumers	Products and services for large users are identified. Then the products and services are detailed by user classes and subclasses	Same consumers	Different consumers
Satisfied need/purchase criteria	The products that satisfy the same need are identified, and then the product groups that are purchased according to the same purchase criteria are identified.	Same needs	Different needs
Distribution channels	The contribution of the distribution channels at the level of the different efficiency indicators is identified	Same channel	Different channels
Competition	Identify the same competitors in the basic activities of the company. The directions for increasing the specialization are identified.	Same competitors	Different competitors
Market	Local, regional and national markets are identified and quantified. Criteria for increasing market share in existing markets and penetration in other markets are identified. Identify the markets from which the company is to retire.	Same market	Different market
Costs	The nature of the nature's activity specific costs, by cost centers, is identified and also detailed	Mostly shared costs	Dominant specific costs
Competences	The specific competences aspects specific toregarding the activity fields are identified.	Same competences	Different competences
Technology	The segments that are based on specific types of technology are identified.	Same technology	Different technology
Synergy	There are identified the activities that can be carried out together, but with greater efficiency, with major implications in improving productivity and reducing costs.	Strong	Relatively weak
Synthesis		**Same segment**	**Different segments**

Source: Proccesing after Atamer, Calori, 1993

within the same productive strategic segments, while the company's strategic segmentation has as its basic purpose the cutting of its strategic segments (Udrescu et al, 2018).

The criteria for identifying the strategic segments, whether they are marketing or structuring the company, as well as the common and differentiation aspects, are summarized in Table 1.

We consider that good segmentation is based on a correctly defined aggregation level. Segmentation should not be too global, but also, not too detailed (Gresoi et al, 2012). Too detailed segmentation leads to distortions in cost sharing and appreciation of synergy elements, and far too global segmentation overestimates the same factors, but slows the decision-making process in relation to the specificity of the competences gained in each activity. Strategic management is good to understand that any strategic segment is the result of supplying demand on request, and technology, costs, competences and synergy are factors that come from the supply direction and the customers, purchasing criteria, distribution and market come from demand analysis. If the demand is detailed, for example, a form of strategic myopia can be reached, in which the activities with the same demand type can be disturbed by very different offers (McEwen, 2008). In turn, the detailing and privileging of the offer can lead to uninspired cuts in its own segments already in operation. The company may think that it can build a new strategic niche, but the niche exists and becomes presentable only when there is a certain demand. This strategic mistake puts the company in the situation of wasting secure resources on an illusory market (Udrescu & Nastase, 2019).

Also, the company's management and production can be a major problem in the strategic segments' inventory. The head of a production unit can lead several strategic segments and, conversely, a single strategic segment can comprise several production operational segments. Any mismatch between the strategic segmentation of the company and its organizational structure can cause confusion, even blockages, affecting the natural requirements of clearly identifying the segments and defining with greater clarity and coherence of the strategies. Neglecting or ignoring the occurrence and intensification of competition between the managers of the operational units inevitably leads to affecting the managerial clairvoyance at different organizational levels. Thus, the opinions and evaluations of the operational managers can become divergent when the problem of identifying the competitors and mastering the specific market techniques is raised.

Since there are no successful infallible methods in strategic segmentation, responsible strategic management engages in iterative approaches, in which the result of any segmentation is permanently and professionally confronted with the effects it produces on the adopted strategy.

SOLUTIONS AND RECOMMENDATIONS

As the case may be, strategic management can decide for the following types of strategy: cost strategy, differentiation strategy, specialization strategy, concentration strategy, entrepreneurial strategy, technological strategy (Mockler, 2001).

The cost strategy prioritizes all the company's efforts towards the primary objectives of reducing, until minimizing, the costs, on cost centers. It covers all types of costs: production, research, marketing, administration. The entire strategic approach starts from the assumption that the company with the lowest costs is also the most competitive company, and the minimization of costs is transformed into a managerial approach of foundation and achievement of competitive advantage. In order to hope for a certain competitiveness, under the conditions of the sustainable economy, the company's strategic management is forced to control the main costs that affect the profit and loss account, throughout the economic cycle: supply, production and sale.

As a rule, the strategy of pursuing a competitive advantage by reducing costs is appropriate on the areas of activity where the effect of the experience is strong, the differentiation of the products is weak, and the market competition is centered on costs and prices. The differentiation strategy consists in achieving, in each of the activity areas in which the company is present on the market, a decisive and sustainable competitive advantage. Such a competitive advantage is ensured by the realization of the company's unique offer. This type of strategy is suitable for both fragmented areas and volume activities. In both the cost strategy and the differentiation strategy, the notion of cost is present, but the role of cost is different. Cost minimization is achieved through cost reduction policies, favorable exploitation of experience standards and the company adopting the diversification strategy will strive to achieve superior performance by managing the costs related to the uniqueness of the offer, by focusing costs in the specific costs category, through which it ensures a superior experience gap than the hard-to-overcome competition.

The specialization strategy is specific to the strategic management that chooses to gain an appropriate market position focusing on a single activity field. In general, specialization becomes a priority both for companies that have weakened their competitive position and for companies that are trying to limit themselves to imposing an extremely competitive activity. Depending on the situation, the strategic management adopts a strategy that either ensures the focus on a single activity, by abandoning other diversified activities, which aims to rapidly improve the competitive competence, or ensures the re-segmentation and centering on a niche where the company is well positioned and can ensure a certain financial balance.

The concentration strategy involves a activity domain's analysis and the adoption of an internal conduct of a domain's preferential support, when the same attention cannot be paid at the same time to all the domains. The basis of these strategies is the belief that it is possible that, in the conditions of the cantonment on a group of clients, the company will obtain a better economic efficiency than if it would be dispersed throughout the activities that characterize it.

The entrepreneurial strategy aims to create and build visions of extraordinary originality. This represents a creative human action regarding the initiation and implementation of new processes, to the detriment of the traditional analysis' actions by using adaptation skills. The expected result consists, as the case may be, in: single markets, unique products, unique resources and unique people (Petters & Waterman, 2011).

The technological strategy involves considering the technological novelty as a factor of competitive advantage. The technological evolution affects the strategic segmentation, ie the identification of the modules that compose the global activity and their analysis on competitive fields. Progressively, technological changes can cause border mutations between activities, either in the sense of distinction and individualization, or in the sense of assimilation and creation of unique segments. As such, the technology strategy can be at the origin of building a competitive advantage either by minimizing costs or by differentiating activity.

FUTURE RESEARCH DIRECTIONS

One of the research directions it would be to build a team and a company with complementary skills. It is important to ensure that the company is populated with quality human resources who are good at the five discovery skills. As the literature highlights, *„discovery-driven leaders need the delivery driven skills of people who excel at execution, not only do effective leaders of innovative teams understand their own constellation of discovery and delivery skills, they actively balance their weaknesses with other people's strengths."* (Dyer et al., 2011)

Another research direction based on the main objectives pointed out above, the authors believe that sustainable strategic management could be a problem solved for both business community and academic field. After analyzing worldwide specialized literature, it could be highlighted the fact that sustainable economy is based on sustainable activities in each field of activity, such as: accounting, engineering, tourism, education, management, marketing, artificial inteligence.

The research directions could continue with management models, that could quantify other future research in a sustainable economy, such as Blue Ocean Strategies and Disruptive Innovations, seen as new instruments for monitoring and measuring innovation's performance.

CONCLUSION

Since Romania has assumed the mission of adopting a political conduct of gradually assuming the environmental requirements contained in the European Union's Strategy for Sustainable Development, the sustainable economy has become a turbulent environment for the traditional Romanian companies. As a consequence, the strategic management of these companies has been in a situation to either perceive the meanings in which the general environmental policies will evolve, and in such cases it is necessary to adapt their own lucrative processes to predictable constraints of the environment, or to have the vision of the lucrative field qualitative change with obvious implications on the competitive advantage's domain.

For companies that have always adapted to the requirements of sustainable development, their strategic management aimed, as appropriate, to impose short, medium or long term strategies, which consisted in the organic incorporation of sustainable development practices, according to their requirements. They have the source in the external environment, in reaching an acceptable level according to taking into account some basic sustainable development indicators, generally accepted indicators, or near, equaling, even exceeding, the leading companies in the field, also based on the indicators established by sustainable development.

Since the sustainable development became the fundamental political option, the company's strategic management has been forced to focus on the following action directions: acquiring the conceptual framework with which sustainable development operates at the local, national and global level; assessing the current situation of natural, anthropic, human and other capital according to which the performances of sustainable development are measured; materializing a vision over time horizons, strictly following the logic of the challenges that come from the companies and institutions that are dedicated to sustainable development; analyzing the specific problems that the current company faces in this way of development in the process of moving to sustainable development, by eliminating the existing gaps in relation to the performance levels of the companies in the top of modernity; formulation of concrete strategies meant to ensure the implementation, monitoring and confirmation of the results in relation to the experience and practice established in the reference social and political environment.

Strategic management and organizational culture are everywhere studied as interdependent elements, with a close link between management, leadership, current and future performance and organizational culture. As soon as a new company is established, as soon as a new management strategy is implemented, we appreciate that conditions are created for the formation of a new organizational culture, which reflects the way of thinking and action of all, but under the authority of strategic management. In such circumstances, the strategic management has the duty that, with the formulation of the new visions and strategies, it will also express its own work conduct, a process by which it is transmitted on the managerial and execution stages subordinated to the own belief of what is about to happen, for the company to survive the changes and enjoy success.

The demands of the sustainable economy have thus become the cause of the entrepreneurial change, but also a fundamental criteria for appreciating the competitive advantage, the strategic management having the mission to first notice the threats of the new environment on the respective company, and by awareness of the strengths and weaknesses, to devise renewal strategies, so as to minimize the obvious vulnerabilities, as well as the possible ones.

The knowledge of the competitive situation and the awareness of the vulnerabilities are premises from which the strategic management can fulfill its forecasting purpose. The new state of affairs, at least at the national level, can suggest to strategic management the option of using benchmarking techniques, learning from leaders and competitors in the field, discovering best practices, copying or customizing them, increasing their effectiveness.

The strategic management of the company, under the pressure of the sustainable economy, becomes aware of the need to change to higher quality in production, to high competitiveness on the market, to a new relationship with the natural environment, opting, as the case may be, for the following types of strategy: cost strategy, strategy differentiation, specialization strategy, concentration strategy, entrepreneurial strategy, technological strategy.

Undoubtedly, the sustainable economy is friendly with the efficient and unmanaged strategic management with the one who does not find the path of qualitative adaptation, which in economic terms means bankruptcy.

REFERENCES

Adamson, P. A. (2010). *Brand Simple*. Publica Publishing House.

Ansoff, I. (1989). *Company's development strategies.* Organization's Edition.

Armstrong, M. (2004). *How to become a better manager.* Meteor Press Publishing House.

Atamer, T., & Calori, R. (1993). *Diagnosis and strategic decisions*. Dunod.

Clayton, C. M. (1997). Innovator' s Dilemma, Harvard Business School Press.

Colins, J. (2010). *Business excellence*. Curtea Veche Publishing House.

Covey, R. S. (2006). *The Ethics of the effective leader or the principle –based leadership.* ALLFA Publishing House.

Druker, P. (2010). *About decision and efficiency*. Curtea Veche Publishing House.

Dumitrescu, M. (2002). *Strategies and Strategic Management*. Economica Publishing House.

Dyer, J., Gregersen, H., & Christensen, C. M. (2011). The Innovators DNA, Mastering the five skills of disruptive innovators. Harvard Business Review Press.

Eppler, M. (2007). *Management's traps*. Polirom Publishing House.

Fisk, P. (2008). *Marketing genius*. Meteor Press Publishing House.

Gheorghe, A., & Udrescu, M. A. (2017). *Aspects regarding organizational behavior in the romanian tourism field*. International Symposium 10 years membership in the European Union- Analyses, methods, models regarding the results of Romania, Bucharest, Romania.

Gheorghe, A., & Udrescu, M. A. (2019). Governance in the EU Member, States in the Era of Big Data. In *25th PGV Network Conference*. Economica Publishing House.

Gordon, M. E. (2012). *Entrepreneurship*. Curtea Veche Publishing House.

Gresoi, S. G., & Gheorghe, A. (2011). Interdependencies between sustainable development and ecology. *International Journal of Academic Research in Accounting, Finance and Management Sciences, 1*(2), 25–32.

Gresoi, S. G., Gheorghe, A., & Buiga, A. (2012). *Production Management-Theoretrical Synthesis and Case Studies*. Terra Nostra Publishing House.

Jenson, R. (2004). *The success pyramid*. Codecs Publishing House.

Maciarello, I. A., & Druker, P. (2016). *Training course for managers*. Litera Publishing House.

Manfred, F., & Kets de Vries, R. (2001), *The leadership mystique: a user's for the human enterprise*. Financial Times.

Marcu, F., & Manea, C. (1978). *Neologisms Dictionary*. Romanian Academy Publishing House.

McEwen, J. W. (2008). *Brand strength*. ALLFA Publishing House.

Mockler, J. R. (2001). *Multinational Strategic Management. An integrative process based on context*. Economica Publishing House.

NCSD. (2008). *The National Center for Sustainable Development, Romania's National Strategy for Sustainable Development*. Horizons 2013-2020-2-30, Bucharest, 11.

Neagu, C. (2017). *Human Resources Management*. Tritonic Publishing House.

Neagu, C., & Udrescu, M. (2008). *Organization's Management*. Tritonic Publishing House.

Newton, R. (2009). *Change management step by step*. All Publishing House.

Pascale, R.T. (1985, Winter). The Paradox of Corporate Culture. *California Management Review*.

Peters, T. J., & Watterman, H. R. (2011). *In search of excellence*. Meteor Press Publishing House.

Prahalad, C. K. (2010). *The treasure from the pyramids basis*. Publica Publishing House.

Schein, E. (1985). *Organizational Culture and leadership*. Jossey-Bass Publishers.

Sexton, D. (2012). *Branding*. Curtea Veche Publishing House.

Sustainable Development Strategy, Europe's Council, 9th June 2006.

Thompson, A., Jr., & Strickland III. (1987). Strategic management. Concept and Cases. Irwin Homewood.

Tracy, B. (2010). *How the best leaders lead*. Curtea Veche Publishing House.

Udrescu, M., & Năstase, D. (2019). *Research, forecasts and seminars in marketing*. The Romanian Academy of Scientists Publishing House.

Udrescu, M., & Popescu-Cruceru, A. (2018). *Logistics and logistic subsystems of the company*. The Romanian Academy of Scientists Publishing House.

Udrescu, M. A., & Gheorghe, A. (2016). Benchmarketing-Fashionable term concerning traditional processes. *Academic Journal of Economic Research*, *2*(2), 100–113.

Udrescu, M. A., & Gheorghe, A. (2016). Management's Involvement in the New Products' Development. Simpozionul Internațional "Research –Forecast- Decision in the Social- Economic System", Bucharest, Romania.

Udrescu, M. A., & Gheorghe, A. (2017). Motivation and organizational behavior. Staff between Value Added and Conflict-Generating Losses. *Academic Journal of Economic Studies (Glasgow, Scotland)*, *3*(2), 55–59.

Udrescu, M. A., Neagu, C., Popescu-Cruceru, A., & Gheorghe, A. (2016). *General Management- Concepts and Case Studies*. Artifex Publishing House.

Ziglar, Z. (2011). *Beyond the peak*. Curtea Veche Publishing House.

ADDITIONAL READING

Gheorghe, A., & Iftime, S. (2013). *Strategic Planning of Ecotourism in Europe and the Development of its Products in Europe, Knowledge Horizons-Economics, 5(1)*. Pro Universitaria Publishing House.

Gresoi, S., & Gheorghe, A. (2013). *Continuous Improvement Strategy- Viable Strategy for Romanian Companies, Knowledge Horizons-Economics, 5(1)*. Pro Universitaria Publishing House.

Militaru, Gh. (2005). *Organizational behavior*. Economica Publishing House.

Parvu, F., & Gheorghe, A. (2014). Increasing Sălaj County tourism development through the implementation of strategies based on the ecotourism products. *Business Excellence and Management.*, *4*(1), 22–27.

Popescu, D. (2013). Organizational behavior, Second Edition, Management Collection, ASE Publishing House, Bucharest, Romania, 101-124.

KEY TERMS AND DEFINITIONS

Organizational Culture (OC): Represents a set made of cultural values found in a company that refer to the employees' mentality, attitudes, and personal beliefs.

Responsible Management (RO): Represents an improved management, targeting both the quality of the managerial act, as well as the socio-economic and environmental benefits, both local and global.

Strategic Management (SM): Represents a accumulation of actions carried out following the decision regarding the implementation of plans and projects, both in the medium and long term, and in the short term, in order to achieve the fundamental objectives of the company.

Sustainable Strategic Management (SSM): Defined as a full connection of the company to a new philosophy of political, environmental and social development, namely sustainable development, which represents the central element of the company's competitive environment.

Chapter 12
Importance of Value of the Company for Development Business

Lavinia Essen Yildirim
Ankara University, Turkey

Diana Mândricel
Titu Maiorescu University, Romania

ABSTRACT

The value of the company is necessary to become the key element in any entity development strategy. In this context, the action of the market contemporary forces determines certain behavior of the companies, which become more and more engaged in the resources, quality, customers, and suppliers, in which the top role is played by the top quality management. At the same time, the value of an enterprise or rather of its shares is no longer calculated as the sum of the values of its assets but determined by its ability to generate economic benefits, and the balance sheet loses interest in the income statement. This chapter analyses the new research directions regarding the value of the company in managing business risks.

INTRODUCTION

The human society, as a whole, often considered and not without reason an extremely complex mechanism, had and has to face the challenges of first stringent problems - the implementation of an integrated system of performance indicators to accurately determine the value of a company. (Stettina & Hörz, 2015; Chan, Shaffer & Snape, 2004).

One aspect of great importance to the existence, perpetuation and rise or fall of companies in the economy of any country is their contribution to creating new value, or, in other words, the value added in order to be more relevant, needs to be examined closely, along with the number of employees (Becker & Huselid, 2006; Alhyari, Alazab, Venkatraman, Alazab & Alazab, 2013).

DOI: 10.4018/978-1-7998-4637-6.ch012

The framework in which the economic information is optimized is represented by the information system, whose decisive role is to provide the necessary information network to the entities involved in the economic process in order to minimize the risk and the uncertainty, thus facilitating the decision making relevant at any managerial level.

Most often the appreciation of the value of a company is based on analysis of profit and loss account. The option for researching the profit and loss account as a performance model, defines the system of evaluation and presentation of the result (Akgün, Keskin & Byrne, 2009).

Enterprises activity is not confined to any country to production in the strict sense; they participate in both exports and imports in order to achieve the purposes of the owners. In addition, it should be noted that between them, the most important place is micro (Arsenault & Faerman, 2014; Fisher, 2010). Due to its' small size and simpler organizational structures, they can make many changes during their existence, that allow them to operate in conditions of economic efficiency. Another important advantage of small and medium size organizations refers to their innovative potential in the technical, technological and managerial view (Agha, Alrubaiee & Jamhour, 2012).

Value analysis of the company is another technique of organizing and processing the values of individuals and organizational culture (Amagoh, 2008; Taticchi, Tonelli & Cagnazzo, 2010). This method provides information about what people value more or less, about what they value as desirable in correspondence with certain intentions, expectations and ideals. In organizations where employees are more concerned with meeting the basic, elementary needs, their behavioral choices are restricted, which leads to a decrease in their contribution to increasing the efficiency of their work (Deutsch & Silcox, 2003; Ashkanasy, 2011). In strong economic firms, employees have higher aspirations, both spiritually and materially, which leads to their participation in organizational performance (Olson, Slater, Tomas & Hult, 2005; Andriole, 2010).

Successful companies increasingly manifest themselves as true open systems, whose position in the market depends not only on their internal resources, but also their relations with configuration and external entities with complementary skills. External network of the company is basically an extension of the internal borders between the two types of networks becoming increasingly difficult to identify.

This chapter proves that if the company ceases to expand at a cost under the cost of trading in the market, but equally the cost of organizing the transaction by another firm, both procedures may allow the organization of production at a price below the market. One can formulate the conclusion that if in a balanced approach and patrimonial, the result measures the variation of the patrimony owned by the company, the economic approach leads to the construction of a result as a performance indicator.

Background

Considered a socio-cultural stake, the accounting based on the information provided reflects both the financial position and the performance of the entity, becoming the main informational source of the information system through its quality as a component of the economic records, along with the operational and statistical records.

In the light of the new conditions generated by digital economy, any company, no matter the field it has as operation, rules the principles of effectiveness and efficiency, competitive party, functional and decisional autonomy, and that of developing activities that suit the market requests (Cocca & Alberti, 2010). Consequently, due to changes fever, due to their rapid succession rhythm, companies are compelled to frequently reorganize their structure, to continuous adapt to new trends determined by the contemporary scientific and technical progress, by the intensification of the contest within the national and international level, by human taste development and change in needs.

An incursion into the specialized literature that addresses performance indicators to accurately determine the value of a company allows the detachment of an entire suite of theories:

- according to the assumed risk theory, it is considered that the economic profit represents a reward of the entrepreneur (the company) for the risk he assumes with the initiation or development of the activity. In this sense, it is argued that if the other factors of production are rewarded (wages, interest), the residual part of the income is the right of the entrepreneur based on the risk of the activity that involves in frequent cases loss. As a result of the risk involved in the activity, the potential profitability of the production must be sufficiently high to encourage the entrepreneur to initiate, develop and conduct such an activity;
- according to this theory, innovation is the source of profit: the entrepreneur who produces and sells a new product, realizes a more efficient manufacturing technology, which is the premise of obtaining a higher profit. This means obtaining profit as a result of reducing costs or by selling higher quality goods, unaffected by the prices existing on the market.

Since the value of an enterprise or rather of its shares is no longer calculated as the sum of the values of its assets, but determined by its ability to generate economic benefits, the balance sheet loses interest in the income statement, which better translates this skill. In such an approach, the result no longer expresses a variation of the patrimony but becomes a performance indicator.

In a competitive environment, performance cannot be judged without being placed in the context of essential economic imperatives: effectiveness and efficiency.

Anyway, the display of efficiency in the economical field may take different shapes, as follows: the output increase per man-shift; reducing the consumption of raw materials, fuel and consumables, reducing the freight costs, increase profitability of the enterprises, improving the quality of the products (Hurley, 2002; Ahearne, Lam, Mathieu & Bolander, 2010). Thus, the efficiency is expressed upon case by its multitude of forms and partial aspects, but especially through them reunite series.

Economic efficiency must represent a basis component of the entire economic activity due to the limited character of the resources which have to be wisely managed so as to ensure the economic progress and the improvement of mankind living standards (Davila, 2012). Within a market economy context, the economic efficiency must be viewed both from the micro and macro economical point of view. The economic efficiency, especially the investment and fixed capital, have a foresight character, fact that guarantees a particular importance in taking economic decisions. Decisions shall be taken based on the existence of several project variants, creating the possibility of choosing the most efficient one. The economic efficiency represents the main qualitative factor of the economic growth as it ensures the absolute boost of the effects using the same effort volume input.

The economical efforts should be analyzed from the following points of view; planning in time, financing sources, report of the import investment versus the total investment, degree of availability of certain resources, renewing potential, consequences of these expenses upstream and downstream the activity where they are meant to be used (Cameron & Quinn, 2011). Last but not the least, we have to bear in mind that the consumed resources are expressed in different measuring units (pc, hrs. / man; m^3, tons etc.)

The concept of efficiency has been practically introduced in all socio-human activities, so, we can easily discuss today about economic, social and ecological efficiency (Tallon & Pinsonneault, 2011). From the social prospect, a system is deemed as efficient if it's capable to focalize within the social and economic circuit all the necessary resources, if it is able to optimally distribute them on different fields and branches, to manage them with maximum effectiveness so as to satisfy the social need at her highest point.

Social efforts materialized in educational, cultural, sanitary and social assistance programmers, correlated with the social, individual and collective effects are defining the concept of social efficiency (Behery, Jabeen & Parakandi, 2014). The physical state of the population, degree of civilization, social security and protection, welfare expressed by the living standard and the quality of socio- ecological life are all upshots justifying the distribution of resources for the mankind benefit.

The actual economic efficiency includes natural environment protection and preservation exploiting the resources in order to study the ecological balance, to adopt sets of measures preventing and eliminating negative effects caused by disturbing factors and maintaining a life friendly environment (Behery, Jabeen & Parakandi, 2014; Basten & Haamann, 2018). Feature of the environment protection, the ecological efficiency expresses the attempts that have to be made in order to meet the natural environment parameters with the normal evolution standards, imposed by the ecological balance.

A minute assessment of any economic activity efficiency implies a systemic approach that sets off economic, political, social or ecological aspects, having in mind the multiple set of effects created up and down the specific subject activity.

THE IMPORTANCE OF VALUE OF THE COMPANY FOR DEVELOPMENT BUSINESS

One of the major tasks of management in perceiving the value of the company is the maintenance of balance for satisfying the investors' interests (shareholders) and workers (personnel). The specific sensitivity of the company, its distinctiveness and rapid transformation of customers' preferences justifies the systemic and dynamic approach of the efficiency, fact that takes into consideration the premises of a rational use of resources and their preservation in order to maintain the eco balance and the mankind health (Hartnell, Ou & Kinicki, 2011).

Any activity plan, (production, investment, promotion of the technical progress, organizational, purchasing and dispatching) implies several achieving methods (Rowland & Hall, 2014). At its turn, each modality has at its incipit point numerous project variants, characterized by a variety of information regarding efforts, effects, the existing report between, duration of completion, period till achieving the expected socio-economic effects (Tong & Arvey, 2015). Next, a system of economic indicators is used to choose the best variant quantitatively and as much as possible qualitative. The need for using a system of indicators is imposed by the complex character of the economic efficiency as each part of it reflects a certain criterion of economic efficiency (Kaplan & Norton, 2006; Tapanainen, 2012).

The cluster of general indicators of the entire economic activity includes indicators that characterize the broad efficiency of the economic activity, despite the level of achieving (workshop, shop, company, national economy, activity field etc.). The main indicators belonging to this group are the profit arte and the expenses at a 1000 Euro production (income).

This particular indicator helps in reflecting the totality of the final effects (from certain activities), as well as the totality of the resources consumed, no matter their nature– human resource, material or financial – exploited for the welfare of that specific activity. The indicator calculated in this manner perfectly expresses the influence of each factor part of the production process and thus, favored the achieving of that precise profit. It might be calculated for the entire commercial unit as well as for each kind or product individually.

In relation to this indicator it is worth mentioning that for some economic analysis it is taken into account instead of production costs the total volume of the production capital allotted which contains the fixed capital and the working capital of the commercial society.

In order to evaluate the value of the company when exploiting the fixed capital, it is normally used a system of indicators related to: dynamics, structural and functional state of the fixed capital; the extensively and the efficient of the equipment based on the synthetically efficiency indicators.

As the economic efficiency growth calls for supplementary investment, the appraisal methodology of the efficiency within the e industry must follow the accuracy of all investment efforts, especially of the multiple economic effects, direct or indirect. In this view, the evaluation of the economic efficiency is achieved by calling a complex system of indicators, system that includes main indicators in the static and dynamic approach, to which we add a number of indicators specific to the industry.

The Economic Value Added (EVA) method was proposed for the first time Stern Stewart & Co. in 1991, and then developed over 90 years as an internal indicator of business performance measurement for determining the efficiency of capital. EVA "provides a common language for managers in discussions about creating value, and because it is widely accepted and used in financial circles, may increase the legitimacy of a company in financial markets as an indicator of the ability of a company to create value, or, conversely, destroy it during a certain period of time" (Anand & Kodali, 2010).

Stern Stewart has developed this model to help managers incorporate two basic principles in making decisions (Chen & Fu, 2008). The first is that the main financial goal of any company should be to increase shareholder value; the second is that the value of a company depends on the amount by which income exceeds the cost of capital.

EVA is defined in the European Management Journal as "the difference between net sales and the amount of operating expenses, taxes and cost of capital (capital charges), where the cost of capital is calculated as a weighted average cost of capital multiplied by total invested capital. Basically, EVA increases when the average cost of capital is lower than the rate of return on assets (return on net assets), and vice versa" (Alstete & Beutell, 2018).

EVA calculation, based on the following indicators: WACC (Weighted Average Cost of Capital - Weighted average cost of capital) - weighted average cost of debt, after tax and equity (cost of equity); ROIC = ratio of capital invested and at night (which is similar rate ROI).

As shown, EVA model was developed initially as an internal measure of performance used by managers to help them make decisions about investments. In practice has shown that an investment project that causes higher incomes than the net cost of its financing and thus generate profit, not necessarily lead to increased company value (Tapanainen, Hallanoro, Päivärinta & Salmela, 2008). A company should be concerned only those investment projects capable of generating a positive EVA or even increasing, because it will increase shareholder value. Thus, it becomes clear that applying the principles of this method companies should change their priorities.

Creating value for shareholders involves maximizing the difference between the market value of the company and the nominal value of shares (initial investment of shareholders), this difference is called market value added (MVA) - market value added or the present value of EVA, and is essentially the difference between the capital that investors have brought in the original company and the amount of money they can get far by selling shares they hold (Yadav & Sagar, 2013). Maximizing the wealth gap actually increases the company's shareholders. The difference between market value and book value of the company is attributable, as shown before intangible assets that are usually neglected by accounting documents of the company.

Market value added is a measure of external performance, while EVA is an internal performance indicator which measures the firm, in terms of the market (Sarabi, Naghizadeh, Liu & Liu, 2016). EVA was created to remove MVA shortcomings, namely that the latter indicator expresses the company's value based on performance in the previous year and the current situation so that a company can register a positive MVA even if investments made in the current or to be made are bad.

Since the value added measure has not been fully achieved either in this way, due to factors that could not be determined (to establish whether the drive way destroy or create value or measurement of intellectual potential), has developed a new method, VAIC (Value added intellectual coefficient), which was designed to assist managers in determining the potential of their companies, based on current performance (Sementelli, 2016).

Companies have recognized the importance of intellectual capital as a key factor for success, looking for ways to measure and control this factor (Jung, Nam, Lee & Kim, 2016). Financial performance measurement is not sufficient that reflects how the profit is due to intellectual capital. In the knowledge economy, wealth is created through a combination of services and products that generate value. Each company has its unique set of knowledge, skills, values and solutions, all intangible resources. Monitoring and management of these resources can be made with value creation efficiency analysis because it is a priority for managers to obtain and maintain productivity and efficiency in the enterprise. VAIC indicates value creation efficiency of all resources, expressing a firm's intellectual abilities. The more qualitative resources (human and intellectual capital) were used, the higher the value creation efficiency of the company.

VAIC depends on the structure of human capital employed and the results they have achieved in the past (patents, licenses, innovation, customer relationship), the value added (VA = operating profit + depreciation + cost of salaries and depreciation), the costs employees (salaries, bonuses, training) and the value of assets involved in the work (Lin, Peng & Kao, 2008).

VAIC analysis is based on two essential resources: capital employed (physical and financial) and intellectual capital. Both are treated as investments and are creating value. Human capital consists of all employees, their organization and their ability to create value that can assess the market. Performance Monitoring equity and intellectual capital based on VAIC analysis, based on financial results: value added (difference between operating revenue and expenses from outside the enterprise). Expenditure on salaries is not included in the calculation because they are treated as investments.

To calculate the value creation efficiency of the two factors used indicators: EEC (capital employed efficiency = VA / EC) - the efficiency of capital employed, HCE (human capital efficiency = VA / HC) - the efficiency of human capital SCE (structural capital efficiency = SC / VA) - structural capital efficiency. SCE is calculated differently for HCE and the ECA, is inversely proportional to the efficiency of human capital (Schneider & Somers, 2006). These indicators show how much value was created from a monetary unit. If the indicators are aggregated to obtain VAIC, it will be shown the overall effectiveness of a company or intellectual abilities.

Another element that contributes to increasing the value of a company is the quality of the products which represents the final expression of the production processes (Henczel, 2002). It is also synthesizing the technical level, the operational and the economical performances, as well the esthetical ones. In substance, the quality represents the level to which the totality of a certain product properties is made worth. It is the expression of the degree in which the society needs are satisfied, by means of the products technical, economical and esthetical parameters.

For an accurate assessment of the quality we select those properties which significantly determine the degree in which the product satisfies the consumer requirements. That constitutes the quality features.

By measuring or evaluating the quality features that essentially contribute to the way the product is estimated, we obtain the quality indicators (Homburg & Pflesser, 2000). Concluding, the quality indicators of the textile products are grouped in: technical, esthetical, hygienic-sanitary and comfort indicators, utilization and operational ones and nevertheless, the economical ones. Every single one is ascribed in standards, tasks books and specifications.

The analytical side, on the contrary, has as an objective the analysis of the profitability of the activity of the company, both at its level as well as at the level of the various elements that compose it. This analysis requires the use of purely internal concepts whose content is freely defined according to the own conventions of each enterprise and which are therefore outside any standardization.

SOLUTIONS AND RECOMMENDATIONS

The practice has shown that besides the financial statements, the scope of the research is also oriented towards the situations that contain non-financial data, which bring more clarity in the performance assessment. In this regard, we note the tools used by management control, in order to impose on managers - and intensify their efforts in setting realistic goals.

In this sense, managerial accounting plays an essential role, being appreciated as a system of reporting the information it classifies according to the areas of responsibility within the organization. Studies have shown that managerial accounting tools have proven to be extremely efficient in performance appraisal.

At the same time, managerial culture highlights the needs and aspirations of an entity's managers and reflects the behavior, personality of stakeholders or strong leaders, influencing the decisions and actions of managers on different hierarchical levels. Managers are those who are directly involved in the process of building and developing organizational culture, discovering strong motivation, which leads to the establishment of norms, standards, and codes of conduct in accordance with their values. It is also why they agree to be evaluated and motivated, as do all the actors involved, in relation to established standards.

Placed in this context, performance is an unstable balance between efficiency and productivity. An enterprise is, in theory, performance when it is both productive and effective. Perfect correspondence is never attainable due to the subjective and unstable nature of external expectations. If efficiency were identical with productivity, this means that the source of expectations would have become endogenous to the enterprise and not external.

FUTURE RESEARCH DIRECTIONS

Absolute economic value does not exist (Behery, Jabeen & Parakandi, 2014). As a result, we are pleased to measure a level of performance in relative value expressed by the deviation, efficiency-productivity. Considering only productivity, entrepreneurs do not they just transplant the organizational models and put them under control through a lot of management rates, thinking that this is the only successful solution. This is a behavior that prevents the identification of the real problems that arise at the enterprise level. If the companies establish their efficiency as a priority, they voluntarily situate themselves in a totally different logic of action, to create and ensure the sustainability of an activity by understanding market expectations. This voluntary behavior favors external action. The chosen solutions derive from a preliminary analysis of the external constraints that must be removed.

As the performance of an enterprise is the result of a double dynamic, theoretically two important rules should be taken into account: the increase of the productivity must be accompanied, to a small extent, by an increase of the efficiency; the higher the productivity, the higher the relative efficiency increase must increase.

An enterprise must be not only effective but also efficient. efficiency information is of particular interest to both managers and owners. Both categories of users, want to know not only the size of the result but also the efficiency of the use of resources.

CONCLUSION

Today, companies develop their activity within an environment which is permanently changing, especially from the technological point of view and due to the market conditions (Basten & Haamann, 2018).

The realities brought into light by the present epoch determined the rise of significant concerns from the economical theoreticians and practitioners side in order to increase the companies' efficiency. They have also generated the occurrence of specialized organizations primarily dealing with managing resources and limiting their consumption correlated with human society needs. Their main focusing direction is towards finding out alternative, durable solutions, so as to ensure that the generations to come have at least equal chances of existence, knowledge and development. The classical approach of organizations, without a complex tactic on long and medium term cannot confer them any chance in expanding the business, the main issue being now the survival of the fittest.

To a large extent, financial reporting is based on estimates and arbitrary rules. Because the accounting records are not accurate, in practice certain conventions are respected to facilitate the interpretation of financial reports by users.

The appreciation of the value of a company should not be limited to the mere finding of profit, but in relation to the efficiency and efficiency of the use of resources. An enterprise is practically performance, if it is profitable, effective and efficient.

REFERENCES

Agha, S., Alrubaiee, L., & Jamhour, M. (2012). Effect of core competence on competitive advantage and organizational performance. *International Journal of Business and Management*, *7*(1), 192–204.

Ahearne, M., Lam, S. K., Mathieu, J. E., & Bolander, W. (2010). Why are some sales people better at adapting to organizational change? *Journal of Marketing*, *74*(3), 65–79. doi:10.1509/jmkg.74.3.065

Akgün, A. E., Keskin, H., & Byrne, J. (2009). Organizational emotional capability, product and process innovation, and firm performance: An empirical analysis. *Journal of Engineering and Technology Management*, *26*(3), 103–130. doi:10.1016/j.jengtecman.2009.06.008

Alhyari, S., Alazab, M., Venkatraman, S., Alazab, M., & Alazab, A. (2013). Performance evaluation of e-government services using balanced scorecard. *Benchmarking*, *20*(4), 512–536. doi:10.1108/BIJ-08-2011-0063

Alstete, J. W., & Beutell, N. J. (2018). Designing learning spaces for management education: A mixed methods research approach. *Journal of Management Development*, *37*(2), 201–211. doi:10.1108/JMD-08-2017-0247

Amagoh, F. (2008). Perspectives on organizational change: Systems and complexity theories. *The Innovation Journal*, *13*(3), 1–14.

Anand, G., & Kodali, R. (2010). A mathematical model for the evaluation of roles and responsibilities of human resources in a lean manufacturing environment. *International Journal of Human Resources Development and Management*, *10*(1), 63–100. doi:10.1504/IJHRDM.2010.029447

Andriole, S. J. (2010). Business impact of Web 2.0 Technologies. *Communications of the ACM*, *53*(12), 67–79. doi:10.1145/1859204.1859225

Arsenault, P., & Faerman, S. R. (2014). Embracing paradox in management: The value of the competing values framework. *Organizational Management Journal*, *11*(3), 147–158. doi:10.1080/15416518.2014.949614

Ashkanasy, N. (2011). International happiness; a multilevel perspective. *The Academy of Management Perspectives*, (February), 23–29.

Becker, B. E., & Huselid, M. A. (2006). Strategic human resources management: Where do we go from here? *Journal of Management*, *32*(6), 898–925. doi:10.1177/0149206306293668

Behery, M., Jabeen, F., & Parakandi, M. (2014). Adopting a contemporary performance management system. *International Journal of Productivity and Performance Management*, *63*(1), 22–43. doi:10.1108/IJPPM-07-2012-0076

Cameron, K. S., & Quinn, R. E. (2011). *Diagnosing and Changing Organizational Culture: Based on the Competing Values Framework*. Jossey-Bass.

Chan, L. L., Shaffer, M. A., & Snape, E. (2004). In search of sustained competitive advantage: The impact of organizational culture, competitive strategy and human resource management practices on firm performance. *International Journal of Human Resource Management*, *15*(1), 17–35. doi:10.1080/0958519032000157320

Chen, H. M., & Fu, P. C. (2008). A systematic framework for performance appraisal and compensation strategy. *Human Systems Management*, *27*(2), 161–175. doi:10.3233/HSM-2008-0674

Cocca, P., & Alberti, M. (2010). A framework to assess performance measurement in SMEs. *International Journal of Productivity and Performance Management*, *59*(2), 186–200. doi:10.1108/17410401011014258

Davila, A. (2012). New trends in performance measurement and management control. *In Performance Measurement and Management Control. Global Issues (Washington, D.C.)*, *25*, 65–87.

Deutsch, P., & Silcox, B. (2003). Learning from other libraries: Benchmarking to assess library performance. *Information Outlook*, *7*(7), 18–25.

Fisher, C. D. (2010). Happiness at Work. *International Journal of Management Reviews*, *12*(4), 384–412. doi:10.1111/j.1468-2370.2009.00270.x

Hartnell, C. A., Ou, A. Y., & Kinicki, A. (2011). Organizational culture and organizational effectiveness: A meta-analytic investigation of the competing values framework's theoretical suppositions. *The Journal of Applied Psychology*, *96*(4), 677–694. doi:10.1037/a0021987 PMID:21244127

Henczel, S. (2002). Benchmarking – measuring and comparing for continuous improvement. *Information Outlook*, *6*(7), 12–20.

Homburg, C., & Pflesser, C. (2000). A Multiple Layer Model of Market-Oriented Organizational Culture: Measurement Issues and Performance Outcomes. *JMR, Journal of Marketing Research*, *37*(4), 449–462. doi:10.1509/jmkr.37.4.449.18786

Hurley, R. F. (2002). Putting people back into organizational learning. *Journal of Business and Industrial Marketing*, *17*(4), 270–281. doi:10.1108/08858620210431679

Kaplan, R. S., & Norton, D. P. (2006). How to implement a new strategy without disrupting your organization. *Harvard Business Review*, *84*(3), 100. doi:10.1108d.2006.05622had.002 PMID:16515159

Lin, C. H., Peng, C. H., & Kao, D. T. (2008). The innovativeness effect of market orientation and learning orientation on business performance. *International Journal of Manpower*, *29*(8), 752–772. doi:10.1108/01437720810919332

Olson, E. M., Slater, S. F., Tomas, G., & Hult, M. (2005). The performance implications of fit among business strategy, marketing organization structure, and strategic behavior. *Journal of Marketing*, *69*(3), 49–65. doi:10.1509/jmkg.69.3.49.66362

Rowland, C., & Hall, R. (2014). Management learning, performance and reward: Theory and practice revisited. *Journal of Management Development*, *33*(4), 342–356. doi:10.1108/JMD-08-2012-0110

Schneider, M., & Somers, M. (2006). Organizations as complex adaptive systems: Implications of complexity theory for leadership research. *The Leadership Quarterly*, *17*(4), 351–365. doi:10.1016/j.leaqua.2006.04.006

Stettina, C. J., & Hörz, J. (2015). Agile portfolio management: An empirical perspective on the practice in use. *International Journal of Project Management*, *33*(1), 140–152. doi:10.1016/j.ijproman.2014.03.008

Tallon, P. P., & Pinsonneault, A. (2011). Competing Perspectives on the Link Between Strategic Information Technology Alignment and Organizational Agility: Insights from a Mediation Model. *Management Information Systems Quarterly*, *35*(2), 463–486. doi:10.2307/23044052

Tapanainen, T., Hallanoro, M., Päivärinta, J., & Salmela, H. (2008). Towards an Agile IT Organization: A Review of Prior Literature. In *Proceedings of the 2nd European Conference on Information Management and Evaluation* (pp. 425-432). London, UK: Academic Conferences Limited.

Taticchi, P., Tonelli, F., & Cagnazzo, L. (2010). Performance measurement and management: A literature review and a research agenda. *Measuring Business Excellence*, *14*(1), 4–18. doi:10.1108/13683041011027418

Tong, Y. K., & Arvey, R. D. (2015). Managing complexity via the Competing Values Framework. *Journal of Management Development*, *34*(6), 653–673. doi:10.1108/JMD-04-2014-0029

Yadav, N., & Sagar, M. (2013). Performance measurement and management frameworks. *Business Process Management Journal*, *19*(6), 947–971. doi:10.1108/BPMJ-01-2013-0003

ADDITIONAL READING

Basten, D., & Haamann, T. (2018). Approaches for Organizational Learning: A Literature Review. *SAGE Open*, *8*(3), 1–20. doi:10.1177/2158244018794224

Jung, J., Nam, C., Lee, E., & Kim, S. (2016). Subculture by autonomy and group cohesion and its effect on job satisfaction of R&D professionals in an R&D organization. *Journal of Management & Organization*, *22*(2), 154–172. doi:10.1017/jmo.2015.20

Sarabi, A., Naghizadeh, P., Liu, Y., & Liu, M. (2016). Risky business: Fine-grained data breach prediction using business profiles. *Journal of Cybersecurity*, *2*(1), 15–28. doi:10.1093/cybsec/tyw004

Sementelli, J. (2016). OD, change management, and the a priori: Introducing parrhesia. *Journal of Organizational Change Management*, *29*(7), 1083–1096. doi:10.1108/JOCM-12-2015-0234

KEY TERMS AND DEFINITIONS

Environmental Characteristics: The external factors that may limit or support a company's activities.

Financial Risks: These types of risk may reflect inadequate or unclear definition of strategies and objectives of the organization.

Organisational Performance: Elements affecting company performance such as financial and marketing factors, return on sales, return on investment, etc.

Chapter 13
The Role of Controlling in the Business Environment

Ibrahim Oba
Ahmadu Bello University, Niger

Mirela Anca Postole
Titu Maiorescu University, Romania

ABSTRACT

Environmental changes and especially the development of the digital economy have posed real existential questions to businesses, provoked strategic reflection, and made the emergence of controlling efficient. The objective of this chapter was to explore the role of controlling in the business environment and generalize a reflection on strategy and controlling in the life of companies. The results show that controlling has a significant role in enhancing the corporate governance pillars in companies, and the successes of corporate governance requires compliance with all elements of internal control.

INTRODUCTION

Controlling, along with accounting, is a management science (Mikalef & Pateli, 2017). The information available to the control centers supports the decisions of the managers and allows the evaluation of the behavior of the actors. In fact, management control has become a discipline related to both management and management accounting, devoted to examining the canonical forms of business structure (Awais & Hussain, 2015).

The concept of controlling appeals to various instruments, of influence and less of direct control within a hierarchy. Verification, of course, can be part of the whole. In this sense, controlling is a result, a consequence of a power situation, coming from within organization or other source (Elbannan, 2009).

However, in the enterprise regarded as a set of parties and at the same time as a unitary whole, controlling is the human activity of continual attempt to make the responsibilities, decisions and actions of different managers coherent (Marlin & Geiger, 2012). The coherence process represents the coordination of the interrelationships between the assembly of parts and the different components, and the result is

DOI: 10.4018/978-1-7998-4637-6.ch013

the degree of coherence achieved. As a result, controlling controls the good balance between the differentiation of the parties and their integration through individual self-control and collective self-control (Fadilah, 2013).

Controlling has evolved, become autonomous with respect to the techniques of control of deviations and adjustment of budgets, and today the theorists and practitioners see it rather as a system of behavior regulation (Young, 2002). It exists in the context of a contractual approach to delegating responsibilities and relies on a set of remote behavior control techniques.

In the long term, controlling refers to strategic planning (Aguilera & Jackson, 2003). This includes a complete study of the possible options, an accounting of the treatments that are retained, a reaffirmation of the structure of the company and consequently of its operating and capital expenditures. The control associated with the strategic planning is oriented mainly to the relevance of the objectives set (Clarke, 2004).

In the short term, controlling is about budgetary control (Bhimani, 2008). It represents the set of piloting techniques that allow to orient the management of the company towards achieving the previously defined objectives. Budgetary control is one of the techniques of management control that allows, starting from a decentralization of responsibilities, ensuring control within a budgetary exercise, of all the activities of the company, translated into monetary units (Johnstone & Rupley, 2011).

Controlling in the French sense has a double meaning: verification (carried out by the management controller) and holding control (exercised by the manager). So, is management control what the management controller does or the purpose of the process that powers it? The purpose is to allow managers to keep management. However, there are value management controllers that can perform both functions (Weygandt, Kimmel & Kieso, 2011).

The objective of this chapter was to explore the role of internal control in enhancing the corporate governance and supervise the functionality of the implementation of the corporate government principles. The results show that the internal control has a significant role in enhancing the corporate governance pillars in companies, and the successes of corporate governance requires compliance with all elements of internal control.

Background

Controlling is a circular system of rules that helps to achieve the objectives of the company, avoiding surprises and signaling in time the dangers that require corrective measures (Zikmund, 2000).

Alongside governance and risk management, internal control is the third major component of corporate governance (Monks & Minow, 2004). A good corporate government depends on risk management to understand the issues with which the organization is confronted and the internal control for fulfilling its objectives (Cheng, 2008).

In practice, every organization wants to implement these three ideals, corporate governance, risk management and the internal control system, whereas internal audit is the key component of its supervision (Hoitash, Hoitash & Bedard, 2009).

More specifically, corporate governance refers to the way in which the rights and responsibilities are distributed among the categories of participants in the company's activity, such as the board of directors, the managers, the shareholders and other groups of interest, also specifying how are decisions taken regarding the company's activity, how are strategic objectives defined, what are the means of fulfilment and how are the financial results monitored (Todorovic, 2013).

Internal auditors, the same way as they must support the company for the identification and monitoring of risks that they face, they must also understand and supervise the functionality of the internal control system, which is the key element for the implementation of the corporate government principles (Mensah, 2003).

Because information is the most valuable resource and it is common knowledge by now that managers expect more from the internal auditors than just an opinion, the duty to foreshadow factors that can stimulate consolidation, development or the financial performance processes of the audited company cannot be denied (Steinthórsdóttir, 2004).

With a transparent reporting system, you can create the necessary conditions to ensure the stability of markets and economic development, while a good organization of the internal audit department will be the key factor for securing the objectives of trading companies (Young, Kim, Black & Jang, 2000). Moreover, an internal audit adds value by the fact that it requires the execution of assurance and counselling missions.

On the other hand, control has evolved and continues to evolve after the appearance of other patterns of control based on the environment where it is used and is, at its turn, in continuous movement, through the improvement of commercial relations and the permanent evolution of the market economy (Shah, Butt & Saeed, 2011).

The community acquis in the field of internal control, recommended by EC, comprised the general principles of internationally and EUR accepted good practice. The adequate manners of transposing them into the internal management and control systems are specific to each country, taking into account the constitutional, administrative, legal provisions specific to each culture and were a new approach of internal control (Aduda, Okiro & Omoro, 2015).

Generally speaking, the concept of control was given a limited connotation, namely, the control of transactions to see if they are compliant with the regulations in force. However, in the context of implementation of the principles of good practice, according to the definition of control, the term must part with this restricted meaning and acquire a new structure on the basis of the principles of corporate governance recommended by the European Commission.

The international practice recommends outlining an internal control system and an internal audit structure as part of the coordination of the general management, capable of managing the risks that entities face (Bar-Yosef & Prencipe, 2011). Moreover, it requires the implementation of the internal audit within organizations and the clear division of its activities from those of internal control.

The optimal operation of entities on the basis of an integrated internal control framework requires the existence of an adequate control environment which promotes ethical values, is transparent, accepts good practice standards and establishes responsibilities in the spirit of the strategies and policies approved by the senior management (Carcello, 2002).

The managerial accountability exercised by the management of an organization requires that, within the limits of internal and external constraints, for the effective, efficient and legal fulfilment of the objectives defined, to communicate and be responsible for the non-fulfilment of the managerial duties according to the type of legal responsibility (Dechow & Ge, 2006).

For the organization of the managerial activity, managers must take into account the following main principles: the general manager / the applicant is responsible for the fulfilment of the entity's objectives; the general manager / the applicant can delegate its authority without being absolved from the general responsibility; the managerial responsibility does not exist without the adequate authority; responsibility requires transparency and liability; the control system must be based on controls and corrective measures within the entity, but also on external controls (Brown & Caylor, 2004).

To ensure the implementation of the managerial control system, a working group is created that comprises the heads of the functional departments within the entity, respectively the line management, for the coordination of a member of the Board (Rankin, Stanton, McGowan, Ferlauto & Tilling, 2012).

Its activity is counselled and monitored by the head of the internal audit department, who is not a member of the working group (Hay, Knechel & Wong, 2004).

A Board of directors that has a well-implemented, controlled and developed risk assessment strategy represents the foundation for defining a risk tolerance and is also intended for all managers and employees of the organization (Xie, Davidson & DaDalt, 2003).

The risk appetite can be identified by several means based on many variables such as financial, time, quality etc. variables. The risk appetite must be identified before the appearance of the risk, because otherwise we will basically accept a deviation that occurred (Abbott, Park & Parker, 2000).

The reliable solution for risk management is finding a balance in which the existing risk – the residual risk – is equal with the risk that we are ready to tolerate – the risk appetite.

Because the resources available in the risk management process are limited and the risks cannot be avoided, each organization must take all necessary accepted measures, considered tolerable for the organization, respectively their risk appetite.

The Role of Controlling in Corporate Governance System

Controlling is relevant for the entire institution as a whole and for each department. While the internal control system is relevant and applicable to all institutions, management's implementation varies greatly depending on the nature of the institution and depends on a number of specific factors. These factors include: the organizational structure, the nature / risk profile, the environment of activity, the size and complexity of the activities, and the applicable regulatory system. Due to the specific situation of the institution, management considers a number of options regarding the complexity of the processes and methodologies used to apply the components of the internal control system (Beiner, Drobetz, Schmid & Zimmerman, 2004).

The control environment includes the general attitude, awareness and measures taken by management and those charged with governance of the internal control system and its importance within the entity (Cho,Ran & Kim, 2003). The control environment determines the tone of the organization, influencing staff awareness. It is the basis of all other components of internal control, ensuring a discipline within the organization to be respected and a structure of the entity so that the internal control system can be effectively applied. In addition, the internal control environment is an effective tool in preventing corruption and fraud (Daily, Dalton & Cannella, 2003).

The purpose of entity risk management is to enable management to identify the element of uncertainty regarding the achievement of the objectives set and the associated risk, and to have the opportunity to increase the capacity to add value, provide more efficient, economical and effective services, and maintain value account such as equity and justice. The risk can be considered negative in the sense of uncertainty, threat, obstruction or positively, as an opportunity (Young, 2002).

Given the economic events in recent years, the most important challenge will be for organizations to find a balance between risk, costs and value, given that a significant benefit is to have as many results as possible with few resources, clear identification of the key risks faced by entities. In this context, the internal control must be effective, avoid additional costs, and save material, financial and human resources (Mikalef & Pateli, 2017). In fact, there may also be a situation to design a good internal control system but it is misunderstood and put into practice by those involved in that entity (wrongly trained personnel with regard to the implementation of internal control) or formally dealt with.

Due to the fact that the improvement of the internal control can be done with the help of the internal audit, and the internal control is universal, then we can state that the internal audit is universal. The internal audit function has become a function of managerial assistance through which internal auditors help managers at all levels to master the other functions and activities.

The internal auditor must document the issues important for providing evidence to support the audit opinion and evidence attesting the execution of the audit in accordance with the law. Documentation means the materials (the documents) prepared by and for the auditor, or acquired and kept by the auditor during the audit (Rankin, Stanton, McGowan, Ferlauto & Tilling, 2012).

The auditor must include in the documents information regarding the planning of the audit activity, the nature, duration and extent of the audit procedures, the results of this activity and the conclusions drawn from the audit evidence obtained (Todorovic, 2013). The documents must contain the auditor's opinion regarding the significant elements that require the exercise of a professional reasoning, together with the conclusions drawn regarding the analyzed issue. In the fields that involve difficult matters of principle or judgment, the documents will contain the relevant facts known by the auditor at the time of outlining the conclusions.

In case of recurrent audit activities, certain files with documents can be considered permanent audit files and updated with new permanent information, unlike the current audit files that contain information regarding a single audit.

The internal auditors must document the relevant information in order to justify the conclusions and the results of the mission (Marlin & Geiger, 2012). The documents used for the documentation of the audit activity must be drawn up by the internal auditor and revised by the management of the internal audit. These documents must include the information obtained and the analyses made and must confirm the findings and the audit recommendations that will be reported.

The organization, elaboration and content of audit files are regulated according to the mission. The internal auditors compile these files with the help of the management and of the decisional bodies for which they make the provisions. The content of these files is estimated to be generally confidential and can be based on facts and on opinions. The access to the audit files can be requested by third parties through various procedures, among which we can list criminal investigations, disputes, tax controls, controls of regulatory courts, examination of public procurements and controls made at the competent professions for self-regulation. Theoretically, all files not covered by professional secrecy between the attorney and its client can be communicated in the event of legal actions. For other procedures, the issue of access to files is less obvious.

The internal audit officer must set the rules that must be followed for the documents, adjusted rules for each type of mission (Mensah, 2003). The normalization of legal files, for example the normalization of questionnaires and audit programs can improve the efficiency of a mission and can facilitate the delegation of tasks. Certain business files can be considered permanent files. These files contain permanent information.

The control of audit files involves the documents of the mission are owned by the entity. Generally, they must remain under the control of the internal audit and only the authorized staff must have access to them; the management and the other members of the entity can request the access to the documents of the mission. This access may be necessary to corroborate or explain the findings and recommendations of the mission or to use the documents of a mission for other purposes. The internal audit officer must authorize these requests in advance; in practice, the external and internal auditors send the business files to one another. The access given to external auditors must be approved by the internal audit officer; there are cases when the requests of access to the business files and to the reports are made by persons outside the entity, other than external auditors. Before accepting the supply of the requested documentation, the internal audit officer must obtain the management's approval and/or, as necessary, the legal counselor's approval.

Every mission must end with a file comprising the most important business documents, the evidence behind the assertions made in the report being crucial (Monks & Minow, 2004). The business documents must be written and have a standard predefined format, a reference number that coincides with the documents from the audit file, the correspondence with the number of the mission from the internal audit plan etc. The documents must contain mandatory information: the name of the entity, the name of the audited service; the name of the auditor, the date; whether it refers to tests: objectives, the structure of tests, the documents or the transactions reviewed, the results and interpretation etc.

The internal audit process should be carried out periodically, step by step, and take into account all aspects, not just the pleasant things. It has to be organized and planned so as to improve internal control and management processes. The audit is there to help line management improve its functional management and risk analysis (Elbannan, 2009).

The internal audit findings and recommendations are useful to the management line in the audited areas, in particular with regard to potential improvements in the risk management process, and which the auditor will evaluate again on the occasion of his return, which will ensure and guarantee a plus of value to the organization.

The management's evolution comprised methods of organization from merely theoretical levels to very practical levels, forms appeared and applied between them which proved the validity of some and invalidated the existence of others (Bhimani, 2008).

Moreover, the approach of the internal audit function must contain the organization of the internal audit department as well as the organization of labor and the management of the competences and of the resources needed for performing the internal audit.

From the analysis of the evolution of the internal audit function to the present, we can appreciate the following elements of involvement in the life of the audited entity, namely: counseling given to the manager; aid to employees without judging them; independence and total objectivity of auditors.

It is unanimously accepted that the internal auditor advises, assists, recommends, but does not decide, his obligation to be a means to improve the control each manager has on his activities and those in coordination, in order to achieve the objectives of the control internal.

Moreover, in an entity where the internal audit is part of the culture of the organization, it is accepted with interest, but in an entity experiencing significant potential risks, with the lack of compliance with the underlying regulations, with low effectiveness and fragility due to the misappropriation of funds, the disappearance of assets or fraud, it is obvious that the respective manager will be judged, appreciated, considered according to the findings of the internal auditor.

A control environment can enhance the effectiveness of the internal audit if it is part of the culture of the organization because it contributed to the exchange of information, favors cooperation during the working process, allows the elaboration and collection of mutually interesting and easy to apply proposals.

The communication is based on a well-defined plan whose purpose is to know the function, to understand it and to act upon the control environment. The targets must be highlighted in the communication plan, the objectives must be confronted with the expectations and the messages must be clearly defined per categories of recipients, the choice of the most appropriate communication media.

Effectiveness is assessed through the internal audit quality control plan, assessments that can be internal and external, according to the Qualification rule 1300 – Insurance and quality improvement program.

The head of the internal audit is responsible for the internal assessments, who also supervises the auditors' competence, the quality of communication, the observance of the audit methodology and the rational choice of investigation instruments, the quality and pertinence of findings and observations, the quality of the audit report and the observance of the terms, the realism of recommendations, their applicability and effectiveness.

External assessments also include an audit of the audit which is conducted by audit revisions which mainly examines: the profile and competence of auditors, the exhaustiveness of the audit plan and its observance, the implementation of the internal audit standards, the methodology, the quality of audit reports and the application of recommendations, the quality of the internal audit manual and of the audit guides, the assessment of the internal audit by the management (Cheng, 2008).

The external assessment can also be conducted through external auditors, by "exchanging experience" with auditors from similar entities from non-competing sectors, or by using a qualified team outside the audit organization once every five years (Awais & Hussain, 2015).

Regardless of the solution chosen, the Qualification rule 1320 – Reports regarding the quality program must be observed, which regulates that "The internal audit officer must communicate the results of the external assessments to the Board" (Mensah, 2003).

Effectiveness is measured through several instruments: indicators, benchmarking and opinion poll. The indicators are those that give the image of appreciation of the activity and of the quality, are essentially a means for enhancing the effectiveness and are calculated on three categories: business indicators, quality indicators and cost indicators.

For example, Benchmarking is the use of qualitative and quantitative criteria to understand where you stand among the members of the same profession, the final purpose of the measurement is to identify the best practices in order to obtain a higher effectiveness, a sort of standardization of methods, of procedures and work rules that provide a high effectiveness.

This practice was developed by the International Institute of Internal Audit under the name of "Global Auditing Information Network" and provides the most popular professional practices to auditors, which can lead to a low interest in research, negligence and a lower spirit of initiative and consideration of the environment.

The survey is another important means of measuring the effectiveness of the internal audit department, however it must be considered very sensitive if it is not developed by specialists, because it can give irrelevant or even contradictory results that can also influence the judgment of beneficiaries.

Normally, for justified reasons, the survey is a good instrument for collecting useful information and data for the internal audit concerning the relationship with the management, the level of understanding of the management regarding the internal audit.

The audit committee is the level reached after an evolution of more than one hundred years, but which has acquired a higher importance at the end of the twentieth century, when the role of movements in business morale came to surface (Marlin & Geiger, 2012).

The audit committee acquired responsibilities for guaranteeing the quality of accounts and reports to shareholders, remunerations and appointments of directors, ensuring the shareholders of the independence of the opinions formulated.

The practice in many countries has revealed the need of existence of audit committees, but we need to clarify two essential elements: the scope of audit committees; the hierarchical position of the internal audit.

The scope is not defined by any professional rule, it is not perceived as being rigorously encountered, but it refers to the effectiveness of the management and resources engaged, to the fact that the processes of the entity are correctly accounted, keeping under control the risks related to conflicts of interests, a free evolution of the entity, unobstructed by the measures of the management.

The hierarchical positioning of the internal audit in terms of the subordination was and is a subject of debate that does not have a unique solution, but proposes variants that can be appropriate or not depending on several elements related to the organizational culture (Awais & Hussain, 2015).

In France, for example, to overcome the deadlock, the internal control committee was developed which also handles the relationship with the management and its concerns, as well as with internal auditors.

At first sight it appears to be confusion, but the internal audit works for all the functions of the entity, hierarchically positioned at the general division, but also acts according to the guidance of the audit committee.

In the next years, the effectiveness of these organizations will probably be measured more precisely, and the involvement of the audit committee in the corporate governance will be better structured and characterized.

SOLUTIONS AND RECOMMENDATIONS

Cost control is the system by which the management ensures that the resources are obtained and used efficiently, effectively and relevantly, in accordance with the organization's objectives, and that the actions in progress are within the meaning of the defined strategy (Mikalef & Pateli, 2017).

But controlling in the field of costs does not stop at the objective control of the economic efficiency of the resources allocated and used by a company. Its perimeter also includes the routine preparation of decisions regarding the performance of the company through costs and results. This is the case of the decision-making orientation of the cost calculation for the establishment of prices, the optimization of the production program based on the cost-results relationship, the choice of the manufacturing processes based on the same relationship, as the basis of the choice between own production and the purchase of products from third parties.

It is important that the audit files intended for the public to be well prepared. For this purpose, we recommend following the steps below: only the requested documents will be made public. As a general rule, audit files containing opinions and recommendations are not communicated. The documents that disclose the argumentation or the strategies of lawyers are generally covered by professional secrecy and their transmission is not crucial; only the copies must be sent, the original must be kept, especially if the documents were drawn up by pencil. If the tribunal requests the original, the internal audit must keep a copy; marking each document with "confidential" and a notation specifying that any disclosure to another person must be the object of a prior approval.

FUTURE RESEARCH DIRECTIONS

Understanding the control environment, the characteristics of the information system as a whole is an important and decisive step for auditors to determine the degree of credibility of the system itself and the information it provides. The overall objective and audit process in a computerized environment does not differ structurally from classical steps and processes. Exceptions only arise from the need for the auditor to know the existing computer system, understand the computer applications used in automatic data processing, and how it satisfies the user's requirements.

From a practical point of view, there are numerous factors that influence the profitable management of the company and the controlling systems at the enterprise level. Both internal and external factors have been identified, which have an important impact on the concept of cost control system, including: company status, manufacturing technology, interdependence of activities, strategic options, environment.

An exhaustive audit of internal control is impossible to achieve and, in essence, is not a goal of the audit process. Selective testing - by sampling - is the frequently encountered technique for assessing internal control as well as for detailed testing of account and transaction values. The auditor will examine the supporting evidence that will support the values and disclosures in the financial statements, based on an assessment of the accounting principles, accounting policies and estimates made by the entity's management to present the financial statements. The test activity should, however, start from the presumption of completeness, integrity and accuracy of the data to be audited. This is ensured by an understanding of the computerized environment and an assessment of internal control at the level of the information system. Although apparently the previously mentioned presumption can be considered as meaningless, practice has demonstrated serious incidents (fraud, data or application alteration, permanent loss of data in a system) that may occur in a computerized environment where the magnitude risks takes another dimension.

Practical reality implies addressing the risk through three factors: threats seen as events or activities (generally outside the audited system) that can affect the vulnerabilities existing in any system, thus causing the impact that is considered to be a short-, medium- long supported by the organization.

Thus, the audit practice does not distinguish between the two types of control (internal and general) because in reality they complement one another and the assessment of this control will give the financial auditor confidence in the data to be audited.

Also today, in a computerized era where the complexity of computerized accounting systems and the volume of transactions have increased significantly, the need for computer assisted auditing techniques is recognized to allow for an increase in the efficiency of the audit engagement.

CONCLUSION

Controlling should ultimately allow the activity to be carried out and decision making so that businesses, regardless of their size, can reach your goals. The essential role of controlling is the definition of criteria and the development of indicators that allow the decision makers to follow the evolution of the company in the light of its strategic objectives. The management indicators must be carefully selected, otherwise the enterprise is at risk move away from its goals without managers realizing it.

Internal Auditor is a manager's support function to enable them to better manage their activities. The assistance, counseling component attached to the internal audit clearly distinguishes it from any control or inspection action and is unanimously recognized as having further evolving tendencies.

The professionalism of the internal auditor is the art and the way to give value to the instruments and techniques used, such as rules, procedures, instructions, information systems, organizational types, etc., representing all the control activities used by the manager the institution or the manager of a job, recognized by the specialists as internal control.

The role of the internal auditor is to assist the manager for the successive practical approaches already developed and to analyze the whole to contribute to improving the internal control and work system with more security and efficiency.

The complex complexity of economic activities emphasizes the need for evolving accounting and audit tools to respond to the "hunger" of relevant user information. Such a responsibility cannot be achieved by classical audit techniques alone. Alliance with computer assisted auditing techniques is natural and beneficial to audit purposes. The symbiosis between audit and information technology was predictable and beneficial.

In conclusion, controlling costs in the conditions of profitable management of the company can be considered a link in the company that supports the management decision making through a rigorous foundation. According with same authors effective internal control system increases good corporate governance since it is a built-in part of the management process (i.e., plan, organize, direct, and control). Internal control keeps an organization on course toward its objectives and the achievement of its mission, and minimizes surprises along the way.

REFERENCES

Abbott, L. J., Park, Y., & Parker, S. (2000). The effects of audit committee activity and independence on corporate fraud. *Managerial Finance Journal, 26*(30), 55–67. doi:10.1108/03074350010766990

Aduda, J., Okiro, K., & Omoro, N. (2015). The Effect of Corporate Governance and Capital Structure on Performance of Firms Listed at the East African Community Securities Exchange. *European Scientific Journal, 11*(7), 18–19.

Aguilera, R. V., & Jackson, G. (2003). The cross-national diversity of corporate governance: Dimensions and determinants. *Academy of Management Review, 28*(3), 447–465. doi:10.5465/amr.2003.10196772

Awais, A., & Hussain, S. (2015). Understanding Corporate Governance and Board of Directors: A Generic Analysis. *Academic Research International Journal, 6*(4), 20–25.

Bar-Yosef, S., & Prencipe, A. (2011). Corporate governance and Earnings Management in Family Controlled Companies. *Journal of Accounting, Auditing & Finance, 26*(2), 199–227. doi:10.1177/0148558X11401212

Beiner, S., Drobetz, W., Schmid, M., & Zimmerman, H. (2004). An integrated framework of corporate governance and firm valuation. *European Financial Management, 12*(2), 249–283. doi:10.1111/j.1354-7798.2006.00318.x

Bhimani, A. (2008). Making Corporate Governance Count: The Fusion of Ethics and Economic Rationality. *The Journal of Management and Governance, 12*(2), 135–147. doi:10.100710997-008-9056-7

Brown, L., & Caylor, M. (2004). Corporate governance and firm operating performance. *Review of Quantitative Finance and Accounting*, *32*(2), 129–144. doi:10.100711156-007-0082-3

Carcello, F. (2002). The effects of uncertainty reporting on lending officers' perceptions of risk and additional information required. *Abacus*, *23*(2), 172–181.

Cheng, S. (2008). Board size and the variability of corporate performance. *Journal of Financial Economics*, *87*(10), 157–176. doi:10.1016/j.jfineco.2006.10.006

Cho, J., Ran, J., & Kim, L. (2003). Subject to' audit opinions and abnormal security returns –Outcomes and ambiguities. *Journal of Accounting Research*, *20*(2), 617–638.

Clarke, T. (2004). The evolution of directors' duties: Bridging the divide between corporate governance and corporate social responsibility. *Journal of General Management*, *32*(3), 79–105. doi:10.1177/030630700703200305

Daily, C., Dalton, D. R., & Cannella, A. A. Jr. (2003). Corporate governance: Decades of dialogue and data. *Academy of Management Review*, *28*(10), 371–382. doi:10.5465/amr.2003.10196703

Dechow, P., & Ge, W. (2006). The persistence of earnings and cash flows and the role of special items: Implications for the accrual anomaly. *Review of Accounting Studies*, *11*(2-3), 253–296. doi:10.100711142-006-9004-1

Elbannan, M. A. (2009). Quality of internal control over financial reporting, corporate governance and credit ratings. *International Journal of Disclosure and Governance*, *6*(2), 127–149. doi:10.1057/jdg.2008.32

Fadilah, S. (2013). The influence of good governance implementation to organization performance: Analysis of factors affecting. *The International Journal of Social Sciences (Islamabad)*, *7*(1), 15–33.

Hay, D. C., Knechel, W. R., & Wong, N. (2004). Audit fees: A meta-analysis of the effect of supply and demand attributes. *Contemporary Accounting Research*, *23*(1), 141–191. doi:10.1506/4XR4-KT5V-E8CN-91GX

Hoitash, U., Hoitash, R., & Bedard, J. C. (2009). Corporate governance and internal control over financial reporting: A comparison of regulatory regimes. *The Accounting Review*, *84*(3), 839–867. doi:10.2308/accr.2009.84.3.839

Johnstone, K., Li, C., & Rupley, K. H. (2011). Changes in corporate governance associated with the revelation of internal control material weaknesses and their subsequent remediation. *Contemporary Accounting Research*, *28*(1), 331–383. doi:10.1111/j.1911-3846.2010.01037.x

Marlin, D., & Geiger, S. W. (2012). The Composition of Corporate Boards of Directors: Does Industry Matter. *Journal of Business & Economics Research*, *10*(3), 100–115. doi:10.19030/jber.v10i3.6854

Mensah, M. L. (2003). The effect of audit quality on earnings management. *Contemporary Accounting Research*, *15*(1), 1–21.

Monks, R., & Minow, N. (2004). *Corporate governance* (3rd ed.). Blackwell Publishing.

Rankin, M., Stanton, P., McGowan, S., Ferlauto, K., & Tilling, M. (2012). *Contemporary issues in accounting* (1st ed.). John Wiley & Sons Australia, Ltd.

Shah, S. Z. A., Butt, S. A., & Saeed, M. M. (2011). Ownership structure and performance of firms: Empirical evidence from an emerging market. *African Journal of Business Management*, *5*(2), 515–523.

Steinthórsdóttir, L. (2004). Internal control–corporate governance, internal audit and strategic renewal. *Monetary Bulletin*, *6*(1), 85–95.

Todorovic, I. (2013). Impact of Corporate Governance on Performance of Companies. *Montenegrin Journal of Economics*, *9*(2), 47–53.

Weygandt, J. J., Kimmel, P. D., & Kieso, D. E. (2011). *Financial accounting* (1st ed.). John Wiley & Sons, Inc.

Xie, B., Davidson, W. N. III, & DaDalt, P. J. (2003). Earnings Management and Corporate Governance: The role of the board and the audit committee. *Journal of Corporate Finance*, *9*(10), 295–316. doi:10.1016/S0929-1199(02)00006-8

Young, F., Kim, W., Black, B. S., & Jang, H. (2000). Predicting firms' corporate governance choices: Evidence from Korea. *Journal of Corporate Finance*, *12*, 660–691.

Young, M. R. (2002). *Accounting irregularities and financial fraud*. Corporate Governance Guide. Aspen Law & Business.

Zikmund, W. G. (2000). *Business research methods* (6th ed.). Dryden Press.

ADDITIONAL READING

Kim, J., & Kim, J. (2018). Corporate Sustainability Management and Its Market Benefits. *Sustainability*, *10*(5), 1455. doi:10.3390u10051455

Mikalef, P., & Pateli, A. (2017). Information technology-enabled dynamic capabilities and their indirect effect on competitive performance: Findings from PLS-SEM and fsQCA. *Journal of Business Research*, *70*, 1–16. doi:10.1016/j.jbusres.2016.09.004

KEY TERMS AND DEFINITIONS

Audit Committee: Committee of responsible for oversight of the financial reporting process, selection of the independent auditor, and receipt of audit results both internal and external.

Auditing: Systematic process of objectively obtaining and evaluating statements about economic actions and events in order to assess the degree of compliance of these statements with pre-established criteria and to communicate results to interested users.

Board of Directors: Group of persons elected by the shareholders of a corporation to govern and manage the affairs of the company.

Corporate Governance: Set of measures taken within the social entity that is an enterprise to favor the economic agents to take part in the productive process, in order to generate some organizational surplus, and to set up a fair distribution between the partners, taking into consideration what they have brought to the organization.

Financial Performance: Level of performance of a business over a specified period of time, expressed in terms of overall profits and losses during that time.

Internal Control: Process which providing reasonable certainty regarding the achievement of the objectives of efficiency and effectiveness of operating activities, reliability of accounting information, compliance with laws and regulations.

Stakeholder: Any group or individual who can affect or is affected by the achievement of the organization's objectives.

Chapter 14
The Role of the Leader in Increasing the Performance of the Entity

Ionica Oncioiu
European Academy of the Regions, Belgium

Alina Stanciu
1 Decembrie 1918 University, Romania

ABSTRACT

Business excellence models represent the entity's framework for synchronizing vision with action decisions in a more systematic and structured manner, which results in an entity's performance increase. This chapter aims to open new research and deepen directions at the intersection of accounting and management, between science and practice, with the role of potentiating performance as a result of managerial accounting and leadership vision.

INTRODUCTION

The new approaches to the concept of performance outweigh the barriers to profitability, and the sustainability factor becomes paramount (Alstete & Beutell, 2018). For the leadership of new economic entities, performance is directly related to Resource Scarcity - resource reduction and Stewardship with a capital S - the new Stewardship concept that includes understanding the cost opportunity. Adaptability to the influence of these trends may not be possible without the direct involvement of theoreticians and practitioners whose concerns are directed towards clarifying the concept of performance in all its aspects, starting from economic, legal, technical and continuing social and environmental issues, thus supporting a multidisciplinary approach by modern entities under the conditions of an "Interconnected Global Economy" (Arsenault & Faerman, 2014).

DOI: 10.4018/978-1-7998-4637-6.ch014

2030 represents the new time horizon that has led entities to shape their Vision, Strategy and Performance Objectives as clearly and convincingly as possible. Although it seems remote as a time horizon, an in-depth knowledge of the resources of each entity with performance potential, including the management system as a whole, methods and techniques implemented to define KPI's Performance Indicators, only build a bridge between Accounting and Management, with a vital role in the evolution of the entity (Lin, Peng & Kao, 2008).

This new global context and the entities' prospect to achieve and maintain Sustainability Performance impose and force the entity's leadership to synchronize managerial decisions with financial-accounting situations as well as industry-specific predictability reports (Tajeddini, 2015). In this way, one can envisage an escalation from a global level to the individual one, towards increasing the competitive advantage, global development, counteraction of the external environment threats, and capitalization of the opportunities through the adoption of pertinent managerial decisions based on economic and financial indicators (Brown & Harvey, 2006; Satell, 2017).

From a conceptual point of view, performance has seen multiple interpretations and approaches from theoreticians and practitioners whose concerns have focused on studying it (Denison, 1990; Akgün, Keskin & Byrne, 2009; Davila, 2012). Specialized practice reveals the interference of the organizational performance concept with other concepts such as management, leadership, profitability, predictability, economic-financial indicators and metrics (Becker & Huselid, 1998). All of these interferences have led to an interdisciplinary approach and a deepening of the concept of performance, depending on the specificity of the field in order to extend its spectrum of applicability (Yadav & Sagar, 2013).

The term "performance" has appeared in literature around the middle of the nineteenth century and has been associated with the start of sports competitions as a result of the participation and winning of such a competition (Bourguignon, 2000). With the twentieth century, the concept begins to deepen, and new approaches are attributed to it by theorists and practitioners of the time, for today, in the digital age, performance is identified with the true measure of value for any business leader and manager (Hartnell, Ou & Kinicki, 2011). Those indicators that are directly related to performance and that affect its level are measurable, can be compared to pre-established benchmarks and can provide solutions for future corrections, added value and competitive advantage (Henczel, 2002).

Moreover, the performance and metric performance indicators have been ranked by industry practitioners in business intelligence techniques, but they are different (Rowland & Hall, 2014). Performance indicators are specific, refer to the expected results in the future, answering the question: Where are we going? - contributing to stakeholder decision-making and sending a signal if there is a variable that could produce inappropriate results. Metrics are generic, focusing strictly on performance results and on the current situation, responding to the question: Where are we today? - focusing on delivering work packages, achieving milestones and achieving performance goals.

The economic era of the Digital Age, characterized by an acceleration of technology innovation, fierce competition in gaining competitive advantage, increasing consumer expectations and emerging market pressure, drives leadership to adapt Vision and Entity Strategy to new performance standards (Adegoke, Walumbwa & Myers, 2012). The challenge is all the more so since the influence of the endogenous and exogenous factors of the entities is continuous, hard to control and in which the concept of Performance brings together under this umbrella other characteristics beyond the economic and financial ones that modern entities must incorporate and develop in their own strategy, such as: adaptability, flexibility, customer orientation, and the recruitment and retention of talent, ability to disrupt (Andriole, 2010).

For theoreticians, on the one hand because the management expertise developed on the basis of years of study and research shows that within each entity there is an own organizational culture that underlies the functioning of the management system and gives the entity its own identity, and for the big multinational corporations, the organizational culture represents the element of differentiation in the competitive market and in the age of globalization. Regardless of the geographical positioning of a multinational entity, its organizational culture attracts the competitive human resource that resonates with the entity's mission and objectives in order to achieve the performance (Arsenault & Faerman, 2014; Davila, 2012).

On the other hand, the integrated performance indicators system would help leadership to lead but at the same time inspire, motivate, in order to have an integrated vision of the clients, the desiderata achieved through the ability to reach the core of the business (Schneider & Somers, 2006; Behery, Jabeen & Parakandi, 2014).

For the leadership of entities facing the pressure to adapt strategic decisions to economic turmoil, the only source capable of providing accounting information of informational value is accounting, "the basic tool for knowledge, management and control of patrimony and the results obtained by economic entities" (Amagoh, 2008).

Achieving performance remains the desideratum of entities, both those present in the competitive market, and new start-ups that break the existing markets, capitalizing on the opportunities offered by an external environment characterized by volatility, uncertainty, complexity and ambiguity, but also the present digitalization, Internet of Things (IoT), 5G Internet, e-platforms. Seen as a reflection of the clear vision of extremely powerful leaders, the overall performance of the entity is attained today against the background of the innovation process. This chapter presents radiography of the new research and deepening directions at the intersection of accounting and management, between science and practice, with the role of potentiating performance as a result of managerial accounting and leadership vision.

Background

Entities nowadays operate in an increasingly dynamic environment where boundaries of territoriality and temporality almost disappeared, everything is global, multinational and related to the future (Alstete & Beutell, 2018). Any development strategy involves taking into account the predictions: 2030 has become very close, and the performance of an entity has exceeded the profitability boundaries.

In this Digital Age, performing entities "play the best books" for three stakes: the first is "sustainable performance", the second "finding and retaining talents", the quality of human resources contributing to the differentiation in a global and aggressive competitive market, while the third is "research & innovation" (Satell, 2017).

In the opinion of industry practitioners and due to the very high pressure of the external environment, high performance organizations are entities that "have exceptional financial results, satisfied customers and employees, high productivity, organizations that encourage innovation and skills development Leadership" (Tong & Arvey, 2015). At these, depending on the entity and the environment in which it operates, it is possible to add specific features: sustainable financial development, long-term orientation and achieving exceptional.

According with Arsenault and Faerman (2014), three directions of performance measurement have been developed: the first direction determines the actual performance of an entity as a result of the endogenous factors that have an influence on the entity's strategic values; the second direction implies the use of a standard aimed at two actions: the evaluation of the present state by the difference between the performed and the standard performance; the third direction to be referred to as the speed of change within entities to adapt to the environment. This rate of change determines economic entities to adopt a real strategic aggressiveness attitude, manifested through the degree of discontinuity of the organizations' strategic movements and the pace of the entities' strategic movements.

As a result, the focus of entity leadership is increasingly directed towards creating an organizational culture geared to excellence and performance, and to the crystallization of elements that define and contribute to the development of such an environment - Performance Indicators / KPI's.

The need for entities to monitor their activities and their results is vital in order to cope with the threats of competitiveness, to be able to respond in real time to these threats through adaptability and flexibility and to gain competitive advantage over direct competitors (Agha, Alrubaiee & Jamhour, 2012).

In the process of achieving high performance and co-opting, retaining and capitalizing on human resources with a high potential, performance management is a determining factor, being the instrument of leadership to "evaluate individual and team objectives in line with the strategic objectives of the company, in order for the company to gain that competitive advantage in a continuously evolving market" (Olson, Slater, Tomas & Hult, 2005).

Practice in the field reveals that performance management is a process whose purpose is to position an entity among those with "high level of performance" by gating the results and improving individual skills and abilities (Cocca & Alberti, 2010).

At the level of an entity, performance management involves aligning the vision of leadership, strategy and culture with actions taken to achieve goals (Hurley, 2002). Alignment is reflected both at an operational level, through operations management - reflected in the achievements of the team, department or project objectives, and at an individual level - reflected in the entity's maturity level and the high level of human resource utilization (Becker & Huselid, 2006). As a consequence, the individual performance assessment increases and its results directly influence the performance management process, leading to the emergence of the premise to develop new performance measurement tools and methods reflected in the development of performance management systems.

The implementation of performance management within an entity meets multiple requirements directly related to the level of achievement of the set goals (Amagoh, 2008). A first requirement refers to the need for leadership to evaluate and manage a low level of performance relative to objectives, which brings about other implications: focusing on the entity's strategic objectives, aligning resources with activities, feedback and future development directions (Chen & Fu, 2008).

Business excellence models have been developed by international or national bodies and are the basis for awarding prestigious awards (Taticchi, Tonelli & Cagnazzo, 2010). Entities using these models do this for self-evaluation because they can identify improvement opportunities and strengths, use the model as a framework for future organizational development, and achieve significant benefits beyond financial indicators: improving innovation and generating ideas, satisfaction customers, organizational growth (employees), employee satisfaction and involvement, product efficiency, effectiveness and reliability (Fisher, 2010).

A key benefit of prize-based models is that it provides a "balanced balance" of criteria and measures against which entities can objectively assess their performance management systems and compare their performance with standard benchmarks globally or with that of other organizations (Arsenault & Faerman, 2014).

The theoretical course with incursions in the sphere of practical applicability so far has been to draw the framework for the next section, which makes the transition to managerial accounting. The transition is one from the whole.

THE ROLE OF MANAGERIAL ACCOUNTING IN INCREASING THE PERFORMANCE OF THE ENTITY FROM THE PERSPECTIVE OF LEADERSHIP

From a managerial point of view, entity leadership monitors the current state, closely related to the environment in which it evolves, to scan the internal environment and validate by mandate the need to implement a Performance Management System to achieve a State Desired Evolution (Englund & Gerdin, 2018). In this sense, a portfolio of Initiatives is developed in which the long-term and medium-term strategic objectives are correlated with the Strategy, Scorecard and Performance Dashboard. In terms of Performance Management, entities apply new methods to increase their competitive advantage: Balanced Scorecard, Dashboard / Dash Board, Benchmarking, Prism Card Performance Skill / Skandia Navigator Framework, EQFM Business Excellence Model (Wickramasinghe & Alawattage, 2007).

Harmonizing with the new requirements of the Global Market and meeting the requirements of more and more sophisticated customers, it drives the leadership of the performing entities towards implementing customer-oriented management models such as CRM (Customer Relationship Management), Benchmarking, Dash-Boards (Verbeeten, 2010).

Under the above-mentioned conditions and considering that the accounting information is the main source of substantiation of the value-creation indicators, it is necessary to apply within the entities the analysis and diagnosis of its economic activity and the application of modern methodologies and techniques for measuring the performance (Alhyari et al., 2013). Applying modern methods and techniques to measure performance has the role of enabling leadership of the best way to implement a tool that enables value creation for the entity along with the development of future-oriented policies and strategies (Deutsch & Silcox, 2003).

Modern methods and techniques for measuring the performance on which management is based in analyzing and substantiating strategic, tactical and operational decisions are: Balanced Scorecard; Dash Board; Benchmarking; Prism Performance Card; Skandia Navigator Framework and EQFM Business Excellence Model (Cameron & Quinn, 2011).

Balanced Scorecard (BSC) is the result of Kaplan and Norton's research in 1992, being the result of a KPMG sponsored research project. If we were to define the BSC, then it "represents a mechanism used by leadership to implement the strategy and expression of the entity's vision" by bringing together both financial and non-financial indicators (De Waal & Kourtit, 2013). BSC offers the perfect framework for performing performance measures, with the goal of achieving competitive advantage.

The utility of the medley proves to be all the more valuable for the entity's leadership as four development dimensions are approached, which Kaplan and Norton highlight: the financial dimension: related to the satisfaction of investor requirements and expressed by: financial indicators used to determine the performance of the entity ; customer dimension: aims to meet customer requirements and is expressed through indicators such as delivery times, quality, performance level and cost from the customer perspective; the size of internal business processes: refers to the quality of internal processes and is expressed by operational measures taken by the leadership at the internal level; development and innovation dimension: expresses the entity's ability to innovatively and continuously develop, engaging in these processes all resources to improve critical processes that can influence performance, and is expressed by indicators such as: the entity's development curve.

Both theoreticians and field practitioners recommend applying BSC at the entity level, as it provides a balance between the qualitative and quantitative outcomes and the main drivers of performance, and, on the other hand, a harmonization of the application of some external measures for shareholders and customers, and internal measures for critical business processes, innovation, development and knowledge (Kaplan & Norton, 2006). This value judgment is supported by Kaplan and Norton through some pertinent allegations that serve to strengthen the BSC's position among modern methods of measuring one entity's performance and deriving from each other: BSC actively contributes to the clarification process and updating the strategy of the entity in which it is implemented by identifying and aligning strategic objectives; BSC requires communication by leadership and understanding by all departments and stakeholders interested in the entity's strategy; The BSC contributes positively to the system's processing of a large amount of both financial and non-financial information, obtaining a concise and essential amount of data in assessing the entity's performance; BSC helps to align long-term strategic objectives with annual budgets; BSC is a method of periodically reviewing performance to improve it through strategic feedback.

The Balanced Scorecard is a method developed to help improve entity performance by focusing on key financial and operational information in the entity's activities (Ahearne, Mathieu & Bolander, 2010). Balanced Scorecards consist of quantitative, visual, tabular and graphical components or key performance indicators, thus reinforcing their ability to improve the performance of an entity, the users of the method become "core of the business ". Both Scorecards and Dashboards are two similar techniques that enable leadership to "analyze, measure, provide more information to agents, and act swiftly, and thereby contribute to enhancing entity performance."

The Dashboard is a leadership tool of the entity, which originates in interwar France (Anand & Kodali, 2010). Its role is to analyze and select those indicators through which the presentation can synthesize the activity developed by the entity. As an instrument in the leadership process, it allows access to both financial and non-financial indicators, which in the context of this versatile economy makes it even more valuable (Homburg & Pflesser, 2000). The relatively low number of indicators makes it easy to understand, simple to interpret, with an addressing sphere at any operational level of the entity.

Dashboards can be: operational (monitors operational processes), tactical (monitors key processes and projects for a small number of employees), and strategic (monitors achievement of objectives). The role of the Dashboard is to connect leadership to the entity's real-time activities, gaining the status of personalized user interface, "helping to measure organization performance, understanding organizational units, business processes"(Chan, Shaffer & Snape, 2004). Dashboards are generated in Excel, with the cost of implementation being reasonable and allowing analysis and monitoring of operational performance every week, day, or even hour.

Designing Dashboards enables efficient communication based on graphs and tables of key risk indicators whose values are above the accepted thresholds. "It is estimated that 40% of the top 2,000 companies in the world use Dashboards in their Business Intelligence programs"(Rowlan & Hall, 2014).

Benchmarking, in the context of today's economic environment, so volatile, uncertain, complex and ambiguous, is the key to controlling entities that have understood and accepted that in order to stay on the market it is necessary, regardless of the field of activity, to consider Vision Pillar - Innovation as essential (Allan,1993). The purpose of applying the Benchmarking method is to establish for the entity the policies and strategies that will need to be adopted and implemented to maintain market position and gain competitive advantage. Benchmarking is the process of comparing your own organization, operations or processes with other organizations in the same industry or a wider market (Davila, 2012).

Some authors bring attention to several variants whereby an entity may decide to apply the Benchmarking method to improve its performance (Alhyari et al., 2013; Deutsch & Silcox, 2003; Galbraith & Lawler, 1993). It may mean applying a: Strategic Benchmarking - used when the organization wants to improve its overall performance by examining strategies and approaches that have made it possible to achieve high performance "by certain entities; Process Benchmarking - is used when trying to improve processes and operations with a decisive role in generating organizational performance; Benchmarking Competitive - Enhanced performance of the entity through comparative analysis of key product and service characteristics obtained by competitors; Functional Benchmarking - entity performance is analyzed against other selected entities in different business sectors.

The purpose of this type of analysis is to improve the performance of functions similar to other entities; Internal Benchmarking - Improves the performance of an entity's department (e.g., a "business unit") as compared to another department within the same entity; External Benchmarking - The entity's performances are analyzed against the best-in-class market; International Benchmarking - An entity's performance analysis is performed by comparison with the performance of other entities on a particular international market.

Leaders' decision to apply Benchmarking to their entity can be taken as a result of the desire to continuously improve performance as a result of preventing threats that may arise or as a result of harnessing some of the external or internal environment (Henczel, 2002). Applying the Benchmarking method involves passing it through a complex process of performance comparison, a process that will take place within a predetermined time, and on which it is imperative to establish stages to justify its performance at the end and to ensure its efficiency reflected in synchronization the leader's vision with the performance of the entity.

Another method by which entities can manage the increase in shareholders' wealth, together with the increased prosperity of the community in which they operate, is Stewardship - the management of the business with care and responsibility (Ashkanasy, 2011).

The challenge is all the more so as modern entities seek to contribute to the prosperity and well-being of their society, what they now carry with the nomination of Corporate Social Responsibility (Lim, 1995).

In Stewardship Asia Center's view, stewardship is a way of managing a company that ensures that the company's business can thrive and have a growth rate that can be sustained, and also ensures that you act in such a way that to increase in the long run both the wealth of its shareholders and the prosperity and well-being of the company in which the company operates (Alstete & Beutell, 2018). At the level of an entity, the Stewardship implies that the people to whom it is entrusted wealth, whatever it is, or of any kind of assets, have the obligation, at the end of their term of office, to hand over those assets in a better condition than the one they inherited, in other words being responsible beyond your own person or beyond the entity you lead, and in the long run beyond your life (Reed, Goolsby & Johnston, 2016).

Stewardship is directly related to the concept of performance, but the performance time with capital, where it is obtained without sacrificing future profits, ensuring that there is a continuity of competencies and relationships that contribute to creating a positive net impact - economic, social and environmental on future generations. But for this, it is imperative to have a very well-defined strategy that traces the "trajectory" of action, investing in capabilities and competencies in R & D, marketing and branding (Barney, 1986).

Another feature of stewardship entities is that they strategically operate with long-term horizons based on trust-based cultures, structures well-aligned with strategy and goals, and supported by strategically-minded thinkers, whose vision is medium and long term, ensuring that succession in leadership positions is assured and prepared early, and that the "legacy" of principles and leadership experience is protected and passed on (Delaney & Huselid, 1996).

Performance Indicators, Value Indicators, Integrated Performance Indicators System implemented by leading leadership, converge to Benchmarking and Stewardship (Satell, 2017). Challenged by the evolution of a fragmented market, the pragmatic adoption of new technologies together with the implementation of an Integrated Performance Indicator System represents new opportunities for new market players to innovate and develop business models that generate profit (Parveen & Noor Ismawati, 2015).

The Performance Pyramid - PP method suggests that a performance pyramid is capable of transforming executive economic information into a hierarchy from top to bottom in a set of operational objectives for business division managers and also from top-level managers, the top management financial ratios to be evaluated on the basis of financial scorecards (Tong & Arvey, 2015).

The Skandia Navigator Framework is classified as a non-financial model that emerged from the need to measure and demonstrate the contribution that the value expressed by intellectual capital can actively contribute to improving the performance of an entity (Davila, 2012).

Through the model, leadership is able to establish a link between the strategic vision of the entity and its objectives that serve as a communication and information tool (Fan, Li & Zheng, 2016). Specifically, the model divides intellectual capital into two main components: human capital and structural capital. The structural capital consists of: the client's capital and the capital of innovation and process, and the Human Capital is represented by knowledge (more precisely) of the adaptability of human capital to different tasks. In the opinion of its initiators, human capital has the highest rate of generating intangible assets, bringing together under the same umbrella, knowledge, experiences, talents and abilities in a continuous transformation of human know-how into structural capital (Mikalef & Pateli, 2017).

The main reason the entity's leadership wants intangible measurement is to develop different non-financial performance indicators (Ball, Li & Shivakumar, 2015). Unlike other scoring methods, Skandia Navigator presents users with a wide scale of measurement of immaterial systems from every perspective. The model has developed very useful tools to achieve intangible performance with various focus points by using a large number of reports and percentages.

The EQFM Business Excellence Model is defined by the European Foundation for Quality Management (EFQM) as the expression of "outstanding practices in organizing and delivering results, all based on a set of eight fundamental concepts": orientation towards results; client, leadership and constancy of purpose, management through processes and facts, people's development and involvement, continuous learning, innovation and improvement, partnership development, and public accountability (Rowland & Hall, 2014).

On the interdependence between management and financial-accounting Alstete and Beutell (2018) find: Support Function Advantage (supporting functions to create added value for activities with cost reduction and use of digitization); Shared Services (use of digitization to increase productivity and work efficiency); Complexity Management (Simplifying Management to Increase Competitiveness); Capability Sourcing (Synchronization between price, source and partnership); Business Process Redesign (getting value added to consumers); R & D / Innovation (supporting R & D investment to increase the competitive potential of the entity and creativity).

SOLUTIONS AND RECOMMENDATIONS

But even if conceptually terminology gives clarity to the approach, field practice reveals difficulties that entities encounter in defining KPI's, which are due to differences in the field of activity (Ahmed, Arshad, Mahmood & Akhtar, 2016). To counteract the appearance of confusion, it is imperative that the entities clearly determine the field of activity for which KPI's specific lineages are to be developed, whether we are talking about the financial area, the human resources or the operations.

In order for this approach to take shape, specialist practice recommends an integrated approach to internal and external resources, and greater focus on the implementation of the concepts of knowledge management, supply chain management, knowledge-sharring, open innovation "," Enterprise resource planning (ERP) "," enterprise interoperability ". In addition to this integrated resource approach, the theoreticians recommend that the entity's leadership develop and apply the concept of "step-by-step linear performance" precisely to reduce the rate of change the entity is subject to in the turbulent environment in order to get closer as much as possible from real competitors.

The impact of Internet of Things (IoT), Cloud Computing, Distributed Intelligence and Robotics on entities over the 2020-2030 period will be very strong. Only an in-depth knowledge of the entity, the operations carried out, the transparency of managerial processes, the use of accounting information and its proper use, the knowledge of the external environment but especially the threats, the innovation in order to increase the performance, the creation and implementation of modern methods of determination its performance and permanent upgrading, all of which can represent the response to the disruptive forces and can ensure the stay in the market.

FUTURE RESEARCH DIRECTIONS

For an entity operating around globalization, digitization, machine learning, it is increasingly difficult to focus its activities without taking into account the complexity of both the internal environment and the external environment. And, as an extra threat, the time for which the performance results recorded keeps its validity decreased vertiginously. Whenever, anywhere, there are entities that gain competitive advantage, which breaks up emerging markets and raises quality standards and leads to a global, global thinking, all around world oriented.

The underlying element of an entity's Performance Measurement and through which the Leadership harmonizes the Vision with the Strategy to reach the objectives is the Performance Indicators / KPI's. The evolution of the economic environment, the emergence of new concepts of globalization, circular economy, green growth, exponentially contributes to the diversification of Performance Indicators on which an entity's leadership directs its attention. The practice of recent years has relevant two major trends: a high degree of the presence of non-financial indicators and a correlation of the entity's strategy with the actions taken to achieve the objectives.

At the entity level, Performance Indicators are the expression of Leadership Vision Harmonization with the Strategy, and their values indicate correlation with established goals, showing whether they have been met or not adding value to the entity. But how is it that, although the concept is so clearly defined, present entities face a lack of performance, or a much lower level than projected and pursued. In order to achieve this, identifying, selecting and implementing Performance Indicators appropriate to the activities of an entity is more than necessary, each of the objectives of the strategy being assigned a relevant Performance Indicator.

If until now the time and cost, as well as their derivatives were the indicators over which the entities have focused, the current challenges have generated the need for entities to expand their performance spectrum and to take into account both economic and non- economic, economic, technical, managerial, and environmental mix.

The process of identifying and selecting relevant and useful KPIs that are embedded in strategic planning processes must be done by respecting a set of rules that both the theory and practice advocates, rules that actively contribute to the imposition quality requirements for these performance indicators, thus answering leadership to the question: "How should a KPI be my value-added?"

Quality requirements refer to criteria of: credibility, opportunity, accessibility, reliability, relevance, consistency, simplicity, neutrality and reactivity.

The continuation of the study is intended to be an insight into these questions faced by the modern, visionary Leadership, which is governed by Stewardship and Sustainable Development. Because in Stewardship's sense "getting the current performance is done without sacrificing future profits".

CONCLUSION

Being global, multinational, sustainable, socially responsible, profitable, talented oriented, credible, performing, involves at the level of the entity a leadership connected to market threats, adaptable, market oriented, customer oriented, effective, identifying with the vision of the entity to its members through the organizational culture it cultivates, but above all a leader who understands and is aware of the functioning of the entity, both managerial and economic. The understanding of the economic and managerial mechanisms of functioning, underpins the making of relevant, real and especially opportune decisions with a role in counteracting the turbulent environment threats and increasing the potential of the entity. And for this, a permanent assessment and re-evaluation of the entity's performance is imperative.

Performance in the present controversial, contradictory, vulnerable and volatile context is similar to achieving the entity's economic and financial objectives while increasing customer satisfaction, while respecting stakeholder interests, in terms of sustainability and stewardship. And this desideratum will contribute to transforming some entities into some performances: "Do not lower your expectation to meet your performance. Increase your level of performance to meet your expectations. "At the same time, more attention needs to be paid to implementing the concepts of" knowledge management "," supply chain management "," knowledge-sharing, "" open innovation, enterprise resource planning (ERP) "," enterprise interoperability ".

The relationship between the value of the accounting information and the Performance Indicators is mandatory, and there can be no predictability and performance without each other. Both concepts gain value over time, both the accounting information as a result of the economic activities and the KPI's as a result of a clear set of future directions for action, and therefore I think that both concepts fall into the core capabilities area ". The core that a leading leadership can base their most important decisions: whether we are talking about new markets, benchmarking, business scaling, market exit, globalization or digitization. There are very large-impact decisions at the level of entities, decisions that can play a heavy role in market positioning, economically grounded decisions can counteract external forces that exert pressure on the entity.

In conclusion, the results that accounting practitioners provide to leadership through financial statements and reports can facilitate access to the entity's current state, to possible upward or downward trends that may influence positively or negatively its evolution.

REFERENCES

Adegoke, O., Walumbwa, F.O., & Myers, A. (2012). Innovation strategy, human resource policy, and firms' revenue growth: The roles of environmental uncertainty and innovation performance. *A Journal of Decision Sciences Institute, 43*(2), 273-301.

Agha, S., Alrubaiee, L., & Jamhour, M. (2012). Effect of core competence on competitive advantage and organizational performance. *International Journal of Business and Management*, *7*(1), 192–204.

Ahearne, M., Lam, S. K., Mathieu, J. E., & Bolander, W. (2010). Why are some sales people better at adapting to organizational change? *Journal of Marketing*, *74*(3), 65–79. doi:10.1509/jmkg.74.3.065

Akgün, A. E., Keskin, H., & Byrne, J. (2009). Organizational emotional capability, product and process innovation, and firm performance: An empirical analysis. *Journal of Engineering and Technology Management*, *26*(3), 103–130. doi:10.1016/j.jengtecman.2009.06.008

Alhyari, S., Alazab, M., Venkatraman, S., Alazab, M., & Alazab, A. (2013). Performance evaluation of e-government services using balanced scorecard. *Benchmarking*, *20*(4), 512–536. doi:10.1108/BIJ-08-2011-0063

Allan, F. (1993). Benchmarking: Practical aspects for information professionals. *Special Libraries*, *84*(3), 123–130.

Alstete, J. W., & Beutell, N. J. (2018). Designing learning spaces for management education: A mixed methods research approach. *Journal of Management Development*, *37*(2), 201–211. doi:10.1108/JMD-08-2017-0247

Amagoh, F. (2008). Perspectives on organizational change: Systems and complexity theories. *The Innovation Journal*, *13*(3), 1–14.

Anand, G., & Kodali, R. (2010). A mathematical model for the evaluation of roles and responsibilities of human resources in a lean manufacturing environment. *International Journal of Human Resources Development and Management*, *10*(1), 63–100. doi:10.1504/IJHRDM.2010.029447

Andriole, S. J. (2010). Business impact of Web 2.0 Technologies. *Communications of the ACM*, *53*(12), 67–79. doi:10.1145/1859204.1859225

Arsenault, P., & Faerman, S. R. (2014). Embracing paradox in management: The value of the competing values framework. *Organizational Management Journal*, *11*(3), 147–158. doi:10.1080/15416518.2014.949614

Ashkanasy, N. (2011). International happiness; a multilevel perspective. *The Academy of Management Perspectives*, (February), 23–29.

Barney, J. B. (1986). Organizational culture: Can it be a source of sustained competitive advantage. *Academy of Management Review*, *11*(3), 656–665. doi:10.5465/amr.1986.4306261

Becker, B. E., & Huselid, M. A. (1998). High performance work systems and firm performance: A synthesis of research and managerial implications. *Research in Personnel and Human Resources Management*, *16*, 53–101.

Becker, B. E., & Huselid, M. A. (2006). Strategic human resources management: Where do we go from here? *Journal of Management*, *32*(6), 898–925. doi:10.1177/0149206306293668

Behery, M., Jabeen, F., & Parakandi, M. (2014). Adopting a contemporary performance management system. *International Journal of Productivity and Performance Management*, *63*(1), 22–43. doi:10.1108/IJPPM-07-2012-0076

Bourguignon, A. (2000). *Performance et contrôle de gestion. Encyclopédie de Comptabilité, Contrôle de gestion et Audit*. Economica.

Brown, D. R., & Harvey, D. (2006). *An Experimental approach to Organization development*. Pearson Education.

Cameron, K. S., & Quinn, R. E. (2011). *Diagnosing and Changing Organizational Culture: Based on the Competing Values Framework*. Jossey-Bass.

Chan, L. L., Shaffer, M. A., & Snape, E. (2004). In search of sustained competitive advantage: The impact of organizational culture, competitive strategy and human resource management practices on firm performance. *International Journal of Human Resource Management*, *15*(1), 17–35. doi:10.1080/0958519032000157320

Chen, H. M., & Fu, P. C. (2008). A systematic framework for performance appraisal and compensation strategy. *Human Systems Management*, *27*(2), 161–175. doi:10.3233/HSM-2008-0674

Cocca, P., & Alberti, M. (2010). A framework to assess performance measurement in SMEs. *International Journal of Productivity and Performance Management*, *59*(2), 186–200. doi:10.1108/17410401011014258

Davila, A. (2012). New trends in performance measurement and management control. *In Performance Measurement and Management Control. Global Issues (Washington, D.C.)*, *25*, 65–87.

De Waal, A. A., & Kourtit, K. (2013). Performance measurement and management in practice. *International Journal of Productivity and Performance Management*, *62*(5), 446–473. doi:10.1108/IJPPM-10-2012-0118

Delaney, J. T., & Huselid, M. A. (1996). The impact of human resource management practices on perceptions of organizational performance. *Academy of Management Journal*, *39*, 949–969.

Denison, D. R. (1990). *Corporate Culture and Organizational Effectiveness*. Wiley.

Deutsch, P., & Silcox, B. (2003). Learning from other libraries: Benchmarking to assess library performance. *Information Outlook*, *7*(7), 18–25.

Englund, H., & Gerdin, J. (2018). Management accounting and the paradox of embedded agency: A framework for analyzing sources of structural change. *Management Accounting Research*, *38*(1), 1–11. doi:10.1016/j.mar.2017.12.001

Fisher, C. D. (2010). Happiness at Work. *International Journal of Management Reviews*, *12*(4), 384–412. doi:10.1111/j.1468-2370.2009.00270.x

Galbraith, J. R., & Lawler, E. E. (1993). *Organizing for the Future: The New Logic for Managing Complex Organizations*. Jossey-Bass.

Hartnell, C. A., Ou, A. Y., & Kinicki, A. (2011). Organizational culture and organizational effectiveness: A meta-analytic investigation of the competing values framework's theoretical suppositions. *The Journal of Applied Psychology*, *96*(4), 677–694. doi:10.1037/a0021987 PMID:21244127

Henczel, S. (2002). Benchmarking – measuring and comparing for continuous improvement. *Information Outlook*, *6*(7), 12–20.

Homburg, C., & Pflesser, C. (2000). A Multiple Layer Model of Market-Oriented Organizational Culture: Measurement Issues and Performance Outcomes. *JMR, Journal of Marketing Research*, *37*(4), 449–462. doi:10.1509/jmkr.37.4.449.18786

Hurley, R. F. (2002). Putting people back into organizational learning. *Journal of Business and Industrial Marketing*, *17*(4), 270–281. doi:10.1108/08858620210431679

Kaplan, R. S., & Norton, D. P. (2006). How to implement a new strategy without disrupting your organization? *Harvard Business Review*, *84*(3), 100. doi:10.1108d.2006.05622had.002 PMID:16515159

Lim, B. (1995). Examining the organizational culture and organizational performance link. *Leadership and Organization Development Journal*, *16*(5), 16–21. doi:10.1108/01437739510088491

Lin, C. H., Peng, C. H., & Kao, D. T. (2008). The innovativeness effect of market orientation and learning orientation on business performance. *International Journal of Manpower*, *29*(8), 752–772. doi:10.1108/01437720810919332

Olson, E. M., Slater, S. F., Tomas, G., & Hult, M. (2005). The performance implications of fit among business strategy, marketing organization structure, and strategic behavior. *Journal of Marketing*, *69*(3), 49–65. doi:10.1509/jmkg.69.3.49.66362

Rowland, C., & Hall, R. (2014). Management learning, performance and reward: Theory and practice revisited. *Journal of Management Development*, *33*(4), 342–356. doi:10.1108/JMD-08-2012-0110

Satell, G. (2017). *A Playbook for Navigating a Disruptive Age*. McGraw Hill Education.

Schneider, M., & Somers, M. (2006). Organizations as complex adaptive systems: Implications of complexity theory for leadership research. *The Leadership Quarterly*, *17*(4), 351–365. doi:10.1016/j.leaqua.2006.04.006

Tajeddini, K. (2015). Exploring the antecedents of effectiveness and efficiency. *International Journal of Hospitality Management*, *49*(7), 125–135. doi:10.1016/j.ijhm.2015.06.007

Taticchi, P., Tonelli, F., & Cagnazzo, L. (2010). Performance measurement and management: A literature review and a research agenda. *Measuring Business Excellence*, *14*(1), 4–18. doi:10.1108/13683041011027418

Tong, Y. K., & Arvey, R. D. (2015). Managing complexity via the Competing Values Framework. *Journal of Management Development*, *34*(6), 653–673. doi:10.1108/JMD-04-2014-0029

Verbeeten, F. (2010). The impact of business unit strategy, structure and technical innovativeness on change in management accounting systems. *International Journal of Management*, *27*(1), 123–143.

Wickramasinghe, D., & Alawattage, C. (2007). *Management accounting change: approaches and perspectives*. Routledge, Taylor & Francis Group.

Yadav, N., & Sagar, M. (2013). Performance measurement and management frameworks. *Business Process Management Journal*, *19*(6), 947–971. doi:10.1108/BPMJ-01-2013-0003

ADDITIONAL READING

Ahmed, A., Arshad, M. A., Mahmood, A., & Akhtar, S. (2016). Holistic human resource development: Balancing the equation through the inclusion of spiritual quotient. *Journal of Human Values*, *22*(3), 165–179. doi:10.1177/0971685816650573

Ball, R., Li, X., & Shivakumar, L. (2015). Contractibility and transparency of financial statement information prepared under IFRS: Evidence from debt contracts around IFRS adoption. *Journal of Accounting Research*, *53*(5), 915–963. doi:10.1111/1475-679X.12095

Fan, J. P. H., Li, J., & Zheng, G. (2016). Revisiting the bright and dark sides of capital flows in business groups. *Journal of Business Ethics*, *134*(4), 509–528. doi:10.100710551-014-2382-6

Mikalef, P., & Pateli, A. (2017). Information technology-enabled dynamic capabilities and their indirect effect on competitive performance: Findings from PLS-SEM and fsQCA. *Journal of Business Research*, *70*, 1–16. doi:10.1016/j.jbusres.2016.09.004

Parveen, F., & Noor Ismawati, J. (2015). Social media usage and organizational performance: Reflections of Malaysian social media managers. *Telematics and Informatics*, *32*(1), 67–78. doi:10.1016/j.tele.2014.03.001

Reed, K., Goolsby, J. R., & Johnston, M. K. (2016). Listening in and out: Listening to customers and employees to strengthen an integrated market-oriented system. *Journal of Business Research*, *69*(9), 3591–3599. doi:10.1016/j.jbusres.2016.01.002

KEY TERMS AND DEFINITIONS

Decision: A person or group of persons' social and deliberate act defining the purpose and the objectives of a certain action, the directions and the ways to achieve that action, all of them determined, according to a certain need, by a process of obtaining information, deliberation, and assessment of the means and consequences of carrying out that action.

Economic Management: The achievement of the budget objectives with minimum costs so that when the activity is completed the revenue exceeds the costs, namely there is a profit that ensures a level of profitability as high as possible both at general level and by product, department or service performed.

Management: The process of manager's coordinating and overseeing the work activities of others so that their activities are completed.

Managerial Dashboard: Contains a set of actual information presented in a predetermined form, relating to the main results of the company's activities or to some of them and to the main factors conditioning their effective and efficient progress.

Organisational Performance: Elements affecting company performance such as financial and marketing factors, return on sales, return on investment, etc.

Chapter 15
Environmental, Social, and Governance Disclosure and Financial Performance:
Evidence From the Rail Industry

İsmail Çağrı Özcan
Ankara Yıldırım Beyazıt University, Turkey

ABSTRACT

The environmental, social, and governance (ESG) disclosure performance of the companies is becoming a major criterion for significant stakeholders like shareholders, creditors, and customers. In line with the increasing interest in ESG activities, a growing respective literature emerges. Despite this evolving attraction, the ESG aspects of the transport industry in general, and the rail industry in particular remain relatively untouched except for a small body of research on airlines. This study aims at filling this gap by analyzing how the ESG disclosure performance of the rail companies affect their financial performance, which the authors measure by return on assets (ROA), return on equity (ROE), and Tobin's Q. Based on a sample of 35 rail companies from nine countries over the 2007-2017 period, the analyses show that ESG disclosure performance has a positive and statistically significant association with the ROA of the rail companies.

1. INTRODUCTION

The business world has been witnessing the advancement of awareness with respect to the sustainability and social issues. Accordingly, apart from financial performance measures such as profit ratios, sale figures, and stock prices, major stakeholders like investors (both small and institutional), creditors, and customers place a higher priority to achievements/activities of the companies regarding the environment and social issues. Kiron et al. (2017) document that the sustainability conduct of a company is an important investment determinant for a large majority of investment firms. Likewise, Plumlee et al. (2015)

DOI: 10.4018/978-1-7998-4637-6.ch015

show how enhanced voluntary environmental disclosure leads to higher market valuation. Similarly, El Ghoul et al. (2011) and Dhaliwal et al. (2014) indicate a negative association between the cost of equity and social responsibility performance.

On the other side, from the corporate governance perspective, financial scandals like Enron, Lehman Brothers, Tyco, Arthur Andersen, Parmalat, and Marconi force financial markets to place more emphasis on corporate governance practices and transparency. As a result of this growing need, firms with enhanced corporate governance performance can not only enjoy a lower cost of debt (Bhojraj and Sengupta, 2003), but also they can lower their cost of equity (Chen et al., 2009).

Despite such growing general attraction on environmental sustainability, social responsibility, and corporate governance, the rail industry failed to draw the academic interest regarding these issues. Traditionally, the mostly unprofitable structure of the rail industry has required governments to retain state ownership to enable the continuation of this strategic public service. Therefore, with the exception of several countries having private rail companies particularly in the freight segment, state-owned rail enterprises have maintained their monopolistic positions for decades. However, the rail privatizations, especially those in the United Kingdom and Japan, created a new business environment for the industry. With the increase of private rail companies, the industry now has to comply with new market forces. As discussed earlier, what they are doing in terms sustainability, social responsibility, and corporate governance is now a major concern of their investors, lenders, and consumers.

This chapter analyzes how the ESG disclosure performance of the publicly traded rail companies affect their profitability and market valuation. We employ a sample of 35 rail companies from 9 countries over the 2007-2017 period. Our findings, based on ordinary least squares (OLS), fixed-effects (FE), and random-effects (RE) estimations, suggest that ESG disclosure performance is positively associated with the return on assets (ROA) whereas we cannot document its statistically significant effect on return on equity (ROE) and Tobin's Q. This chapter is organized as follows. Section 2 reviews the relevant literature, explains the methodology used and outlines the dataset. Section 3 reports the empirical finding of the analyses. Section 4 provides the conclusion and discusses the policy implications.

2. LITERATURE REVIEW, METHODOLOGY, AND DATA

The ESG disclosure activities of the rail companies remain mostly untouched in the relevant literature. A quick review reveals only two related studies. Özcan (2018) examines the determinants of governance disclosure of the publicly traded rail companies. His findings indicate that the board size, the representation of outside directors, financial leverage, and firm size have positive association with governance disclosure whereas rail companies established in civil law countries tend to underperform their counterparts from common law countries in term of governance disclosure. In a more in-depth study, Özcan (2020) documents that government ownership has a positive effect on the ESG disclosure scores of the publicly traded rail companies. The goal of this chapter is to contribute to the literature by filling this gap. Particularly, we intend to explore the impact of ESG disclosure performance of the publicly traded rail companies on their profitability and market valuation. Our model to test these associations is as follows:

$$Y = f\,(\text{ESG Disclosure, Growth, Size, Leverage, Tangibility}) \quad (1)$$

In (1), we adopt three separate dependent variables for Y. The first two, return on assets (ROA) and return on equity (ROE), are profitability measures whereas the third one is for the market valuation. We use the pretax income to calculate both ROA and ROE to handle the different taxations among countries. ROA and ROE are equal to the ratio of pretax income to total assets and ratio of pretax income to equity, respectively. To measure the valuation of the rail companies, we adopt Tobin's Q, which is equal to the sum of the market capitalization of equity and total debt divided by total assets.

Our policy variable in (1) is the ESG disclosure performance of the rail companies. Bloomberg publishes ESG disclosure scores of the companies, which are computed by weighting the environmental, social, and governance disclosure performance. As noted in the introduction, the value of the ESG disclosure performance is growing and appreciated by many stakeholders. The literature also provides evidence on the increasing significance of ESG activities.

Alexander and Bucholz (1978) test the association between corporate social responsibility (CSR) and stock market returns. Their findings show that CSR performance is not associated with both stock returns and stock risks. They conclude that this finding is an indication of the efficient stock markets suggested by Fama (1970). The analysis of Boyle et al. (1997) suggests interesting policy implications. They examine whether signing an agreement regarding an ethical initiative make a difference among participating and non-participating defense contractors. Contrary to their initial expectation, they find that both participating and non-participating defense contractors experience negative price movements in the stock markets. Boyle et al. (1997) bring two explanations. The first one is that the markets assume this ethical initiative as a signal of a future sanction for the participating firms. Their second explanation is that the investors may simply punish the non-participating firms for not behaving ethically. Waddock and Graves (1997) examine the linkage between corporate social performance and financial performance. They report two-way causation such that prior profitability is a determinant of CSP and CSP is affected by prior profitability. Using a sample coming from Compustat and employing CSR performance statistics of the Kinder, Lydenberg, and Domini, McWilliams and Siegel (2000) document that CSR performance has a positive effect on the accounting profits of the companies. The findings of Brammer et al. (2006) indicate a striking result against the majority of the relevant literature. They show, using a sample of UK firms, that corporate social performance has a negative effect on the stock market returns. When they further analyze after disaggregating the corporate social performance data, they reveal that higher environmental and community variables tend to decrease stock returns whereas employment variable is positively associated with it. Renneboog et al. (2008) provide an overview of the relevant literature on socially responsible investments. They conclude that, against the positive association between the corporate social responsibility and shareholder value, the direction of the causality is not certain. Edmans (2011) analyzes how employee satisfaction affects stock market returns of the companies. He constructs a sample coming from the "100 Best Companies to Work for in America". His findings suggest that these companies have higher stock returns than their industry averages. Weber (2014) examines the effect of ESG reporting activities on the financial market returns of Chinese firms over the 2005-2012 period. He shows that firms publishing ESG reports tend to get higher returns than those not publishing. Fatemi et al. (2015) present a hypothetical model to test the effects of corporate social responsibility expenditures of the firms on their valuation. Their model reveals that such expenditures can have a positive association with the firm valuation subjected to couple preconditions. Harjoto and Jo (2015) report that firms with higher corporate social responsibility performance have a higher valuation and lower cost of capital based on a sample of US public firms over the 1993-2009 period. Fatemi et al. (2017) analyze how various ESG features contribute to firm value. They use two dimensions of the ESG activities namely ESG performance and ESG disclosure. Their analyses, based on a sample of 1640 firm-year observations from 403 US companies over the 2006-2011 period, indicate that whereas ESG disclosure tends to reduce firm valuation (Tobin's Q), ESG strength has a positive association with it.

If ESG disclosure performance really matters for the stakeholders, then we can expect that railroad companies with higher ESG performance should help these companies enjoy lower borrowing costs, increased sales, attracted capital expecting a lower return on equity. In this book chapter, following a similar logic, we expect that the ESG disclosure score will have a positive effect on all of our three our dependent variables.

In addition to ESG disclosure performance, we employ four control variables coming from the financial statements of the rail companies. Our first control variable is the growth. The relevant literature adopts various parameters to measure the growth rate of the firms. The larger group of comparable research use sale growth [(Abor, 2005), (Margaritis and Psillaki, 2010), (Fosu, 2013), (Zeitun and Tian, 2014), and (Le and Phan, 2017)]. Alternatively, Memon et al. (2012) employ asset growth to measure the growth of the companies. Previous findings confirm the positive effect of growth on firm financial performance. With respect to profitability, Zeitun and Tian (2014), Memon et al. (2012), and Le and Phan (2017) indicate a positive linkage between firm growth and ROA. Similarly, Abor (2005) and Le and Phan (2017) report the positive effect of firm growth on ROE. Regarding the valuation impacts, Le and Phan (2017) show how firm growth adds to Tobin's Q. Lastly, the analyses of Margaritis and Psillaki (2010) suggest higher growth rates stimulate firm efficiency. When calculating the growth rate of rail companies, we stick to the majority of the relevant literature. The explanatory variable we employ to measure growth is the ratio of current sales to the last year's sales figure and we anticipate that the coefficient of the growth variable will be positive.

Our second control variable is the size. Size is a significant factor especially for the network industries where economies of scale matter. Therefore, we can expect that larger rail companies tend to be more profitable and valuable than smaller ones. In the comparable studies, size is measured by total sales [(Majumdar and Chhibber, 1999), (Abor, 2005), (Margaritis and Psillaki, 2007), (Margaritis and Psillaki, 2010), and (Memon et al., 2012)] or total assets [(Kyereboah-Coleman, 2007), (El-Sayed Ebaid, 2009), (Khan, 2012), (Zeitun and Tian, 2014), (Hasan et al., 2014), (Fosu, 2013), and (Bandyopadhyay and Barua, 2016)]. In this book chapter, we measure the size of the publicly traded rail companies by their net sales (in the natural logarithm). Our expectation is to get a positive coefficient for the size variable.

Our third control variable aims at measuring the financial leverage of the rail companies. The capital structure has been one of the hottest topics in the finance literature for decades. The debate mainly started with the seminal work of Modigliani and Miller (1958), who point out that the value of the firm is free from its capital structure. Afterward, several capital structure theories challenge the theory of "capital structure irrelevance" proposed by Modigliani and Miller. The trade-off theory, for example, argues that firms can benefit from additional debt if the cost of extra debt is less than its tax advantage. Free cash flow theory, on the other hand, claims that debt can be used to not to waste firms' money into unfeasible projects. Pecking order theory, on the other hand, claims that the internal financing should be the first option rather than debt.

The relevant literature consists of supporting evidence for each of these capital structure theories. On the one hand, a group of studies document how higher levels of debt are associated with the lower firm performance [(Majumdar and Chhibber, 1999), (Khan, 2012), (Pouraghajan et al., 2012), and (Le and Phan, 2017)]. These studies report the negative impact of higher financial leverage on various performance measures like RAO, ROE, and Tobin's Q. Another group of research indicates the positive impact of higher borrowing levels on efficiency [(Margaritis and Psillaki, 2007) and (Margaritis and Psillaki, 2010)] and ROA [(Memon et al., 2012) and (Fosu, 2013)]. In this study, we measure the financial leverage by dividing the total liabilities to the total assets. We expect that the leverage variable will get a negative coefficient.

Tangibility is our last control variable. Previous literature suggests both negative and positive effect of tangibility on the financial performance of the firms. The underlying assumption for the negative linkage is that more tangible firms may lose their flexibility in financial decisions especially at the time of economic crises and downturns. The findings of Memon et al. (2012) reveal that tangibility ratio has a negative association with the ROA based on a sample from the Pakistani textile industry. Contrarily, keeping higher shares of long-term assets against short-term ones can be a tool to handle agency conflicts from the agency theory point of view. Because knowing that firms have high ratios of durable assets, creditors can easily lend money and they can ask lower interest rates. Regarding the positive impact of tangibility, both Margaritis and Psillaki (2007) and Margaritis and Psillaki (2010) show how tangibility contributes to firm efficiency. Unlike these papers reporting either a negative or a positive effect, Zeitun and Tian (2014) show tangibility has a negative association with both ROA and the ratio of the market value of equity to its book value. The findings of Zeitun and Tian (2014) also suggest that higher tangibility tends to rise the ratio of earnings before interest, taxes, and depreciation to the total assets. In this study, we calculate the tangibility ratio by dividing the fixed assets to the total assets. Following an agency theory perspective, we expect that the tangibility ratio will get a positive coefficient.

Table 1. Descriptive Statistics

Variable	Definition	Expected Sign	Mean	Std. Dev.	Minimum	Maximum
ROA	The ratio of pretax income to total assets		0.06068	0.04329	-0.02699	0.27409
ROE	The ratio of pretax income to equity		0.17446	1.70785	-19.29167	12.93701
Tobin's Q	The sum of the market capitalization of equity and total debt divided by total assets.		0.82473	0.35399	0.23818	5.34991
ESG Disclosure	ESG scores published by Bloomberg Data Base	+	30.24697	11.74335	5.37	56.61
Sales growth	The ratio of net sales to its last year figure	+	1.04602	0.15938	0.74749	2.85691
Size	The natural logarithm of net sales of each rail company (adjusted for inflation)	+	21.53799	1.10617	16.72228	23.42558
Financial leverage	The ratio of total liabilities to total assets	-	0.66082	0.18141	0.12281	1.04086
Tangibility	The share of long term assets in the total assets	+	0.85099	0.09968	0.36996	0.96704

Table 2. Correlation Matrix of the Variables

	ROA	ROE	Tobin's Q	ESG Disclosure	Growth	Size	Leverage	Tangibility
ROA	1.0000							
ROE	-0.0187	1.0000						
Tobin's Q	0.5854	0.0486	1.0000					
ESG Disclosure	0.1326	0.0317	0.0341	1.0000				
Growth	0.1306	-0.0098	0.2961	-0.0893	1.0000			
Size	0.2592	0.0354	0.0880	0.5886	-0.0721	1.0000		
Leverage	-0.3062	-0.0049	-0.3460	0.1043	0.1870	0.1732	1.0000	
Tangibility	-0.2308	-0.0114	-0.0366	0.0402	-0.0391	0.0570	-0.3124	1.0000

We gather our sample from Bloomberg database, which supplies the financial data we need for the 35 publicly traded rail companies. Table 1 depicts the descriptive statistics of our sample. The correlation matrix of the variables is presented in Table 2. We also calculate the variance inflation factors (VIFs) to check for a possible multicollinearity problem. After looking at the mean VIF (1.29) and the maximum VIF (1.58), we can conclude that multicollinearity remains within tolerable margins.

3. EMPIRICAL RESULTS

Table 3 shows the results of our OLS, FE, and RE estimations. For each of the regression types, we adopt ROA, ROE, and Tobin's Q as the dependent variable, respectively. The first three rows of Table 3 present the estimations where we regress ROA on the explanatory variables. Our policy variable ESG gets positive and statistically significant coefficients in each of the OLS, FE, and RE estimations. Holding other explanatory variables constant, a 1 point increase in the ESG disclosure performance of a rail company is expected to increase its ROA by 0.0009, 0.0006, and 0.0008 units according to our OLS, FE, and RE estimations, respectively. We should note that the coefficients in the OLS and RE estimations are statistically significant at the 5% level whereas that of the FE model is significant at the 10% significance level. Regarding the control variables, we document that both the financial leverage and tangibility have a negative effect on ROA in all of the three estimations. In the OLS estimation, our findings also suggest a positive association between firm size and ROA. But we should note that this finding is not supported by both FE and RE estimations.

Columns 4, 5, and 6 of Table 3 reports the results of the estimations when we use ROE as the dependent variable. Our findings suggest that the ESG disclosure performance of the publicly traded rail companies do not have a statistically significant impact on ROE. Columns 4, 5, and 6 also reveal that the associations between our control variables and ROE are also statistically insignificant.

Unlike the first six columns of Table 3 where we examine the profitability effects, Columns 7, 8, and 9 report the results of the OLS, FE, and FE estimations when we adopt market valuation, which we measure by Tobin's Q, as the dependent variable. Our findings reveal that the effect of ESG disclosure performance on Tobin's Q is statistically insignificant for the publicly traded rail companies. With respect to the control variables, our findings indicate that financial leverage has a negative association with

Table 3 Regression Results

	ROA			ROE			Tobin's Q		
	OLS (1)	**FE (2)**	**RE (3)**	**OLS (4)**	**FE (5)**	**RE (6)**	**OLS (7)**	**FE (8)**	**RE (9)**
ESG Disclosure	0.00087** (2.39)	0.00065* (1.82)	0.00076** (2.22)	0.00026 (0.02)	0.01107 (0.71)	0.00364 (0.37)	0.00079 (0.38)	0.00384 (1.59)	0.00201 (0.95)
Growth	0.00603 (0.29)	0.02446 (1.57)	0.02427 (1.57)	-0.61660 (0.97)	-0.02166 (0.03)	-0.10476 (0.17)	0.48238*** (4.09)	0.54246*** (5.24)	0.52416*** (5.03)
Size	0.00697** (1.99)	-0.00490 (0.38)	0.00511 (0.70)	0.04668 (0.44)	0.71932 (1.27)	0.03339 (0.34)	0.04652*** (2.19)	-0.33354*** (3.85)	0.03185 (1.14)
Leverage	-0.10320*** (5.64)	-0.07903* (1.92)	-0.07306** (2.12)	-0.16100 (0.29)	-1.27496 (0.71)	-0.13720 (0.25)	-0.75253*** (6.99)	-0.31023 (1.09)	-0.62821*** (4.01)
Tangibility	-0.13527*** (4.16)	-0.13365* (1.88)	-0.10411* (1.70)	-0.19033 (0.19)	-3.21979 (1.04)	-0.25183 (0.26)	-0.55261*** (2.93)	-0.56678 (1.19)	-0.45702 (1.63)
Constant	0.09805 (1.06)	0.28366 (0.99)	0.03059 (0.19)	0.72456 (0.26)	-11.97869 (0.96)	-0.24365 (0.11)	0.44146 (0.83)	8.01229*** (4.19)	0.33321 (0.54)
R^2	0.2	0.09	0.16	0.06	0.00	0.03	0.27	0.00	0.22
F-value	4.48	2.73		1.14	0.85		6.65	8.68	
Prob > F	0.0000	0.02		0.3158	0.5187		0.0000	0.0000	
Wald Test			16.02			0.73			46.27
Prob > Chi^2			0.0068			0.9811			0.0000
Number of groups		35	35		35	35		34	34
Number of observations	331	331	331	331	331	331	320	320	320

Tobin's Q as in the case of ROA. What is noteworthy in the last three columns is the positive linkage between growth of the rail companies and their Tobin's Q. We should note that we fail to document a similar finding when we use ROA and ROE as the dependent variables. This means that while the growth rate of the rail companies does not have an immediate impact on their profitability, the stock market appreciates such positive progress, evaluate it as a good signal for the future financial performance, and reflect it into the stock prices.

4. CONCLUSION

The way of doing business is changing very rapidly. On the one hand, the business actors and the consumers are increasingly placing more weight on social and sustainability issues. On the other hand, corporate scandals like Enron and Lehman Brothers advance the agency debate. Accordingly, corporate governance mechanisms become a tool to reduce agency conflicts which in turn create value for the shareholders, creditors, and the managers of the companies. For all these reasons, ESG disclosure attracts more and more attention from the practitioners and academicians.

This study examines the effect of ESG disclosure performance on the profitability and market valuation of the publicly traded rail companies. We adopt a dataset coming from 35 rail companies from nine countries over the 2007-2017 period. We should underline that the privatization wave in the last three decades makes the conduct of such analysis possible since around half of our sample consist of privatized rail companies. In the OLS, FE, and RE estimations, we employ ROA, ROE, and Tobin's Q as the dependent variables whereas our control variables include size, growth, financial leverage, and tangibility in addition to ESG disclosure score, which is our policy variable. Our findings suggest that ESG disclosure performance is positively associated with ROA whereas we cannot document a similar effect on ROE and Tobin's Q.

Our analyses brings important policy insights. Since higher ESG disclosure performance tends to increase ROA, we can conclude that the managements of the rail companies should place more weight to ESG activities. In a new business environment where sustainability efforts, social initiatives, and corporate governance activities attract more attention from major stakeholders, improving ESG disclosure performance should be among significant policy objectives to improve profitability.

A possible future research might involve a qualitative analysis that examines how major stakeholders such as creditors, suppliers, and investment bankers incorporate the ESG performance of the rail companies (in particular or transport companies in general) into their decision making processes.

REFERENCES

Abor, J. (2005). The effect of capital structure on profitability: An empirical analysis of listed firms in Ghana. *The Journal of Risk Finance*, *6*(5), 438–445. doi:10.1108/15265940510633505

Alexander, G. J., & Buchholz, R. A. (1978). Corporate social responsibility and stock market performance. *Academy of Management Journal*, *21*(3), 479–486. doi:10.5465/255728

Bandyopadhyay, A., & Barua, N. M. (2016). Factors determining capital structure and corporate performance in India: Studying the business cycle effects. *The Quarterly Review of Economics and Finance*, *61*, 160–172. doi:10.1016/j.qref.2016.01.004

Bhojraj, S., & Sengupta, P. (2003). Effect of corporate governance on bond ratings and yields: The role of institutional investors and outside directors. *The Journal of Business*, *76*(3), 455–475. doi:10.1086/344114

Boyle, E. J., Higgins, M. M., & Rhee, G. S. (1997). Stock market reaction to ethical initiatives of defense contractors: Theory and evidence. *Critical Perspectives on Accounting*, *8*(6), 541–561. doi:10.1006/cpac.1997.0124

Brammer, S., Brooks, C., & Pavelin, S. (2006). Corporate social performance and stock returns: UK evidence from disaggregate measures. *Financial Management*, *35*(3), 97–116. doi:10.1111/j.1755-053X.2006.tb00149.x

Chen, K. C., Chen, Z., & Wei, K. J. (2009). Legal protection of investors, corporate governance, and the cost of equity capital. *Journal of Corporate Finance*, *15*(3), 273–289. doi:10.1016/j.jcorpfin.2009.01.001

Dhaliwal, D., Li, O. Z., Tsang, A., & Yang, Y. G. (2014). Corporate social responsibility disclosure and the cost of equity capital: The roles of stakeholder orientation and financial transparency. *Journal of Accounting and Public Policy*, *33*(4), 328–355. doi:10.1016/j.jaccpubpol.2014.04.006

Edmans, A. (2011). Does the stock market fully value intangibles? Employee satisfaction and equity prices. *Journal of Financial Economics*, *101*(3), 621–640. doi:10.1016/j.jfineco.2011.03.021

El Ghoul, S., Guedhami, O., Kwok, C. C., & Mishra, D. R. (2011). Does corporate social responsibility affect the cost of capital? *Journal of Banking & Finance, 35*(9), 2388–2406. doi:10.1016/j.jbankfin.2011.02.007

El-Sayed Ebaid, I. (2009). The impact of capital-structure choice on firm performance: Empirical evidence from Egypt. *The Journal of Risk Finance, 10*(5), 477–487. doi:10.1108/15265940911001385

Fama, E. F. (1970). Efficient capital markets: A review of theory and empirical work. *The Journal of Finance, 25*(2), 383–417. doi:10.2307/2325486

Fatemi, A., Fooladi, I., & Tehranian, H. (2015). Valuation effects of corporate social responsibility. *Journal of Banking & Finance, 59*, 182–192. doi:10.1016/j.jbankfin.2015.04.028

Fatemi, A., Glaum, M., & Kaiser, S. (2017). ESG performance and firm value: The moderating role of disclosure. *Global Finance Journal.*

Fosu, S. (2013). Capital structure, product market competition and firm performance: Evidence from South Africa. *The Quarterly Review of Economics and Finance, 53*(2), 140–151. doi:10.1016/j.qref.2013.02.004

Harjoto, M. A., & Jo, H. (2015). Legal vs. normative CSR: Differential impact on analyst dispersion, stock return volatility, cost of capital, and firm value. *Journal of Business Ethics, 128*(1), 1–20. doi:10.100710551-014-2082-2

Hasan, M. B., Ahsan, A. M., Rahaman, M. A., & Alam, M. N. (2014). Influence of capital structure on firm performance: Evidence from Bangladesh. *International Journal of Business and Management, 9*(5), 184. doi:10.5539/ijbm.v9n5p184

Khan, A. G. (2012). The relationship of capital structure decisions with firm performance: A study of the engineering sector of Pakistan. *International Journal of Accounting and Financial Reporting, 2*(1), 245. doi:10.5296/ijafr.v2i1.1825

Kiron, D., Unruh, G., Kruschwitz, N., Reeves, M., Rubel, H., Meyer, A., & Felde, Z. (2017). *Corporate sustainability at a crossroads: Progress toward our common future in uncertain times*. MIT Sloan Management Review & Boston Consulting Group.

Kyereboah-Coleman, A. (2007). The impact of capital structure on the performance of microfinance institutions. *The Journal of Risk Finance, 8*(1), 56–71. doi:10.1108/15265940710721082

Le, T. P. V., & Phan, T. B. N. (2017). Capital structure and firm performance: Empirical evidence from a small transition country. *Research in International Business and Finance, 42*, 710–726. doi:10.1016/j.ribaf.2017.07.012

Majumdar, S. K., & Chhibber, P. (1999). Capital structure and performance: Evidence from a transition economy on an aspect of corporate governance. *Public Choice, 98*(3/4), 287–305. doi:10.1023/A:1018355127454

Margaritis, D., & Psillaki, M. (2007). Capital structure and firm efficiency. *Journal of Business Finance & Accounting, 34*, 1447–1469.

Margaritis, D., & Psillaki, M. (2010). Capital structure, equity ownership and firm performance. *Journal of Banking & Finance, 34*(3), 621–632. doi:10.1016/j.jbankfin.2009.08.023

McWilliams, A., & Siegel, D. (2000). Corporate social responsibility and financial performance: Correlation or misspecification? *Strategic Management Journal*, *21*(5), 603–609. doi:10.1002/(SICI)1097-0266(200005)21:5<603::AID-SMJ101>3.0.CO;2-3

Memon, F., Bhutto, N. A., & Abbass, G. (2012). Capital structure and firm performance: A case of textile sector of Pakistan. *Asian Journal of Business and Management Sciences*, *1*, 9–15.

Modigliani, F., & Miller, M. H. (1958). The cost of capital, corporation finance and the theory of investment. *The American Economic Review*, *48*(3), 261–297.

Özcan, İ. Ç. (2018). *Halka Açık Demiryolu Şirketlerinin Yönetişim Aydınlatma Notlarının Belirleyicileri. İşletme Araştırmaları Dergisi*, *10*(4), 1242–1254.

Özcan, İ. Ç. (2020). Determinants of Environmental, Social, and Governance Reporting of Rail Companies: Does State Ownership Matter? In F. Manes-Rossi & R. Levy Orelli (Eds.), *New Trends in Public Sector Reporting. Public Sector Financial Management*. Cham: Palgrave Macmillan; doi:10.1007/978-3-030-40056-9_8

Plumlee, M., Brown, D., Hayes, R. M., & Marshall, R. S. (2015). Voluntary environmental disclosure quality and firm value: Further evidence. *Journal of Accounting and Public Policy*, *34*(4), 336–361. doi:10.1016/j.jaccpubpol.2015.04.004

Pouraghajan, A., Malekian, E., Emamgholipour, M., Lotfollahpur, V. & Bagheri, M. M. 2012. The relationship between capital structure and firm performance evaluation measures: Evidence from the Tehran Stock Exchange. *International Journal of Business and Commerce, 1*, 166-181.

Renneboog, L., Ter Horst, J., & Zhang, C. (2008). Socially responsible investments: Institutional aspects, performance, and investor behavior. *Journal of Banking & Finance*, *32*(9), 1723–1742. doi:10.1016/j.jbankfin.2007.12.039

Waddock, S. A., & Graves, S. B. (1997). The corporate social performance–financial performance link. *Strategic Management Journal*, *18*(4), 303–319. doi:10.1002/(SICI)1097-0266(199704)18:4<303::AID-SMJ869>3.0.CO;2-G

Weber, O. (2014). Environmental, social and governance reporting in China. *Business Strategy and the Environment*, *23*(5), 303–317. doi:10.1002/bse.1785

Zeitun, R. & Tian, G. 2014. Capital structure and corporate performance: evidence from Jordan.

Compilation of References

Abbas, J. (2020). Impact of total quality management on corporate green performance through the mediating role of corporate social responsibility. *Journal of Cleaner Production, 242*, 118458. doi:10.1016/j.jclepro.2019.118458

Abbott, L. J., Park, Y., & Parker, S. (2000). The effects of audit committee activity and independence on corporate fraud. *Managerial Finance Journal, 26*(30), 55–67. doi:10.1108/03074350010766990

Abor, J. (2005). The effect of capital structure on profitability: An empirical analysis of listed firms in Ghana. *The Journal of Risk Finance, 6*(5), 438–445. doi:10.1108/15265940510633505

Abrahamson, E. (1991). Managerial fads and fashions: The diffusion and rejection of innovations. *Academy of Management Review, 16*(3), 586–612. doi:10.5465/amr.1991.4279484

Abrahamson, E. (1996). Management fashion, academic fashion, and enduring truths. *Academy of Management Review, 21*(3), 616–618.

Accenture. (2016). *The United Nations Global Compact. CEO Study on Sustainability. Transforming Partnerships for the SDGs*. Author.

Adams, J. S., Taschian, A., & Shore, T. H. (1996). Ethics in family and non-family owned firms: An exploratory study. *Family Business Review, 9*(2), 157–170. doi:10.1111/j.1741-6248.1996.00157.x

Adamson, P. A. (2010). *Brand Simple*. Publica Publishing House.

Adegoke, O., Walumbwa, F.O., & Myers, A. (2012). Innovation strategy, human resource policy, and firms' revenue growth: The roles of environmental uncertainty and innovation performance. *A Journal of Decision Sciences Institute, 43*(2), 273-301.

Adler, R. W. (2000). Strategic investment decision appraisal techniques: The old and the new. *Business Horizons, 43*(6), 15–22. doi:10.1016/S0007-6813(00)80017-8

Aduda, J., Okiro, K., & Omoro, N. (2015). The Effect of Corporate Governance and Capital Structure on Performance of Firms Listed at the East African Community Securities Exchange. *European Scientific Journal, 11*(7), 18–19.

Aerts, W., Cormier, D., & Magnan, M. (2005). Intra-industry imitation in corporate environmental reporting: An international perspective. *Journal of Accounting and Policy, 25*(3), 299–331. doi:10.1016/j.jaccpubpol.2006.03.004

Agasisti, T., Arnaboldi, M., & Azzone, G. (2008). Strategic management accounting in universities: The Italian experience. *Higher Education, 55*(1), 1–15. doi:10.100710734-006-9032-6

Agboli, M., & Ukaegbu, C. C. (2006). Business environment and entrepreneurial activity in Nigeria: Implications for industrial development. *The Journal of Modern African Studies, 44*(1), 1–30. doi:10.1017/S0022278X05001394

Aggarwal, P. (2013). Sustainability reporting and its impact on corporate financial performance: A literature review. *Indian Journal of Commerce & Management Studies*, *4*(3), 51–59.

Agha, S., Alrubaiee, L., & Jamhour, M. (2012). Effect of core competence on competitive advantage and organizational performance. *International Journal of Business and Management*, *7*(1), 192–204.

Aguilera, R. V., & Jackson, G. (2003). The cross-national diversity of corporate governance: Dimensions and determinants. *Academy of Management Review*, *28*(3), 447–465. doi:10.5465/amr.2003.10196772

Ahearne, M., Lam, S. K., Mathieu, J. E., & Bolander, W. (2010). Why are some sales people better at adapting to organizational change? *Journal of Marketing*, *74*(3), 65–79. doi:10.1509/jmkg.74.3.065

Ahmad, N., & Seymour, R. G. (2008). *Defining Entrepreneurial Activity: Definitions Supporting Frameworks for Data Collection.* OECD Statistics Working Papers. OECD Publishing.

Akgün, A. E., Keskin, H., & Byrne, J. (2009). Organizational emotional capability, product and process innovation, and firm performance: An empirical analysis. *Journal of Engineering and Technology Management*, *26*(3), 103–130. doi:10.1016/j.jengtecman.2009.06.008

Alamri, A. M. (2018). Strategic Management Accounting and the Dimensions of Competitive Advantage: Testing the Associations in Saudi Industrial Sector, *International Journal of Academic Research in Accounting. Finance and Management Sciences*, *8*(2), 48–64.

Aldrich, H. E. (2011). *An Evolutionary Approach to Entrepreneurship: Selected Essays by Howard E. Aldrich.* Edward Elgar.

Alestalo, M., & Kuhnle, S. (1986). 1 The Scandinavian Route: Economic, Social, and Political Developments in Denmark, Finland, Norway, and Sweden. *International Journal of Sociology*, *16*(3-4), 1–38. doi:10.1080/15579336.1986.11769909

Alexander, G. J., & Buchholz, R. A. (1978). Corporate social responsibility and stock market performance. *Academy of Management Journal*, *21*(3), 479–486. doi:10.5465/255728

Alhyari, S., Alazab, M., Venkatraman, S., Alazab, M., & Alazab, A. (2013). Performance evaluation of e-government services using balanced scorecard. *Benchmarking*, *20*(4), 512–536. doi:10.1108/BIJ-08-2011-0063

Alkaraan, F., & Northcott, D. (2006). Strategic capital investment decision-making: A role for emergent analysis tools? A study of practice in large UK manufacturing companies. *The British Accounting Review*, *38*(2), 149–173. doi:10.1016/j.bar.2005.10.003

Allan, F. (1993). Benchmarking: Practical aspects for information professionals. *Special Libraries*, *84*(3), 123–130.

Allen, A., & Ramanna, K. (2013). Towards an understanding of the role of standard setters in standard setting. *Journal of Accounting and Economics*, *55*(1), 1–66. doi:10.1016/j.jacceco.2012.05.003

Almutairi, A. R., Dunn, K. A., & Skantz, T. (2009). Auditor tenure, auditor specialization, and information asymmetry. *Managerial Auditing Journal*, *24*(7), 600–623. doi:10.1108/02686900910975341

Alstete, J. W., & Beutell, N. J. (2018). Designing learning spaces for management education: A mixed methods research approach. *Journal of Management Development*, *37*(2), 201–211. doi:10.1108/JMD-08-2017-0247

Al-Thuneibat, A. A., Al Issa, R. T. I., & Baker, R. A. A. (2011). Do audit tenure and firm size contribute to audit quality? Empirical evidence from Jordan. *Managerial Auditing Journal*, *26*(4), 317–334. doi:10.1108/02686901111124648

Al-Tuwaijri, S. A., Christensen, T. E., & Hughes, K. E. II. (2004). The relations among environmental disclosure, environmental performance, and economic performance: A simultaneous equations approach. *Accounting, Organizations and Society*, *29*(5-6), 447–471. doi:10.1016/S0361-3682(03)00032-1

Alvarez, S. A., & Barney, J. B. (2005). How Do Entrepreneurs Organize Under Conditions of Uncertainty? *Journal of Management*, *31*(5), 776–793. doi:10.1177/0149206305279486

Alzola, M. A. (2017). Beware of the watchdog: Rethinking the normative justification of gatekeeper liability. *Journal of Business Ethics*, *140*(4), 705–721. doi:10.100710551-017-3460-3

Amagoh, F. (2008). Perspectives on organizational change: Systems and complexity theories. *The Innovation Journal*, *13*(3), 1–14.

Amir, E., & Lev, B. (1996). Value-relevance of nonfinancial information: The wireless communication industry. *Journal of Accounting and Economics*, *2*(1-3), 3–30. doi:10.1016/S0165-4101(96)00430-2

Anand, G., & Kodali, R. (2010). A mathematical model for the evaluation of roles and responsibilities of human resources in a lean manufacturing environment. *International Journal of Human Resources Development and Management*, *10*(1), 63–100. doi:10.1504/IJHRDM.2010.029447

Andayani, W., Atmini, S., Sadewo, D., & Mwangi, J. (2008). *Corporate social responsibility, good corporate governance and the intellectual property: An external strategy of the management to increase the company's value*. National Conference on Management Research, Makassar. Retrieved from https://ssrn.com/abstract=1327513

Anderson, J. C., & Frankle, A. W. (1980). Voluntary Social Reporting: An Iso-Beta Portfolio Analysis. *The Accounting Review*, *55*(3), 467–479.

Andon, P., & Baxter, J. (2011). Introducing and contextualising customer lifetime valuation: A management accounting teaching resource. *Accounting Education*, *20*(1), 39–61. doi:10.1080/09639284.2010.543342

Andriole, S. J. (2010). Business impact of Web 2.0 Technologies. *Communications of the ACM*, *53*(12), 67–79. doi:10.1145/1859204.1859225

Angelini, P., Di Salvo, R., & Ferri, G. (1998). Availability and cost of credit for small businesses: Customer relationships and credit cooperatives. *Journal of Banking & Finance*, *22*(6-8), 925–954. doi:10.1016/S0378-4266(98)00008-9

Anik, R., Nadjadji, A., & Suwignjo, P. (2010). Analysis of internal and external factors for competitive advantage of Indonesian contractors. *Journal of Economics and Engineering*, *2*(4), 51–68.

Anna, A. L., Chandler, G. N., Jansen, E., & Mero, N. P. (2000). Women business owners in traditional and non-traditional industries. *Journal of Business Venturing*, *15*(3), 279–303. doi:10.1016/S0883-9026(98)00012-3

Ansoff, I. (1989). *Company's development strategies*. Organization's Edition.

Aras, G., Tezcan, N., & Furtuna, O. K. (2018). Multidimensional comprehensive corporate sustainability performance evaluation model: Evidence from an emerging market banking sector. *Journal of Cleaner Production*, *185*, 600–609. doi:10.1016/j.jclepro.2018.01.175

Aren, S., & Aydemir, S. D. (2015). The moderation of financial literacy on the relationship between individual factors and risky investment intention. *International Business Research*, *8*(6), 17–28. doi:10.5539/ibr.v8n6p17

Aren, S., Aydemir, S. D., & Sehitoglu, Y. (2016). Behavioral biases on institutional investors: A literature review. *Kybernetes*, *45*(10), 1668–1684. doi:10.1108/K-08-2015-0203

Argento, D., Culasso, F., & Truant, E. (2019). From Sustainability to Integrated Reporting: The Legitimizing Role of the CSR Manager. *Organization & Environment*, *32*(4), 484–507. doi:10.1177/1086026618769487

Argyris, C. (1990). *Overcoming organizational defences: Facilitating organizational learning*. Allyn and Bacon.

Armstrong, C. S., Guay, W. R., & Weber, J. P. (2010). The role of information and financial reporting in corporate governance and debt contracting. *Journal of Accounting and Economics*, *50*(2-3), 179–234. doi:10.1016/j.jacceco.2010.10.001

Armstrong, M. (2004). *How to become a better manager*. Meteor Press Publishing House.

Armstrong, M. B., Ketz, J. E., & Owsen, D. (2003). Ethics education in accounting: Moving toward ethical motivation and ethical behavior. *Journal of Accounting Education*, *21*(1), 1–16. doi:10.1016/S0748-5751(02)00017-9

Arsenault, P., & Faerman, S. R. (2014). Embracing paradox in management: The value of the competing values framework. *Organizational Management Journal*, *11*(3), 147–158. doi:10.1080/15416518.2014.949614

Ashkanasy, N. (2011). International happiness; a multilevel perspective. *The Academy of Management Perspectives*, (February), 23–29.

Astebro, T., & Thompson, P. (2009). *Entrepreneurs: Jacks of All Trades or Hobos?* Economics Research Working Paper Series, 48. Miami, FL: Florida International University.

Atamer, T., & Calori, R. (1993). *Diagnosis and strategic decisions*. Dunod.

Atkinson, A. A., Kaplan, R. S., Matsumura, E. M., & Young, S. M. (2012). *Management accounting – Information for decision-making and strategy execution* (6th ed.). Pearson Prentice Hall.

Audretsch, D. B. (2003). *Entrepreneurship. A Survey of the Literature. Enterprise Papers, 14*. European Commission.

Aupperle, K. E., Carroll, A. B., & Hatfield, J. B. (1985). An Empirical Examination of the Relationship between Corporate Social Responsibility and Profitability. *Academy of Management Journal*, *28*, 446–463.

Awais, A., & Hussain, S. (2015). Understanding Corporate Governance and Board of Directors: A Generic Analysis. *Academic Research International Journal*, *6*(4), 20–25.

Ayağ, Z. (2005). A fuzzy AHP-based simulation approach to concept evaluation in a NPD environment. *IIE Transactions*, *37*(9), 827–842. doi:10.1080/07408170590969852

Bachmann, P., & Ingenhoff, D. (2016). Legitimacy through CSR disclosures? The advantage outweighs the disadvantages. *Public Relations Review*, *42*(3), 386–394. doi:10.1016/j.pubrev.2016.02.008

Baines, A., & Langfield-Smith, K. (2003). Antecedents to management accounting change: A structural equation approach. *Accounting, Organizations and Society*, *28*(7-8), 675–698. doi:10.1016/S0361-3682(02)00102-2

Balachandran, B., & Faff, R. (2015). Corporate governance, firm value and risk: Past, present, and future. *Pacific-Basin Finance Journal*, *35*(A), 1-12.

Ball, R., Li, X., & Shivakumar, L. (2015). Contractibility and transparency of financial statement information prepared under IFRS: Evidence from debt contracts around IFRS adoption. *Journal of Accounting Research*, *53*(5), 915–963. doi:10.1111/1475-679X.12095

Bandyopadhyay, A., & Barua, N. M. (2016). Factors determining capital structure and corporate performance in India: Studying the business cycle effects. *The Quarterly Review of Economics and Finance*, *61*, 160–172. doi:10.1016/j.qref.2016.01.004

Barnea, A., & Rubin, A. (2010). Corporate Social Responsibility as a conflict between shareholders. *Journal of Business Ethics*, *97*(1), 71–86. doi:10.100710551-010-0496-z

Barney, J. B. (1986). Organizational culture: Can it be a source of sustained competitive advantage. *Academy of Management Review*, *11*(3), 656–665. doi:10.5465/amr.1986.4306261

Baron, R. A. (2007). Entrepreneurship: A Process Perspective. In J. R. Baum, M. Frese, & R. A. Baron (Eds.), *The Psychology of Entrepreneurship* (pp. 19–39). Erlbaum.

Baroto, M. B., Abdullah, M. M. B., & Wan, H. L. (2012). Hybrid strategy: A new strategy for competitive advantage. *International Journal of Business and Management*, *7*(20), 120–133.

Barth, M. E. (2013). Global comparability in financial reporting: What, why, how, and when? *China Journal of Accounting Studies*, *1*(1), 2–12. doi:10.1080/21697221.2013.781765

Barth, M. E., Konchitchki, Y. L., & Landsman, W. R. (2013). Cost of capital and earnings transparency. *Journal of Accounting and Economics*, *55*(2–3), 206–224. doi:10.1016/j.jacceco.2013.01.004

Barth, M. E., Landsman, W. R., Young, D., & Zhuang, Z. (2014). Relevance of Differences between Net Income based on IFRS and Domestic Standards for European Firms. *Journal of Business Finance & Accounting*, *41*(3-4), 297–506. doi:10.1111/jbfa.12067

Barth, M., Landsman, W., & Lang, M. (2008). International accounting standards and accounting quality. *Journal of Accounting Research*, *46*(3), 467–498. doi:10.1111/j.1475-679X.2008.00287.x

Bar-Yosef, S., & Prencipe, A. (2011). Corporate governance and Earnings Management in Family Controlled Companies. *Journal of Accounting, Auditing & Finance*, *26*(2), 199–227. doi:10.1177/0148558X11401212

Bassen, A., Meyer, K., & Schlange, J. (2006). The Influence of corporate social responsibility on the cost of capital. *SSRN Electronic Journal*. Retrieved from https://ssrn.com/abstract=984406

Bazerman, M., Morgan, K., & Loewenstein, G. (1997). The impossibility of auditor independence. *Sloan Management Review*, *38*(4), 89–94.

Beasley, M. S., Buckless, F. A., Glover, S. M., & Prawitt, D. F. (2009). *Auditing Cases. An Interactive Learning Approach* (4th ed.). Prentice Hall.

Becchetti, L., Rocco, C., & Hasan, I. (2007). *Corporate Social Responsibility and Shareholder's Value: An Event Study Analysis*. Working Paper. Federal Reserve Bank of Atlanta. Retrieved from https://www.frbatlanta.org/research/publications/wp/2007/06.aspx

Becker, B. E., & Huselid, M. A. (1998). High performance work systems and firm performance: A synthesis of research and managerial implications. *Research in Personnel and Human Resources Management*, *16*, 53–101.

Becker, B. E., & Huselid, M. A. (2006). Strategic human resources management: Where do we go from here? *Journal of Management*, *32*(6), 898–925. doi:10.1177/0149206306293668

Behery, M., Jabeen, F., & Parakandi, M. (2014). Adopting a contemporary performance management system. *International Journal of Productivity and Performance Management*, *63*(1), 22–43. doi:10.1108/IJPPM-07-2012-0076

Beiner, S., Drobetz, W., Schmid, M., & Zimmerman, H. (2004). An integrated framework of corporate governance and firm valuation. *European Financial Management*, *12*(2), 249–283. doi:10.1111/j.1354-7798.2006.00318.x

Berger, A., & Udell, G. F. (1995). Relationship lending and lines of credit in small business finance. *The Journal of Business*, *68*(3), 351–381. doi:10.1086/296668

Berger, A., & Udell, G. F. (1998). The economics of small business finance: The roles of private equity and debt markets in the financial growth cycle. *Journal of Banking & Finance*, *22*, 613–673. doi:10.1016/S0378-4266(98)00038-7

Berger, A., & Udell, G. F. (2003). Small business and debt finance. In Z. Acs & D. Audretsch (Eds.), *Handbook of entrepreneurship*. Kluwer Academic Publishing.

Bhattacharya, S., & Thakor, A. V. (1993). Contemporary banking theory. *Journal of Financial Intermediation*, *3*(1), 2–50. doi:10.1006/jfin.1993.1001

Bhimani, A. (2008). Making Corporate Governance Count: The Fusion of Ethics and Economic Rationality. *The Journal of Management and Governance*, *12*(2), 135–147. doi:10.100710997-008-9056-7

Bhimani, A., & Langfield-Smith, K. (2007). Structure, formality and the importance of financial and nonfinancial information in strategy development and implementation. *Management Accounting Research*, *18*(1), 3–31. doi:10.1016/j.mar.2006.06.005

Bhojraj, S., & Sengupta, P. (2003). Effect of corporate governance on bond ratings and yields: The role of institutional investors and outside directors. *The Journal of Business*, *76*(3), 455–475. doi:10.1086/344114

Blackwell, D., & Winters, D. (1997). Banking relationships and the effect of monitoring on loan pricing. *Journal of Financial Research*, *20*(2), 275–289. doi:10.1111/j.1475-6803.1997.tb00249.x

Bodenhorn, H. (2003). Short-term loans and long-term relationships: Relationship lending in Early America. *Journal of Money, Credit and Banking*, *35*(4), 485–506. doi:10.1353/mcb.2003.0025

Boiral, O., Heras-Saizarbitoria, I., Brotherton, M., & Bernard, J. (2019). Ethical issues in the assurance of sustainability reports: Perspectives from assurance providers. *Journal of Business Ethics*, *159*(4), 1111–1125. doi:10.100710551-018-3840-3

Boot, A. W. (2000). Relationship banking: What do we know? *Journal of Financial Intermediation*, *9*(1), 7–25. doi:10.1006/jfin.2000.0282

Boot, A. W., & Thakor, A. V. (1994). Moral hazard and secured lending in an infinitely repeated credit market game. *International Economic Review*, *35*(4), 899–920. doi:10.2307/2527003

Bortree, D. S. (2009). The impact of green initiatives on environmental legitimacy and admiration of the organization. *Public Relations Review*, *35*(2), 133–135. doi:10.1016/j.pubrev.2009.01.002

Botosan, C. A. (1997). Disclosure level and the cost of equity capital. *The Accounting Review*, *72*, 323–349.

Bourguignon, A. (2000). *Performance et contrôle de gestion. Encyclopédie de Comptabilité, Contrôle de gestion et Audit*. Economica.

Boyle, E. J., Higgins, M. M., & Rhee, G. S. (1997). Stock market reaction to ethical initiatives of defense contractors: Theory and evidence. *Critical Perspectives on Accounting*, *8*(6), 541–561. doi:10.1006/cpac.1997.0124

Bozec, Y. (2008). Ownership Concentration, Separation of Voting Rights from Cash Flow Rights, and Earnings Management: An Empirical Study in Canada. *Canadian Journal of Administrative Sciences*, *25*(1), 1–15. doi:10.1002/cjas.52

Brammer, S., Brooks, C., & Pavelin, S. (2006). Corporate social performance and stock returns: UK evidence from disaggregate measures. *Financial Management*, *35*(3), 97–116. doi:10.1111/j.1755-053X.2006.tb00149.x

Brem, A., Maier, M., & Wimschneider, C. (2016). Competitive advantage through innovation: The case of Nespresso. *European Journal of Innovation Management*, *19*(1), 133–148. doi:10.1108/EJIM-05-2014-0055

Brevoort, K. P., & Wolken, J. D. (2008). *Does Distance Matter in Banking? Finance and Economics Discussion Series, Division of Research & Statistics and Monetary Affairs*. Federal Reserve Board. Retrieved from https://www.federalreserve.gov/Pubs/FEDS/2008/200834/200834pap.pdf

Brinkmann, J. (2002). Marketing ethics as professional ethics: Concepts, approaches and typologies. *Journal of Business Ethics*, *41*(1/2), 159–177. doi:10.1023/A:1021318710382

Bromwich, M. (1990). The case for strategic management accounting: The role of accounting information for strategy in competitive markets. *Accounting, Organizations and Society*, *15*(1-2), 27–46. doi:10.1016/0361-3682(90)90011-I

Bromwich, M., & Bhimani, A. (1994). *Management accountant pathways to progress*. The Chatered Institute of Management Accountants.

Brouthers, K. D., & Roozen, F. A. (1999). Is it time start thinking about strategic accounting? *Long Range Planning*, *32*(3), 311–322. doi:10.1016/S0024-6301(99)00035-7

Brown, D. R., & Harvey, D. (2006). *An Experimental approach to Organization development*. Pearson Education.

Brown, L., & Caylor, M. (2004). Corporate governance and firm operating performance. *Review of Quantitative Finance and Accounting*, *32*(2), 129–144. doi:10.100711156-007-0082-3

Brown, V. L., Gissel, J. L., & Neely, D. G. (2016). Audit quality indicators: Perceptions of junior-level auditors. *Managerial Auditing Journal*, *31*(8/9), 949–980. doi:10.1108/MAJ-01-2016-1300

Brüggemann, U., Hitz, J.-M., & Sellhorn, T. (2013). Intended and unintended consequences of mandatory IFRS adoption: A review of extant evidence and suggestions for future research. *European Accounting Review*, *22*(1), 1–37. doi:10.1080/09638180.2012.718487

Bula, H. O. (2012). Evolution and Theories of Entrepreneurship: A Critical Review on the Kenyan Perspective. *International Journal of Business and Commerce*, *1*(11), 81–96.

Burchell, J., & Cook, J. (2008). Stakeholder dialogue and organisational learning: Changing relationships between companies and NGOs. *Business Ethics (Oxford, England)*, *17*(1), 35–46. doi:10.1111/j.1467-8608.2008.00518.x

Burns, C.J.M., Houghton, L., & Stewart, H., (2019). Sustainability – A key to Australian finance directors improving their organisation's CSR culture. *Corp Soc Resp Env Ma.*, 1– 13.

Busenitz, L. W., & Barney, J. B. (1997). Differences between entrepreneurs and managers in large organizations: Biases and heuristics in strategic decision-making. *Journal of Business Venturing*, *12*(1), 9–30. doi:10.1016/S0883-9026(96)00003-1

Bushee, B. J. (1998). Do institutional investors prefer near-term earnings over long-run value? *Contemporary Accounting Research*, *18*(2), 207–246. doi:10.1506/J4GU-BHWH-8HME-LE0X

Cadez, S., & Guilding, C. (2008). An exploratory investigation of integrated contingency model of strategy management accounting. *Accounting, Organizations and Society*, *33*(7-8), 836–863. doi:10.1016/j.aos.2008.01.003

Cairns, D., Massoudi, D., Taplin, R., & Tarca, A. (2011). IFRS fair value measurement and accounting policy choice in the United Kingdom and Australia. *The British Accounting Review*, *43*(1), 1–21. doi:10.1016/j.bar.2010.10.003

Cameron, K. S., & Quinn, R. E. (2011). *Diagnosing and Changing Organizational Culture: Based on the Competing Values Framework*. Jossey-Bass.

Camilleri, M. A. (2018). Theoretical insights on integrated reporting: The inclusion of non-financial capitals in corporate disclosures. *Corporate Communications*, *23*(4), 567–581. Advance online publication. doi:10.1108/CCIJ-01-2018-0016

Campa, D. (2013). "Big 4 fee premium" and audit quality: Latest evidence from UK listed companies. *Managerial Auditing Journal*, *28*(8), 680–707. doi:10.1108/MAJ-11-2012-0784

Canning, M., O'Dwyer, B., & Georgakopoulos, G. (2019). Processes of auditability in sustainability assurance – The case of materiality construction. *Accounting and Business Research*, *49*(1), 1–27. doi:10.1080/00014788.2018.1442208

Carcello, F. (2002). The effects of uncertainty reporting on lending officers' perceptions of risk and additional information required. *Abacus*, *23*(2), 172–181.

Carey, P., & Simnett, R. (2006). Audit partner tenure and audit quality. *The Accounting Review*, *81*(3), 653–676. doi:10.2308/accr.2006.81.3.653

Carlson, J. R., Carlson, D. S., & Ferguson, M. (2010). Deceptive Impression Management: Does deception pay in established workplace relationships? *Journal of Business Ethics*, 497–514.

Carlsson-Wall, M., Kraus, K., & Lind, J. (2015). Strategic management accounting in close interorganisational relationships. *Accounting and Business Research*, *45*(1), 27–54. doi:10.1080/00014788.2014.965128

Carr, C., Kolehmainen, K., & Mitchell, F. (2010). Strategic investment decision making practices: A contextual approach. *Management Accounting Research*, *21*(3), 167–184. doi:10.1016/j.mar.2010.03.004

Carr, C., & Tomkins, C. (1996). Strategic investment decisions: The importance of SCM. A comparative analysis of 51 case studies in U.K., U.S. and German companies. *Management Accounting Research*, *7*(2), 199–217. doi:10.1006/mare.1996.0012

Carroll, A. B., & Buchholtz, A. K. (2006). Business & Society: Ethics and Stakeholder Management (6th ed.). Mason: Thomson South-Western.

Carroll, G. R., & Khessina, O. M. (2005). The Ecology of Entrepreneurship. In S. A. Alvarez, R. Agarwal, & O. Sorenson (Eds.), *Handbook of Entrepreneurship Research: Disciplinary Perspectives* (pp. 167–200). Springer. doi:10.1007/0-387-23622-8_9

Carson, E. (2009). Industry specialization by global audit firm networks. *The Accounting Review*, *84*(2), 355–382. doi:10.2308/accr.2009.84.2.355

Caves, R., & Uekusa, M. (1976). *Industrial organization in Japan*. Brookings Institution.

Chan, L. L., Shaffer, M. A., & Snape, E. (2004). In search of sustained competitive advantage: The impact of organizational culture, competitive strategy and human resource management practices on firm performance. *International Journal of Human Resource Management*, *15*(1), 17–35. doi:10.1080/0958519032000157320

Chan, Y. S. S., & Leung, P. (2006). The Effects of Accounting Students' Ethical Reasoning and Personal Factors on Their Sensitivity. *Managerial Auditing Journal*, *21*(4), 436–457. doi:10.1108/02686900610661432

Chapin, F. S. III, Torn, M. S., & Tateno, M. (1996). Principles of ecosystem sustainability. *American Naturalist*, *148*(6), 1016–1037. doi:10.1086/285969

Chebaane, S., & Othman, H. B. (2014). The Impact of IFRS Adoption on Value Relevance of Earnings and Book Value of Equity: The Case of Emerging Markets in African and Asian Regions. *Procedia: Social and Behavioral Sciences*, *145*, 70–80. doi:10.1016/j.sbspro.2014.06.012

Cheng, B., Ioannou, I., & Serafeim, G. (2014). Corporate social responsibility and access to finance. *Strategic Management Journal*, *35*(1), 1–23. doi:10.1002mj.2131

Cheng, S. (2008). Board size and the variability of corporate performance. *Journal of Financial Economics*, *87*(10), 157–176. doi:10.1016/j.jfineco.2006.10.006

Chen, H. M., & Fu, P. C. (2008). A systematic framework for performance appraisal and compensation strategy. *Human Systems Management*, *27*(2), 161–175. doi:10.3233/HSM-2008-0674

Chen, H., Tang, Q., Jiang, Y., & Lin, Z. (2010). The role of international financial reporting standards in accounting quality: Evidence from the European Union. *Journal of International Financial Management & Accounting*, *21*(3), 220–278. doi:10.1111/j.1467-646X.2010.01041.x

Chenhall, R. H. (2008). Accounting for the horizontal organization: A review essay. *Accounting, Organizations and Society*, *33*(4-5), 517–550. doi:10.1016/j.aos.2007.07.004

Chen, K. C., Chen, Z., & Wei, K. J. (2009). Legal protection of investors, corporate governance, and the cost of equity capital. *Journal of Corporate Finance*, *15*(3), 273–289. doi:10.1016/j.jcorpfin.2009.01.001

Chen, K. Y., Lin, K. L., & Zhou, J. (2005). Audit quality and earnings management for Taiwan IPO firms. *Managerial Auditing Journal*, *20*(1), 86–104. doi:10.1108/02686900510570722

Chen, Y., Hsu, J., Huang, M., & Yang, P. (2013). Quality, size, and performance of audit firms. *The International Journal of Business and Finance Research*, *7*(5), 89–105.

Chin, C., & Chi, H. (2009). Reducing restatements with increased industry expertise. *Contemporary Accounting Research*, *26*(3), 729–765. doi:10.1506/car.26.3.4

Chiucchi, M. S. (2013). Intellectual capital accounting in action: Enhancing learning through interventionist research. *Journal of Intellectual Capital*, *14*(1), 48–68. doi:10.1108/14691931311289011

Cho, C. H., Guidry, R. P., Hageman, A. M., & Patten, D. M. (2012). Do actions speak louder than words? An empirical investigation of corporate environmental reputation. *Accounting, Organizations and Society*, *37*(1), 14–25. doi:10.1016/j.aos.2011.12.001

Cho, C. H., Michelon, G., & Patten, D. M. (2012). Impression management in sustainability reports: An empirical investigation of the use of graphs. *Accounting and the Public Interest*, *12*(1), 16–37. doi:10.2308/apin-10249

Cho, C. H., & Patten, D. M. (2007). The role of environmental disclosures as tools of legitimacy: A research note. *Accounting, Organizations and Society*, *32*(7-8), 7–8, 639–647. doi:10.1016/j.aos.2006.09.009

Cho, C. H., Phillips, J., Hageman, A. M., & Patten, D. M. (2009). Media richness, user trust, and perceptions of corporate social responsibility. An experimental investigation of visual website disclosures. *Accounting, Auditing & Accountability Journal*, *22*(6), 933–952. doi:10.1108/09513570910980481

Cho, C. H., Roberts, R. W., & Patten, D. M. (2010). The language of US corporate environmental disclosure. *Accounting, Organizations and Society*, *35*(4), 431–443. doi:10.1016/j.aos.2009.10.002

Choi, J., Kim, C. F., Kim, J., & Zang, Y. (2010). Audit office size, audit quality, and audit pricing. *Auditing*, *29*(1), 73–97. doi:10.2308/aud.2010.29.1.73

Choi, Y.-S., Peasnell, K., & Toniato, J. (2013). Has the IASB been successful in making accounting earnings more useful for prediction and valuation? UK evidence. *Journal of Business Finance & Accounting*, *40*(7–8), 741–768. doi:10.1111/jbfa.12025

Cho, J., Ran, J., & Kim, L. (2003). Subject to' audit opinions and abnormal security returns –Outcomes and ambiguities. *Journal of Accounting Research*, *20*(2), 617–638.

Chu, T. C. (2002). Facility location selection using fuzzy TOPSIS under group decisions. *International Journal of Uncertainty, Fuzziness and Knowledge-based Systems, 10*(06), 687–701. doi:10.1142/S0218488502001739

Cinquini, L., & Tenucci, A. (2010). Strategic management accounting and business strategy: A loose coupling? *Journal of Accounting and Organizational Change, 6*(2), 228–259. doi:10.1108/18325911011048772

Ciulla, J. B. (2007). The importance of leadership in shaping business values. In *Corporate Ethics and Corporate Governance* (pp. 67–77). Springer. doi:10.1007/978-3-540-70818-6_5

Clarke, T. (2004). The evolution of directors' duties: Bridging the divide between corporate governance and corporate social responsibility. *Journal of General Management, 32*(3), 79–105. doi:10.1177/030630700703200305

Clarkson, P. M., Overell, M. B., & Chapple, L. (2011). Environmental Reporting and its Relation to Corporate Environmental Performance. *Abacus, 47*(1), 27–60. doi:10.1111/j.1467-6281.2011.00330.x

Clayton, C. M. (1997). Innovator' s Dilemma, Harvard Business School Press.

Coad, A. (1996). Smart work and hard work: Explicating a learning orientation in strategic management accounting. *Management Accounting Research, 7*(4), 387–408. doi:10.1006/mare.1996.0022

Cocca, P., & Alberti, M. (2010). A framework to assess performance measurement in SMEs. *International Journal of Productivity and Performance Management, 59*(2), 186–200. doi:10.1108/17410401011014258

Cohen, A. (1962). Yield on new underwritten corporate bonds. *The Journal of Finance, 42*, 585–605.

Colins, J. (2010). *Business excellence.* Curtea Veche Publishing House.

Collins, D. W., & Kothari, S. P. (1998). An analysis of intertemporal and cross-sectional determinants of earnings responses coefficients. *Journal of Accounting and Economics, 11*(2-3), 143–181. doi:10.1016/0165-4101(89)90004-9

Collis, D. J., & Rukstad, M. G. (2008). Can you say what your strategy is? *Harvard Business Review, 86*(4), 82-90.

Combe, A. (2012). Marketing and flexibility: Debates past, present and future. *European Journal of Marketing, 46*(10), 1257–1267. doi:10.1108/03090561211248116

Cooper, R. (1996). Costing techniques to support corporate strategy: Evidence from Japan. *Management Accounting Research, 7*(2), 219–246. doi:10.1006/mare.1996.0013

Coram, P. J., Monroe, G. S., & Woodliff, D. R. (2009). The Value of Assurance on Voluntary Nonfinancial Disclosure: An Experimental Evaluation. *Auditing, 28*(1), 137–151. doi:10.2308/aud.2009.28.1.137

Covey, R. S. (2006). *The Ethics of the effective leader or the principle –based leadership.* ALLFA Publishing House.

Coyle, G. (2004). *The Analytic Hierarchy Process (AHP).* Available from: http://www.booksites.net/download/coyle/stuent_files/AHP_Technique.pdf

Craswell, A., Francis, J., & Taylor, S. (1995). Auditor brand name reputations and industry specializations. *Journal of Accounting and Economics, 20*(3), 297–322. doi:10.1016/0165-4101(95)00403-3

Cravens, K. S., & Guilding, C. (1999). Strategic brand valuation: A cross-functional perspective. *Business Horizons, 42*(4), 53–62. doi:10.1016/S0007-6813(99)80064-0

Cravens, K. S., & Guilding, C. (2001). An empirical study of the application of strategic management accounting techniques. *Advances in Management Accounting, 10*, 95–124.

Cuervo, A., Ribeiro, D., & Roig, S. (Eds.). (2007). Entrepreneurship: Concepts, Theory, and Perspective. Springer.

Cuganesan, S., Dunford, R., & Palmer, I. (2012). Strategic management accounting and strategy practiceswithin a public sector agency. *Management Accounting Research, 23*(4), 245–260. doi:10.1016/j.mar.2012.09.001

Cummings, S., & Daellenbach, U. (2009). A guide to the future of strategy? The history of Long Range Planning. *Long Range Planning, 42*(2), 234–263. doi:10.1016/j.lrp.2008.12.005

D'Auria, C., Foglia, A., & Reedtz, P. M. (1999). Bank interest rates and credit relationships in Italy. *Journal of Banking & Finance, 23*(7), 1067–1093. doi:10.1016/S0378-4266(98)00131-9

Daily, C., Dalton, D. R., & Cannella, A. A. Jr. (2003). Corporate governance: Decades of dialogue and data. *Academy of Management Review, 28*(10), 371–382. doi:10.5465/amr.2003.10196703

Dalal-Clayton, D. B., & Bass, S. (2002). *National Sustainable Development Strategies: Experience and Dilemmas. Environmental Planning Issues, 6.* IIED.

Daru, M. (2016). Total Quality Management (TQM): A strategy for competitive advantage. *International Journal of Research in IT and Management, 6*(9), 51–55.

Daske, H., & Gebhardt, G. (2006). International financial reporting standards and experts' perceptions of disclosure quality. *Abacus, 42*(3/4), 461–498. doi:10.1111/j.1467-6281.2006.00211.x

Davila, A. (2012). New trends in performance measurement and management control. *In Performance Measurement and Management Control. Global Issues (Washington, D.C.), 25*, 65–87.

De Paul University. (2007). *Ethics 101.* Viewed 8 April 2017. Retrieved from https://business.depaul.edu/about/centers-institutes/institute-business-professional-ethics/ Documents/EthicsManual.pdf

De Waal, A. A., & Kourtit, K. (2013). Performance measurement and management in practice. *International Journal of Productivity and Performance Management, 62*(5), 446–473. doi:10.1108/IJPPM-10-2012-0118

Dechow, P., & Ge, W. (2006). The persistence of earnings and cash flows and the role of special items: Implications for the accrual anomaly. *Review of Accounting Studies, 11*(2-3), 253–296. doi:10.100711142-006-9004-1

Dechow, P., Sloan, R., & Sweeney, A. (1996). Causes and consequences of earnings manipulation: An analysis of firms subject to enforcement actions by the SEC. *Contemporary Accounting Research, 13*(1), 1–36. doi:10.1111/j.1911-3846.1996.tb00489.x

Deegan, C. (2002). The legitimizing effect of social and environmental disclosures: A theoretical foundation. *Accounting, Auditing & Accountability Journal, 15*(3), 282–311. doi:10.1108/09513570210435852

Deepa, N., & Ganesan, K. (2018). Multi-class classification using hybrid soft decision model for agriculture crop selection. *Neural Computing & Applications, 30*(4), 1025–1038. doi:10.100700521-016-2749-y

Deepa, N., & Ganesan, K. (2019). Hybrid Rough Fuzzy Soft classifier based Multi-Class classification model for Agriculture crop selection. *Soft Computing, 23*(21), 10793–10809. doi:10.100700500-018-3633-8

Deepa, N., Ganesan, K., & Sethuramasamyraja, B. (2019). Predictive mathematical model for solving multi-criteria decision-making problems. *Neural Computing & Applications, 31*(10), 6733–6746. doi:10.100700521-018-3505-2

DeFond, M. L. (2010). Earnings quality research: Advances, challenges and future research. *Journal of Accounting and Economics, 50*(2-3), 402–409. doi:10.1016/j.jacceco.2010.10.004

DeFond, M., & Zhang, J. (2014). A review of archival auditing research. *Journal of Accounting and Economics, 58*(2-3), 275–326. doi:10.1016/j.jacceco.2014.09.002

Degryse, H., & van Cayseele, P. (2000). Relationship lending within a bank-based system: Evidence from European Small Business Data. *Journal of Financial Intermediation*, *9*(1), 90–109. doi:10.1006/jfin.1999.0278

Delaney, J. T., & Huselid, M. A. (1996). The impact of human resource management practices on perceptions of organizational performance. *Academy of Management Journal*, *39*, 949–969.

Dell'ariccia, G., & Marquez, R. (2004). Information and bank credit allocation. *Journal of Financial Economics*, *72*(1), 185–214. doi:10.1016/S0304-405X(03)00210-1

Denison, D. R. (1990). *Corporate Culture and Organizational Effectiveness*. Wiley.

Dent, J. F. (1996). Global competition: Challenges for management accounting and control. *Management Accounting Research*, *7*(2), 247–269. doi:10.1006/mare.1996.0014

Deutsch, P., & Silcox, B. (2003). Learning from other libraries: Benchmarking to assess library performance. *Information Outlook*, *7*(7), 18–25.

Dhaliwal, D., Li, O. Z., Tsang, A., & Yang, Y. G. (2014). Corporate social responsibility disclosure and the cost of equity capital: The roles of stakeholder orientation and financial transparency. *Journal of Accounting and Public Policy*, *33*(4), 328–355. doi:10.1016/j.jaccpubpol.2014.04.006

Diab, S. M. (2014). Using the competitive dimensions to achieve competitive advantage: A study on Jordanian private hospitals. *International Journal of Academic Research in Business and Social Sciences*, *4*(9), 138–150. doi:10.6007/IJARBSS/v4-i9/1136

Diamond, D. W. (1984). Financial intermediation and delegated monitoring. *The Review of Economic Studies*, *51*(3), 393–414. doi:10.2307/2297430

Diamond, D. W., & Verrecchia, R. E. (1991). Disclosure, liquidity, and the cost of capital. *The Journal of Finance*, *46*(4), 1325–1359. doi:10.1111/j.1540-6261.1991.tb04620.x

Dinçer, H., Yüksel, S., Kartal, M. T., & Alpman, G. (2019). Corporate Governance-Based Evaluation of Alternative Distribution Channels in the Turkish Banking Sector Using Quality Function Deployment with an Integrated Fuzzy MCDM Method. In *Intergenerational Governance and Leadership in the Corporate World: Emerging Research and Opportunities* (pp. 39–77). IGI Global. doi:10.4018/978-1-5225-8003-4.ch003

Dixon, R. (1998). Accounting for strategic management: A practical application. *Long Range Planning*, *31*(2), 272–279. doi:10.1016/S0024-6301(98)00011-9

Dixon, R., & Smith, D. (1993). Strategic Management Accounting. *Omega*, *21*(6), 605–618. doi:10.1016/0305-0483(93)90003-4

Dolinsky, C., & Feinberg, R. A. (1986). Linguistic barriers to consumer information processing: Information overload in the Hispanic population. *Psychology and Marketing*, *3*(4), 261–271. doi:10.1002/mar.4220030405

Donnelly, D. P., Quirin, J. J., & O'Byran, D. (2003). Auditor acceptance of dsyfunctional audit behavior: An explanatory model using auditors' personal characteristics. *Behavioral Research in Accounting*, *15*(1), 87–110. doi:10.2308/bria.2003.15.1.87

Douglas, E. J., & Shepherd, D. (1997). *Why entrepreneurs create businesses: a utility maximizing response. Frontiers of Entrepreneurship Research*. Babson College.

Doukakis, L. C. (2010). The persistence of earnings and earnings components after the adoption of IFRS. *Managerial Finance*, *36*(11), 969–980. doi:10.1108/03074351011081286

Dowling, J., & Pfeffer, J. (1975). Organizational legitimacy: Social values and organizational behavior. *Pacific Sociological Review*, *18*(1), 122–136. doi:10.2307/1388226

Drucker, P. F. (1985). *Innovation and Entrepreneurship: Practice and Principles*. Harper Business.

Druker, P. (2010). *About decision and efficiency*. Curtea Veche Publishing House.

Dubini, P. (1988). *Motivational and environmental influences on business start-ups: some hints for public policies. Frontiers of Entrepreneurship Research*. Babson College.

Duellman, S., Hurwitz, H., & Sun, Y. (2015). Managerial overconfidence and audit fees. *Journal of Contemporary Accounting & Economics*, *11*(2), 148–165. doi:10.1016/j.jcae.2015.05.001

Dumay, J., Bernardi, C., Guthrie, J., & Demartini, P. (2016). Integrated reporting: A structured literature review. *Accounting Forum*, *40*(3), 166–185. doi:10.1016/j.accfor.2016.06.001

Dumitrescu, M. (2002). *Strategies and Strategic Management*. Economica Publishing House.

Dyer, J., Gregersen, H., & Christensen, C. M. (2011). The Innovators DNA, Mastering the five skills of disruptive innovators. Harvard Business Review Press.

Dyllick, T., & Hockerts, K. (2002). Beyond the business case for corporate sustainability. *Business Strategy and the Environment*, *11*(2), 130–141. doi:10.1002/bse.323

Eccles, R. G., Ioannou, I., & Serafeim, G. (2014). The Impact of a Corporate Culture of Sustainability on Corporate Behavior and Performance. *Management Science*, *60*(11), 2835–2857. doi:10.1287/mnsc.2014.1984

Edmans, A. (2008). Does the stock market fully value intangibles? Employee satisfaction and equity prices. *SSRN Electronic Journal*. Retrieved from http://ssrn.com/abstract=985735

Edmans, A. (2011). Does the stock market fully value intangibles? Employee satisfaction and equity prices. *Journal of Financial Economics*, *101*(3), 621–640. doi:10.1016/j.jfineco.2011.03.021

Edwards, J., & Fischer, K. (1994). Banks, finance and investment in Germany. *Econpapers*. Retrieved from https://EconPapers.repec.org/RePEc:cup:cbooks:9780521566087

El Ghoul, S., Guedhami, O., Kwok, C. C. Y., & Mishra, D. V. (2011). Does corporate social responsibility affect the cost of capital? *Journal of Banking & Finance*, *35*(9), 2388–2406. doi:10.1016/j.jbankfin.2011.02.007

Elbannan, M. A. (2009). Quality of internal control over financial reporting, corporate governance and credit ratings. *International Journal of Disclosure and Governance*, *6*(2), 127–149. doi:10.1057/jdg.2008.32

Elkington, J. (2017). Towards the sustainable corporation: Win-win-win business strategies for sustainable development. *California Management Review*, *36*(2), 90–100. doi:10.2307/41165746

Elsas, R., & Krahnen, J. P. (1998). Is relationship lending special? Evidence from creditfile data in Germany. *Journal of Banking & Finance*, *22*(10-11), 1283–1316. doi:10.1016/S0378-4266(98)00063-6

El-Sayed Ebaid, I. (2009). The impact of capital-structure choice on firm performance: Empirical evidence from Egypt. *The Journal of Risk Finance*, *10*(5), 477–487. doi:10.1108/15265940911001385

Elyasini, E., & Goldberg, L. G. (2004). Relationship lending: A survey of the literature. *Journal of Economics and Business*, *56*(4), 315–330. doi:10.1016/j.jeconbus.2004.03.003

Englund, H., & Gerdin, J. (2018). Management accounting and the paradox of embedded agency: A framework for analyzing sources of structural change. *Management Accounting Research*, *38*(1), 1–11. doi:10.1016/j.mar.2017.12.001

Environmental Leader. (2008). Retrieved from http://www.environmentalleader.com/2008/09/28/ sustainability-and-its-impact-on-brand-value/

Eppler, M. (2007). *Management's traps*. Polirom Publishing House.

Erdem, F., & Gül Başer, G. (2010). Family and business values of regional family firms: A qualitative research. *International Journal of Islamic and Middle Eastern Finance and Management*, *3*(1), 47–64. doi:10.1108/17538391011033861

Eryesil, K., Esmen, O., & Beduk, A. (2015). The role of strategic flexibility for achieving sustainable competition advantage and its effect on business performance. *World Academy of Science, Engineering and Technology*, *9*(10), 587–593.

European Commission. (2011). *A renewed EU strategy 2011-14 for corporate social responsibility*. Available from: https://www.europarl.europa.eu/meetdocs/2009_2014/documents/com/com_com(2011)0681_/com_com(2011)0681_en.pdf

Ewert, R., & Ernst, C. (1999). Target costing, co-ordination and strategic cost management. *European Accounting Review*, *8*(1), 23–49. doi:10.1080/096381899336131

Fadilah, S. (2013). The influence of good governance implementation to organization performance: Analysis of factors affecting. *The International Journal of Social Sciences (Islamabad)*, *7*(1), 15–33.

Fama, E. F. (1970). Efficient capital markets: A review of theory and empirical work. *The Journal of Finance*, *25*(2), 383–417. doi:10.2307/2325486

Fama, E. G. (1985). What's different about banks. *Journal of Monetary Economics*, *15*(1), 29–36. doi:10.1016/0304-3932(85)90051-0

Fatemi, A., Fooladi, I., & Tehranian, H. (2015). Valuation effects of corporate social responsibility. *Journal of Banking & Finance*, *59*, 182–192. doi:10.1016/j.jbankfin.2015.04.028

Fatemi, A., Glaum, M., & Kaiser, S. (2017). ESG performance and firm value: The moderating role of disclosure. *Global Finance Journal*.

Fauré, B., & Rouleau, L. (2011). The strategic competence of accountants and middle managers in budget making. *Accounting, Organizations and Society*, *36*(3), 167–182. doi:10.1016/j.aos.2011.04.001

Feeney, O., & Pierce, B. (2007). Today's management accountant: Honest bean counter and savvy business advisor? *Accountancy Ireland*, *39*, 16–21.

Feeser, H. R., & Dugan, K. W. (1989). *Entrepreneurial motivation: a comparison of high and low growth high tech founders. Frontiers of Entrepreneurship Research*. Babson College.

Feldman, S. J., Soyka, P. A., & Ameer, P. G. (1997). Does improving a firm's environmental management system and environmental performance result in a higher stock price? *Journal of Investing*, *6*(4), 87–97. doi:10.3905/joi.1997.87

Fernandez-Feijoo, B., Romero, S., & Ruiz, S. (2018). Financial auditor and sustainability reporting: Does it matter? *Corporate Social Responsibility and Environmental Management*, *25*(3), 209–224. doi:10.1002/csr.1449

Ferrell, L., & Ferrell, O. (2009). *Essential Managers: Ethical Business*. Dorling Kindersley.

Finucane, M. L., Alhakami, A., Slovic, P., & Johnson, S. M. (2000). The effect heuristic in jodgements of risk and benefits. *Journal of Behavioral Decision Making*, *13*(1), 1–17. doi:10.1002/(SICI)1099-0771(200001/03)13:1<1::AID-BDM333>3.0.CO;2-S

Fischhoff, B., Slovic, P., & Lichtenstein, S. (1977). Knowing with certainty: The appropriateness of extreme confidence. *Journal of Experimental Psychology. Human Perception and Performance*, *3*(4), 552–564. doi:10.1037/0096-1523.3.4.552

Fisher, C. D. (2010). Happiness at Work. *International Journal of Management Reviews, 12*(4), 384–412. doi:10.1111/j.1468-2370.2009.00270.x

Fisher, L. (1959). Determinants of risk premiums on corporate bonds. *Journal of Political Economy, 67*(3), 217–237. doi:10.1086/258172

Fisk, P. (2008). *Marketing genius*. Meteor Press Publishing House.

Flower, J. (2015). The international integrated reporting council: A story of failure. *Critical Perspectives on Accounting, 27*, 1–17. doi:10.1016/j.cpa.2014.07.002

Fombrun, C., & Shanley, M. (1990). What's in a name? Reputation building and corporate strategy. *Academy of Management Journal, 33*, 233–258.

Fosu, S. (2013). Capital structure, product market competition and firm performance: Evidence from South Africa. *The Quarterly Review of Economics and Finance, 53*(2), 140–151. doi:10.1016/j.qref.2013.02.004

Frame, W. S., Srinivasan, A., & Woosley, L. (2001). The Effect of credit scoring on small business lending. *Journal of Money, Credit and Banking, 33*(3), 813–825. doi:10.2307/2673896

Francis, J., & Yu, M. (2009). The effect of Big 4 office size on audit quality. *The Accounting Review, 84*(5), 1521–1552. doi:10.2308/accr.2009.84.5.1521

Freedman, M., & Jaggi, B. (1986). An analysis of the impact of corporate pollution disclosures included in annual financials statements on investors' decisions. *Advances in Public Interest Accounting, 1*, 193–212.

Freeman, R. E. (1984). *Strategic management: a stakeholder approach*. Pitman Publishing Inc.

Frese, M., & Gielnik, M. M. (2014). The Psychology of Entrepreneurship. *Annual Review of Organizational Psychology and Organizational Behavior, 1*(1), 413–438. doi:10.1146/annurev-orgpsych-031413-091326

Fuerman, R. D., & Kraten, M. (2009). The big 4 audit report: Should the public perceive it as a label of quality? *Accounting and the Public Interest, 9*(1), 148–165. doi:10.2308/api.2009.9.1.148

Fu, R., Kraft, A., & Zhang, H. (2012). Financial reporting frequency, information asymmetry, and the cost of equity. *Journal of Accounting and Economics, 54*(2–3), 132–149. doi:10.1016/j.jacceco.2012.07.003

Furrer, O., Thomas, H., & Goussevskaia, A. (2008). The structure and evolution of the strategic management field: A content analysis of 26 years of strategic management research. *International Journal of Management Reviews, 10*(1), 1–23. doi:10.1111/j.1468-2370.2007.00217.x

Gaglio, C. M. (1997). Opportunity recognition: review, critique, and suggested research directions. In J. Katz (Ed.), *Advances in Entrepreneurship, Firm Emergence and Growth* (pp. 139–202). JAI Press.

Gaglio, C., & Katz, J. (2001). The Psychological Basis of Opportunity Identification: Entrepreneurial Alertness. *Small Business Economics, 16*(2), 95–111. doi:10.1023/A:1011132102464

Galbraith, J. R., & Lawler, E. E. (1993). *Organizing for the Future: The New Logic for Managing Complex Organizations*. Jossey-Bass.

Gazzola, P., & Ratti, M. (2014). Transparency in Italian non profit organizations. *The Annals of the University of Oradea – Economic Sciences, 23*(1), 123-133.

Gertler, M., & Gilchrist, S. G. (1994). Monetary policy, business cycles and the behaviour of small manufacturing firms. *The Quarterly Journal of Economics, 109*(2), 309–340. doi:10.2307/2118465

Ghaffari, F., Kyriacou, O., & Brennan, R. (2008). Exploring the Implementation of Ethics in U.K. Accounting Programs. *Issues in Accounting Education*, *23*(2), 183–198. doi:10.2308/iace.2008.23.2.183

Gheorghe, A., & Udrescu, M. A. (2017). *Aspects regarding organizational behavior in the romanian tourism field.* International Symposium 10 years membership in the European Union- Analyses, methods, models regarding the results of Romania, Bucharest, Romania.

Gheorghe, A., & Udrescu, M. A. (2019). Governance in the EU Member, States in the Era of Big Data. In *25th PGV Network Conference*. Economica Publishing House.

Ghosh, A., & Olsen, L. (2008). Environmental uncertainty and managers' use of discretionary accruals. *Accounting, Organizations and Society*, *34*(2), 188–205. doi:10.1016/j.aos.2008.07.001

Global Reporting Initiative (GRI). (2019). *Information About GRI*. Retrieved from https://www.globalreporting.org/information/about-gri/Pages/default.aspx

Global Reporting Initiative. (2011). Sustainability Reporting Guidelines. Global Reporting Initiative. *G3*, 1.

Gnyawali, D., & Fogel, D. (1994). Environments for entrepreneurship development: Key dimensions and research implications. *Entrepreneurship Theory and Practice*, *18*(4), 43–62. doi:10.1177/104225879401800403

Godfrey, P. C. (2005). The relationship between corporate philanthropy and shareholder wealth: A risk management perspective. *Academy of Management Review*, *30*(4), 777–798. doi:10.5465/amr.2005.18378878

Gomez, L. M., & Chalmeta, R. (2011). Corporate responsibility in US corporate websites: A pilot study. *Public Relations Review*, *37*(1), 93–95. doi:10.1016/j.pubrev.2010.12.005

Gómez-Navarro, T., García-Melón, M., Guijarro, F., & Preuss, M. (2018). Methodology to assess the market value of companies according to their financial and social responsibility aspects: An AHP approach. *The Journal of the Operational Research Society*, *69*(10), 1599–1608. doi:10.105741274-017-0222-7

Goodpaster, K. E. (1991). Business ethics and stakeholder analysis. *Business Ethics Quarterly*, *1*(1), 53–73. doi:10.2307/3857592

Goodwin, J., & Wu, D. (2014). Is the effect of industry expertise on audit pricing an office-level or a partner-level phenomenon? *Review of Accounting Studies*, *19*(4), 1532–1578. doi:10.100711142-014-9285-8

Gore, A. (1993). *Earth in the balance*. Houghton Mifflin Company.

Goss, A., & Roberts, G. S. (2006). The cost of virtue: corporate social responsibility and the cost of debt Financing. *SSRN Electronic Journal*. Retrieved from http://ssrn.com/abstract=955041

Goss, A., & Roberts, G. S. (2011). The impact of corporate social responsibility on the cost of bank loans. *Journal of Banking & Finance*, *35*(7), 1794–1810. doi:10.1016/j.jbankfin.2010.12.002

Graafland, J., Van de Ven, B., & Stoffele, N. (2003). Strategies and instruments for organising CSR by small and large businesses in the Netherlands. *Journal of Business Ethics*, *47*(1), 45–60. doi:10.1023/A:1026240912016

Graham, J. R., Harvey, C. R., & Rajgopal, S. (2005). The economic implications of corporate financial reporting. *Journal of Accounting and Economics*, *40*(1-3), 3–73. doi:10.1016/j.jacceco.2005.01.002

Greenbaum, S., Kanatas, G., & Venezia, I. (1989). Equilibrium loan pricing under the bank-client relationship. *Journal of Banking & Finance*, *13*(2), 221–235. doi:10.1016/0378-4266(89)90061-7

Gresoi, S. G., & Gheorghe, A. (2011). Interdependencies between sustainable development and ecology. *International Journal of Academic Research in Accounting, Finance and Management Sciences*, *1*(2), 25–32.

Gresoi, S. G., Gheorghe, A., & Buiga, A. (2012). *Production Management-Theoretrical Synthesis and Case Studies*. Terra Nostra Publishing House.

GRI G4. (2013). Sustainability Reporting Guidelines, Reporting principles and standard disclosures. Author.

GRI. (2016). Retrieved from https://www.globalreporting.org/standards/media/1036/gri-101-foundation-2016.pdf

GRI. (2019). Retrieved from https://www.globalreporting.org/standards/gri-standards-download-center/

Gronewold, U., & Donle, M. (2011). Organizational error climate and auditors' predispositions toward handling errors. *Behavioral Research in Accounting*, *23*(2), 69–92. doi:10.2308/bria-10061

Guilding, C., Cravens, K. S., & Tayles, M. (2000). An international comparison of strategic management accounting practices. *Management Accounting Research*, *11*(1), 113–135. doi:10.1006/mare.1999.0120

Guilding, C., & McManus, L. (2002). The incidence, perceived merit and antecedents of customer accounting: An exploratory note. *Accounting, Organizations and Society*, *27*(1-2), 45–59. doi:10.1016/S0361-3682(01)00030-7

Gupta, K. P., & Manrai, R. (2019). Prioritizing Factors Affecting the Adoption of Mobile Financial Services in Emerging Markets—A Fuzzy AHP Approach. In *Performance Prediction and Analytics of Fuzzy, Reliability and Queuing Models* (pp. 55–81). Springer. doi:10.1007/978-981-13-0857-4_4

Hababou, M., & Martel, J. M. (1998). A multicriteria approach for selecting a portfolio manager. *INFOR*, *36*(3), 161–176. doi:10.1080/03155986.1998.11732354

Habib, A., & Hossain, M. (2013). CEO/CFO characteristics and financial reporting quality: A review. *Research in Accounting Regulation*, *25*(1), 88–100. doi:10.1016/j.racreg.2012.11.002

Hambrick, D. C. (2016). Upper echelons theory. *The Palgrave Encyclopedia of Strategic Management*. https://link.springer.com/referenceworkentry/10.1057/978-1-349-94848-2_785-1

Hambrick, D. C., & Mason, P. (1984). Upper echelons: The organization as a reflection of its top managers. *Academy of Management Review*, *9*(2), 193–206. doi:10.5465/amr.1984.4277628

Hammann, E., Habisch, A., & Pechlaner, H. (2009). Values that create value: Socially responsible business practices in SMEs: Empirical evidence from German companies. *Business Ethics (Oxford, England)*, *18*(1), 37–51. doi:10.1111/j.1467-8608.2009.01547.x

Hamzaçebi, C., & Pekkaya, M. (2011). Determining of stock investments with grey relational analysis. *Expert Systems with Applications*, *38*(8), 9186–9195. doi:10.1016/j.eswa.2011.01.070

Harjoto, M. A., & Jo, H. (2015). Legal vs. normative CSR: Differential impact on analyst dispersion, stock return volatility, cost of capital, and firm value. *Journal of Business Ethics*, *128*(1), 1–20. doi:10.100710551-014-2082-2

Hartnell, C. A., Ou, A. Y., & Kinicki, A. (2011). Organizational culture and organizational effectiveness: A meta-analytic investigation of the competing values framework's theoretical suppositions. *The Journal of Applied Psychology*, *96*(4), 677–694. doi:10.1037/a0021987 PMID:21244127

Hart, S. (1995). A natural-resource-based view of the firm. *Academy of Management Review*, *20*(4), 986–1014. doi:10.5465/amr.1995.9512280033

Hasan, M. B., Ahsan, A. M., Rahaman, M. A., & Alam, M. N. (2014). Influence of capital structure on firm performance: Evidence from Bangladesh. *International Journal of Business and Management*, *9*(5), 184. doi:10.5539/ijbm.v9n5p184

Hassel, L., Nilsson, H., & Nyquist, S. (2005). The value relevance of environmental performance. *European Accounting Review*, *14*(1), 41–61. doi:10.1080/0963818042000279722

Hay, D. C., Knechel, W. R., & Wong, N. (2004). Audit fees: A meta-analysis of the effect of supply and demand attributes. *Contemporary Accounting Research*, *23*(1), 141–191. doi:10.1506/4XR4-KT5V-E8CN-91GX

Heal, G. M. (2004). *Corporate social responsibility – an economic and financial framework*. SSRN Electronic Journal. Retrieved from doi:10.2139srn.642762

Hébert, R. F., & Link, A. N. (1989). In Search of the Meaning of Entrepreneurship. *Small Business Economics*, *1*, 39–49. doi:10.1007/BF00389915

Henczel, S. (2002). Benchmarking – measuring and comparing for continuous improvement. *Information Outlook*, *6*(7), 12–20.

Herremans, I., Akathaporn, P., & McInnes, M. (1993). An Investigation of Corporate Social Responsibility Reputation and Economic Performance. *Accounting, Organizations and Society*, *18*(October- November), 587–604. doi:10.1016/0361-3682(93)90044-7

Hickman, L., & Cote, J. (2019). CSR reporting and assurance legitimacy: A client–assuror dyad investigation. *Journal of Applied Accounting Research*, *20*(4), 372–393. doi:10.1108/JAAR-01-2018-0009

Hiller, K., Mahlendorf, M. D., & Weber, J. (2014). Management accountants' occupational prestige within the company: A social identity theory perspective. *European Accounting Review*, *23*(4), 671–691. doi:10.1080/09638180.2013.849204

Hoitash, R., Markelevich, A., & Barragato, C. A. (2007). Auditor fees and audit quality. *Managerial Auditing Journal*, *22*(8), 761–786. doi:10.1108/02686900710819634

Hoitash, U., Hoitash, R., & Bedard, J. C. (2009). Corporate governance and internal control over financial reporting: A comparison of regulatory regimes. *The Accounting Review*, *84*(3), 839–867. doi:10.2308/accr.2009.84.3.839

Homburg, C., & Pflesser, C. (2000). A Multiple Layer Model of Market-Oriented Organizational Culture: Measurement Issues and Performance Outcomes. *JMR, Journal of Marketing Research*, *37*(4), 449–462. doi:10.1509/jmkr.37.4.449.18786

Hong, H. G. (2008). What Drives Corporate Social Responsibility? *SSRN Electronic Journal*. Retrieved from http://ssrn.com/abstract=1212645

Horngren, C. T., Datar, S. M., & Rajan, M. V. (2012). *Cost accounting – A managerial emphasis* (14th ed.). Pearson Prentice Hall.

Horrigan, J. (1966). The determination of long-term credit standing with financial ratios. *Journal of Accounting Research*, *4*(Supplement), 44–62. doi:10.2307/2490168

Horton, J., Serafeim, G., & Serafeim, I. (2013). Does mandatory IFRS adoption improve the information environment? *Contemporary Accounting Research*, *30*(1), 388–423. doi:10.1111/j.1911-3846.2012.01159.x

Hoshi, T., Kashyap, A., & Scharfstein, D. (1990). The role of banks in reducing the costs of financial distress in Japan. *Journal of Financial Economics*, *27*(1), 67–88. doi:10.1016/0304-405X(90)90021-Q

Houque, M. N. (2012). The effect of IFRS adoption and investor protection on earnings quality around the world. *The International Journal of Accounting*, *47*(3), 333–355. doi:10.1016/j.intacc.2012.07.003

Hoyle, J. (1978). Mandatory auditor rotation: The arguments and an alternative. *Journal of Accountancy*, *145*(5), 69–78.

Hsieh, T., Wang, Z., & Demirkan, S. (2018). Overconfidence and tax avoidance: The role of CEO and CFO interaction. *Journal of Accounting and Public Policy*, *37*(3), 241–253. doi:10.1016/j.jaccpubpol.2018.04.004

Huang, J. Y., Shen, K. Y., Shieh, J. C., & Tzeng, G. H. (2019). Strengthen Financial Holding Companies' Business Sustainability by Using a Hybrid Corporate Governance Evaluation Model. *Sustainability*, *11*(3), 582. doi:10.3390u11030582

Hughes, K. II. (2000). The value relevance of nonfinancial measures of air pollution in the electric utility industry. *The Accounting Review*, *75*(2), 209–228. doi:10.2308/accr.2000.75.2.209

Hung, Y. H., Huang, T. L., Hsieh, J. C., Tsuei, H. J., Cheng, C. C., & Tzeng, G. H. (2012). Online reputation management for improving marketing by using a hybrid MCDM model. *Knowledge-Based Systems*, *35*, 87–93. doi:10.1016/j.knosys.2012.03.004

Hurley, R. F. (2002). Putting people back into organizational learning. *Journal of Business and Industrial Marketing*, *17*(4), 270–281. doi:10.1108/08858620210431679

Hyytinen, A., & Pajarinen, M. (2002). *Small business finance in Finland. A Descriptive study*. ETLA, The Research Institute of the Finnish Economy, Discussion papers 812: 1-59.

Iatridis, G. (2010). International Financial Reporting Standards and the quality of financial statement information. *International Review of Financial Analysis*, *19*(3), 193–204. doi:10.1016/j.irfa.2010.02.004

Iatridis, G. (2012). Hedging and earnings management in the light of IFRS implementation: Evidence from the UK stock market. *The British Accounting Review*, *44*(1), 21–35. doi:10.1016/j.bar.2011.12.002

Iç, Y. T., & Yurdakul, M. (2010). Development of a quick credibility scoring decision support system using fuzzy TOPSIS. *Expert Systems with Applications*, *37*(1), 567–574. doi:10.1016/j.eswa.2009.05.038

International Federation of Accountants (IFAC). (2006). *Approaches to the Development and Maintenance of Professional Values, Ethics and Attitudes in Accounting Education Programs*. Information Paper. New York. Retrieved from http://www.ifac.org

Ireland, R. D., Hitt, M. A., & Sirmon, D. G. (2003). A Model of Strategic Entrepreneurship: The Construct and its Dimensions. *Journal of Management*, *29*(6), 963–989. doi:10.1016/S0149-2063(03)00086-2

Islam, A. (2015). Entrepreneurship and the Allocation of Government Spending Under Imperfect Markets. *World Development*, *70*, 108–121. doi:10.1016/j.worlddev.2015.01.002

Ittner, C. D., & Larcker, D. F. (1998). Innovations in Performance Measurement: Trends and Research Implications. *Journal of Management Accounting Research*, *10*, 205–238.

Jackling, B., Cooper, B. J., Leung, P., & Dellaportas, S. (2007). Professional Accounting Bodies' Perceptions of Ethical Issues, Causes of Ethical Failure and Ethics Education. *Managerial Auditing Journal*, *22*(9), 928–944. doi:10.1108/02686900710829426

Jackson, A. B., Moldrich, M., & Roebuck, P. (2008). Mandatory audit firm rotation and audit quality. *Managerial Auditing Journal*, *23*(5), 420–437. doi:10.1108/02686900810875271

Jamnik, A. (2011). Ethical code in the public accounting profession. *Journal of International Business Ethics*, *1*(1), 80–90.

Jarzabkowski, P. (2004). Strategy as practice: Recursiveness, adaptation, and practices-in-use. *Organization Studies*, *25*(4), 529–560. doi:10.1177/0170840604040675

Jarzabkowski, P., & Paul Spee, A. (2009). Strategy-as-practice: A review and future directions for the field. *International Journal of Management Reviews*, *11*(1), 69–95. doi:10.1111/j.1468-2370.2008.00250.x

Jeanjean, T., & Stolowy, H. (2008). Do accounting standards matter? An exploratory analysis of earnings management before and after IFRS adoption. *Journal of Accounting and Public Policy*, *27*(6), 480–490. doi:10.1016/j.jaccpubpol.2008.09.008

Jenkins, D. S., & Velury, U. K. (2012). Auditor tenure and the pricing of discretionary accruals in the Post-SOX Era. *Accounting and the Public Interest*, *12*(1), 1–15. doi:10.2308/apin-10204

Jenkins, H. (2009). A 'business opportunity' model of corporate social responsibility for small-and medium-sized enterprises. *Business Ethics (Oxford, England)*, *18*(1), 21–36. doi:10.1111/j.1467-8608.2009.01546.x

Jensen, K. L., & Payne, J. L. (2005). Audit procurement: Managing audit quality and audit fees in response to agency costs. *Auditing*, *24*(2), 27–48. doi:10.2308/aud.2005.24.2.27

Jenson, R. (2004). *The success pyramid*. Codecs Publishing House.

Johnson, B. R. (1990). Toward a multidimensional model of entrepreneurship: The case of achievement motivation and the entrepreneur. *Entrepreneurship Theory and Practice*, *14*(3), 39–48. doi:10.1177/104225879001400306

Johnson, E., Kuhn, J. R., Apostolu, B., & Hassell, J. M. (2013). Auditor perceptions of client narcissism as a fraud attitude risk factor. *Auditing*, *32*(1), 203–219. doi:10.2308/ajpt-50329

Johnstone, K., Li, C., & Rupley, K. H. (2011). Changes in corporate governance associated with the revelation of internal control material weaknesses and their subsequent remediation. *Contemporary Accounting Research*, *28*(1), 331–383. doi:10.1111/j.1911-3846.2010.01037.x

Jones, C. A., & Levy, D. L. (2007). North American business strategies towards climate change. *European Management Journal*, *25*(6), 428–440. doi:10.1016/j.emj.2007.07.001

Jones, D. A., & Smith, K. J. (2012). Comparing the value relevance, predictive value, and persistence of other comprehensive income and special items. *The Accounting Review*, *86*(6), 2047–2073. doi:10.2308/accr-10133

Jo, S. (2011). Factors shaping activists' perceptions of corporate organizations: An empirical case from South Korea. *Public Relations Review*, *37*(2), 178–180. doi:10.1016/j.pubrev.2011.01.002

Joyner, B. E., Payne, D., & Raiborn, C. A. (2002). Building values, business ethics and corporate social responsibility into the developing organization. *Journal of Developmental Entrepreneurship*, *7*(1), 113.

Kahneman, D. (2018). *An Interview with Daniel Kahneman*. Retrieved from https://www.theguardian.com/books/2015/jul/18/daniel-kahneman-books-interview

Kahneman, D., & Tversky, A. (1972). Subjective probability: A judgement of representativeness. *Cognitive Psychology*, *3*(3), 430–454. doi:10.1016/0010-0285(72)90016-3

Kahneman, D., & Tversky, A. (1973). On the psychology of prediction. *Psychological Review*, *80*(4), 237–251. doi:10.1037/h0034747

Kahneman, D., & Tversky, A. (1979). Prospect theory: An analysis of decision under risk. *Econometrica*, *47*(2), 263–291. doi:10.2307/1914185

Kaplan, R. S., & Norton, D. P. (2001). Transforming the balanced scorecard form performance measurement to strategic management: Part II. *Accounting Horizons*, *15*(2), 147–160. doi:10.2308/acch.2001.15.2.147

Kaplan, R. S., & Norton, D. P. (2006). How to implement a new strategy without disrupting your organization. *Harvard Business Review*, *84*(3), 100. doi:10.1108d.2006.05622had.002 PMID:16515159

Kaplan, R., & Urwitz, G. (1979). Statistical models of bond ratings: A methodological inquiry. *The Journal of Business*, *52*(2), 231–261. doi:10.1086/296045

Kelly, P. T. (2004). *An Examination of the Moral Reasoning of Accounting Students* (Doctor of Philosophy Thesis). University of Connecticut.

Kerr, D. S., & Smith, L. M. (1995). Importance of and approaches to incorporating ethics into the accounting classroom. *Journal of Business Ethics*, *14*(1), 987–995. doi:10.1007/BF00872114

Khan, A. G. (2012). The relationship of capital structure decisions with firm performance: A study of the engineering sector of Pakistan. *International Journal of Accounting and Financial Reporting*, *2*(1), 245. doi:10.5296/ijafr.v2i1.1825

Kim, S., & Lee, Y. J. (2011). The complex attribution process of corporate social responsibility motives. *Public Relations Review*, *38*(1), 168–170. doi:10.1016/j.pubrev.2011.09.024

Kim, S., & Reber, B. H. (2008). Public relations' place in corporate social responsibility: Practitioners define their role. *Public Relations Review*, *34*(4), 337–342. doi:10.1016/j.pubrev.2008.07.003

Kiron, D., Unruh, G., Kruschwitz, N., Reeves, M., Rubel, H., Meyer, A., & Felde, Z. (2017). *Corporate sustainability at a crossroads: Progress toward our common future in uncertain times*. MIT Sloan Management Review & Boston Consulting Group.

Kirzner, I. M. (1979). *Perception, Opportunity, and Profit: Studies in the Theory of Entrepreneurship*. The University of Chicago Press.

Kitchen, N. (2010). Systemic pressures and domestic ideas: A neoclassical realist model of grand strategy formation. *Review of International Studies*, *36*(1), 117–143. doi:10.1017/S0260210509990532

Klein, A. (2002). Audit committee, board of director characteristics and earnings management. *Journal of Accounting and Economics*, *33*(3), 375–400. doi:10.1016/S0165-4101(02)00059-9

Knechel, W. R., & Vanstraelen, A. (2005). The relationship between auditor tenure and audit quality implied by going concern opinions. *Auditing*, *26*(1), 113–131. doi:10.2308/aud.2007.26.1.113

Knechel, W. R., Vanstraelen, A., & Zerni, M. (2014). Does the identity of engagement partners matter? An analysis of audit partner reporting decisions. *Contemporary Accounting Research*, *32*(4), 1443–1478. doi:10.1111/1911-3846.12113

Koerber, C.P. (2015). Corporate responsibility standards: current implications and future possibilities for peace through commerce. *Journal of Business Ethics*, *89*(4), 461–480.

Koiranen, M. (2002). Over 100 years of age but still entrepreneurially active in business: Exploring the values and family characteristics of old Finnish family firms. *Family Business Review*, *15*(3), 175–187. doi:10.1111/j.1741-6248.2002.00175.x

Kothari, S. P., Leone, A. J., & Wasley, C. E. (2005). Performance matched discretionary accrual measures. *Journal of Accounting and Economics*, *39*(1), 163–197. doi:10.1016/j.jacceco.2004.11.002

Kou, G., Peng, Y., & Wang, G. (2014). Evaluation of clustering algorithms for financial risk analysis using MCDM methods. *Information Sciences*, *275*, 1–12. doi:10.1016/j.ins.2014.02.137

Kou, G., & Wu, W. (2014). An analytic hierarchy model for classification algorithms selection in credit risk analysis. *Mathematical Problems in Engineering*, *2014*, 2014. doi:10.1155/2014/297563

KPMG & ACCA. (2011). *Business briefing series – 20 issues on building a sustainable business.* Author.

KPMG Survey of Corporate Responsibility Reporting. (2017). Retrieved rom https://home.kpmg/xx/en/home/insights/2017/10/the-kpmg-survey-of-corporate-responsibility-reporting-2017.html

KPMG. (2013). *The KPMG survey of corporate social responsibility reporting 2013.* Retrieved from https://assets.kpmg.com/content/dam/kpmg/pdf/2015/08/kpmg-survey-of-corporate-responsibility-reporting-2013.pdf

Krajewski, L. J., & Ritzman, L. P. (2005). *Operations Management* (7th ed.). Prentice Hall.

Kumar, K., & Lim, L. (2015). Was Andersen's audit quality lower than its peers? A comparative analysis of audit quality. *Managerial Auditing Journal*, *30*(8/9), 911–962. doi:10.1108/MAJ-10-2014-1105

Kyereboah-Coleman, A. (2007). The impact of capital structure on the performance of microfinance institutions. *The Journal of Risk Finance*, *8*(1), 56–71. doi:10.1108/15265940710721082

Laha, S., & Biswas, S. (2019). A hybrid unsupervised learning and multi-criteria decision making approach for performance evaluation of Indian banks. *Accounting*, *5*(4), 169–184. doi:10.5267/j.ac.2018.11.001

Laiken, M. (2001). *Models of organizational learning: Paradoxes and best practices in the post industrial workplace.* NALL Working Paper, 25. University of Toronto. Retrieved January 12, 2020, from https://nall.oise.utoronto.ca/res/25MarilynLaiken.pdf

Lambert, C., & Pezet, E. (2011). The making of the management accountant – Becoming the producer of truthful knowledge. *Accounting, Organizations and Society*, *36*(1), 10–30. doi:10.1016/j.aos.2010.07.005

Landsman, W. R., Maydew, E. L., & Thornock, J. R. (2012). The information content of annual earnings announcements and mandatory adoption of IFRS. *Journal of Accounting and Economics*, *53*(1-2), 34–54. doi:10.1016/j.jacceco.2011.04.002

Langfield-Smith, K. (2008). Strategic management accounting: How far have we come in 25 years? *Accounting, Auditing & Accountability Journal*, *21*(2), 204–228. doi:10.1108/09513570810854400

Langlois, L., & Lapointe, C. (2010). Can ethics be learned? Results from a three-year action-research project. *Journal of Educational Administration*, *48*(2), 147–163. doi:10.1108/09578231011027824

Lang, M., Raedy, J. S., & Wilson, W. (2006). Earnings management and cross listing: Are reconciled earnings comparable to US earnings? *Journal of Accounting and Economics*, *42*(1-2), 255–283. doi:10.1016/j.jacceco.2006.04.005

Lazear, E. P. (2004). Balanced Skills and Entrepreneurship. *The American Economic Review*, *94*(2), 208–211. doi:10.1257/0002828041301425

Lazear, E. P. (2005). Entrepreneurship. *Journal of Labor Economics*, *23*(4), 649–680. doi:10.1086/491605

Lennox, C. S., & Wu, X. (2018). A review of the archival literature on audit partners. *Accounting Horizons*, *32*(2), 1–35. doi:10.2308/acch-51942

Le, T. P. V., & Phan, T. B. N. (2017). Capital structure and firm performance: Empirical evidence from a small transition country. *Research in International Business and Finance*, *42*, 710–726. doi:10.1016/j.ribaf.2017.07.012

Leuz, C., Nanda, D., & Wysocki, P. D. (2003). Earnings management and investor protection: An international comparison. *Journal of Financial Economics*, *69*(3), 505–527. doi:10.1016/S0304-405X(03)00121-1

Leventis, S., & Caramanis, C. (2005). Determinants of audit time as a proxy of audit quality. *Managerial Auditing Journal*, *20*(5), 460–478. doi:10.1108/02686900510598821

Lichtenstein, S., & Fischhoff, B. (1977). Do those who know more also know more about how much they know? *Organizational Behavior and Human Performance*, *20*(2), 159–183. doi:10.1016/0030-5073(77)90001-0

Ligteringen, E., & Zadek, S. (2005). The Future of Corporate Responsibility Standards. *Business and the Environment*, *16*(6), 121–123.

Li, H. (2019). Repetitive disclosures in the MD&A. *Journal of Business Finance & Accounting*, *46*(9-10), 1063–1096. doi:10.1111/jbfa.12405

Lim, B. (1995). Examining the organizational culture and organizational performance link. *Leadership and Organization Development Journal*, *16*(5), 16–21. doi:10.1108/01437739510088491

Lin, C. H., Peng, C. H., & Kao, D. T. (2008). The innovativeness effect of market orientation and learning orientation on business performance. *International Journal of Manpower*, *29*(8), 752–772. doi:10.1108/01437720810919332

Lindahl, F. W., & Schadewitz, H. (2008). Accounting quality and the law. *SSRN Electronic Journal*. Retrieved from https://ssrn.com/abstract=1275971

Lin, S., Riccardi, W., & Wang, C. (2012). Does accounting quality change following a switch from U.S.GAAP to IFRS? Evidence from Germany. *Journal of Accounting and Public Policy*, *31*(6), 641–657. doi:10.1016/j.jaccpubpol.2012.10.006

Liu, H. T. (2011). Product design and selection using fuzzy QFD and fuzzy MCDM approaches. *Applied Mathematical Modelling*, *35*(1), 482–496. doi:10.1016/j.apm.2010.07.014

Li, X., Kim, J. B., Wu, H., & Yu, Y. (2019). Corporate Social Responsibility and Financial Fraud: The Moderating Effects of Governance and Religiosity. *Journal of Business Ethics*. Advance online publication. doi:10.100710551-019-04378-3

Llewellyn, S., & Tappin, E. (2003). Strategy in the public sector: Management in the wilderness. *Journal of Management Studies*, *40*(4), 955–982. doi:10.1111/1467-6486.00366

Lloret, A. (2015). Modeling corporate sustainability strategy. *Journal of Business Research*, *69*(2), 418–425. doi:10.1016/j.jbusres.2015.06.047

Lobo, G. L., & Zhou, J. (2001). Disclosure quality and earning management. *Asia-Pacific Journal of Accounting & Economics*, *8*(1), 1–20. doi:10.1080/16081625.2001.10510584

Longhofer, D., & Santos, J. (2000). The importance of bank seniority for relationship lending. *Journal of Financial Intermediation*, *9*(1), 57–89. doi:10.1006/jfin.1999.0272

Lord, B. R. (1996). Strategic management accounting: The emperor's new clothes? *Management Accounting Research*, *7*(3), 347–366. doi:10.1006/mare.1996.0020

Lougee, B., & Wallace, J. (2008). The Corporate Social Responsibility (CSR) Trend. *Journal of Applied Corporate Finance*, *20*(1), 96–108. doi:10.1111/j.1745-6622.2008.00172.x

Louwers, T. J., Ramsay, R. J., Sinason, D. H., & Strawser, J. R. (2007). *Auditing and Assurance Services* (2nd ed.). McGraw-Hill Irwin.

Low, M., Davey, H., & Hooper, K. (2008). Accounting Scandals, Ethical Dilemmas and Educational Challenges. *Critical Perspectives on Accounting*, *19*(1), 222–254. doi:10.1016/j.cpa.2006.05.010

Lozano, R., (2019). Analysing the use of tools, initiatives, and approaches to promote sustainability in corporations. *Corp Soc Resp Env Ma.*, 1– 17.

Maciarello, I. A., & Druker, P. (2016). *Training course for managers*. Litera Publishing House.

Mahtani, U. S., & Garg, C. P. (2018). An analysis of key factors of financial distress in airline companies in India using fuzzy AHP framework. *Transportation Research Part A, Policy and Practice*, *117*, 87–102. doi:10.1016/j.tra.2018.08.016

Majumdar, S. K., & Chhibber, P. (1999). Capital structure and performance: Evidence from a transition economy on an aspect of corporate governance. *Public Choice*, *98*(3/4), 287–305. doi:10.1023/A:1018355127454

Malmendier, U., & Tate, G. (2004). *CEO overconfidence and corporate investment.* NBER Working Paper, No. 10807.

Malmendier, U., & Tate, G. (2005). CEO overconfidence and corporate investment. *The Journal of Finance*, *60*(6), 2661–2700. doi:10.1111/j.1540-6261.2005.00813.x

Malmendier, U., & Tate, G. (2008). Who makes acquisitions? CEO overconfidence and the market's reaction. *Journal of Financial Economics*, *89*(1), 20–43. doi:10.1016/j.jfineco.2007.07.002

Manetti, G., & Taccofondi, S. (2012). The role of stakeholders in sustainability reporting assurance. *Journal of Business Ethics*, *107*(3), 363–377. doi:10.100710551-011-1044-1

Manfred, F., & Kets de Vries, R. (2001), *The leadership mystique: a user's for the human enterprise*. Financial Times.

Marcu, F., & Manea, C. (1978). *Neologisms Dictionary*. Romanian Academy Publishing House.

Margaritis, D., & Psillaki, M. (2007). Capital structure and firm efficiency. *Journal of Business Finance & Accounting*, *34*, 1447–1469.

Margaritis, D., & Psillaki, M. (2010). Capital structure, equity ownership and firm performance. *Journal of Banking & Finance*, *34*(3), 621–632. doi:10.1016/j.jbankfin.2009.08.023

Margolis, J. D., Elfenbein, H. A., & Walsh, J. P. (2002). *Does It Pay to Be Good? A Meta-Analysis and Redirection of Research on the Relationship between Corporate Social and Financial Performance*. Available from: https://books.google.com.hk/books/about/Does_it_Pay_to_be_Good.html?id=hE3OnQAACAAJ&redir_esc=y

Margolis, J. D., & Walsh, J. P. (2001). *People and Profits*. Lawrence Erlbaum Associates. doi:10.4324/9781410600622

Mariotti, S., & Glackin, C. (2010). *Entrepreneurship*. Prentice Hall.

Marlin, D., & Geiger, S. W. (2012). The Composition of Corporate Boards of Directors: Does Industry Matter. *Journal of Business & Economics Research*, *10*(3), 100–115. doi:10.19030/jber.v10i3.6854

Marra, A., Mazzola, P., & Prencipe, A. (2011). Board Monitoring and Earnings Management Pre- and Post-IFRS. *The International Journal of Accounting*, *46*(2), 205–230. doi:10.1016/j.intacc.2011.04.007

Martin, R. L. (2002). The virtue matrix: Calculating the return on corporate responsibility. *Harvard Business Review*, *80*, 68–75. PMID:11894384

Ma, Y., & Tayles, M. (2009). On the emergence of strategic management accounting: An institutional perspective. *Accounting and Business Research*, *39*(5), 473–495. doi:10.1080/00014788.2009.9663379

McAdam, P., & Rummel, O. (2004). Corruption: A non-parametric analysis. *Journal of Economic Studies (Glasgow, Scotland)*, *31*(6), 509–523. doi:10.1108/01443580410569253

McCaffrey, M. (2015). The economics of peace and war in the Chinese military classics. *Economics of Peace and Security Journal*, *10*(1), 23–31. doi:10.15355/epsj.10.1.23

McEwen, J. W. (2008). *Brand strength*. ALLFA Publishing House.

McGuire, J. B., Sundgren, A., & Scheeweis, T. (1988). Corporate social responsibility and firm financial performance. *Academy of Management Journal*, *31*, 354–372.

McLachlan, J., & Gardner, J. (2004). A Comparison of Socially Responsible and Conventional Investors. *Journal of Business Ethics*, *52*(1), 11–25. doi:10.1023/B:BUSI.0000033104.28219.92

McManus, L. (2013). Customer accounting and marketing performance measures in the hotel industry: Evidence from Australia. *International Journal of Hospitality Management*, *33*, 140–152. doi:10.1016/j.ijhm.2012.07.007

McManus, L., & Guilding, C. (2008). Exploring the potential of customer accounting: A synthesis of the accounting and marketing literatures. *Journal of Marketing Management*, *24*(7-8), 771–795. doi:10.1362/026725708X345515

McWillams, A., & Siegel, D. (2001). Corporate Social Responsibility: A theory of the firm perspective. *Academy of Management Review*, *26*(1), 117–127. doi:10.5465/amr.2001.4011987

McWilliams, A., & Siegel, D. (2001). Corporate social responsibility and financial performance: Correlation or misspecification? *Strategic Management Journal*, *21*(5), 603–609. doi:10.1002/(SICI)1097-0266(200005)21:5<603::AID-SMJ101>3.0.CO;2-3

Mechelli, A., & Cimini, R. (2014). Is comprehensive income value relevant and does location matter? A European study. *Accounting in Europe*, *16*(25), 1–35. doi:10.1080/17449480.2014.890777

Memon, F., Bhutto, N. A., & Abbass, G. (2012). Capital structure and firm performance: A case of textile sector of Pakistan. *Asian Journal of Business and Management Sciences*, *1*, 9–15.

Mensah, M. L. (2003). The effect of audit quality on earnings management. *Contemporary Accounting Research*, *15*(1), 1–21.

Menz, K.-M. (2009). Corporate social responsibility: Is it rewarded by the corporate bond market? A critical note. *SSRN Electronic Journal*. Retrieved from http://ssrn.com/abstract=1332349

Messier, W. F., Glover, S. M., & Prawitt, D. F. (2008). *Auditing and Assurance Services. A Systematic Approach* (5th ed.). McGraw-Hill Irwin.

Meyer, B., Ferrari, D., & Zoebeli, D. (2012). *Transparency of NPOs' financial reporting: A quantitative study of annual reports (Switzerland)*. Retrieved from https://www.ffhs.ch/?action=get_file&id=583&resourc e_link_id=7bc

Michelon, G., Pilonato, S., & Ricceri, F. (2014). CSR reporting practices and the quality of disclosure: An empirical analysis. *Critical Perspectives on Accounting*, 33.

Milanzi, M. C. (1997). Business Ethics in Eastern and Southern Africa. *Journal of Business Ethics*, *16*(14), 1549–1553. doi:10.1023/A:1005811014294

Milne, M. J., & Gray, R. (2013). W(h)ither Ecology? The Triple Bottom Line, the Global Reporting Initiative, and Corporate Sustainability Reporting. *Journal of Business Ethics*, *118*(1), 13–29. doi:10.100710551-012-1543-8

Mintzberg, H., Ahlstrand, B. W., & Lampel, J. (1998). *Strategy Safari: The Complete Guide Through the Wilds of Strategic Management*. Harlow, UK: Financial Times.

Mockler, J. R. (2001). *Multinational Strategic Management. An integrative process based on context*. Economica Publishing House.

Modigliani, F., & Miller, M. H. (1958). The cost of capital, corporation finance and the theory of investment. *The American Economic Review*, *48*(3), 261–297.

Mohammed, A., Harris, I., & Govindan, K. (2019). A hybrid MCDM-FMOO approach for sustainable supplier selection and order allocation. *International Journal of Production Economics*, *217*, 171–184. doi:10.1016/j.ijpe.2019.02.003

Monks, R., & Minow, N. (2004). *Corporate governance* (3rd ed.). Blackwell Publishing.

Morsing, M., & Spence, L. J. (2019). Corporate social responsibility (CSR) communication and small and medium sized enterprises: The governmentality dilemma of explicit and implicit CSR communication. *Human Relations*, *72*(12), 1920–1947. doi:10.1177/0018726718804306

Mörttinen, L. (2000). *Essays on loan pricing and the credit channel of monetary policy. Research Reports. Kansantaloustieteen laitoksen tutkimuksia, 85.*

Motlanthe, K. (2011). *Address at the University of the Witwatersrand, Johannesburg (February 17, 2011): The Presidency Republic of South Africa*. Available: http://www.thepresidency.gov.za/pebble. asp?relid=4682

Mukherjee, A., & Nuñez, R. (2018). Doing well by doing good: Can voluntary CSR reporting enhance financial performance? *Journal of Indian Business Research*, *11*(2), 100–119. doi:10.1108/JIBR-07-2018-0199

Muttakin, M. B., Khan, A., & Mihret, D. G. (2017). Business group affiliation, earnings management and audit quality: Evidence from Bangladesh. *Managerial Auditing Journal*, *32*(4/5), 427–444. doi:10.1108/MAJ-01-2016-1310

Nagy, A. (2012). Audit partner specialization: The case of Andersen followers. *Managerial Auditing Journal*, *27*(3), 251–262. doi:10.1108/02686901211207483

Nakatani, I. (1984). The role of financial corporate grouping. In M. Aoki (Ed.), *Economic analysis of the Japanese firm* (pp. xx–xx). North Holland.

Naliaka, V. W., & Namusonge, G. S. (2015). Role of inventory management on competitive advantage among manufacturing firms in Kenya: A case study of UNGA Group Limited. *International Journal of Academic Research in Business and Social Sciences*, *5*(5), 87–104.

NCSD. (2008). *The National Center for Sustainable Development, Romania's National Strategy for Sustainable Development*. Horizons 2013-2020-2-30, Bucharest, 11.

Neagu, C. (2017). *Human Resources Management*. Tritonic Publishing House.

Neagu, C., & Udrescu, M. (2008). *Organization's Management*. Tritonic Publishing House.

Newton, R. (2009). *Change management step by step*. All Publishing House.

Nixon, B., & Burns, J. (2012). The paradox of strategic management accounting. *Management Accounting Research*, *23*(4), 229–244. doi:10.1016/j.mar.2012.09.004

Nyamori, R. O., Perrera, M. H. B., & Lawrence, S. R. (2001). The concept of strategic change and implications for management accounting research. *Journal of Accounting Literature*, *20*, 62–83.

O'Leary, C. (2009). An Empirical Analysis of the Positive Impact of Ethics Teaching on Accounting Students. *Accounting Education*, *18*(4–5), 505–520. doi:10.1080/09639280802532158

Ogbonna, G. N., & Ebimobowei, A. (2012). Effect of Ethical Accounting Standards on the Quality of Financial Reports of Banks in Nigeria. *Current Research Journal of Social Sciences*, *4*(1), 69–78.

Olifant, N. (2009). *S'bu Ndebele's R1, 1-million gift*. https://www.iol.co.za/news/politics/sbundebele

Olson, E. M., Slater, S. F., Tomas, G., & Hult, M. (2005). The performance implications of fit among business strategy, marketing organization structure, and strategic behavior. *Journal of Marketing*, *69*(3), 49–65. doi:10.1509/jmkg.69.3.49.66362

Orlitzky, M., Schmidt, F. L., & Rynes, S. L. (2003). Corporate Social and Financial Performance: A Meta-analysis. *Organization Studies*, *24*(3), 403–441. doi:10.1177/0170840603024003910

Oskamp, S. (1965). Overconfidence in case-study judgments. *Journal of Consulting Psychology*, *29*(3), 261–265. doi:10.1037/h0022125 PMID:14303514

Otero-Neira, C., Tapio Lindman, M., & Fernández, M. J. (2009). Innovation and performance in SME furniture industries: An international comparative case study. *Marketing Intelligence & Planning*, *27*(2), 216–232. doi:10.1108/02634500910944995

Owen, D., & O'Dwyer, B. (2004). *Assurance statement quality in environmental, social and sustainability reporting: A critical evaluation of leading edge practice.* ICCSR Research Paper Series, No. 23-2004.

Özcan, İ. Ç. (2018). *Halka Açık Demiryolu Şirketlerinin Yönetişim Aydınlatma Notlarının Belirleyicileri. İşletme Araştırmaları Dergisi*, *10*(4), 1242–1254.

Özcan, İ. Ç. (2020). Determinants of Environmental, Social, and Governance Reporting of Rail Companies: Does State Ownership Matter? In F. Manes-Rossi & R. Levy Orelli (Eds.), *New Trends in Public Sector Reporting. Public Sector Financial Management.* Cham: Palgrave Macmillan; doi:10.1007/978-3-030-40056-9_8

Painter-Morland, M., & Werhane, P. (2008). *Cutting Edge Issues in Business Ethics Continental challenges to Tradition and practice.* Springer.

Pascale, R.T. (1985, Winter). The Paradox of Corporate Culture. *California Management Review.*

Pasewark, W. R., & Riley, M. E. (2010). It's a Matter of Principle: The Role of Personal Values in Investment Decisions. *Journal of Business Ethics*, *93*(2), 237–253. doi:10.100710551-009-0218-6

Pava, L., & Krausz, J. (1996). The Association between Corporate Social Responsibility and Financial Performance. *Journal of Business Ethics*, *15*(3), 321–357. doi:10.1007/BF00382958

Peltoniemi, J., & Vieru, M. (2013). Personal Guarantees, Loan Pricing and Lending Structure in Finnish Small Business Loans. *Journal of Small Business Management*, *51*(2), 235–255. doi:10.1111/jsbm.12015

Peng, Y., Wang, G., Kou, G., & Shi, Y. (2011). An empirical study of classification algorithm evaluation for financial risk prediction. *Applied Soft Computing*, *11*(2), 2906–2915. doi:10.1016/j.asoc.2010.11.028

Perrini, F., & Castaldo, S. (2008). Editorial introduction: Corporate social responsibility and trust. *Business Ethics (Oxford, England)*, *17*(1), 1–2. doi:10.1111/j.1467-8608.2008.00514.x

Petersen, M., & Rajan, R. (1994). The benefits of lending relationships: Evidence from small business data. *The Journal of Finance*, *49*(1), 3–37. doi:10.1111/j.1540-6261.1994.tb04418.x

Petersen, M., & Rajan, R. (1995). The effect of credit market competition on lending relationships. *The Quarterly Journal of Economics*, *110*(2), 407–433. doi:10.2307/2118445

Peters, T. J., & Watterman, H. R. (2011). *In search of excellence.* Meteor Press Publishing House.

Pineda, P. J. G., Liou, J. J., Hsu, C. C., & Chuang, Y. C. (2018). An integrated MCDM model for improving airline operational and financial performance. *Journal of Air Transport Management*, *68*, 103–117. doi:10.1016/j.jairtraman.2017.06.003

Pingle, M. (1995). Imitation Versus Rationality: An Experimental Perspective on Decision Making. *Journal of Socio-Economics*, *24*(2), 281–315. doi:10.1016/1053-5357(95)90023-3

Pingle, M., & Day, R. H. (1996). Modes of economizing behavior: Experimental evidence. *Journal of Economic Behavior & Organization*, *29*(2), 191–209. doi:10.1016/0167-2681(95)00059-3

Piot, C. (2007). Auditor concentration in a joint-auditing environment: The French market 1997-2003. *Managerial Auditing Journal*, *22*(2), 161–176. doi:10.1108/02686900710718663

Pires, R.A.R., Alves, M.C.G., & Rodrigues, L. L. (2015). Strategic management accounting: definitions and dimensions. In XVIII Congreso AECA Innovación y internacionalización: factores de éxito para la pyme. *Cartagena*, 1-17.

Pivato, S., Misani, N., & Tencati, A. (2008). The impact of corporate social responsibility on consumer trust: The case of organic food. *Business Ethics (Oxford, England)*, *17*(1), 3–12. doi:10.1111/j.1467-8608.2008.00515.x

Plumlee, M., Brown, D., Hayes, R. M., & Marshall, R. S. (2015). Voluntary environmental disclosure quality and firm value: Further evidence. *Journal of Accounting and Public Policy*, *34*(4), 336–361. doi:10.1016/j.jaccpubpol.2015.04.004

Pope, P., & McLeay, S. (2011). The European IFRS experiment: Objectives, research challenges and some early evidence. *Accounting and Business Research*, *41*(3), 233–266. doi:10.1080/00014788.2011.575002

Pop, O., Dina, G. C., & Martin, C. (2011). Promoting the corporate social responsibility for a green economy and innovative jobs. *Procedia: Social and Behavioral Sciences*, *15*, 1020–1023. doi:10.1016/j.sbspro.2011.03.232

Porter, M. E. (1991). Essay: America's green strategy. *Scientific American*, *264*(4), 4. doi:10.1038cientificamerican0491-168

Pouraghajan, A., Malekian, E., Emamgholipour, M., Lotfollahpur, V. & Bagheri, M. M. 2012. The relationship between capital structure and firm performance evaluation measures: Evidence from the Tehran Stock Exchange. *International Journal of Business and Commerce, 1*, 166-181.

Prado-Lorenzo, J. M., Gallego-Alvarez, I., & Garcia-Sanchez, I. M. (2009). Stakeholder engagement and corporate social responsibility reporting: The ownership structure effect. *Corporate Social Responsibility and Environmental Management*, *16*(2), 94–107. doi:10.1002/csr.189

Prahalad, C. K. (2010). *The treasure from the pyramids basis*. Publica Publishing House.

Prajogo, C., & McDermott, P. (2011). Examining competitive priorities and competitive advantage in service organisations using Importance-Performance Analysis matrix. *Managing Service Quality*, *21*(5), 465–483. doi:10.1108/09604521111159780

Presley, T. J., & Abbott, L. J. (2013). AIA submission: CEO overconfidence and the incidence of financial restatement. *Advances in Accounting, Incorporating. Advances in International Accounting*, *29*(1), 74–84. doi:10.1016/j.adiac.2013.03.007

Preston, L., & O'Bannon, D. (1997). The Corporate Social-Financial Performance Relationship. *Business & Society*, *36*(4), 5–31. doi:10.1177/000765039703600406

Ranjith, V. (2016). Business Models and Competitive Advantage. *Procedia Economics and Finance*, *37*, 203–207. doi:10.1016/S2212-5671(16)30114-9

Rankin, M., Stanton, P., McGowan, S., Ferlauto, K., & Tilling, M. (2012). *Contemporary issues in accounting* (1st ed.). John Wiley & Sons Australia, Ltd.

Reheul, A. M., Van Caneghem, T., Van den Bogaerd, M., & Verbruggen, S. (2017). Auditor gender, experience and reporting in nonprofit organizations. *Managerial Auditing Journal*, *32*(6), 550–577. doi:10.1108/MAJ-01-2016-1296

Renneboog, L., Horst, J., & Zhang, C. (2007). *Socially responsible investments: methodology, risk exposure and performance*. Finance Working Paper No. 175/2007. Retrieved from http://ssrn.com/abstract_id=985267

Renneboog, L., Ter Horst, J., & Zhang, C. (2008). Socially responsible investments: Institutional aspects, performance, and investor behavior. *Journal of Banking & Finance*, *32*(9), 1723–1742. doi:10.1016/j.jbankfin.2007.12.039

Rhoua, Y., & Singal, M. (2020). A review of the business case for CSR in the hospitality industry. *International Journal of Hospitality Management*, *84*, 102330. doi:10.1016/j.ijhm.2019.102330

Richardson, A. (2011). Myth, Paradigms and Academic Accounting Research: A Comment on Reading and Understanding Academic Research in Accounting. *Global Perspectives on Accounting Education*, *8*, 67–77.

Richardson, A., & Welker, M. (2001). Social disclosure, financial disclosure and the cost of equity capital. *Accounting, Organizations and Society*, *26*(7-8), 597–616. doi:10.1016/S0361-3682(01)00025-3

Rittenberg, L. E., & Schwieger, B. J. (2005). *Auditing. Concepts for a Changing Environment* (5th ed.). Thomson South-Western.

Rodgers, W., Choy, H., & Guiral-Contreras, A. (2008). Do investors value a firm's commitment to social activities? The Moderating Role of Intangibles and the Impact of the Sarbanes-Oxley Act. *SSRN Electronic Journal*. Retrieved from http://ssrn.com/abstract=1311473

Rodriguez, P., Siegel, D. S., Hillman, A., & Eden, L. (2006). Three Lenses on the Multinational Enterprise: Politics, Corruption and Corporate Social Responsibility. *Journal of International Business Studies*, *37*(6), 733–746. doi:10.1057/palgrave.jibs.8400229

RomaniaC. S. R. Index. (2018). Available from: https://www.theazores.ro/wp-content/uploads/2018/02/Romania_CSR_Index_Detailed_Report.pdf

Romanus, R. N., Maher, J. J., & Fleming, D. M. (2008). Auditor industry specialization, auditor changes, and accounting restatements. *Accounting Horizons*, *22*(4), 389–413. doi:10.2308/acch.2008.22.4.389

Roslender, R., & Hart, S. J. (2003). In search of strategic management accounting: Theoretical and field study perspectives. *Management Accounting Research*, *14*(3), 255–279. doi:10.1016/S1044-5005(03)00048-9

Roslender, R., & Hart, S. J. (2006). Interfunctional Cooperation in progressing accounting for brands: The case for brand management accounting. *Journal of Accounting & Organizational Change*, *2*(3), 229–247. doi:10.1108/18325910610690072

Roslender, R., & Hart, S. J. (2010). Taking the customer into account: Transcending the construction of the customer through the promotion of self-accounting. *Critical Perspectives on Accounting*, *21*(8), 739–753. doi:10.1016/j.cpa.2010.04.002

Rossouw, D., Prozesky, M., du Plessis, C., & Prinsloo, F. (2010). *Ethics for accountants & auditors*. OUP Catalogue.

Rothenburg, E. (2003). Incorporating business ethics into introductory accounting courses. *The CPA Journal*, *6*(8).

Rowland, C., & Hall, R. (2014). Management learning, performance and reward: Theory and practice revisited. *Journal of Management Development*, *33*(4), 342–356. doi:10.1108/JMD-08-2012-0110

Ruf, B. M., Muralidhar, K., Brown, R. M., Janney, J. J., & Paul, K. (2001). An Empirical Investigation of the Relationship between Change in Corporate Social Performance and Financial Performance: A Stakeholder Theory Perspective. *Journal of Business Ethics*, *32*(2), 143–156. doi:10.1023/A:1010786912118

Rusko, R., Hietanen, L., Kohtakangas, K., Kemppainen-Koivisto, R., Siltavirta, K., & Järvi, T. (2017). Educational and Business Co-Operatives: The Channels for Collective Creativity and Entrepreneurial Teams. In Collective Creativity for Responsible and Sustainable Business Practice (pp. 242-259). IGI Global.

Russo, M. V., & Foults, P. A. (1997). A resource-based perspective on corporate environmental performance and profitability. *Academy of Management Journal*, *40*, 534–559.

Saaty, T. L. (2004). Decision making— The Analytic Hierarchy and Network Processes (AHP/ANP). *Journal of Systems Science and Systems Engineering*, *13*(1), 1–35. doi:10.100711518-006-0151-5

Sachitra, V., Chong, S. C., & Khin, A. A. (2016). Sources of competitive advantage measurement in the minor export Crop Sector in Sri Lanka result from pilot study. *Asian Journal of Agricultural Extension. Economia e Sociologia*, *12*(2), 1–15.

Sager, W.H. (2003, June 14). Professional conduct: symbol of a profession. *National Public Accountan*t.

SAICA. (2011). *CA (SA) Training Programme*. Available: https://www.saica. co.za/Training/Training/CASATraining-Programme/tabid/1657/language/enUS/Default.aspx

Saiz-Alvarez, J. M. (2015). Solidarity Entrepreneurship in the European Knowledge Economies: Keys for a New Paradigm to Be Applied into Developing Nations. In Entrepreneurship in the Contemporary Knowledge-based Global Economy. Hershey, PA: Information Science Reference (IGI Global).

Saiz-Alvarez, J. M. (2018). *Business Strategies and Advanced Techniques for Entrepreneurship 4.0*. IGI Global. doi:10.4018/978-1-5225-4978-9

Saiz-Alvarez, J. M., Coduras, A., & Cuervo-Arango, C. (2013). Entrepreneurial Strategy, Innovation, and Cognitive Capabilities. What Role for Intuitive SMEs? *Journal of Small Business Strategy*, *21*(2), 25–35.

Saiz-Alvarez, J. M., Coduras, A., & Cuervo-Arango, C. (2014). An Entrepreneurial Well-being Model based on GEM Data for Spain. *International Journal of Interactive Multimedia and Artificial Intelligence*, *2*(5), 38–47. doi:10.9781/ijimai.2014.255

Sarasvathy, S. D. (2001). *Effectuation. Elements of Entrepreneurial Expertise*. Edward Elgar.

SASB. (2018). Retrieved from https://materiality.sasb.org/

Satell, G. (2017). *A Playbook for Navigating a Disruptive Age*. McGraw Hill Education.

Sauer, D. A. (1997). The Impact of Social-Responsibility Screens on Investment Performance: Evidence from the Domini 400 Social Index and Domini Equity Mutual Fund. *Review of Financial Economics*, *6*(2), 137–149. doi:10.1016/S1058-3300(97)90002-1

Scheinberg, S., & McMillan, I. C. (1988). *An all country study of motivations to start a business, Frontiers of Entrepreneurship Research*. Babson College.

Schein, E. (1985). *Organizational Culture and leadership*. Jossey-Bass Publishers.

Schleicher, T., Tahoun, A., & Walker, M. (2010). IFRS adoption in Europe and investment-cash flow sensitivity: Outsider versus insider economies. *The International Journal of Accounting*, *45*(2), 143–168. doi:10.1016/j.intacc.2010.04.007

Schneider, M., & Somers, M. (2006). Organizations as complex adaptive systems: Implications of complexity theory for leadership research. *The Leadership Quarterly*, *17*(4), 351–365. doi:10.1016/j.leaqua.2006.04.006

Schotten, P. C., & Morais, D. C. (2019). A group decision model for credit granting in the financial market. *Financial Innovation*, *5*(1), 6. doi:10.118640854-019-0126-4

Schrand, C. M., & Zechman, S. L. C. (2012). Executive overconfidence and the slippery slope to financial misreporting. *Journal of Accounting and Economics*, *53*(1-2), 311–329. doi:10.1016/j.jacceco.2011.09.001

Schultz, T. W. (1980). Investment in Entrepreneurial Ability. *The Scandinavian Journal of Economics*, *82*(4), 437–448. doi:10.2307/3439676

Schumpeter, J. A. (1934). *The Theory of Economic Development: An Inquiry into Profits, Capital, Credit, Interest, and the Business Cycle*. Harvard University Press.

Schumpeter, J. A. (1977). *Capitalism, Socialism, and Democracy*. Harper Collins Publishers. (Original work published 1942)

Schumpeter, J. A. (1997). *Theorie der wirtschaftlichen Entwicklung: Eine Untersuchung über Unternehmergewinn, Kapital, Kredit, Zins und den Konjunkturzyklus*. Duncker Humblot. (Original work published 1911) doi:10.3790/978-3-428-07725-0

Schwindenhammer, S. (2013). Patterns and Explanations of Corporate Voluntary Norm Compliance: Results from a Structured Focused Comparison of German G500 in the Global Reporting Initiative. *German Policies Studies*, *9*(2), 123–160.

Scott, T. W., & Tiessen, P. (1999). Performance measurement and managerial teams. *Accounting, Organizations and Society*, *24*(3), 263–285. doi:10.1016/S0361-3682(98)00060-9

Sengupta, P. (1998). Corporate disclosure quality and the cost of debt. *The Accounting Review*, *73*, 459–474.

Sexton, D. (2012). *Branding*. Curtea Veche Publishing House.

Shada, M. K., Laia, F. W., Fatt, C. L., Klemeš, J. J., & Bokhari, A. (2019). Integrating sustainability reporting into enterprise risk management and its relationship with business performance: A conceptual framework. *Journal of Cleaner Production*, *208*, 415–425. doi:10.1016/j.jclepro.2018.10.120

Shah, S. Z. A., Butt, S. A., & Saeed, M. M. (2011). Ownership structure and performance of firms: Empirical evidence from an emerging market. *African Journal of Business Management*, *5*(2), 515–523.

Shane, S., & Venkataraman, S. (2000). The Promise of Entrepreneurship as a Field of Research. *Academy of Management Review*, *25*(1), 217–226. doi:10.5465/amr.2000.2791611

Shank, J. K., & Govindarajan, V. (1992). Strategic cost management: The value chain perspective. *Journal of Management Accounting Research*, *4*, 179–198.

Sharfman, M. P. (1996). The Construct Validity of the Kinder, Lydenberg & Domini Social Performance Ratings Data. *Journal of Business Ethics*, *15*(3), 287–296. doi:10.1007/BF00382954

Sharma, U., & An, Y. (2018). Accounting and accountability in Fiji: A review and synthesis. *Australian Accounting Review*, *28*(3), 421-427.

Sharpe, S. (1990). Asymmetric information, bank lending, and implicit contracts: A stylized model of customer relationship. *The Journal of Finance*, *45*, 1069–1089.

Shaw, W. H. (2008). *Business Ethics*. Wadsworth Inc.

Shefrin, H. (2007). *Behavioral corporate finance: Decisions that create value*. McGraw-Hill/Irwin.

Shen, K. Y., Sakai, H., & Tzeng, G. H. (2019, June). Multi-graded Hybrid MRDM Model for Assisting Financial Performance Evaluation Decisions: A Preliminary Work. In *International Joint Conference on Rough Sets* (pp. 439-453). Springer. 10.1007/978-3-030-22815-6_34

Shepherd, D. A., & Patzelt, H. (2011). The New Field of Sustainable Entrepreneurship: Studying Entrepreneurial Action Linking "What Is To Be Sustained" with "What Is To Be Developed?". *Entrepreneurship Theory and Practice*, *35*(1), 137–163. doi:10.1111/j.1540-6520.2010.00426.x

Sierra-García, L., Zorio-Grima, A., & García-Benau, M. A. (2013). Sustainable development and assurance of corporate social responsibility reports published by Ibex-35 companies. *Corporate Social Responsibility and Environmental Management*, *20*(6), 359–370. doi:10.1002/csr.1303

Sigalas, Ch., Economou, V. P., & Georgopoulos, N. B. (2013). Developing a measure of competitive advantage. *Journal of Strategy and Management*, *6*(4), 320–342. doi:10.1108/JSMA-03-2013-0015

Sijbom, R. B. L., Janssen, O., & Van Yperen, N. W. (2015). Leaders' Receptivity to Subordinates' Creative Input: The Role of Achievement Goals and Composition of Creative Input. *European Journal of Work and Organizational Psychology*, *24*(3), 462–478. doi:10.1080/1359432X.2014.964215

Silva, O. (2007). The Jack-of-All-Trades entrepreneur: Innate talent or acquired skill? *Economics Letters*, *97*(2), 118–123. doi:10.1016/j.econlet.2007.02.027

Simmonds, K. (1981). Strategic management accounting. *Management Accounting*, *59*, 26–30.

Simmonds, K. (1982). Strategic management accounting for pricing: A case example. *Accounting and Business Research*, *47*(47), 206–214. doi:10.1080/00014788.1982.9728809

Simnett, R., Vanstrealen, A., & Chua, W. F. (2009). Assurance on sustainability reports: An international comparison. *The Accounting Review*, *84*(3), 937–967. doi:10.2308/accr.2009.84.3.937

Simon, H. (1957). *Administrative Behavior: A Study of Decision-making Processes in Administrative Organization*. Macmillan.

Simon, H. A. (1955). A behavioral model of rational choice. *The Quarterly Journal of Economics*, *69*(1), 99–118. doi:10.2307/1884852

Sinthupundaja, J., Chiadamrong, N., & Kohda, Y. (2019). Internal capabilities, external cooperation and proactive CSR on financial performance. *Service Industries Journal*, *39*(15-16), 1099–1122. doi:10.1080/02642069.2018.1508459

Slager, R., Gond, J.-P., & Moon, J. (2012). Standardization as Institutional Work: The Regulatory Power of a Responsible Investment Standard. *Organization Studies*, *33*(5-6), 763–790. doi:10.1177/0170840612443628

Smit, S., & Steenkamp, G. (2015). The competencies developed in an undergraduate accounting course before SAICA's SAICA competency framework was effective: A student's perspective. *Journal of Economic and Financial Sciences*, *8*(2), 666–688. doi:10.4102/jef.v8i2.115

Soloman, R., & Hansen, K. (1995). *It's Good Business*. Atheneum.

Song, Y., & Peng, Y. (2019). A MCDM-Based Evaluation Approach for Imbalanced Classification Methods in Financial Risk Prediction. *IEEE Access: Practical Innovations, Open Solutions*, *7*, 84897–84906. doi:10.1109/ACCESS.2019.2924923

South African Institute of Chartered Accountants (SAICA). (2006). *Code of professional conduct*. https://www.saica.co.za/documents/Code_of_Professional_Conduct_2006.pdf

Spence, L. J., & Lozano, J. F. (2000). Communicating about ethics with small firms: Experiences from the UK and Spain. *Journal of Business Ethics*, *27*(1-2), 43–53. doi:10.1023/A:1006417425446

Spicer, B. H. (1978). Investors, Corporate Social Performance and Information Disclosure: An Empirical Study. *The Accounting Review*, *53*, 94–111.

Stanley, J. D., & DeZoort, F. T. (2007). Audit firm tenure and financial restatements: An analysis of industry specialization and fee effects. *Journal of Accounting and Public Policy*, *26*(2), 131–159. doi:10.1016/j.jaccpubpol.2007.02.003

Stanwick, P. A., & Stanwick, S. D. (1998). The Relationship Between Corporate Social Performance, and Organizational Size, Financial Performance, and Environmental Performance: An Empirical Examination. *Journal of Business Ethics*, *17*(2), 195–204. doi:10.1023/A:1005784421547

Steinthórsdóttir, L. (2004). Internal control–corporate governance, internal audit and strategic renewal. *Monetary Bulletin, 6*(1), 85–95.

Stephan, U., Uhlaner, L. M., & Stride, C. (2015). Institutions and Social Entrepreneurship: The Role of Institutional Voids, Institutional Support, and Institutional Configurations. *Journal of International Business Studies, 46*(3), 308–331. doi:10.1057/jibs.2014.38

Stettina, C. J., & Hörz, J. (2015). Agile portfolio management: An empirical perspective on the practice in use. *International Journal of Project Management, 33*(1), 140–152. doi:10.1016/j.ijproman.2014.03.008

Stevenson, H. H., & Jarillo, J. C. (1990). A Paradigm of Entrepreneurship: Entrepreneurial Management. *Strategic Management Journal, 11*, 17–27.

Sustainable Development Strategy, Europe's Council, 9th June 2006.

Svanberg, J., & Ohman, P. (2013). Auditors' time pressure: Does ethical culture support audit quality? *Managerial Auditing Journal, 28*(7), 572–591. doi:10.1108/MAJ-10-2012-0761

Tajeddini, K. (2015). Exploring the antecedents of effectiveness and efficiency. *International Journal of Hospitality Management, 49*(7), 125–135. doi:10.1016/j.ijhm.2015.06.007

Tallon, P. P., & Pinsonneault, A. (2011). Competing Perspectives on the Link Between Strategic Information Technology Alignment and Organizational Agility: Insights from a Mediation Model. *Management Information Systems Quarterly, 35*(2), 463–486. doi:10.2307/23044052

Tan, H. P., Plowman, D., & Hancock, P. (2008). The evolving research on intellectual capital. *Journal of Intellectual Capital, 9*(4), 585–608. doi:10.1108/14691930810913177

Tapanainen, T., Hallanoro, M., Päivärinta, J., & Salmela, H. (2008). Towards an Agile IT Organization: A Review of Prior Literature. In *Proceedings of the 2nd European Conference on Information Management and Evaluation* (pp. 425-432). London, UK: Academic Conferences Limited.

Taticchi, P., Tonelli, F., & Cagnazzo, L. (2010). Performance measurement and management: A literature review and a research agenda. *Measuring Business Excellence, 14*(1), 4–18. doi:10.1108/13683041011027418

Tayles, M., Pike, R. H., & Sofian, S. (2007). Intellectual capital, management accounting practices and corporate performance: Perceptions of managers. *Accounting, Auditing & Accountability Journal, 20*(4), 522–548. doi:10.1108/09513570710762575

TCFD. (2017). *Final Report: Recommendations of the Task Force on Climate-related Financial Disclosures*. Retrieved from https://www.fsb-tcfd.org/publications/final-recommendations-report/

Tendeloo, B., & Vanstrelen, A. (2005). Earnings management under German GAAP versus IFRS. *European Accounting Review, 14*(1), 155–180. doi:10.1080/0963818042000338988

Thakor, A. V. (1995). Financial intermediation and the market for credit. *Handbooks in OR and MS, 9, 1073-1103.*

Thakor, A. V., & Callaway, R. (1983). Costly Information Production Equilibria in the Bank Credit Market with Applications to Credit Rationing. *Journal of Financial and Quantitative Analysis, 18*(2), 229–256. doi:10.2307/2330921

Thompson, A., Jr., & Strickland III. (1987). Strategic management. Concept and Cases. Irwin Homewood.

Thong, T. Y., Ding, D. K., & Lim, C. Y. (2008). Firm diversification and earning management: Evidence from seasoned equity offerings. *Review of Quantitative Finance and Accounting, 30*(1), 69–92. doi:10.100711156-007-0043-x

Tillmann, K., & Goddard, A. (2008). Strategic management accounting and sense-making in a multinational company. *Management Accounting Research*, *19*(1), 80–102. doi:10.1016/j.mar.2007.11.002

Todorovic, I. (2013). Impact of Corporate Governance on Performance of Companies. *Montenegrin Journal of Economics*, *9*(2), 47–53.

Tong, Y. K., & Arvey, R. D. (2015). Managing complexity via the Competing Values Framework. *Journal of Management Development*, *34*(6), 653–673. doi:10.1108/JMD-04-2014-0029

Torkabadi, A. M., Pourjavad, E., & Mayorga, R. V. (2018). An integrated fuzzy MCDM approach to improve sustainable consumption and production trends in supply chain. *Sustainable Production and Consumption*, *16*, 99–109. doi:10.1016/j.spc.2018.05.008

Torugsa, N. A., O'Donohue, W., & Hecker, R. (2012). Capabilities, proactive CSR and financial performance inSMEs: Empirical evidence from an Australian manufacturing industry sector. *Journal of Business Ethics*, *109*(4), 483–500. doi:10.100710551-011-1141-1

Tracy, B. (2010). *How the best leaders lead*. Curtea Veche Publishing House.

Transparency International Global Corruption Barometer. (2010). Available at http: www transparency. org/policy research/survey indices/gcp/2010/

Tversky, A., & Kahneman, D. (1986). Rational choice and framing of decisions. *Journal of Business, 59*(4), 251-278.

Tversky, A., & Kahneman, D. (1974). Judgement under uncertainty: Heuristics and biases", *Science. New Series*, *185*(4157), 1124–1131. PMID:17835457

Udrescu, M. A., & Gheorghe, A. (2016). Management's Involvement in the New Products' Development. Simpozionul Internațional "Research –Forecast- Decision in the Social- Economic System", Bucharest, Romania.

Udrescu, M. A., & Gheorghe, A. (2016). Benchmarketing-Fashionable term concerning traditional processes. *Academic Journal of Economic Research*, *2*(2), 100–113.

Udrescu, M. A., & Gheorghe, A. (2017). Motivation and organizational behavior. Staff between Value Added and Conflict-Generating Losses. *Academic Journal of Economic Studies (Glasgow, Scotland)*, *3*(2), 55–59.

Udrescu, M. A., Neagu, C., Popescu-Cruceru, A., & Gheorghe, A. (2016). *General Management- Concepts and Case Studies*. Artifex Publishing House.

Udrescu, M., & Năstase, D. (2019). *Research, forecasts and seminars in marketing*. The Romanian Academy of Scientists Publishing House.

Udrescu, M., & Popescu-Cruceru, A. (2018). *Logistics and logistic subsystems of the company*. The Romanian Academy of Scientists Publishing House.

UNEP FI Asset Management Working Group Support. (2014). *Integrated Governance, A New Model of Governance for Sustainability*. Author.

UNEP. (2012). *The Business Case for the Green Economy*. Sustainable Return on Investment.

Velilla, J., Molina, J. A., & Ortega, R. (2018). Why Older Workers Become Entrepreneurs? International Evidence Using Fuzzy Set Methods. *The Journal of the Economics of Ageing*, *12*, 88–95. doi:10.1016/j.jeoa.2018.03.004

Verbeeten, F. (2010). The impact of business unit strategy, structure and technical innovativeness on change in management accounting systems. *International Journal of Management*, *27*(1), 123–143.

Verenich, V. (2014). The Splendors and Miseries of Constitutional Reasoning in Times of Global Crisis: A Critical Look from the Realist Perspectives of Semiotics. *International Journal for the Semiotics of Law-Revue internationale de Sémiotique juridique, 27*(4), 687-711.

Verschoor, C. C. (1998). A Study of The Link Between Corporation's Financial Performance and Its Commitment to Ethics. *Journal of Business Ethics, 17*(13), 1509–1516. doi:10.1023/A:1006020402881

Vidal, P., Torres, D., Guix, B., & Rodríguez, M. P. (2005). *The Social Responsibility of Non-Profit Organisations. A conceptual Approach and Development of SRO model.* Observatori del Tercer Sector.

Vidaver-Cohen, D., & Brønn, P. S. (2015). Reputation, responsibility, and stakeholder support in Scandinavian firms: A comparative analysis. *Journal of Business Ethics, 127*(1), 49–64. doi:10.100710551-013-1673-7

Vincent, D. R., Deepa, N., Elavarasan, D., Srinivasan, K., Chauhdary, S. H., & Iwendi, C. (2019). Sensors Driven AI-Based Agriculture Recommendation Model for Assessing Land Suitability. *Sensors (Basel), 19*(17), 3667. doi:10.339019173667 PMID:31450772

Waddock, S. (2015). Building a new institutional infrastructure for corporate responsibility. *The Academy of Management Perspectives, 22*(3), 87–108. doi:10.5465/amp.2008.34587997

Waddock, S. A., & Graves, S. B. (1997). The corporate social performance–financial performance link. *Strategic Management Journal, 18*(4), 303–319. doi:10.1002/(SICI)1097-0266(199704)18:4<303::AID-SMJ869>3.0.CO;2-G

Wagner, J. (2003). Testing Lazear's jack-of-all-trades view of entrepreneurship with German micro data. *Applied Economics Letters, 10*(11), 687–689. doi:10.1080/1350485032000133273

Wang, G., & Ma, J. (2012). A hybrid ensemble approach for enterprise credit risk assessment based on Support Vector Machine. *Expert Systems with Applications, 39*(5), 5325–5331. doi:10.1016/j.eswa.2011.11.003

Watts, G., Fernie, S., & Dainty, A. (2019). Paradox and legitimacy in construction: How CSR reports restrict CSR practice. *International Journal of Building Pathology and Adaptation, 37*(2), 231–246. doi:10.1108/IJBPA-05-2018-0037

Watts, R., & Zimmerman, J. (1978). Towards a Positive Theory of the Determination of Accounting Standards. *The Accounting Review, 53*(1), 112–134.

Weber, O. (2014). Environmental, social and governance reporting in China. *Business Strategy and the Environment, 23*(5), 303–317. doi:10.1002/bse.1785

Weinstein, A. (2012). *Superior customer value: strategies for winning and retaining customers* (3rd ed.). CRC Press-Taylor & Francis Group.

Weinstein, D., & Yafeh, Y. (1998). On the costs of a bank centered financial system: Evidence from the changing main bank relations in Japan. *The Journal of Finance, 53*(2), 635–672. doi:10.1111/0022-1082.254893

Weinstein, M. (1981). The systematic risk of corporate bonds. *Journal of Financial and Quantitative Analysis, 41*(3), 257–278. doi:10.2307/2330238

Welch, I. (1997). Why is bank debt senior? A theory of asymmetry and claim priority based on influence costs. *Review of Financial Studies, 10*(4), 1203–1236. doi:10.1093/rfs/10.4.1203

Wells, V. K., Ponting, C. A., & Peattie, K. (2011). Behaviour and climate change: Consumer perceptions of responsibility. *Journal of Marketing Management, 27*(7-8), 808–833. doi:10.1080/0267257X.2010.500136

West, R. (1970). An alternative approach to predicting corporate bond ratings. *Journal of Accounting Research, 7*(1), 118–127. doi:10.2307/2674717

Weygandt, J. J., Kimmel, P. D., & Kieso, D. E. (2011). *Financial accounting* (1st ed.). John Wiley & Sons, Inc.

Whittington, O. R., & Pany, K. (2008). *Principles of Auditing & Other Assurance Services* (16th ed.). McGraw-Hill Irwin.

Wickramasinghe, D., & Alawattage, C. (2007). *Management accounting change: approaches and perspectives.* Routledge, Taylor & Francis Group.

Williams, G. (2007). Some determinants of the socially responsible investment decision: A cross-country study. *Journal of Behavioral Finance*, *8*(1), 43–57. doi:10.1080/15427560709337016

Woo, C. Y., Cooper, A. C., & Dunkelberg, W. C. (1988). *Entrepreneurial typologies: definitions and implications, Frontiers of Entrepreneurship Research.* Babson College.

Wu, H. Y., Tzeng, G. H., & Chen, Y. H. (2009). A fuzzy MCDM approach for evaluating banking performance based on Balanced Scorecard. *Expert Systems with Applications*, *36*(6), 10135–10147. doi:10.1016/j.eswa.2009.01.005

Wu, T. C., & Hsu, M. F. (2012). Credit risk assessment and decision making by a fusion approach. *Knowledge-Based Systems*, *35*, 102–110. doi:10.1016/j.knosys.2012.04.025

Wu, Z., & Chua, J. H. (2012). Second-order gender effects: The case of U.S. small business borrowing cost. *Entrepreneurship Theory and Practice*, *36*(3), 443–463. doi:10.1111/j.1540-6520.2012.00503.x

Xie, B., Davidson, W. N. III, & DaDalt, P. J. (2003). Earnings Management and Corporate Governance: The role of the board and the audit committee. *Journal of Corporate Finance*, *9*(10), 295–316. doi:10.1016/S0929-1199(02)00006-8

Xiong, Y. (2006). Earning management and its measurement; a theoretical perspective. *The Journal of American Academy of Business, Cambridge*, *9*(1), 214–219.

Xu, D. L., & Yang, J. B. (2006). Intelligent decision system and its application in business innovation self-assessment. *Decision Support Systems*, *42*(2), 664–673. doi:10.1016/j.dss.2005.03.004

Yadav, N., & Sagar, M. (2013). Performance measurement and management frameworks. *Business Process Management Journal*, *19*(6), 947–971. doi:10.1108/BPMJ-01-2013-0003

Young, F., Kim, W., Black, B. S., & Jang, H. (2000). Predicting firms' corporate governance choices: Evidence from Korea. *Journal of Corporate Finance*, *12*, 660–691.

Young, M. R. (2002). *Accounting irregularities and financial fraud.* Corporate Governance Guide. Aspen Law & Business.

Zainon, S., Hashim, M., Yahaya, N., & Atan, R. (2013). Annual Reports of Non-profit Organizations (NPOs): An Analysis. *Journal of Modern Accounting and Auditing*, *9*(2), 183–192.

Zbuchea, A. (2013). Are customers rewarding responsible businesses? An overview of the theory and research in the field of CSR. *Management Dynamics in the Knowledge Economy*, *1*(3), 367–385.

Zeghal, D., Chtourou, S., & Fourati, M. Y. (2012). The effect of mandatory adoption of IFRS on earning quality: Evidence from the European Union. *Journal of International Accounting Research*, *11*(2), 1–25. doi:10.2308/jiar-10221

Zéghal, D., Chtourou, S., & Mnif, S. Y. (2011). An analysis of the effect of mandatory adoption of IAS/IFRS on earnings Management. *Journal of International Accounting, Auditing & Taxation*, *20*(2), 61–72. doi:10.1016/j.intaccaudtax.2011.06.001

Zeghal, D., & Mhedhbi, K. (2016). An analysis of the factors affecting the adoption of international accounting standards by developing countries. *The International Journal of Accounting*, *41*(4), 373–386. doi:10.1016/j.intacc.2006.09.009

Zeitun, R. & Tian, G. 2014. Capital structure and corporate performance: evidence from Jordan.

Zerni, M. (2012). Audit partner specialization and audit fees: Some evidence from Sweden. *Contemporary Accounting Research*, *29*(1), 312–340. doi:10.1111/j.1911-3846.2011.01098.x

Zhang, Y., & Lee, M. (2019). A Hybrid Model for Addressing the Relationship between Financial Performance and Sustainable Development. *Sustainability*, *11*(10), 2899. doi:10.3390u11102899

Ziglar, Z. (2011). *Beyond the peak*. Curtea Veche Publishing House.

Zikmund, W. G. (2000). *Business research methods* (6th ed.). Dryden Press.

Zingales, L. (2000). In search of new foundations. *The Journal of Finance*, *55*(4), 1623–1653. doi:10.1111/0022-1082.00262

Zitzler, E., & Thiele, L. (1998, September). Multiobjective optimization using evolutionary algorithms—a comparative case study. In *International conference on parallel problem solving from nature* (pp. 292-301). Springer.

Zolfani, S. H., Aghdaie, M. H., Derakhti, A., Zavadskas, E. K., & Varzandeh, M. H. M. (2013). Decision making on business issues with foresight perspective; an application of new hybrid MCDM model in shopping mall locating. *Expert Systems with Applications*, *40*(17), 7111–7121. doi:10.1016/j.eswa.2013.06.040

Zorn, T., & Collins, E. (2006). Green is the new black: are CSR and sustainable business just fads? *Proceedings of the 20th ANZAM (of Management) Conference on "Management: Pragmatism, Philosophy, Priorities*". Retrieved from http://library-resources.cqu.edu.au:8888/access/detail.php?pid=cqu:961

Related References

To continue our tradition of advancing information science and technology research, we have compiled a list of recommended IGI Global readings. These references will provide additional information and guidance to further enrich your knowledge and assist you with your own research and future publications.

Abtahi, M. S., Behboudi, L., & Hasanabad, H. M. (2017). Factors Affecting Internet Advertising Adoption in Ad Agencies. *International Journal of Innovation in the Digital Economy*, *8*(4), 18–29. doi:10.4018/IJIDE.2017100102

Agrawal, S. (2017). The Impact of Emerging Technologies and Social Media on Different Business(es): Marketing and Management. In O. Rishi & A. Sharma (Eds.), *Maximizing Business Performance and Efficiency Through Intelligent Systems* (pp. 37–49). Hershey, PA: IGI Global. doi:10.4018/978-1-5225-2234-8.ch002

Alnoukari, M., Razouk, R., & Hanano, A. (2016). BSC-SI: A Framework for Integrating Strategic Intelligence in Corporate Strategic Management. *International Journal of Social and Organizational Dynamics in IT*, *5*(2), 1–14. doi:10.4018/IJSODIT.2016070101

Alnoukari, M., Razouk, R., & Hanano, A. (2016). BSC-SI, A Framework for Integrating Strategic Intelligence in Corporate Strategic Management. *International Journal of Strategic Information Technology and Applications*, *7*(1), 32–44. doi:10.4018/IJSITA.2016010103

Altındağ, E. (2016). Current Approaches in Change Management. In A. Goksoy (Ed.), *Organizational Change Management Strategies in Modern Business* (pp. 24–51). Hershey, PA: IGI Global. doi:10.4018/978-1-4666-9533-7.ch002

Alvarez-Dionisi, L. E., Turner, R., & Mittra, M. (2016). Global Project Management Trends. *International Journal of Information Technology Project Management*, *7*(3), 54–73. doi:10.4018/IJITPM.2016070104

Anantharaman, R. N., Rajeswari, K. S., Angusamy, A., & Kuppusamy, J. (2017). Role of Self-Efficacy and Collective Efficacy as Moderators of Occupational Stress Among Software Development Professionals. *International Journal of Human Capital and Information Technology Professionals*, *8*(2), 45–58. doi:10.4018/IJHCITP.2017040103

Aninze, F., El-Gohary, H., & Hussain, J. (2018). The Role of Microfinance to Empower Women: The Case of Developing Countries. *International Journal of Customer Relationship Marketing and Management, 9*(1), 54–78. doi:10.4018/IJCRMM.2018010104

Arsenijević, O. M., Orčić, D., & Kastratović, E. (2017). Development of an Optimization Tool for Intangibles in SMEs: A Case Study from Serbia with a Pilot Research in the Prestige by Milka Company. In M. Vemić (Ed.), *Optimal Management Strategies in Small and Medium Enterprises* (pp. 320–347). Hershey, PA: IGI Global. doi:10.4018/978-1-5225-1949-2.ch015

Aryanto, V. D., Wismantoro, Y., & Widyatmoko, K. (2018). Implementing Eco-Innovation by Utilizing the Internet to Enhance Firm's Marketing Performance: Study of Green Batik Small and Medium Enterprises in Indonesia. *International Journal of E-Business Research, 14*(1), 21–36. doi:10.4018/IJEBR.2018010102

Atiku, S. O., & Fields, Z. (2017). Multicultural Orientations for 21st Century Global Leadership. In N. Baporikar (Ed.), *Management Education for Global Leadership* (pp. 28–51). Hershey, PA: IGI Global. doi:10.4018/978-1-5225-1013-0.ch002

Atiku, S. O., & Fields, Z. (2018). Organisational Learning Dimensions and Talent Retention Strategies for the Service Industries. In N. Baporikar (Ed.), *Global Practices in Knowledge Management for Societal and Organizational Development* (pp. 358–381). Hershey, PA: IGI Global. doi:10.4018/978-1-5225-3009-1.ch017

Ávila, L., & Teixeira, L. (2018). The Main Concepts Behind the Dematerialization of Business Processes. In M. Khosrow-Pour, D.B.A. (Ed.), Encyclopedia of Information Science and Technology, Fourth Edition (pp. 888-898). Hershey, PA: IGI Global. doi:10.4018/978-1-5225-2255-3.ch076

Bartens, Y., Chunpir, H. I., Schulte, F., & Voß, S. (2017). Business/IT Alignment in Two-Sided Markets: A COBIT 5 Analysis for Media Streaming Business Models. In S. De Haes & W. Van Grembergen (Eds.), *Strategic IT Governance and Alignment in Business Settings* (pp. 82–111). Hershey, PA: IGI Global. doi:10.4018/978-1-5225-0861-8.ch004

Bashayreh, A. M. (2018). Organizational Culture and Organizational Performance. In W. Lee & F. Sabetzadeh (Eds.), *Contemporary Knowledge and Systems Science* (pp. 50–69). Hershey, PA: IGI Global. doi:10.4018/978-1-5225-5655-8.ch003

Bedford, D. A. (2018). Sustainable Knowledge Management Strategies: Aligning Business Capabilities and Knowledge Management Goals. In N. Baporikar (Ed.), *Global Practices in Knowledge Management for Societal and Organizational Development* (pp. 46–73). Hershey, PA: IGI Global. doi:10.4018/978-1-5225-3009-1.ch003

Benmoussa, F., Nakara, W. A., & Jaouen, A. (2016). The Use of Social Media by SMEs in the Tourism Industry. In I. Lee (Ed.), *Encyclopedia of E-Commerce Development, Implementation, and Management* (pp. 2159–2170). Hershey, PA: IGI Global. doi:10.4018/978-1-4666-9787-4.ch155

Berger, R. (2016). Indigenous Management and Bottom of Pyramid Countries: The Role of National Institutions. In U. Aung & P. Ordoñez de Pablos (Eds.), *Managerial Strategies and Practice in the Asian Business Sector* (pp. 107–123). Hershey, PA: IGI Global. doi:10.4018/978-1-4666-9758-4.ch007

Bharwani, S., & Musunuri, D. (2018). Reflection as a Process From Theory to Practice. In M. Khosrow-Pour, D.B.A. (Ed.), Encyclopedia of Information Science and Technology, Fourth Edition (pp. 1529-1539). Hershey, PA: IGI Global. doi:10.4018/978-1-5225-2255-3.ch132

Bhatt, G. D., Wang, Z., & Rodger, J. A. (2017). Information Systems Capabilities and Their Effects on Competitive Advantages: A Study of Chinese Companies. *Information Resources Management Journal*, *30*(3), 41–57. doi:10.4018/IRMJ.2017070103

Bhushan, M., & Yadav, A. (2017). Concept of Cloud Computing in ESB. In R. Bhadoria, N. Chaudhari, G. Tomar, & S. Singh (Eds.), *Exploring Enterprise Service Bus in the Service-Oriented Architecture Paradigm* (pp. 116–127). Hershey, PA: IGI Global. doi:10.4018/978-1-5225-2157-0.ch008

Bhushan, S. (2017). System Dynamics Base-Model of Humanitarian Supply Chain (HSCM) in Disaster Prone Eco-Communities of India: A Discussion on Simulation and Scenario Results. *International Journal of System Dynamics Applications*, *6*(3), 20–37. doi:10.4018/IJSDA.2017070102

Biswas, A., & De, A. K. (2017). On Development of a Fuzzy Stochastic Programming Model with Its Application to Business Management. In S. Trivedi, S. Dey, A. Kumar, & T. Panda (Eds.), *Handbook of Research on Advanced Data Mining Techniques and Applications for Business Intelligence* (pp. 353–378). Hershey, PA: IGI Global. doi:10.4018/978-1-5225-2031-3.ch021

Bücker, J., & Ernste, K. (2018). Use of Brand Heroes in Strategic Reputation Management: The Case of Bacardi, Adidas, and Daimler. In A. Erdemir (Ed.), *Reputation Management Techniques in Public Relations* (pp. 126–150). Hershey, PA: IGI Global. doi:10.4018/978-1-5225-3619-2.ch007

Bureš, V. (2018). Industry 4.0 From the Systems Engineering Perspective: Alternative Holistic Framework Development. In R. Brunet-Thornton & F. Martinez (Eds.), *Analyzing the Impacts of Industry 4.0 in Modern Business Environments* (pp. 199–223). Hershey, PA: IGI Global. doi:10.4018/978-1-5225-3468-6.ch011

Buzady, Z. (2017). Resolving the Magic Cube of Effective Case Teaching: Benchmarking Case Teaching Practices in Emerging Markets – Insights from the Central European University Business School, Hungary. In D. Latusek (Ed.), *Case Studies as a Teaching Tool in Management Education* (pp. 79–103). Hershey, PA: IGI Global. doi:10.4018/978-1-5225-0770-3.ch005

Campatelli, G., Richter, A., & Stocker, A. (2016). Participative Knowledge Management to Empower Manufacturing Workers. *International Journal of Knowledge Management*, *12*(4), 37–50. doi:10.4018/IJKM.2016100103

Căpusneanu, S., & Topor, D. I. (2018). Business Ethics and Cost Management in SMEs: Theories of Business Ethics and Cost Management Ethos. In I. Oncioiu (Ed.), *Ethics and Decision-Making for Sustainable Business Practices* (pp. 109–127). Hershey, PA: IGI Global. doi:10.4018/978-1-5225-3773-1.ch007

Carneiro, A. (2016). Maturity in Health Organization Information Systems: Metrics and Privacy Perspectives. *International Journal of Privacy and Health Information Management*, *4*(2), 1–18. doi:10.4018/IJPHIM.2016070101

Chan, R. L., Mo, P. L., & Moon, K. K. (2018). Strategic and Tactical Measures in Managing Enterprise Risks: A Study of the Textile and Apparel Industry. In K. Strang, M. Korstanje, & N. Vajjhala (Eds.), *Research, Practices, and Innovations in Global Risk and Contingency Management* (pp. 1–19). Hershey, PA: IGI Global. doi:10.4018/978-1-5225-4754-9.ch001

Chandan, H. C. (2016). Motivations and Challenges of Female Entrepreneurship in Developed and Developing Economies. In N. Baporikar (Ed.), *Handbook of Research on Entrepreneurship in the Contemporary Knowledge-Based Global Economy* (pp. 260–286). Hershey, PA: IGI Global. doi:10.4018/978-1-4666-8798-1.ch012

Charlier, S. D., Burke-Smalley, L. A., & Fisher, S. L. (2018). Undergraduate Programs in the U.S: A Contextual and Content-Based Analysis. In J. Mendy (Ed.), *Teaching Human Resources and Organizational Behavior at the College Level* (pp. 26–57). Hershey, PA: IGI Global. doi:10.4018/978-1-5225-2820-3.ch002

Chaudhuri, S. (2016). Application of Web-Based Geographical Information System (GIS) in E-Business. In U. Panwar, R. Kumar, & N. Ray (Eds.), *Handbook of Research on Promotional Strategies and Consumer Influence in the Service Sector* (pp. 389–405). Hershey, PA: IGI Global. doi:10.4018/978-1-5225-0143-5.ch023

Choudhuri, P. S. (2016). An Empirical Study on the Quality of Services Offered by the Private Life Insurers in Burdwan. In U. Panwar, R. Kumar, & N. Ray (Eds.), *Handbook of Research on Promotional Strategies and Consumer Influence in the Service Sector* (pp. 31–55). Hershey, PA: IGI Global. doi:10.4018/978-1-5225-0143-5.ch002

Dahlberg, T., Kivijärvi, H., & Saarinen, T. (2017). IT Investment Consistency and Other Factors Influencing the Success of IT Performance. In S. De Haes & W. Van Grembergen (Eds.), *Strategic IT Governance and Alignment in Business Settings* (pp. 176–208). Hershey, PA: IGI Global. doi:10.4018/978-1-5225-0861-8.ch007

Damnjanović, A. M. (2017). Knowledge Management Optimization through IT and E-Business Utilization: A Qualitative Study on Serbian SMEs. In M. Vemić (Ed.), *Optimal Management Strategies in Small and Medium Enterprises* (pp. 249–267). Hershey, PA: IGI Global. doi:10.4018/978-1-5225-1949-2.ch012

Daneshpour, H. (2017). Integrating Sustainable Development into Project Portfolio Management through Application of Open Innovation. In M. Vemić (Ed.), *Optimal Management Strategies in Small and Medium Enterprises* (pp. 370–387). Hershey, PA: IGI Global. doi:10.4018/978-1-5225-1949-2.ch017

Daniel, A. D., & Reis de Castro, V. (2018). Entrepreneurship Education: How to Measure the Impact on Nascent Entrepreneurs. In A. Carrizo Moreira, J. Guilherme Leitão Dantas, & F. Manuel Valente (Eds.), *Nascent Entrepreneurship and Successful New Venture Creation* (pp. 85–110). Hershey, PA: IGI Global. doi:10.4018/978-1-5225-2936-1.ch004

David, F., van der Sijde, P., & van den Besselaar, P. (2016). Enterpreneurial Incentives, Obstacles, and Management in University-Business Co-Operation: The Case of Indonesia. In J. Saiz-Álvarez (Ed.), *Handbook of Research on Social Entrepreneurship and Solidarity Economics* (pp. 499–518). Hershey, PA: IGI Global. doi:10.4018/978-1-5225-0097-1.ch024

David, R., Swami, B. N., & Tangirala, S. (2018). Ethics Impact on Knowledge Management in Organizational Development: A Case Study. In N. Baporikar (Ed.), *Global Practices in Knowledge Management for Societal and Organizational Development* (pp. 19–45). Hershey, PA: IGI Global. doi:10.4018/978-1-5225-3009-1.ch002

Delias, P., & Lakiotaki, K. (2018). Discovering Process Horizontal Boundaries to Facilitate Process Comprehension. *International Journal of Operations Research and Information Systems*, *9*(2), 1–31. doi:10.4018/IJORIS.2018040101

Denholm, J., & Lee-Davies, L. (2018). Success Factors for Games in Business and Project Management. In *Enhancing Education and Training Initiatives Through Serious Games* (pp. 34–68). Hershey, PA: IGI Global. doi:10.4018/978-1-5225-3689-5.ch002

Deshpande, M. (2017). Best Practices in Management Institutions for Global Leadership: Policy Aspects. In N. Baporikar (Ed.), *Management Education for Global Leadership* (pp. 1–27). Hershey, PA: IGI Global. doi:10.4018/978-1-5225-1013-0.ch001

Deshpande, M. (2018). Policy Perspectives for SMEs Knowledge Management. In N. Baporikar (Ed.), *Knowledge Integration Strategies for Entrepreneurship and Sustainability* (pp. 23–46). Hershey, PA: IGI Global. doi:10.4018/978-1-5225-5115-7.ch002

Dezdar, S. (2017). ERP Implementation Projects in Asian Countries: A Comparative Study on Iran and China. *International Journal of Information Technology Project Management*, *8*(3), 52–68. doi:10.4018/IJITPM.2017070104

Domingos, D., Martinho, R., & Varajão, J. (2016). Controlled Flexibility in Healthcare Processes: A BPMN-Extension Approach. In M. Cruz-Cunha, I. Miranda, R. Martinho, & R. Rijo (Eds.), *Encyclopedia of E-Health and Telemedicine* (pp. 521–535). Hershey, PA: IGI Global. doi:10.4018/978-1-4666-9978-6.ch040

Domingos, D., Respício, A., & Martinho, R. (2017). Reliability of IoT-Aware BPMN Healthcare Processes. In C. Reis & M. Maximiano (Eds.), *Internet of Things and Advanced Application in Healthcare* (pp. 214–248). Hershey, PA: IGI Global. doi:10.4018/978-1-5225-1820-4.ch008

Dosumu, O., Hussain, J., & El-Gohary, H. (2017). An Exploratory Study of the Impact of Government Policies on the Development of Small and Medium Enterprises in Developing Countries: The Case of Nigeria. *International Journal of Customer Relationship Marketing and Management*, *8*(4), 51–62. doi:10.4018/IJCRMM.2017100104

Durst, S., Bruns, G., & Edvardsson, I. R. (2017). Retaining Knowledge in Smaller Building and Construction Firms. *International Journal of Knowledge and Systems Science*, *8*(3), 1–12. doi:10.4018/IJKSS.2017070101

Edvardsson, I. R., & Durst, S. (2017). Outsourcing, Knowledge, and Learning: A Critical Review. *International Journal of Knowledge-Based Organizations*, *7*(2), 13–26. doi:10.4018/IJKBO.2017040102

Edwards, J. S. (2018). Integrating Knowledge Management and Business Processes. In M. Khosrow-Pour, D.B.A. (Ed.), Encyclopedia of Information Science and Technology, Fourth Edition (pp. 5046-5055). Hershey, PA: IGI Global. doi:10.4018/978-1-5225-2255-3.ch437

Ejiogu, A. O. (2018). Economics of Farm Management. In *Agricultural Finance and Opportunities for Investment and Expansion* (pp. 56–72). Hershey, PA: IGI Global. doi:10.4018/978-1-5225-3059-6.ch003

Ekanem, I., & Abiade, G. E. (2018). Factors Influencing the Use of E-Commerce by Small Enterprises in Nigeria. *International Journal of ICT Research in Africa and the Middle East, 7*(1), 37–53. doi:10.4018/IJICTRAME.2018010103

Ekanem, I., & Alrossais, L. A. (2017). Succession Challenges Facing Family Businesses in Saudi Arabia. In P. Zgheib (Ed.), *Entrepreneurship and Business Innovation in the Middle East* (pp. 122–146). Hershey, PA: IGI Global. doi:10.4018/978-1-5225-2066-5.ch007

El Faquih, L., & Fredj, M. (2017). Ontology-Based Framework for Quality in Configurable Process Models. *Journal of Electronic Commerce in Organizations, 15*(2), 48–60. doi:10.4018/JECO.2017040104

El-Gohary, H., & El-Gohary, Z. (2016). An Attempt to Explore Electronic Marketing Adoption and Implementation Aspects in Developing Countries: The Case of Egypt. *International Journal of Customer Relationship Marketing and Management, 7*(4), 1–26. doi:10.4018/IJCRMM.2016100101

Entico, G. J. (2016). Knowledge Management and the Medical Health Librarians: A Perception Study. In J. Yap, M. Perez, M. Ayson, & G. Entico (Eds.), *Special Library Administration, Standardization and Technological Integration* (pp. 52–77). Hershey, PA: IGI Global. doi:10.4018/978-1-4666-9542-9.ch003

Faisal, M. N., & Talib, F. (2017). Building Ambidextrous Supply Chains in SMEs: How to Tackle the Barriers? *International Journal of Information Systems and Supply Chain Management, 10*(4), 80–100. doi:10.4018/IJISSCM.2017100105

Fernandes, T. M., Gomes, J., & Romão, M. (2017). Investments in E-Government: A Benefit Management Case Study. *International Journal of Electronic Government Research, 13*(3), 1–17. doi:10.4018/IJEGR.2017070101

Fouda, F. A. (2016). A Suggested Curriculum in Career Education to Develop Business Secondary Schools Students' Career Knowledge Management Domains and Professional Thinking. *International Journal of Technology Diffusion, 7*(2), 42–62. doi:10.4018/IJTD.2016040103

Gallardo-Vázquez, D., & Pajuelo-Moreno, M. L. (2016). How Spanish Universities are Promoting Entrepreneurship through Your Own Lines of Teaching and Research? In L. Carvalho (Ed.), *Handbook of Research on Entrepreneurial Success and its Impact on Regional Development* (pp. 431–454). Hershey, PA: IGI Global. doi:10.4018/978-1-4666-9567-2.ch019

Gao, S. S., Oreal, S., & Zhang, J. (2018). Contemporary Financial Risk Management Perceptions and Practices of Small-Sized Chinese Businesses. In I. Management Association (Ed.), Global Business Expansion: Concepts, Methodologies, Tools, and Applications (pp. 917-931). Hershey, PA: IGI Global. doi:10.4018/978-1-5225-5481-3.ch041

Garg, R., & Berning, S. C. (2017). Indigenous Chinese Management Philosophies: Key Concepts and Relevance for Modern Chinese Firms. In B. Christiansen & G. Koc (Eds.), *Transcontinental Strategies for Industrial Development and Economic Growth* (pp. 43–57). Hershey, PA: IGI Global. doi:10.4018/978-1-5225-2160-0.ch003

Gencer, Y. G. (2017). Supply Chain Management in Retailing Business. In U. Akkucuk (Ed.), *Ethics and Sustainability in Global Supply Chain Management* (pp. 197–210). Hershey, PA: IGI Global. doi:10.4018/978-1-5225-2036-8.ch011

Giacosa, E. (2016). Innovation in Luxury Fashion Businesses as a Means for the Regional Development. In L. Carvalho (Ed.), *Handbook of Research on Entrepreneurial Success and its Impact on Regional Development* (pp. 206–222). Hershey, PA: IGI Global. doi:10.4018/978-1-4666-9567-2.ch010

Giacosa, E. (2018). The Increasing of the Regional Development Thanks to the Luxury Business Innovation. In L. Carvalho (Ed.), *Handbook of Research on Entrepreneurial Ecosystems and Social Dynamics in a Globalized World* (pp. 260–273). Hershey, PA: IGI Global. doi:10.4018/978-1-5225-3525-6.ch011

Gianni, M., & Gotzamani, K. (2016). Integrated Management Systems and Information Management Systems: Common Threads. In P. Papajorgji, F. Pinet, A. Guimarães, & J. Papathanasiou (Eds.), *Automated Enterprise Systems for Maximizing Business Performance* (pp. 195–214). Hershey, PA: IGI Global. doi:10.4018/978-1-4666-8841-4.ch011

Gianni, M., Gotzamani, K., & Linden, I. (2016). How a BI-wise Responsible Integrated Management System May Support Food Traceability. *International Journal of Decision Support System Technology*, *8*(2), 1–17. doi:10.4018/IJDSST.2016040101

Glykas, M., & George, J. (2017). Quality and Process Management Systems in the UAE Maritime Industry. *International Journal of Productivity Management and Assessment Technologies*, *5*(1), 20–39. doi:10.4018/IJPMAT.2017010102

Glykas, M., Valiris, G., Kokkinaki, A., & Koutsoukou, Z. (2018). Banking Business Process Management Implementation. *International Journal of Productivity Management and Assessment Technologies*, *6*(1), 50–69. doi:10.4018/IJPMAT.2018010104

Gomes, J., & Romão, M. (2017). The Balanced Scorecard: Keeping Updated and Aligned with Today's Business Trends. *International Journal of Productivity Management and Assessment Technologies*, *5*(2), 1–15. doi:10.4018/IJPMAT.2017070101

Gomes, J., & Romão, M. (2017). Aligning Information Systems and Technology with Benefit Management and Balanced Scorecard. In S. De Haes & W. Van Grembergen (Eds.), *Strategic IT Governance and Alignment in Business Settings* (pp. 112–131). Hershey, PA: IGI Global. doi:10.4018/978-1-5225-0861-8.ch005

Grefen, P., & Turetken, O. (2017). Advanced Business Process Management in Networked E-Business Scenarios. *International Journal of E-Business Research*, *13*(4), 70–104. doi:10.4018/IJEBR.2017100105

Haider, A., & Saetang, S. (2017). Strategic IT Alignment in Service Sector. In S. Rozenes & Y. Cohen (Eds.), *Handbook of Research on Strategic Alliances and Value Co-Creation in the Service Industry* (pp. 231–258). Hershey, PA: IGI Global. doi:10.4018/978-1-5225-2084-9.ch012

Haider, A., & Tang, S. S. (2016). Maximising Value Through IT and Business Alignment: A Case of IT Governance Institutionalisation at a Thai Bank. *International Journal of Technology Diffusion*, *7*(3), 33–58. doi:10.4018/IJTD.2016070104

Hajilari, A. B., Ghadaksaz, M., & Fasghandis, G. S. (2017). Assessing Organizational Readiness for Implementing ERP System Using Fuzzy Expert System Approach. *International Journal of Enterprise Information Systems, 13*(1), 67–85. doi:10.4018/IJEIS.2017010105

Haldorai, A., Ramu, A., & Murugan, S. (2018). Social Aware Cognitive Radio Networks: Effectiveness of Social Networks as a Strategic Tool for Organizational Business Management. In H. Bansal, G. Shrivastava, G. Nguyen, & L. Stanciu (Eds.), *Social Network Analytics for Contemporary Business Organizations* (pp. 188–202). Hershey, PA: IGI Global. doi:10.4018/978-1-5225-5097-6.ch010

Hall, O. P. Jr. (2017). Social Media Driven Management Education. *International Journal of Knowledge-Based Organizations, 7*(2), 43–59. doi:10.4018/IJKBO.2017040104

Hanifah, H., Halim, H. A., Ahmad, N. H., & Vafaei-Zadeh, A. (2017). Innovation Culture as a Mediator Between Specific Human Capital and Innovation Performance Among Bumiputera SMEs in Malaysia. In N. Ahmad, T. Ramayah, H. Halim, & S. Rahman (Eds.), *Handbook of Research on Small and Medium Enterprises in Developing Countries* (pp. 261–279). Hershey, PA: IGI Global. doi:10.4018/978-1-5225-2165-5.ch012

Hartlieb, S., & Silvius, G. (2017). Handling Uncertainty in Project Management and Business Development: Similarities and Differences. In Y. Raydugin (Ed.), *Handbook of Research on Leveraging Risk and Uncertainties for Effective Project Management* (pp. 337–362). Hershey, PA: IGI Global. doi:10.4018/978-1-5225-1790-0.ch016

Hass, K. B. (2017). Living on the Edge: Managing Project Complexity. In Y. Raydugin (Ed.), *Handbook of Research on Leveraging Risk and Uncertainties for Effective Project Management* (pp. 177–201). Hershey, PA: IGI Global. doi:10.4018/978-1-5225-1790-0.ch009

Hassan, A., & Privitera, D. S. (2016). Google AdSense as a Mobile Technology in Education. In J. Holland (Ed.), *Wearable Technology and Mobile Innovations for Next-Generation Education* (pp. 200–223). Hershey, PA: IGI Global. doi:10.4018/978-1-5225-0069-8.ch011

Hassan, A., & Rahimi, R. (2016). Consuming "Innovation" in Tourism: Augmented Reality as an Innovation Tool in Digital Tourism Marketing. In N. Pappas & I. Bregoli (Eds.), *Global Dynamics in Travel, Tourism, and Hospitality* (pp. 130–147). Hershey, PA: IGI Global. doi:10.4018/978-1-5225-0201-2.ch008

Hawking, P., & Carmine Sellitto, C. (2017). Developing an Effective Strategy for Organizational Business Intelligence. In M. Tavana (Ed.), *Enterprise Information Systems and the Digitalization of Business Functions* (pp. 222–237). Hershey, PA: IGI Global. doi:10.4018/978-1-5225-2382-6.ch010

Hawking, P., & Sellitto, C. (2017). A Fast-Moving Consumer Goods Company and Business Intelligence Strategy Development. *International Journal of Enterprise Information Systems, 13*(2), 22–33. doi:10.4018/IJEIS.2017040102

Hawking, P., & Sellitto, C. (2017). Business Intelligence Strategy: Two Case Studies. *International Journal of Business Intelligence Research, 8*(2), 17–30. doi:10.4018/IJBIR.2017070102

Haynes, J. D., Arockiasamy, S., Al Rashdi, M., & Al Rashdi, S. (2016). Business and E Business Strategies for Coopetition and Thematic Management as a Sustained Basis for Ethics and Social Responsibility in Emerging Markets. In M. Al-Shammari & H. Masri (Eds.), *Ethical and Social Perspectives on Global Business Interaction in Emerging Markets* (pp. 25–39). Hershey, PA: IGI Global. doi:10.4018/978-1-4666-9864-2.ch002

Hee, W. J., Jalleh, G., Lai, H., & Lin, C. (2017). E-Commerce and IT Projects: Evaluation and Management Issues in Australian and Taiwanese Hospitals. *International Journal of Public Health Management and Ethics*, *2*(1), 69–90. doi:10.4018/IJPHME.2017010104

Hernandez, A. A. (2018). Exploring the Factors to Green IT Adoption of SMEs in the Philippines. *Journal of Cases on Information Technology*, *20*(2), 49–66. doi:10.4018/JCIT.2018040104

Hernandez, A. A., & Ona, S. E. (2016). Green IT Adoption: Lessons from the Philippines Business Process Outsourcing Industry. *International Journal of Social Ecology and Sustainable Development*, *7*(1), 1–34. doi:10.4018/IJSESD.2016010101

Hollman, A., Bickford, S., & Hollman, T. (2017). Cyber InSecurity: A Post-Mortem Attempt to Assess Cyber Problems from IT and Business Management Perspectives. *Journal of Cases on Information Technology*, *19*(3), 42–70. doi:10.4018/JCIT.2017070104

Igbinakhase, I. (2017). Responsible and Sustainable Management Practices in Developing and Developed Business Environments. In Z. Fields (Ed.), *Collective Creativity for Responsible and Sustainable Business Practice* (pp. 180–207). Hershey, PA: IGI Global. doi:10.4018/978-1-5225-1823-5.ch010

Ilahi, L., Ghannouchi, S. A., & Martinho, R. (2016). A Business Process Management Approach to Home Healthcare Processes: On the Gap between Intention and Reality. In M. Cruz-Cunha, I. Miranda, R. Martinho, & R. Rijo (Eds.), *Encyclopedia of E-Health and Telemedicine* (pp. 439–457). Hershey, PA: IGI Global. doi:10.4018/978-1-4666-9978-6.ch035

Iwata, J. J., & Hoskins, R. G. (2017). Managing Indigenous Knowledge in Tanzania: A Business Perspective. In P. Jain & N. Mnjama (Eds.), *Managing Knowledge Resources and Records in Modern Organizations* (pp. 198–214). Hershey, PA: IGI Global. doi:10.4018/978-1-5225-1965-2.ch012

Jabeen, F., Ahmad, S. Z., & Alkaabi, S. (2016). The Internationalization Decision-Making of United Arab Emirates Family Businesses. In N. Zakaria, A. Abdul-Talib, & N. Osman (Eds.), *Handbook of Research on Impacts of International Business and Political Affairs on the Global Economy* (pp. 1–22). Hershey, PA: IGI Global. doi:10.4018/978-1-4666-9806-2.ch001

Jain, P. (2017). Ethical and Legal Issues in Knowledge Management Life-Cycle in Business. In P. Jain & N. Mnjama (Eds.), *Managing Knowledge Resources and Records in Modern Organizations* (pp. 82–101). Hershey, PA: IGI Global. doi:10.4018/978-1-5225-1965-2.ch006

Jamali, D., Abdallah, H., & Matar, F. (2016). Opportunities and Challenges for CSR Mainstreaming in Business Schools. *International Journal of Technology and Educational Marketing*, *6*(2), 1–29. doi:10.4018/IJTEM.2016070101

James, S., & Hauli, E. (2017). Holistic Management Education at Tanzanian Rural Development Planning Institute. In N. Baporikar (Ed.), *Management Education for Global Leadership* (pp. 112–136). Hershey, PA: IGI Global. doi:10.4018/978-1-5225-1013-0.ch006

Janošková, M., Csikósová, A., & Čulková, K. (2018). Measurement of Company Performance as Part of Its Strategic Management. In R. Leon (Ed.), *Managerial Strategies for Business Sustainability During Turbulent Times* (pp. 309–335). Hershey, PA: IGI Global. doi:10.4018/978-1-5225-2716-9.ch017

Jean-Vasile, A., & Alecu, A. (2017). Theoretical and Practical Approaches in Understanding the Influences of Cost-Productivity-Profit Trinomial in Contemporary Enterprises. In A. Jean Vasile & D. Nicolò (Eds.), *Sustainable Entrepreneurship and Investments in the Green Economy* (pp. 28–62). Hershey, PA: IGI Global. doi:10.4018/978-1-5225-2075-7.ch002

Jha, D. G. (2016). Preparing for Information Technology Driven Changes. In S. Tiwari & L. Nafees (Eds.), *Innovative Management Education Pedagogies for Preparing Next-Generation Leaders* (pp. 258–274). Hershey, PA: IGI Global. doi:10.4018/978-1-4666-9691-4.ch015

Joia, L. A., & Correia, J. C. (2018). CIO Competencies From the IT Professional Perspective: Insights From Brazil. *Journal of Global Information Management, 26*(2), 74–103. doi:10.4018/JGIM.2018040104

Juma, A., & Mzera, N. (2017). Knowledge Management and Records Management and Competitive Advantage in Business. In P. Jain & N. Mnjama (Eds.), *Managing Knowledge Resources and Records in Modern Organizations* (pp. 15–28). Hershey, PA: IGI Global. doi:10.4018/978-1-5225-1965-2.ch002

K., I., & A, V. (2018). Monitoring and Auditing in the Cloud. In K. Munir (Ed.), *Cloud Computing Technologies for Green Enterprises* (pp. 318-350). Hershey, PA: IGI Global. doi:10.4018/978-1-5225-3038-1.ch013

Kabra, G., Ghosh, V., & Ramesh, A. (2018). Enterprise Integrated Business Process Management and Business Intelligence Framework for Business Process Sustainability. In A. Paul, D. Bhattacharyya, & S. Anand (Eds.), *Green Initiatives for Business Sustainability and Value Creation* (pp. 228–238). Hershey, PA: IGI Global. doi:10.4018/978-1-5225-2662-9.ch010

Kaoud, M. (2017). Investigation of Customer Knowledge Management: A Case Study Research. *International Journal of Service Science, Management, Engineering, and Technology, 8*(2), 12–22. doi:10.4018/IJSSMET.2017040102

Kara, M. E., & Fırat, S. Ü. (2016). Sustainability, Risk, and Business Intelligence in Supply Chains. In M. Erdoğdu, T. Arun, & I. Ahmad (Eds.), *Handbook of Research on Green Economic Development Initiatives and Strategies* (pp. 501–538). Hershey, PA: IGI Global. doi:10.4018/978-1-5225-0440-5.ch022

Katuu, S. (2018). A Comparative Assessment of Enterprise Content Management Maturity Models. In N. Gwangwava & M. Mutingi (Eds.), *E-Manufacturing and E-Service Strategies in Contemporary Organizations* (pp. 93–118). Hershey, PA: IGI Global. doi:10.4018/978-1-5225-3628-4.ch005

Khan, M. A. (2016). MNEs Management Strategies in Developing Countries: Establishing the Context. In M. Khan (Ed.), *Multinational Enterprise Management Strategies in Developing Countries* (pp. 1–33). Hershey, PA: IGI Global. doi:10.4018/978-1-5225-0276-0.ch001

Khan, M. A. (2016). Operational Approaches in Organizational Structure: A Case for MNEs in Developing Countries. In M. Khan (Ed.), *Multinational Enterprise Management Strategies in Developing Countries* (pp. 129–151). Hershey, PA: IGI Global. doi:10.4018/978-1-5225-0276-0.ch007

Kinnunen, S., Ylä-Kujala, A., Marttonen-Arola, S., Kärri, T., & Baglee, D. (2018). Internet of Things in Asset Management: Insights from Industrial Professionals and Academia. *International Journal of Service Science, Management, Engineering, and Technology*, *9*(2), 104–119. doi:10.4018/IJSSMET.2018040105

Klein, A. Z., Sabino de Freitas, A., Machado, L., Freitas, J. C. Jr, Graziola, P. G. Jr, & Schlemmer, E. (2017). Virtual Worlds Applications for Management Education. In L. Tomei (Ed.), *Exploring the New Era of Technology-Infused Education* (pp. 279–299). Hershey, PA: IGI Global. doi:10.4018/978-1-5225-1709-2.ch017

Kożuch, B., & Jabłoński, A. (2017). Adopting the Concept of Business Models in Public Management. In M. Lewandowski & B. Kożuch (Eds.), *Public Sector Entrepreneurship and the Integration of Innovative Business Models* (pp. 10–46). Hershey, PA: IGI Global. doi:10.4018/978-1-5225-2215-7.ch002

Kumar, J., Adhikary, A., & Jha, A. (2017). Small Active Investors' Perceptions and Preferences Towards Tax Saving Mutual Fund Schemes in Eastern India: An Empirical Note. *International Journal of Asian Business and Information Management*, *8*(2), 35–45. doi:10.4018/IJABIM.2017040103

Lassoued, Y., Bouzguenda, L., & Mahmoud, T. (2016). Context-Aware Business Process Versions Management. *International Journal of e-Collaboration*, *12*(3), 7–33. doi:10.4018/IJeC.2016070102

Lavassani, K. M., & Movahedi, B. (2017). Applications Driven Information Systems: Beyond Networks toward Business Ecosystems. *International Journal of Innovation in the Digital Economy*, *8*(1), 61–75. doi:10.4018/IJIDE.2017010104

Lazzareschi, V. H., & Brito, M. S. (2017). Strategic Information Management: Proposal of Business Project Model. In G. Jamil, A. Soares, & C. Pessoa (Eds.), *Handbook of Research on Information Management for Effective Logistics and Supply Chains* (pp. 59–88). Hershey, PA: IGI Global. doi:10.4018/978-1-5225-0973-8.ch004

Lederer, M., Kurz, M., & Lazarov, P. (2017). Usage and Suitability of Methods for Strategic Business Process Initiatives: A Multi Case Study Research. *International Journal of Productivity Management and Assessment Technologies*, *5*(1), 40–51. doi:10.4018/IJPMAT.2017010103

Lee, I. (2017). A Social Enterprise Business Model and a Case Study of Pacific Community Ventures (PCV). In V. Potocan, M. Ünğan, & Z. Nedelko (Eds.), *Handbook of Research on Managerial Solutions in Non-Profit Organizations* (pp. 182–204). Hershey, PA: IGI Global. doi:10.4018/978-1-5225-0731-4.ch009

Lee, L. J., & Leu, J. (2016). Exploring the Effectiveness of IT Application and Value Method in the Innovation Performance of Enterprise. *International Journal of Enterprise Information Systems*, *12*(2), 47–65. doi:10.4018/IJEIS.2016040104

Lee, Y. (2016). Alignment Effect of Entrepreneurial Orientation and Marketing Orientation on Firm Performance. *International Journal of Customer Relationship Marketing and Management*, *7*(4), 58–69. doi:10.4018/IJCRMM.2016100104

Leon, L. A., Seal, K. C., Przasnyski, Z. H., & Wiedenman, I. (2017). Skills and Competencies Required for Jobs in Business Analytics: A Content Analysis of Job Advertisements Using Text Mining. *International Journal of Business Intelligence Research, 8*(1), 1–25. doi:10.4018/IJBIR.2017010101

Leu, J., Lee, L. J., & Krischke, A. (2016). Value Engineering-Based Method for Implementing the ISO14001 System in the Green Supply Chains. *International Journal of Strategic Decision Sciences, 7*(4), 1–20. doi:10.4018/IJSDS.2016100101

Levy, C. L., & Elias, N. I. (2017). SOHO Users' Perceptions of Reliability and Continuity of Cloud-Based Services. In M. Moore (Ed.), *Cybersecurity Breaches and Issues Surrounding Online Threat Protection* (pp. 248–287). Hershey, PA: IGI Global. doi:10.4018/978-1-5225-1941-6.ch011

Levy, M. (2018). Change Management Serving Knowledge Management and Organizational Development: Reflections and Review. In N. Baporikar (Ed.), *Global Practices in Knowledge Management for Societal and Organizational Development* (pp. 256–270). Hershey, PA: IGI Global. doi:10.4018/978-1-5225-3009-1.ch012

Lewandowski, M. (2017). Public Organizations and Business Model Innovation: The Role of Public Service Design. In M. Lewandowski & B. Kożuch (Eds.), *Public Sector Entrepreneurship and the Integration of Innovative Business Models* (pp. 47–72). Hershey, PA: IGI Global. doi:10.4018/978-1-5225-2215-7.ch003

Lhannaoui, H., Kabbaj, M. I., & Bakkoury, Z. (2017). A Survey of Risk-Aware Business Process Modelling. *International Journal of Risk and Contingency Management, 6*(3), 14–26. doi:10.4018/IJRCM.2017070102

Li, J., Sun, W., Jiang, W., Yang, H., & Zhang, L. (2017). How the Nature of Exogenous Shocks and Crises Impact Company Performance?: The Effects of Industry Characteristics. *International Journal of Risk and Contingency Management, 6*(4), 40–55. doi:10.4018/IJRCM.2017100103

Lu, C., & Liu, S. (2016). Cultural Tourism O2O Business Model Innovation-A Case Study of CTrip. *Journal of Electronic Commerce in Organizations, 14*(2), 16–31. doi:10.4018/JECO.2016040102

Machen, B., Hosseini, M. R., Wood, A., & Bakhshi, J. (2016). An Investigation into using SAP-PS as a Multidimensional Project Control System (MPCS). *International Journal of Enterprise Information Systems, 12*(2), 66–81. doi:10.4018/IJEIS.2016040105

Malega, P. (2017). Small and Medium Enterprises in the Slovak Republic: Status and Competitiveness of SMEs in the Global Markets and Possibilities of Optimization. In M. Vemić (Ed.), *Optimal Management Strategies in Small and Medium Enterprises* (pp. 102–124). Hershey, PA: IGI Global. doi:10.4018/978-1-5225-1949-2.ch006

Malewska, K. M. (2017). Intuition in Decision-Making on the Example of a Non-Profit Organization. In V. Potocan, M. Ünğan, & Z. Nedelko (Eds.), *Handbook of Research on Managerial Solutions in Non-Profit Organizations* (pp. 378–399). Hershey, PA: IGI Global. doi:10.4018/978-1-5225-0731-4.ch018

Maroofi, F. (2017). Entrepreneurial Orientation and Organizational Learning Ability Analysis for Innovation and Firm Performance. In N. Baporikar (Ed.), *Innovation and Shifting Perspectives in Management Education* (pp. 144–165). Hershey, PA: IGI Global. doi:10.4018/978-1-5225-1019-2.ch007

Martins, P. V., & Zacarias, M. (2017). A Web-based Tool for Business Process Improvement. *International Journal of Web Portals*, *9*(2), 68–84. doi:10.4018/IJWP.2017070104

Matthies, B., & Coners, A. (2017). Exploring the Conceptual Nature of e-Business Projects. *Journal of Electronic Commerce in Organizations*, *15*(3), 33–63. doi:10.4018/JECO.2017070103

McKee, J. (2018). Architecture as a Tool to Solve Business Planning Problems. In M. Khosrow-Pour, D.B.A. (Ed.), Encyclopedia of Information Science and Technology, Fourth Edition (pp. 573-586). Hershey, PA: IGI Global. doi:10.4018/978-1-5225-2255-3.ch050

McMurray, A. J., Cross, J., & Caponecchia, C. (2018). The Risk Management Profession in Australia: Business Continuity Plan Practices. In N. Bajgoric (Ed.), *Always-On Enterprise Information Systems for Modern Organizations* (pp. 112–129). Hershey, PA: IGI Global. doi:10.4018/978-1-5225-3704-5.ch006

Meddah, I. H., & Belkadi, K. (2018). Mining Patterns Using Business Process Management. In R. Hamou (Ed.), *Handbook of Research on Biomimicry in Information Retrieval and Knowledge Management* (pp. 78–89). Hershey, PA: IGI Global. doi:10.4018/978-1-5225-3004-6.ch005

Mendes, L. (2017). TQM and Knowledge Management: An Integrated Approach Towards Tacit Knowledge Management. In D. Jaziri-Bouagina & G. Jamil (Eds.), *Handbook of Research on Tacit Knowledge Management for Organizational Success* (pp. 236–263). Hershey, PA: IGI Global. doi:10.4018/978-1-5225-2394-9.ch009

Mnjama, N. M. (2017). Preservation of Recorded Information in Public and Private Sector Organizations. In P. Jain & N. Mnjama (Eds.), *Managing Knowledge Resources and Records in Modern Organizations* (pp. 149–167). Hershey, PA: IGI Global. doi:10.4018/978-1-5225-1965-2.ch009

Mokoqama, M., & Fields, Z. (2017). Principles of Responsible Management Education (PRME): Call for Responsible Management Education. In Z. Fields (Ed.), *Collective Creativity for Responsible and Sustainable Business Practice* (pp. 229–241). Hershey, PA: IGI Global. doi:10.4018/978-1-5225-1823-5.ch012

Muniapan, B. (2017). Philosophy and Management: The Relevance of Vedanta in Management. In P. Ordóñez de Pablos (Ed.), *Managerial Strategies and Solutions for Business Success in Asia* (pp. 124–139). Hershey, PA: IGI Global. doi:10.4018/978-1-5225-1886-0.ch007

Muniapan, B., Gregory, M. L., & Ling, L. A. (2016). Marketing Education in Sarawak: Looking at It from the Employers' Viewpoint. In B. Smith & A. Porath (Eds.), *Global Perspectives on Contemporary Marketing Education* (pp. 112–130). Hershey, PA: IGI Global. doi:10.4018/978-1-4666-9784-3.ch008

Murad, S. E., & Dowaji, S. (2017). Using Value-Based Approach for Managing Cloud-Based Services. In A. Turuk, B. Sahoo, & S. Addya (Eds.), *Resource Management and Efficiency in Cloud Computing Environments* (pp. 33–60). Hershey, PA: IGI Global. doi:10.4018/978-1-5225-1721-4.ch002

Mutahar, A. M., Daud, N. M., Thurasamy, R., Isaac, O., & Abdulsalam, R. (2018). The Mediating of Perceived Usefulness and Perceived Ease of Use: The Case of Mobile Banking in Yemen. *International Journal of Technology Diffusion*, *9*(2), 21–40. doi:10.4018/IJTD.2018040102

Naidoo, V. (2017). E-Learning and Management Education at African Universities. In N. Baporikar (Ed.), *Management Education for Global Leadership* (pp. 181–201). Hershey, PA: IGI Global. doi:10.4018/978-1-5225-1013-0.ch009

Naidoo, V., & Igbinakhase, I. (2018). Opportunities and Challenges of Knowledge Retention in SMEs. In N. Baporikar (Ed.), *Knowledge Integration Strategies for Entrepreneurship and Sustainability* (pp. 70–94). Hershey, PA: IGI Global. doi:10.4018/978-1-5225-5115-7.ch004

Nayak, S., & Prabhu, N. (2017). Paradigm Shift in Management Education: Need for a Cross Functional Perspective. In N. Baporikar (Ed.), *Management Education for Global Leadership* (pp. 241–255). Hershey, PA: IGI Global. doi:10.4018/978-1-5225-1013-0.ch012

Ndede-Amadi, A. A. (2016). Student Interest in the IS Specialization as Predictor of the Success Potential of New Information Systems Programmes within the Schools of Business in Kenyan Public Universities. *International Journal of Information Systems and Social Change*, *7*(2), 63–79. doi:10.4018/IJISSC.2016040104

Nedelko, Z., & Potocan, V. (2016). Management Practices for Processes Optimization: Case of Slovenia. In G. Alor-Hernández, C. Sánchez-Ramírez, & J. García-Alcaraz (Eds.), *Handbook of Research on Managerial Strategies for Achieving Optimal Performance in Industrial Processes* (pp. 545–561). Hershey, PA: IGI Global. doi:10.4018/978-1-5225-0130-5.ch025

Nedelko, Z., & Potocan, V. (2017). Management Solutions in Non-Profit Organizations: Case of Slovenia. In V. Potocan, M. Üngan, & Z. Nedelko (Eds.), *Handbook of Research on Managerial Solutions in Non-Profit Organizations* (pp. 1–22). Hershey, PA: IGI Global. doi:10.4018/978-1-5225-0731-4.ch001

Nedelko, Z., & Potocan, V. (2017). Priority of Management Tools Utilization among Managers: International Comparison. In V. Wang (Ed.), *Encyclopedia of Strategic Leadership and Management* (pp. 1083–1094). Hershey, PA: IGI Global. doi:10.4018/978-1-5225-1049-9.ch075

Nedelko, Z., Raudeliūnienė, J., & Črešnar, R. (2018). Knowledge Dynamics in Supply Chain Management. In N. Baporikar (Ed.), *Knowledge Integration Strategies for Entrepreneurship and Sustainability* (pp. 150–166). Hershey, PA: IGI Global. doi:10.4018/978-1-5225-5115-7.ch008

Nguyen, H. T., & Hipsher, S. A. (2018). Innovation and Creativity Used by Private Sector Firms in a Resources-Constrained Environment. In S. Hipsher (Ed.), *Examining the Private Sector's Role in Wealth Creation and Poverty Reduction* (pp. 219–238). Hershey, PA: IGI Global. doi:10.4018/978-1-5225-3117-3.ch010

Nycz, M., & Pólkowski, Z. (2016). Business Intelligence as a Modern IT Supporting Management of Local Government Units in Poland. *International Journal of Knowledge and Systems Science*, *7*(4), 1–18. doi:10.4018/IJKSS.2016100101

Obaji, N. O., Senin, A. A., & Olugu, M. U. (2016). Supportive Government Policy as a Mechanism for Business Incubation Performance in Nigeria. *International Journal of Information Systems and Social Change*, *7*(4), 52–66. doi:10.4018/IJISSC.2016100103

Obicci, P. A. (2017). Risk Sharing in a Partnership. In *Risk Management Strategies in Public-Private Partnerships* (pp. 115–152). Hershey, PA: IGI Global. doi:10.4018/978-1-5225-2503-5.ch004

Obidallah, W. J., & Raahemi, B. (2017). Managing Changes in Service Oriented Virtual Organizations: A Structural and Procedural Framework to Facilitate the Process of Change. *Journal of Electronic Commerce in Organizations*, *15*(1), 59–83. doi:10.4018/JECO.2017010104

Ojasalo, J., & Ojasalo, K. (2016). Service Logic Business Model Canvas for Lean Development of SMEs and Start-Ups. In N. Baporikar (Ed.), *Handbook of Research on Entrepreneurship in the Contemporary Knowledge-Based Global Economy* (pp. 217–243). Hershey, PA: IGI Global. doi:10.4018/978-1-4666-8798-1.ch010

Ojo, O. (2017). Impact of Innovation on the Entrepreneurial Success in Selected Business Enterprises in South-West Nigeria. *International Journal of Innovation in the Digital Economy*, *8*(2), 29–38. doi:10.4018/IJIDE.2017040103

Okdinawati, L., Simatupang, T. M., & Sunitiyoso, Y. (2017). Multi-Agent Reinforcement Learning for Value Co-Creation of Collaborative Transportation Management (CTM). *International Journal of Information Systems and Supply Chain Management*, *10*(3), 84–95. doi:10.4018/IJISSCM.2017070105

Ortner, E., Mevius, M., Wiedmann, P., & Kurz, F. (2016). Design of Interactional Decision Support Applications for E-Participation in Smart Cities. *International Journal of Electronic Government Research*, *12*(2), 18–38. doi:10.4018/IJEGR.2016040102

Pal, K. (2018). Building High Quality Big Data-Based Applications in Supply Chains. In A. Kumar & S. Saurav (Eds.), *Supply Chain Management Strategies and Risk Assessment in Retail Environments* (pp. 1–24). Hershey, PA: IGI Global. doi:10.4018/978-1-5225-3056-5.ch001

Palos-Sanchez, P. R., & Correia, M. B. (2018). Perspectives of the Adoption of Cloud Computing in the Tourism Sector. In J. Rodrigues, C. Ramos, P. Cardoso, & C. Henriques (Eds.), *Handbook of Research on Technological Developments for Cultural Heritage and eTourism Applications* (pp. 377–400). Hershey, PA: IGI Global. doi:10.4018/978-1-5225-2927-9.ch018

Parry, V. K., & Lind, M. L. (2016). Alignment of Business Strategy and Information Technology Considering Information Technology Governance, Project Portfolio Control, and Risk Management. *International Journal of Information Technology Project Management*, *7*(4), 21–37. doi:10.4018/IJITPM.2016100102

Pashkova, N., Trujillo-Barrera, A., Apostolakis, G., Van Dijk, G., Drakos, P. D., & Baourakis, G. (2016). Business Management Models of Microfinance Institutions (MFIs) in Africa: A Study into Their Enabling Environments. *International Journal of Food and Beverage Manufacturing and Business Models*, *1*(2), 63–82. doi:10.4018/IJFBMBM.2016070105

Patiño, B. E. (2017). New Generation Management by Convergence and Individual Identity: A Systemic and Human-Oriented Approach. In N. Baporikar (Ed.), *Innovation and Shifting Perspectives in Management Education* (pp. 119–143). Hershey, PA: IGI Global. doi:10.4018/978-1-5225-1019-2.ch006

Pawliczek, A., & Rössler, M. (2017). Knowledge of Management Tools and Systems in SMEs: Knowledge Transfer in Management. In A. Bencsik (Ed.), *Knowledge Management Initiatives and Strategies in Small and Medium Enterprises* (pp. 180–203). Hershey, PA: IGI Global. doi:10.4018/978-1-5225-1642-2.ch009

Pejic-Bach, M., Omazic, M. A., Aleksic, A., & Zoroja, J. (2018). Knowledge-Based Decision Making: A Multi-Case Analysis. In R. Leon (Ed.), *Managerial Strategies for Business Sustainability During Turbulent Times* (pp. 160–184). Hershey, PA: IGI Global. doi:10.4018/978-1-5225-2716-9.ch009

Perano, M., Hysa, X., & Calabrese, M. (2018). Strategic Planning, Cultural Context, and Business Continuity Management: Business Cases in the City of Shkoder. In A. Presenza & L. Sheehan (Eds.), *Geopolitics and Strategic Management in the Global Economy* (pp. 57–77). Hershey, PA: IGI Global. doi:10.4018/978-1-5225-2673-5.ch004

Pereira, R., Mira da Silva, M., & Lapão, L. V. (2017). IT Governance Maturity Patterns in Portuguese Healthcare. In S. De Haes & W. Van Grembergen (Eds.), *Strategic IT Governance and Alignment in Business Settings* (pp. 24–52). Hershey, PA: IGI Global. doi:10.4018/978-1-5225-0861-8.ch002

Perez-Uribe, R., & Ocampo-Guzman, D. (2016). Conflict within Colombian Family Owned SMEs: An Explosive Blend between Feelings and Business. In J. Saiz-Álvarez (Ed.), *Handbook of Research on Social Entrepreneurship and Solidarity Economics* (pp. 329–354). Hershey, PA: IGI Global. doi:10.4018/978-1-5225-0097-1.ch017

Pérez-Uribe, R. I., Torres, D. A., Jurado, S. P., & Prada, D. M. (2018). Cloud Tools for the Development of Project Management in SMEs. In R. Perez-Uribe, C. Salcedo-Perez, & D. Ocampo-Guzman (Eds.), *Handbook of Research on Intrapreneurship and Organizational Sustainability in SMEs* (pp. 95–120). Hershey, PA: IGI Global. doi:10.4018/978-1-5225-3543-0.ch005

Petrisor, I., & Cozmiuc, D. (2017). Global Supply Chain Management Organization at Siemens in the Advent of Industry 4.0. In L. Saglietto & C. Cezanne (Eds.), *Global Intermediation and Logistics Service Providers* (pp. 123–142). Hershey, PA: IGI Global. doi:10.4018/978-1-5225-2133-4.ch007

Pierce, J. M., Velliaris, D. M., & Edwards, J. (2017). A Living Case Study: A Journey Not a Destination. In N. Silton (Ed.), *Exploring the Benefits of Creativity in Education, Media, and the Arts* (pp. 158–178). Hershey, PA: IGI Global. doi:10.4018/978-1-5225-0504-4.ch008

Radosavljevic, M., & Andjelkovic, A. (2017). Multi-Criteria Decision Making Approach for Choosing Business Process for the Improvement: Upgrading of the Six Sigma Methodology. In J. Stanković, P. Delias, S. Marinković, & S. Rochhia (Eds.), *Tools and Techniques for Economic Decision Analysis* (pp. 225–247). Hershey, PA: IGI Global. doi:10.4018/978-1-5225-0959-2.ch011

Radovic, V. M. (2017). Corporate Sustainability and Responsibility and Disaster Risk Reduction: A Serbian Overview. In M. Camilleri (Ed.), *CSR 2.0 and the New Era of Corporate Citizenship* (pp. 147–164). Hershey, PA: IGI Global. doi:10.4018/978-1-5225-1842-6.ch008

Raghunath, K. M., Devi, S. L., & Patro, C. S. (2018). Impact of Risk Assessment Models on Risk Factors: A Holistic Outlook. In K. Strang, M. Korstanje, & N. Vajjhala (Eds.), *Research, Practices, and Innovations in Global Risk and Contingency Management* (pp. 134–153). Hershey, PA: IGI Global. doi:10.4018/978-1-5225-4754-9.ch008

Raman, A., & Goyal, D. P. (2017). Extending IMPLEMENT Framework for Enterprise Information Systems Implementation to Information System Innovation. In M. Tavana (Ed.), *Enterprise Information Systems and the Digitalization of Business Functions* (pp. 137–177). Hershey, PA: IGI Global. doi:10.4018/978-1-5225-2382-6.ch007

Rao, Y., & Zhang, Y. (2017). The Construction and Development of Academic Library Digital Special Subject Databases. In L. Ruan, Q. Zhu, & Y. Ye (Eds.), *Academic Library Development and Administration in China* (pp. 163–183). Hershey, PA: IGI Global. doi:10.4018/978-1-5225-0550-1.ch010

Ravasan, A. Z., Mohammadi, M. M., & Hamidi, H. (2018). An Investigation Into the Critical Success Factors of Implementing Information Technology Service Management Frameworks. In K. Jakobs (Ed.), *Corporate and Global Standardization Initiatives in Contemporary Society* (pp. 200–218). Hershey, PA: IGI Global. doi:10.4018/978-1-5225-5320-5.ch009

Renna, P., Izzo, C., & Romaniello, T. (2016). The Business Process Management Systems to Support Continuous Improvements. In W. Nuninger & J. Châtelet (Eds.), *Handbook of Research on Quality Assurance and Value Management in Higher Education* (pp. 237–256). Hershey, PA: IGI Global. doi:10.4018/978-1-5225-0024-7.ch009

Rezaie, S., Mirabedini, S. J., & Abtahi, A. (2018). Designing a Model for Implementation of Business Intelligence in the Banking Industry. *International Journal of Enterprise Information Systems, 14*(1), 77–103. doi:10.4018/IJEIS.2018010105

Riccò, R. (2016). Diversity Management: Bringing Equality, Equity, and Inclusion in the Workplace. In J. Prescott (Ed.), *Handbook of Research on Race, Gender, and the Fight for Equality* (pp. 335–359). Hershey, PA: IGI Global. doi:10.4018/978-1-5225-0047-6.ch015

Romano, L., Grimaldi, R., & Colasuonno, F. S. (2017). Demand Management as a Success Factor in Project Portfolio Management. In L. Romano (Ed.), *Project Portfolio Management Strategies for Effective Organizational Operations* (pp. 202–219). Hershey, PA: IGI Global. doi:10.4018/978-1-5225-2151-8.ch008

Rostek, K. B. (2016). Risk Management: Role and Importance in Business Organization. In D. Jakóbczak (Ed.), *Analyzing Risk through Probabilistic Modeling in Operations Research* (pp. 149–178). Hershey, PA: IGI Global. doi:10.4018/978-1-4666-9458-3.ch007

Rouhani, S., & Savoji, S. R. (2016). A Success Assessment Model for BI Tools Implementation: An Empirical Study of Banking Industry. *International Journal of Business Intelligence Research, 7*(1), 25–44. doi:10.4018/IJBIR.2016010103

Ruan, Z. (2016). A Corpus-Based Functional Analysis of Complex Nominal Groups in Written Business Discourse: The Case of "Business". *International Journal of Computer-Assisted Language Learning and Teaching, 6*(2), 74–90. doi:10.4018/IJCALLT.2016040105

Ruhi, U. (2018). Towards an Interdisciplinary Socio-Technical Definition of Virtual Communities. In M. Khosrow-Pour, D.B.A. (Ed.), Encyclopedia of Information Science and Technology, Fourth Edition (pp. 4278-4295). Hershey, PA: IGI Global. doi:10.4018/978-1-5225-2255-3.ch371

Ryan, J., Doster, B., Daily, S., & Lewis, C. (2016). A Case Study Perspective for Balanced Perioperative Workflow Achievement through Data-Driven Process Improvement. *International Journal of Healthcare Information Systems and Informatics, 11*(3), 19–41. doi:10.4018/IJHISI.2016070102

Safari, M. R., & Jiang, Q. (2018). The Theory and Practice of IT Governance Maturity and Strategies Alignment: Evidence From Banking Industry. *Journal of Global Information Management*, *26*(2), 127–146. doi:10.4018/JGIM.2018040106

Sahoo, J., Pati, B., & Mohanty, B. (2017). Knowledge Management as an Academic Discipline: An Assessment. In B. Gunjal (Ed.), *Managing Knowledge and Scholarly Assets in Academic Libraries* (pp. 99–126). Hershey, PA: IGI Global. doi:10.4018/978-1-5225-1741-2.ch005

Saini, D. (2017). Relevance of Teaching Values and Ethics in Management Education. In N. Baporikar (Ed.), *Management Education for Global Leadership* (pp. 90–111). Hershey, PA: IGI Global. doi:10.4018/978-1-5225-1013-0.ch005

Sambhanthan, A. (2017). Assessing and Benchmarking Sustainability in Organisations: An Integrated Conceptual Model. *International Journal of Systems and Service-Oriented Engineering*, *7*(4), 22–43. doi:10.4018/IJSSOE.2017100102

Sambhanthan, A., & Potdar, V. (2017). A Study of the Parameters Impacting Sustainability in Information Technology Organizations. *International Journal of Knowledge-Based Organizations*, *7*(3), 27–39. doi:10.4018/IJKBO.2017070103

Sánchez-Fernández, M. D., & Manríquez, M. R. (2018). The Entrepreneurial Spirit Based on Social Values: The Digital Generation. In P. Isaias & L. Carvalho (Eds.), *User Innovation and the Entrepreneurship Phenomenon in the Digital Economy* (pp. 173–193). Hershey, PA: IGI Global. doi:10.4018/978-1-5225-2826-5.ch009

Sanchez-Ruiz, L., & Blanco, B. (2017). Process Management for SMEs: Barriers, Enablers, and Benefits. In M. Vemić (Ed.), *Optimal Management Strategies in Small and Medium Enterprises* (pp. 293–319). Hershey, PA: IGI Global. doi:10.4018/978-1-5225-1949-2.ch014

Sanz, L. F., Gómez-Pérez, J., & Castillo-Martinez, A. (2018). Analysis of the European ICT Competence Frameworks. In V. Ahuja & S. Rathore (Eds.), *Multidisciplinary Perspectives on Human Capital and Information Technology Professionals* (pp. 225–245). Hershey, PA: IGI Global. doi:10.4018/978-1-5225-5297-0.ch012

Sarvepalli, A., & Godin, J. (2017). Business Process Management in the Classroom. *Journal of Cases on Information Technology*, *19*(2), 17–28. doi:10.4018/JCIT.2017040102

Satpathy, B., & Muniapan, B. (2016). Ancient Wisdom for Transformational Leadership and Its Insights from the Bhagavad-Gita. In U. Aung & P. Ordoñez de Pablos (Eds.), *Managerial Strategies and Practice in the Asian Business Sector* (pp. 1–10). Hershey, PA: IGI Global. doi:10.4018/978-1-4666-9758-4.ch001

Saygili, E. E., Ozturkoglu, Y., & Kocakulah, M. C. (2017). End Users' Perceptions of Critical Success Factors in ERP Applications. *International Journal of Enterprise Information Systems*, *13*(4), 58–75. doi:10.4018/IJEIS.2017100104

Saygili, E. E., & Saygili, A. T. (2017). Contemporary Issues in Enterprise Information Systems: A Critical Review of CSFs in ERP Implementations. In M. Tavana (Ed.), *Enterprise Information Systems and the Digitalization of Business Functions* (pp. 120–136). Hershey, PA: IGI Global. doi:10.4018/978-1-5225-2382-6.ch006

Seidenstricker, S., & Antonino, A. (2018). Business Model Innovation-Oriented Technology Management for Emergent Technologies. In M. Khosrow-Pour, D.B.A. (Ed.), Encyclopedia of Information Science and Technology, Fourth Edition (pp. 4560-4569). Hershey, PA: IGI Global. doi:10.4018/978-1-5225-2255-3.ch396

Senaratne, S., & Gunarathne, A. D. (2017). Excellence Perspective for Management Education from a Global Accountants' Hub in Asia. In N. Baporikar (Ed.), *Management Education for Global Leadership* (pp. 158–180). Hershey, PA: IGI Global. doi:10.4018/978-1-5225-1013-0.ch008

Sensuse, D. I., & Cahyaningsih, E. (2018). Knowledge Management Models: A Summative Review. *International Journal of Information Systems in the Service Sector, 10*(1), 71–100. doi:10.4018/IJISSS.2018010105

Sensuse, D. I., Wibowo, W. C., & Cahyaningsih, E. (2016). Indonesian Government Knowledge Management Model: A Theoretical Model. *Information Resources Management Journal, 29*(1), 91–108. doi:10.4018/irmj.2016010106

Seth, M., Goyal, D., & Kiran, R. (2017). Diminution of Impediments in Implementation of Supply Chain Management Information System for Enhancing its Effectiveness in Indian Automobile Industry. *Journal of Global Information Management, 25*(3), 1–20. doi:10.4018/JGIM.2017070101

Seyal, A. H., & Rahman, M. N. (2017). Investigating Impact of Inter-Organizational Factors in Measuring ERP Systems Success: Bruneian Perspectives. In M. Tavana (Ed.), *Enterprise Information Systems and the Digitalization of Business Functions* (pp. 178–204). Hershey, PA: IGI Global. doi:10.4018/978-1-5225-2382-6.ch008

Shaikh, A. A., & Karjaluoto, H. (2016). On Some Misconceptions Concerning Digital Banking and Alternative Delivery Channels. *International Journal of E-Business Research, 12*(3), 1–16. doi:10.4018/IJEBR.2016070101

Shams, S. M. (2016). Stakeholder Relationship Management in Online Business and Competitive Value Propositions: Evidence from the Sports Industry. *International Journal of Online Marketing, 6*(2), 1–17. doi:10.4018/IJOM.2016040101

Shamsuzzoha, A. (2016). Management of Risk and Resilience within Collaborative Business Network. In R. Addo-Tenkorang, J. Kantola, P. Helo, & A. Shamsuzzoha (Eds.), *Supply Chain Strategies and the Engineer-to-Order Approach* (pp. 143–159). Hershey, PA: IGI Global. doi:10.4018/978-1-5225-0021-6.ch008

Shaqrah, A. A. (2018). Analyzing Business Intelligence Systems Based on 7s Model of McKinsey. *International Journal of Business Intelligence Research, 9*(1), 53–63. doi:10.4018/IJBIR.2018010104

Sharma, A. J. (2017). Enhancing Sustainability through Experiential Learning in Management Education. In N. Baporikar (Ed.), *Management Education for Global Leadership* (pp. 256–274). Hershey, PA: IGI Global. doi:10.4018/978-1-5225-1013-0.ch013

Shetty, K. P. (2017). Responsible Global Leadership: Ethical Challenges in Management Education. In N. Baporikar (Ed.), *Innovation and Shifting Perspectives in Management Education* (pp. 194–223). Hershey, PA: IGI Global. doi:10.4018/978-1-5225-1019-2.ch009

Sinthupundaja, J., & Kohda, Y. (2017). Effects of Corporate Social Responsibility and Creating Shared Value on Sustainability. *International Journal of Sustainable Entrepreneurship and Corporate Social Responsibility*, *2*(1), 27–38. doi:10.4018/IJSECSR.2017010103

Škarica, I., & Hrgović, A. V. (2018). Implementation of Total Quality Management Principles in Public Health Institutes in the Republic of Croatia. *International Journal of Productivity Management and Assessment Technologies*, *6*(1), 1–16. doi:10.4018/IJPMAT.2018010101

Smuts, H., Kotzé, P., Van der Merwe, A., & Loock, M. (2017). Framework for Managing Shared Knowledge in an Information Systems Outsourcing Context. *International Journal of Knowledge Management*, *13*(4), 1–30. doi:10.4018/IJKM.2017100101

Soares, E. R., & Zaidan, F. H. (2016). Information Architecture and Business Modeling in Modern Organizations of Information Technology: Professional Career Plan in Organizations IT. In G. Jamil, J. Poças Rascão, F. Ribeiro, & A. Malheiro da Silva (Eds.), *Handbook of Research on Information Architecture and Management in Modern Organizations* (pp. 439–457). Hershey, PA: IGI Global. doi:10.4018/978-1-4666-8637-3.ch020

Sousa, M. J., Cruz, R., Dias, I., & Caracol, C. (2017). Information Management Systems in the Supply Chain. In G. Jamil, A. Soares, & C. Pessoa (Eds.), *Handbook of Research on Information Management for Effective Logistics and Supply Chains* (pp. 469–485). Hershey, PA: IGI Global. doi:10.4018/978-1-5225-0973-8.ch025

Spremic, M., Turulja, L., & Bajgoric, N. (2018). Two Approaches in Assessing Business Continuity Management Attitudes in the Organizational Context. In N. Bajgoric (Ed.), *Always-On Enterprise Information Systems for Modern Organizations* (pp. 159–183). Hershey, PA: IGI Global. doi:10.4018/978-1-5225-3704-5.ch008

Steenkamp, A. L. (2018). Some Insights in Computer Science and Information Technology. In *Examining the Changing Role of Supervision in Doctoral Research Projects: Emerging Research and Opportunities* (pp. 113–133). Hershey, PA: IGI Global. doi:10.4018/978-1-5225-2610-0.ch005

Studdard, N., Dawson, M., Burton, S. L., Jackson, N., Leonard, B., Quisenberry, W., & Rahim, E. (2016). Nurturing Social Entrepreneurship and Building Social Entrepreneurial Self-Efficacy: Focusing on Primary and Secondary Schooling to Develop Future Social Entrepreneurs. In Z. Fields (Ed.), *Incorporating Business Models and Strategies into Social Entrepreneurship* (pp. 154–175). Hershey, PA: IGI Global. doi:10.4018/978-1-4666-8748-6.ch010

Sun, Z. (2016). A Framework for Developing Management Intelligent Systems. *International Journal of Systems and Service-Oriented Engineering*, *6*(1), 37–53. doi:10.4018/IJSSOE.2016010103

Swami, B., & Mphele, G. T. (2016). Problems Preventing Growth of Small Entrepreneurs: A Case Study of a Few Small Entrepreneurs in Botswana Sub-Urban Areas. In N. Baporikar (Ed.), *Handbook of Research on Entrepreneurship in the Contemporary Knowledge-Based Global Economy* (pp. 479–508). Hershey, PA: IGI Global. doi:10.4018/978-1-4666-8798-1.ch020

Tabach, A., & Croteau, A. (2017). Configurations of Information Technology Governance Practices and Business Unit Performance. *International Journal of IT/Business Alignment and Governance*, *8*(2), 1–27. doi:10.4018/IJITBAG.2017070101

Talaue, G. M., & Iqbal, T. (2017). Assessment of e-Business Mode of Selected Private Universities in the Philippines and Pakistan. *International Journal of Online Marketing*, *7*(4), 63–77. doi:10.4018/IJOM.2017100105

Tam, G. C. (2017). Project Manager Sustainability Competence. In *Managerial Strategies and Green Solutions for Project Sustainability* (pp. 178–207). Hershey, PA: IGI Global. doi:10.4018/978-1-5225-2371-0.ch008

Tambo, T. (2018). Fashion Retail Innovation: About Context, Antecedents, and Outcome in Technological Change Projects. In I. Management Association (Ed.), Fashion and Textiles: Breakthroughs in Research and Practice (pp. 233-260). Hershey, PA: IGI Global. doi:10.4018/978-1-5225-3432-7.ch010

Tambo, T., & Mikkelsen, O. E. (2016). Fashion Supply Chain Optimization: Linking Make-to-Order Purchasing and B2B E-Commerce. In S. Joshi & R. Joshi (Eds.), *Designing and Implementing Global Supply Chain Management* (pp. 1–21). Hershey, PA: IGI Global. doi:10.4018/978-1-4666-9720-1.ch001

Tandon, K. (2016). Innovative Andragogy: The Paradigm Shift to Heutagogy. In S. Tiwari & L. Nafees (Eds.), *Innovative Management Education Pedagogies for Preparing Next-Generation Leaders* (pp. 238–257). Hershey, PA: IGI Global. doi:10.4018/978-1-4666-9691-4.ch014

Tantau, A. D., & Frăţilă, L. C. (2018). Information and Management System for Renewable Energy Business. In *Entrepreneurship and Business Development in the Renewable Energy Sector* (pp. 200–244). Hershey, PA: IGI Global. doi:10.4018/978-1-5225-3625-3.ch006

Teixeira, N., Pardal, P. N., & Rafael, B. G. (2018). Internationalization, Financial Performance, and Organizational Challenges: A Success Case in Portugal. In L. Carvalho (Ed.), *Handbook of Research on Entrepreneurial Ecosystems and Social Dynamics in a Globalized World* (pp. 379–423). Hershey, PA: IGI Global. doi:10.4018/978-1-5225-3525-6.ch017

Trad, A., & Kalpić, D. (2016). The E-Business Transformation Framework for E-Commerce Architecture-Modeling Projects. In I. Lee (Ed.), *Encyclopedia of E-Commerce Development, Implementation, and Management* (pp. 733–753). Hershey, PA: IGI Global. doi:10.4018/978-1-4666-9787-4.ch052

Trad, A., & Kalpić, D. (2016). The E-Business Transformation Framework for E-Commerce Control and Monitoring Pattern. In I. Lee (Ed.), *Encyclopedia of E-Commerce Development, Implementation, and Management* (pp. 754–777). Hershey, PA: IGI Global. doi:10.4018/978-1-4666-9787-4.ch053

Trad, A., & Kalpić, D. (2018). The Business Transformation Framework, Agile Project and Change Management. In M. Khosrow-Pour, D.B.A. (Ed.), Encyclopedia of Information Science and Technology, Fourth Edition (pp. 620-635). Hershey, PA: IGI Global. doi:10.4018/978-1-5225-2255-3.ch054

Trad, A., & Kalpić, D. (2018). The Business Transformation and Enterprise Architecture Framework: The Financial Engineering E-Risk Management and E-Law Integration. In B. Sergi, F. Fidanoski, M. Ziolo, & V. Naumovski (Eds.), *Regaining Global Stability After the Financial Crisis* (pp. 46–65). Hershey, PA: IGI Global. doi:10.4018/978-1-5225-4026-7.ch003

Turulja, L., & Bajgoric, N. (2018). Business Continuity and Information Systems: A Systematic Literature Review. In N. Bajgoric (Ed.), *Always-On Enterprise Information Systems for Modern Organizations* (pp. 60–87). Hershey, PA: IGI Global. doi:10.4018/978-1-5225-3704-5.ch004

van Wessel, R. M., de Vries, H. J., & Ribbers, P. M. (2016). Business Benefits through Company IT Standardization. In K. Jakobs (Ed.), *Effective Standardization Management in Corporate Settings* (pp. 34–53). Hershey, PA: IGI Global. doi:10.4018/978-1-4666-9737-9.ch003

Vargas-Hernández, J. G. (2017). Professional Integrity in Business Management Education. In N. Baporikar (Ed.), *Management Education for Global Leadership* (pp. 70–89). Hershey, PA: IGI Global. doi:10.4018/978-1-5225-1013-0.ch004

Vasista, T. G., & AlAbdullatif, A. M. (2017). Role of Electronic Customer Relationship Management in Demand Chain Management: A Predictive Analytic Approach. *International Journal of Information Systems and Supply Chain Management, 10*(1), 53–67. doi:10.4018/IJISSCM.2017010104

Vergidis, K. (2016). Rediscovering Business Processes: Definitions, Patterns, and Modelling Approaches. In P. Papajorgji, F. Pinet, A. Guimarães, & J. Papathanasiou (Eds.), *Automated Enterprise Systems for Maximizing Business Performance* (pp. 97–122). Hershey, PA: IGI Global. doi:10.4018/978-1-4666-8841-4.ch007

Vieru, D., & Bourdeau, S. (2017). Survival in the Digital Era: A Digital Competence-Based Multi-Case Study in the Canadian SME Clothing Industry. *International Journal of Social and Organizational Dynamics in IT, 6*(1), 17–34. doi:10.4018/IJSODIT.2017010102

Vijayan, G., & Kamarulzaman, N. H. (2017). An Introduction to Sustainable Supply Chain Management and Business Implications. In M. Khan, M. Hussain, & M. Ajmal (Eds.), *Green Supply Chain Management for Sustainable Business Practice* (pp. 27–50). Hershey, PA: IGI Global. doi:10.4018/978-1-5225-0635-5.ch002

Vlachvei, A., & Notta, O. (2017). Firm Competitiveness: Theories, Evidence, and Measurement. In A. Vlachvei, O. Notta, K. Karantininis, & N. Tsounis (Eds.), *Factors Affecting Firm Competitiveness and Performance in the Modern Business World* (pp. 1–42). Hershey, PA: IGI Global. doi:10.4018/978-1-5225-0843-4.ch001

von Rosing, M., Fullington, N., & Walker, J. (2016). Using the Business Ontology and Enterprise Standards to Transform Three Leading Organizations. *International Journal of Conceptual Structures and Smart Applications, 4*(1), 71–99. doi:10.4018/IJCSSA.2016010104

von Rosing, M., & von Scheel, H. (2016). Using the Business Ontology to Develop Enterprise Standards. *International Journal of Conceptual Structures and Smart Applications, 4*(1), 48–70. doi:10.4018/IJCSSA.2016010103

Walczak, S. (2016). Artificial Neural Networks and other AI Applications for Business Management Decision Support. *International Journal of Sociotechnology and Knowledge Development, 8*(4), 1–20. doi:10.4018/IJSKD.2016100101

Wamba, S. F., Akter, S., Kang, H., Bhattacharya, M., & Upal, M. (2016). The Primer of Social Media Analytics. *Journal of Organizational and End User Computing, 28*(2), 1–12. doi:10.4018/JOEUC.2016040101

Wang, C., Schofield, M., Li, X., & Ou, X. (2017). Do Chinese Students in Public and Private Higher Education Institutes Perform at Different Level in One of the Leadership Skills: Critical Thinking?: An Exploratory Comparison. In V. Wang (Ed.), *Encyclopedia of Strategic Leadership and Management* (pp. 160–181). Hershey, PA: IGI Global. doi:10.4018/978-1-5225-1049-9.ch013

Wang, F., Raisinghani, M. S., Mora, M., & Wang, X. (2016). Strategic E-Business Management through a Balanced Scored Card Approach. In I. Lee (Ed.), *Encyclopedia of E-Commerce Development, Implementation, and Management* (pp. 361–386). Hershey, PA: IGI Global. doi:10.4018/978-1-4666-9787-4.ch027

Wang, J. (2017). Multi-Agent based Production Management Decision System Modelling for the Textile Enterprise. *Journal of Global Information Management*, *25*(4), 1–15. doi:10.4018/JGIM.2017100101

Wiedemann, A., & Gewald, H. (2017). Examining Cross-Domain Alignment: The Correlation of Business Strategy, IT Management, and IT Business Value. *International Journal of IT/Business Alignment and Governance*, *8*(1), 17–31. doi:10.4018/IJITBAG.2017010102

Wolf, R., & Thiel, M. (2018). Advancing Global Business Ethics in China: Reducing Poverty Through Human and Social Welfare. In S. Hipsher (Ed.), *Examining the Private Sector's Role in Wealth Creation and Poverty Reduction* (pp. 67–84). Hershey, PA: IGI Global. doi:10.4018/978-1-5225-3117-3.ch004

Wu, J., Ding, F., Xu, M., Mo, Z., & Jin, A. (2016). Investigating the Determinants of Decision-Making on Adoption of Public Cloud Computing in E-government. *Journal of Global Information Management*, *24*(3), 71–89. doi:10.4018/JGIM.2016070104

Xu, L., & de Vrieze, P. (2016). Building Situational Applications for Virtual Enterprises. In I. Lee (Ed.), *Encyclopedia of E-Commerce Development, Implementation, and Management* (pp. 715–724). Hershey, PA: IGI Global. doi:10.4018/978-1-4666-9787-4.ch050

Yablonsky, S. (2018). Innovation Platforms: Data and Analytics Platforms. In *Multi-Sided Platforms (MSPs) and Sharing Strategies in the Digital Economy: Emerging Research and Opportunities* (pp. 72–95). Hershey, PA: IGI Global. doi:10.4018/978-1-5225-5457-8.ch003

Yusoff, A., Ahmad, N. H., & Halim, H. A. (2017). Agropreneurship among Gen Y in Malaysia: The Role of Academic Institutions. In N. Ahmad, T. Ramayah, H. Halim, & S. Rahman (Eds.), *Handbook of Research on Small and Medium Enterprises in Developing Countries* (pp. 23–47). Hershey, PA: IGI Global. doi:10.4018/978-1-5225-2165-5.ch002

Zanin, F., Comuzzi, E., & Costantini, A. (2018). The Effect of Business Strategy and Stock Market Listing on the Use of Risk Assessment Tools. In *Management Control Systems in Complex Settings: Emerging Research and Opportunities* (pp. 145–168). Hershey, PA: IGI Global. doi:10.4018/978-1-5225-3987-2.ch007

Zgheib, P. W. (2017). Corporate Innovation and Intrapreneurship in the Middle East. In P. Zgheib (Ed.), *Entrepreneurship and Business Innovation in the Middle East* (pp. 37–56). Hershey, PA: IGI Global. doi:10.4018/978-1-5225-2066-5.ch003

About the Contributors

Ionica Oncioiu holds a Ph.D. in economy and accounting. Her research interests include the development of SMEs innovation, Project Management, Accounting Information Systems, Asset Management and E-Commerce Marketing. She has had more than 10 years of experience in this area and has published 10 textbooks and more than 70 papers in scholarly peer reviewed international journals.

Sorinel Căpuşneanu is a PhD. associate professor at Titu Maiorescu University of Bucharest. Also, he is the Editor in Chief of Academic Journal of Economic Studies. His research focus is the area of Management Accounting, Management Performance, Management Information Systems, Audit and Controlling, and Business Ethics. He is the author of the following books: Elements of Cost Management, Economica Publishing House (2008) and Management Accounting. Performance Assessment Tool, University Publishing House (2013) and co-author of Ethics and Decision-Making for Sustainable Business Practices (Chapter 7 Business Ethics and Cost Management in SME's. Theories of Business Ethics and Cost Management Ethos) published by IGI-Global (USA, 2017). He has participated in numerous national and international conferences and has made a remarkable contribution to managerial accounting by publishing several articles.

Dan Ioan Topor is a PhD. lecturer at the 1 Decembrie 1918 University of Alba-Iulia, Faculty of Economic Sciences. His research focus is the area of Management Accounting, Management Performance and Management Information Systems, Audit and Controlling, and Business Ethics. He is the author of the following books: New dimensions of cost-related cost information for winemaking (2014) and Basics of Accounting (2016). He has published numerous articles on Managerial Accounting and Management Control and has participated in numerous national and international conferences.

Dana Maria Constantin is a PhD. lecturer at the University of Bucharest, Department of Meteorology and Hydrology. Her research focus is the area of biometeorology, bioclimatology, meteorology, climatology. She is the author of the book: The relation between the climate and the environment pollution in the area of Slatina (2013). She has published numerous articles on meteorology and climatology, and she has participated in numerous national and international conferences.

* * *

Cristian-Marian Barbu, PhD, is a graduate of the Academy of Economic Studies in Bucharest, Romania, and after passing the Bachelor exam in 1997, he received the degree of Economist. He received his PhD degree in Economics from the Academy of Economic Studies in Bucharest in 2005 with the dissertation entitled „Agricultural sustainable economic development in the mountain areas in Romania". After graduation, he took the academic career and started working in higher education in 1998, in „ARTIFEX" University of Bucharest. He held the positions of instructor, starting with 1998, teaching assistant starting with 2000, lecturer starting with 2003, associate professor starting with 2008, and University professor starting with 2017. His expertise in teaching and research, as tenured teaching staff in higher education, since 2003, in Political Economics, Microeconomics, Macroeconomics, Prices and Competition, Economic Policies, made him allocate time to research and the dissemination of the findings, which resulted into books, monographs, studies, and articles published, as well as participation in national and international conferences, and research grants. In his capacity of tenured teaching staff in higher education, he wrote specialized handbooks, as author and co-author, which have been aids for students and enriched the data in the field. During his academic career, he has been involved in research in national research projects and in partnerships with economic agents (contracts with the business companies). He also disseminated his findings in specialized /ISI indexed journals, and during national and international scientific events. The topics of the books, articles, papers and studies published by Mr. Cristian-Marian BARBU reflect his preoccupation about micro and macroeconomics, economic balance, analysis of correlations between the result indicators and the effort indicators, agriculture – a major sector of national economy, economic policies, macroeconomic studies and analyses, comparative analyses regarding the agricultural potential of Romania, analyses regarding various segments of national economy at various moments in time, analyses regarding the cost and /or performance in economic entities, aspects regarding the economic-financial crisis, the need of a paradigm to return to nature and to good sense, price and price policy in the strategic planning of the enterprise, environment and monitoring of prejudice to the economic environment etc.

Prabadevi Boopathy is an Assistant Professor (Sr.) in School of Information Technology and Engineering, VIT University, India. She received her PhD in Information Technology with Networking as specialisation from Vellore Institute Technology, Vellore, India in 2018. She completed her undergraduation and post-graduation under Anna University, Chennai in 2010 and 2012 respectively. She has published around 25 international journal papers and many international conference papers. She is currently working in the areas of Decision support systems and Machine Learning. She received an active researcher award from Vellore Institute of Technology for three consecutive years.

Daniel Constantin Diaconu is Associate Professor at the University of Bucharest. He worked in parallel in the private sector but also in the state administration. The management of the water resource as well as of the ecosystem services provided by this resource being one of the fields in which the activity is carried out.

Sibel Dinç Aydemir received her undergraduate degree in Business Administration from Hacettepe University in 2002. She has worked as Assistant Treasury Specialist at Isbank between the years 2004 and 2007. She earned her MBA and PhD degrees in Business Administration from Gebze Technical University in 2011 and 2015 respectively. Her research interests primarily include behavioral finance, individual financial behavior, financial literacy, attitudinal and emotional factors' role on financial risk-taking.

Razvan Catalin Dobrea studied Technological Engineering and Economical Sciences, holds a Master Degree in English Communication and Economical Research and sa PD degree in Management from the Bucharest University of Economic Studies. He is expert in project management with exquisite results in both theoretical and application directions. Is an evaluating expert for various projects with European financing or with financing from the World Bank. Currently is involved into various projects regarding the strategical coordination of the planning across administrative territorial units in Romania.

Cristian Constantin Drăghici is an associate professor at the Faculty of Geography, Department of Human and Economic Geography, University of Bucharest and researcher at the Research Center for Integrated Analysis and Territorial Management, University of Bucharest. The scientific activity is mainly focused on advanced research in integrated analysis and territory management. Also a significant part of the researches made so far have as main subject the tourism sector and how it can positively influence the economic development at local and regional level.

Alina Gheorghe is a University Lecturer at Artifex University from Bucharest. The author is a doctor in Economic Sciences. The authors' scientific concerns are aiming to integrate business management and administration policies through applicability. Research directions include business administration in niche and mass tourism through their mutual correlation, respecting the requirements of sustainable development. At the same time, a particular interest has been directed towards current and future management strategies. The scientific works resulted in a set of over 30 researches published in national and international publishing houses. The author is also a member in the editorial board of some international journals.

Diana Andreea Mândricel is teaching at the Titu Maiorescu University. She is the author of 5 books, over 40 articles to various national and international conferences.

Deepa N. is currently working as Assistant Professor(Senior) in School of Information Technology and Engineering, Vellore Institute of Technology, Vellore, Tamil Nadu, India. She has pursued her Master of Engineering in Computer science and Engineering from Anna University. She completed her Doctoral degree in Vellore Institute of Technology, Vellore. She is having more than 15 years of Teaching Experience. She has guided the number of undergraduate and postgraduate student projects. She has published papers in many refereed International journals with high impact factor. Her areas of interest are Machine Learning, Soft computing, Data mining, Artificial Intelligence, Predictive Analytics.

Vannie Naidoo is a full-time staff member at the University of KwaZulu-Natal, South Africa, in the Faculty of Management and Law. Her field of teaching is in management, corporate strategy, project management and entrepreneurship. The research areas pursued by Dr Naidoo are in the areas of management, marketing, service marketing, entrepreneurship and social media and e-learning or learning with new technologies. She has presented papers at international conferences throughout the world and has written on various issues in management and marketing in journal articles and books.

İsmail Çağrı Özcan is an assistant professor at Ankara Yıldırım Beyazıt University (Department of Aviation Management). He received his MBA and Ph.D. in Business Administration degrees from Hacettepe University and Master of Public Policy degree from the University of California, Los Angeles.

Between August 2014 and August 2016, he was a Visiting Post-Doc Researcher at Regional Economics Applications Laboratory of University of Illinois, Urbana-Champaign. His research has appeared at journals such as Journal of Air Transport Management, European Journal of Transport and Infrastructure Research, International Journal of Transport Economics, and Case Studies on Transport Policy.

Janne Peltoniemi is Head of BBA-ERP programme, co-Head of MBA-ERP programme, SAP Next-Gen Chapter Leader and Principal Lecturer at the Centria University of Applied Sciences in Kokkola (Finland) and Head of BBA-ERP programme. His main research interests are in the fields of accounting, finance, small business finance, debt markets, stock markets, corporate social responsibility and lately in strategic finance. He holds a master's degree in Business Administration (Accounting) from the University of Oulu (Finland)and a Ph.D. in Business Administration (Accounting and Finance) from the University of Oulu (Finland). In the sustainability field, his research focus is on corporate finance related issues in corporate social responsibility.

Daniel Peptenatu is an associate professor at the Faculty of Geography, Department of Human and Economic Geography, University of Bucharest and the director of the Research Center for Integrated Analysis and Territorial Management, University of Bucharest. The scientific activity is focused in the main advanced researches in the integrated analysis and the management of the territory, one of the proposed objectives being created and promoted some methodologies of integrated analysis of the territory.

Rauno Rusko is university lecturer at the University of Lapland. His research activities focus on cooperation, coopetition, strategic management, supply chain management and entrepreneurship mainly in the branches of information communication technology, forest industry and tourism. His articles appeared in the European Management Journal, Forest Policy and Economics, International Journal of Business Environment, Industrial Marketing Management, International Journal of Innovation in the Digital Economy and International Journal of Tourism Research among others.

Alina Stanciu is a highly skilled professional with extended expertise in Management and Public Relation gained in multinational environment in the past 10 years. Experienced in Business 2 Business Strategy and New Business with a strong understanding of management concepts, leadership, business policies and talent acquisition, having solid track record in building and motivating strong teams. Involved in external relations with business organizations, persuasive and empathic character with strong communication skills.

Mircea Alecsandru Udrescu is a PhD. Professor at Artifex University of Bucharest. The author has a degree in Economics and Military Sciences being a PhD programme coordinator in Logistics. The authors' scientific concerns are aiming to integrate management and marketing into functional logistics. Its research directions support the ideas according to which logistics is becoming more and more individualized as a science of the future, whose activity object is the dimensioning and correlation of the flows of information and goods, in order to continuously adapt the company to the environmental conditions, in which the successive elements are subordinated to the synchronization requirements, in compliance with the requirements of efficiency and sustainable development. The author is a member of different fundamental research groups in the fields of logistics, marketing and management, has led different departments and educational systems, is a member of the Romanian Academy of Sciences and a member of the Romanian Statistical Society. The authors' scientific concerns and research have resulted in more than 20 books and manuals, as well as in about four hundred articles and published communications.

Markku Vieru is Professor of Accounting at the University of Lapland at the Multidimensional Tourism Institute (MTI) in Rovaniemi (Finland). His main research interests lie in the area of financial economics, accounting and tourism business. He holds a master's degree in Business Administration (Accounting) from the University of Vaasa (Finland) and a Ph.D. in Business Administration (Accounting) from the University of Oulu (Finland). He is adjunct professor of financial accounting at the University of Oulu.

Lavinia Yildirim is a PhD student in Ankara University where her major is management in the Faculty of Political Science.

Index

www.ingramcontent.com/pod-product-compliance
Lightning Source LLC
LaVergne TN
LVHW062142300926
849161LV00010B/2601
* 9 7 8 1 7 9 9 8 4 6 3 7 6 *